Technology and Communist Culture

edited by
Frederic J. Fleron, Jr.

The Praeger Special Studies program—utilizing the most modern and efficient book production techniques and a selective worldwide distribution network—makes available to the academic, government, and business communities significant, timely research in U.S. and international economic, social, and political development.

Technology and Communist Culture

The Socio-Cultural Impact of Technology under Socialism

Praeger Publishers New York London

PRAEGER SPECIAL STUDIES IN INTERNATIONAL POLITICS AND GOVERNMENT

Library of Congress Cataloging in Publication Data

Main entry under title:

Technology and Communist culture.

    (Praeger special studies in international politics
and government)
    Includes bibliographical references and index.
    1. Technological innovations—Communist countries.
I. Fleron, Frederic J., 1937-
HC710.T4T42   1977   301.24'3'091717   77-7810
ISBN 0-03-021821-7

PRAEGER SPECIAL STUDIES
200 Park Avenue, New York, N.Y., 10017, U.S.A.

Published in the United States of America in 1977
by Praeger Publishers,
A Division of Holt, Rinehart and Winston, CBS, Inc.

789   038   987654321

Printed in the United States of America

For generations to come we will not
know the decency and the poised ease
of living any day for that day's sake,
or be graceful here like the wild
flowers blooming in the fields,
but must live drawn out and nearly
broken between past and future
because of our history's wages,
bad work left behind us,
demanding to be done again.

Wendell Berry,
"The Wages of History"

This book is the result of a project conceived in the fall of 1973 during the deliberations of the Planning Group on Comparative Communist Studies of the American Council of Learned Societies (ACLS). As a member of the group from 1969 until its dissolution in 1975 and an active participant in two of its several projects (the 1971 Arden House Conference on Political Culture and Comparative Communist Studies and the 1970 St. Croix Conference on Peasant Rebellion and Communist Revolution in Asia), I was stimulated to broaden the conceptualization and application of ideas that had intrigued me for some time but had not yet crystallized in my own thinking. It is therefore a great pleasure to record here my sincere appreciation and intellectual debt to a distinguished and stimulating group of scholars who served on the group during my tenure: Donald L. M. Blackmer, R. V. Burks, Mark G. Field, John W. Lewis, Nicolas Spulber, Robert C. Tucker, Gordon B. Turner, and Ezra F. Vogel. While we did not agree in all things during our many deliberations, I am grateful to them for the opportunity to organize a conference to pursue collectively the exploration of ideas about which many of them had considerable skepticism.

The essays in this book are a selection of papers presented at the Conference on Technology and Communist Culture that I convened during August 22-28, 1975, under the auspices of the ACLS Planning Group on Comparative Communist Studies at the Rockefeller Foundation Study and Conference Center, Villa Serbelloni, Bellagio (Lake Como), Italy. I am grateful to the Rockefeller Foundation for the opportunity to convene the conference in the lovely surroundings of the Villa Serbelloni and most appreciative of the warm hospitality of William and Betsy Olson during our stay at the villa.

The conference was attended by 20 scholars, many of whom were invited to prepare papers as background for the discussions. Because of limitation of space, not all of those papers could be included in this volume. I wish to record my sincere thanks and appreciation to all of the conference participants for their contributions, which made our meeting such an enriching experience. In addition to the authors of chapters in this conference volume, the participants included Pavel Apostol, Joseph Berliner, Genevieve Dean, Colin C. Gallagher, Philip Hanson, David E. Powell, Jon Sigurdson, Albrecht Wellmer, and George S. Wheeler.

I am grateful to R. V. Burks, Erik P. Hoffmann, and William Leiss, who so kindly served with me as an advisory committee during an intermediate planning stage of the conference.

It was my desire that half of the participants would be scholars from socialist countries, and a number of invitations were extended; but in the end only one was accepted. Hopefully, the time is rapidly approaching when scholars from both sides will be able to discuss these issues around the same table.

During the development of my ideas on the relationship between technology and culture in socialist societies, I was greatly stimulated by the writings of, and my discussions with, a number of friends, colleagues, and associates, who contributed in one way or another to the sharpening of my own perceptions and who were generous in their critical and constructive analyses of my attempts to commit those ideas to paper. In this regard I wish to express special thanks to William N. Dunn, Andrew L. Feenberg, Erik P. Hoffmann, William Leiss, Peter Linebaugh, Frank Marini, and Gene L. Mason. I am grateful as well for the opportunity to discuss these issues with a number of colleagues in Eastern Europe and the Soviet Union.

Finally, and most importantly, I must record my deepest appreciation to Lou Jean, my intellectual companion and gracious editor.

While it is a pleasure to acknowledge the support, criticism, and encouragement of all of these persons, I wish to make it clear that I assume full responsibility for the selection of conference participants, for the selection of papers for this conference volume, and especially for the ideas expressed in my introductory and concluding essays.

CONTENTS

PART III: THE IMPACT OF TECHNOLOGY
AND TECHNICAL RATIONALITY ON
SOCIALIST SOCIETIES

LIST OF TABLES AND FIGURES

INTRODUCTION
Frederic J. Fleron, Jr.

BACKGROUND

Communist revolutions are much more than political revolutions; they are cultural revolutions in the broadest sense. They seek not only to seize and to wield power in societies, but also to transform the basic relationships among people and thereby to create the "new communist man." For this reason, as Robert C. Tucker has argued, it should prove useful to view modern communism as a culture-transforming movement.[1] The participants in the 1971 Arden House Conference on Communist Studies and Political Culture, Harrison, New York, agreed that such an orientation might well open up new possibilities for the comparative study of communist societies.[2]

However, that view does not originate in recent Western scholarship. Lenin himself, both in State and Revolution (1917) and "On Co-operation" (1923), pointed to the necessity for full-scale cultural revolution in Russia in order to realize the ideals of Bolshevism. Lenin's words are so forceful and unambiguous that they are worth considering at length:

> From the point of view of the "enlightened" (primarily, literate) European there is not much left for us to do to induce absolutely everyone to take not a passive, but an active part in co-operative operations. Strictly speaking, there is "only" one thing we have left to do and that is to make our people so "enlightened" that they understand all the advantages of everybody participating in the work of the co-operatives, and organize this participation. "Only" that. There are no other devices needed to advance to socialism. But to achieve this "only," there must be a veritable revolution—the entire people must go through

1

a period of cultural development.

> Our opponents told us repeatedly that we were
> rash in undertaking to implant socialism in an insuf-
> ficiently cultured country. But they were misled by our
> having started from the opposite end to that prescribed
> by theory (the theory of pedants of all kinds), because
> in our country the political and social revolution preced-
> ed the cultural revolution, that very cultural revolution
> which nevertheless now confronts us.

> This cultural revolution would now suffice to make
> our country a completely socialist country; but it pre-
> sents immense difficulties of a purely cultural (for we
> are illiterate) and material character (for to be cultured
> we must achieve a certain development of the material
> means of production, must have a certain material base).[3]

Starting from the Leninist perspective that communist revolutions are culture-transforming movements, we will examine the impact of technology, especially the complex technology of the more
advanced capitalist countries, on the process of cultural transformation in communist societies. Before that, however, the concept of
communist culture must be clarified.

Gabriel Almond suggested in his memorandum to the Arden
House conference that

> while there has been an assumption in the communist
> movement that the model of "Communist man" would be
> the same regardless of differences in culture in the vari-
> ous parts of the world in which the movement acquires
> a foothold, in actual fact the content of "Communist
> man" varies from one communist party to the next,
> from one communist country to the next.

To be sure, there are some common elements within these models,
based on the view of human development derived from Marx. At the
same time there do exist some differences, which Tucker suggests
can be explained by the fact that "communism in practice tends to be
an amalgam of an innovated cultural system and elements of a national cultural ethos."[4] There is also a third, crucial element in the
amalgam—imported culture. When we examine the culture of any
particular communist society, we must identify three analytically
distinct elements: the innovated cultural system (the indigenous progressive Marxist movement); the national cultural ethos (the traditions of society); and aspects of imported foreign culture (the objects
of cultural diffusion). The fact that these basic elements may be
fruitfully isolated analytically must not obscure the equally impor-

tant fact that they are in reality highly and very intricately interrelated and interdependent.

National cultural ethos refers to the historical and cultural
traditions of the socialist country in the prerevolutionary period. It
includes religious factors; the patterns of authority structures; the
level of economic development; the system of social stratification;
and certain traditions in science, philosophy, and the arts. The innovated cultural system of communism is the system of thought pertaining to the goals of socialist society plus some notions of the
means to be employed in achieving those ends, however vague and
elusive those ends may be at times. [5]

The third element of the amalgam, imported foreign culture,
is the result of cultural diffusion from some donor countries to the
recipient socialist countries. Such cultural diffusion may include any
of the elements of culture mentioned above. Needless to say, cultural diffusion has been an important and increasingly powerful (or, perhaps, increasingly possible) mode of historical change in many societies, either with or without the approval of the recipient cultures.
Technology appears to be one of the more readily diffused elements
of culture: indeed, its spread from the more to the less technologically developed societies has been a hallmark of the modern age. We
must be careful at the outset to distinguish between at least two distinct aspects of technology: machines or tools themselves and technical rationality. The diffusion potential of these two elements is quite
different, and as we shall begin to see below, the interrelationship
between them is quite complex. Machines and tools are the concrete
artifacts of human experience and invention. Technical rationality is
that mode of purposive rational action that accompanies the implementation and use of a particular machine technology. In his 1972
study The Domination of Nature, William Leiss has described as
follows the distinction between technical artifacts and rationality:

> "Techniques" comprise not only tools but equally as
> importantly the organization and training of human la-
> bor: Lewis Mumford illustrated this point well in his
> argument that the first great machine in history con-
> sisted of the forced-labor gangs that built the Egyptian
> pyramids, together with the stage administration which
> planned and supervised their work. [Cf. Mumford, The
> Myth of the Machine, Ch. 9.] The purposeful organiza-
> tion and combination of productive techniques, directed
> either by public or private authorities, has been called
> "technical rationality. "[6]

The particular attributes of capitalist technical rationality can
be described for present purposes as a broad set of basic cultural
values including the dichotomization of means and ends, of work

activity and product; the acceptance of means-ends efficiency as a
primary goal; the compartmentalization of knowledge; the separation
of mental and manual labor; the human domination of nature; efficiency defined in nonhuman terms; the hierarchical control of production;
and, underlying it all, the assumption of the priority and insatiability
of human material wants.

Now it appears likely that the transfer of machine technology
from one society to another as an element of cultural diffusion can
take place relatively easily; what is involved is essentially the physical movement of the machine itself. Whether or not that machine will
be utilized and operated to full advantage and efficiency will depend
in large part on the availability in the recipient country of elements
of technical rationality and what we shall call cultural infrastructure
congruent with that particular machine technology. To anticipate the
main argument of this paper, it would appear that the transfer of
elements of technical rationality and cultural infrastructure is a much
more complex and difficult process than the transfer of the machine
technology. What makes this problem particularly vexing is that
while it is possible to distinguish analytically between machine technology and the mode of purposive rational action (technical rationality) surrounding its usage, in fact these two elements of technology
are so closely enmeshed that the transfer of the machinery brings
great pressures for the transfer of technical rationality.

One caveat before proceeding further: When we concentrate on
aspects of imported foreign culture in any socialist society, we must
remember that the process of cultural diffusion was in operation
long before any particular communist regime came to power and
that, therefore, aspects of foreign culture entered these countries
in the prerevolutionary as well as the postrevolutionary period. For
example, in early eighteenth-century Russia, the borrowings by
Peter the Great from Western culture included not only Western
technology but also Western administrative practice, leading to the
famous Table of Ranks or chin. [7] Peter was also greatly concerned
with appearances and insisted that Russians become cleanshaven
and adopt Western styles of dress. In order to do what Westerners
did, apparently Russians had to look the way Westerners looked.

Again, in the latter part of the nineteenth-century, Russia
borrowed extensively from Western technology. In the cases of
China and Cuba, the presence of Western culture was not so much
a matter of conscious choice as it was the product of Western imperialism and economic exploitation. Regardless of the circumstances
of the transfer of technology, by the time of the communist revolution in these countries, those technological and other forms of borrowed culture had to some degree become part of the national cultural ethos that the innovated cultural system of communism had to confront.

The nature of the communist culture-transforming process depends in major part on the state of development of the society at the time of the communist acquisition of power. As Tucker has suggested, a dominant theme of Marx and Engels was as follows:

> Industrialization, urbanization, machine technology, the conquest of nature, the breakdown of traditional society in the backward countries, and the internationalization of society were all the work of the bourgeois era. The bourgeois revolution of modernization was the preparation of society for communism. The mission of the communist revolution was not to modernize society further, but to humanize it, to reintegrate man with himself and nature and make him, collectively, the "sovereign of circumstances."[8]

What happens to communism as a culture-transforming process, however, when these aspects of bourgeois society are not present at the time of the communist revolution, as indeed they have not been in most instances?

This question is obviously related to the question of "socialism in one country." Had history marched along the general path Marx expected, the world socialist revolution would have confronted the bourgeois world only as tradition, not as some coexisting and competing society. Mondialization would have created circumstances in which socialism could flower upon the base of this materially highly developed world culture. Socialism would not in any circumstance "borrow" from bourgeois society in any meaningful sense of the word, because bourgeois society would already have been historically transcended. In the absence of that development, however, one of the main culture transformations undertaken immediately after the isolated revolution is modernization itself—a bourgeois process that was frequently modeled on capitalist forms.[9] In those circumstances then it is perhaps no wonder that this aspect of the innovative cultural system of communism necessarily has bourgeois limitations.

In the Soviet case, industrialization and machine technology were not sufficiently present prior to 1917 to have "conquered nature" and broken down traditional society. Certainly there were the beginnings of these processes in small pockets of Russia, but Russian society in general could not have been described in those terms.[10] For Lenin and the Bolsheviks, then, a central part of the thoroughgoing cultural revolution was full-scale industrialization and expansion of production capacity, which was accomplished with the importation of foreign technology and systems of factory organization to increase worker productivity.

The advantages of backwardness, as they are sometimes called, that accrue to "late modernizers" are a mixed blessing. On the one hand, the highly developed and sophisticated technology of the West, that is, Western Europe and the United States, can be imported in order to change greatly the shape of the recipient "backward" economic system and to increase productive capacity in a relatively short period of time. On the other hand, the recipient society frequently lacks the cultural infrastructure present in the donor society to support such advanced technology. Sometimes this "infrastructure" is considered as a set of prerequisites to industrial development and sometimes as necessary accompanying character-istics (including what some might call consequences) of that develop-ment. Some such characteristics seem to be linked inextricably to industrialization itself, and some others seem more closely tied to the particular requirements of capitalism and its specific form of industrial development. In either case and without attempting here to sort out the elements among those two pairs of possibilities, we can note that the concept of capitalist infrastructure usually refers to (1) a materialistic and secular world view that can reject traditional and mystical values, that relies increasingly on the "scientific" ex-amination and explanation of reality, and that accepts material change and "innovation" as the rule in life; (2) a social structure that is ordered hierarchically according to materialistic achievement norms, has objectified labor so that there is a high degree of (not necessarily and not usually vertical) social mobility, and is disci-plined by the regularization of activity in quantified time;[11] (3) a system of "social overhead" that fulfills the material requirements of industrialization, such as an extensive training and educational system, mass communication and transportation systems, and de-veloped inanimate power sources and systems; and (4) a pervasive acceptance of industrial technical rationality, meaning those speci-fic mechanisms by which labor and life (styles) are adapted to the machine in the industrial production process and in which the re-quirements of the machine spill over directly into social values and organization, including, for example, the acceptance of means-ends efficiency as a primary goal.

Some of these infrastructural "prerequisites" themselves can be borrowed from the advanced nations, as Alexander Gerschenkron points out in the following passage:

> Illiteracy and low standards of education and the resulting
> difficulty in training skilled labor and efficient engineers,
> can be overcome to some extent by immigration from
> more advanced countries and to some extent by using the
> training facilities of those countries. The same is true,

even more importantly, of the lack of a store of technical knowledge. It can be imported from abroad. In this
sense, however, one can say that in a backward country
there exists a "prerequisite" to industrial development
which "the" advanced country did not have at its disposal, that is, the existence of the more advanced countries as sources of technical assistance, skilled labor,
and capital goods. [12]

Other of these prerequisites must be compensated for by the development of functional equivalents that are indigenously feasible, as
in the case of Russia, where the state acted as a surrogate entre-
preneur. [13]

Still another compensating mechanism is politically to force
the development of those requisite infrastructural elements in the
"backward" society. The particular mix of these three alternative
means of supporting capitalist industrialism will, of course, be
determined by national-historical factors. The case of Russia/USSR
makes but one, although a very instructive, example—perhaps the
more instructive because the Soviet Union was in a position to force
its particular mix on many other communist states.

This historical form of state capitalism in tsarist Russia, the
postrevolutionary aim of confining or limiting the bourgeois-culture
effects of modernization, and the growth-maximizing objectives of
the Soviet Union in competition with capitalism, led to capital-intensive techniques and gigantomania in the industrial sector. In the more
advanced science-based technologies of the West, capital-intensive
techniques were highly developed, and it was natural that the Soviet
leaders again turned to the West as a source of technological innovation, as their tsarist predecessors had done decades before them.
Antony Sutton has documented in detail the breadth of Western technical transfer to the Soviet Union. [14] Machine technology was not the
only aspect of technical transfer, however, and could not be completely separated from its infrastructural entanglements:

Technical transfers are linked to the social conditions
extant in donor and recipient societies alike. Whenever
techniques invented in particular social matrices are
exported to vastly different settings, there is a risk
that great psychological and value changes may occur.
This is particularly true when the techniques in question
are derived from the application of the social sciences.
Most technical transfers made for development purposes
do in fact rely on social sciences: transfers in education,
manpower strategy, administration, research, community organization, and so on.

> Transfers of technique for development purposes
> made by persons of one society or subdivision thereof
> to those of another have special effects on the culture
> and politics of recipients. The transfer itself is not
> merely a technique, but a value-laden political act with
> far-reaching implications. [15]

As I have argued elsewhere, Frederick Winslow Taylor's
"scientific management" served as the basis for Soviet factory organization in an effort to increase worker productivity. [16] John A.
Armstrong has observed that

> The persistent impact of Taylorism in the Soviet Union
> is remarkable. . . . While some of the early Bolshevik
> industrial directors distrusted Taylorism because of its
> capitalist origins, like Alexander I a century earlier
> most believed Russia had to borrow any advanced tech-
> niques available.[17]

Armstrong goes on to point out that given Soviet emphasis on
engineering approaches and "the ruthless social control by other
agencies, a certain portion of the administrative apparatus (chiefly
industrial ministries and enterprises) could virtually disregard human factors."[18] This appears to be in sharp contrast to aspects of
the Chinese and Cuban experiences.

In her summary of discussions at the Sussex Study Group on
Science and Technology in China's Development, Genevieve Dean
emphasized that "The relative success or failure of the strategies
chosen for technological modernization in China must then be judged,
not only in terms of economic 'development', but also in terms of
the broader economic, social and political objectives associated
with particular technological choices."[19] Examples of these broader
objectives are the elimination of the "three big differences" between
industry and agriculture, city and countryside, and mental and
manual labor. Realization of these objectives cannot be accomplished
through the development of concentrated capital-intensive technology,
but rather requires a technology of smaller-scale capital development and perhaps even a more labor-intensive technology, which
would be more consistent with the decentralization of enterprise
administration, the growth of local "self-reliance," and more equit-
ably distributed employment opportunities for the entire population
of working age.

It is clear that concern for social and political objectives
would lead to the choice of technological alternatives quite different
from those chosen primarily on the basis of growth-maximizing ob-

jectives. The latter choice would lead to extensive borrowing from the more advanced science-based technologies of the West and would resemble the Soviet path of technological development. The former choice would require a more "nativist" path of technical development— a point well made in 1973 by Rensselaer W. Lee III in an important article on technological nativism in China. [20]

If there are differences within the transferred machine technology and technical rationality in the sense that some aspects are in conflict with communist goal culture and others are not, then which ones are chosen? The communist response has been varied. The Soviets apparently have not clearly made this distinction and have borrowed almost any advanced technique available in the areas of machine technology, management forms, and patterns of technical rationality. The Chinese record is mixed. While using labor-intensive techniques in the consumer goods sector, they have tended to utilize capital-intensive and skill-intensive techniques in the producer goods sector. [21] Even in the latter, however, they have rejected some elements of capitalist technical rationality and sought to develop new organizational forms, such as the Two Participations and the Triple Combination, which are more consonant with their political and social goals.

The Yugoslav experiments with worker self-management are also techniques for overcoming elements of technical rationality and organization as developed in the context of capitalist industrialism, that is, to reduce hierarchy in the production process by increasing the participation of workers in managerial decision making. It would be interesting to examine one aspect of this problem by looking at the effects the multinational corporations based in capitalist countries have had when they have built plants in Communist countries, such as the Fiat automobile plant in the USSR. These effects include impacts on patterns of work organization, plant management, and commodity consumption. Are the organizational and administrative forms in these industries merely transplanted into those enterprises in recipient communist societies, or have there developed "nativist" forms of management and organization of work?

In the case of Cuba, Richard Fagen has referred to the Cuban view of "technology as the motor of abundance and a component of the new man. "[22] Castro has pointed to the crucial role of modern science and technology in the creation of wealth. In Fagen's view, "this commitment to bringing technology to bear on production is manifested in . . . a series of programs designed to increase productivity by borrowing, modifying, or developing an appropriate scientific style of labor. "[23] While interested in the process of technical transfer, however, the Cubans have been very much aware of the cultural consequences of their ability to create abundance through

science and technology while building a new communist culture and
creating the new Cuban man. From an analysis of Castro's speeches,
Fagen has pieced together the Cubans' conception of their dilemma
as follows:

> (1) The ideal Communist society is defined as a cultural
> system in which every man acts as a true brother to every
> other man. (2) It is not possible to achieve such a cultural
> system until abundance replaces want as the collective
> situation of the citizenry. (3) The very process of creating
> abundance, however, can easily destroy the potential of
> the abundant society for being a truly Communist society.
> (4) Thus a society must strive to achieve abundance by
> creating and nourishing those values and motivations—
> shared feelings about collective responsibility and gain,
> and an ethic of societal service—that will one day become
> internalized as the general character structure of Com-
> munist man. Above all, abundance achieved by appealing
> to individual aggrandizement, by rewarding egoismo (self-
> centeredness), leads inexorably not to Communism but
> to increased exploitation of man by man, increased indi-
> vidual alienation, and rising levels of social disorganiza-
> tion. [24]

This suggests that it is not merely technological "methods" that may
be in conflict with communist goals, but also that some originally
bourgeois goals that remain under communism, most especially the
notion of material wealth in the form of "abundant" individual consumption, may themselves be in conflict or contradiction with other
communist goals. This problem may derive from Marx, who stressed
"abundance" right alongside his keen insights into commodity fetishism.

Ends and means are never more than analytically separable,
but for certain analyses that distinction may be quite useful.
Here it seems appropriate to apply Anthony F. C. Wallace's important distinction between two elements of culture, goal culture and
transfer culture, to the innovated cultural system of communism.
The goal culture is the idealized image of a future communist society in which the new communist man lives in harmony with nature
and in cooperation with his fellow man. The transfer culture is the
system of techniques and procedures for achieving the goal culture. [25]
This distinction has found its way into recent discussions about communist political culture. [26] The focus of our interest is on one of
several elements of communist culture; this element is the ways in
which technology and technical rationality have been incorporated

into the transfer culture of several communist societies and the way those elements of transfer culture impact on the goal culture. This focus includes a concern for both transferred and nativist innovated elements of machine technology and technical rationality.

One of the major problems in the study of science and technology is that there is no unified body of theory upon which to draw. What theory does exist has been developed within the various disciplinary compartments of the social sciences. One result of this insulation has been that the process commonly referred to as "technical transfer" has been viewed in the very narrow sense of transfer of specific technical innovations from a donor to a recipient society. The study of the impact of that particular technical transfer has been limited to the way particular aspects of the <u>economic</u> system are affected, for example, the extent to which technical advances have widened the area of effective technical choice and reduced the objective constraints on central planners or the effect of continuing and extensive technical transfer on the level of native technological innovation within the recipient society. These questions are important indeed, but they focus on only one dimension of the process of technical transfer. [27]

A much broader perspective of the implications of technical transfer could be obtained by viewing this process as one dimension of cultural diffusion. In 1959, in the introductory article to the new journal <u>Technology and Culture</u>, Melvin Kranzberg quoted Edward B. Tylor's century-old definition of culture as "that complex whole which includes knowledge, belief, art, morals, laws, customs, and any other capabilities and habits acquired by man as a member of society."[28] As an artifact of human experience, technology must be viewed as an element of culture. The process of technological transfer, therefore, can be viewed as an aspect of the more general process of cultural diffusion. Placing the problem of technical transfer in the broader context of cultural diffusion would permit us to adopt a more appropriate use of the term technology, not in its narrow sense as industrial science, but in its broader sense as technique. William Leiss has expressed this broader meaning of technology as "the authoritative mode of the organization of human labor for the purpose of satisfying needs.[29] Professor A. Zvorikine of the USSR Academy of Sciences Institute of Philosophy has defined technology as "the means of work, the means of human activity developing within a system of social production and social life," a definition which he feels correctly reckons with both the material and social aspects of technology.[30]

In his study of technological transfer in Eastern Europe, Alexander Woroniak made the following suggestion:

Technology can be and has been conceptualized in a number of ways, each of which suggests different theoretical and operational approaches. The simplest version views technology as involving only changes in artifacts. A more sophisticated approach adds to the physical objects the labor and the managerial know-how. Finally, technology can be viewed as a "sociotechnological" phenomenon, by adding to the material and artifact changes the cultural, social, and psychological factors as well. [31]

In this study we start from the assumption of this broadest definition of technology as a "sociotechnical" phenomenon and an integral part of the basic values of every culture. Thus technological change in any culture has direct consequences for other cultural values. Margaret Mead states this as follows:

A change in any one part of the culture will be accompanied by changes in other parts, and . . . only by relating any planned detail of change to the central values of the culture is it possible to provide for the repercussions which will occur in other aspects of life. [32]

Some of the more basic and interesting questions related to technological change concern the impact of technology on other cultural values, and vice versa.

In order to be in a position really to understand the impact of technology on culture, we must know more than we do now about the impact of culture on technology and its development. Only by coming to grips with the question of the extent to which a particular technology in its formative stages is a reflection, embodiment, or reification of dominant cultural values will we be able to progress to a solution of the problems of the impact of technology on culture and the possibility of developing radically alternative technologies. Since the late 1950s, many fashionable volumes have been written concerning the impact of technology on culture—including, among the most popular and widely read, the works of Jacques Ellul, Emmanuel Mesthene, John Kenneth Galbraith, R. J. Forbes, Daniel Bell, and Zbigniew K. Brzezinski—but precious little has been written about the other side of the question, which is the impact of culture on the formative stages of technology at each of its successive stages of development—industrialization, mechanization, and automation and technetronics.

The important result of this decidedly one-sided approach has been a proliferation of theories that must be characterized as representing one form or another of technological determinism. In an important recent analysis, William Leiss suggested that

the confusions prevalent in the recent literature arise
from a failure to treat the particular question (namely,
the social consequences of technological progress)
within the context of a more general phenomenon (namely, the attempt to shape social behavior according to
rational standards and freely-chosen goals).[33]

Leiss suggests:

If technology is the organization of knowledge for practical purposes, what we need to know is: Who organizes
it? and how is it organized? Or, if we look at Forbes'
definition [of technology as "the product of interaction
between man and environment, based on the wide range
of real or imagined needs and desires which guided man
in his conquest of Nature"], we must ask: Who guided
the conquest of nature? and for what purposes? Lass-
well's conception, accepted by Ellul [technology as "the
ensemble of practices by which one uses available resources in order to achieve certain valued ends"],
prompts us to inquire: What ends? and how are they
selected?[34]

Technological determinist theories do not raise such questions
and hence do not permit us to evaluate the two-way dialectical interaction between technology and the cultural milieu. Instead these
theories "mark a retreat in the realm of social theory by isolating
the rationality of technology from the rationality of the whole" cultural milieu.[35] Leiss further contends:

The essential error in these theories is to isolate one
aspect of this totality (technology) and then to relate it
back to the totality in a mechanical fashion; accordingly, the cause-and-effect network is resolved upon analysis into a set of circular propositions. The result is
that a "technological veil" (to use Marcuse's term) is
cast over the social process which obscures both the
general dynamic of advanced societies and the specific
role of technology in that dynamic.[36]

One of the exceptions is the work of Stephen A. Marglin, who
has been centrally concerned with the cultural sources of technology
and technological innovation.[37] Stanley Aronowitz succinctly summarized Marglin's explanation of the emergence of technologies that
relied on the minute division of labor for accelerating output as
follows:

Contrary to most opinion, he denies the determining
role of either efficiency or the drive to maximize profit in the choice of production methods. Instead, specialization of tasks is seen as a product of the recognition by capitalists of the importance of devising technologies that maintain the crucial role of management
in organizing production. With the reduction of artisan
skills to relatively simple tasks, no individual worker
or group of workers is able to master the intricacies of
either the production process or the market, and the
capitalist's centrality to the process of production and
distribution of commodities, which consists in his ability to coordinate the relationship between the producers
and the market, remains secure. [In effect what Marglin has attempted to do is] to demonstrate that the organization of production according to this premise historically procedes the appearance of complex machinery
and was transferred to the machines socially.[38]

This argument can be linked with that of Schlomo Avineri to
provide a more complete picture of the historical evolution of the
factory system and production methods. It was, as Gorz and Marglin point out, the tradesmen who organized the artisans and crafts-
men into factory-type units for purposes of control.[39] Once organized in that fashion and given the increase in demand for goods
brought about by the discovery of new trade routes, it followed that
ways were developed to increase productive capacity. Hence the
beginnings of industrialization. "The industrial revolution for Marx
is not the beginning of the capitalist process, but rather its culmination. Capitalism precedes industrialization."[40] This, of course,
is precisely the same point argued by Lukács in his famous 1925 review of N. I. Bukharin's Historical Materialism:

The social preconditions of modern mechanized techniques
thus arose first; they were the product of a hundred-year
social revolution. The technique is the consummation of
modern capitalism, not its initial cause. It only appeared
after the establishment of its social prerequisites; when
the dialectical contradictions of the primitive forms of
manufacture had been resolved, when "At a given stage of
its development, the narrow technical base on which manufacture rested, came into conflict with requirements of
production that were created by manufacture itself" (Capital I). It goes without saying that technical development

is thereby extraordinarily accelerated. But this reciprocal interaction by no means surpasses the real
historical and methodological primacy of the economy
over technique. [41]

The core of this argument is that (1) the organization of production precedes the development of complex machinery; (2) this
organization of production was accomplished for purposes of control
of the workers; and (3) this social control was transferred to the
machine technology, and the system of production developed soon
afterward. The industrial revolution of the eighteenth and nineteenth
centuries is the source of the substantiation. Cooper describes this
as follows:

> In England after the bourgeois revolution in the second
> half of the 17th century capitalist manufacture became
> the dominant form of production but the system of tech-
> nology remained as before in the feudal formation, i.e.,
> hand tools remained the basic instruments of labour. In
> manufacture, however, a progressive breaking down of
> the labour process into a series of distinct operations
> took place; a process which led to the specialization of
> workers and to the differentiation and specialization of
> hand tools: "Differentiation, specialization and simplifi-
> cation of instruments of labour, brought about by the
> division of labour . . . are one of the technological,
> material preconditions for the development of machine
> production as one of the elements revolutionizing the
> mode of production and production relations." [Marx,
> Critique of Political Economy] Manufacture, by break-
> ing down the labour process into relatively simple,
> repetitive elements, created the conditions facilitating
> the transfer of the specialized hand tool from the human
> hand to a working mechanism, thereby forming what
> Marx termed the "working machine." It was the working
> machine, in Marx's view, which served as the starting
> point of the Industrial Revolution. This step did not
> occur simply as a result of the action of purely techni-
> cal forces, but was promoted by motive forces of a
> social nature. [42]

Most interestingly, it seems that a similar process occurred
in the early twentieth century, just prior to the introduction of mechanization. [43] Aronowitz describes this as follows:

> The substance of the professional engineer's job at the
> turn of the century was to organize the labor process
> in a way that yielded the highest possible profit. In
> many cases, his efforts were directed at finding ways
> to break down traditional skills into their components
> and to describe the limits of these discrete components
> as new jobs.[44]

It would seem not unlikely that a similar abstract dissection of
thought patterns played an important part in the development of cybernetics.

This is very much a part of the thinking of Taylor's "scientific
management" theory and flows from a dominant spirit of the times
described by Siegfried Giedion:

> The position is clear. Competition is growing. Wage-
> cutting has proved impractical as a means of lowering
> production costs. The machine tools are at hand. They
> will become continually further differentiated and more
> specialized, but few real improvements seem likely to
> raise productivity.[45]

The focus, then, shifted from new inventions to methods of organization within the plant that could lower costs and increase productivity.
Our primary point here can be made by briefly examining the main
contributions of two of the most outstanding contributors to the movement for rationalizing operations within the factory, Taylor and
Frank B. Gilbreth.

Probably the best place to start with Taylor is to recognize
that he viewed the factory as a completely closed organism; it was a
goal in itself. Taylor was only concerned with mechanical efficiency
and how things were manufactured, not with questions of what was
produced and why. It is common knowledge that Taylor was preoccupied with matters of human efficiency—how the human body can increase its productive capacity with a maximum of ease and a minimum of fatigue. What this meant in reality, Giedion suggests, is
that "the human body is studied to discover how far it can be transformed into a mechanism."[46] This study involved the minute scrutiny of the physical movements of the worker in performing his tasks.
After numerous experiments with time and motion studies of workers,
the most efficient way to perform each task was discovered and re-
corded as the job description for each worker. When it came to deciding which task would be performed when by each worker, Taylor
insisted on the "military type of organization":

> One of the cardinal principles of the military type of
> management is that every man in the organization shall
> receive his orders directly through the one superior
> who is over him. The general superintendent of the
> works transmits his orders on tickets or written card-
> boards through the various officers to the workmen
> in the same way that orders through a general in com-
> mand of a division are transmitted. [47]

The net result, Giedion suggests, is the automatization of the mass
of the workers, whereby "human movements become levers in the
machine."

Taylor's methods of time-motion study were greatly refined by
Gilbreth's cyclograph, or "motion recorder," which could photograph-
ically capture the forms of the worker's movements invisible to the
naked eye. "The light patterns reveal all hesitation or habits inter-
fering with the worker's dexterity and automaticity. In a word, they
embrace the sources of error as well as the perfect performance."[48]
On the basis of these refined methods, Gilbreth could be much more
precise in the contents of the Taylor-type "military dispatches" to
the workers. His Concrete System (1908) sets forth some 400 rules
for the process of ferroconcrete building. Gilbreth describes the
book as "almost a stenographic report of what a successful contractor said to his workmen."[49]

The foregoing suggests that the process of the "mechanization
of man" involved the breaking down of traditional skills into component parts, with each of these components described as a new job
(in effect an increased division of labor), and the observation and
recording of the minutiae of motions required to perform each task,
with these descriptions becoming the only acceptable ways to perform the task. All of this having been accomplished, the next logical
step was to replace the "human mechanism" with an inanimate mechanism.

If similar motive forces of a social nature (that is, requirements for control) stand behind the development of the next highest
stage of technological development—automation and cybernetics, the
quarternary level—then one must seriously question the ability of
automation to perform the function of human liberation that many
Western and socialist theorists attribute to it. Automation is clearly
liberating in certain respects. The drudgery, monotony, and physical
danger can be and has to some extent been reduced. Theoretically,
at least, the reduction of unrewarding toil can result in the opportunity for more creative and satisfying activities, although the substance
and range of those opportunities are of course socially determined.

Automation is not, however, without its drawbacks and real hazards, not all of which can be anticipated. One highly visible one is its requirements for inanimate energy. Many sources of energy in the world (wind, solar, tidal) are virtually without limit, but the sources that have been utilized and most of the ones immediately projected for harnessing to fill the rapidly escalating demands are either quantitatively limited (fossil fuels), ecologically disastrous (some forms of extraction and transportation of fossil fuels, nuclear energy, and some hydropower), and/or decidedly incompatible in their development with a free society (nuclear power).

The choice of power sources is an excellent example of the economic and social choices behind technological development. If capitalists opt in favor of solar, wind, and tidal energy, they can reap profits only from the techniques used to harness these free energy sources, and there is always the "danger" that these techniques will become part of the public domain. With nuclear energy (as, of course, with the fossil fuels), on the other hand, both the techniques for harnessing the energy source and the energy source itself can be controlled—for purposes of social control and for profit making. In addition, of course, the breeder reactor constitutes a real breakthrough, both technically and economically. The technological result is the production by the power plant, after approximately nine years, of fissionable raw material in quantities greater than the plant itself requires. The economic result is the capitalist's dream: self-reproducing resources that can be owned and controlled. The sun, wind, and tides satisfy the technical criterion of nondepletable resources, but since they cannot be owned, they do not satisfy the economic and social requirements of capitalism.

The social consequences of a nuclear energy policy are beginning to be painted in stark relief in the West, with research indicating, for example, that workers on nuclear power generators are subjected to strict regimentation and hierarchical controls because of safety factors; that a highly trained special military unit is required to guard such installations (called "nuclear parks" in the United States); and that the potential for blackmail is so high as to necessitate the suspension of civil liberties in the search for alleged thieves of materials such as plutonium, which could be used in the production of nuclear energy. [50]

For socialist theorists, and not without good reason, automation is a key component of the scientific and technological revolution. Of course, they feel that only under socialism can the revolutionary and liberatory potential of automation be fully realized. Under capitalism the "synthesis of revolutionary science and technology meets insurmountable obstacles." [51] As another Soviet source has put it, "the new scientific and technical revolution is beyond the capabilities

of modern rotting capitalism. As the CPSU program notes, socialism alone is capable of fully implementing its potential and utilizing
it in the interest of the whole of society. "52

There is an important element of this question of the liberatory role of automation that Soviet theorists have apparently continued to underplay, however. The capitalist industrial system is related to a particular mode of purposive rational action, that is; the
particular form of technical rationality that has developed through the
last 200 years of the industrial revolution in the capitalist West.

Although this concept of capitalist technical rationality is
quite a difficult one, it nevertheless seems to have some usefulness
in referring to a broad set of basic social attitudes, and as such
would include the dichotomization of means and ends, of work activity and product; the compartmentalization of knowledge; the separation of manual and mental labor; the human domination of nature;
efficiency defined in nonhuman terms; the hierarchical control of
production; and, underlying it all, the assumption of the priority and
insatiability of human material wants.

It is this technical rationality, perhaps more than the technological hardware itself, that has the greatest impact as cultural diffusion. Insofar as the communist countries, especially the USSR, have
accepted capitalist technical rationality as well as capitalist hardware, there arises the very real possibility that this process of cultural diffusion will inhibit the qualitative transcending of capitalist
industrial technology in the form of automation. That is, if automation is developed within the framework of a capitalist technical rationality, it may merely deepen the potential contradiction between
automation and liberation. So directed, the transfer culture of communism may come to acquire a degree of cultural autonomy that will
prove subversive of communist goal culture and, as in capitalist
states, prevent the realization of the liberating potential of automation. Such a development would not surprise the founders of the
Frankfurt School of Critical Social Theory, who argued that as technology develops it becomes an almost autonomous and mystical
force in society. 53

THE FOCUS OF THE CONFERENCE

The focus of the 1975 Bellagio Conference on Technology and
Communist Culture was the extent to which particular aspects of
imported machine technology and technical rationality have proven
to be more or less incompatible with the goal cultures of communist
societies and the ways in which these societies have attempted to
deal with this problem by means of selective adoption of foreign
technology and innovative indigenous developments.

The concept of communist "goal culture" has remained rather elusive. In referring to the future forms of communist society, the authors of Fundamentals of Marxism-Leninism[54] suggest that "It is pointless to guess at the definite forms this system will assume, but some of its general outlines can be discerned with a considerable degree of certainty." We can at least sketch those general outlines of communist goal culture that are common to Marx, Mao, Lenin, Khrushchev, Castro, Tito, and Brezhnev: full freedom of development of the human personality in the sociable and cooperative context of an egalitarian classless society; the elimination of private property and the selfishness and exploitation that go with it; the end of the domination and subordination that result from the discriminatory distinctions between mental and manual labor, town and countryside, and industry and agriculture that accompany the capitalist division of labor; the elimination of toil and drudgery through advanced economic and technical development and the cooperative, creative character of communist production for use value. The differences among various national communist movements and regimes exist not in regard to such general principles of goal culture, but to some extent in the more concrete forms they take in actuality and even more in the realm of transfer culture which is concerned with how to make real these (more or less concrete) ideals of the goal culture.

For purposes of illustration, let us examine two of these principles in order to identify the types of problems that may be encountered in the interaction between goal culture and transfer culture.

In an earlier ACLS Planning Group Conference on Peasant Rebellion and Communist Revolution in Asia, the discussions of several participants focused on the question of the separation between town and country and on how this separation would be overcome in the future by communist society. In his examination of utopian socialist themes in Maoism, Maurice Meisner suggested that the great differences among Marx, the utopian socialists and Russian populists, the Soviets, and the Maoists on this question were in the means employed to realize the common goal of elimination of differences between town and country. Meisner quotes Marx in the Grundrisse as saying that modern history "is the urbanization of the countryside, not, as among the ancients, the ruralisation of the city." For Marx the separation of town and country represented one important aspect of the social division of labor in presocialist societies. While in the short run urbanization was viewed as a historically progressive development, in the long run the solution of the problem was abolition of the distinction. Meisner suggests that the revolutionary role assigned to the peasant in Maoist theory and practice indicates that Mao "has been intent on reversing the direction of the modern historical process." Maoists, according to Meisner, re-

ject the theory of stages according to which urbanized and industrialized (capitalist) society becomes a necessary and hence progressive
stage of development in every country, including China—a necessary
stage of development prior to the elimination of the differences between town and country. Meisner concludes his paper as follows:

> The inversion of the Marxist view of the relationship be-
> tween town and countryside in modern revolutionary
> theory is by no means a distinctively Chinese Marxist
> phenomenon. Along with similar intellectual affinities
> with utopian socialist thought, it is found in contempo-
> rary Marxist ideologies in other areas of the world—
> most notably in the Castroist version of Marxism-Len-
> inism, in the neo-Marxist writings of Frantz Fanon, and
> the "African socialism" of Julius Nyerere. For Castro,
> for example, "the city is a cemetary of revolutionaries;"
> and for Fanon, the peasantry is the only revolutionary
> class, since the foreign-built towns are populated by a
> privileged and conservative proletariat as well as a
> parasitic bourgeoisie. [55]

In contemporary Soviet theory, one can find statements concerning the elimination of the social and economic distinctions between town and country, "but there is no ground for assuming that
large cities, as centres of industry and culture, will disappear." [56]
Meisner observes that while Soviet practice has

> perhaps confirmed Marx's original characterization
> of modern history as the "urbanization of the country-
> side," it has contributed nothing to the realization of
> Marx's goal of abolishing the distinction between town
> and countryside. Indeed if anything, the Soviet model
> of industrialization—and the urban elites it has spawned—
> has widened the gap between town and countryside. [57]

This may be seen by the Soviets as another reflection of the
fact that their particular circumstances necessarily keep them for a
while yet in that "short run."

Another concrete example of goal culture, and one that clearly
illustrates the conflict between goal culture and transfer culture, is
the cooperative character of communist production in developing a
more human culture. In their famous work The ABC of Communism,
N. I. Bukharin and E. Preobrazhensky discuss the goal culture of
communism, in which human culture will climb to heights never
attained before. It will no longer be a class culture, but will become

a genuinely human culture. "[58] A very important part of this more
human culture of communism is the replacement of occupational
specialization, which restricts the development of the human personality with cooperative forms of production:

> The cooperative character of communist production is
> likewise displayed in every detail of organization. Un-
> der communism, for example, there will not be perm-
> anent managers of factories, nor will there be persons
> who do one and the same kind of work throughout their
> lives. Under capitalism, if a man is a bootmaker, he
> spends his whole life in making boots (the cobbler
> sticks to his last); if he is a pastrycook he spends all
> his life baking cakes; if he is the manager of a factory,
> he spends his days in issuing orders and in administra-
> tive work; if he is a mere labourer, his whole life is
> spent in obeying orders. Nothing of this sort happens
> in communist society. Under communism people re-
> ceive a manysided culture, and find themselves at
> home in various branches of production: to-day I work
> in an administrative capacity, I reckon up how many
> felt boots and how many French rolls must be produced
> during the following month; to-morrow I shall be work-
> ing in a soap factory, next month perhaps in a steam
> laundry, and the month after in an electric power sta-
> tion. This will be possible when all the members of
> society have been suitably educated. [59]

This characterization of cooperative work under communism
is reminiscent of passages from Lenin's State and Revolution, written just two years before in 1917, during his "Walden-like" days at
Razliv. To any observer of the Soviet scene, however, it is quite
obvious that Soviet industrialization since 1917 has in fact resulted
in a great increase in occupational specialization. As Kendall Bailes
pointed out in a 1974 paper, this conflict between the necessity for
specialists on the one hand and the desire for the elimination of occupational specialization on the other has led to certain tensions in
Soviet society, which were manifested at the time of the First Five-
Year Plan in the trials surrounding the Industrial Party Case. [60]
Many Western analysts suggest that this dilemma represents one of
the important trade-offs the communists must continue to make between the apparently contradictory demands of goal culture and transfer culture. Whether or not occupational specialization will continue
to increase in Soviet society as it has in the past remains to be seen;
but since occupational specialization is so very much a part of the

infrastructure of capitalist industrialism, which the Soviet Union has consistently used as part of its transfer culture in order to create the material abundance necessary to achieve full communism, it is quite likely that it will persist for a long time to come and thereby perpetuate the strains between goal culture and transfer culture.

While occupational specialization illustrates the problem of conflict between goal culture and transfer culture, it is by no means the only aspect of the cultural infrastructure of capitalist industrialism that is relevant to this discussion, which must also be concerned with division of labor, hierarchical forms of management, worker competition, material incentives, differential wage scales, compartmentalization of knowledge, and so on. These are among the various elements of technical rationality and cultural infrastructure accompanying capitalist machine technology. They exist in socialist societies to varying degrees, along with the borrowed technological hardware, as elements of communist transfer culture, and they thereby represent contradictions to communist goal culture. An important task of this conference was a reasoned analysis of which of these elements is necessary to the use of capitalist machine technology and, indeed, which additional elements may be required.

It is quite possible, as some have suggested, that the existence of elements of capitalist technical rationality and infrastructure represent certain trade-offs between the economic requirements of efficiency on the one hand and the desire for congruency between ideological forms and practice on the other. According to this interpretation, communists desire capitalist machine technology for its ability to produce the material abundance necessary for the emergence of a classless society and the withering away of the state. They have discovered, however, that it is impossible to use this machine technology efficiently, that is, to have the same high output in relation to input that it does under capitalism, without utilizing capitalist forms of technical rationality and cultural infrastructure. In fact, some observers contend that despite increased diffusion of capitalist infrastructure and technical rationality into some socialist economies, the hardware still does not produce under socialism all that it produces under capitalism: it does not have a multiplier effect, and it does not give rise to new types of hardware of greater productive power.[61] This is not a universally held interpretation among Western scholars, and several of the contributors to this book directly challenge this notion of the necessity of such trade-offs, especially William Leiss, Andrew L. Feenberg, Robert F. Dernberger, and William N. Dunn.

The fact remains, nevertheless, that there has been a continuing diffusion of the forms of capitalist technical rationality and infrastructure into socialist societies (some much more than others)

over the years and that these have had sociocultural effects at the
level of transfer culture that appear to be subversive of, or dysfunctional to, communist goal culture and therefore are ideologically
embarrassing. Further, even one of the more optimistic theorists
of the scientific and technological revolution, Radovan Richta, suggests that "there is no getting round some awkward civilization problems stemming from the ill effects of the manually-operated machine
system on human beings, especially where arduous and stereotype
operations are involved."[62]

This matter of not being able to get around some of the awkward civilization problems of capitalist industrialism is much more
profound than even Richta will admit. While the solution of the problem is far from easy, the reason for its existence is fairly easy to
identify: machine technology does not and cannot exist in a vacuum.
It was developed in a particular context of cultural infrastructure and
technical rationality. Nathan Rosenberg put it as follows:

> We are now coming to realize that modern technology
> has a long umbilical cord. Innumerable unsuccessful
> foreign aid projects in the past twenty years—including
> Russian-sponsored as well as American-sponsored
> projects—have confirmed that when modern technology
> is carried to points remote from its source, without
> adequate supporting services, it will often shrivel and
> die. This is partly because the technology emerged in
> a particular context, often in response to highly narrow
> and specific problems, such as may have been defined
> by a particular natural resource deposit. But, more
> important, the technology functions well only when it
> is maintained and nourished by an environment offering
> it a range of services which are essential to its contin-
> ued operation.[63]

The question is not really whether or not the context of development
and the environment of usage are important for the successful operation of transferred technology, but rather, how much and which elements of the capitalist infrastructure and technical rationality must
accompany capitalist machine technology during the process of technology transfer.

In Chapter 1, on communism and the paradox of development,
Andrew L. Feenberg suggests the following succinct formulation of
this central issue:

> The diffusion of Western technology into different social
> systems highlights in something resembling an experi-

mental setting the paradox of development associated with it, which is the contradiction between this technology and human freedom. As this technology has developed willy-nilly in Western capitalist societies, it has become extremely difficult to separate in it what is universal—essential to any technological society—and what is contingent on Western culture and the specific requirements of the capitalist system. Only when this distinction has been made will it be possible to decide the fate of freedom in a developed technological society and determine on what general sort of technology it will have to be based. The communist experiments with Western capitalist technology can be seen as so many attempts to solve this problem in practice, some more promising than others.

In any case, the very existence of these experiments forbids the apriority of the many theories of "modernization" and "technological rationality," which take industrial societies as a single phenomenon, whatever the political system, and derive all their repressive features from "imperatives" of development. Rather, only aposteriori will it be possible to distinguish with any certainty the aspects of Western technology that are actually "technically determined" and those that are culturally or economically determined.

In order to proceed toward a clarification of this problem, the conference agenda and this volume were planned around three related sets of issues: Marxist perspectives on technology, technical transfer and innovation in socialist countries, and the impact of technology and technical rationality on socialist societies.

MARXIST PERSPECTIVES ON TECHNOLOGY

In their monumental work on the social and human implications of the scientific and technological revolution, Radovan Richta and his associates in Czechoslovakia focused on the scientific and technological revolution as "a cultural revolution of unprecedented proportions."[64] At the core of their analysis is a discussion of the transcendence of the traditional views of science and technology, which were products of capitalist industrial civilization. Central to any evaluation of the impact of technology on culture, therefore, is a comparative analysis of theoretical communist perspectives on science and technology, their relation to the economic base of society and to the relations and forces of production.

The place of science in the Bolshevik theory of cultural revolution in Russia has been described by Loren R. Graham as follows:

> The revolutionaries who came to power in Soviet Russia
> believed they would create a new culture. The adherents
> of the theory of proletarian culture believed the new cul-
> ture would begin to develop quickly, during the initial
> period of the dictatorship of the proletariat. Others,
> aware that this period should be relatively short, pre-
> dicted a novel culture only after the creation of a so-
> cialist state. A number of other revolutionary thinkers
> believed that the new culture would contain important
> elements of past cultures. All, however, subscribed
> in some degree to the belief that culture is a derivative
> superstructure above the economic base and that a modi-
> fication of the base inevitably results in a transformation
> of culture. Science was one of the layers of culture—
> perhaps the highest layer—and would also acquire unique
> characteristics. These characteristics would include
> a new theory of the place of science in society, a more
> fertile economic environment for technological growth,
> unprecedented governmental support for research, a
> superior organizational scheme of research institutes,
> and methodology for the planning of science. A socialist
> science would eventually evolve, a science superior to
> all its capitalist competitors. That transformation would
> be difficult, but the final product would be worth the
> cost. [65]

Communist attitudes toward science and technology have not been constant or uniform, and the historical development of communist theories of science and technology appears to be infused with a feeling of ambivalence. Soviet theory and practice can be divided into three distinct stages: (1) Early Bolshevik theory viewed science and technology as the great transformers of society. Lenin's enchantment with electrification and with Taylor's scientific management were but two manifestations of these early attitudes. (2) This early optimism about the transforming powers of science and technology was followed by a period of disillusionment beginning in the late 1920s, in which pure science was subordinated to "praktikat." (3) In the post-Stalin era, the Soviet leadership has increasingly come to realize that science and technology require considerable autonomy to realize their full growth and development potential. [66] Symptomatic of this third period is the "discovery" of the new status of science, described by Richta as follows:

> Science has penetrated the foundations of contemporary
> society, infused the dynamics of historical movement so
> thoroughly that the whole pattern of change appears as
> a "research revolution" and the coming age as one of
> "scientific civilization." If we free the innumerable
> reflections on this subject from the fog of popular illu-
> sions that see science as a magic wand without identi-
> fying the social and human sources of its power, we
> discover that the crux lies in the new status of science.
> This type of human activity, which has hitherto served
> primarily as a factor of social consciousness, is now
> fully and self-evidently proving its worth as a produc-
> tive force. [67]

In the Soviet case, part of this new role of science was its shift from
the superstructure to the base, as the 1961 Party program announced
that science was becoming a productive force—a position that had
been elaborated by Max Horkheimer some 25 years earlier. [68]

The Chinese communists were never as fully committed as the
Bolsheviks to science and technology as the great transformers of
society, but they had strong tendencies in that direction up until the
period of the Great Proletarian Cultural Revolution (GPCR). Since
then, however, they have entered the second Soviet stage of development, with a great emphasis on "praktikat," at least in areas such
as medicine, consumer goods, and agriculture (for example, the
"barefoot" doctors and agronomists). To what extent they have
entered the third Soviet phase in some sectors is still open to question. [69]

We must also explore the relationship of science and technology with the economic base and parts of the superstructure. While
the Soviets have tended to view technology as essentially science-
based (along the model of the capitalist West, albeit with an allegedly transformed science), the Chinese have viewed technology as "the
summation of labor in action," eschewing the idea that technology is
science-based. Labor, not science, is the source of technical creativity. The Chinese model has proceeded on the nativist assumption
that "the development of technology in China should depart as far as
possible from foreign industrial models." [70] As a result, the Chinese
have explicitly rejected, while the Soviets have explicitly accepted,
the originally bourgeois notion of technology as science-based. [71]

The differences between the Chinese and the Soviets concerning
the sources of technology are reflected in their different approaches
to the organization and planning of scientific and technological research. If, as Richta suggests, "science is emerging as the leading
variable in the national economy and the vital dimension in the

growth of civilization, "[72] then the consequences for the organization
of scientific research are likely to be quite different from a system
based on the Maoist virtues of self-reliance and struggle in industrial development. The Soviet position on the status of scientific research is probably most clearly stated in Keldysh's Proportion,
which stipulates the proper relationship between science, technology,
and production in the period of the socialist scientific and technological revolution as follows:

> In the new historical situation . . . it is necessary that
> our technology should grow and develop faster than
> heavy industry and that the natural sciences, represent-
> ing the main basis of technological advance and the main
> source of the most profound technological ideas, should
> exceed the rate of development of technology. [73]

It follows from Keldysh's Proportion that scientific work
should have the highest priority. [74] Hence, beginning in the early
1960s, the earlier restrictions on the Soviet Academy of Sciences
to insure that it concentrated on "practical work" were relaxed, and
pure scientific research began to enjoy increased autonomy as the
leading force in the scientific and technological revolution. [75] Of
course, Soviet scientific research is still planned and integrated
closely with the state's economic plan, but it is no longer subordinated to "praktikat." The Technical Services Department was retained as a branch of the academy, but no longer dominated it. The
academy emerged as a center for fundamental scientific research.
Since 1965 there have been increased efforts to integrate scientific
research more closely with production, but this has not gone so far
as to subordinate pure scientific research to "praktikat."[76]
     This is in sharp contrast to the Chinese model, which rejects
"bourgeois" science-based technology as an alien form. The concept of the technical revolution means something very different to
the Chinese following the Maoist model than it does to Richta and
some Soviet theorists. For the former it means technical democracy,
the advance of production over technology and technology over
science. [77] For the Soviets, it means technology over production and
science over technology. The Maoist model starts with the interaction between technology and culture rather than with pure science.
The result is a great emphasis on "praktikat," which carries beyond
science to education generally. If one starts with the relationship
that must exist between technology and cultural attitudes, then these
relationships become the measures by which everything else gets
evaluated, including education, science, research, and organization
of production methods. The Chinese appear to have been willing to

accept various kinds of disruptions, problems, and uncertainties in order to maintain the priority of sociopolitical goals, an important example being the complete reorganization of the Chinese Academy of Sciences. The academy's 120 institutes were reduced in number to only 20, with the remaining 100 converted into practical institutes and attached to factories. This has broader implications for education generally, when every factory comes to have a school and every school has a factory. Factory workers run the high schools and universities, and this includes monitoring the effect of the science and technology courses on the students' general attitudes and development and making sure that these are kept in harmony. [78] The Taching oilfield is celebrated as the epitome of the proper relationship between science, technology, and socialist cultural norms. The production method employed was the "three-in-one method" of "combining cadres, technicians, and workers into a harmonious team with full cooperation and equality." [79] The basic differences between the Soviet and Chinese models of the organization and planning of the scientific and technological research styles of technological innovations in those countries. The Chinese model leads one to question the extent to which basic scientific research can be limited in an effort to achieve sociopolitical goals without significant consequences for technological development. On the other hand, the Soviet model leads one to question the extent to which the emphasis on basic scientific research and the "bourgeois" approach to science-based technology has grave consequences for the communist goal culture. The Soviet and Chinese models probably form the two poles between which other communist systems can be located, even if not linearly, and that is our reason for emphasizing them in this limited discussion.

Since a number of these questions regarding Soviet and Chinese perspectives on science and technology have been explored in the literature already discussed, the three chapters by Leiss, Feenberg, and Cooper discuss different dimensions of Marxian perspectives on technology, primarily in relation to cultural and political factors in the transition from capitalism to socialism. Leiss, in Chapter 2, discusses ideal typical formulations of the role of technology under capitalism and socialism. Feenberg, in Chapter 1, discusses the relevance of Marx and the Marxian theory of the transition. Cooper, in Chapter 3, guides us through contemporary Soviet theories about the role of technology in the transition, as discussed in theories of the "scientific and technological revolution."

Leiss focuses on the role of technology in social change—a role, he argues, that "can only be understood in relation to the crucial areas of contradiction in modern society." The areas within which these important social contradictions unfold are what he terms the "predominant modes of social reproduction": commodity production, bureaucratic authority, and domination over nonhuman nature. Concerning the relationship between communist goal culture and transfer culture, Leiss argues that "the efficacy of techniques can only be judged concretely in relation to explicit goals and the processes that seem appropriate to them. In any case, the choice of techniques will depend upon the specific conditions of time and place, taking into account such contingent factors as inherited cultural traditions." He concludes, in contrast to the argument presented in this introduction, that the problem of transfer of technology from capitalist to socialist states "is not some incompatibility between transferred techniques and ultimate purposes, but rather the exacerbation of internal social contradictions through the transfer of technologies." In Leiss's formulation, the transfer of technology itself does not present any inherent difficulties in communist transfer culture in relation to the goal culture.

This argument is supported by Feenberg, who argues that modern technology is itself contradictory in essence, at one and the same time making possible a transition to socialism and also providing a basis for forms of elite rule incompatible with socialism. By this account, the success of socialism would mean the resolution of this contradiction in the technology in favor of a new type of industrial apparatus designed to be employed by a very different type of labor force. Thus, there are no "technological imperatives" in modern technology that are inherently "subversive" of communist goal culture. Rather, modern technology is ambivalent with regard to ends—its impact on the development of society depends on the context of social and political power in which it is itself developed and transformed.

TECHNOLOGY TRANSFER AND INNOVATION IN SOCIALIST COUNTRIES

The experience of the several communist states with regard to technological transfer has been mixed. In the case of Czechoslovakia a significant industrial base had already been established by the time of communist control. This was not the case in the USSR, China, and much of Eastern Europe. The Soviets were at a decided disadvantage in their early efforts to industrialize because there was no other communist society on which they could rely for assistance, let alone one with a more advanced industrial sector. As a result of that circumstance and of their desire to prove themselves economically and politically competitive in the short run, the Soviets had to rely on the more industrially advanced capitalist countries as sources of technological imports. During the period of rapid industrialization beginning in the late 1920s, they appeared to give preference to large-scale U.S. methods, as follows:

> Certainly the high regard for U.S. technology is well documented in Soviet sources. For example, the admiration of the American engineer Hugh Cooper, who supervised the building of both Muscle Shoals (a dam on the main stream of the Tennessee River) and the Dnepr River hydro-electric system (a key project in the Soviet First Five-Year Plan) was symbolic of the Soviet view of American technical assistance. Moreover, the American approach to mass production in machine-building was chosen in the First Five-Year Plan over the European small-scale operations. The Soviet tractor and automobile industry were applications of American mass production techniques. [80]

The extent of Soviet borrowing from capitalist technology has led one scholar to conclude that "Western technical assistance was the major causal factor in Soviet economic growth for the period 1928-1945."[81] As John P. Hardt points out, however, this interpretation is disputed by Richard Moorsteen and Raymond P. Powell, who have argued "in a 1966 study that the major part of Soviet economic growth can be attributed to increments in capital and labor, rather than technological progress."[82] It is not necessary to resolve this dispute in order to conclude that technological transfer from capitalist countries was of major importance to Soviet economic development.

In order to understand technology transfer and thereby approach a realistic assessment of its impact on the recipient society, it must be realized that the international transfer of technology is a complex process that can take a variety of forms that may have quite different economic and social consequences. The British economist Philip Hanson has suggested an important threefold distinction in forms of technology transfer. First, technology transfer may be vertical or horizontal. That is, the technology may be transferred "between stages of the product cycle (e. g., going from applied research to development and from development to production)" or it may be transferred "between places or institutions at a given stage of the product cycle."[83]

Second, the technology may be transferred in either embodied or disembodied forms. "For our present purposes we can think of embodied transfer as the transfer of technology embodied in products, especially machines. Disembodied transfer will then refer to

useful technical knowledge carried by persons or documents. Embodied transfer, to be effective, usually needs to be accompanied by
some disembodied transfer."[84]

Third, the channels of technology transfer may be either ne-
gotiable or nonnegotiable.

Among the mechanisms of technology transfer employed by the
Soviet Union at one time or another in its transactions with the capitalist West are (1) "reverse engineering," or copying Western technology originally purchased as prototypes, (2) the purchase of embodied technology, (3) the purchase of licenses, (4) joint-stock companies, and (5) industrial cooperation. These mechanisms are not
easily interchangeable because they are each dependent on a different set of circumstances, not only in the international political and
economic situation, but also in the political and economic conditions
of both donor and recipient. From recent analyses and reports it
seems clear that an important shift has taken place in Soviet, and
perhaps also Chinese, mechanisms of receiving transferred technology.

Marshall I. Goldman has suggested that the preferred Soviet

> technique (except during the early 1930s, the Lend Lease
> years, and 1959-63, when they undertook to buy whole
> factories) was to buy one or two prototypes of a finished
> product and then reproduce both the product and the fac-
> tory process. In this way the Russians reproduced an
> array of products ranging from coal-mining equipment
> and scotch tape to trucks and Polaroid cameras.[85]

This approach has some very serious shortcomings, however, especially if the purpose of such "borrowing" is to close the technology
gap:

> As technological change became more rapid, it was
> almost certain that the copy and the process would be
> obsolete by the time the Russians had managed to dupli-
> cate the production stage. Because of the difficulty in-
> volved in trying to reproduce someone else's work,
> moreover, such products also tended to be outdated,
> more expensive and qualitatively inferior to the ori-
> ginal. Consequently, the decision was made to go back
> to the practice of buying whole factories and licenses
> rather than prototypes.[86]

In order for the Soviets to purchase whole factories and licenses in significant quantity to have a positive impact on the rate of

technological development, enormous amounts of convertible currency were necessary—amounts far in excess of what the Soviets had and have available, given their desire not to rely solely on their substantial gold reserves to finance these transactions. One mechanism developed was the joint-stock company, in which both the Western and Eastern partner would contribute a certain percentage of equity. In the long run the joint-stock company has proved an unsatisfactory mechanism since the Eastern partner is reluctant to give the Western partner more than 49 percent equity and the Western partner is not likely to risk large sums of foreign investment in which it has less than 51 percent interest. However, according to Goldman,

> Although the Russians have been squeamish about allowing Western or Japanese firms to operate and share equity profits inside the territory of the U.S.S.R. (even the Occidental Petroleum and Pullman deals involve only the sale and barter of equipment and technology), they have no qualms about Russian firms engaging in such "unorthodox" practices in the West. [87]

In addition to the control and doctrinal problems for both sides, there is the problem of available capital. This is not a one-sided problem, as assumed by many Western observers of communism, who argue that it is the communists who are short of venture capital for joint-stock companies and who must be extended credits by the West in order to purchase embodied Western technology. The international economic situation has deteriorated so rapidly in the last few years that it appears to threaten the economic capability of the capitalist states either to supply substantial international credits, even at the prevailing market rate of interest, or to supply large amounts of venture capital for joint-stock companies. Factors contributing to this deteriorating position of the United States, for example, are a twice-recently depreciated currency; a crippling inflation rate; a serious balance of payments deficit; an intolerable unemployment rate; a negligible GNP growth; an economy that is operating at least one-fifth below its productive capacity; sectors of the production system, such as operating with antiquated machinery and processes; and a critical shortage of capital. This last point is particularly relevant to our present discussion:

> One projection based on present maximum estimates of [U.S.] energy-demand indicates that energy production could consume as much as 80% of all available capital in 1985. . . . Thus, compounded effects of a trend toward enterprises that inefficiently convert capital into

energy production threaten to overrun the system's
capacity to produce its most essential factor—capital.
This may well explain why, according to a recent New
York Stock Exchange report, we are likely to be $650
billion short in needed capital in the next decade.[88]

All of this suggests that the matter of venture capital and the economic crisis are not merely socialist problems, but rather worldwide
economic problems.

Despite these problems with traditional methods of technology
transfer from the West, the Soviets seem determined to catch up
with (and overtake) capitalism in terms of technological development.
Philip Hanson feels that there is greater awareness now by the Soviets that "catching up" with West is difficult—indeed, that it may be
increasingly difficult given the types and rates of changes in technologies. Hanson writes as follows:

It is possible that the proliferation of technologies in the
past two decades or so has made it increasingly hard to
keep up with the new products and processes simply by
screening the literature and buying individual machines
to use as prototypes. To absorb foreign technology in this
way may require an inordinate number of technologists
working in the design, testing and de-bugging of products
adapted from foreign prototypes. On paper, at least,
the USSR has about three times as many graduate engineers as the US, and yet there are many signs that the
civilian economy is short of competent personnel. No
doubt many Soviet engineers are poorly trained and
wastefully used, and no doubt many of the better ones
are in the defense sector. However, it might also be
that the Soviet effort to "keep up" with the latest foreign technology without very large outright purchasing
of hardware and know-how simply swallows up too much
skilled manpower. As the sheer number of products and
processes in existence, many of them subject to con-
tinual modification, goes up and up, it may be increasingly cost-effective for the Soviets to shorten lead-
times and save resources by the direct purchase of
western technology. . . . If this is so, the pressure
on them to expand such buying further and extend their
scientific and technological cooperation with the West is
considerable.[89]

Since the mid-1960s there has emerged a new mechanism of
East-West technology transfer that appears to alleviate many of the

economic, doctrinal, and control problems of the more traditional
mechanisms discussed above and also permits the communists to
"keep up" better with the capitalist West. That mechanism is most
generally known as "industrial cooperation" and has been defined by
the United Nations Economic Commission for Europe (ECE) as
follows:

> Industrial co-operation in an East-West context denotes
> the economic relationships and activities arising from
> (a) contracts extending over a number of years between
> partners belonging to different economic systems which
> go beyond the straightforward sale or purchase of goods
> and services to include a set of complementary or reci-
> procally matching operations (in production, in the
> development and transfer of technology, in marketing,
> etc.); and from (b) contracts between such partners
> which have been identified as industrial co-operation
> contracts by Governments in bilateral or multilateral
> agreements. [90]

Industrial cooperation can take at least six different forms:
licensing with payment in resultant products; supply of complete
plants or production lines with payments in resultant products; co-
production and specialization; subcontracting; joint ventures; and
joint tendering, joint construction, or similar projects. [91] While
there is not space here to explore this important subject in detail, a
few examples of Hungarian experiences will serve to indicate why
industrial cooperation has become an increasingly important and
more frequently utilized mechanism of technology transfer.

In a 1974 study, "Some Legal and Financial Aspects of Industrial Co-operation," the Hungarian economist Egon Kemenes described three industrial cooperation relationships between Hungarian
and Western firms that clearly indicate some advantages of this
mechanism to both sides:

> In the framework of a co-operation contract concluded
> between TECHNOIMPEX Hungarian Machine Industries
> Foreign Trade Company and the CSEPEL Machine-Tool
> Factory, on the one side, and the FRG firm Hermann
> Kolb on the other, the FRG firm has ceded to the Hungar-
> ian enterprise, free of charge, the license of the drilling
> head used in radial drilling machines, further the tech-
> nical documentation and know-how relating thereto; in
> return the Hungarian enterprise has undertaken to sell
> radial drills equipped with the above-mentioned special
> drilling heads to Messrs. Hermann Kolb, viz.: 40 ma-

chines in 1974, 60 machines in 1975, 20 in 1976. Further deliveries will depend on the market situation. The total value of the 120 machines is, 5.5 million marks.

There is an obvious difference between the said contract and a simple subcontractor's agreement relating to the supply of accessories: in a way it is just the reverse of the latter, as the major part of the value of deliveries is made up by the radial drill which had been delivered and is manufactured by the Hungarian company. The special drilling head—whose license is owned by the FRG firm—is but a component of the machine which, however, represents the latest advance in its field.

Neither is this a case of joint production of equal proportions; in fact the respective contributions of the two partners are rather asymmetric. More precisely, there are two asymmetries, on two fields: as to the value of the finished product to the benefit of the Hungarian enterprise, while on the field of the technological level, to the benefit of the FRG firm. The two asymmetries offset each other: this is how the reciprocity of interests becomes manifest.

It is equally clear that the long duration of the contract is important for both parties. This, again, is one of the factors in a co-operation contract.

Thanks to this contract, the FRG firm obtained additional capacities without costly investment, without the need of financing them either from its own means or from credits.

A similar co-operation contract has been concluded by TECHNOIMPEX together with the Esztergom (North-Transdanubia) plant of the Machine-Tool Works and the West-Berlin firm Fritz Werner, concerning knee-type milling machines. The West-Berlin firm grants the Hungarian enterprise the production license, the technological documentation, and the electrical equipment of the machines. However, in this case the finished product is marketed both in the Western and Eastern countries.

A further example in the range of the food-processing industry is the co-operation between MIRELITE enterprise (Hungarian Deepfreezing Industry) and the Swedish firm FINDUS. (Both firms are engaged in producing deep-frozen foods.) The Swedish firm has handed over its production methods and technical experience to the Hungarian company and in return it receives items

produced with the help of these processes. This way
the product range of the Swedish firm is widened by
the Hungarian fruits and vegetables. This co-operation deal, too, is characterized by large-scale production and long duration.

These few examples explain why payment is
effected in many cases by supplies of products. [92]

As of 1974 it was estimated that at least 1,000 industrial cooperation agreements had been developed between CEMA and Western
countries. Only about 160 of these agreements involved the USSR,
but the Soviet agreements tend to be much larger in scope and magnitude. [93] There is evidence, however, to indicate that in the future the
Soviets will rely increasingly on the compensation mechanisms in
certain forms of industrial cooperation described above. [94] In sum-
marizing the advantages of industrial cooperation mechanisms, a
1973 ECE report concluded as follows:

East-west industrial co-operation, in addition to any advantages it may offer in terms of the speedier transfer
of technology or the mutual opportunities for enlargement
of markets, has a positive contribution to make to the
dynamism of east-west trade to the extent that it (a) enables trade in the most dynamic categories of manufactures (especially research—or skill-intensive products)
to grow faster than would otherwise be the case; and (b)
provides financial or payments arrangements which make
possible a faster growth of east European imports. [95]

The advantages to the communists of industrial cooperation,
especially those forms involving compensation mechanisms, are
clear from the Hungarian examples. Cooperation obviates the necessity for hard-currency payment and the extension of foreign credits.
It makes available to the Eastern partner the latest technical innovations in the West, thereby releasing skilled personnel from costly
R&D commitments. It also provides Western markets for the Eastern
products.

Industrial cooperation has its liabilities and disadvantages as
well. Insofar as the communists fail to develop their own R&D capacity, they must always lag behind the West in technical innovations.
To be sure, industrial cooperation reduces the time lag between
Western innovation and Eastern implementation, but it is also subject to the whims of the international political environment. In addition, it has been suggested that industrial cooperation tends to lock
the communists into the Western production cycle and the vicissitudes

of Western markets, especially when the Eastern partner sells finished products in Western markets.

In addition, where an industrial cooperation arrangement calls
for compensation by the Eastern partner in finished products (as
opposed to raw materials), the Western partner has a decided interest in quality control of production, and in the case of the USSR this
is "a function which cannot be effectively exercised by non-Soviet
personnel under existing Soviet regulations. Before the Western
participant could direct any meaningful quality control, Soviet policies would have to be altered to permit a management role for the
Western enterprise."[96] While there does not yet appear to be any
official Soviet acceptance of such reforms, there is some evidence
in Soviet pronouncements "suggesting that new forms are being considered which, while stopping short of an equity or ownership position for the Western partner, might provide a measure of participation which would approximate long term contractual arrangements
traditional in the West."[97] Where the communists accept Western
definitions of standards of quality control and monitoring of production, there will be some heavy costs. One set of costs relates to
foreign personnel acquiring detailed knowledge of the Eastern partner's economy and production processes. This is an intelligence
cost. For our present purposes, however, there is a more important cost. In these areas of joint control, the communists would be
prevented by contract from experimenting with new forms of technical rationality in an effort to develop truly socialist forms of technical rationality that would be more congruent with the goal culture of
communism.

The foregoing discussion suggests the spectre of technological
interdependence between capitalist and socialist societies. In Chapter 4, on "Technology Transfer and Change in the Soviet Economic
System," Hardt and Holliday assess the shift in the Soviet preferences in technology transfer mechanisms from a traditional approach
that "relied on short-term arrangements designed to rapidly achieve
specific domestic production goals with minimal personal contacts
with Western managers, engineers, and technicians" toward what
they term a "modified systems approach" to technology transfer.
This new approach is characterized by the following elements: "a
long-term or continuous connection; complex or project-oriented
industrial cooperation; systems-related construction, production,
management, and distribution; and Western involvement in the
training and the decision-making process both in the Soviet Union
and abroad." They suggest that the traditional approach was designed
to achieve Soviet economic and technological independence from the
West, whereas the modified systems approach indicates the acceptance of a much greater degree of economic and technological inter-

dependence. Their case studies of Western technology transfer to the Soviet automotive industry (the Gorkiy Automobile Plant built during the late 1920s with the assistance of the Ford Motor Company, the Volga Automobile Plant—VAZ—built during the 1960s with the assistance of Fiat, and the Kama River Truck Plant—KamAZ—currently being constructed with massive assistance from many Western firms) clearly illustrate this shift in the Soviet approach to technology transfer.

Hardt and Holliday suggest that the shift from independence to interdependence is a relatively recent development by the Soviets and has been taking place on a step-by-step basis since the early 1970s. The implications of this shift for communist transfer culture and goal culture in the USSR will be discussed in the concluding chapter to this volume. Suffice it to state here that Hardt and Holliday present convincing evidence that the modified systems approach is gaining momentum in the USSR and will have the effect of locking the Soviets into some long-range commitments regarding interdependence. Elsewhere Philip Hanson has presented a more cautious conclusion "with no firm views about the future development of East-West economic interdependence but with at least some grounds for expecting it to increase, so far as Soviet interests are concerned."[98]

Supporting the view of increased Soviet interdependence is a 1974 statement by Ivan D. Ivanov, chief of the Economic Division at the Institute of United States Studies of the Soviet Academy of Sciences: "the traditional ways and means of trading have been supplemented, step by step, with new, nontraditional arrangements based mainly on the internationalization in production and research and development (R and D)."[99]

Another dimension of increased interdependence is the changing communist attitude toward capitalist multinational corporations, which Jozef Wilzcynski has described as "the move from traditional prejudice to modern collaboration."[100]

The transfer of technology into China has been different in several respects. Up until 1957-58 the Chinese appeared keen on industrializing by the Soviet path and had the added advantage of being able to rely on Soviet technical and managerial assistance in realizing this program. From 1952 to 1960, China's annual imports from communist countries were much greater than her imports from noncommunist countries. In 1961 the latter surpassed the former for the first time since 1951. This transfer of technology from communist states, especially from the USSR, included machinery, whole plants, and entire industrial complexes, with a sizable increase in transfer taking place during the period of the Great Leap (1957-60). In 1960 the Soviet Union withdrew its technicians from China, and trade between the two countries fell off substantially. Since 1961 imports from noncommunist countries have surpassed those from communist countries, and the gap widens annually. In addition, Chinese imports of machinery and equipment fluctuated significantly between 1965 and 1970.[101] Since 1970 there has been a rapid increase in the machinery and equipment imports of the People's Republic. Nevertheless, China seems far from moving in the direction of technological and economic interdependence with the capitalist West, as the Soviet Union has in recent years. In sharp contrast to the Soviets, the Chinese have not accepted industrial cooperation in its various forms as a focal mechanism for technology transfer. Instead, as Hans Heyman has stated, "for China today, the more significant forms of foreign technology acquisition are industrial exhibitions, prototype copying, and purchase of complete plants."[102]

In Chapter 5, on "Economic Development and Modernization in Contemporary China," Robert F. Dernberger analyzes Chinese experience with the transfer of machinery and equipment. He suggests that the People's Republic has fluctuated between two seemingly contradictory policies of self-reliance and the import of foreign technology. Chinese policy does not represent so much a conflict between theory and practice as it does a policy of compromise based on a scheme of dual technological development as follows:

> On the one hand there is the modern sector—the core of China's industrialization, consisting of large-scale, capital-intensive projects, relying heavily on imported technology; on the other hand, there is the rural, small-scale sector, which is very significant in both its contribution to total supply and to China's development potential. . . . This simultaneous commitment to both rural, small-scale, "native" industries and urban, large-scale, modern industries is neither schizophrenic behavior nor dishonest propaganda. It is merely sound development policy.

Dernberger's conclusions concerning the impact of this large-scale borrowing of modern industrial machinery and equipment are particularly noteworthy. While he does not reject the notion of "technological imperatives" and their impact on the infrastructure of the borrowing country, he argues emphatically (in contrast to Richard Baum in Chapter 7) that Chinese borrowing did not result in large-scale corruption of the Maoist cultural revolution. Instead the impact of these "imperatives" has so far been limited to the large-scale, modern, urban, industrial sector, which, Dernberger argues, is only "a relatively small segment of China's total society."

The question of technological innovation in communist societies has been viewed by many Western analysts in the context of the dichotomy between economic efficiency and political control, suggesting that a choice must be made for one or the other.[103] That is not a satisfactory posing of the issue, however, since this approach prejudges the compatibility of efficiency and political control (or cohesion) and discounts the goal culture factors, which in some of these countries are given great weight and which were a major concern of the Bellagio conference. In addition, "economic efficiency" is a relative, not an absolute, concept. That is to say, economic efficiency is relative to time and place; it all depends on how one defines the parameters of the system and which factors thereby become exogenous and which ones endogenous. One cannot arbitrarily isolate a narrow range of purely economic factors and then argue that these are the absolute standard for any calculation of economic "efficiency." Indeed, that has been the tendency of capitalist economists, who, through disclaimers such as ceteris paribus and assumptions such as infinite growth, construct artificial parameters of ideal economic models. Likewise, innovation in the strictly economic sense does not deal with qualitative factors. It is a strange social calculus that regards a new antimissile missile, a new electric comb, a new chemical fertilizer, and a new heart pacer each as one innovation per 100,000 population—and yet that is the usual method of calculating innovation economically.

While there is little doubt that internal organizational and political factors contribute to an explanation of differences among countries in their ability to engage in technological innovation, consideration of these factors is beyond the scope of this project.

The following rather pessimistic view of Soviet technological innovation up to 1946 has been presented by Sutton:

> No major plant under construction between 1930 and 1945 has been identified as a purely Soviet effort. No usable technology originated in Soviet laboratories except in the case of synthetic rubber.[104]

The record of Soviet technological innovation since 1946 has been quite different. John P. Hardt writes as follows:

> Soviet achievements since World War II in military and space technology, presumably independent of technology transfers from the West, raise doubts of the current validity—even accepting its earlier basis—of the view that Soviet industry is incapable of generating necessary

technological change. Certain civilian sectors have also
made important technological innovations. Huge Soviet
expenditures on research and development have apparently created a new capability for generating technology.[105]

It is quite possible that the great advances in Soviet aerospace and
military technical innovation can be traced to quite different organizational methods and incentives to innovate in those sectors.

Robert W. Campbell has pointed to the possibility of management spillovers from the Soviet aerospace and military programs to
other sectors of the economy. The U.S. experience suggests that
the space program and technologically advanced defense program are
"unprecedentedly complex programmes to manage, and present
novel problems in controlling quality, designing for reliability, and
coordinating the efforts of a very large number of participants in a
context of urgency and uncertainty."[106] He assumed that "The Soviet
Union, in managing its space and military programmes, has surely
confronted the same requirements for managerial innovation and the
presumptive Soviet success in meeting these requirements strikes
one as a sharp contrast to the ineffectiveness with which analagous
problems are handled elsewhere in the economy." In examining "the
extent to which Soviet planners have succeeded in harnessing the
organizational and managerial experience of the space and military
efforts to improving planning and management elsewhere in the
economy," Campbell concluded (1) that "the space and military programmes have indeed been the source of important breakthroughs";
(2) that "there is a lot more indication of spillover of managerial
innovations than of innovations in processes, materials, hardware";
(3) that "it seems to have been very difficult for the Russians to identify innovations in space and military programmes and bring them to
the attention of an authority able to cut across the secrecy barrier
and to get them transferred"; and (4) that "the most serious bottlenecks in the diffusion process seems to be on the receiving end.
Apparently, many managerial weaknesses persist in the general
economy not because there is no known technique for handling a problem, but because the incentive system is such that management has
no real interest in improving aspects of its performance."[107]
Richard Baum's reference to the defense sector as the "technological vanguard" of Chinese industry suggests that this difference in
innovation systems among sectors of socialist economies may not be
limited to the Soviet experience.[108]

While the record of Chinese Communist success in technological innovation is still quite unclear, it is clear that the principles
underlying the sources of technological innovation diverge significantly from both the Western science-based model and the Soviet

science-based plus centralized planning model. As we have noted, the Chinese model starts from the assumption that labor is the source of technical creativity. Rensselaer W. Lee III has described this Chinese model as follows:

> "Technology," according to a statement written during the Great Leap, "does not fall from the skies," but is the summation of labor in action. Hence, the argument runs, technology is nothing mysterious and can be easily grasped by the masses of people. As the property of the masses, theories develop primarily on the basis of innovations and creations made in response to practical problems of production. To argue that theory is primarily deductive and develops according to autonomous inner laws is, the communists argue, to defend the class nature of ideas, to deny the creative intelligence of the laborer, and to confine his role to the mere working out in practice of designs formulated by specialists. [109]

The concrete consequences of the practice of technical democracy could be significant indeed:

> The postulated dependence of new technology upon the creations of the masses in China has led in practice to the institutionalized participation of workers in technical designing of new equipment, processes, and products. [110]

The result is the Tachai Scale System in agriculture and the Taching Three-in-One Combination in industry (described below).

In Chapter 6 of this book, Lee compares and contrasts the Soviet and Chinese Communist methods of mass innovation. He suggests that the Soviet approach to mass innovation represents an effort to develop a truly communist form of technical rationality and consists of three distinct elements or dimensions:

> Mass innovation in the USSR is a multidimensional concept—one that embodies legal, social, and ideological as well as technical principles. To the extent that it serves purposes and involves agencies that are external to the technical-administrative components of the productive system, it may be seen as a form of "Communist" technical rationality.

The second element of the Soviet approach is as follows:

> A second manifestation of "Communist technical ration-
> ality" lies in the realm of what might be called "social
> control"—use of "extrabureaucratic" (and extralegal)
> agencies to promote mass innovation and to assure the
> flow and implementation of technical novelty within
> Soviet industry.

The third element is as follows:

> The third, and possibly the most explicit example of
> communist technical rationality in the sphere of inno-
> vation is the linkage, in Soviet thought, of creative la-
> bor to the ideological "goal culture"—to the normative
> order that reflects the legitimating political value of
> the Soviet regime. Mass technical creativity is hailed
> as a vehicle for creating the outlines of the future com-
> munist society, a society in which the social distinc-
> tions between intellectual elites and manual laborers
> have been abolished and in which the productive process
> is dominated by a new type of individual, the "worker
> intellectual."

Despite some superficial similarities, Lee concludes from his
comparative analysis that there are basic differences between Chinese "technical democracy" and Soviet "creative labor." These
differences in the Soviet and Chinese approaches to mass participation are very much related to differences in perception of the industrialization process itself and the connection between goal culture
and transfer culture. Lee argues as follows:

> Unlike the Soviets, at least since the 1930s, the Chinese
> Communists have felt that the disappearance of major
> social distinctions, such as those between mental and
> manual labor, between city and village, can be implicit
> in the industrialization process itself. That is, these
> changes need not await a "postindustrial" stage of high
> automation and vast material wealth.

The implications of these differences will be discussed in the afterword.

At the beginning of our discussion of technical innovation, we
mentioned the problem of the relativity of the notion of efficiency to
both time and place. As a result, any calculation of efficiency must

take into account the parameters that define the given situation or calculus. Chinese technical democracy as a form of mass innovation illustrates the importance and relevance of this point to the present discussion. In Chapter 7, Richard Baum argues that "the vast majority of technical innovations successfully designed and implemented by ordinary workers have been relatively simple, relatively unsophisticated, relatively inexpensive, and only marginally useful." To the extent that this is an accurate depicting of the record, one might be tempted to conclude that Chinese mass innovation techniques are inefficient at best. As Baum is quick to point out, however:

> "Such mass-oriented mousetrap technology may be
> marginal only in a short-term, narrow economic sense,
> since there may well be significant social and educational
> utilities inherent in the process of participating in inno-
> vation that are not easily reflected in short-term econom-
> ic calculations."

The relativity of calculations of efficiency to the sociocultural context is further analyzed in Chapter 2 by William Leiss, in his discussion of socialist transformations of capitalist modes of social reproduction, and in Chapter 1 by Andrew L. Feenberg, in his discussion of new criteria of efficiency and social purpose under socialism.

THE IMPACT OF TECHNOLOGY AND
TECHNICAL RATIONALITY ON SOCIALISM

In the chapter on estranged labor from the 1844 manuscripts, Karl Marx states, "It is just in his work upon the objective world . . . that man first really proves himself to be a species being. This production is his active species life." Thus, for Marx, man's potential as a free individual and as a species being are both rooted in the nature of his productive activity. Nothing less than the harmonious, egalitarian, cooperative society and the liberated human individual (neither of which can exist without the other) are at stake in the communist attempts to revolutionize work to fulfill Marx's vision.

Some communist efforts in the organization and management of production have indeed been revolutionary in Marx's sense. One of the most notable has been Yugoslavia's worker self-management, which is institutionalized in the form of workers' councils, the theory of which Mihailo Marković describes as:

the fundamental cells of direct workers' democracy. Within the limits posed by the existing legislation and accepted general policies, these bodies would have full freedom to decide what to produce, what kind of services to offer, with whom to cooperate, how to organize work, in which direction to develop, and how to distribute income after making whatever contribution is necessary for the needs of the whole society.[111]

William N. Dunn concludes the following from his Chapter 8 analysis of "The Social Context of Technology Assessment in Eastern Europe":

Self-management may hold one of the keys to the recovery of socialist praxis under conditions of rapid scientific and technological change. . . . Demands for industrialization and economic development, which are intimately tied to the theme of scientific and technological revolution, have promoted strong tendencies toward the rationalization of production and management throughout Eastern Europe.

In spite of these pressures, Yugoslavia has so far

proved capable of achieving high rates of growth under conditions of minimal and selective external dependence on capital and technology.

This enables Dunn to make the following strong claim:

The case of Yugoslavia thus demonstrates that social organization is the form of mediation between technology and socialist practice.

Other very important revolutionizing organizational forms are the Chinese developments in the area of technological process innovation. The Two Participations, or two-group rotation system, involves cadre participation in productive labor and worker participation in management. The Taching System in industry (also called the Triple Combination or Three-Thirds System) is a " 'three-in one method' of combining cadres, technicians, and workers into a harmonious team with full cooperation and equality."[112] A third innovation is the Tachai Scale System, under which "workers receive points based on periodic self and group evaluations. While personal and civic qualities have taken precedence over productivity, evaluations are made according to five criteria: high skills; enthusiasm and motivation for work; support by the masses; honesty; and class consciousness. "[113]

Along with others we have not here analyzed, such as Soviet collectivization of agriculture, the early Cuban forms of agricultural production management, centralized economic planning, and social and economic service organization, these innovative organizational forms, some of which seem to have obvious democratizing effects, have been used in conjunction with a variety of forms of technological hardware. Nevertheless, especially in China, they seem to have been more successful in those economic spheres in which advanced capitalist industrial technology was not firmly rooted or widely adopted. This observation is not to provide an answer to one of the major questions posed for this conference, but rather serves as a kind of hypothesis about the relationship of revolutionary organizational and management forms of production with the various types of imported and native technology used in that productive process.

Such methods of organization and management of production introduce political and social elements that may clash with the so-called technological imperatives of production. It raises prominently the question of whether or not foreign technological hardware can be utilized in communist societies where there are strong social and political (some would call them "ideological") imperatives regarding social organization. One interesting aspect of this problem is the type of production processes that have been used in whole plants that have been transferred from various capitalist to communist states. Both Pepsi Cola and Fiat have transferred whole plants into the Soviet Union, and perhaps there is little conflict of the hierarchical organization of management and production required to operate those plants with existing Soviet practices. However, it is interesting to speculate on the outcome of an attempt to operate a Fiat or Ford assembly line according to the Taching Triple Combination.

Obviously not all communist experiences with organizing and managing production have been revolutionizing. It is also important to examine the instances in which the fulfillment of Marx's hope for the liberation of man's productive capacity and creativity seem at best remote. These are the routes to communism that have become overgrown with the briars of bureaucratization and the ensnaring forms of what we have been calling capitalist technical rationality.

Primary among these is the division of labor and the apparently concomitant hierarchy required to unite separate functions into a coherent productive process. Mihailo Marković has suggested that "one of the consequences of the growing division of labor is that management has become a profession unto itself, with enormous economic and political power. "[114] The increased professionalization

of management in the Soviet Union has resulted in an increased separation of the management of labor from labor itself. This has resulted in increased status differentials between managers and workers and has contributed in no small part to the emergence of a mana-
gerial-technical elite in Soviet society that is almost bound to follow
from practices of centralized management and one-man authority
(edinonachalie).

    This existence of a technical and/or managerial elite may be
attributed to political choices (presumably based on control of production), or it may be attributed to the development of certain technological forms themselves—the "technological imperatives" argument. The fact that those two are not isolatable is well, if not inten-
tionally, illustrated by Roger Garaudy as follows:

> This staggering increase in our technical mastery of na-
> ture entrusts to a few handfuls of men a fund of knowl-
> edge and organization that gives them a terrifying power.
> This technocratic cleavage between the managers and the
> masses is the law in monopolistic regimes in which the
> concentration of resources is a class matter. In funda-
> mentally different conditions, the objective difficulties
> created by this situation raise problems for the develop-
> ment of a true socialist democracy. [115]

    The well-known theories, starting with Djilas, that see this
elite as a new class were not themselves the subject of this conference, but several of the contributions shed light on the proposition
that at least some forms of technological development require an
intellectual, technological, or managerial elite. This seems inconsistent with the communist goal of an egalitarian society.

    The concentration of knowledge among an elite group of tech-
nical or management experts also seems to have exacerbated the
discriminatory division between mental and manual labor. The Chinese have most self-consciously addressed this problem and have
stressed institutional mechanisms by which the cleavages between
the social roles associated with each are greatly reduced, if not
eliminated. Mark G. Field (Chapter 10) contrasts Soviet and Chinese
perceptions of the role of specialists in their respective health care
delivery systems. William N. Dunn (Chapter 8) describes the process of deprofessionalization in Yugoslavia and the wide range of
views on egalitarianism versus elitism throughout Eastern Europe.
It is interesting that some Marxist theorists of the new scientific and
technological revolution, like some Western theorists, seem to
leave the elimination of that social division to technology itself and
argue that automation will cause an inversion in the numerical ratio

of manual to mental workers, gradually eliminating the former. In Chapter 6 Rensselaer W. Lee, III compares the Soviet and Chinese views on this point.

The historical elimination of this classic antinomy is seen to be possible only under socialism. As early as 1930 the Soviet theorist B. Kuznetsov wrote: "Thorough going and full automation is incompatible with the very production relations of capitalism; it liquidates the opposition between mental and physical labor and abolishes the objective conditions of capitalist subordination."[116] More recently the eminent Soviet sociologist M. N. Rutkevich wrote that "the progress of technology and culture demands an accelerated rise in the number of scientists, engineers, technicians, teachers, physicians and other experts, as well as of categories of white-collar personnel in the service occupations." One democratizing aspect of the inversion, according to Rutkevich, is that "the relatively faster increase in the numbers of the non-manual category . . . brings about the entry of workers and collective farmers and their children into its ranks."[117]

In addition to these social effects of automation, Richta suggests that the nature of work itself is transformed:

> As far as one can judge from the rather scanty evidence available at present, complex automation always goes further in that it proceeds to abolish human operation in the control phase, too; it cuts the job-setting maintenance and repair personnel, freeing man altogether from direct participation in the production process. It relieves him of his role as a mere cog in the machine system and offers him the position of inspired creator, master of the technological system, able to stand apart from the immediate manufacturing process. The hub of human activity is shifted to the preparatory phases of production. This is the soil for a sharp rise in technological-engineering and technical-managerial personnel with the emphasis on creative technologists, technicians, designers, automation experts, system analysts and scientists, and of management personnel, industrial psychologists, sociologists, people concerned with industrial aesthetics, hygiene, etc.[118]

Even the most optimistic among these theorists realize that this route to socialism through automation will not be easy:

> There is nothing to be gained by shutting our eyes to the fact that an acute problem of our age will be to

close the profound cleavage in industrial civilization
which, as Einstein realized with such alarm, places
the fate of the defenceless mass in the hands of an educated elite, who wield the power of science and technology. Possibly this will be among the most complex
undertakings facing socialism. With science and technology essential to the common good, circumstances
place their advance primarily in the hands of the conscious, progressive agents of this movement—the professionals, scientists, technicians and organizers, and
skilled workers. And even under socialism we may
find tendencies to elitism, a monopoly of educational
opportunities, exaggerated claims on higher living
standards and the like; these groups forget that the
emancipation of the part is always bound up with the
emancipation of all. [119]

How the whole might be emancipated through revolutionary forms of
political, social, and economic organization is a question of primary
concern to several of the contributors to this book.

One crucial area of the present scientific and technological
revolution where Garaudy's "technocratic cleavage" between managers and the masses is manifested is the area of collecting, processing, and transmitting information. The desire for increasingly
greater amounts of information not only increases the reliance on
more sophisticated technological hardware—computers—to process
the information, but it also requires increasingly complex theories
and modes of thought for the interpretation of that information—cybernetics and systems theory. For Garaudy this represents another
great inversion of the scientific and technological revolution, whereby "the cybernetic principle is superseding the mechanical principle."[120]

The Soviet leaders have exhibited a great interest in both aspects of the "information revolution." In addition to importing computer hardware and software and developing large computer networks
throughout the country,[121] they speak openly of the "systems approach in management"[122] and even have given financial support to
the founding of the International Institute of Applied Systems Analysis at Laxenburg, Austria, of which the chairman of the Institute
Council is Alexei Kosygin's son-in-law, Dzherman M. Gvishiani.
These apparently represent Soviet attempts to solve what R. V.
Burks has termed the "growing informational problem" of "coping
with the extraordinary complexity and interdependence of a highly
specialized industrial society."[123]

Recent western research has focused on aspects of information processing in Soviet party administration and economic management, but much remains to be explored. [124] More sweeping yet, and crucial to our interests in information processing and technical rationality, is Daniel Bell's suggestion that the "systems revolution" is vital to the spread of technocratic thinking, since it introduces a new form of rationalization. [125] Whether or not this new form of rationalization is compatible with communist goal culture and other elements of transfer culture is a problem requiring further study. Preliminary research has only gone so far as to point out the similarities and differences between some Soviet and U.S. systems theorists. [126]

The faith of some Marxists (Richta and Garaudy, for example) in the liberatory role of technology leads them to place a positive value on the cybernetic revolution. Richta's discussion of the relationship between the rationalization of information processing and the working out of a system of civilization regulators is a good case in point. Civilization regulators are the

> means and rules for adjusting the economic, and also the social, political, psychological and cultural conditions for promoting man's creative activity and directing his interest to socialism, so that the approaches to the scientific and technological revolution may be opened in a planned way. . . .
> Regulation of the regulators is in fact a higher form of management, adapted to more versatile and powerful movements in society. Furthermore, it is the sole means by which to make the process of modern civilization amenable to planning and control. Since it allows the flow of information to be rationalized and then taken over by technical devices . . . it provides a sound basis for widespread application of modern computer technology. . . . This technology in its turn again and again breaks through the circle of processes hitherto susceptible to management and transforms the nature of management as such. This two-way counter-motion will ultimately allow a reversal of the inherent propensity of the industrial system born of capitalism to erect a hierarchy and bureaucracy. [127]

Marković agrees that there is this "debureaucratizing" impact of the rationalization of information processing and cybernation:

> Of all the various strata of contemporary bureaucracy the only one which will surely survive are the experts

who make and test the alternative programs within the
framework of the goals, criteria, and established priorities of the accepted general politics. [128]

However, since increasingly greater amounts of information will be
in the hands of many fewer people, the remaining professional politicians and highly skilled administrators and executives will

still maintain considerable power and influence. Unlike
other citizens they have free access to all information.
They have more time than others to study the data and
to try to establish certain general trends. By mere
selection and interpretation of data, by the choice of certain possibilities and elimination of others in the process of the preparation of alternative solutions, and
finally, by a biased presentation of the results of accepted programs, professional politicians will retain
considerable capacity to induce a desired course of
action. [129]

This raises the specter of control by a knowledge elite and thereby
makes all the more crucial the problem of control of the knowledge
elite.
          In Chapter 9 Erik P. Hoffmann presents a case study of the
impact of computers on the relationship between technology, values,
and political power in the USSR. He considers whether or not the
increased technical skills of the younger generation of Soviet information specialists will enable them to enhance their political power
vis-a-vis the traditional party leadership. He is pessimistic about
the ability of the technical specialists to convert their technical
knowledge into political power, but he goes on to suggest that potential conflict between the technocrat and the apparatchik is not the
only context in which the role of technical expertise may be evaluated:

One need not assess the role of computer specialists in
terms of elite conflict between knowledge elites and
political elites, or between distinct ascending and descending elite groupings that perform different functions and possess different skills. Rather, the problem
may be conceptualized as one in which technocratic consciousness becomes pervasive and subtly influences
policy makers' and information specialists' thinking
about politics. This has almost certainly begun to happen in the Soviet Union, for example, through the influ-

ence of cybernetics and systems analysis, through the
professionalization of economic thought, and in the
persistent official emphasis on the concepts of "rationality," "efficiency," and "the scientific management
of society."

This important contention will be discussed in more detail in the
Afterword.

The consequences for communist goal culture of what Silviu
Brucan terms the "symbiosis between Marxism—the nineteenth-century breakthrough in social thinking—and cybernetics—the twentieth-
century breakthrough in scientific methodology"[130] are still uncertain, although we must inquire into the possibility that the feedback
mechanisms of systems analysis and cybernetics might open up a
new rationality, or at least a new decision-making process, in
society. At the same time we must carefully examine those aspects
that seem incompatible with liberatory elements in some communist
transfer cultures, and hence ultimately subversive of communist
goal culture.

One of the many social costs of modernization is the disruption of the natural environment, such as the pollution of air and
water by industrial and consumer wastes. Any country that increases
its industrial production is confronted with the problems of ecological disruptions. Given what we now know about the ecosystem of the
earth, these disruptions cause much more than mere aesthetic dis-
pleasure—they ultimately impact on the ability of the human race to
survive. Hence the liberty and survival of the species is tied to its
relationship to nature.

The Soviet pollution of Lake Baikal is frequently pointed to as
a case of ecological disaster in a communist society. The deepest
body of fresh water in the world, Lake Baikal was so free of mineral
content that it contained myriad varieties of plant and animal life,
some dating back to prehistoric times. Pulp paper mills have dumped
their wastes into the lake and brought it to a state of biological death
close to that of Lake Erie.[131] This "tragedy of the commons" appears to be the result of both bureaucratic obstinacy and a set of
attitudes that make nature merely an object of human manipulation.
The latter is reflected in a 1968 speech by Brezhnev: "For us communists, builders of the most advanced society in the history of mankind, scientific-technological progress is one of the main ways of
speeding up the plans of the party regarding the transformation of
nature."[132] David E. Powell concluded a recent study of environmental problems in the USSR by suggesting that solution of those
problems "will require a fundamental re-ordering of priorities,

from the almost pathological fixation on production to a more balanced attitude, showing as much concern for ecology as for production indices."[133]

William Leiss pushes this argument even further when he contends quite forcefully:

> that the customs, beliefs, and social practices that
> express a particular relationship of man to nature are
> necessarily bound to a larger totality in which their con-
> crete significance for everyday life is grounded. Exter-
> nal nature, the surrounding environment, is the materi-
> al basis for the satisfaction of human needs. Therefore
> the attitude toward the environment forms an integral
> part of the general political economy of every society,
> that is, the set of rules according to which human needs
> are socially legitimated and possibilities for their satis-
> faction are proportionately distributed.[134]

One important issue discussed during the conference was the
various ways whereby attitudes toward the environment interact with
the totality of concrete life-activity in communist cultures. There
are basic attitudes from both the traditional culture and the innovated cultural system that interact with the instrumentalist technical
rationality imported from the West, which views nature as something to be conquered and manipulated for the immediate pleasure of
mankind. William Leiss discusses this problem in Chapter 2, on
"Technology and Instrumental Rationality in Capitalism and Socialism."

Chinese communist attitudes and practices concerning the relationship between technology and ecology again appear in sharp contrast to those in the Soviet Union. Rather than starting from the
machine or the product and then organizing all productive and social
relations outward from the machine, the Taching model starts from
a particular source of energy (in this case an oilfield). This involves,
most importantly, a definition of technology that is not just the movement from animate to inanimate sources of energy but also involves
a system of nonhierarchical production relations. That is, social
and political factors become part of the efficiency calculation. No
detailed study of the implications for the technology-ecology nexus
of the Taching model has been undertaken in the West. It is possible,
however, that models of technology that start from the point of view
of the energy source rather than that of the machine or the product
will have a much different impact on the environment. At least such
a radical departure from dominant Western forms of technical rationality holds the possibility that the human race will be more harmoniously integrated into the ecosystem.

The ecology problem is particularly important, since it shows most dramatically that the questions that have been raised here are not simply the result of conflict between ends and means, but rather have come from a more basic crisis in values—a crisis that has been heightened in the socialist states as some contemporary Western notions of consumption have come to predominate in them. Technology is a means to achieve abundance, but how is it possible to realize abundance without commodity fetishism? How is it possible to utilize technology as an element of transfer culture—as a means—without allowing it to acquire an independence and autonomy of its own? These are basic questions and difficult to answer; Daniel Bell has suggested:

> In the technocratic mode, the ends have become simply efficiency and output. The ends have become means and they exist in themselves. The technocratic mode has become established because it is the mode of efficiency—of production, of program, of "getting things done." For these reasons, the technocratic mode is bound to spread in our society. [135]

Differences in communist reactions to imported technology are related in part to different perceptions of the symbolic value of technology. To the Chinese, Western technology is an alien invention; to the Soviets, it is a symbol of progress. Some communists express ultimate faith in the liberating role of technology. Garaudy expressed this faith with the famous axiom, "A little technology removes us from man and a lot of technology can lead us back to him." [136] Richta's faith in technology takes the following form: "When technology is weak, it confines and masters man; when, however, it is perfected and versatile, it gives him entry to his own independent development." [137]

These expressions of optimism are to be contrasted with the less sanguine view of the Czech sociologist Ladislav Tondl, who has written of the Janus head of technology as follows:

> The marriage of technology with such concepts as "control" and "organization," and with the concept of "enclaves of a growing organization, raises the question of what we have called the "Janus head" of technology. Also, since, in the domains of energy and information, perpetual motion is not possible, the application of technology leads directly, or more often indirectly, to an increase of entropy, both outside and even inside of these enclaves. In other words, the application of technology to various domains of social life, and at the same

time the collective solution of socially significant crises,
ushers in not only benefits, not only the attainment of
difficult goals, the realization of new conceptions of
civilization; but also simultaneously with such benefits
(or in contradiction to them), an increase in unforeseen
dangers, difficulties, and problems.

The many heads (Januskopf) of technology means
that technology not only increases and multiplies human
capacities, not only enlarges the spectrum of human
possibilities, not only develops the creative powers of
man; but it also subdues these same creative powers,
and restricts and destroys them. Industrialization has
brought not only many blessings with it, but also the
pitfalls of the agglomeration of cities, atmospheric
pollution, and the destruction of nature, man included.
Modern mass communication brings with it not only
quick and basic sources of information, and naturally
new forms of entertainment, but also the dangers of
uniformity and regimentation, the destruction of our
creative powers, etc. The abundance of rational information in the fields of science and technology can dull
our capacity and sensitivity for information stemming
from our own experiences and emotions. Moreover,
the order and organization brought about by technological progress in one sphere often leads to the neglect
of another field. [138]

The essays that follow examine various communist attempts to solve
this paradox of technological development.

NOTES

1. Robert C. Tucker, "Culture, Political Culture, and Communist Society, " Political Science Quarterly 88 (1973): 173-90.

2. The Conference on Political Culture and Comparative Communist Studies was convened by Robert C. Tucker at Arden House
in November 1971 under the auspices of the Planning Group on Comparative Communist Studies of the American Council of Learned
Societies. A Digest of the conference appears in the Newsletter on
Comparative Studies of Communism 5 (1972): 2-17.

3. V. I. Lenin, "On Co-operation, " Collected Works, vol. 33
(4th ed. , Moscow: Progress, 1966), pp. 469-70, 474-75.

4. Tucker, op. cit., p. 190.

5. In the past half-century a number of studies have been published that focus on the cultural patterns of socialist societies emerging from the interaction, and frequently intense conflict between those two forces. Major works on Russia include René Fueloep-Miller, The Mind and Face of Bolshevism (1928), Geoffrey Gorer and John Rickman, The People of Great Russia: A Psychological Study (1949), Nathan Leites, The Operational Code of the Politburo (1951), Margaret Mead, Soviet Attitudes toward Authority (1951), Nathan Leites, A Study of Bolshevism (1953), and Dinko Tomasic, The Impact of Russian Culture on Soviet Communism (1953). In a somewhat narrower vein, the more recent studies by Alfred G. Meyer (The Soviet Political System, 1965) and Frederick C. Barghoorn (Politics in the USSR, 1966) focus on conflicts between traditional and innovated forms of political culture.

A number of recent studies have examined aspects of the interaction between traditional and innovated forms of Chinese culture and political culture from quite different perspectives. These include John W. Lewis, "The Study of Chinese Political Culture," World Politics 18 (1966), and the several works discussed therein; William Hinton, Fanshen: A Documentary of Revolution in a Chinese Village (1966); Lucian Pye, The Spirit of Chinese Politics (1966); Ralph C. Crozier, China's Cultural Legacy and Communism (1970); Richard H. Solomon, Mao's Revolution and the Chinese Political Culture (1971); John Bryan Starr, Ideology and Culture: An Introduction to the Dialectic of Contemporary Chinese Politics (1973); and James R. Townsend, Politics in China (1974). To date, only one major study has appeared that analyzes the interaction of the traditional and innovated cultures of any of the other socialist societies, and that is Richard R. Fagen, The Transformation of Political Culture in Cuba.

6. William Leiss, The Domination of Nature (New York: Braziller, 1972), p. 199. For other discussions of the concept of technical rationality, see Herbert Marcuse, One-Dimensional Man (Boston: Beacon, 1964), and Herbert Marcuse, An Essay on Liberation (Boston: Beacon, 1969). The Appendix to Leiss's book is an important critique of Marcuse's usage of the concept. For a comparison of the use of the concept in the writings of Karl Marx and Max Weber, see Leiss's chapter to the present volume (Chapter 2) and Anthony Giddens, Capitalism and Modern Social Theory: An Analysis of the Writings of Marx, Durkheim and Max Weber (Cambridge: Cambridge University Press, 1971), pp. 215-16. A very important recent discussion of technical rationality is "Cultural-Marxism: The Contradictions of Industrial 'Rationality'," in Trent Schroyer, The Critique of Domination: The Origins and Development of Critical Theory (New York: Braziller, 1973).

7. Marc Raeff, "The Russian Autocracy and Its Officials," in Russian Thought and Politics, ed. Hugh McLean, Martin E. Malia,

and George Fischer, Harvard Slavic Studies, vol. 4 (Cambridge, Mass.: Harvard University Press, 1957), pp. 78-79.

8. Robert C. Tucker, The Marxian Revolutionary Idea (New York: Norton, 1969), p. 106.

9. For an important and instructive elaboration of this point in terms of the "dialectics of backwardness," see Alfred G. Meyer, Leninism (Cambridge: Harvard University Press, 1957), chap. 12.

10. See Theodore Von Laue, Sergei Witte and the Industrialization of Russia (New York: Atheneum, 1969). For a Soviet critique of Von Laue's interpretation, see I. F. Gindin, "Russia's Industrialization under Capitalism as Seen by Theodore Von Laue," Istoriia SSSR, no. 4 (1971). An English translation appears in Soviet Studies in History 11 (1972). 0 55.

11. On the significance of quantified time in this context, see E. P. Thompson, "Time, Work-Discipline, and Industrial Capitalism," Past and Present 38 (1967): 56-97; Herbert G. Reid, "American Social Science in the Politics of Time and the Crisis of Technocorporate Society: Toward a Critical Phenomenology," Politics and Society 3 (1973): 201-43; Staffan B. Linder, The Harried Leisure Class (New York: Columbia University Press, 1970).

12. Alexander Gerschenkron, Economic Backwardness in Historical Perspective (New York: Praeger, 1965), pp. 46-47.

13. See ibid.; John P. McKay, Pioneers for Profit: Foreign Entrepreneurship and Russian Industrialism, 1885-1913 (Chicago: University of Chicago Press, 1970), especially pp. 283-85; Von Laue, op. cit., especially pp. 95-114.

14. Antony Sutton, Western Technology and Soviet Economic Development, 1917-1965 (3 vols.; Stanford, Calif.: Hoover Institution Publications, 1968-73). For a mixed review of these controversial volumes focusing on a sharp criticism of the third volume, see Samuel Lieberstein, "Technology, Work, and Sociology in the USSR: The NOT Movement," in Technology and Culture 16 (1975): 508-10.

15. Denis Goulet, The Cruel Choice: A New Concept in the Theory of Development (New York: Atheneum, 1973), p. 171.

16. Frederic J. Fleron, Jr., and Lou Jean Fleron, "Administrative Theory as Repressive Political Theory: The Communist Experience," Newsletter on Comparative Studies of Communism 6 (Stanford, Calif.,1972): 4-41. This paper also appears in Telos 12 (1972): 63-92.

17. John A. Armstrong, The European Administrative Elite (Princeton, N.J.: Princeton University Press, 1973), p. 189. Emphasis added.

18. Ibid., p. 190.

19. Genevieve Dean, "Science, Technology and Development: China as a 'Case Study'," The China Quarterly 51 (1972): 521.

20. Rensselaer W. Lee III, "The Politics of Technology in Communist China," Comparative Politics 5, no. 2 (1973): 237-60.

21. Dean, op. cit., p. 528.

22. Fagen, The Transformation of Political Culture in Cuba, op. cit., p. 141.

23. Ibid.

24. Ibid., p. 140.

25. Anthony F. C. Wallace, Culture and Personality (2nd ed., New York: Random House, 1970), p. 192.

26. Tucker, "Culture, Political Culture, and Communist Society," op. cit., p. 186; Chalmers Johnson, "Comparing Communist Nations," in Change in Communist Systems, ed. Chalmers Johnson (Stanford, Calif.: Stanford University Press, 1970), p. 7.

27. Antony Sutton, op. cit.; Peter Solomon, "Technological Innovation and Soviet Industrialization," in Social Consequences of Modernization in Communist Societies, ed. Mark G. Field (Baltimore: Johns Hopkins University Press, 1976), pp. 207-33; R. V. Burks, "Technology and Political Change in Eastern Europe," in Johnson, Change in Communist Systems, op. cit., pp. 265-311.

28. Melvin Kranzberg, introductory article, Technology and Culture 1 (1959): 1.

29. William Leiss, "Nature, Technology, and Domination," postscript to forthcoming French edition of The Domination of Nature, op. cit.

30. A. Zvorikine, "Technology and the Laws of Its Development," Technology and Culture 3 (1962): 443.

31. Alexander Woroniak, "Technological Transfer in Eastern Europe: Receiving Countries," in East-West Trade and the Technology Gap, ed. Stanislaw Wasowski (New York: Praeger, 1970), p. 87.

32. Margaret Mead, Cultural Patterns and Technical Change, (New York: Mentor, 1955), p. 13.

33. William Leiss, "The Social Consequences of Technological Progress: Critical Comments on Recent Theories," Canadian Public Administration 13, no. 3 (1970): 247.

34. Ibid., p. 250.

35. Ibid., p. 261.

36. Ibid., p. 253.

37. See Stephen A. Marglin, "What Do Bosses Do? The Origins and Functions of Hierarchy in Capitalist Production," Review of Radical Political Economics 6, no. 2 (1974): 33-60.

38. Stanley Aronowitz, False Promises: The Shaping of American Working-Class Consciousness (New York: McGraw-Hill, 1973), p. 155.

39. See André Gorz, "Technical Intelligence and the Capitalist Division of Labor," Telos 12 (1972): 27-41; and Marglin, op. cit.

40. Shlomo Avineri, The Social and Political Thought of Karl Marx (Cambridge: Cambridge University Press, 1970), p. 154.

41. Georg Lukács, "Technology and Social Relations," in Marxism and Human Liberation: Essays on History, Culture and Revolution by Georg Lukacs, ed. E. San Juan, Jr. (New York: Dell, 1973), p. 56. This essay was originally published in Archiv für die Geschichte des Socialismus und der Arbeiterbewegung 11 (1925).

42. Julian M. Cooper, "The Concept of the Scientific and Technical Revolution in Soviet Theory" (unpublished CREES Discussion Paper Number 9, Centre For Russian and East European Studies, University of Birmingham, England, 1973), p. 17. This paper is an earlier version of the essay by Cooper that appears in this volume (Chaper 3). The present version omits the quoted passage. Emphasis added.

43. For details, see Aronowitz, op. cit., p. 156, and Siegfried Giedion, Mechanization Takes Command: A Contribution to Anonymous History (New York: Norton, 1969), pp. 96ff.

44. Aronowitz, op. cit., p. 156.

45. Giedion, op. cit., p. 96.

46. Ibid., p. 98.

47. Ibid., p. 99.

48. Ibid., p. 103.

49. Ibid., p. 102.

50. See Alvin M. Weinberg, "Social Institutions and Nuclear Energy," Science 177 (1972): 27-34.

51. B. Kuznetsov, Kommunism i tekhnika budushchego (Moscow: AN SSSR, 1940), p. 15.

52. V. I. Gromeka and V. S. Vasil'yev. "Bourgeois Theorists on the Scientific and Technical Revolution," USA: Economics, Politics, Ideology (Moscow) no. 1 (1971), p. 73.

53. See Max Horkheimer and T. W. Adorno, Dialectic of Enlightenment (New York: Herder and Herder, 1972). Originally published in 1944 as Dialektik der Aufklärung.

54. Fundamentals of Marxism-Leninism (Moscow: Foreign Languages Publishing House, 1961), p. 870.

55. Maurice Meisner, "Utopian Socialist Themes in Maoism," in Peasant Rebellion and Communist Revolution in Asia, ed. John W. Lewis (Stanford, Calif.: Stanford University Press, 1974), p. 250.

56. Fundamentals of Marxism-Leninism, op. cit., p. 816.

57. Meisner, op. cit., p. 232.

58. N. I. Bukharin and E. Preobrazhensky, The ABC of Communism: A Popular Explanation of the Program of the Communist Party of Russia (Ann Arbor: University of Michigan Press, 1966), p. 77.

59. Ibid., pp. 71-72.

60. Kendall Bailes, "The Politics of Technology: Stalin and Technocratic Thinking among Soviet Engineers," American Historical Review 79 (1974): 445-69.

61. See Burks, op. cit., pp. 265-311.

62. Radovan Richta, et al., Civilization at the Crossroads: Social and Human Implications of the Scientific and Technological Revolution (White Plains, N.Y.: International Arts and Sciences Press, 1969), p. 111.

63. Nathan Rosenberg, Perspectives on Technology (Cambridge: Cambridge University Press, 1976), p. 167.

64. Richta, op. cit., p. 55. Emphasis in original.

65. Loren R. Graham, The Soviet Academy of Sciences and the Communist Party, 1927-1932 (Princeton, N.J.: Princeton University Press, 1967), pp. 190-91.

66. This periodization was first suggested to me by David Joravsky in a 1974 conversation. A similar approach can be found in Maurice Richter, "Chinese Science Policy: A Comparative Analysis," Bulletin of Atomic Scientists 32 (1976): 14.

67. Richta, op. cit., p. 212.

68. Julian M. Cooper discusses this development in Chapter 3 of this book, "The Scientific and Technical Revolution in Soviet Theory." See also Richta, op. cit., pp. 39-43, and I. G. Kurakov, Science, Technology and Communism: Some Questions of Development (Oxford: Pergamon, 1966), pp. 1-13.

69. For a general overview of Chinese science policy, see Richard P. Suttmeier, Research and Revolution: Science Policy and Societal Change in China (Lexington, Mass.: Lexington Books, 1974).

70. Lee, op. cit., p. 303.

71. Of course, this subject has not been free of controversy in the People's Republic of China. Indeed, the relationship of Western science to Chinese technological development was one of the central issues of conflict between the Maoists and Liuists. For discussion of this conflict in the context of the role of science and technology in Chinese cultural transformation, see Lowell Dittmer, Liu Shao-ch'i and the Chinese Cultural Revolution: The Politics of Mass Criticism (Berkeley: University of California Press, 1974), especially chap. 7. Suttmeier, op. cit., chap. 4, also analyzes this controversy.

72. Richta, op. cit., p. 39.

73. Richta, op. cit., p. 41, gives original sources from Pravda.

74. See ibid., pp. 41-44, and Roger Garaudy, The Crisis of Communism: The Turning Point of Socialism (New York: Grove, 1970), pp. 23-32, for discussion of the significance of Keldysh's Proportion for the new scientific and technological revolution from

the Marxist point of view. Richta gives as the source of this idea of
the inversion of the relationship between science and technology a
1961 article in Pravda by M. V. Keldysh, president of the USSR
Academy of Sciences: "Sovetskaya nauka i stroitelstvo kommunizma,"
Pravda, June 13, 1961. He also indicates that "we can find an indication of a similar idea in S. Kuznets, Six Lectures on Economic
Growth, Glencoe 1959, p. 30. J. D. Bernal gives it mathematical
expression: the advance of technology corresponds to the first deri-
vation of the production curve, that of science to its second deriva-
tion." See Richta, op. cit., p. 41n. It appears, however, that this
idea can be traced back much further, at least to N. I. Bukharin's
criticism of Stalin's First Five-Year Plan in the early 1930s. According to Stephen F. Cohen, Bukharin argued "repeatedly in 1929-
33 that a technological revolution must be the basis of genuine industrialization, and that therefore 'the scientific-research network must
grow faster than even the leading branches of socialist heavy industry.' " Stephen F. Cohen, Bukharin and the Bolshevik Revolution: A
Political Biography, 1888-1938 (New York: Knopf, 1973), p. 353.
(Emphasis in original.) The sources for several such statements by
Bukharin are indicated in ibid., p. 467.

    75. See D. A. Senior, "The Organization of Scientific Re-
search," Survey 52 (1964), for details up to 1964 and several important chapters in E. Zaleski, J. P. Kozlowski, H. Weinert, R. W.
Davies, M. J. Berry, and R. Amann, Science Policy in the USSR
(Paris: Organization for Economic Cooperation and Development,
1969).

    76. Linda Lubrano Greenberg, "Soviet Science Policy and the
Scientific Establishment," Survey 81 (1971): 51-63.

    77. For an interesting discussion of this idea, see Richard P.
Suttmeier, "Thinking About Science Policy: A Chinese Comparison,"
paper presented at the VIII World Congress of Sociologists, Toronto,
1974.

    78. I am grateful to John W. Lewis for suggesting this formu-
lation of Chinese science-education-production policy in the present
context. In addition to the literature on China already cited, discus-
sion of several additional aspects of this policy can be found in C. K.
Jen, "Science and the Open-Doors Educational Movement," China
Quarterly 64 (1975): 741-47; Richard P. Suttmeier, "Science Policy
Shifts, Organizational Change and China's Development," China
Quarterly 62 (1975): 207-41, especially p. 228; Jan S. Prybyla,
"Notes on Chinese Higher Education: 1974," China Quarterly 62
(1975): 271-96.

    79. Barry M. Richman, Industrial Society in Communist
China (New York: Vintage, 1969), p. 238. To my knowledge, there
is no study of the Taching oilfield available in English other than the

official Chinese publication Taching: Red Banner on China's Industrial Front (Peking: Foreign Languages Publishing House, 1972).

80. John P. Hardt and George D. Holliday, U. S.-Soviet Commercial Relations: The Interplay of Economics, Technology Transfer, and Diplomacy, U.S., Congress, House, Committee on Foreign Affairs, Subcommittee on National Security Policy and Scientific Developments, 93rd Cong., 1st sess. (Washington, D.C.: Government Printing Office, 1973), p. 30.

81. Antony C. Sutton, Western Technology and Soviet Economic Development, 1930 to 1945, (Stanford, Calif.: Hoover Institution Publications, 1971), vol. 2, p. 339.

82. U.S.-Soviet Commercial Relations, op. cit., p. 30.

83. Philip Hanson, "International Technology Transfer from the West to the U.S.S.R.," in Soviet Economy in a New Perspective, U.S., Congress, Joint Economic Committee, 94th Cong., 2nd sess. (Washington, D.C.: Government Printing Office, 1976), p. 786.

84. Ibid., p. 787.

85. Marshall I. Goldman, Detente and Dollars: Doing Business with the Soviets (New York: Basic Books, 1975), p. 33.

86. Ibid., p. 33.

87. For details, see ibid., p. 133.

88. Barry Commoner, "As the West Sinks Slowly into the Sun . . . ," New York Times, November 20, 1974, p. 43.

89. Philip Hanson, "The Russian Connection," New Scientist, January 23, 1975, p. 197.

90. United Nations, Economic Commission for Europe, Analytical Report on Industrial Co-operation among ECE Countries (Geneva: United Nations, 1973), p. 2. This definition is retained in the more recent work of the Senior Advisors to ECE Governments on Science and Technology. It reappears in Proceedings of the UN/ECE Seminar on the Management of the Transfer of Technology within Industrial Co-operation (Geneva: United Nations, 1975), p. 17. As far as I know, these two reports are the most detailed studies of industrial cooperation between Eastern Europe (including the USSR) and the capitalist West. A more recent brief survey appears to be based largely on these two ECE reports. See Maureen R. Smith, "Industrial Cooperation Agreements: Soviet Experience and Practice," in U.S., Congress, Joint Economic Committee, Soviet Economy in a New Perspective (Washington, D.C.: Government Printing Office, 1976), pp. 767-85.

91. Analytical Report on Industrial Co-operation among ECE Countries, op. cit., p. 2.

92. Egon Kemenes, "Some Legal and Financial Aspects of Industrial Co-operation," Marketing in Hungary, no. 3 (1974),

pp. 11-12. This journal describes itself as a quarterly market research review published by the Hungarian Chamber of Commerce and the Institute for Economic and Market Research. It frequently carries articles on industrial cooperation and other aspects of technology transfer.

93. See Smith, op. cit., p. 771.

94. Ibid., p. 782.

95. Analytical Report on Industrial Co-operation among ECE Countries, op. cit., p. 29.

96. Smith, op. cit., p. 784.

97. Ibid.

98. Philip Hanson, "The Import of Western Technology," in Archie Brown and Michael Kaser, eds., The Soviet Union Since the Fall of Khrushchev (New York: Free Press, 1975), p. 44. The question of interdependence is also discussed by Marshall I. Goldman, "Autarchy or Integration—The U.S.S.R. and the World Economy," in Soviet Economy in a New Perspective, op. cit., pp. 81-96. Goldman argues that there is "reason to believe that given the nature of the new technology the Soviet Union is currently purchasing, the Soviet Union will find it more difficult than it has in the past to isolate itself." Ibid., p. 93. Indeed, he suggests, "based on the record to date, there is strong evidence to indicate that the Soviet Union may already find itself interdependent." Ibid., p. 95.

99. Ivan D. Ivanov, "Soviet-American Economic Cooperation: Recent Development, Prospects and Problems," Annals of the American Academy of Political and Social Science 414 (1974): 19.

100. Jozef Wilczynski, "Multinational Corporations and East-West Economic Co-operation," Journal of World Trade Law 9 (1975): 266. For another treatment of the role of multinationals in East-West economic interdependence, see U.S., Congress, Senate, Committee on Foreign Relations, Subcommittee on Multinational Corporations, Western Investment in Communist Economies: A Selected Survey on Economic Interdependence, by John P. Hardt, George D. Holliday, and Young C. Kim, Committee Print (Washington, D.C.: Government Printing Office, 1974).

101. See William Whitson, "China's Quest for Technology," Problems of Communism 22 (1973): 16-30. Chapter 5 in this volume, by Robert F. Dernberger, describes this process in some detail and on the basis of more recent data than was available to Whitson.

102. Hans Heymann, Jr., "Acquisition and Diffusion of Technology in China," in China: A Reassessment of the Economy, U.S., Congress, Joint Economic Committee (Washington, D.C.: Government Printing Office, 1975), p. 680. Heymann discusses the Chinese experience with these three forms of technology acquisition.

103. See John R. Thomas, "Technology and Nationalism,"
Survey 65 (1967): 100; R. V. Burks, "The Political Implications of
Economic Reform," in Plan and Market: Economic Reform in
Eastern Europe, ed. Morris Bornstein (New Haven, Conn.: Yale
University Press, 1973), pp. 373-401; R. V. Burks, "The Political
Hazards of Economic Reform," in Reorientation and Commercial
Relations of the Economies of Eastern Europe, U.S., Congress,
Joint Economic Committee (Washington, D.C.: Government Printing
Office, 1974), pp. 51-78.

104. Sutton, Western Technology and Soviet Economic Development, 1930-1945, op. cit., p. 346.

105. U.S.-Soviet Commercial Relations, op. cit., p. 31.

106. Robert W. Campbell, "Management Spillovers from
Soviet Space and Military Programmes," Soviet Studies 23 (1972):
586.

107. Ibid., pp. 586, 606, 607.

108. Richard Baum, "Technology, Economic Organization,
and Social Change: Maoism and the Chinese Cultural Revolution," in
China in the Seventies, ed. B. Staiger (Wiesbaden: Otto Harrassowitz, 1975), p. 160.

109. Lee, "The Politics of Technology in Communist China,"
op. cit., p. 314.

110. Ibid., p. 317.

111. Mihailo Marković, From Affluence to Praxis: Philosophy
and Social Criticism (Ann Arbor: University of Michigan Press,
1974), p. 235.

112. Richman, op. cit., p. 238.

113. William N. Dunn, "Revolution and Modernization in
Socialist Economic Organizations," in Comparative Socialist Systems: Essays on Politics and Economics, ed. Carmelo Mesa-Lago
and Carl Beck (Pittsburgh: University of Pittsburgh Center for International Studies, 1975), p. 187.

114. Marković, op. cit., p. 263.

115. Roger Garaudy, Marxism in the Twentieth Century (New
York: Scribner's, 1970), p. 26.

116. B. Kuznetsov, "Dialektika, estestvennie nauki i tekhnicheskaia rekonstruktsiia," Plankhoz, nos. 10-11 (1930), p. 315.

117. M. N. Rutkevich, "Elimination of Class Differences and
the Place of Non-Manual Workers," Soviet Sociology, no. 3 (1964),
pp. 4-5, 11. Cited by Lipset and Dobson, "Social Stratification and
Sociology in the Soviet Union," Survey 88 (1973): 171.

118. Richta, op. cit., pp. 112-13.

119. Ibid., p. 250.

120. Roger Garaudy, The Crisis in Communism, op. cit.,
p. 24.

121. See Victor Glushkov, "Remove Departmental Barriers to Automated Management Systems," Izvestiia, March 8, 1974, p. 2.

122. G. Pospelov, "The Systems Approach," Pravda, March 21, 1974, p. 2.

123. Burks, "Technology and Political Change in Eastern Europe," op. cit., p. 271.

124. See Richard Judy, "Information, Control, and Soviet Economic Management," in Mathematics and Computers in Soviet Economic Planning, ed. John P. Hardt, et al. (New Haven, Conn.: Yale University Press, 1967), pp. 1-48; Erik P. Hoffmann, "Soviet Metapolicy: Information-Processing in the Communist Party of the Soviet Union," Journal of Comparative Administration 5 (1973): 200-32; Donald V. Schwartz, "Information and Administration in the Soviet Union: Some Theoretical Considerations," Canadian Journal of Political Science 7 (1974): 228-47; Erik P. Hoffmann, "Soviet Information Processing: Recent Theory and Experience," Soviet Union 2 (1975): 22-49.

125. Daniel Bell, "Technocracy and Politics," Survey 7 (1971): 17.

126. See Donald V. Schwartz, "Recent Soviet Adaptations of Systems Theory to Administrative Theory," Journal of Comparative Administration 5 (1973): 233-64; Donald V. Schwartz, "Decision-making, Administrative Decentralization, and Feedback Mechanisms: Comparisons of Soviet and Western Models," Studies in Comparative Communism 7 (1974): 146-83.

127. Richta, op. cit., pp. 238-39.

128. Marković, op. cit., p. 227.

129. Ibid., p. 228.

130. Silviu Brucan, The Dissolution of Power: A Sociology of International Relations and Politics (New York: Knopf, 1971), p. xii.

131. For details of ecological problems in the USSR, see Marshall I. Goldman, The Spoils of Progress: Environmental Pollution in the Soviet Union (Cambridge, Mass.: MIT Press, 1972); Philip R. Pryde, Conservation in the Soviet Union (Cambridge: Cambridge University Press, 1972); David E. Powell, "The Social Costs of Modernization: Ecological Problems in the USSR," World Politics 23 (1971): 618-34; Donald R. Kelley, Kenneth R. Stunkel, and Richard R. Wescott, The Economic Superpowers and the Environment: The United States, the Soviet Union, and Japan (San Francisco, Calif.: Freeman, 1976).

132. Quoted in Burks, "Technology and Political Change in Eastern Europe," op. cit., p. 276.

133. Powell, op. cit., p. 634.

134. William Leiss, "Nature, Technology, and Domination," op. cit.

135. Daniel Bell, The Coming of Post-Industrial Society: A Venture in Social Forecasting (New York: Basic Books, 1973), pp. 354-55.

136. Garaudy, The Crisis of Communism, op. cit., p. 20.

137. Richta, op. cit., p. 180.

138. Ladislav Tondl, "The Janus Head of Technology," in Contemporary East European Philosophy, vol. 4, ed. Edward D'Angelo, David H. DeGrood, and Dale Riepe (Bridgeport, Conn.: Spartacus, 1971), pp. 296-97.

PART

1

MARXIST PERSPECTIVES ON TECHNOLOGY

1

TRANSITION OR CONVERGENCE: COMMUNISM AND THE PARADOX OF DEVELOPMENT
Andrew L. Feenberg

THE PARADOX OF DEVELOPMENT

According to an ancient tradition of Western political theory, societies cannot achieve both civic virtue and material prosperity. For centuries the rise and fall of the Roman Republic served as a cautionary tale illustrating pessimistic maxims. "Roman liberty," said Saint-Just, "was drowned in gold and delights."[1] There is a flaw in human nature: released by riches from a common struggle with nature, men become greedy and soft and lose the spirit of self-sacrifice required for life in a free society. This is the dilemma Mandeville mockingly formulated long ago in his famous doggerel:

> . . . Fools only strive
> To make a Great an honest Hive . . .
> Bare Vertue can't make Nations live
> In Splendour; they, that would revive
> A Golden Age, must be as free,
> For Acorns, as for Honesty. [2]

I shall call "the paradox of development" the view that the highest values pursued in public and private life are thus mutually exclusive.

Since Max Weber, something very much like this traditional view has been frequently reformulated in modern social theory. New and much stronger reasons are advanced to show that the satisfaction of material needs in industrial societies is fundamentally incompatible with the progress of human freedom. Today the argument goes (very roughly) that the technology that provides prosperity requires a scale of enterprise, a planning of production and markets, and an application of scientific knowledge so far beyond the control

and attainments of the ordinary citizen as to render him a mere cog
in an alienated mechanism. In such recent reformulations of the
paradox of development, the emphasis is less on moral flaws in
human nature than on the growing gap between the cognitive capacities of the individual and the complex problems of a technological
society. This condition, it is said, is today a general one, regardless of the prevailing political system, be it capitalist democracy or
communism.

Marx's work belongs to a different tradition, one that seeks in
various ways to reconcile the goals of freedom and prosperity.
Marx's concept of socialism is specifically designed to overcome the
paradox of development, with its contradiction of public and private
goods.[3] It is worth emphasizing that Marx's vision of socialism includes the introduction or preservation of democratic liberties much
as we know them: the republic, universal suffrage, and civil rights.
Socialism was to extend democracy into the world of work, not substitute economic rights for political ones as is sometimes supposed.
Did Marx anticipate the subversive impact of modernization on human
freedom? Had he any understanding of the new technological basis
for the paradox of development, different from the old moral basis
and so insidious that it renders traditional political rights obsolete
while reducing the promise of industrial democracy to the point of
absurdity?

It is ironic that the strongest arguments advanced today against
the very possibility of Marx's kind of socialism rest on an analysis
of the imperatives of modern technology. Marx, of course, attempted to establish the historical limits of capitalism precisely on this
basis. Where Marx saw democratic planning as the inevitable response to the new scale of enterprise and the complexity of economic
interdependencies, the modern critics of Marxism argue that East
and West alike are now administered by centralized bureaucracies
in response to these very problems. This is the fundamental thesis
of convergence theory, which underlies most contemporary approaches
to the study of modernization in the existing communist societies,
including the study of technology transfer from capitalist to communist nations. The bureaucratization of the world is a predictable
consequence of the internationalization of Western technology through
transfer and imitation. Societies presently in the "acorns and honesty" stage—like the People's Republic of China—will eventually
confront the paradox of development in full force.

Two types of technological determinism are associated with
this convergence theory. First, it asserts that the pattern of technical progress is fixed, one and the same for all societies. No reciprocal influence of cultural causes along the general line of technological development is admitted, the latter being derived from the

progress of science and the logic of technology.

Second, this theory asserts that social organization must adapt to technical progress at each stage of development, according to "imperative" requirements of technology. Given these assumptions, all societies can be ordered along a single continuum of modernization, the more advanced exemplifying future stages of the less advanced. To quote Marx himself, "De te fabula narratur": the advanced societies are a destiny for their poorer neighbors. [4]

While still predominant, this sort of convergence theory has been challenged for assuming "ethnocentrically" that the inevitable outcome of modernization in any culture is a society like that of the United States. It is, on the face of it, implausible that the differing cultural values of different societies should have as little impact on their patterns of development as is assumed by convergence theory. Surely the response to modernization may influence its course. This seems all the more likely in communist societies, which are self-consciously committed to the development of a new culture and a future utterly unlike the present. Robert C. Tucker therefore suggests that we take the

> culture transforming and culture building process as
> the central content of "development" in its communist
> forms. Instead of treating communism as a modernizing
> movement, we will see certain ingredients of what
> Westerners call "modernization" as present in the pro-
> cesses of directed cultural change observable in com-
> munist societies. We will, in short, take care not to
> assume that the communists are recapitulating our
> developmental history in their peculiar manner; our
> theoretical perspective itself will become culture con-
> scious.[5]

Viewed in this light, the subject of technology transfer is an exceptionally interesting one. The diffusion of Western technology into different social systems highlights in something resembling an experimental setting the paradox of development associated with it, which is the contradiction between this technology and human free-dom. Since this technology has developed willy-nilly in Western capitalist societies, it has become extremely difficult to separate in it what is universal—essential to any technological society—and what is contingent on Western culture and the specific requirements of the capitalist system. Only when this distinction has been made will it be possible to decide the fate of freedom in a developed tech-nological society and determine on what general sort of technology

it will have to be based. The communist experiments with Western
capitalist technology can be seen as so many attempts to solve this
problem in practice, some more promising than others.

In any case, the very existence of these experiments forbids
the apriority of the many theories of "modernization" and "technological rationality," which take industrial societies as a single phenomenon, whatever the political system, and derive all their repressive features from "imperatives" of development. [6] Rather, only by
experience will it be possible to distinguish with any certainty the
aspects of Western technology that are actually "technically determined" and those that are culturally or economically determined.

The difficulty of such research is considerable. It is not possible to prove from the mere fact of technology transfer that the recipient organism will grow to resemble the donor. The significant question is whether the transferred technology takes its place in a general
process of cultural change leading to a different type of industrial
society from that in which it originated, or whether, on the contrary,
it merely contributes to a process of modernization convergent with
that in the West. It is extremely difficult to formulate such judgments. A new type of industrial society cannot emerge ready-made
from a revolution, especially not in a backward society. Present
investigation can hope to find nothing more conclusive than indications of a divergent path of development. What constitutes such an
indication, and how is its importance to be weighed relative to the
convergent features of the society? This chapter will attempt to
clarify the methodological problems involved in making judgments
about such questions.

The first of these problems is the status of convergence theory
itself. What does it mean that Western research on communist societies accepts Western models of development as normative? What
does it mean that the paradox of development is accepted as a universal limit to progress that every people in the world must eventually
encounter? I will argue that the thesis of convergence is less a conclusion of research than an ethnocentric starting point for it. It is a
starting point that is implicit in methods and approaches, becoming
explicit in their application. As in Kantian epistemology, empirical
studies arrive at the very general conclusions they have unconscious-
ly "read into" the data. The application of a conceptual framework,
while necessary, leads the researcher to emphasize certain facts at
the expense of others. With a different method, these emphasized
facts might be ignored or regarded as less significant. Thus the
data do less to prove the conclusions than the conclusions do to define and shape the data. It is doubtless an inescapable fact of research that one cannot learn anything at all without making assump-

tions and that it is far more difficult than is generally supposed to get more out of information than one puts into it in selecting and organizing it.

In the specific case of the study of technology transfer and modernization in communist societies, these epistemological dilemmas raise difficulties of a cultural order. We are engaged in the study of societies not our own, in which the meaning of institutional arrangements and events is often interpreted by participants according to codes we neither sympathize with nor accept. What is particularly serious is not just the empty circularity that threatens all interpretative knowledge; of society, but still more the antagonism of capitalist and communist codes of interpretation, which overlap in all dimensions and which each claims to be normative for the other.

It is my contention that some of the most basic assumptions that underlie many studies of communist societies are ethnocentric, derived uncritically from the nature of the advanced capitalist environment of the researcher. I will discuss assumptions concerning wealth and technology that to varying degrees have influenced communist studies, guiding them fatefully toward the thesis of convergence.[7] I will show that these assumptions are based on the taking as normative for society in general, capitalist ways of organizing technological progress and understanding human welfare. It is not surprising that, having derived its basic concepts uncritically from advanced capitalism, this method arrives at the thesis of convergence, according to which advanced capitalism is a general model of development for all others. A method that rests on these bases cannot help but misunderstand alien cultural worlds and reject alternative social options.

I will argue that it is precisely in its normative dimension that the thesis of convergence begs rather than answers the question that needs to be posed about the future of communist societies. Starting with Marx's work, Marxism has challenged the promise that there is only one model of industrial progress, one path to abundance. Marx situated the breaking-off point, at which alternatives emerge, quite early in the history of modern technological development, with the mechanization of industry. Thereafter, Marx asserted, radically different industrial futures are possible, depending on whether the dominant political option is capitalist or socialist. Thus properly formulated, the question to which the study of communism should address itself is that of the possibility of alternative paths of modernization, leading perhaps, under different social systems, to different consequences for human freedom.

In this essay I will discuss this very general question in the context of a narrower one, namely, how research on communist

societies might test the signs of an evolution leading beyond convergence, beyond the paradox of development. In Marxist theory such an
evolution is called the "transition to socialism." This concept refers
to a process of social change affecting values, human relations, and
technologies and leading, over a period of generations, from capitalism to Marx's vision of socialism. All the existing communist societies claim to be making this transition, although most Western observers are profoundly sceptical of such claims.

How can we decide this dilemma—transition or convergence—
one way or the other? We cannot simply compare an "ideal-type" of
socialism to the existing state of affairs in communist societies,
since none of them claim to have gone beyond the early stages of the
transition. There is, furthermore, considerable potential for mis-
understanding associated with any ideal-typical presentation of socialist models. Such presentations may aid in clarifying concepts,
but by the same token they may also seem to imply that socialism is
a preestablished policy that could be imposed on society from above
by a government. In the framework of Marx's theory it is clear that
this cannot be, that socialism is not a policy but a process of change
far deeper than anything that could be accomplished by politics, although the latter may of course contribute decisively to initiating
this process. Marx did not suggest that idealistic individuals could
succeed in the voluntaristic imposition of their personal utopias, but
he attempted to identify and further an actual process of cultural
change that would ultimately produce a new type of society in which
new patterns of behavior would flow spontaneously from new conditions of life. [8]

What is of interest, then, in the Marxist approach is that it
not only admits the difference between the ideal and the reality of
socialism but suggests the existence of a historical "law" leading
from the one to the other. This "law" may or may not actually apply
to any real society, but its logic can be formulated as a general
model of the dynamics of cultural change in societies making the
transition to socialism. This model can then be compared with the
realities in order to test the claims and counterclaims of the theses
of convergence and transition.

What I will do throughout the rest of this essay is to elaborate
such a conceptual framework for the study of the cultural dynamics
of communist societies, based on the Marxist theory of the transition
to socialism. The use I intend to make of this Marxist concept is
strictly methodological. I will not be concerned with whether the
transition to socialism is inevitable—obviously a question that concerned Marx—but rather with whether anything resembling it is
actually occurring. I will argue that, when reformulated as a theory
of the dynamics of cultural change in communist societies, signifi-

cant features of this theory of transition can be applied to some of these societies. This result suggests that the grim antinomies of the paradox of development may yet be transcended in a new type of industrial society.

THE MARXIAN CRITIQUE OF INDUSTRIAL SOCIETY

It is obvious that the question of alternative paths of modernization can be posed and answered without reference to Marx and Marxism. There have been suggestive attempts to do so, for example the work of Ivan Illich. What then is the interest in returning to Marx in considering this question? What is his relevance after all these years to a question that, it is said, he considered only briefly in his youth in his unfinished theory of alienation? The problem today, so goes the argument, is not the narrow one of economic justice that concerned Marx but the much more basic one of the role of knowledge in society.

There are in fact interpretations of Marxism in which his whole contribution to the critique of industrial society is seen as a moral one. It is true that Marx was an emphatic critic of the evils of industrialism, of child labor, of the mutilating effects of the machines on workers, of the poverty of the proletariat, and so on. Were his contributions confined to such moral denunciations, they would indeed be irrelevant to the contemporary debate over the future of technological society.

This is the position of Daniel Bell, for example, whose seminal article "Two Roads from Marx"[9] still defines the horizon of most discussions of Marxism, both in the mainstream and to some extent on the left of the academy as well. It is worth briefly considering the thesis of this article to establish the relevance of a new look at Marx's critique of industrial society and his cure for its ills.

Bell argues that Marx passed from an early humanistic concern with the alienation of labor to sterile analyses of economic exploitation in his mature writings. "Alienation, initially conceived by Marx to be a process whereby an individual lost his capacity to express himself in work, now became seen as exploitation, or the appropriation of a laborer's surplus product by the capitalist."[10] The narrowed focus of these later works misled the socialist movement into believing that the overthrow of the property relations associated with capitalism would automatically solve all the other problems of workers, including oppression on the job and in society at large. Thus Marxism cut off the route to an independent critique of these other problems, which are quite as important as exploitation and independent of it. "Marxist thought . . . [developed] along

one road, the narrow road of primitivist economic conceptions of
men, property, and exploitation, while another road, which might
have led to new, humanistic conceptions of work and labour, was
left unexplored. "[11]

It is essential to Bell's thesis that Capital, the chief work of
Marx's maturity, not contain a serious discussion of alienation in the
Marxian sense, as the worker's loss of control over the conditions
and products of his or her labor. Bell does argue that "other than as
literary references in Capital, to the dehumanization of labor and the
fragmentation of work, this first aspect of the problem was glossed
over by Marx. "[12] I will show that this assertion is entirely and
textually inaccurate, that in Capital Marx does present an analysis
of the capitalist organization of labor and that this analysis is relevant to contemporary discussions of technology and freedom. Indeed,
Marx sets out to account for the characteristic phenomena identified
by theorists of technological society as the nemesis of freedom: the
scientization of production and administration, the disqualification
of the labor force, and its consequent subordination to the mechanical and bureaucratic systems that organize its common efforts. I
will argue that Capital was in fact the first systematic attempt to
carry out the program Bell lays down in the following passage for a
modern social theory freed from the ideological furies of Marxism
itself:

> The time has come, perhaps, to move away from the
> transmogrified personifications, with their simplistic
> views of social behavior and their simple-minded solu-
> tions for "history." If one is to deal meaningfully with
> the loss of self, of the meaning of responsibility in
> modern life, one must begin again with concrete prob-
> lems, and among the first of these is the nature of the
> work process itself, the initial source of alienation. [13]

Bell's error is to reduce Marxism to a critique of the unjust
distribution of wealth. What Bell fails to see is that for Marx the
relations of distribution are derivative of the more fundamental relations of production. Under capitalism, ownership of wealth is not
just possession of unequal rights as a consumer but, more importantly, it is possession of unequal rights of control over and access
to the means of production, which is capital. Considered in its social aspect, the personal wealth of the individual capitalist is inextricably bound up with the "divorce" of workers from the means of
production, hence also their subordination in the labor process to
the owners of wealth. The continuum of incomes masks a sharp dis-

continuity of power between those who own the instruments of labor
and those who must work under the control of the former to earn a
living. Marx wrote as follows:

> The worker's propertylessness, and . . . the appropri-
> ation of alien labour by capital . . . are fundamental
> conditions of the bourgeois mode of production, in no
> way accidents irrelevant to it. These modes of distribu-
> tion are the relations of production themselves, but sub
> specie distributionis.[14]

In Marx's analysis this feature of the capitalist system is related to another, conceptually deeper characteristic of it. All economic systems, Marx argues, consist of a specific combination of
workers, nonworking owners, and means of production. Two very
different types of relationships bind the members of the first two
categories to the third. Marx distinguishes between what he calls the
"relation of appropriation" of workers to the means of production,
that is, their access to and control over the land and tools of their
trade, and the "relation of ownership, " which concerns access to and
control over the product. In precapitalist economic systems, as
Marx explains them, these two relations are nonhomologous. The
serf, for example, has a time-honoured right to appropriate the
means of production, but ownership lies in the hands of the lord. Under capitalism, for the first time, these two relations are homologous: the capitalist both owns the means of production and controls
their appropriation by workers, the workers participating negatively
in these relations. [15] It is because of this homologous relation of
appropriation and ownership that distribution of wealth and control
of the labor process are conjoined in the capitalist system.

In Capital Marx argues that this unusual feature of capitalism
results from its unique organization of cooperative labor. The capitalist brings together a labor force, provides it with tools, and sets
it to work on a prearranged project. The capitalist appears as the
veritable source and unity of this production process. The workers
relate to each other only through the capitalist, who has hired them
all. They relate to the tools, again, only through the capitalist who
provides them. They relate to the project, also, only through the
plan of the capitalist. It is because the workers neither own their
own tools nor form a natural community based on some traditional
mode of appropriation that they can be so organized. In the process
a new "post" in the social division of labor is created, that of the
capitalist or his managerial representatives who do the organizing.
Thus to the "divorce" of the workers from the means of production
also corresponds a new role for the owners of these means: direct
control of the labor process. [16]

As Marx conceives it, capital is more than a sum of wealth: a characteristic organization of labor is also one of its essential determinants. This organization of labor includes a sharp division of mental and manual functions in the production process. The first fully developed manufacturing capitalism elaborated this division of labor through the incorporation and parceling of the traditional handicraft methods of production. The goal was to reduce the skill levels of the workers, simplifying tasks into mechanical routines that could be quickly learned. Cheap, unskilled labor could then replace costly, skilled labor.

With this type of division of labor the position of capitalist is truly a necessary one. Manual labor having been degraded to a mechanical routine, all the mental functions of production are concentrated in the hands of the capitalist as organizer. It is thus just insofar as the capitalist division of labor restricts the mental horizon associated with each job that capital itself emerges as the "subject" of production. The cultural incapacity of workers, their inability to understand and master production on the basis of their narrow experience of it, becomes the secure foundation on which the power of capital is built. Marx wrote as follows:

> Intelligence in production expands in one direction because it vanishes in many others. What is lost by the detail labourers, is concentrated in the capital that employs them. It is a result of the division of labour in manufactures, that the labourer is brought face to face with the intellectual potencies of the material process of production, as the property of another, and as a ruling power. This separation begins in simple cooperation, where the capitalist represents to the single workman, the oneness and the will of the associated labour. It is developed in manufacture which cuts down the labourer into a detail labourer. It is completed in modern industry, which makes science a productive force distinct from labour and presses it into the service of capital. [17]

Note especially that in this passage Marx does not criticize capitalism for the inhuman effects of this division of labor. The point is not that work becomes boring and uncreative; the point is rather a political one, that capital establishes its reign over labor through a division of labor that disqualifies the worker and renders the worker helpless before the massed forces of knowledge embodied in capital.

The introduction of machinery completes the radical separation of mental and manual labor, the intellectual and physical forces of production, which was already begun in manufacture. In machine industry, the specifically capitalist organization of the labor process "for the first time acquires technical and palpable reality."[18] Here "the labourer becomes a mere appendage to an already existing material condition of production."[19] Where in the handicraft era the worker possessed all the knowledge required for production as subjective capacity, now this knowledge has become an objective power owned by another. Machine industry thus represents the adequate form of mature capitalism. In it the subordination of the worker to the conditions of labor is in no way accidental or external but has become a necessary consequence of the mechanical crystallization of the knowledge associated with production. Marx wrote as follows in his draft of Capital, the Grundrisse:

> The development of the means of labour into machinery is not an accidental moment of capital, but is rather the historical reshaping of the traditional, inherited means of labour into a form adequate to capital. The accumulation of knowledge and of skill, of the general productive forces of the social brain, is thus absorbed into capital, as opposed to labour, and hence appears as an attribute of capital. . . . In machinery, knowledge appears as alien, external to him [the worker]; and living labour as subsumed under self-activating objectified labour.[20]

To summarize, for Marx the capitalist system is characterized not just by a specific form of ownership (and associated form of exchange), but also by at least three other essential "moments." These are, as discussed above, a specific form of appropriation, based on direct control of the labor process by capitalists or their representatives; a specific division of mental and manual labor, designed to reduce to an absolute minimum the levels of knowledge and skill required by the ordinary worker; and the increasing objectification of the accumulated knowledge of the human species in the means of production, in machines. In the absence of major countervailing trends of some sort, these attributes characterize a social system that is less and less manageable for its members, increasingly and radically "alienated" in the sense that the workers come more and more under the power of the economic and social world they contribute to creating through their own combined efforts.

The core of Marx's critique of capitalism can be summed up as an argument to the effect that the division of labor associated with technological advancement in this system removes all economic incentives for society to teach and for workers to learn enough knowledge about the social world to participate fully in making the im-

portant social decisions that concern them. The acquisition of knowledge follows the patterns established by a specialized breakdown of
tasks designed to insure capitalist control of the labor process. It
rarely goes beyond this minimum. The result is what I will call a
"knowledge deficit," an enlarging gap between the level of culture
required by most positions in the division of labor and that required
to make significant social decisions. The paradox of development is
the consequence at the political level of this knowledge deficit produced in the economy. [21]

Before proceeding in the next section to a discussion of the
"crisis" of capitalism and the remedies proposed by Marx to deal
with alienation in industrial society, I would like to draw some general conclusions about the relevance of Marx. It should be clear from
this brief description of his position that it is a great deal more complex and interesting than Bell's presentation would lead one to believe. Marx is not only, nor even centrally, concerned with economic justice in the distribution of wealth; nor is it true that Marx's
Marxism is narrowly focused on economics while recent social
science first explored the more important problems of labor organization and the distribution of knowledge in society. For Marx,
questions of distribution of wealth are derivative from questions of
labor organization. Thus the abolition of "exploitation," of capital
as a form of ownership, could not, as Bell suggests, suffice to establish Marxian socialism. This legal act would not even abolish
capital as Marx defines it.

I can now answer one of the questions I posed in the introduction to this essay. Was Marx aware of the consequences of modern
technology for human freedom? The answer is clearly that he was.
In fact, it was Marx who first reformulated what I have called the
paradox of development in terms of the growing gap between the cognitive capacities of the individual and the complexity of social life.
Concern with these matters did not have to await the innovations of
modern sociology.

What distinguishes Marx's approach from that of recent
critics of technological society is his refusal to accept the inevitability of the link between alienated administration of the economy and
the employment of industrial technology. This link—the paradox of
development in modern dress—is real enough under capitalism, but
Marx ascribes it not to the nature of technology but to the capitalist
division of mental and manual labor. Thus according to Marx the
paradox of development in modern societies is not rooted in technological imperatives but in the capitalist system, which cannot increase social wealth without diminishing the control over their work
and the lives of the great mass of mankind.

CRISIS AND TRANSITION

Whatever the merits of Marx's diagnosis of the ills of capitalism, economically backward societies on the receiving end of technology transfers exhibit many of the symptoms described by Marx. The massive introduction of advanced, science-based technologies transforms the economic life of such societies and generates an instant knowledge deficit of enormous proportions. The gap between individual capacities and the demands of technology has political consequences similar to those anticipated by Marx, in particular the rise of managerial control from above. Thus in one of its most interesting dimensions, its reflections on the social role of knowledge in industrial society, Marx's theory provides a description of problems actually confronting communist societies today.

Some of these societies, for example the People's Republic of China, are very concerned about precisely these sorts of problems. They are attempting to implement Marx's own remedy, the gradual abolition of the division of mental and manual labor, with, as a long range consequence, the transformation of "capitalist" technology into "socialist" technology. This is, of course, the essence of the promised "transition to socialism, " much as Marx initially described it. [22]

However, we are bound to observe a critical difference between what is happening today and Marx's expectations. Marx related capitalism and socialism as antecedent and consequent, positing two imperative dynamics of change connecting them, one leading to the crisis of capitalism, the other to the transition to socialism. Both of these anticipated dynamics of change are supposed to be rooted in the ultimate incompatibility of large-scale industrial production with class society. It is true that Marx sometimes admitted the possibility of failure, of the crisis of capitalism leading not to socialism but to the breakdown of civilization itself, to barbarism. More often, he described the historical development as a law-governed process of change, overriding, in the final analysis, all countertendencies and historical accidents. [23] What he did not anticipate is the present situation, in which quite stable capitalist societies promise to endure for a very long time, side by side with communist ones.

In fact, capitalism has not collapsed in crisis but peacefully and profitably negotiates the sale of its accumulated know-how to coexisting communist states. Just as capitalism seems to be a great deal more secure as a social system than Marx expected, so Marx's own kind of socialism is a great deal weaker and more threatened in the countries of its triumphant revolutionary victory than he would have anticipated. Neither imperative dynamic, capitalist crisis or socialist transition, seems to be taking an imperative

form. The reconstruction of Marx's theory undertaken here will
therefore move from the imperative to the declarative mode, trans-
lating Marx's language of historical law and tendency into that of
ideal-typical description. At the end of this section I will suggest
indices that can be used to apply to communist societies this model
of the transition to socialism.

The Crisis of Capitalism

Marx's theory of capitalist development is based on the dynamics of the defining "moments" of capitalism, several of which were
described in the preceding section. The "breakdown" of capitalism
anticipated by Marx results from the reaction of the working class
to the catastrophic social consequences of the contradictory interaction of these moments. Actually, Marx's theory leads to the identification of a whole series of crisis tendencies, but here only one of
these is directly relevant. This is the crisis tendency rooted in the
conflict between the increasing objectification of human knowledge in
machines and the capitalist mode of "appropriation," or control of
the labor process, and its associated division of manual and mental
labor. On the one hand, Marx argues, more "intelligent" means of
production embodying a deepening knowledge of nature, to be used to
maximum advantage, will eventually require more intelligent producers. On the other hand, capitalism must resist any increase in
the skill and knowledge of the producers in the interest of maintaining tight control of the labor process and, ultimately, of the sociopolitical process as well.

This crisis tendency can be restated as a "contradiction" between the social and technical dimensions of capitalist production.
Marx points out that under capitalism the economy is organized "from
above," not by the producers themselves but by capitalists who control the means of production. For Marx, capitalist control of the
labor process has a double character. On the one hand it has a clear
technical necessity, demanded by the conditions for the successful
cooperation of large numbers of people: this is the work of supervision inseparable from large-scale production. On the other hand,
this same system of control is designed to produce an income for the
capitalist, a goal that flows from no technical necessity and that is
not voluntarily served by the workers. [24]

These distinct social and technical functions are condensed in
the characteristic organization of labor that capital imposes on the
production process. Labor must be organized in the "interests" of
the capitalist class, that is, in the service of the goal of a privately
appropriated profit. The capitalist cannot count on the good will and

cooperation of the workers in pursuing this end because their claims on the wealth of the enterprise compete with the capitalist's own. Labor discipline must therefore be imposed from above. [25] The sharp division of mental and manual labor is the most powerful basis for this imposition. Through it the capitalist can fulfill the technical functions of supervision in the specific manner most appropriate to generating profits for the enterprise and concentrating them in the capitalist's own hands.

This same double character of the role of the capitalist also has effects on the innovation process. Marx argues that in capitalist society innovation is responsive not just to the pursuit of increased power over nature, but also to the pursuit of increased power over the labor force. Progress is governed simultaneously by at least these two criteria, both of which must be satisfied if an innovation is to be introduced. The social criterion orients the innovation process toward technologies that disqualify the labor force and subordinate it to the mechanical conditions of production, making it easier to control. There is thus a sense in which innovation under capitalism is class-determined; it proceeds not so much from the logic of technology as from the interests of capital. Marx says of science that it "is the most powerful weapon for repressing strikes, those periodical revolts of the working class against the autocracy of capital."[26] Marx claims that "it would be possible to write quite a history of inventions, made since 1830, for the sole purpose of supplying capital with weapons against the revolts of the working class."[27] Technology is thus shaped in its development by the social purposes of capital, particularly by the need to maintain and further a division of labor that keeps the labor force safely under control.

Considerations such as these suggest the ultimate vulnerability of the capitalist system. Might not the pursuit of technical progress at some point come into conflict with the pursuit of power over the worker? Is it not possible that at some point new technologies might render dysfunctional the division of mental and manual labor on which capital relies and thereby transform it from a source of social progress into an obstacle? Marx replies that with the development of machine technology the maintenance of the old division of labor becomes a source of gigantic waste for society as a whole. Nevertheless, capital cannot overthrow this division of labor without abolishing the base of its own power. The consequences would appear first in the economy, in the wage demands of a skilled labor force; the further results of such a revolution in the organization of labor would be revolution in society in general.

Marx describes the growing conflict between the social and technical dimensions of the role of the capitalist in production as follows:

> Although then, technically speaking, the old system of
> division of labour is thrown overboard by machinery,
> it hangs on in the factory, as a traditional habit handed
> down from Manufacture, and is afterwards systemati-
> cally remoulded and established in a more hideous form
> by capital, as a means of exploiting labour-power. . . .
> Machinery is put to a wrong use, with the object of trans-
> forming the workman, from his very childhood, into a
> part of a detail-machine. In this way, not only are the
> expenses of his re-production considerably lessened,
> but at the same time his helpless dependence upon the
> factory as a whole, and therefore upon the capitalist,
> is rendered complete. Here as everywhere else, we
> must distinguish between the increased productiveness
> due to the development of the social process of produc-
> tion, and that due to the capitalist exploitation of that
> process. [28]

The skills and knowledge of the working population, which are
the cultural infrastructure of society, stand here in contradiction
with the mechanical infrastructure of production. Two of the defining
moments of capitalism have come into contradiction: that which leads
to the increasing objectification of human knowledge in machinery and
that which generates a radical division of mental and manual labor. A
new "law" of economic life has arisen with the new technology, a law
that commands "fitness of the labourer for varied work, consequently the greatest possible development of his varied aptitudes."[29] Modern industry "by its very nature . . . necessitates variation of labour, fluency of function, universal mobility of the labourer."[30] However, by its very nature capitalism requires just the opposite, an
ignorant and docile labor force tied to highly specialized tasks. This
is the "absolute contradiction between the technical necessities of
Modern Industry, and the social character inherent in its capitalistic
form."[31] This contradiction manifests itself in the inability of the
labor force to follow the constantly shifting winds of innovation and
investment. The empirical evidence of it is everywhere, Marx claims,
in the unemployment and waste of energy and intelligence of millions
of workers.[32]

Marx's argument in these passages might be restated as two
different propositions, a "maximum" and a "minimum" thesis. The
maximum thesis comes across in the imperative formulation of this
crisis tendency, according to which capitalism will fall victim to
devastating and politically unmanageable problems of unemployment
and social waste. In the dispute over this version of Marx's argument,
the implications of his still more interesting minimum thesis have

been ignored. This latter holds that industrial technology is compatible with a radically different division of labor than that under which it first develops. The minimum thesis thus asserts not the inevitability of socialism but its possibility. Assertion of its possibility, of course, is a logically prior and more fundamental point. Marx argues it by distinguishing those aspects of capitalist production that are socially relative, hence dispensable in a different social context, and those that open up new technical possibilities only partially explored by capitalism. On these terms, if the capitalist division of labor is socially relative, rooted in the control problems of this form of economic organization, then it will be possible to replace it with another division of labor in a society freed from these control problems.

This is the interesting point for the argument developed in this essay. Thus where Marx claims that "Modern Industry, indeed, compels society, under penalty of death" to adopt a new division of labor, let us merely say that modern industry permits society

> to replace the detail-worker of today, crippled by lifelong repetition of one and same trivial operation, and thus reduced to a mere fragment of a man, by the fully developed individual, fit for a variety of labours, ready to face any change of production, and to whom the different social functions he performs, are but so many modes of giving free scope to his own natural and acquired powers. [33]

Here Marx is describing the end of the knowledge deficit and the end of the paradox of development that is its political consequence. The remainder of this section will be devoted to constructing the hypothetical social conditions that might make possible such a change in the status of the worker in the economy and society.

The Transition to Socialism

The Marxist vision of history is based on the proposition that "it is . . . the law of division of labour that lies at the basis of the division into classes."[34] Lower-class individuals raised to day-to-day economic activity and manual labor cannot understand and participate in the work of organizing society as a whole. Overall organization thus becomes the specialized concern of ruling groups, who impose it on the lower classes through an elaborate system of control. Only drastic reductions in the gaps between the levels and types of knowledge and skills involved in basic productive activities and the work of social organization can make possible an end to class society. In Marx's long-range view of industrial societies, the massive objectification of human knowledge in machines will require a corresponding rise in the level of knowledge and skill of the labor force. The gradual breakdown of the old division of labor under the impact of the new technologies will be the basis for revolution initiating the transition to a classless society.

In its broadest outlines this idea of socialism as classlessness has been anticipated in millenarian and utopian speculation for centuries. Indeed, in one form or another it may have existed throughout the entire history of class society as its mythic critique. What Marx sets out to show is that the industrial working class is the first class in history that has the capability of realizing this ideal, and of doing so not on the basis of an ethical or ideological impulse in contradiction with its needs, but rather in the pursuit of its concrete interests as a class. Capitalism thus creates not only the technical possibility of a classless society, but also a social group in the working class with an interest in this prospect.

Marx's use of the concept of "interest" in this connection is designed to give an objective, imperative form to the process of the transition to socialism. Thus, just as the interests of capitalists are supposed to govern for the cultural and technological development of capitalism, so the interests of workers would form the red thread guiding the lengthy transitional process. These interests, in which Marx places his confidence, are summed up over and over again in Marxism as the abolition of the proletariat. Concretely, this seems to mean two chief things: (1) the abolition of the division of mental and manual labor and the transformation of technology into the basis for highly productive, interesting, and inherently worthwhile labor and (2) the abolition of the wage system in favor of distribution according to need.

What is Marx's justification for reformulating as class interests, goals that in the past have always been presented as ethical or religious ideals? According to Marx, socialist society contains in the very principle it realizes, that is, universal labor, the motive and means of its own evolution into a radically different type of industrial society. So long as all must work, the only way that individuals can hope to improve their personal lot dramatically is through contributing to a general progress from which all will benefit. Furthermore, universal labor means that the overall organizing functions of society are transformed into work like any other, performed in accordance with a plan agreed upon by all. Those who do the productive work thus also take final responsibility for the organization of the society. Marx argues that, considered as a "ruling class," workers are unique. All previous ruling classes had in common a disinterest and disdain for the quality of work because they were released from the obligation to do it by the subordination of workers. The workers themselves are the only ones who cannot shift the burden of productive activity onto the shoulders of other, subordinate classes. They will therefore undertake to humanize the world of work.

Marx develops this approach along two lines. First, such a society would handle control problems very differently from the way they are handled by class societies in general and capitalism in particular. As discussed above, capitalist control of the labor process must be exercised in conflict with workers as a class. It therefore requires a sharp division of mental and manual labor as a means of imposing labor discipline on an indifferent or hostile labor force. Under socialism, Marx argues, no fundamental conflict of interest would divide organizers and organized into a ruling and a ruled class. The workers would elect those who perform the overall organizing functions of society and collectively impose social self-discipline on themselves. Having assumed collective responsibility for production, the workers would mutually enforce on each other a discipline of work that they might individually be inclined to evade. Resistance to labor discipline becomes an individual matter and no longer takes the form of class struggle as under capitalism. Under these conditions, an ever-increasing measure of voluntary cooperation could be assumed, and thus the problems of control would be immensely simplified. [35]

Of course, Marx is not so utopian as to imagine that the need for labor discipline would rapidly disappear. Marx notes that both the culture and the technology of the transitional period would at first be products of the capitalist system. In consequence, individual egoism and unrewarding work would be the rule. Work motivations would therefore have to be maintained in this phase of socialist development by individual incentives such as wages. What is new is that the release of the industrial system from the struggle between capitalists and workers would in turn permit the release of workers from the harsh discipline of the capitalist division of labor with all its attendant consequences, including the knowledge deficit, the associated paradox of development, and alienation.

This first consequence of workers' self-administration would make possible a second and still more significant change in human life. Under socialism, workers would control not only day-to-day production, but also the long-term reproduction of society. Marx argues that they would use this control to change the very natures of technology and work, which for the first time in history would become major preoccupations of a ruling class with a motive to alter them. Marx seems to have believed that the possession and exercise of class power is decisive in determining the general course of technological development over long periods. An undemocratic class

power (that of the capitalist class, Marx would argue), eliminates
technologies that threaten its interests, while a democratic power
would similarly emphasize developments favorable to it. Over time
the application of such different social criteria of development would
yield alternative industrial systems, adapted to different class interests and based on different cultures.

It is important to note that Marx does not presuppose the transformation of technology and work as preconditions for workers organizing themselves as a ruling class, but rather anticipates such
changes as a result of working class rule. In the Marxist perspective,
the working class would begin with the capitalist inheritance and, in
the process of using and reproducing it, would subject it to the demands of a new class power. The transformation of capitalist technology is conceived as a lengthy process in which changing social
relations would create the conditions for a democratic reproduction
of the mechanical base. Presumably, new social criteria of innovation,
responding to the interests of the producers, would prevail over the
values embodied in capitalist technology.

Considered as a dynamic of technological change, the transition
to socialism is rooted in the conflict of socialist and capitalist social
criteria of development, the one responding to the "interests" of
workers in humane work settings and the other embodied in the inherited technology of the old society, with its inhuman division of
labor. Marx believed that eventually, under these conditions, the
workers would produce a new technology in which work would be "one
of life's prime wants" and not a burdensome obligation. This goal
would be achieved when labor

> is of a scientific and at the same time general character,
> not merely human exertion as a specifically harnessed
> natural force, but exertion as subject, which appears in
> the production process not in a merely natural, spontan-
> eous form, but as an activity regulating all the forces of
> nature. [36]

Such a transformation of technology and work would be the
basis for the socialist principle of distribution according to need.
Where man has become the "subject" of production, labor can become a domain of self-expression that no longer has to be motivated
by extrinsic rewards. In such a society the gratification of need
could be disassociated from the performance of socially validated
services. This would be the achievement of the "higher phase" of
socialism.

As reconstructed here, Marx's theory of the transition to socialism can be summarized in the following three propositions:

1. Systems of control from above (class rule) require a division of labor and criteria of innovation incompatible with the full and democratic development of the individuality of the workers;

2. A system of workers' self-administration would require the development of a quantitatively different division of labor compatible with the employment of highly educated and socially responsible workers;

3. Such a self-administered system would be oriented toward long-range patterns of technological development that would further the ever-fuller actualization of human potentialities at work.

Socialism is thus not just workers' self-administration, but self-administration on behalf of the creation of a radically new type of industrial society.

If Marx's argument is once again divided into maximum and minimum theses, it will be possible to reformulate his imperative propositions as declarative ones. Marx's maximum thesis argues that the transition to socialism would be a necessary consequence of workers' self-administration, that self-administration would inevitably lead to the socialist transformation of technology. This imperative formulation will be examined more closely below and need not detain us here. Marx's more basic minimum thesis might be formulated to say that workers' self-administration is compatible with changes in the division of labor and eventually in technologies as well, in conformity with the concept of the transition to socialism. This "compatibility" can be given a specific economic significance.

At the basis of the concept of the transition to socialism is the hypothesis that, suitably adapted, the technology developed by capitalism can be efficiently employed by workers in the context of a new division of labor and in function of new social purposes. Marx foresaw no necessary economic losses from the changeover that could not be compensated by the release of the technology from the contradiction between its technical and social facets. Under socialism the "subjective" forces of production—human skill and intelligence—formerly wasted by capitalism, could be rapidly developed as a new source of wealth. The transition to socialism can thus be understood not as an attempt to impose impractical, ideological goals on a satisfactory technical base, but rather as an alternative method of maximizing the contribution of technology to human welfare in a different social context.

So formulated, the theory of the transition to socialism is an attempt to show the possibility of an alternative type of industrial society, one based on a much fuller development of individual capa-

cities than is capitalism. This would be a society in which the very
pursuit of economic efficiency would raise the cultural capacities of
individuals to the level of the social responsibilities they would have
to fulfill. It would be a society, therefore, in which the paradox of
development would be overcome, in which there would be no necessary trade-off between the pursuit of economic well-being and democratic participation.

The Distribution of Knowledge

Marx cast his theory of the transition to socialism in an imperative form because he believed that socialist societies would possess
definite structural properties compelling them forward along essentially predictable lines. The objective "interests" of the working
class Marx posits are themselves consequences of these structural
properties, in sum, of the implications of cooperative self-administration for systems of control and criteria of innovation.

The weak point of this imperative formulation, however, is
precisely this concept of interest. It does not really succeed in providing a convincing link between the minimum changes that would be
associated with the establishment of a system of self-administration
and the long-range goal of transforming technology. Concretely, it
may be asked what would necessarily orient workers toward the new
concepts of labor and welfare that Marx identifies with socialism.
While his theory suggests the economic viability of reducing the
knowledge deficit somewhat, what would motivate workers to emphasize the development of their individual capacities and knowledge to
the highest degree, as opposed, for example, to choosing the insatiable pursuit of commodities that is characteristic of advanced capitalist societies? In fact, there is a good deal of evidence from the
existing communist societies that the trade-offs involved in this
choice are controversial ones. Thus the "interests" of workers under communism seem to be relatively ambiguous and may not guar-
antee a socialist evolution.

For the purposes of this paper it is not necessary to establish
Marx's maximum thesis. Of central concern here is only the possibility that workers in some communist societies might influence technological choices and futures in an original direction corresponding
in its main outlines with Marx's concept of the transition. What is
of relevance to this problem is not the "interests" of workers in socialist society generally considered, but the empirically identifiable
interests they actually defend in specific cases. Where these latter
approximate to the hypothetical "interests" Marx imputes to workers,
they may become the basis for the adaptation of technology to social-

ist purposes. The observable tendency of workers in a communist society to perceive their interests much as Marx anticipated they would, might well serve as an <u>index</u> of the existence of a transitional process.

These considerations suggest the usefulness of a closer look at Marx's hypothetical construction of the interests of workers under socialism, not for the purpose of criticizing or defending Marx's model, but rather in order to reformulate it as an ideal-type of the sorts of interests associated with the transition to socialism. Marx's <u>Grundrisse</u> provides a basis for this approach.

Capitalist society distributes wealth in the form of ever more varied commodities, but Marx argues, this commodity form is only a limited reflection of the actual enrichment of the human species represented by the growth of the needs and faculties of the consumers of commodities. It is this latter that is "real" wealth, the development of human attributes and capacities as dimensions of individual self-actualization, mediated by material goods to be sure, but not identical with them. The extension of transport and communications is a clear example of Marx's new standard of wealth. Peasants confined mentally and physically to the small villages of their ancestors are "poor" by Marx's standard, compared with the modern individuals situated at the nexus of cosmopolitan interactions. Instead of appearing in the form of goods external to the individual, wealth now appears as the developed powers of that individual. A socialist society would be oriented toward just such an enlargement of human experience and individuality as an end in itself, without subordinating these forms of wealth to the pursuit of a profit on the sale of the material goods associated with their acquisition.[37]

For Marx the industrial economy creates unique opportunities to apply the expanded powers of the individual to increasing productivity, and therefore, under socialism, there are economic motivations for the enlargement of human capacities. Once a society has been gripped by this dynamic relation of consumption to production—the pursuit of "real" wealth contributing to its production—radical changes in the economy will occur. Marx argues that, under socialism, workers would increasingly be able to unfold their powers and potentialities at work in a socially productive manner. There is a sense, then, in which training and education, variety of experience and occupation would become a higher type of "consumer" good. Nevertheless, the labor process would always remain a "realm of necessity" beyond which the individual would seek freely to apply the powers developed at work. Marx believed that workers would therefore strive to reduce the time spent working while simultaneously increasing their learning time in the leisure created by technical advances. "The saving of labour time (is) equal to an increase

of free time, i.e. time for the full development of the individual,
which in turn reacts back upon the productive power of labour as itself the greatest productive power."[38] Socialist patterns of consumption, established in the interests generated by socialist society, develop the "wealth" of the individual personality and the productivity
of labor in a self-reinforcing cycle.

This remarkable hypothesis can serve in the construction of an
ideal type of the transition to socialism if it is translated out of the
objectivistic language of "interest" into the more empirical language
of "culture." Margaret Mead and her coworkers have shown in Cultural Patterns and Technical Change that attitudes toward the economy and perceived self-interest in different cultures are relevant to
development problems.[39] I would therefore prefer to abandon for the
purpose of this discussion Marx's term "interest" and to substitute
for it my own concept of "economic perceptions," referring to empirically identifiable cultural differences.

By economic perceptions I mean the way in which individuals
customarily perceive their own welfare in a given society, what they
regard as economic goals, and what they consider to be legitimate or
desirable economic means. Economic perceptions govern such
things as the goods individuals seek to obtain as economic rewards
and whether they expect these goods to be delivered publicly or as
privately consumable commodities; attitudes toward such things as
workmanship, authority relations on the job, savings and leisure,
the occupational expectations associated with various jobs and with
sex and age, and so on.

Economic perceptions are culturally relative, differing from
one society to another. While there may be some common core of
minimum economic expectations sought in all industrial societies
(food, shelter, transport), the form in which people demand these
basic goods, as well as the various other economic ends they pursue, may differ radically according to cultural traditions and contexts. These cultural differences may have major implications for
the process of technological development and technology transfer.

In any society, it is through economic perceptions that economic "realities" take on their specific significance. In particular,
culturally relative conceptions of efficiency and interpretations of
the boundaries between economic "internalities" and "externalities"
govern the reception and adaptation of transferred technology. Thus,
to give an example, a polluting industrial process may be considered
efficient in a society that regards the environment surrounding factories as waste land, but it may be considered extremely inefficient
in another society that is used to farming that land.

Marx's theory of the interests associated with the transition
to socialism may be reformulated as a hypothesis about the sorts of

economic perceptions that would support a transitional process. These perceptions would have to motivate an emphasis on education and training that would be out of all proportion to anything observed in capitalist societies at comparable levels of development. In the case of communist societies, one index of whether they are involved in a process of transition or convergence would be whether they pursue an initial commitment to raising the technical level of the labor force far beyond the minimum levels required to handle the transferred technology they receive. Of course, this would seem to involve onerous and wasteful investments in manpower, once a solution had been found to the early problems of producing a labor force capable of dealing with transferred technology.

This objection, however, is rooted in the culturally relative distinction between investment and welfare that is associated with capitalism. We tend ethnocentrically to consider these as unambiguous categories, because in our own system of economic perceptions the goals of production are signified in terms of capitalist concepts of wealth. Here wealth takes the primary form of material goods available for private consumption. Education and other public services are seen primarily as investments, not as major positive components of personal welfare. What I would argue is that in a socialist culture, the activities that capitalist society places under the category of investment and evaluates in terms of efficiency in the production of material goods would be placed under the category of consumption and evaluated as contributions to individual welfare. In such a society, inputs of skill no longer appear as subtractions from welfare but as components of it. Economic and technological development would thus be conditioned by very different factors than those that dominate Western capitalist societies.

In such a society, skilled labor would be far more abundant than it has been at corresponding stages in the Western process of modernization. Under these conditions, the use of such inputs would not provoke sharply increased labor costs because they would not be in short supply but widely available as a "free" resource on which the economy could draw at will. An economy developing under these conditions might reach efficient solutions to technical problems in different ways from ours, moving generally toward an alternative type of industrialization. In some cases skills might be employed in relation to technologies that it would be economically irrational to introduce in a capitalist society. Different patterns of consumption and leisure pursuits would occupy the labor force of such a society, and in it, management and politics in general might take on a qualitatively different character. This would, in short, be a socialist system of production.

Transfer and Transition

These Marxian models of the crisis of capitalism and the transition to socialism have far-reaching implications for the study of communist societies involved in the transfer of technology. None of these societies is truly self-administered in Marx's sense of the term. In all of them bureaucratic elites hold great and relatively independent power over the labor force. Nevertheless, in some communist countries workers have succeeded in winning a share of influence over production and politics through special institutional arrangements (self-management) and popular struggles (cultural revolution).

The transfer of technology plays an important role in the contest of the bureaucracy and the working class. Our own technology is peculiarly adapted to a centralized, elitist administration. Elites may therefore attempt to base their power on the "post" of capital in the division of mental and manual labor to which this technology has been adjusted in its development under capitalism. They may then use their position in the technical organization of production to consolidate their power as a privileged stratum, developing as far as possible practices and systems of control that are convergent with capitalist ones. [40]

On the other side, workers doubtless see in technology transfer a means of accelerating the process of economic development that alone can free them from the more or less harsh poverty of their societies. Where, under these conditions, the workers choose to resist the growing power the bureaucracy derives from transfers, they can only do so by initiating struggles against the capitalist division of labor and its associated distribution of knowledge. Such struggles, if successful, should further the transition to socialism. Thus where workers are demanding such things as a reduction in the economic and social gap between management and workers, liberalized work rules, a democratized system of university admissions, access to skills and knowledge beyond the minimum economic needs of their jobs, expulsion of unrepresentative leaders from positions of administrative power, and participation in economic innovation, it may still be possible for a divergent path of industrialization to prevail.

From the Marxian models, we can learn what are the indices of an emerging transitional process. These indices all seem economically irrational or administratively ineffective from the standpoint of capitalist models, and so when they are encountered in isolation, they may be dismissed by researchers as momentary aberrations. The contribution of the theory of the transition is to bring them all together around the concept of an emerging, original pattern of culture. Taken together, these indices should suffice to indicate the initiation of a transition to socialism. No communist country exhibits them all, but various combinations of some of them can be identified, indicating the degree to which convergent or transitional processes are predominant. At this point I would like to summarize briefly the indices that flow from my analysis.

1. Capitalism's highly articulated reward structures based on private consumption have an economic function in the allocation of skilled labor in a system in which knowledge is an investment good. One would expect a transitional society to develop an alternative, emphasizing public models of consumption of goods and services and "ideological" motivations for the acquisition and application of skills. The effect would be the compression of the wage hierarchy into a narrower range than would normally be considered effective in a capitalist society.

2. The transitional society must be organized to insure the continuing and enlarged access of workers to the kinds of knowledge required to perpetuate and increase their power in society. By our accepted standards of economic efficiency, optimal investments in the training of manpower produce a knowledge deficit that a socialist society would attempt to overcome. Evidence of the cultural and technical "overqualification" of the labor force is thus significant as an indication of a different orientation. Similarly, meritocratic methods of educational selection, while most efficient economically in a capitalist context, contradict the cultural objectives of socialism by perpetuating parental cultural advantages in the children and con-tributing to the creation of a self-conscious and partially "hereditary" technocratic stratum. A more democratic distribution of knowledge, governed by class criteria to some degree, would improve the pros-pects for the transition.

3. In many domains, the workers cannot immediately abolish the division of mental and manual labor. They must therefore rely on the exercise of authority by highly trained professional and mana-gerial personnel during the transitional period. This authority con-tributes to the transitional process, in which its long-range impact is the enlargement of the workers' initiative and control throughout society. One way this result can be achieved is by insuring that in these instances the training and job definitions discourage techno-cratic and encourage democratic attitudes on the part of those strata with authority. Most important in this regard are the rules and roles that are governing for the exercise of authority. These rules and roles concern such things as the procedures and criteria of innovation, the position of science in society, the restrictions on and context of the exercise of managerial authority, the taste and ideology of workers in mass communications and education, and so on. It should be possible to ascertain empirically whether democratic

and socialist behavior has been imposed on those with authority or whether their authority is exercised along capitalist lines, as the basis of an alienated distribution of power.

4. There must be formal institutions in a transitional society, through which the workers can intervene in the activities of those with power and authority. Workers' control in the economy and the free election of political leaders would be the best evidence of this.[41] Where the workers have no such institutions or very imperfect ones, their degree of power may be indicated to some extent by the responsiveness of union and party organs to complaints, pressures, and movements from below. It goes without saying that, except in conditions of extreme national danger, freedom of speech and criticism of the government are indications that the mass of the population has some degree of power over its own affairs.

Most basically, what is reflected in these four indices of the transition is the growth of a new culture, as measured by the development of self-administration and the economic perceptions associated with a socialist distribution of knowledge. Marxism argues that these factors have momentous implications for long-range technological development. Elite control from above, by this argument, is not rooted in the imperatives of technology but is properly a political alternative reflected in technological choices. Different and democratic choices can only come from those involved in productive work, since they alone can develop the economic perceptions that would so orient the criteria of technological progress. If any of the existing communist societies are involved to some degree in the transition to socialism, this will therefore appear through the application of these indices. The contest between workers and elites over the adaptation of transferred technology will prove to be one of the most sensitive areas for such a study.

TRANSITION OR CONVERGENCE?

I would like now to apply the methodological framework developed above to some of the other papers prepared for this book. The authors' discussions of elite roles, of the prospects for democratization, and of worker participation in management and innovation all bear on the indices of the transition presented here. A great many of these papers assume or predict convergence between the communist and the capitalist societies, although within limits reflecting significant secondary differences. I will show that in the case of the People's Republic of China, by contrast with that of the Soviet Union, these conclusions are reached by the application of methods that exclude a priori the possibility of a transition to socialism.

Several of the papers on the USSR, for example Chapter 4, by John P. Hardt and George D. Holliday, and Chapter 9, by Erik P. Hoffmann, consider the implications of technology transfer for the maintenance of the undemocratic features of Soviet society. These papers consider the impact of transfers in terms of the imperatives built into specific products and processes, such as the automobile, the computer, and so on. Sometimes these imperatives conflict with more or less vital aspects of the Soviet system. For example, the best use of computers requires freer flows of more accurate information than is customary in the USSR. The authors seem to assume that if it were necessary to democratize Soviet society to adapt it to such imperatives, then the dominant elites would prefer to enforce backwardness and avoid the risks of progress. Hence the possibility of transfers rests on their having relatively limited impacts on the system. From this it can be concluded that the very fact of transfer is in some sense evidence of its political nullity as a democratizing force. This confirms my own conclusions about the political role of transfers in elite strategies of power.

The method on the basis of which the authors defend and develop these views is a nondeterministic one. They treat technological imperatives as flowing from the nature of specific technologies and not from technology as such, and they show these imperatives to be clearly subordinated as causal factors to the policies of those with power and to the structural constraints of the recipient social system. This is, I believe, correct as far as it goes, but I would argue that convergence is validated by this method precisely because the only political constraints imposed on transferred technology in the USSR come from an unrepresentative bureaucracy. The issue was never that of alternative models of industrialization, of transition or convergence, or of what might be created under the impact of popular demands corresponding to the indices outlined above. The USSR and the United States have already converged in one essential respect, which is the rule of an elite basing itself on the diversion of mental and manual labor. The difference between the Western and Soviet styles of administration is not so very great as to exclude the easy exchange of technologies.

Several of the papers on China, for example Chapter 7, by Richard Baum and Chapter 6, by Rensselaer W. Lee III, arrive at the thesis of convergence on the basis of far more speculative concepts of modernization. For them, technological imperatives derive not just from specific technologies but from the overall process of economic development in any society. There is a significant difference in method here, but strangely, these two opposed methodological choices lead the writers on China and the USSR to approximately the same point, the point of convergence. While the writers on the

Soviet Union are very sensitive to questions of political power in its impact on economic development, the writers on China minimize the role of politics in influencing technology. Nevertheless, such opposite perspectives yield similar results in contact with different communist systems.

Baum and Lee bring forward impressive evidence of the more egalitarian and democratic character of China as compared with the Soviet Union. Their research suggests that China is gripped by very deep struggles over the transition to socialism, as this concept has been developed above. They argue, however, that many of the most novel features of the PRC system derive not so much from "ideological" considerations as from economic backwardness. Thus, further technology transfers and economic development will destroy rather than generalize what enclaves of socialist experimentation may now exist in the unique social system of that nation.

Where a discussion of political struggle over technology, culture, and management in the People's Republic might point toward radical alternatives emerging there, the application of modernization theory liquidates this possibility a priori. This methodological framework has the effect of "containing" the remarkable implications of the struggles and reforms described by the authors. The fact that the politics of the Chinese case are given so little weight in determining long-range trends seems to be linked to their mass character, which defies ordinary methods of analysis and prognostication. Nevertheless, the discussions do recognize and describe a radically different kind of political process from the bureaucratic one identified in the papers on the USSR.

There is a dilemma here, which is that some basic disagreements are masked by the fact that different methods produce identical conclusions when applied to different cases. If the general approach to technological imperatives in the papers on the USSR could be combined with the concept of politics that emerges from the papers on the PRC, the results might be surprising. This could be a first step toward showing that the adaptation of transferred technology under the constraints of workers' power would lead in wholly new directions. This alternative is foreclosed by the methodological choices of the authors, specifically by the deterministic modernization theories that form the background to the discussions of the People's Republic.

The deterministic approach assumes that technology is responsive only to those values implicit in its own logic of development. The intent of communist societies to overcome the paradox of development by altering the direction of technological progress is dismissed as futile and utopian. What is at issue is whether technology is the sort of thing that a people can integrate into its own social system and culture, bending it to original values, or whether it is an invariant element that, once introduced, will bend the recipient social system to its own imperatives.

Richard Baum has suggested a terminology that is helpful in stating the deterministic position. The imperatives of technology as formulated by modernization theory he calls "techno-logic," and the goals socialists attempt to impose upon the process of modernization he calls "ideo-logic."[42] Techno-logic, in modernization theory, has a kind of power and necessity that ideo-logic lacks. Techno-logic is always presented as something "real," substantial, objective, almost spontaneous in character, like a natural process. Ideo-logic is a matter of human will and goals. It is "voluntaristic"; that is, it lacks ultimate force in contact with techno-logic.

This invidious comparison of terms is supported by a characteristic methodological procedure: whenever ideo-logic contributes to economic development, it is said to coincide momentarily with the imperatives of modernization at that stage. Hence in the long run ideo-logic can accomplish nothing original but is destined to be outmoded by the very process of development it furthers. On the other hand, any socioeconomic change that does not accord with the standard pattern of modernization is attributed to the influence of ideo-logic, described as irrational, and dismissed as a passing aberration imposed by misguided political leaders. The impotence of ideo-logic is thus a matter of definition.[43] Its causal efficacy only appears independently where it is probably doomed to fail because it stands in the way of progress.

There is no notion here that in a different social system with a different standard of efficiency, progress may be subversive of a development leading to convergence, that technological choices may be "over-determined" in simultaneous response to both technical and social criteria. As a result, no integral cultural and economic system responding to new and democratic goals is conceivable in this framework, only a contradiction, doubtless temporary, between rather impractical "voluntaristic" intentions and technological imperatives.

In a 1974 article William N. Dunn developed sophisticated models to describe the consequences of this supposed contradiction between efficiency and revolutionary values in communist societies.[44] Dunn applies Amitai Etzioni's concept of "dual compliance" to the problems of communist industrial organizations, which, he asserts, are caught in the crossfire of conflicting goals. Dunn assumes that the pursuit of an "ideo-logical" end such as egalitarianism has economic costs, while the pursuit of economic efficiency has, correspondingly, "social" costs, in the sense that egalitarianism must be sacrificed to productivity. Under these conditions, goal-seeking behavior is characterized by fluctuating emphasis as one or the other goal gains temporary predominance.

Because Dunn does not envisage deep changes in economic perceptions and technologies, his preferred formal treatment (the "complex participation model") lacks a real historical dimension and is stated in terms of cyclical changes in emphasis and equilibrim. Communist societies would thus exhibit essentially Western patterns of modernization during cyclical emphases on efficiency. These patterns would be unaffected by the time lost to technological progress during periods of emphasis on revolutionary values. In this process, the criterion of economic efficiency is never adapted to the demands of a different culture, and so socialist criteria of progress simply inhibit the achievement of maximum efficiency in a series of temporary trade-offs of noneconomic for economic values. The unexamined assumption here is the deterministic image of technology and an uncritically accepted standard of efficiency, derived from capitalist models.

Such assumptions are not the monopoly of the critics of socialism. Some humanistic socialists in the West concede that a production system controlled by workers would be less "efficient" than capitalism. Socialism, they argue, would lower labor productivity in favor of increasing returns of "soft" variables, such as job satisfaction and equality. They thus implicitly affirm the thesis of technological determinism and its associated dual compliance model of the relation of "values" to the economy.

In the previous section I tried to show that the real issue is not whether socialism is as efficient as capitalism by the standards of the latter. Instead, the real issue is the cultural one of the way individuals living under these different systems perceive their own welfare. In both systems it stands to reason that means-ends rationality will be pursued ruthlessly, in the one to increase profits and in the other to enhance the material well-being of the workers, including, of course, their satisfaction at work. The pursuit of efficiency entails sacrifices, but—and this is the critical point—if each system has a different end in view, then very different sacrifices may be made.

Soft variables are "soft" under capitalism not because they cannot be reconciled with a high productivity of labor, nor because they are objectively less vital or desirable than "hard" ones, but simply because they are not the privileged ends served by capitalist production. These same things might be "hard" variables in another system with a different culture and economic perceptions. Where one of the ends of production is the development and application of actualized human capacities, no sacrifice of productivity is involved in serving this end, even if the purported drop in the volume of material goods produced should in fact occur.

This is no merely verbal point. Where the actualization of human capacities is culturally signified as an end and not simply as a means to the production of material goods, it will be pursued spontaneously by the individuals as a positive component of their own welfare and need not be imposed on them by market incentives or political or moral coercion in opposition to their own perceived interests. Since technology is routinely adapted to changing economic goals in the pursuit of efficiency, there is no reason of principle why it should not be made to conform to the needs of such a culture; it is not destined to remain a fixed and antagonistic element never fully assimilated by the culture into which it is inserted.

The implicit determinism of all these positions lies in the assumption that culture plays no significant role in shaping the history of technological development but can only motivate or obstruct progress along a fixed and unilinear track. As a result, the mechanical subsystem produced by capitalist technological progress can be abstracted from the rest of the social system in which it developed and considered separately as normative for development in all societies.[45] Technology is presented as the pure application of the laws of nature to problems of production, quite as independent of human will as the movements of the heavenly bodies. Some of the aura of science can then be transferred back to the machines that depend on its principles. The iron necessity characteristic of the laws of nature is "read into" the process of technological development and through it into society as a whole. From this point of view, the very idea of an alternative path of industrialization appears to be an absurdity.

The conception of the mechanical subsystem of society as an independent force with a self-propelling dynamic of its own reflects the uncritical acceptance of the structure of capitalist society. The specifically capitalist division of labor, as discussed above, accomplishes just this separation of the means of production from the producers, of machines from men. We live in a society that is based on this separation and that extends it to the limit of precision. A definition of technology that abstracts the mechanical conditions of production from living labor and from its cultural contexts therefore resonates ethnocentrically with our own experience of economic reality. Abstracted and hypostasized technology as an independent and determining factor responds to the categorial underpinnings of our own world, but clearly this is a culturally relative assumption derived uncritically from the structure of capitalism.

In the case of technology transfer, this deterministic image of technology is constantly reinforced by the visible, short-run consequences of transfers. The imported technology is designed to require and reproduce the post of capital in the division of labor. Hence the less transformation it undergoes upon importation, the more suitable it is as a power base for an elite. In contrast, workers acting on a socialistic basis cannot simply accept transferred technology as is but must subject it to complex and problematical adaptations. The fact that the technology requires greater transformation in its adaptation to the needs of the workers than it does in adapting to the needs of an elite gives the impression that in a movement such as the Chinese Cultural Revolution a solid substantial reality— technology with its built in criteria of efficiency—is in conflict with a mere subjective ideology.

The methodological problems involved in studying technology transfer are thus singularly complex. In the case of the People's Republic of China, for example, there are obvious problems of adaptation and struggles crystallize around them. At first socialist objectives can be expected to intervene as political goals in these struggles. It cannot be assumed, however, that because these objectives first arise as political goals they are mere voluntaristic intentions, opposed to the inherent logic of technology. This position would be validated if the goals were simply subjective notions in the heads of a few political leaders; but in fact they are advanced in mass struggles such as the Cultural Revolution, by millions of Chinese. The critique would still be validated if the masses were usually as foolish as those workers who, in the Great Leap Forward, "exceeded bourgeois limits" on engine speeds by burning out the engines. Much of what Chinese radicals and workers demand corresponds with the potentialities of Chinese society and the conditions for the initiation of the transition to socialism. Their ability to accomplish their purposes can only be judged by the study of concrete cases in the light of an aposteriori methodology that does not automatically foreclose the options.

From the standpoint of such a methodology, goals corresponding to the transition to socialism have the status of objective realities, sociopolitical and ultimately cultural constraints, as real and potentially powerful as any imposed by capitalists or by the Soviet political leadership. These goals may prove to be the basis on which the workers will transform imported capitalist technology into a new system that will be as well adjusted to their needs as it originally was to the needs of capitalists. Thus it can be argued that the "interests" of Chinese workers, like those of the Soviet leadership, may fundamentally influence technological development.

Similarly, the so-called techno-logic cannot impose itself independently of a political process that has some resemblance to that of the "ideo-logical" struggle. The "goals" inscribed in the techno-logic, abstracted from the Western capitalist type of modernization and read back into the supposedly autonomous movement of technological development, are and always have been the goals of particular social groups, that is, of those groups that profit from an alienated process of modernization.

In the People's Republic such groups exist; there is a bureaucracy that could extend its power indefinitely at the expense of the workers. The Chinese administration, as has the Soviet, may attempt to base its power on the post of capital in the division of mental and manual labor. On several occasions this bureaucracy has already been taken as the target of direct mass struggles with the objective of defeating its attempts to structure the social system around the power it acquires through access to special skills and knowledge. Remarkable changes in Chinese society have occurred in response to these struggles, some of which have been lasting changes. Thus the struggle of techno-logic and ideo-logic is not a struggle between abstract categories but between actual social groups that are organized in specific ways, have specific economic perceptions, and pursue concrete political and cultural objectives. All of these characteristics are subject to empirical study, and such study shows that the issue—transition or convergence—is not yet finally decided.

THE AMBIVALENT HERITAGE

For this concluding section I have saved certain issues raised by Frederic J. Fleron, Jr., that point toward philosophical considerations far broader in their implications than the scope of this chapter. As presented in the introduction to this book, Fleron's theoretical model of the impact of technology transfer on communist societies straddles the gap between Marxism and modernization theory. On the one hand, of the two theses that I take to be definitive for technological determinism, Fleron rejects the notion that there is only one possible path of technological development. Nevertheless, he continues to argue that, however developed or introduced, technologies govern the rest of the social system. On the other hand, of the two corresponding and opposed theses characterizing the Marxist position, Fleron accepts the idea of the class determination of technological development while rejecting the companion hypothesis that technology can be readapted under different political and cul-

tural conditions to a class power other than the one under which it
originated. In short, Fleron is a Marxist for the past and a determinist for the future.

     With such a starting point, Fleron must arrive at conclusions
about communist societies similar to those of modernization theory.
He notes, for example, that Chinese innovations in the introduction
of industrial democracy seem most widely applicable in backward
sectors of the economy. This "raises prominently the question of
whether or not foreign technological hardware can be utilized in
communist societies where there are strong social and political . . .
imperatives regarding social organization." Fleron wants to suggest
the possibility of a wholly original path of development that would not
be based on the transfer of technology but on native methods embodying appropriate values at the outset. Nowhere is this occurring, nor
is there any likelihood that it ever will; not even in China, the one
communist country that professes to be worried about the cultural
consequences of the transfer of technology. We are left with a rather
gloomy projection of universal convergence in a social order of which
Fleron manifestly disapproves.

     The basis of Fleron's position is the proposition that "ends and
means are never more than analytically separable." In other words,
capitalist means (transferred technology) cannot be bent to the service of socialist goals. Fleron shares this conception of the relationship of means and ends with both liberal and anarchist critics of
Marxism, who deny for different reasons that mankind can be liberated by a "proletarian dictatorship." The left-wing application of
this means-ends concept takes the form of the refusal of all continuity between capitalism and a free communitarian society, the insistence that the latter can only be built on the basis of the most complete, radical, and immediate break with the past. Although it is
ethically appealing, this position must sacrifice Marx's idea of a
transitional process rooted in people and things as they are, but
leading beyond this horizon to a new society, which is a considerable
advance over traditional utopian speculation.

     Marx believed that socialists could give a new overall direc-
tion to social development by delicately balancing a temporary acceptance of some major features of capitalism against the immediate
transformation of other aspects of that system more vulnerable to a
direct assault. An overemphasis on the break with the past, or voluntarism, would lead to social chaos, while an overemphasis on continuity would disorganize and demoralize the revolution itself. Between these extremes there is supposed to lie a strategic path,
leading from one link in the chain to the next until the entire social
system has been renewed.

Modesty in projecting immediate changes is a function of a realistic sense of the limits of revolutionary action and moral imperatives. Marx's special and lasting contribution to the socialist movement was not so much a theory of "total revolution," with which workers could do nothing in any case, as the discovery of the function of partial objectives in a revolutionary process of cultural change extending over generations. [46] What has always distinguished Marxism from anarchism has been the assertion that the first link in the chain, the starting point for general social transformation, is political power. What equally distinguishes it from doctrines based on the identity of means and ends is the concept of the transition to socialism as a practical process of political and cultural change, proceeding not from morality or ideology but from interest and power.

The concept of the transition to socialism is thus, in one of its many dimensions, a political concept. That is, it belongs not to the domain of moral imperatives but to that of the art of the possible. It is true that Marxism attempts to "enlarge the field of the possible" in a way that is often considered moralistic, but it is important to understand the distinction made within Marxism itself between transitional and moral practice. As noted above, Marx was not concerned with "realizing an ideal" but rather with initiating a historical process in which certain real interests would assert themselves at the expense of others. The means employed in support of the "progressive" interests at each stage might bear little relation to the ultimate result expected of the process governed by these interests. The means, then, would not necessarily be in conformity with the end pursued, as in moral practice. Indeed, they might temporarily contradict that end or even be drawn from the heritage of bourgeois society.

From a methodological viewpoint this "nonmoral" approach to the transition to socialism is extremely suggestive. Marx's conception is characterized by a whole series of contradictions between means and ends that he would doubtless have described as dialectical. Examples of these contradictions are as follows:

     1. Fundamental political institutions such as voting would be taken over from capitalist democracy and developed as the basis for a far more democratic socialist state. This socialist state would not be an end in itself but merely a means to the end of abolishing the state altogether.

     2. Similarly, even such a basic capitalist institution as the wage system would be retained during the transition, although the socialist goal is distribution according to need.

     3. The technology of alienation taken over from capitalism would not be abolished directly but used as a means for

the production of an entirely different technological apparatus,
a technology of liberation in which work would become "one of
life's prime wants. "

   This approach seems to involve Marxism in ominous conflicts
of methods and goals. Marx's critics have argued from the actual
evolution of the Soviet Union that these conflicts are fatal to the
Marxist theory, that the path of social development is not altered
but irreversibly fixed by these tortuous methods.[47] There are undoubtedly difficulties in Marx's theory, but the USSR has made a
poor test case for socialism, given its initial backwardness and isolation. Marx's theory continues to be more convincing as a combination of political realism and revolutionary idealism than any of its
competitors.
   What Marx sought to do was to find mediations between capitalism and socialism, demonstrating the possibility of the latter. He
argued that workers under capitalism could make a revolution that
would have been impossible for all earlier lower classes precisely
because capitalism itself produces a technology, a culture, and
some social institutions that workers can take over and use for their
own ends during the transitional era. This heritage of mediating elements then becomes the basis for the realization of new social purposes quite different from those that inspired its creation; the old
forms are given a new class content as a step toward their total
dissolution.
   Does this mean that Marx regarded the "bourgeois heritage"
as neutral, equally adapted to the needs of a capitalist and socialist
society alike? The answer to this question is clearly negative. For
example, from capitalism the workers would obtain a technological
apparatus designed to be operated by a disqualified labor force under
the control of an autocratic management—in other words, a technology adapted to the culture of capitalism. Of course it contains neutral elements, but the system as a whole introjects cultural values
antagonistic to the goals of socialism. [48] Thus the technology is not
neutral; and yet workers can use it, or at least Marx assumed they
could, to produce the goods required for their continued survival
while they changed it to suit their new criteria of efficiency and
social purpose.
   The reshaping of the inherited technology may be understood
as a process of bootstrapping. The technology would not simply be
put to new uses in a different social context, but more importantly,
it would be employed to produce new technological means, fully
adapted to the culture of socialism. It is vital to distinguish clearly
between this developmental approach and the notion that the technology developed under capitalism is simply neutral, that the same

means can be used for different ends. Marx's position suggests the further relationship: not what different ends may be directly served by a given technology, but what new technological means it may produce, in a technically and culturally feasible sequence leading from one type of industrial society to quite a different type.

Marx accepted means that were not in conformity with his goals, but he did not justify this by postulating an abstract indifference of ends and means and assuming the neutrality of the latter. The intermediary position he took up requires a new concept, which I will call "ambivalence" of means with respect to ends. [49] The thesis of ambivalence on which his concept of the transition to socialism was based can be summed up in the following three propositions:

1. In the short run workers can, and indeed must, use many inherited (or transferred) elements while consolidating their power.

2. Workers can transform these elements in the course of using them over an extended period, until finally they have made a radically different technological base, one adjusted to their needs as a class.

3. What ultimately determines which of the ambivalent potentialities of the heritage is developed most completely is the class power under which the system operates and which sets the standards and goals of progress for society.

In the case of technology transfer, very little is changed from Marx's original formulation of the problems and solutions. Although created under the cultural and economic constraints of capitalism, the imported technology may be bent to new ones in a new context. It may then be routinely and efficiently employed in the service of cultural values quite different from those that presided over its creation. Here too, Marxism would reject the notion that technologies are simply given and completed entities that either are or are not suited to socialist society. It would regard them instead as starting points in a process of cultural change. [50]

This is the theory, but what of the actual chances of socialism as a solution to the paradox of development in the world today? Even confining discussion to the existing communist societies, surely these chances are better than Fleron admits, perhaps not in the USSR, but conceivably in China, Cuba, or Yugoslavia. In these countries the transition to socialism may be engaged in important domains, even though it is clearly obstructed in others. Of course, the most important of the areas in which it is obstructed is in the growth of political democracy, that other vital aspect of the ambivalent heritage of capitalist society. Nevertheless, there are still relevant contexts in

which the Marxist theory of the transition seems to have applications, in spite of the many ambiguities surrounding its implementation.

NOTES

1. Louis Antoine Léon de Saint-Just, L'esprit de la révolution
(Paris: U. G. E. , 1963), p. 63.

2. Bernard de Mandeville, The Fable of the Bees (Baltimore:
Penguin, 1970), p. 76.

3. Throughout this paper I will use the term "socialist" to refer to Marx's vision of a classless society and the term "communist"
to refer to those existing societies that claim that title. I realize
that this usage contradicts Marx's own preferences, but I hardly
think he would be more pleased to see his vision confused with some
of the attempts to realize it historically.

4. Karl Marx, Capital (New York: Modern Library, 1906), p.
13.

5. Robert C. Tucker, "Culture, Political Culture, and Communist Society," Political Science Quarterly, 88 (1973): 186-87.

6. For a critique of the concept of technological imperatives,
see William Leiss, "The Social Consequences of Technological Progress," Canadian Public Administration 13, no. 3 (1970): 246-62.

7. Briefly noted here, these assumptions are as follows: (1)
Technology is conceptualized as an autonomous, socially neutral,
and value-free element of culture, determining society as a whole
according to "imperatives" of modernization. (2) Efficiency and welfare are conceptualized in terms of the productivity of human labor
in manufacturing material goods for private consumption.

8. Thus Marx and Engels write in The German Ideology, "Communism is for us not a state of affairs still to be established, not an
ideal to which reality [will] have to adjust. We call communism the
real movement which abolishes the present state of affairs. The
conditions of this movement result from premises now in existence."
Quoted in Loy D. Easton, and Kurt H. Guddat, eds. , Writings of the
Young Marx on Philosophy and Society (Garden City: Doubleday, 1967),
p. 426. The same points are made still more forcefully in Marx's
article, "Critical Notes on 'The King of Prussia and Social Reform,' "
Ibid. , pp. 349-50, 355-58.

9. Daniel Bell, The End of Ideology: On the Exhaustion of
Political Ideals in the Fifties (New York: Free Press, 1962): 355-92.

10. Ibid. , p. 362.

11. Ibid. , pp. 386-87

12. Ibid. , p. 367. This is also, of course, the position of the
Althusserian school in France.

13. Ibid., p. 387. A number of important works on the development of technology and labor have appeared recently that approach the problems from a Marxist perspective. See, for example, Harry Braverman, Labor and Monopoly Capital (New York: Monthly Review, 1974); André Gorz, ed., Critique de la division du travail (Paris: Seuil, 1973); Stephen A. Marglin, "What Do Bosses Do? The Origins and Functions of Hierarchy in Capitalist Production" The Review of Radical Political Economics 6, no. 2 (1974); M. Regini and E. Reyneri, Lotte operaie e organizzazione del lavoro (Padua: Marsilio, 1971); Radovan Richta, et al., Civilization at the Crossroads: Social and Human Implications of the Scientific and Technological Revolution (White Plains: International Arts and Sciences, 1969); Russian and Czech Academies of Science, Man, Science, Technology (Prague: Academia, 1973).

14. Karl Marx, Grundrisse (Baltimore: Penguin, 1973), p. 823.

15. For further discussion of this point, see Nicos Poulantzas, Pouvoir politique et classes sociales (Paris: Maspero, 1968), vol. 1, pp. 20-24.

16. It is altogether remarkable that not only Bell but several generations of "orthodox" Marxists could fail to understand the importance of the discussions in Part 4 of Volume 1 of Capital on precisely these matters. Over 200 pages are devoted to this subject, which Bell regards as altogether unmentioned.

17. Marx, Capital, pp. 396-97.

18. Ibid., p. 462.

19. Ibid., p. 421.

20. Marx, Grundrisse, op. cit., pp. 694-95.

21. Throughout this chapter I abstract from a second major feature of the Marxist theory, which I call the "solidarity deficit." Marxism emphasizes the decreasing force of collective incentives under capitalism, as traditional social units break down. The individual that emerges as an independent and isolated economic agent is motivated by individual incentives. The effect of the solidarity deficit is similar to that of the knowledge deficit: the atomized individuals can only be organized for common action by external controls from above. Just as socialism must overcome the cognitive effects of capitalism in the knowledge deficit, so it must overcome the characterological consequences summed up in the solidarity deficit. For an interesting discussion of Cuban attempts to deal with the latter, see Arthur MacEwan, "Incentives, Equality, and Power in Revolutionary Cuba," Socialist Revolution, no. 23 (April 1975).

22. Marx's two principal discussions of the transition to socialism are contained in "The Civil War in France" and "The Critique of the Gotha Program." Important for understanding recent Marxist discussions of the transition are the problems raised by

Paul Sweezy and Charles Bettelheim in On the Transition to Socialism (New York: Monthly Review, 1971), especially pp. 132-34 in connection with this paper. In this chapter I will attempt my own rather
freewheeling reconstruction of the Marxist theory of the transition,
based on scattered and fragmentary remarks by Marx and Engels.

23. Marx's theory of the inevitability of revolution rests on
the following conditions: (1) that socialism be the "immanent negation"
of capitalism, not contingent on noncapitalist factors for its occur-
ence; (2) that the economic evolution of capitalist society produce
adequate motivations for proletarian revolution, in terms of poverty,
oppression, war, and so on; and (3) that these conditions be continually and periodically reproduced so that the working class, no matter
how often it may fail to grasp them as motives for revolution, always
has another chance to do so.

24. "The control exercised by the capitalist is not only a special function, due to the nature of the social labour-process, and
peculiar to that process, but it is, at the same time, a function of
the exploitation of a social labour-process, and is consequently
rooted in the unavoidable antagonism between the exploiter and the
living and labouring raw material he exploits. " Marx, Capital, op.
cit., vol. 1, p. 363.

25. "Personified capital, the capitalist, takes care that the
labourer does his work regularly and with the proper degree of intensity. " Ibid., vol. 1, p. 338.

26. Ibid., vol. 1.

27. Ibid., vol. 1, pp. 475-76.

28. Ibid., vol. 1, p. 461. My emphasis.

29. Ibid., p. 534.

30. Ibid.

31. Ibid., p. 535.

32. Ibid., vol. 1, pp. 533-34.

33. Ibid., vol. 1, p. 534. My emphasis.

34. Friedrich Engels, "Socialism: Utopian and Scientific, "
in Karl Marx and Friedrich Engels, Selected Works (New York: International Publishers, 1969), p. 431. For a further discussion of
this approach, see Andrew L. Feenberg, review of Lénine et la révolution culturelle by Carmen Claudin-Urondo, in Theory and Society 2, no. 4 (1975): 599-600.

35. Marx's principal discussion of these matters is in "The
Critique of the Gotha Program, " op. cit., pp. 323-25. Lenin presents striking formulations of the concept of social self-discipline
in his Selected Works (New York: International Publishers, 1967),
vol. 2, pp. 646, 731-32. Marxism's treatment of this concept of
democratic economic organization is simply an application and extension of traditional democratic theories of political organization.

It may be compared with Immanuel Kant's theory of "unsocial socia-
bility" in "Perpetual Peace." See Kant, On History (New York: Bobbs-
Merrill, 1963), pp. 112-13.

36. Marx, Grundrisse, op. cit., p. 612.

37. "In fact, however, when the limited bourgeois form is
stripped away, what is wealth other than the universality of individual needs, capacities, pleasures, productive forces, etc., created
through universal exchange? The full development of human mastery
over the forces of nature, those of so-called nature as well as of
humanity's own nature? The absolute working-out of his creative potentialities, with no presupposition other than the previous historic
development, which makes this totality of development, i.e. the
development of all human powers as such the end in itself, not as
measured on a predetermined yardstick? Where he does not reproduce himself in one specificity, but produces his totality? Strives not
to remain something he has become, but is in the absolute movement
of becoming?" Ibid., p. 488.

38. Ibid., pp. 711-12.

39. Margaret Mead, ed., Cultural Patterns and Technical
Change (New York: Mentor, 1955).

40. For further discussion of this concept of the bureaucratic
elite from a Marxist perspective, see Charles Bettelheim, Les luttes
de classes en USSR (Paris: Maspero/Seuil, 1974), pp. 115-21.

41. The commitment of early Marxism to democratic management in the work place is made clear in Friedrich Engels, "On Authority," in Marx and Engels: Basic Works on Politics and Philosophy,
ed. L. Feuer (New York: Anchor, 1959), pp. 483-84. "The Civil War
in France" is the most famous text in which Marx and Engels state
their commitment to universal suffrage.

42. Richard Baum, "Technology, Economic Organization, and
Social Change: Maoism and the Chinese Cultural Revolution," in
China in the Seventies, ed. B. Staiger (Wiesbaden: Otto Harrasso-
witz, 1975).

43. This is an example of the sort of circular and self-verify-
ing argumentation criticized in the introduction to this chapter.

44. William N. Dunn, "The Economics of Organizational
Ideology: the Problem of Dual Compliance in the Worker-Managed
Socialist Firm," Journal of Comparative Administration 5, no. 4
(1974).

45. William Leiss writes, "The essential error in these
theories is to isolate one aspect of this totality (technology) and then
to relate it back to the totality in a mechanical fashion; accordingly,
the cause-and-effect network is resolved upon analysis into a set of
circular propositions." Leiss, op. cit., p. 253.

46. This is one of the most basic arguments of Georg Lukács in History and Class Consciousness (Cambridge: MIT Press, 1971). For a discussion of Lukács in this connection, see Andrew L. Feenberg, "Lukács and the Critique of 'Orthodox' Marxism," Philosophical Forum 3, nos. 3-4 (1972): 435-40.

47. Left-wing adversaries of Marxism such as Jean-François Lyotard go so far as to accuse it of being a reactionary doctrine for this reason.

48. At the Bellagio Conference I suggested a terminology with which to distinguish the neutral from the socially determined aspects of what might be called the "technosphere." I would reserve the term "technique" for specific technical elements such as the lever, the wheel, the electric circuit, and so on, all of which are in themselves neutral applications of objective knowledge of nature. These elements are like the vocabulary of a language; they can be strung together to form a variety of "sentences" with different meanings and purposes. "Technologies," defined as developed ensembles of technical elements, are greater than the sums of their parts. They meet social criteria of purpose in the very selection and arrangement of the intrinsically neutral units from which they are built up. These social criteria can be understood as "embodied" in the technology and not simply as an extrinsic use to which a neutral tool might be put.

49. The concept of "ambivalence" employed here is derived from F. Feher, "Is the Novel Problematic?" Telos, no. 15 (Spring 1973).

50. I am presently working on what I call a "pluralistic model of cultural change," with which I hope to develop further many of the ideas presented in this chapter. I summarize this model in the following basic points: (1) Cultural change in industrial societies results from the shifting patterns of conflict and accord between the values embodied in technology, ideology, and economic perceptions. (2) A cultural change is accomplished by bringing all three of these relatively independent factors into accord with the same basic values. (3) Cultural change affects not only the beliefs and attitudes of the members of society but equally the technological realities that underlie the economy. Thus, like the other factors, technology not only causes but responds to cultural change, through adaptation, rationalization, and innovation, by which it is brought into accord with the dominant cultural values. (4) Social groups stand behind different factors of change and attempt to use the factors under their control to gain control over the others. (5) Cultural change is thus the consequence of the resolution of certain types of social conflict on the terms of one or another social group.

2

TECHNOLOGY AND INSTRUMENTAL RATIONALITY IN CAPITALISM AND SOCIALISM
William Leiss

There is an enduring problem in our understanding of modern technology and its social significance. On the one hand, we have abundant empirical knowledge about the history of technical innovations, including the conditions of their development and their diffusion within and among different nations. On the other hand (the speculative side of the matter), the evaluation of the social consequences of technological change remains trapped in the seemingly arbitrary polarization between subjective feelings of pessimism or optimism, between warnings of doom and complacent advocacy of the "technological fix." In other words, as soon as we move from the level of empirical investigation, concerning such matters as rates of innovation and technology transfer, to the level of general social theory, we encounter a great number of extravagant claims about the overall impact of modern technology on social change. There are those who emphasize the beneficent aspects of this process, chiefly the expanding realm of personal choice and individual freedom, which, it is claimed, flows from the achievements of technology. At the other extreme, there are those who see modern technology as a corrosive force that penetrates and undermines the institutional bases for healthy human development. Both views are fatalistic, in that they regard social institutions as being forced to adjust to changes brought about by technological innovations, and both consistently ignore the reciprocal influence that conflicting social interests exert

I am indebted to Ian Angus, Andrew L. Feenberg, and Irving Zeitlin for stimulating discussions on the subject matter of this essay and to Frederic J. Fleron, Jr., for his encouragement and support of my work.

on the process of innovation and application. [1] Neither of these formulations permit us to reconcile the widely divergent claims about the
social significance of modern technology.

Under these circumstances it would not be surprising if many
observers concluded that the best solution would be to discourage
speculative thought on this subject altogether. Such a solution might
be attractive on account of its simplicity, but in my view it would not
be a satisfactory response. The inconclusive results in the domain of
general social theory are not entirely the result of conceptual inco-
herence or intellectual laziness but are also symptoms of real, unresolved social contradictions. The existing literature on what is
called "the social consequences of technological progress" has
yielded inconclusive results so far, primarily because the contradictory possibilities for the future shape of modern societies—societies
that are different from earlier ones partly because of their encouragement of and reliance upon rapid, continuous technological innovation—have not yet worked themselves out. Another way of putting
this is to say that the very diverse possibilities for future human
development that are implicit in modern technology are unfolding in
an anarchic social setting, that is, in a setting wherein there is no
general agreement on the basic ends or goals in the service of which
our new technical means are to be employed.

The interaction of means and ends as a problem of general social theory is the basic issue to be discussed in this chapter. It is of
course a point at issue in the understanding of any culture, and not
only the cultures that fall under the rubric of "modern societies."
More specifically, evaluation of a culture may involve one or more
of the following approaches: (1) the manifest goals or purposes in a
culture may be regarded as either worthy or unworthy in themselves;
(2) it may be asserted that there are inconsistencies or contradictions in the ensemble of goals that are concealed or unrecognized
within that culture; (3) it may be asserted that the chosen means are
either adequate or manifestly inappropriate and self-defeating for the
realization of the goals; or (4) an attempt may be made to show that
arising out of the choice of means are unintended consequences that
will damage or destroy the ecological viability of that culture. To
some extent the first and the third approaches necessitate the formulation of criteria that are "external" to a culture, while the second
and fourth focus on its "internal" coherence. These are loose desig-
nations, however, and the two sets tend to shade into each other.
Both goals and techniques may also be discussed or pursued by individuals "abstractly," that is, in isolation from each other and from
direct connection with a social milieu.

In this chapter the discussion of the means-ends problem for
modern societies will proceed on the basis of a working hypothesis,

namely that the uncertainty or lack of agreement about the role of technology in social change is partly a symptom of real, unresolved social contradictions. I distinguish between "contradictions" and "conflicts" as follows: Social conflicts are opposing demands (peaceful or violent) on the direction of social policy by groups because of their immediate or present-day understanding of their own interests. These may or may not be capable of resolution without "basic" or "structural" alterations in existing institutions. Contradictions are conflicts of interest that have become "sedimented" in the structure of the dominant institutions and that can be resolved only by alterations in that structure. For example, a social class that reproduces its power and wealth mainly by confining a subject labor force to specific localities, as did the feudal aristocracy of medieval Europe, has a contradictory interest vis-a-vis another class (the emergent bourgeoisie), which strives to establish a "free market" for labor. Similarly, it is often argued that there is a contradiction between political democracy and an extreme inequality of economic power.

Naturally this is not meant to be a hard-and-fast distinction. At any time a social group's perception of its interest will affect its judgments concerning the extent of the institutional modifications necessary for realizing them, and of course these perceptions also change over time. In addition, the composition of the groups themselves is somewhat flexible, leading to the total or partial absorption of previously conflicting interests, such as the transformation of part of the feudal aristocracy into the bourgeoisie or the "embourgeoisement" of elements of the working class in capitalist societies. Then too, what in fact constitutes a "structural" alteration in institutions, as opposed to a modification in institutional practices, is often not easy to determine. In authoritarian "socialist" regimes, conflicts of interest between a ruling elite and the ruled population are masked rather than resolved by institutional changes in the modes of control over social wealth.

In the light of these qualifications, the original distinction between conflicts and contradictions can be modified. Social contradictions are unstable sets of intersecting, actual, and potential conflicts. In other words, they are ensembles of areas of conflict the specific character of which is always changing, whose interconnectedness is not necessarily understood by the actors or groups involved. It is thus the generality in the scope and understanding of a social problem reflected in an institutional arrangement, and not some abstract, "essential" characteristic such as ownership of the means of production, that distinguishes a contradiction from a conflict.

An example of a contradiction in advanced capitalist societies is the antagonism between the actual and potential capacity in individuals for the responsible exercise of initiative and personal responsibility, on the one hand, and the pervasive authoritarianism that is sedimented in institutions and structures of behavior, on the other. Political, economic, and social institutions all have deeply entrenched modes of authoritarian control, as do the existing patterns of interpersonal behavior, such as the relations between men and women. At the same time, modern society has attempted to overcome the traditional obstacles to individual self-development through acceptance of public responsibility for education, welfare, civil liberties, and so forth. This is an ongoing contradiction that cannot have a definitive resolution, at least in the foreseeable future. The opposing tendencies, however, continually reveal new dimensions and modify institutional practices and individual behavior.

In what follows, I shall try to give a preliminary justification for the argument that the role of technology in social change can only be understood in relation to the crucial areas of contradiction in modern society. To do so, I shall first set forth a series of conceptual distinctions for the following terms: techniques, technology (or technologies), instrumental rationality, and technological rationality. Next I shall show how these are connected with the predominant modes of social reproduction (commodity production, bureaucratic authority, and domination over nonhuman nature), which are the arenas within which the crucial social contradictions unfold. This analysis provides a framework for evaluating the role of modern technology in the developing opposition between capitalist and socialist forms of social organization. As stated earlier, the problem of means-ends rationality provides the general context for the discussion, and the concluding section attempts to show the particular relevance of that context for an understanding of the social significance of modern technology.

TECHNOLOGY AND INSTRUMENTAL RATIONALITY

Techniques are solutions to practical or theoretical problems arising out of the environmental forces that impinge upon organisms. In plant and animal life, techniques are adaptive responses to environmental forces, while among social animals they may be intergenerationally transmitted through learning patterns. [2] Considered as solutions to problems, techniques are for the most part the outcome of individual responses and are relevant only to individual settings. Those that transcend such limited settings and become incorporated into the behavioral patterns of groups represent transmissive solutions and thereby have an evolutionary significance for a particular species.

In human society, techniques encompass all sorts of activities: There are techniques for saving souls as well as for manufacturing steel. Their origination has a degree of relative autonomy from their contextual settings: there have been many instances in which a technical solution has lain dormant or has been forgotten and subsequently rediscovered, to be put to use later under much different circumstances. They may arise either as a result of random selection governed by environmental interactions that remain uncomprehended or as the outcome of reflective activity and an explicit desire to control the play of environmental forces.

Those transmissive techniques that attain a certain level of general significance in particular societies or historical epochs become technologies. The main reason for distinguishing between techniques and technologies is that only the general modes of social organization, and not the specific properties of techniques themselves, determine which types of techniques will be encouraged and promoted and which will be downplayed or perhaps forbidden. For example, techniques of magic have been developed and practiced in many different cultures, and there is a specific rationality that is appropriate to them.[3] In some cultures such techniques have a socially legitimate public function, which may be institutionalized in formal roles and training. In others, such as our own, they may be widely practiced in private life but have no legitimate public function. This has nothing to do with the degree of "operational perfection" attained by the techniques themselves but rather reflects changes in the predominant modes of social reproduction.

The rationality of the selection of techniques in a culture can only be judged in relation to the socially legitimate goals for individual behavior in that culture.[4] In this sense it was reasonable for the culture of medieval Europe to invest far more individual talent and energy in elaborating techniques of salvation, rather than those of material production. The predominant social patterns determine what kinds of techniques will be valued more highly than others and whether the privileged techniques will remain relatively unchanged or will be continually refined and developed. For example, in many types of what we call "primitive" society, warfare is one of the established, legitimate modes of social reproduction (as a determinant of roles, personal development of individuals, and so forth). The techniques of combat and weaponry are adjusted to the cultural function of ritual warfare, and in most cases of this type they do not change over long periods.

The viability of any culture's social patterns can be judged externally in terms of the "reproductive success" of that culture, that is, of its ability to survive and maintain its identity in relation to its competitors. So long as this general requirement is met, we can say that its techniques are appropriate, no matter how bizarre or irrational they may seem from the viewpoint of a different time or culture. In terms of the general ecological form of human societies, the hunter-gatherer ecology and its associated techniques seemed to possess a long-term viability until it succumbed to an alternative pattern involving the domestication of plants and animals and the development of progressively larger social units.[5] The long-term viability of this successor pattern is, of course, not yet known.

The fact that similar techniques have different significance in various cultures and that the same techniques have different social functions at various times in a culture can be reflected conceptually in the distinction between techniques and technologies. This is because the selection and "weighting" of a technique both conditions and is conditioned by other social factors, such as class, status, and role determinations. The development and utilization of techniques never occurs independently of determinations of who can utilize them and for what. Such determinations reflect and affect the social division of labor and the tempo of social change.

Technologies, therefore, are combinations of techniques, and the combinations represent choices among alternative uses or goals in the service of which the techniques are applied. In most cases it is inaccurate to refer simply to "technology," because very often this term carries the implication that there is some fixed character in a society's technological apparatus itself. This is shown most clearly in the recent influential theories of the relation between "technology" and contemporary society. In these theories it is assumed (usually without benefit of argument) that "modern technology" itself must necessarily be associated with certain particular forms of social organization, for example large-scale production units managed through hierarchical lines of authority. The conclusion drawn from this assumption is that society must adapt itself to the "imperatives of technology" in order to realize the inherent benefits that would otherwise lay dormant in the technological apparatus.[6]

What I am suggesting is that there are almost always alternative technologies potentially present in any ensemble of techniques. Certain technologies are "released" and put into practice, and others are suppressed, by the particular features of the institutional forms that predominate in a given society at a given time. In themselves, techniques are inherently "abstract." That is, they set out a solution for a problem involving the relationship between means and ends, and it is a matter of indifference, so far as the technique itself is concerned, who performs the relevant operations and under what conditions. So far as a society or culture is concerned, however, this is not at all a matter of indifference. In established social patterns, techniques are almost always combined with class, status, and role determinations that specify who can perform the operations associated with techniques and under what culturally legitimated conditions. This combination is what I call a technology, and it is "concrete" (as opposed to the abstractness of a technique) because it is only in this context that techniques become operational and productive beyond the purely private sphere of existence.

A technology has a social character, albeit not a fixed one, incorporating tools or techniques in an operational context that normally will be congruent with the predominant institutional structures and social determinations of a culture. Certainly techniques can be incorporated or combined in a variety of ways in different cultures, and it is also true that cultures have differential capacities for adopting new techniques and for recombining techniques within alternative technologies. Finally, as I shall try to show in the following pages, technologies are in turn incorporated into more general forms of social reproduction, and in the latter they often embody structural contradictions that give rise to alternative possibilities for their application.

Any treatment of "technology" that regards a culture's response to the operational attributes of techniques themselves as the most significant aspect of that culture's institutional viability—as is the case in some of the literature on technology transfer—is inadequate. In discussions of this point I have heard propositions such as "a hammer is a hammer" advanced as an apparently self-evident refutation of the idea that techniques can only be evaluated as an integral aspect of a social matrix. The simple analytical logic of such propositions cannot compensate for their triviality, however. In a culture in which role determinations prohibit women from hunting, a spear is more than the sum of its technical attributes. The same is true of a sword in a society that restricts participation in warfare to the members of a closed social class. In modern society the dominant forms of social reproduction have shaped the applications of industrial technology in accordance with authoritarian, hierarchical modes of authority; one of the consequences of this pattern is the pervasive alienated character of labor activity, which is by no means an inherent attribute of the technology itself.

Just as techniques are incorporated into technologies, so are the latter in turn incorporated into wider frameworks that I have called "modes of social reproduction." These are the predominant forms of institutional organization in the spheres of economy, politics, and social relations. The distribution and significance of power, authority, property, class, and status relationships and roles are the concrete attributes of these institutional forms. The prevailing choices among alternative technologies in any society can only be understood in relation to these attributes. The section of this chapter on modes of social reproduction offers an elaboration of this hypothesis with specific reference to modern society. Before turning

to this task, however, I will give an overview of the concept of social
rationality that was developed in the theoretical literature on the relationship of technology and modern society.

THE CONCEPT OF SOCIAL RATIONALITY

A new tradition in Western thought emerged in the seventeenth
century with thinkers (notably Francis Bacon) who advocated the
union of experimental science with the technical arts and crafts. Bacon argued that this union would result in a dramatic increase of
material prosperity and a concomitant reduction in the social tensions, which he thought resulted primarily from an insufficiency of
goods. By the early nineteenth century the industrial applications of
technical innovations prompted other thinkers to see in the growth of
industrial technologies the principal source of social progress. Saint-
Simon and his followers suggested that political leadership be vested
in the hands of the captains of industry and predicted that by this
means a more rational organization of society would come into being.

It was Marx who developed the most comprehensive version of
the argument that capitalism undermined many of the irrational aspects of earlier forms of social organization, such as "nature-wor-
ship," and laid the foundations for a "civilized" and enlightened human society. For Marx, of course, this superior rationality of capitalism was still embedded in irrational social forms (represented
by commodity fetishism, for example), whose most general character was the private appropriation and control of socially created
wealth. This fact notwithstanding, capitalism was for Marx a necessary stage in the evolution of a "rational" society.

Marx's theory was more comprehensive than earlier ones in
another respect. Marx contended that there was an emerging incommensurability between the increasing technical rationality of production, on the one hand, and the repressive political and social structure, on the other, that prevented most individuals from developing
their intellectual and emotional capacities to the fullest extent.

The instrumental rationality embodied in modern science, technology, and industry would remain one-sided and distorted if it were
not accompanied by a matching growth and maturity of human faculties that would govern the disposition of the fruits of technical ingenuity. In effect, Marx raised the question of the commensurability of
means and ends in modern society. He suggested that a necessary
condition for modern society was the emergence of the "general intellect," by which he meant the capacity, distributed widely among
the population, for regulating the new productive apparatus and
directing it toward humane goals. [7]

In the ensuing period the most significant modification of Marx's argument, and one that was to have a great impact on twentieth century thought, was made by Max Weber. In his discussion of what he called "economically rational action" and the place of technique or technology therein, Weber explicitly separated the two realms of means and ends as follows:

> The term "technology" applied to an action refers to this totality of means employed as opposed to the meaning or end to which the action is, in the last analysis, oriented. Rational technique is a choice of means which is consciously and systematically oriented to the experience and reflection of the actor, which consists, at the highest level of rationality, in scientific knowledge. [8]

Not only does this formulation neatly divide the realms of means and ends, but it also advances an "objective" criterion of rationality in the domain of technique itself. The rationality of technique has two aspects in Weber's view: (1) conscious self-reflection on the part of the human agent and (2) an implicit notion of progress, according to which scientific knowledge (one can only assume that Weber means specifically the modern natural sciences) is the highest expression of human rationality in the technical sphere.

We might assume, on a generous interpretation of this passage, that there are other sociocultural settings apart from modern society in which the first-mentioned aspect of rational technique has been present. In other words, we might assume that in most human societies choices about means have been "consciously and systematically oriented to the experience and reflection" of human agents. There are, however, many crucial ambiguities hidden in the second aspect seen by Weber. The chief difficulty is in determining how to interpret it in the light of his famous distinction between "formal" and "substantive" (or "material") rationality.

Formal rationality pertains to the sphere of means. Weber himself admits that "the concept of substantive rationality is full of difficulties." It seems to refer to the relationship between the production of "utilities" in the economy and the "ultimate ends" or values of a society. [9] The distinction, therefore, seems to be made explicitly in order to preserve the dichotomy between means and ends. Weber argues that different social systems will have very different conceptions of ultimate ends and that there is no basis for asserting the intrinsic superiority of one system of ends (goals, values), or of its perception of the "rational" means to be used in the attainment of those ends, over others. "In principle, there is an

indefinite number of possible standards of value which are 'rational'
in this sense. . . . There is no question in this discussion of attempting value judgments in this field, but only of determining and
delimiting what is to be called 'formal'. "[10] The crucial element in
Weber's discussion, therefore, is his attempt to separate out a
sphere of social action (called formal rationality) on which objectively valid judgments could be made. Only the rigorous separation of
means and ends makes this possible. "For purposes of the theoretical definition of technical rationality, it is wholly indifferent whether
the product of a technical process is in any sense useful. . . . In the
present terminology there could well be a rational technique even of
achieving ends which no one desires. "[11] Weber qualified this principle by saying that in practice the concrete goals of economic activity
(the production of "useful" goods) would limit and define the tasks of
technical rationality. Of course, any society is free to choose to produce whatever appears to be useful to its members.

　　　What are some of the problematical issues raised by this
theory? The first problem concerns Weber's conception of modern
scientific knowledge as the "highest level of rationality." In this conception he collapses the distinction between science and technology,
and this is problematical. In addition, we also must consider Edmund Husserl's contention that modern science represents a particular form of the understanding of nature, or a particular form of
rationality, but not the "highest level" (whatever that might mean),
generated by certain operative assumptions and intrinsically oriented
toward determinate ends. [12] For Husserl, these ends are the elaboration of a conceptual system in which the behavior of natural phenomena are understood solely as instances of invariant laws that may be
expressed in mathematical form. This point is not, strictly speaking, a logical objection to Weber's implicit identification of modern
science with what he calls "rational technique." The purpose of
Husserl's work was precisely to raise the question of the means-
ends relationship. In effect, he challenged the notion of formal rationality itself, since his argument suggested that we could not be
content with a situation in which we have no way of evaluating the
consequences in everyday life of the applications of formal-rational
techniques.

　　　The problem opened up by Husserl's work was further clarified
in the writings of the Frankfurt School theorists Max Horkheimer,
Theodor Adorno, and Herbert Marcuse. They used the term "instrumental rationality" to designate more generally what was implied in
the Weberian conception of formal or technical rationality. [13] I will
comment only on that aspect of their contribution that is directly
relevant to the main issue under discussion here. They tried to show
why the separation of the means-ends relationship that is inherent

in the concept of formal rationality is a regressive step in social thought. In this context, the specific uses to which technical rationality are put are not a matter of indifference or incidental concern, but rather are an integral part of a dangerous tendency toward either a terroristic and totalitarian society or a nonterroristic, "administered" society in which human individuality is threatened. Weber himself shared these concerns, of course, and acknowledged that there seemed to be no possible solution for this dilemma. It is noteworthy that at the end of his career Horkheimer reached a position very similar to Weber's: Social theory could only register a lament about the destruction of spontaneity and individuality in the "totally administered" industrial society, both capitalist and socialist.

Whatever the relative strengths and weaknesses of the Frankfurt School's position might be, it did serve to identify a crucial problem in the influential Weberian conception of social rationality. As originally stated, it points to two kinds of rationality, formal and substantive; there is thus an abstract symmetry in the distinction. In actual fact, however, there are no criteria for assessing the "substance" of rationality itself in the substantive or material sphere. In short, the division of rationality into these two domains is misleading. "Substantive rationality" has no objective content whatsoever, although this is not the case with formal rationality, which by definition is supposed to be a domain in which objective measurements of relative efficacy are possible. There is an inherent incommensurability with respect to the two aspects of the sphere of rationality. The actual result of Weber's distinction is that the meaning of the term rationality is confined solely to the domain of technical means; in effect, it defines rationality as formal rationality. The real effect of the concept of formal rationality is to destroy the possibility of even imagining a process of rational goal selection.

Weber adopted a strict cultural relativism, according to which there could be no "rational" debate over ultimate values. It was just this delimitation that allowed him to posit an "autonomous" sphere of technical rationality. The long-run difficulty in this perspective is its failure to see that it is precisely the methodical pursuit of purely instrumentalist solutions to particular, dissociated problems that calls for the formation of an institutional framework for rational goal selection. Our productive-destructive technological capacity can now for the first time threaten a vast, indeterminate alteration in our biological, genetic, and ecological situation. Under these circumstances the pursuit of rational (technical) solutions to particular problems involves so many possible hidden "negative externalities" that we must seek a social forum capable of assessing their appropriateness, in other words, a forum to assess the desirability of the ends in the service of which the practical solutions are proposed. Whether or not we can achieve this is unclear, but we can at least recognize the nature of the dilemma.

In 1973 Laurence Tribe independently developed a critique of instrumental rationality that is also rooted in the means-ends problem. Tribe's basic point is that the exclusive focus on practical outcomes or achievements in formal rationality makes us ignore the effects of the changes on individuals—on their conceptions of themselves, their values, and their understanding of their place in the community of human and nonhuman beings—wrought by the process of social transformation:

> In most areas of human endeavor—from performing a symphony to orchestrating a society—the processes and rules that constitute the enterprise and define the roles played by its participants matter quite apart from any "end state" that is ultimately produced. Indeed, in many cases it is the process itself that matters most to those who take part in it. [14]

Tribe argues further that individuals and societies, in choosing certain technical solutions to problems (or the material products of technical innovations), decisively alter the quality of the experiences they and their successors are likely to have. Over time this has a reciprocal impact on the kinds of subsequent choices they are likely to make.

Tribe rejects the Weberian dichotomy as an analytical tool and maintains that we must regard "virtually every human action" as being "at once both operational (or 'instrumental') and self-forming (or 'constitutive')."[15] A better conception, in his view, "requires a reciprocity of subject and object in which society conceives of the chooser as fluid and of choices as continually shaping and redefining who and what the chooser is."[16] This compelling argument brings us back full circle to Marx's anticipation of our contemporary dilemma, mentioned earlier. Underlying Marx's view, as I have already suggested, is a similar conception of the necessary complementarity of the instrumental and goal-determining dimensions of human existence. What this means concretely is that the instrumental achievement of modern technical rationality—its greater productivity and efficiency in the provisioning of material goods—demands a corresponding growth in the maturity of the individuals for whom those goods are intended, a growth in their ability to use them wisely and responsibly.

It may be admitted that there is no generally accepted standard by which to judge the degree of wisdom and responsibility in the use of things. All I wish to do here is isolate the problem, not offer a solution for it. This admitted shortcoming does not in my view lessen the force of the critique of the concept of technical rationality. Since it arbitrarily isolates one aspect of a holistic social practice, and since simply by virtue of a conceptual dichotomy it deprives the realm of ends of any possible claim to rationality, the notion of formal rationality is itself arbitrary. By whatever label it is known, whether as formal, technical, technological, or instrumental rationality, this notion merely serves to obscure the most fateful choices and issues posed in modern societies.

MODES OF SOCIAL REPRODUCTION

Techniques and technologies are elements in the institutional and socialization patterns through which societies reproduce themselves. Those patterns must maintain a certain degree of internal coherence, as well as provide a basis for resistance to external pressures, in order to insure the reproductive success of an ecological or cultural pattern. This criterion of cultural viability is not sufficient, however, because we also need to understand the "logic" inherent in the process of change within broad patterns, such as "sedentary ecology" or "Western civilization." For example, if we accept the concept of Western civilization as designating a cultural unity in at least some important senses, then we must seek to explain the earlier transition from feudal to capitalist organization or the contemporary transition from capitalist to incipient socialist modes of organization. Since it is obvious that there are radical differences in the kinds of techniques that are most significant in the various phases of Western civilization, it is necessary to understand why and how these differences have come about.

The most influential explanation has been the one made by Marx, namely that there are inherent contradictions within the forms of organization of social life and that historical change results from the friction among those contradictions. He designated the principal organizational forms as the "forces of production" and the "relations of production." Marx's scheme is well known, and I will not elaborate it here; nor will I discuss the important modifications of it, such as those found in J. Habermas's work.[17] Rather, I shall develop a variation of it in terms of the conceptual distinctions being made in this paper.

As a social system, capitalism is characterized by at least the following significant, interrelated modes of social reproduction: (1) generalized market exchange, incorporating technologies of production and consumption; (2) a particular form of political domination;

and (3) domination over nonhuman nature. The relationship among
the three is not one of logical necessity; that is, each is possible in
the absence of the others. Their historical association, however,
gave rise to the specific development of capitalism in Western civilization. The actual utilization of techniques and technologies in this
social form, such as techniques of production, has been conditioned
by the general logic of this social system. Their association marks
capitalism as a unique social form, although of course each mode
has its roots in previous developments. Taken together, they form
a type of society the negative features of which are the maintenance
of inequality of power (domination) and wealth (exploitation), the
distortion of human needs in a high-intensity market economy, and
a purely utilitarian orientation toward nonhuman nature. Its positive
features are a vastly increased productivity of labor, the creation
of institutional frameworks for greater individual freedom, and a
better understanding of natural phenomena.

I shall begin by briefly discussing each of the three modes of
social reproduction, taken separately and in relation to each other.
I shall also try to show what are the developing contradictions within the modes of social reproduction.

Generalized Market Exchange

Capitalism organizes social activity in such a way that market
exchanges gradually become the exclusive basis for production and
consumption. Of course, there are both nonmarket and market exchanges in precapitalist societies (in "primitive" cultures as well as
in premodern civilizations), but until the coming of capitalism there
had never been a market economy, that is, a system of material
production in which all the "factors of production" (especially labor
and land) are drawn into the sphere of market transactions.[18] Heretofore, markets were always a subordinate part of economic life,
and for the bulk of the population production for use was more significant than production for exchange. On the other hand, the ideal
limit of a generalized market economy is a situation in which every
producer has a specialized function and likewise depends exclusively
on market purchases for the satisfaction of his or her needs.

One can imagine a generalized market economy in which all
producers would have equal economic power, (that is, equal control
over the means of production) and in which, as a result, there would
be no significant disparities of wealth as a result of market transactions. This image of a society of equal commodity producers was put
forth by Jean Jacques Rousseau in his Social Contract and was the
social foundation of the universal participatory democracy he

advocated. It is the hidden basis of the misleading ideology of the "equivalence" of market transactions advanced since the seventeenth century by the apologists for bourgeois society. Of course, that image always remained very different from the reality of capitalist society. Here I must anticipate some of the subsequent discussion in noting that capitalism developed the generalized market economy in the context of the existing, pervasive relations of domination and exploitation, for it is this that explains why labor became a commodity, that is, why most producers were forced to sell their labor, not the products of their labor. The interest in constantly reproducing the unequal distribution of wealth governs the capitalist form of generalized market exchange.

The reproduction of the unequal distribution of wealth through the appropriation of surplus value is the basic "imperative" of the capitalist technologies of production and consumption. This social imperative determines the specific application of the techniques therein. In other words, the choice of which techniques and how they have been utilized is primarily the outcome, not of the inherent "rationality" of the techniques, but of the serviceability of the chosen techniques for the maintenance of the unequal distribution of wealth. In a wide-ranging historical study in progress, Stephen Marglin is attempting to show in detail how the factory organization of capitalist production was shaped in the first instance by the interest in extending control over the labor force, not for "efficiency" of production. [19] The application of technical expertise in "planned obsolescence" is an obvious example. This is not inconsistent with the rising productivity of the capitalist economy; it simply means that productive efficiency is a secondary objective.

Actually, it is self-evident that in the capitalist technology of production the inherent virtues of techniques must be subordinated to the conditions of profitable production. The greater energy efficiency of rail over road and air transport is easily demonstrable, but it is effective market demand that determines which shall be the predominant form at any time—and also, in these cases, how funds for research and development of technical innovations are allocated. There is a capitalist technology of consumption as well. [20] This involves the organization of consumer behavior in such a way that the consumer can respond "efficiently" in the ordering of preferences to changing, highly complex characteristics of goods, such as the use of appropriate techniques for assembling, comparing, and evaluating information about commodities. By imposing this requirement on each individual consumer, however, the capitalist market system in its advanced technical stage insures, by virtue of the inherent complexity of the products, that individual purchasing decisions based on adequate information will be impossible in practice.

The capitalist technology of production and consumption, then, subordinates the application of techniques to the social imperative of "adequate" returns to capital. Each dimension of this technology has a potentially contradictory aspect. In production activity, the fragmentation of tasks and the lack of participation in decision making (maintenance of hierarchical control) eliminate or severely constrict the possibilities of deriving satisfaction from work for the majority of people, with the result that all striving for satisfaction is oriented toward consumption activity. In the contemporary capitalist marketplace, which is a "high-intensity market setting" by virtue of the huge number and rapidly changing assortment of goods, the complexity and variety of the things, together with the bewildering claims about them in advertising messages, results in a state of confusion about individual needs, and especially about the relationship between needs and the things that are supposed to satisfy them. [21] If I am correct in arguing that these are potentially structural contradictions in the capitalist technology of production and consumption, then the refinement of techniques in the further development of that technology will exacerbate those problems. That is, it will increase the degree of personal dissatisfaction in the predominant kinds of producing and consuming activities in capitalist society.

Social and Political Domination

The evolution of Western capitalism as a form of political domination was a gradual transition from control based on the monopoly of landed property by a social class to control based on a monopoly of the ownership or management of capital. This "continuum" of domination meant that the generalized market economy could not be an association of equal commodity producers but rather another form of exploitation by a minority of the labor of the majority and the appropriation by that minority of surplus value. This resulted in the persistence of a radical inequality of power and wealth even as the social production of material goods increased enormously.

The characteristic political form of capitalist society is representative democracy. The radical inequality of wealth and power has endured through the evolution of this political form, as is documented in the empirical studies showing the interconnections of economic and political power, the "circulation of elites," and the remarkable stability in income and wealth shares among the population even throughout the developing welfare-state phase of capitalism. [22] What has sustained this social and political domination in recent times is the real material progress for the population as a whole and the expectations of continued material betterment that are associated with the religion of endless economic growth.

The capitalist form of generalized market exchange requires a disposable labor force that can be continually shifted about and retrained for different productive settings. This contrasts sharply with the type of control over labor characteristic of feudalism. The form of hierarchical control appropriate to these requirements is the bureaucratic apparatus organized along functional lines, or "rational authority" in the Weberian sense. The successful political innovations in the modern period generally are just those that can be accommodated to the structures of bureaucratic organization. In other words, the predominant tendency is for the techniques of political participation to be subordinated to the general form of bureaucratic decision making. For example, pressures for more equitable treatment from historically disadvantaged groups (such as women) usually result in the creation of new departments and hiring practices within established bureaucracies while the prevailing distribution of wealth and power remains unaffected.

The potential contradictions in capitalist political domination arise out of the long-range alterations in the everyday life-situations of individuals that the capitalist economy effects. Factors such as the changing occupational structure of the work force, the rising level of education, and the growing interest in "job satisfaction" could form the basis for demands for real popular participation at the immediate levels of decision making (such as work place and community). These demands, unlike electoral politics, would be inconsistent with the prevailing bureaucratic-hierarchical forms. Since these bureaucratic forms are the principal shield for the structure of privilege and domination that persists underneath the ideological manipulations of representative democracy, a mounting challenge to them would represent the emergence of a qualitatively different kind of politics.

Domination over Nonhuman Nature

In every human culture there are directions for the orientation of the social group toward the world of nonhuman nature (topography, flora, and fauna). These patterns determine the ways in which it may be appropriated for the satisfaction of needs, and they also encompass the categories through which its symbolic significance for the group is interpreted. Western capitalism was the first social form with a growing tendency to regard all of nonhuman nature in exclusively utilitarian terms, as being nothing but a warehouse of resources for human use, and to systematically denigrate any other symbolic significance in the human relationship to it. In other words, there arose a vision of nonhuman nature as mere "material" that could be subjected to complete and unchallengeable control through the progress of human scientific and technical ingenuity. [23]

The idea of "man" as the "lord of nature" is of course very old and has its roots in aspects of the Judeo-Christian tradition. Beginning with the seventeenth-century efforts of influential thinkers such as Francis Bacon, however, this idea was transformed into a secular vision. Modern science came to be regarded as the vehicle through which "man's" domination over nature would be achieved. The social and cultural innovation that allowed modern science to assume this role was the liberation of scientific research from its historical subordination to religious and philosophical categories. The gradual fusion of mathematics, experimental science, and technical innovations (such as improved instruments of measurement) occurred simultaneously with the growing command of the capitalist production technology. The mutual reinforcement of these developments laid the basis for the immensely productive integration of science and industry beginning in the nineteenth century. [24]

The cultural victory of modern natural science over religion and philosophy marked the triumph of a radical sense of human separateness from, and indeed superiority over, natural processes. All precapitalist cultures had institutionalized prohibition of appropriation of nature for human use: there were sacred places and animals, ritual procedures, and such were cultural expressions of a sense of identity with other living things and a desire to harmonize human purposes with the course of nature as a whole.

In other words, techniques of appropriation for use were subordinated to a culture's cosmological or philosophical understanding of nature—all of which seems "irrational" from the viewpoint of the modern scientific outlook. By way of contrast, the champions of modern science argued that investigation of nature should be motivated by the search not for insight into nature's "purposes" or the proper station of the human race in nature, but rather for experimental evidence showing how the multiplicity of natural events could be understood as resulting from the operation of general laws or principles. Comprehension of these general principles led to greater human "control" over nature in the sense that a natural event could be reproduced at will once its preconditions were known. The advocates of science argued for the superiority of the techniques that would achieve this goal, as opposed to competing techniques such as numerological metaphysics or the search for a single all-powerful substance (the philosopher's stone). The superiority of the techniques that characterize our science seems self-evident, but this was not so in the seventeenth century, when there were figures of great learning and talent who supported those "irrational" alternatives. [25] The explanation for this is that disputes over the best tech-

niques actually represented differences over the goals that were to
be achieved by the investigation of natural processes.

The science-based notion of domination over nature, with its
goal of achieving the greatest possible control over nature in the
sense defined above, gradually emerged victorious over other conceptions that incorporated different goals (such as the religion-based
search for salvation) on account of its affinity with other powerful social currents, especially the expanding material productivity of the
generalized exchange economy.

What are the potential contradictions in the attempt to achieve
domination over nonhuman nature? The major problem is that the
exclusive focus on purely instrumental goals (control over nature)
and the exclusively utilitarian orientation toward the rest of nature
prevent us from clarifying the "final" objectives of this activity. In
other words, it becomes an end in itself. In concrete terms, cease-
less economic growth and expansion of the sphere of commodities
become self-justifying ideologies for capitalist societies; we lack
any objective criteria for determining whether this is an adequate
route to the satisfaction of needs, since every attained level of
material wealth only seems to elicit further demands. (For the established socialist societies there is the problem of resolving the
ambiguities in the concept of "abundance": How much and what kind
of wealth represents the state of abundance that was framed as an
objective in nineteenth-century socialist theory?) At some point,
it seems to me, modern societies must face these problems, but to
do so they will require criteria for well-being that must transcend
the purely instrumental orientation toward the rest of nature.

A discussion of such possible criteria of well-being would take
us too far from the topic of this paper, but I would like to suggest
one line of argument without being able to defend it here. The prodi-
gious growth of human productive capacities in the modern period
has made a tremendous impact on the biological systems of the natural environment and, among other things, poses an immediate threat
to the future viability of countless plant and animal species. A resolve to "reconcile" or accommodate human demands on the environment with the life-requirements of other species might provide some
guidance for establishing limits to those demands and therefore one
basis for criteria of well-being. This is in no way a plea for "returning" to an archaic, mystical, and therefore "unscientific," orientation to nature; respecting the needs of other species is no more than
prudent or enlightened self-interest. A group of natural scientists
recently suggested that there is a need for an "ethic of biotic diversity," that is, for a policy of maintaining the widest possible range of
other species on the planet, to insure the future well-being of the
human race. [26] At any rate I think it is evident that an alternative

orientation toward the sphere of nonhuman nature, whatever its characteristics turn out to be, will be required to replace the ideology of domination over nonhuman nature that has evolved in capitalist society.

The union of these three modes of social reproduction—generalized market exchange, political domination, and domination over nonhuman nature—forms the most general developmental tendency, or "system-imperative," of capitalism. Under its hegemony, techniques are selected and shaped in a way that on balance perpetuates this form of society and hinders the emergence of alternate forms. If this conception is correct, it should give an insight into the unifying principle that governs the adoption and rejection of technical innovations (on balance and in the long run) in the economic, political, and social domains of capitalist society. This principle is the maintenance of an expanding commodity marketplace and of hierarchical-bureaucratic authority under conditions that permit the enlarged reproduction of capital.

Evolution into Socialism

Socialist theory and practice emerged in the nineteenth century as the determinate negation of capitalism, that is, as the social form that would fall heir to the positive accomplishments wrought by capitalism while overcoming its negative aspects. I use the term "determinate negation" to indicate that socialist theory (and at least some aspects of the actual socialist movement) envisaged the new society not as an arbitrarily chosen alternative to capitalism but rather as the outcome of developmental tendencies set in motion by capitalism itself and as the overcoming of certain of its specific features that were considered to be deleterious, namely alienation, commodity fetishism, and class domination, through different modes of social organization and activity. I shall consider briefly the transformations of the three capitalist modes that socialism and communism are supposed to accomplish.

Generalized market exchange should gradually give way to a different organization of economic life. Marx outlined a well-known conception of this in his Critique of the Gotha Program; rather than commenting on this or any other received formulation, however, I shall present my own version of this expected transformation. Socialist technologies of production and consumption should overcome the two principal negative features of the high-intensity market setting existing in present-day advanced capitalist societies. These features are the alienation that is rooted in the lack of any direct control over producing activity, resulting in a failure to derive satisfaction from labor, and the confusion about human needs that arises in relation to the complexity and variety of commodities, resulting in a failure to derive lasting satisfaction from consumption, as indicated by the apparent insatiability of material wants. To overcome these negative features, socialism must institute a long-range strategy to reduce (not eliminate) the scope of market activity and promote opportunities for involvement in direct production for use (for example, in craft activities). To be sure, this form of production would be less "efficient" as judged by purely technical standards; but this alternative is a qualitatively different mode of social reproduction, the objective of which is not to maximize the number of things in a marketplace available for consumption but to make possible a different form of the satisfaction of needs.

Secondly, hierarchical-bureaucratic authority should give way to participatory, decentralized forms of decision making. In institutional settings this means self-management of enterprises, increasing regional or sectional autonomy, and community control over planning and development. This too would be less efficient according to present standards and would result in a lower aggregate total of material production than now exists in the most technically advanced societies. The presumption is, however, that there would be adequate compensation for this in the increasing sense of satisfaction derived from active participation in decision-making activities in all the domains in which social change has a direct impact on the everyday life-situations of individuals and groups.

The third sphere, that of the relation to nonhuman nature, has received far less attention than the other two, but I think that eventually it will be recognized as equally significant. There is a sense of satisfaction in lessening the massive human transformation of the natural environment so as to preserve generous "undeveloped" spaces and the viability of other forms of life.[27] A reduction in the enormous quantity and variety of toxic residuals that are dumped into the environment through industrial production, the ultimate ecological impact of which cannot be calculated with any assurance, would also result in diminishing the quantity of material objects, but it may appear to be the more prudent course. Many individuals may come to experience an increasing degree of esthetic satisfaction in the presence of undeveloped natural environments and in the knowledge that the self-imposed restrictions on the human transformation of the environment respect the needs of other forms of life. This would represent a rejection of the ideology of domination over nonhuman nature and the appearance of a new orientation based on a sense of "participation" in the community of living entities.

Considered negatively, therefore, socialism is the striving to overcome alienation, commodity fetishism, bureaucratic authority,

and domination over nonhuman nature. Considered positively, it is
the creation of opportunities for individuals to derive satisfaction and
a sense of well-being from the activity of labor, from participation
in decision making, and from recognition of the needs of other living
entities. One cannot describe abstractly the kinds of techniques that
might be appropriate for these objectives. The main point I wish to
make is that the efficacy of techniques can only be judged concretely
in relation to explicit goals and the processes that seem appropriate
for them. In any case, the choice of techniques will depend upon the
specific conditions of time and place, taking into account such contingent factors as inherited cultural traditions. What is described here
is not a sudden "conversion" from one social form to another very
different one, but rather a long and complex historical transformation. There may be revolutionary moments in the realms of political
power and technical innovation, but never with respect to transforming the modes of social reproduction.

I have been discussing two opposing types of social systems on
a highly abstract level. This was done for purposes of clarification,
and naturally I am not supposing that in reality we find two opposite,
self-contained social forms called "capitalism" and "socialism."
I mentioned some of the developing contradictions within capitalism
and the expectation that alternative patterns of activity can emerge
out of those contradictions. In the actual world situation today there
is a state of dialectical tension between the capitalist and socialist
modes within all societies, regardless of whether their dominant
ideologies are capitalism, socialism, or communism and regardless
of the stages of their industrial development. The characteristics of
that tension and the degree to which it is explicit at the level of political controversy vary from country to country, but it is present
in some form everywhere.

In any case, what will result from the resolution of that tension cannot be predicted: there is no strict necessity in the social
dialectic. In all of the present-day capitalist societies, there are
many individuals who support the goals that I have outlined above
under the rubric of socialism. There are also nominally socialist
societies that have institutionalized much of what I have called the
capitalist modes of social reproduction. The dominant ideologies on
both sides mask the real confrontation of opposing modes by confining debate to the level of meaningless abstractions. In the former,
capitalism is assumed to be equivalent to, or a necessary precondition of, "individual freedom," while in the latter, "collective ownership of the means of production" is assumed to be equivalent to socialism.

Such empty formulations inhibit our understanding of contemporary social change. On account of them there is, for example, a

failure to recognize the substantial level of latent public support for socialist goals and processes that exists in many capitalist societies and a corresponding failure to acknowledge the degree of reliance on capitalist strategies in many nominally socialist societies. This is partly a strategic or tactical stance and is to be expected. These opposing modes have not developed in isolation from each other as pristine forms; instead they have grown up side by side as powerful competitors for individual and collective allegiance, and for the foreseeable future each will continue to shape in part the evolution of the other. The "convergence" theory is superficial; beneath the facade of opposing "social systems," the dialectical tension between the opposing modes of social organization within each nation is played out in the context of contending domestic and international pressures.

A number of qualifications with respect to the preceding argument must be noted here. First, the capitalist modes of social reproduction have been presented as they have actually developed (at least in my view) in modern history, but the socialist ones are so far largely, but not entirely, a theoretical construction. The latter are "utopian" in that they are nowhere firmly entrenched in social practice; yet at the same time they represent real historical possibilities and are thus not merely articles of faith. There are many persons who are deeply committed to the clarification and realization of those possibilities and to better understanding of the impact the processes through which this commitment is expressed have on the nature of the intended ends themselves.

Second, the typology of interrelated modes of social reproduction is not meant to be exhaustive. In addition to the two sets I have mentioned, one might argue, the modern terroristic or totalitarian societies represent another distinctive type with its own distinguishing characteristics. In any case, it must be emphasized that these are all "ideal types," presented in this way for purposes of analysis, and that in reality the distinctions among them are a good deal fuzzier.

Third, I did not intend to imply by omission that the socialist modes are devoid of actual or potential contradictions. Since they are in a very early stage of development, however, what may turn out to be the contradictory elements are difficult to determine with any degree of confidence. With respect to the three modes that have been discussed, some speculation may be hazarded as far as all technically advanced societies are concerned: (1) There is likely to be considerable reliance on various forms of market mechanisms for some time to come, especially in view of the global interlocking of national economies, which will conflict with attempts to overcome alienated labor and commodity fetishism. (2) It will be no simple task to devise adequate frameworks for participatory decision mak-

ing, in view of the high degree of institutional coordination, both in
domestic and in international politics, that is necessary at the present stage of social development. (3) The notion of basing our orientation toward nonhuman nature on the vision of ourselves as participants in a wider community of living entities offers few if any actual
guidelines for changed social behavior. Some persons' interpretations of what is entailed by this notion may conflict sharply with
those of others. In the questions of implementation pertaining to all
of these domains, great difficulties may be expected to arise. It is
indeed likely, therefore, that contradictions will emerge, although
eventually they may become nonantagonistic, that is, not based on
social class divisions.

THE TRANSFER OF TECHNIQUES
AND TECHNOLOGIES

The historian Lynn White, Jr., has argued persuasively that
an adequate long-range view of the history of technical innovations
requires us to comprehend the broad cultural significance of those
innovations. [28] This perspective has motivated my own attempt to
clarify problems of contemporary social change by means of the conceptual distinctions developed above. I should now like to bring this
perspective to bear on one of the basic themes of this collection,
namely the impact of "technology transfer" (as conventionally understood) on what has been called the "goal culture" of socialism and
communism. Can these distinctions help us to understand what are
the critical issues here?
    One issue is whether it is sufficient to restrict our attention to
selecting the most "efficient" techniques for any purpose and then
judging a society's institutions largely in terms of whether or not it
can accommodate them at any particular time. There is abundant
evidence to show that cultures do interpret "alien" techniques as
harmful to the integrity of their established modes of social reproduction. Margaret Mead noted many instances of this in her survey
of the cultural impact of technical assistance programs as follows:

> When pest-control is imperative, people will neverthe-
> less release the rats from their traps. Where immuniza-
> tion of cattle is necessary, farmers will hide their cat-
> tle. And where land reform is introduced without ac-
> companying measures for a reformed credit system,
> the land will again be concentrated in the hands of a
> few within a few years. And since change is proposed
> in the interests of human welfare, it is important to

> see to it that it is introduced constructively or, at any
> rate, with a minimum of disruption and destruction of
> established interrelationships and values. [29]

The reason is that technical change does incorporate values,
the first of which is the value of change itself. It is by no means
self-evident for all cultures that change is "good"; acceptance of
regular technical change is itself a particular cultural predisposi-
tion. White maintains that a widespread acceptance of technical
change was present throughout the medieval period of Western civilization;[30] whatever the reasons for this might be, it clearly was a
factor in preparing the ground for the rapid acceleration of such
change in the modern period.

This is by no means the whole story. In the contemporary
period many cultures have quickly accepted new technical devices
(transistor radios, modern medicine), and it is not necessarily the
case that all their traditional techniques will be destroyed and replaced as a result. In general I think that the nature of the response
to new techniques is a function of the internal strength and resilience
of the culture. Few, if any, cultures in the history of human development have been entirely "closed," and there is much evidence in
the anthropological literature of regular technical transfer throughout. The matter of chief importance is for a culture to maintain its
economic and political independence so that it can determine its own
priorities in the process of change and regulate the pace at which
new techniques and technologies are combined with the old.

Even in a state of relative dependence, however, a resilient
culture can adapt new techniques to its purposes. In short, I do not
think there is any technique that is in itself inherently incompatible
with the general framework of established patterns of goals and
processes in any society. A culture may be the passive recipient of
the products of alien techniques that it cannot itself produce without
drastically altering its established patterns; for example, steel tools
are used by the surviving hunter-gatherer peoples. In this case, however, the key question is whether the use of the technique is adapted
to the general framework of the established patterns or helps to undermine them. Which of these alternatives comes to pass is not
primarily a function of the technique itself but of the degree of sophistication and "maturity" of the modes of reproduction (the resil-
iency of the culture). The adoption of a new technique may upset the
ecological balance. For example, the immunization of cattle may
lead to a sudden increase in the size of herds, with resultant over-
grazing and deterioration of the land. This need not necessarily occur, however, if there is sufficient awareness of ecological factors
that countervailing measures (still within the established modes) may

be implemented. This is a general problem in all cultures, even the most technically advanced: we do not yet know the long-range impact on the biosphere of the residuals from present industrial production, some of which—such as the effects of fluorocarbons in the upper atmosphere—involve possible dangers of great magnitude.

The transfer of technologies is a far different matter, since these are always shaped by their intrinsic relation to modes of social reproduction. The difference may be seen in developments concerning automobile production in the Soviet Union. On the surface, what seems to be happening is a simple transfer of techniques in the arrangement with Fiat; but this has occurred in the context of the reinforcement of two capitalist modes. In the first place, there has been a gradual adoption of the general capitalist technology of consumption, where a dramatic increase in the available supply of privately owned consumer durables and the kinds of satisfactions derived therefrom can serve as "compensation" for the dissatisfactions experienced in other spheres of life. An expansion of private consumption can compensate for the widespread estrangement from political life that results from the unyielding sway of bureaucratic-hierarchical authority.[31] In the second place, the importation of management techniques reinforces the capitalist technology of production, that is, the maintenance of the bureaucratic-hierarchical authority in the workplace. Neither of these patterns is necessarily involved in the techniques for producing automobiles; if the cars were destined for public motor pools rather than for private ownership, the capitalist technology of consumption would not be reinforced.[32] As far as the technology of production is concerned, the Swedish innovation of replacing assembly lines with semiautonomous work stations, with its promise of gradually extending the scope of workers' self-management, is an alternative technology that could have been chosen as being more compatible with the general nature of socialist goals.

The problem here is not some incompatibility between transferred techniques and ultimate purposes but rather the exacerbation of internal social contradictions through the transfer of technologies. In this case the ideological interpretation of socialism as "collective ownership of the means of production" inhibits an understanding of the ongoing dialectical tension between capitalist and socialist strategies, that is, between the bureaucratic-hierarchical and the participatory modes of organization of social activity. In the case of the Soviet arrangement with Fiat, the existing resolution of that dialectical tension generally within Soviet society is affected not by the techniques of automobile production in themselves but by the reinforcement of capitalist strategies.

CONCLUSION

In opposition to the fashionable thesis concerning the so-called "imperatives" of technology, I have argued above that there are no imperatives embodied in techniques or in their transfer from one setting to another. There are no imperatives embodied in technologies or their transfer, because technologies do not have a fixed, unidimensional "essence" or character. Rather, they are themselves developing unstable resolutions of diverse and partly contradictory elements. Within technologies there are "mixtures" of means and ends, of techniques and goals, determined in relation to reproductive modes. The formulation of criteria for the selection of techniques and the struggle for the clarification of goals and societal interaction processes are two different but related expressions of the internal dynamics of technological change itself.

One of the outstanding contemporary social problems is the tendency to substitute abstract criteria in the selection of techniques for the clarification of goals. This is the characteristic vice of technocratic thinking. The criterion of "efficiency of allocation of resources" is a prime example in those cases in which it has served to conceal the problem of adverse spillover effects, hidden costs, and externalities.[33] Especially when it is used in an exclusively quantitative form, such as in measurements of the "productivity" of labor, it tends to exclude the consideration of intangibles or "soft variables" such as satisfaction and the need for creative self-expression. No matter how powerful this tendency might be, sooner or later the problem of goal clarification asserts itself in the striving of individuals for ways of expressing a sense of well-being, which presupposes a clear awareness of personal goals and of the necessity for resolving the interpersonal conflicts arising out of incompatible goals. Certainly provisional criteria for the selection of techniques are necessary; but they should be an adjunct to the process of goal clarification, not a substitute for it.

The danger that we may fall victim to an increasing obscurity of goals in our preoccupation with the innovation of techniques is a major theme of the twentieth century dystopian novels, particularly Yevgeny Zamyatin's We. In this story an entire society (the "United State") is mobilized for the construction of a spaceship that will carry the message of the attainment of its collective goals to other planets. The great irony in Zamyatin's novel is that this enormous technical accomplishment is to serve as the vehicle of a fraudulent message, since the activity of rational goal seeking itself has been destroyed by the social organization that was formed to create that vehicle and its message. The complete identification of individual and collective life, which is consummated by the program for universal lobotomies, renders meaningless the very concept, "happiness," that is the foundation of this society's institutionalized goals. A program of intensive social conditioning is designed to produce identical "units" ("numbers" in Zamyatin's terminology) who experience a feeling of anguish at the slightest deviation of their personal lives from the prescribed public routine. "Happiness" is simply the label given to absolute social unity; its meaning is in fact identical with absolute unity, and thus the concept of happiness has no positive content of its own, and nothing would be changed if any other arbitrary designation were substituted for the term happiness. The collective goals of the United State are incoherent and meaningless: the actual social objective is the organized reproduction of identical units for all eternity.

Zamyatin's story uses the technique of exaggeration to show the importance of a rational process of goal setting in society. Technical innovations assist the realization of the objectives incorporated in technologies, but they should never be seen as a substitute for the creation of adequate processes of social interaction for the rational clarification of goals.

NOTES

1. The best example of the first-mentioned approach is Emmanuel G. Mesthene, Technological Change: Its Impact on Man and Society (New York: New American Library, 1970), and of the second, Jacques Ellul, The Technological Society (New York: Vintage Books, 1964). For a discussion of these sources see William Leiss, "The Social Consequences of Technological Progress: Critical Comments on Recent Theories," Canadian Public Administration, 13, no. 3 (1970): 246-62, which was reprinted with minor changes under the title "The False Imperatives of Technology" in David Shugarman, ed., Thinking About Change (Toronto: University of Toronto Press, 1974), pp. 105-21.

2. This formulation differs from Ellul's notion of technique in The Technological Society (the original title of which is La Technique). Ellul's terminology is vague and misleading, as I have tried to show in Leiss, op. cit. It is basically an idiosyncratic variant of "instrumental rationality," which is discussed later in this chapter.

3. See Tom Settle, "The Rationality of Science versus the Rationality of Magic," Philosophy of the Social Sciences 1 (1971): 173-94; C. Lenhardt, "Magic and Domination," in A. Kontos, ed., Domination (Toronto: University of Toronto Press, 1975), pp. 163-84.

4. See Max Weber, The Theory of Social and Economic Organiza-tion, ed. T. Parsons (New York: Free Press of Glencoe, n. d.), p. 161.

5. See the opening essay in Marshall Sahlins, Stone Age Eco-nomics (Chicago: Aldine, 1972), for a provocative assessment of the hunter-gatherer ecology.

6. Examples of these theories are discussed in Leiss, "The Social Consequences of Technological Progress," op. cit., and in William Leiss, "The Social Function of Knowledge in the Liberal Tradition," in On Liberalism, ed. M. McGrath (New York: Marcel Dekker, 1977).

7. Karl Marx, Grundrisse (Baltimore: Penguin, 1973), pp. 409-10, 706. The implications of Marx's concept of the "general intellect" are discussed in William Leiss, "The Social Function of Knowledge," op. cit.

8. Weber, op. cit., pp. 160-61. As the translator points out in the note to page 160, Weber's term Technik connotes both "tech-nique" and "technology."

9. Ibid., p. 185. For other comments on this point see Anthony Giddens, Capitalism and Modern Social Theory: An Analysis of the Writings of Marx, Durkheim and Max Weber (Cambridge: Cam-bridge University Press, 1971), pp. 183-84, 216; P. H. Partridge et al., "The Rationality of Societies," in Rationality and the Social Services, ed. S. I. Benn and G. W. Mortimore (London: Routledge and Kegan Paul, 1976), pp. 359-83; and David Shugarman, "Ration-ality in Contemporary Political Thought," (Ph. D. diss., University of Toronto, 1976), especially p. 47.

10. Weber, op. cit., pp. 185-86.

11. Ibid., p. 162.

12. This is developed by Edmund Husserl, The Crisis of Euro-pean Sciences and Transcendental Phenomenology, trans. D. Carr (Evanston: Northwestern University Press, 1970), part 2. For a commentary see Herbert Marcuse, "On Science and Phenomenology," Boston Studies in The Philosophy of Science, vol. 2 (New York: Hu-manities Press, 1965), pp. 279-91.

13. Max Horkheimer, Eclipse of Reason (New York: Seabury Press, 1975); Max Horkheimer and T. W. Adorno, Dialectic of En-lightenment (New York: Herder & Herder, 1972); Herbert Marcuse, One-Dimensional Man (Boston: Beacon, 1964) and "Indus-trialism and Capitalism in the Work of Max Weber," in Negations (Boston: Beacon, 1968), pp. 201-26. See also William Leiss, The Domination of Nature (Boston: Beacon, 1974), chaps. 5-7.

14. Laurence Tribe, "Technology Assessment and the Fourth Discontinuity: The Limits of Instrumental Rationality," Southern California Law Review 46 (1973): 631.

15. Ibid., p. 635.

16. Ibid., p. 651.

17. For example, J. Habermas, Toward a Rational Society (Boston: Beacon, 1970), pp. 94ff.

18. Karl Polanyi, The Great Transformation (Boston: Beacon, 1957); C. B. Macpherson, The Political Theory of Possessive Individualism (New York: Oxford University Press, 1962); C. B. Macpherson, Democratic Theory (Oxford: Clarendon, 1973).

19. See Stephen Marglin, "What Do Bosses Do? The Origins and Functions of Hierarchy in Capitalist Production," Review of Radical Political Economy 6, no. 2 (1974), 33-60.

20. Kelvin Lancaster, "Change and Innovation in the Technology of Consumption," American Economic Review Annual Proceedings, May 1966, pp. 14-23; Herbert Gintis, "A Radical Analysis of Welfare Economics," Quarterly Journal of Economics 86 (1972): 572-99.

21. For a full discussion of these points see William Leiss, The Limits to Satisfaction: An Essay on the Problem of Needs and Commodities (Toronto: University of Toronto Press, 1976).

22. For the United States there are the following well-known studies: Mills, The Power Elite; G. Kolko, Wealth and Power in America; and W. Domhoff, Who Rules America? For Canada there are Porter, The Vertical Mosaic, and Clement, The Canadian Corporate Elite. I am assuming, without arguing the point here, that inherited inequalities and concentrations of economic power and wealth are reciprocally related to political domination of the majority by minority classes and elites.

23. See The Domination of Nature, part 1, for a discussion of the origins and development of this conception.

24. See, for example, Peter Mathias, "Who Unbound Prometheus? Science and Technical Change, 1600-1800," in Science and Society, 1600-1900, ed. Peter Mathias (Cambridge: Cambridge University Press, 1972).

25. A full account may be found in Lynn Thorndike, A History of Magic and Experimental Science (8 vols., New York: Columbia University Press, 1923-58), vol. 7.

26. Science 184, no. 4137 (1974): 646.

27. It should be obvious that I am referring to the existing situations of the developed, industrialized nations, including those that are designated as "socialist" as well as capitalist. For the "underdeveloped" nations, the key question is what form development should assume and what should be its specific objectives. See Denis Goulet, The Cruel Choice: A New Concept in the Theory of Development (New York: Athenaeum, 1971).

28. Lynn White, Jr., "Technology Assessment from the Stance of a Medieval Historian," American Historical Review 79 (1974): 1-13.

29. Margaret Mead, Cultural Patterns and Technical Change (New York: Mentor, 1955), pp. 178-89.

30. Lynn White, Jr., "Cultural Climates and Technological Advance in the Middle Ages," Viator 2 (1971): 171-201.

31. André Gorz, Socialism and Revolution (New York: Doubleday, 1973), p. 198.

32. The choice of the private automobile form of personal transportation may be disadvantageous on other grounds, especially the high infrastructure costs. This is a separate problem. For details of the historical development of automobile production in the Soviet Union and its relationship to technology transfer, see Chapter 4 of this book, by John P. Hardt and George D. Holliday.

33. E. J. Mishan, The Costs of Economic Growth (New York: Praeger, 1967).

3

THE SCIENTIFIC AND TECHNICAL REVOLUTION IN SOVIET THEORY

Julian M. Cooper

Since the mid-1950s the concept of the "scientific and technical revolution" has come to occupy a central place in the Soviet understanding of the nature of the present epoch. In 1961 a reference to the scientific and technical revolution (STR) was included in the new Party Programme, and since then almost every major pronouncement of the Party leadership has made reference to this process and linked it with the attainment of the Soviet society's socialist goals. At the Twenty-Fourth Congress of the CPSU in 1971, the practical realization of the STR was clearly posed as the primary task of the period ahead as follows:

> Scientific and technical progress is the main lever for
> building the material and technical basis of communism.
> . . . All the prospects are that the revolution in the
> development of the productive forces, touched off by
> science and its discoveries, will become increasingly
> significant and profound. The task we face is one of
> historical importance: to organically fuse the achieve-
> ments of the STR with the advantages of the socialist
> economic system, to unfold more broadly our own, in-
> trinsically socialist, forms of fusing science with pro-
> duction.[1]

On a wider plane, the strategic importance of the STR in the worldwide movement toward socialism has received mounting emphasis since the 1969 Conference of Communist and Workers Parties, the final document of which declared that: "The STR . . . has become one of the main sectors of the historic competition between capitalism and socialism."[2]

It is undoubtedly true that the term "STR" has become something of a cliche in recent years and in popular writings has become a synonym for scientific and technical progress in general. However, there is a rapidly growing body of serious theoretical literature that seeks to analyze the revolutionary upsurge in science and technique of the last 25 years and place it in a broader historical perspective. This theoretical discussion has received little attention in the West. The Soviet writings on the STR can also be regarded as a continuation of a long tradition of Marxist theory on the general theme of science, technique and society, a tradition that has especially strong roots in the USSR. This paper reviews Soviet thought on this theme and the attempt to develop a general theory of the present-day scientific and technical revolution.

SOME BASIC CONCEPTS

Discussion of the nature of the STR requires preliminary consideration of the definitions of some basic concepts, and this is particularly important here because the definitions accepted by Soviet scholars frequently differ from those employed in much Western work. This task of conceptual clarification has received considerable attention and has been the source of much controversy. The definition of the term tekhnika has exercised many Soviet researchers.[3] For a long time the definition provided by A. A. Zvorykin was widely accepted: "Technique is the totality of means of labor in the system of social production."[4] This definition is now generally acknowledged as too narrow. One major study of the STR published in 1967 employed the following broader definition: "By technique we understand artificially created means of activity of people."[5] The main content of technique is seen as artificially created means of labor employed in material production. The various elements of technique are termed "technical means." In present day Soviet writings, technique as such, as opposed to the social consequences of its use, is regarded as neutral with respect to social systems and class; thus such notions as "capitalist technique" or "proletarian technique" are rejected. The Soviet term tekhnologiya has a quite different meaning from technique; it generally refers to processes of production or the sciences associated with such processes.[6]

In the course of development of any given type of technical means, both evolutionary and revolutionary stages occur. Gradual improvements are introduced, and the accumulation of such improvements is regarded as characterizing the evolutionary form of development. In time the effect of such gradual changes diminishes as the technical and technological principles on which the technical means are based are exhausted. Now only the creation of new means founded

on new principles will permit the desired continued advance of performance; the technical means must pass through a revolutionary
stage of development. This revolution is in a particular branch of
technique, however—a revolution in technique. A technical revolution in the wider sense is one that encompasses the entire technical
system of society.[7]

Turning from technique to science, we find similar problems
of definition. For a long period in both Marxist and also in many non-
Marxist writings, the dominant view has been that science is a system of knowledge. Typical of this approach is the definition offered
by M. M. Karpov: "Science is a historically developing system of
verified, logically noncontradictory knowledge about the laws of nature, society, and thought."[8] This approach is now considered one-
sided by many Soviet scholars. As I. A. Maizel points out in a useful review of the problem, the traditional view only regarded science
from the point of view of ideas, thereby neglecting its social aspect.[9]
Overreaction to this position led Volkov to the conclusion that "science is not knowledge itself, but the activity of society for the production of knowledge, i.e., scientific production."[10]

Maizel himself has proposed that any definition of science
should now recognize that it is a complex social phenomenon embracing both scientific activity and scientific knowledge; that is, it
is a unity of the two aspects.[11] This position now has wide support.
It is considered that any given science, regarded as a system of
knowledge, passes through evolutionary and revolutionary stages of
development. Revolutions occur when new discoveries are made
that cannot be adequately explained within the prevailing structure
of concepts, and this contradiction can only be resolved by developing new concepts raising cognition to a higher level.[12] This is a
revolution in science. It is also held that there can be revolutionary
changes in the totality of sciences, giving rise to completely new
modes of scientific thought, and also revolutionary changes in science regarded as a social activity, that is, changes in its technical
apparatus or organizational forms.

SCIENCE, TECHNIQUE, AND SOCIETY

The roles of science and technique in the revolutionary transformation of society following the socialist revolution have been a
central theme of Marxist-Leninist theory developed in the Soviet
Union since 1917, and from the earliest writings to the recent discussion of the theory of the STR, a definite continuity of thought is
apparent. This section is devoted to a brief review of some of the
contributions, in order to provide a background to the later debate.

Lenin's views on the vital importance of scientific and technical development for the creation of the economic basis of socialist
society are well known. The concepts "revolution in science" and
"technical revolution" both appear in his writings. On many occasions he stressed the necessity of adopting all that was best of the
science and technique developed in the capitalist world, firmly rejecting the position of A. Bogdanov and others, who maintained that
science was by its very nature bourgeois or proletarian because it
represented the "organic collective experience" of the dominant
class. According to Bogdanov the victorious Russian proletariat was
faced with the task of creating its own "proletarian science"; but
Lenin, in rejecting the ideas of the Proletkult tendency, also administered a rebuff to such Bogdanovite views, which soon ceased to
have any influence in the realm of the natural sciences. [13] Lenin's
position in relation to technique is summarized by his statement that
"the sole economic basis of socialism is large-scale machine industry. He who forgets this is not a communist."[14] The main direction
of technical development in the circumstances of Russia was considered to be electrification, but for Lenin electrification was by no
means a purely technical matter; it was an essentially socioeconomic
question having profound political and cultural implications in terms
of consolidating the political position of the proletariat, strengthening its alliance with the poor and middle peasants, and transforming
all aspects of the backward Russian society. This theoretical understanding was at the heart of the Party's programme of socialist industrialization.

The concept "technical revolution" and the directions of technical development associated with the creation of the material and
technical basis of communist society were discussed by a number of
writers from an early date, and some of these pioneering works contain analyses and predictions establishing a direct continuity with
more recent contributions. The idea of a technical revolution made
possible by the existence of new production relations was quite widely propagated, notably in the works of N. I. Bukharin. He presented
a theory of the revolutionary process that involved four phases: an
ideological revolution in the revolutionary class of the old social
formation; a political revolution in which the revolutionary class
seizes power; an economic revolution in which the new dominant
class uses its political power to break up the old production relations and replace them by new socialist relations; and a technical
revolution—"a revolution not in the relations between people, but in
the relations between the human collective and external nature." The
technical revolution leads to the creation of a new technical basis of
society appropriate to the new production relations. [15] This theory

situated the technical revolution in a broad historical context, but it did so in a very schematic and mechanistic manner that understandably met with opposition from both Soviet and foreign Marxists. [16]

In the early 1920s there were a number of attempts to analyze the technical basis of the future communist society, some of which showed remarkable foresight. Notable in this respect were the contributions of A. Bogdanov and Ivan D. Ivanov. The former, in his popular textbook of political economy, outlined the prospects for socialism of atomic energy, automatic self-regulating machines, and modern communications and transport systems. This vision of the socialist future was infused with unbounded optimism for the possibilities opened up by scientific and technical progress: "The first characteristic feature of the collective system [that is, socialism] is the actual power of society over nature, developing without limit on the basis of scientifically-organised technique."[17] In Bogdanov's view, the use of machines with automatic regulators would provide the conditions necessary for raising the intellectual content of work in order to eliminate the distinction between mental and manual labor. A similar position was outlined by Ivanov in a highly original contribution in 1923. According to Ivanov, the technical basis of communist society would take the form of an integrated, centralized system of automatic machines. "Reducing physical labor to a minimum," Ivanov concluded, "the new form will push the working class upwards into the sphere of mental labor, transforming the workers into a proletarian technical intelligentsia."[18]

The themes introduced in the writings of the early 1920s remained a concern of Soviet economists, scientists, and political leaders throughout the years before World War II. Immense optimism with regard to the contribution of scientific and technical progress to socialist and communist construction was central to the theoretical understanding and practical activity of the Party leadership in its struggle for industrialization. This view was common both in the core of Party leaders around Stalin and also in the main opposition tendencies, although technical determinism was apparent in some contributions. Leon Trotsky, for example, in 1925, while chairman of the scientific and technical administration of VSNKh, declared that the transition from socialism to communism wholly depended on the technical progress of society.[19] In the following year, noting the possibilities of atomic energy, he prophesied revolutions in science and technique. "This alone [atomic energy] gives us the right to declare that scientific and technical thought is approaching a great turning point, that the revolutionary epoch in the development of human society will be accompanied by a revolutionary epoch in the sphere of the cognition of matter and the mastering of it. . . . Unbounded technical possibilities will open out before liberated mankind."[20]

One of the most prolific and perceptive writers on questions relating to science, technique, and society was Bukharin, especially during the First Five-Year Plan, when he occupied the post of chairman of the scientific and technical administration of heavy industry. The criticisms advanced in relation to his earlier work apply equally to these contributions of 1929-33; technical development tended to be seen in abstraction from the determining role of social relations, and in general a bias toward technical determinism is evident. Nevertheless, Bukharin's work of this period is of theoretical interest, insofar as the tendencies of development of science and technique under socialism and capitalism are analyzed in terms that in some respects prefigure those of later discussions.

Under capitalism, Bukharin wrote in 1931, enormous technical changes were taking place, "verging on technical revolution." These changes involved "the growing application of science to the process of production," the material expression of which was the organization of large-scale factory laboratories and research institutes. "Modern capitalist economy is pregnant with a new technical revolution," he continued, "but this technical revolution cannot develop unless it breaks through its capitalist shell."[21] The Soviet Union, on the other hand, was rushing through several phases of technical development, the old historical heritage of the technical basis of tsarist Russia; the period of "capitalist technique," typified by imported equipment; and "the period in which socialism begins to develop its own technical foundations." Bukharin was at pains to stress the summary nature of this periodization and that "it must be noted that all technique (the machine, technical method, etc.) when introduced into the system of socialist production relations by that very fact becomes socialist technique."[22]

A central theme of much of Bukharin's theoretical and practical work at this time was science—its social function, organization, and planning. Science was regarded not as a self-sufficient body of ideas but as an "activity of vast practical importance," fulfilling a range of social functions connected with the reproduction of social life.[23] Running through his work was an appreciation of the importance of the interrelationship between theory (science) and practice (material production), and the view that the character of the relationship between theory and practice differed from one social formation to another. Under capitalism, he believed, science could not attain "its fusion with practice," but socialism made possible and required a "new social synthesis of science and practice."[24] In the context of the First Five-Year Plan, Bukharin, at the Second All-Union Conference on the Planning of Research in heavy industry in 1932, called for measures to improve the links between science and production; for the "scientification" (onauchivanie) of production and the "engineerification" (ob'inzhenerivanie) of science.[25]

During the First Five-Year Plan period, interest in science and technique and its historical role reached a high level in response to practical demands. There was also interest in the state of science and technique under capitalism during the economic crisis, which for Soviet writers provided irrefutable evidence of the incompatibility of capitalist production relations with the new, developing productive forces. A significant contribution of this time was an article by B. Kuznetsov in 1930 that linked the revolution in technique with the revolution in science. The Soviet Union was, he claimed, "on the threshold of a new technical revolution" made possible by the existence of new production relations. The technical revolution associated with the development of capitalist factory production had been linked with the mechanical natural sciences, but in Kuznetsov's view the new revolution would be associated with sciences founded on dialectical materialism. Capitalist production relations imposed ever-greater constraints on the development of the productive forces and the degree to which new problems of science could be solved. For example, "thoroughgoing and full automation is incompatible with the very production relations of capitalism; it liquidates the antithesis between mental and physical labor and abolishes the objective conditions of capitalistic subordination. [26]

In the course of the Second Five-Year Plan period, theoretical work in this area increasingly suffered the deadening effects of the "cult of personality" of Stalin, but in the immediate prewar years there was some revival of discussion and a number of interesting contributions appeared. The automation of production (avtomatizatsiya) was posed as one of the basic practical tasks of the Third Five-Year Plan, and all the works of the period accept the idea that automation has a crucial role in the creation of the material and technical basis of communist society. Automation, it was generally held, would create the conditions for the elimination of the antithesis between physical and mental labor.[27] One of the writers stressing the importance of automation was Modest I. Rubinshtein, in an interesting book published in 1940. In all previous discussion, the technical revolution had been linked with the building of socialism, the first stage of communism. Socialism would make possible the full application of the technical possibilities arising under capitalism but fettered by its exploitative production relations. Rubinshtein for the first time introduced the concept of the material and technical basis of the transition from socialism to communism. Automation, he declared, was "one of the primary links of the technical revolution corresponding to the transition from socialism to communism."[28] This idea was further developed by Kuznetsov in another original work of the same year: not only would the transition to communism involve a technical revolution, but the new techniques would be

founded on the theories associated with the revolution in the natural
sciences that had begun in the 1890s.[29] Thus, while not explicitly
using the term, Kuznetsov was clearly envisaging a scientific and
technical revolution.

The war and the constraints imposed by dogmatism in the social sciences of the late Stalin years temporarily interrupted this
promising line of research, but by the mid-1950s, Soviet thinking on
science, technique, and society was beginning to revive. This process was aided by the publication in the USSR in 1956 of J. D. Bernal's
pioneering study, Science in History. This book to some extent provided a bridge between the early Soviet work of the First Five-Year
Plan period and the post-Stalin years. Furthermore, by 1955 there
was concern in the Party about the state of technical development in
the country, a concern that gave a stimulus to theoretical work and
found its expression at the July Plenum of the Party Central Committee, when N. A. Bulganin, in his main report on raising the technical
level of Soviet industry, declared that "the summit of the present
stage in the development of science and technique is the discovery of
methods of obtaining and using the energy of the atom. We stand at
the threshold of a new scientific and technical revolution, the significance of which far surpasses the industrial revolutions associated
with the appearance of steam and electricity."[30] This was apparently
the first use of the term "scientific and technical revolution" in Soviet public discussion and heralded the start of a new stage of theoretical work on the theme of science, technique, and society.

THEORY OF THE SCIENTIFIC
AND TECHNICAL REVOLUTION

Early Work

Between 1955 and 1964 the first Soviet books and articles on
the STR were published, and the work of this period, while mainly
of a descriptive nature, helped to establish the study of the STR as
a relatively independent line of research. Pioneering works were
those of V. Danilevskii[31] and G. Osipov.[32] The most significant
contribution, however, was probably that of the members of the
Academy of Sciences Institute of the History of the Natural Sciences
and Technique in Moscow (ПЕиТ). In a collective work, Istoriya
tekhniki, written with the participation of A. A. Zvorykin and S. V.
Shukhardin, the essential features of the STR were analyzed, providing a framework for future theoretical work at the institute.
Writers at this time tended to list significant directions of technical

development, notably automation and atomic energy, when characterizing the STR. The new Program of the CPSU, adopted at the Twenty-
Second Party Congress, also reflected this approach when it stated
that "humanity is entering a period of scientific and technical revolution connected with the mastering of nuclear power, the conquest of
space, the development of chemistry, the automation of production,
and other achievements of science and technique."[33] This official
acknowledgement of the existence and significance of the STR provided a stimulus to research, and in 1962 a sector of the history of
the present-day STR was established at the IIEiT. It was this sector,
headed since its foundation by S. V. Shukhardin, that first attempted
to formulate a general theory of the STR and its place in history; the
results were outlined at a conference on the history of the STR organized by the institute in 1964.

General Theory

A. A. Kuzin and Shukhardin, in their paper presented to this
conference, attempted to analyze the role of technical revolutions in
history and the significance of the new STR.[34] This analysis formed
the basis of a subsequent book, which until 1973 remained the most
comprehensive work of its kind.[35] Here we consider the IIEiT theory
of the STR as a whole, on the basis of a number of works produced
by Kuzin and Shukhardin during the last ten years, looking first at
their understanding of the nature of the previous technical revolutions preceding the STR itself.

Central to the theory of Shukhardin and his team at IIEiT is
the distinction between the technical revolution and the "production"
revolution, a distinction illustrated by the example of the Industrial
Revolution in England. For Marx it was the invention of the "working machine" that began the Industrial Revolution; but this invention,
incorporated in textile machinery and later in the modern machine
tool, did not constitute the revolution as such. This was a broader
process, connected with changes in the class structure of society,
the formation of the industrial proletariat, and the establishment of
the full domination of capitalist production relations. Shukhardin and
his colleagues prefer the term "production revolution" to "industrial
revolution," the latter being a particular case of the former. The
period between the initial technical inventions and the production
revolution can be regarded as one of preliminary preparation, during
which the technical possibilities of establishing a new system of technique are created. This preparatory period is the technical revolution, "the essence of which consists in the appearance and introduction of inventions bringing about a revolution in the means of labor,

the forms of energy, production technology, and the general material
conditions of the production process. The technical revolution is the
process of creation and introduction of the technical means that prepare the transition to a new technological mode of production. "[36]
However, and this is regarded as the crucial point, the technical
revolution will lead to a production revolution only if new production
relations exist; and their creation requires a social revolution. The
production revolution is defined as "a process in which a new mode
of production is created on the foundation of the new technical means,
characterized by a new division of labor, a new place of the producer,
and new social relations of production. "[37]

The concepts of technical and production revolutions are employed by the IIEiT researchers in their analysis of the history of
socioeconomic formations. These revolutions are identified in precapitalist formations, but this part of their work has a rather schematic character. More important is the analysis of the transition
from feudalism to capitalism, which draws heavily on Marx's notebooks of 1861-63, published for the first time in part in 1968. [38] A
key quotation, providing support for the position advanced by Shukhardin, is the following:

> Machine labor, as a revolutionizing element, is brought
> to life directly by the preponderance of need over the
> possibility of satisfying it with the former means of
> production. This preponderance of demand (over supply)
> appeared as a result of the discoveries made earlier on
> the basis of craft production and also as a result of the
> colonial system founded in the period of dominance of
> manufacture and the world market created to some ex-
> tent by this system. Together with the already accom-
> plished revolution in the productive forces, which ap-
> pears as a technological revolution (revolyutsiya tekh-
> nologicheskaya), a revolution in the production rela-
> tions also takes place. [39]

On the basis of their analysis of the Industrial Revolution and
earlier production and technical revolutions, Shukhardin and Kuzin
summarized the general regularities of these processes as follows:

> Each socioeconomic formation has a characteristic sys-
> tem of technique and technological mode of production,
> and in each formation the producer occupies a definite
> place in production. The birth of elements of new tech-
> nique takes place within the old mode of production. The
> establishment of the mode of production of the new forma-

tion passes through two stages. In the period of the first
phase it uses the old material and technical basis inherited from the previous formation, and the old system of
technique and technological mode of production still exist. (The production relations change, as does the mode
of uniting the producers with the means of production.)
As a result of the technical revolution and then the production revolution, the new material and technical basis
is created and the new mode of production is victorious.
The second phase means the full establishment of the
mode of production of the new formation. [40]

This is the theoretical framework within which the IIEiT researchers
situated the concept of the STR, and one that remains basically unchanged since 1964, as can be seen from the contribution of Shukhardin and Kuzin to an important collective work published in 1974. [41]

We now turn to the theory of the STR put forward by Shukhardin
and his team at the IIEiT. The central concern of many Soviet writers on the STR has been to define the essence of this revolution, that
is, to determine its fundamental meaning and character. The starting point of the IIEiT work is an analysis of the labor process. In
this process, workers fulfill a range of functions: technological
(changing the form, composition, or structure of the object of labor),
energetic, transportational, logical (selection, calculation, and
processing of information), and control-regulation. In the course of
technical development, fulfillment of these functions is progressively transferred from human to technical means. Thus the invention
and application of the working machine freed the human race from
the direct fulfillment of the technological function, while the use of
the mill and later the steam engine freed it from the direct fulfillment of the energetic function.

In the opinion of Shukhardin, the STR takes this process a
stage further. Now it is the logical and control functions that are
being transferred from human to technical means. While the machine of the Industrial Revolution consisted of three basic elements—
the working machine, a motor, and a transmission mechanism—the
new automatic machines have a fourth element, in the form of a control mechanism that regulates the action of the machine as a whole
and thereby frees its operators from the direct fulfillment of working
functions in the production process. Thus in their 1967 book, the
IIEiT workers concluded that "the replacement of the direct production functions of man, including his logical and control-regulation
functions, by technical means is the essence of the present-day STR,
as a result of which the technical conditions for the transition from
machine-factory production to comprehensively automated produc-

tion appear."[42] This definition of the essence of the STR has been restated by Shukhardin in a number of subsequent works, although in some recent formulations the use of self-regulating machines freeing man from the mental functions of production is described as the "kernel" of the STR rather than its essence.[43]

The definition of the STR's essence provided by the IIEiT workers makes no direct reference to science and the scientific revolution. The essence is found in the realm of human and technical means alone. Instead, the process of the transformation of science into a direct productive force of society is regarded as an important secondary aspect of the essence of the STR.[44] The following main directions of the revolution are identified: the extension of the use of electric power; the peaceful use of atomic energy; the development of radioelectronics, particularly computer and control instruments; the creation of artificial materials; and space research.

On the chronological limits of the STR, Shukhardin considers that the USSR had reached its threshold by 1941 but that the war and the subsequent reconstruction delayed its start until the early 1950s, a significant landmark being the creation of a fully automated engineering factory in 1949-50. Whereas in the Soviet Union and other socialist countries the STR is considered to be a planned, consciously guided process, in the capitalist countries it is seen as developing spontaneously, fueled by the striving for monopoly profits and the urgent demands to counter the growing economic and military strength of the socialist world. In the United States the STR is considered to have started in about 1953, the Korean War creating favorable conditions for the adoption of advanced technique. Under U.S. influence the STR quickly spread to other industrially advanced capitalist countries between 1955 and 1965.[45]

As noted above, an important component of the theory put forward by Shukhardin and his colleagues is the distinction between the technical and production revolutions, the latter growing out of the former following a successful social revolution. The production revolution marks the transition to a new technological mode of production, five of which are identified: simple craft production associated with agriculture, simple craft production separate from agriculture, manufacture, machine-factory production, and comprehensively automated production characteristic of communist society.[46] An important feature of the technological mode of production is the relationship between the worker and the technical means—relations of subordination or domination, which can be seen in both technological and social senses. A worker may be technologically subordinate to the technical means if his or her movements and actions are determined by the movements and actions of the machine itself. Conversely, the action of the machine may be subordinated to that

of the worker. These relations of subordination have a determining
social aspect, insofar as the use of technical means takes place within a system of production relations having a class character. Fundamental changes in these production relations can only be achieved by
revolutionary political action. Under capitalism, the subordination
of the worker to capital is reinforced by the technological subordination of the worker to the technical means. The new technique of comprehensively automated production provides the material basis for
ending the technological subordination of the worker, but this can
only be realized if the production relations change in such a manner
as to end the social subordination of the worker. Hence the conclusion that, while the STR can take place under both capitalism and
socialism, the subsequent production revolution can only be realized
under the latter within the context of the new nonexploitative production relations formed after the socialist revolution. [47]

In their work the IIEiT team have devoted much attention to the
role of the STR in the transition from socialism to communism. In
the first phase of communism, new relations of production are established; but the technical basis of society remains as under capitalism, that is, it is machine-factory production. Under the conditions
of socialist planning and the political leadership of the Communist
Party guided by Marxist-Leninist theory, the transition from the
technical revolution to the new production revolution is regarded not
as a sharp break but rather as a question of the progressive introduction of the achievements of the STR in a planned regime, a process that will lead to the gradual introduction of comprehensively
automated production, with its attendant social consequences. As
automated production begins to dominate over machine production,
very large increases of productivity will be possible, such that the
scarcity of an ever-wider range of products will be overcome,
creating the conditions for a transition to new distributional relations.
The new technical means will require the adoption of new forms of
production organization and will fundamentally alter the nature of
work and the division of labor, as people are gradually freed from
the necessity of fulfilling direct production functions. One of the
main social consequences will be the progressive elimination of the
distinction between mental and physical labor. Work will acquire
an ever more scientific and creative character, while at the same
time scientific and other intellectual activities will increasingly
merge with production. These processes will make possible, and
necessary, the full all-round development of all individuals in society—the great humanist goal of communism.

It must be stressed, however, that these social-economic
consequences are not seen as following automatically in the wake of
technical changes. The realization of the STR itself and of the social

changes the STR makes possible is regarded as necessarily requiring conscious, mass action within a framework of progressively enhanced socialist democracy.

During the 1960s the IIEiT theory of the STR found quite wide acceptance, but it was by no means the only view and was at times sharply criticized, notably for an alleged neglect of the social consequences of the revolution. Some writers, including Meleshchenko and Marakhov, of the institute's Leningrad division, criticized the Shukhardin team for putting too great an emphasis on automation in defining the essence of the STR and also for its cursory treatment of science and its role. For Meleshchenko, "The essence and principle novelty of the STR consists in the fact that in it the present-day scientific and technical revolutions are organically combined."[48] In the course of the decade, emphasis gradually shifted from concern with the STR in the narrow sense of a phenomenon in the realm of science, technique, and production to the STR as a broad social phenomenon. The tendency on the part of some writers to exaggerate the importance of purely scientific and technical developments prompted criticism on a number of occasions, notably in the pages of the journal Voprosy filosofii. For example, an editorial in July 1968 cautioned as follows:

> In evaluating the social consequences of the STR there
> must be no place for illusions either as to the all-power-
> fulness of technique and the new achievements of science
> or, similarly, their underestimation. . . . Scientific
> and technical progress will not automatically lead to a
> change of the system of production relations, although
> it acts—at times radically—on their elements.[49]

This view was restated with even greater force in a further editorial of December 1971, which called for a more comprehensive and concrete analysis of the social essence of the STR. Technical development, it pointed out, is not an end in itself but must answer to social needs. A tendency towards "technological" interpretations was criticized, as was a bias towards a scientistic understanding of the social consequences of the STR. This stress on the analysis of the social aspects of the STR and criticism of alleged technocratic and scientistic tendencies must be seen in the broader context of a general move at this time to intensify the ideological struggle against both bourgeois and revisionist positions in the social sciences.

"Man—Science—Technique"

One of the most important works yet to appear on the STR has been the joint Soviet-Czech book, Chelovek—nauka—tekhnika (Man—

Science—Technique), written by members of the IIEiT, of the Institute of Philosophy of the USSR Academy of Sciences, and of the Institute of Philosophy and Sociology of the Czechoslovak Academy of Sciences. Published in 1973, this book attempts to outline a comprehensive Marxist-Leninist analysis of the STR and its social consequences. The analysis moves progressively from the STR in a narrow sense, within the system of science-technique-production, to the general system, the STR and society. At each stage the dialectical interrelationships between aspects of the component systems and subsystems are explored, notably the systems of science-technique, man-technique, science-production, and man-environment. Within the science-technique system, it is concluded that the main distinguishing features of the STR are, first, the merging of the revolutionary changes in science and technique into a single process and, second, the fact that science necessarily "runs ahead" of technique as the leading factor.

The essence of the transformation of the material and technical bases of society brought about by the STR is analyzed in terms very similar to those put forward by Shukhardin. At each stage of the development of the productive forces there is a certain correlation between the production functions fulfilled by human beings alone and those fulfilled with the aid of technical means. The Industrial Revolution was associated with the transfer of the technological production function to the machine; with the STR the fulfillment of logical and control-regulation functions is similarly transferred, the "kernel" of this development being the automation and cyberneticization of production.

This change in the roles of human beings and technique has broader, social implications, however. Each major change in technique either directly or indirectly exerts an influence on the human being as the main productive force and entails new forms of production organization, new labor skills, altered conditions of work, and so on. One of the most important social consequences of the revolution in the productive forces brought about by the STR is the change in the position of the worker in the production process. With the formation of large-scale machine production under capitalism, the worker was transformed into an "appendage of the machine"; but with the development of comprehensively automated production, the worker ceases to fulfill direct production functions but instead oversees automatic processes. This does not mean that human beings are banished from production altogether, because creative, scientific work is still essential for creating new processes and managing the productive system. Up to this stage of the analysis, attention is devoted to the science-technique-production system without regard to the social system within which these processes occur; but as soon as one begins to consider changes in the place and role of human beings in production, the social relations cannot be ignored insofar as the possibilities of realizing fundamental changes involving people depend directly and indirectly on the nature of these social relations.

In Chelovek—nauka—tekhnika, the analysis of the STR in a narrow sense serves as the starting point for a detailed investigation of the STR as a social process taking place within different social systems. The authors stress the complexity of analyzing the specific social effects of this revolution because it is as yet still at a very early stage. For this reason the role of the STR in social development cannot be understood simply by looking at direct empirical facts. A deeper analysis is required, it is emphasized, taking the STR in its "pure form." It is stressed that a complex dialectical interrelationship exists between the individual and society, on the one hand, and science and technique, on the other. The development of the productive forces, including science and technique, is a precondition and basis for a whole complex of conditions determining the character of society, the mode of life, and interpersonal relationships, while at the same time scientific and technical progress and the development of the productive forces as a whole are influenced by the development of society, relations between people, and the development of the human personality. Science and technique do not directly shape society and social relations, but they do so in a multiplicity of mediated ways and, similarly, there are diverse, complex interrelations between society and the development of the productive forces. It is stressed that only such a complex, dialectical analysis is adequate. One-sided emphasis on the determining role of science and technique, on the one hand, or social relations, on the other, leads to erroneous theories founded on technical determinism or subjective interpretations of the processes of social development.

Certain significant social and economic consequences stem from the changed place of the worker in production that is brought about by the STR. These include changes in the content and productivity of labor; changes in the social structure of society, involving quantitative and qualitative changes in the structure and occupational skills of the working class and the intelligentsia; a growing requirement that the management, planning, and organization of the affairs of society be carried out on the scale of the society as a whole; the necessity of preventing and overcoming damage to the environment; the development of individuals with the ability and creativity to master the achievements of the STR and move it further forward (this entails a major restructuring of the educational system); and the ever-growing opportunities for people to develop their creative faculties, as the mental functions of the direct production process are

progressively transferred to technical means. These consequences
can only be realized in the interests of people under socialism, it is
stressed, since as capitalist relations do not permit the all-round
development of the mass of working people, the planning and management of socioeconomic processes on the scale of society, and the
full development of science and technique in the interests of society
as a whole. The perspectives of the STR under the two systems are
thus seen as being fundamentally different and opposed. Under socialism the STR facilitates the building of the material and technical
basis adequate to communist society and helps to create the conditions appropriate to securing the full all-round development of the
individual. Under capitalism the STR can only lead to an extension
and intensification of the inherent contradictions of the system,
hastening the time of its necessary revolutionary replacement by
socialism.

The analysis made by the authors of this major study concludes
with a comprehensive definition of the concept of the scientific and
technical revolution as follows:

> The STR is a fundamental transformation of science and
> technique, of their connection and social functions,
> leading to a universal revolution in the structure and
> dynamic of the productive forces of society in the sense
> of a change in the role of man in the system of productive
> force on the basis of the comprehensive technological
> application of science as a direct productive force, pene-
> trating all component parts of production and transform-
> ing the physical conditions of human life. By its essence
> the STR expresses the regularities of the epoch of the
> transition from capitalism to communism. [50]

The Debate Continues

Since the appearance of Chelovek—nauka—tekhnika, the problem of defining the essence of the STR has continued to exercise
many Soviet scholars, and it is evident that there is still a wide
range of positions on this central, extremely difficult question. Some
of the recent contributions reviewed here have offered new solutions
and, looking beyond the present-day STR, have raised the possibility
of yet another new STR as a necessary stage in the process of building a developed communist society.

An interesting alternative view of the essence of the STR has
been put forward on a number of occasions by G. Danilin, of the
recently created Institute of Scientific Information on the Social Sci-

ences of the Academy of Sciences. Danilin believes that the time has
come for the elaboration of a unified Marxist methodology for analyzing the essence of the STR and considers that attempts to draw up
general theoretical models of the entire system of relations between
the STR and society are premature so long as this task has not been
satisfactorily resolved. The existing approaches to defining the
essence of the revolution are regarded as inadequate. Danilin devotes particular attention to criticizing monofactorial approaches
that have quite wide currency. According to this method, one basic
determining factor is at the root of the revolutionary changes in the
productive forces. Two cases are cited: the view that the electronic
computer is the revolutionizing element of technique and the view
that the essence of the STR lies in automation and in the transfer of
control functions to a new "fourth link" of the machine. On the former, Danilin considers that computers can only bring about an informational revolution and not a revolution in the entire productive
forces of society. Practical conclusions are drawn, as follows:

> The artificial symbiosis of traditional technological proc-
> esses with computers does not possess the mystical ca-
> pacity to revolutionize the productive forces. . . . Over-
> estimation of the role of electronic computers in the
> development of the productive forces is equivalent to
> losing time and a diversion of the resources needed for
> the realization of the potentialities of the STR.[51]

The "fourth link" approach of Shukhardin and his IIEiT colleagues is
the main target of Danilin's criticism, however. He stresses that
automation, in the shape of automatic, self-regulating devices
linked to traditional mechanical technology, cannot give rise to any
fundamental change in the technical mode of production and therefore cannot revolutionize the productive forces of society as a whole.
The root of the problem, in Danilin's view, lies in the fact that the
"fourth link," and not the "working machine," is taken as the starting point of the analysis. In general Danilin considers that Shukhardin's approach is shortsighted because mechanical technology is
near the limits of its potentialities and automation of such technology
cannot give rise to any significant improvement in its productivity.

Outlining what he regards as the only correct approach, Danilin draws on Marx's analysis of the Industrial Revolution. The
starting point, he believes, must be the revolution in the implements
of labor. In order to bring about a revolution in the productive forces, these implements must be founded on new technological principles. In other words, there must be a qualitative change in the laws
of nature materialized in the implements of labor. Here Danilin

cites Marx's observation that the revolution in the productive forces
appears as a technological revolution. The criterion for a revolution
in the productive forces can only be, in Danilin's view, a fundamental
change in the dynamic of the productivity of social labor, and this
represents the socioeconomic expression of the revolution.

The present-day STR is analyzed on the basis of these principles. After about 200 years of development, the possibilities of
mechanical implements of labor are nearing exhaustion, and as a
result the process of transition to the application of various types of
nonmechanical technology has begun. These nonmechanical forms of
movement of matter (at molecular, atomic, and subatomic levels)
can only be used technologically if control functions are transferred
to technical means. This combination of nonmechanical technology
with the principles of automatic control will permit the achievement
of a fundamental change in the productivity of technique. When it is
applied in all spheres of material production, it will give rise to a
great increase in the productivity of social labor.[52] Despite this difference in the definition of the essence of the STR, Danilin appears
to agree basically with the IIEiT analysis of the place of this revolution in the transition from capitalism to communism.

A similar shift of emphasis is also apparent in Marakhov's
recent contributions, in which the STR is seen above all as a "technological revolution," insofar as it draws on a new level of cognition
of the laws and qualities of matter. This alone is considered insufficient for a full understanding, however, because the STR is also a
social phenomenon. The use of technique is not an end in itself but is
undertaken in order to raise the productivity of social labor and to
switch the fulfillment of productive functions from human to technical means. Like Danilin, Marakhov cites Marx's statement that the
revolution in the productive forces takes the form of a technological
revolution that brings about changes in the production relations. The
deep essence of the STR is seen to lie in the social sphere and consists of the changing functions of the technical means of labor and
the consequent changed position of the worker in production and also
in relation to the forces of nature.

Enlarging on this last point, Marakhov puts forward the view
that the STR can be understood as a revolution in the control (upravlenie) of the natural processes used in production and even as a revolution in control in a wide sense. This revolution in control is
founded on the revolution in science, which began at the end of the
nineteenth century. Here Marakhov cites Marx's observation that as
capital develops, so does the subordination of the general process of
life to the control of the "general intellect." That is, science increasingly exercises a control function. All the achievements of the STR
put human beings in a new controlling position in relation to the

means of labor and to technological processes; in this lies the social essence of the STR. Thus, Marakhov concludes that the STR has a dual essence embracing both the revolution in the scientific foundations of technique and technological processes and the changes in their social function.[53]

Perhaps the most original contribution made by Marakhov in recent works has been his prediction of yet another, new scientific and technical revolution. Why is a new STR necessary and inevitable? Marakhov writes as follows:

> The paradox of the situation consists in the fact that the present-day STR poses a dilemma for man. It has turned out to be a double-edged weapon; that is, it embraces enormous constructive forces but also powerful destructive forces. It is not only that powerful means of destruction have been created on the basis of the achievements of the STR, but also that even the peaceful development of scientific and technical progress and of the STR in particular brings with it both positive and, in corresponding social and economic conditions, negative results. The latter are linked with the accelerating process of exhaustion of stocks of some useful minerals, pollution of the environment, high rates of industrial processing of oxygen, the utilization of fresh water, etc.[54]

The STR, in Marakhov's opinion, forces the human race to look at the natural processes of the planet in a new way. A new style of philosophical thought is emerging in which humanity sees itself as the owner of the planet as a whole and thinks on a global scale. Here the influence of the social system makes itself acutely felt, Marakhov believes, insofar as optimal solutions to the problem of the interrelationship of society and nature cannot be attained if capitalist relations are dominant. An optimal relationship between society and nature requires technical means of a definite kind, the general character of which can even now be determined, and the acute need for which will promote research into practical solutions. The new technique and technological processes must be such as to permit society and nature to interact harmoniously. Self-renewal of resources must be the guiding principle in society's controlling and regulating activity in the sphere of its interaction with nature. This task can only be solved after further scientific and technical progress, amounting to a new STR. This new revolution will be connected with the use of physical and biological laws of nature, giving rise to a machineless technique and the maintenance of a "closed circuit" between society and nature. The present-day STR, Marakhov adds, can be seen as a transitional phenomenon creating the conditions for the new STR, although for a long time the two revolutions may proceed simultaneously. The new STR will create the new material and technical basis appropriate to "developed communist society."

In the last two years the possibility of another STR has been raised by other writers, and this new development in the theory of the STR has been associated with a tendency to provide a more cautious assessment of the uniqueness and significance of the current STR. G. S. Gudozhnik, in an original contribution to the debate, also supports the idea of a new STR and believes that the qualitative leap associated with it will, in the general scale of history, be a more fundamental change than the present-day revolution. He sees the essence of the revolution in the productive forces in two aspects of labor: its historic form (slave labor, hired or wage labor, and free labor) and its stage of development according to functions fulfilled, three of which are identified—mediation, regulation, and control. According to Gudozhnik, the Industrial Revolution and the STR belong to the same phase which is characterized by the dominance of the regulating function of labor. The STR, however, is a higher stage of development, the full potential of which can be realized only after the transition from wage labor to free labor under socialism. The development of the control function of labor will, he believes, represent the essence of the new STR, which can be realized only in the communist formation. [55]

The present-day STR has also been placed in a broader perspective by Smirnov, who has attempted to show by an historical analysis that the organic fusion of revolutions in science and technique is not a phenomenon specific to the present but a regular feature of all technical revolutions. Smirnov's analysis leads to the conclusion that the STR will lead to a further stage of revolutionary development of science associated with a new biological-cybernetic style of scientific thought. While he does not explicitly develop the idea, this new scientific revolution will be followed by a new technical revolution. Smirnov outlines a regular pattern of revolutions in science and technique—a revolution in the technological mode of production, giving rise to a general technical revolution, and both of these revolutions merging with an "extensive-practical" revolution in the sciences. At the final stage of the revolution in the technological mode of production, the development of science becomes increasingly separated from the solving of practical tasks and eventually a "theoretical-intensive" revolution in the sciences takes place, as a new scientific revolution giving birth to a new style of scientific thought. In this stage science runs ahead of practice, and its achievements can only later be applied on the basis of a new revolution in

the technological mode of production. Smirnov concludes that the
merging of the revolutions in science and technique into a single
flow "is by no means a 'privilege' of the present stage of history. "[56]

The tendency to downgrade the present-day STR has not been
the only shift of emphasis apparent in the recent literature. Another
development, already noted in the discussion of the contributions of
Danilin and Marakhov, has been the new emphasis on the importance
of changes in production technology and the scientific laws associated
with it: the "scientific and technical revolution" is increasingly being
seen as a "scientific and technological revolution. " This development
is found in its most explicit form in an article by V. N. Shevchenko,
a philosopher of the Moscow higher technical school. Following an
analysis that seeks to elucidate the use of the term "technology" in
both Soviet and Western literature of recent years, he concludes
that "scientific and technological revolution" is a more precise
formulation than that usually employed. Whereas in the conventional
Soviet usage "technology" refers to production processes and the
sciences associated with them, Shevchenko adopts a broader definition according to which technology is the application of scientific
knowledge for the achievement of practical aims. The main feature
of the STR, he believes, is the "scientification" (onauchivanie) of all
aspects of social life, including the management of all natural, production and social processes. [57]

This brief review of recent contributions to the ongoing discussion on the essence and role of the STR should be sufficient to indicate that one cannot yet speak of a single, generally accepted Soviet
theory of the scientific and technical revolution and its social consequences. However, on a number of basic questions there does appear
to be broad agreement. All writers accept the reality of the present-
day revolutionary transformation of science and technique and the
fact that it is an integral component of the general revolutionary
transition from capitalism to communism. Furthermore, all agree
that science is to an ever-greater extent being transformed into a
direct productive force and that the STR gives rise to profound social consequences, above all connected with the changing place of the
worker in the production process. Finally, all contributors accept
that the outcome of the STR depends on the nature of the social relations of the society in which it is taking place. Under socialism the
planned realization of the STR is a vital lever in the construction of
the new material and technical basis of communist society; but under
capitalism the spontaneous development of the STR can only lead to
an intensification of inherent, antagonistic contradictions that can
only be resolved by the revolutionary overthrow of capitalist production relations.

Science as a Direct Productive Force

One vital strand of theory has so far been neglected, and that
is the process of the transformation of science into a direct productive force. This question has provoked considerable controversy in
Soviet writings, but there is quite widespread agreement that this
process is an important aspect of the STR. This section is devoted to
a brief review of the background of the recent discussion and indicates the main positions put forward.

The transformation of science into a direct productive force
was discussed by Marx, notably in his notebooks containing early
drafts of Capital. The relevant sections of these works were not
published in the Soviet Union until 1939 and 1958, and as they are not
well known in English, two key quotations are provided here. The
first statement by Marx on this question appeared in the 1857-58
notebooks, the Grundrisse, as follows:

> The development of basic capital is an indicator of the
> degree to which general social knowledge has been
> transformed into a direct productive force and hence
> is an indicator of the degree to which the conditions
> of human life itself have been subordinated to the con-
> trol of the general intellect and been transformed in
> accordance with it. [58]

Marx is here referring to developed capitalism, ripe for the
transition to socialism. The notebooks of 1861-63 return to this
question. After referring to the harnessing of natural forces in production, which takes place only with the widespread use of machines,
Marx continues as follows:

> The application of natural agents . . . coincides with
> the development of science as an independent (samos-
> toyatel'nyi) factor of the production process. If the pro-
> duction process becomes a sphere of the application of
> science, then, conversely, science becomes a factor
> (or, so to speak, a function) of the production process.
> Each discovery becomes the basis for a new invention
> or a new improvement of production methods. The
> capitalist mode of production is the first to put the
> natural sciences at the service of the direct production
> process and, conversely, the development of produc-
> tion gives the means for the theoretical conquest of na-
> ture. Science receives acknowledgment as being a
> means of production of wealth and a means of enrich-

ment. In this mode of production, for the first time
practical problems are posed that can only be solved
scientifically. . . . Capital does not create science,
but it exploits it, appropriating it for the needs of the
production process. Thereby there takes place simultaneously the separation of science, as science applied
to production, from direct labor, whereas in previous
stages of production the limited volume of knowledge
and experience was directly connected with labor itself and did not develop as an independent force separated from it. [59]

These two quotations provide the starting point for many Soviet analyses of the process of the transformation of science into a direct productive force.

The acknowledgement that science can be considered a component of the productive forces of society has had a mixed history in
Soviet theoretical work. In the 1920s a number of writers explicitly
referred to science as a productive force. [60] Thus, V. Adoratskii,
in a book published in 1923, wrote, "Scientific theoretical thought,
insofar as it plays a role in the process of material production,
enters into the productive forces as an indispensable member." [61]
A similar position was put forward by the economist Efimov in
1927, [62] and in 1929 Bukharin wrote that "science is an immense
additional productive force of society." [63]

From about the mid-1930s, notably after the publication of
Stalin's essay on dialectical and historical materialism, which presented a very narrow and oversimplified account of the content of the
productive forces, it was no longer possible to consider science in
this way. It was not until the early 1950s that it again became possible to raise the question of the role of science as a productive force
of society. Strumilin argued for a revision of the prevailing view in
1951 and again at greater length in 1954. [64] At first this position met
with opposition, but this was short-lived. The new Party Program
adopted by the 22nd Congress included a reference to the process of
science being transformed into a direct productive force, and since
then efforts have been directed towards analyzing the nature of this
process and its role in the STR.

It is difficult to briefly summarize the Soviet discussion on the
problem of the transformation of science into a direct productive
force because of the great diversity of views put forward and the
absence of any single, widely accepted position. In 1967 IIEiT organized a symposium on the problem with a view to obtaining greater
unanimity, but as Shukhardin later admitted, the meeting simply revealed the existence of completely opposed viewpoints. [65] The main

disputed issues are (1) the question of how science can be transformed into a productive force; (2) the chronological limits of this
process; and (3) the relationship of the process to the STR. On the
first point, two polar positions can be identified. According to one
view, science can become a productive force not as an independent
element but as knowledge materialized in the material productive
forces. That is, science can become a productive force only through
technique, technology, or people engaged in production. According to
the second view, science should be regarded as a direct productive
force on its own account without the mediation of technique, which is
to say that it acts as a productive force as the direct ideal force of
knowledge. While in a number of early works a variant of the first
position, according to which science becomes a direct productive
force through its embodiment in technique, was often put forward,
but more recently greater attention has been devoted to the human
being as the bearer of the spiritual potential of production and as the
main channel by which science becomes a direct productive force. [66]

One of the first general theories of this process was advanced
by Kuzin and Shukhardin on a number of occasions in the 1960s.
According to their view, science only becomes a fully independent
productive force when the worker is banished from the direct production process—when technical means, embodying the achievements of
science, take over not only the physical productive functions, but
also the mental (logical and control) functions. At that point science
is transformed into a fully independent element of the productive
forces, fully separated from live labor. [67] This position has been
sharply criticized by a number of writers. Maizel', for example,
has termed it "technicist," because the main channel for the inclusion of science in the productive forces is technical rather than human. His view is as follows:

> Science functions as a direct productive force only in
> people, practically using means of labor, and not in
> production techniques isolated from living labor. Just
> as the productive forces do not reduce to technique, so
> the problem of the transformation of science into a
> direct productive force is not exhausted by the interre-
> lationship between science and technique. It is a much
> broader and more complex problem, a problem of the
> development of man as an element of the productive
> forces. [68]

Another critic of the IIEiT position has been V. G. Marakhov.
He puts great stress on the fact that science is a spiritual productive
force and rejects the view that the content of the process of the trans-

formation of science into a direct productive force consists in the embodiment of the findings of science in the material productive forces. The reality of such a process is not denied, but it is regarded as being an indicator of the degree to which science has become a direct productive force, an indicator of the degree of "scientification" of production. In Marakhov's view, science is a collective social product that, unlike other productive forces, does not lose its power when applied in production but may, on the contrary, gain in power through verification and modification in practice. The transformation of science into a direct productive force means that, from being the servant of production, science becomes its leading force as its theoretical basis. He further disagrees with the IIEiT view that science is being transformed into an independent element of the productive forces, on the grounds that one cannot separate science completely from the human being as the bearer of scientific knowledge; its independence is relative, not absolute.[69]

The collective Soviet-Czech work Chelovek—nauka—tekhnika puts forward a theory that combines elements of a number of approaches. Science is seen as serving as a productive force in two ways. First, it may take the form of an ideal productive force in a direct form, with the human being as its bearer realizing his or her spiritual potential in production and fulfilling ideal information functions (logical, controlling, regulating). Second, science may act as a productive force in its transformed, embodied form, with technique or technology as its bearer.[70] This position is also adopted by L. I. Uvarova in a more recent book. Uvarova, the author of an original work on the role of science in the development of technical means,[71] considers that science functions in production both as materialized knowledge embodied in technical objects and as a spiritual productive force—an obligatory attribute of people engaged in the fulfillment of labor operations.[72] This compromise position is probably the one enjoying most support at the present time.

It is generally accepted that the process of the transformation of science into a direct productive force began with the establishment of capitalist large-scale machine production and that with the onset of the STR the process has entered a new stage, as science becomes an ever more indispensable factor in the development of production and "runs ahead" of the development of technique. It is also generally accepted that this process is an integral component of the present-day STR and one of its most important features. This view, recently restated vigorously by N. V. Markov,[73] is not, however, universally upheld. Danilin, for example, has attacked the view that the process of transformation of science into a direct productive force is an aspect of the essence of the STR.[74] Soviet theoretical work on this

theme has progressed far since the early 1950s, but it is clear that
there are still many unresolved questions requiring further research.

CONCLUSION

The theory of the STR as developed in the Soviet Union represents a serious attempt to understand the role of science and technique in the rapidly changing situation of the modern world. This
theoretical work has also made a contribution to Marxist-Leninist
theory on such questions as the nature of the productive forces and
their interaction with the production relations of society and the
transition from one social formation to another. Comparing the
literature of the Stalin years with that of more recent origin, one is
struck by the richness of the best of the latter, which is characterized by a subtlety of analysis unknown in the earlier period. Examination of the relevant literature of the 1920s and early 1930s reveals
very clearly the harm done to Marxist theory in the Soviet Union
during the two decades beginning in the mid-1930s. Many of the
ideas and insights of these early works have resurfaced in the debate on the STR, and early confident predictions have been strikingly
confirmed by practice.

There has undoubtedly been a tendency in Soviet writings on
the STR to exaggerate the determining role of science and technique
in the development of society. This tendency was present in some of
the prewar contributions, and at that time it was given some impetus by the role granted to rapid technical development in the industrialization process, a role aptly summarized by Stalin's well-known
injunction that "technique decides everything." In the debate on the
STR, one-sided stress on the technical revolution in a narrow sense
and exaggerated accounts of the role of automation in particular (or,
in the earliest works, nuclear power) clearly reflect broader technocratic tendencies in society, and this is occasionally admitted by
Soviet writers. Kudrove writes as follows:

> Up to now in the circle of engineers and factory econ-
> omists, it has been possible to meet a simplified . . .
> representation of the STR. Some of them think that it
> will unfold all by itself without special effort on their
> part and that the STR will itself see to everything in
> the very best way. One cannot but see here its fetish-
> isation, a false representation of it as a panacea which
> will automatically solve all problems. [75]

This one-sided emphasis on science and technique must in part stem
from the real problems facing the Soviet economy in accelerating

the rate of technical progress: the STR debate has clearly played a role in heightening awareness of the need to intensify efforts in this direction. Technocratic conceptions have been criticized frequently in the literature of the last four to five years, and now much greater emphasis tends to be placed on the role of the human being as the active agent of social progress.

The review of the Soviet discussion on the STR also reveals that there are still many disputed questions. As indicated, a number of basic elements of the theory are generally accepted, but a range of key issues remains unresolved, notably the central question of the definition of the essence of the STR. There has been a tendency, notably in the work of the 1960s, to build up elaborate theories on very shaky foundations. This has also been admitted in some more recent works. G. I. Karkhin, for example, writing in 1970, considered that the shortcomings of a body of recent research stemmed

> to a great extent from weaknesses of a purely methodological character, and especially when attempts are made to sketch a map of the very latest aspects of social and economic life with the aid of a template, devised according to a deductive scheme. Frequently repeated definitions of such categories as "science and technique" and "automation," formally logical arguments unsupported by facts, and a striving for "scientific" theorizing reduces the value of work of this kind. [76]

This tendency to base arguments on "repeated definitions" has been less in evidence in the more recent work, which has also been marked by a move away from monocausal explanations and the adoption of more subtle analyses, which proceed from a recognition that the phenomena concerned have determinations of a complex, systemic character.

It is relevant here to note briefly the Soviet critiques of bourgeois and revisionist interpretations of the STR. Two main strands of bourgeois thought are identified. [77] The first, an optimistic, scientistic direction, is seen as that which regards scientific and technical progress as a means of overcoming the contradictions of capitalism and also as a force promoting the "convergence" of the two social systems. The second, a pessimistic tendency, is represented by those who doubt the ability of capitalism to adapt to the STR and who are negatively disposed toward modern science and technique. Abstract, humanist alternatives are posed instead, frequently involving demands for changes in individual moral values in isolation from the reality of the objective social situation. In the Soviet view, these apparently opposed positions are in fact intimate-

ly related because they are both founded on a common methodology
of technical determinism. Technique is seen as the sole motive
force of present-day social development, to which both social and
ideological relations passively adapt. The difference between the
two tendencies is simply that the former assesses the influence of
science and technology positively and the latter negatively.

Within a Marxist problematic, Soviet theorists also reject
leftist interpretations which pose the possibility of realizing fundamental socialist social and political measures without regard to the
stage of development of the material and technical basis of society.
Upholders of this viewpoint, which is often ascribed to Maoism, are
inclined to deny any necessary connection between the STR and the
transition from capitalism to communism. Revisionism of the right
is seen as taking the opposite view. The STR's role in social development is exaggerated, and social, political and ideological factors
are depreciated. Thus, according to the Soviet view, conscious,
mass political action is essential for the attainment of socialist
goals, but this action must at each stage be related to the material
possibilities of society.

Turning to the central theme of the Bellagio Conference, it
will be apparent from the above review that Soviet theorists see no
necessary incompatibility between the use of technique developed
under capitalism and the struggle to create a socialist society. That
new technical means frequently involve organizational and other social changes is not denied; what is denied is that the content and social meaning of these changes are uniquely determined by the fact
that the innovations derive from a different social system. In fact,
far from being a force subverting the attainment of socialist goals,
the importation and use of advanced technical means is regarded as
a mechanism for accelerating the transition to communism, irrespec-
tive of the capitalist nature of the country of origin. It could be argued, moreover, that this position will have even greater validity as
the STR proceeds, insofar as the new technical means imported will
increasingly be those appropriate to the comprehensively automated
mode of production of the developing communist society—means that
capitalism itself will find growing difficulty in employing effectively.
Thus an "incompatibility" thesis would, from this perspective, have
had more relevance to the machine-technique epoch of the prewar
years. Soviet theorists similarly reject the neo-Weberian idea of an
all-pervasive "technological rationality" and hence also the view
that this rationality can undermine efforts to achieve and maintain
socialist goals and values. [78] To suggest that elements of the productive forces, in this case science and technique, can, on their own
and in isolation from the production relations and out of the context
of the social totality, have unidirectional social, political, or ideo-

logical effects is, according to the Soviet view, to fall into an essentially technical-determinist mode of thought. Such an approach negates the complex, mediated dialectical connections and relations between productive forces and production relations, and between the basis and superstructure of society. As Lenin constantly stressed, in the last resort the fundamental question for Marxist-Leninists is always, Whose interests are served? Thus in each particular case the social significance of the present-day upsurge of scientific and technical development in both capitalist and socialist countries is crucially dependent upon the nature of the social system within which it is taking place and on the interests of its dominant class.

A characteristic feature of all Soviet literature on science, technique, and society since the Revolution has been the profound optimism expressed about the positive role of science and technique in the development of society and for the liberation of mankind. This confidence, tempered in some recent works by an acknowledgment that negative consequences can arise, is in marked contrast to the widespread pessimism with regard to the social effects of science and technique that has been expressed in the West with mounting emphasis in the last five to ten years. The STR, it is now conceded, may be a "double-edged weapon," but the solution to the problems created is held to lie not in curbing its growth but in strengthening social control over it and pushing science and technique further forward to provide new technological solutions to the negative and harmful social consequences now being manifested. These problems, it is stressed in many recent Soviet contributions, cannot be solved without harnessing science (both natural and social) in order to enhance human control over all aspects of human life on earth. This conclusion of the Soviet theorists of the STR accords well with the vision of the great German Marxist, August Bebel, expressed in 1879: "Socialism is science applied in all fields of human activity."[79]

NOTES

1. Materialy XXIV s''ezda KPSS (Moscow: Politizdat, 1971), p. 57. Emphasis in original.

2. Mezhdunarodnoe soveshchanie kommunisticheskikh i rabochikh partii. Dokumenty i materialy (Moscow: Politizdat, 1969), p. 303.

3. Tekhnika is translated throughout as "technique" in order to distinguish the term from tekhnologiya, translated as "technology."

4. A. A. Zvorykin, Voprosy filosofii, no. 6 (1953), p. 34.

5. Sovremennaya nauchno-tekhnicheskaya revolyutsiya—istoricheskoe issledovanie (2nd ed.; Moscow: Nauka, 1970), p. 13.

6. S. V. Shukhardin, Osnovy istorii tekhniki (Moscow: AN SSSR, 1961), pp. 80-82.

7. Sovremennaya nauchno-teckhnicheskaya revolyutsiya, op. cit., pp. 17-21.

8. M. M. Karpov, Osnovnye zakonomernosti razvitiya estestvoznaniya (Rostov: RGU, 1963), p. 15.

9. I. A. Maizel', Nauka, avtomatizatsiya, obshchestvo (Moscow: Nauka, 1972).

10. G. N. Volkov, Sotsiologiya nauki (Moscow: Politizdat, 1968), p. 121.

11. I. A. Maizel', op. cit., p. 45.

12. Sovremennaya nauchno-tekhnicheskaya revolyutsiya, op. cit., pp. 90-93.

13. See P. A. Rachkov, Nauka i obshchestvennyi progress (Moscow: MGU, 1963), pp. 192-97.

14. V. I. Lenin, Polnoe sobranie sochinenii, vol. 44 (5th ed.; Moscow: Politizdat, 1964), p. 50.

15. See N. I. Bukharin, Historical Materialism (Ann Arbor: University of Michigan Press, 1969), pp. 255-62; N. I. Bukharin, Ekonomika perekhodnogo perioda (Moscow: Gosudarstvennoe izdatel' stvo, 1920), pp. 100-101.

16. One of the best-known critiques was that of Georg Lukács written in 1925: Georg Lukács, Political Writings, 1919-1929 (London: New Left, 1972), pp. 135-42. Originally published as a book review in Archiv für die Geschichte des Socialismus and der Arbeiterbewegung 11 (1925), this essay also appeared as "Technology and Human Relations" in Georg Lukács, Marxism and Human Liberation (New York: Delta, 1973), pp. 49-60.

17. A. Bogdanoff, A Short Course of Economic Science (London: Communist Party of Great Britain, 1923), pp. 378-80. Emphasis in original.

18. Ivan D. Ivanov, Vestnik sotsialisticheskoi akademii, Book 4 (1923), p. 181.

19. Leon Trotsky, Marxism and Science (Sri Lanka: Colombo, 1973), p. 29.

20. Ibid., pp. 40-41.

21. N. I. Bukharin, Socialist Reconstruction and the Struggle for Technique (Moscow: Cooperative Publishing Society of Foreign Workers in the USSR, 1932), p. 10. Emphasis in original. This is an English translation of a speech of August 1931.

22. Ibid., p. 12.

23. N. I. Bukharin, Science at the Crossroads (London: Kniga, 1933), p. 20.

24. Ibid., pp. 27-31.

25. Sotsialisticheskaya rekonstruktsiya i nauka, no. 1 (1933), p. 27.

26. B. Kuznetsov, "Dialektika, estestvennye nauki i tekhnicheskaya rekonstruktsiya," Planovoe khozyaistvo, nos. 10-11 (1930), p. 315.

27. See, for example, S. Batishchev, "Trud v Kommunisticheskom obshchestve," Pod znamenem Marksizma, no. 3 (1939), p. 78.

28. Modest I. Rubinshtein, O material'no-tekhnicheskoi baze perekhod ot sotsializma k kommunizmu (Moscow: Politizdat, 1940), p. 51.

29. B. Kuznetsov, Kommunizm i tekhnika budushchego (Moscow: AN SSSR, 1940), p. 15.

30. N. A. Bulganin, report to the July 1955 plenum of the Communist Party Central Committee, Pravda, July 17, 1955, p. 2.

31. V. Danilevskii, "Na poroge novoi nauchno-tekhnicheskoi revolyutsii," Neva, no. 4 (1956).

32. G. Osipov, Tekhnika i obshchestvennyi progress (Moscow: AN SSSR, 1959).

33. Programma kommunisticheskoi partii sovetskogo soyuza (Moscow: Pravda, 1961), p. 27.

34. Voprosy istorii estestvoznaniya i tekhniki, no. 19 (1965).

35. Sovremennaya nauchno-tekhnicheskaya revolyutsiya, op. cit.

36. Ibid., pp. 33-34.

37. Ibid., p. 34

38. See Voprosy istorii estestvoznaniya i tekhniki, no. 25 (1968). These notebooks have since been published in full: Karl Marx and Friedrich Engels, Sochineniya, vol. 47 (Moscow: Politizdat, 1973).

39. Ibid., p. 461.

40. Voprosy istorii estestvoznaniya i tekhniki, no. 19 (1965), p. 5.

41. Partiya i sovremennaya nauchno-tekhnicheskaya revolyutsiya v SSSR (Moscow: Politizdat, 1974), pp. 29-34.

42. Sovremennaya nauchno-tekhnicheskaya revolyutsiya, p. 124.

43. Filosofskie nauki, no. 5 (1973), p. 93.

44. Ibid.

45. Sovremennaya nauchno-tekhnicheskaya revolyutsiya, pp. 225-27.

46. Partiya i sovremennaya nauchno-tekhnicheskaya revolyutsiya v SSSR, op. cit., p. 32.

47. Ibid., pp. 33-34.

48. Voprosy filosofii, no. 7 (1968), p. 18.

49. Ibid., p. 25.

50. Chelovek—nauka—tekhnika (Moscow: Politizdat, 1973), p. 352.

51. Mezhdunarodnyi simpozium uchenykh i spetsialistov chlenov SEV i SFRYu, "Nauchno-tekhnicheskaya revolyutsiya i sotsial'nyi progress" (Moscow, 1974), sect. 1, p. 14.

52. Filosofskie nauki, no. 2 (1974), p. 107.

53. See Filosofskie nauki, no. 5 (1973), pp. 87-89; and Voprosy filosofii, no. 8 (1974), pp. 92-94.

54. Filosofskie nauki, no. 5 (1973), p. 90.

55. Filosofskie nauki, no. 2 (1974), pp. 96-101.

56. Voprosy istorii, no. 1 (1975), p. 20. See also Smirnov, Voprosy filosofii, no. 3 (1975), pp. 75-84.

57. Filosofskie nauki, no. 3 (1975), pp. 97-107.

58. Karl Marx and Friedrich Engels, Sochineniya, vol. 46, part 2 (Moscow: Politizdat, 1969), p. 215. Emphasis in original.

59. Ibid., vol. 47 (1973), pp. 553-54. Emphasis in original.

60. This early acknowledgment is rarely mentioned by Soviet writers today. An exception is B. A. Chagrin, Ocherk istorii sotsiologicheskoi mysli v SSSR, 1917-1969 (Leningrad: Nauka, 1971), pp. 87-88, from which the Adoratskii quotation is taken.

61. V. Adoratskii, Nauchnyi kommunizm Karla Marksa, part 1 (Moscow: Krasnaya Nov', 1923), p. 98.

62. Vestnik kommunisticheskoi akademii, no. 22 (1927), pp. 159-60.

63. N. I. Bukharin, Pravda, January 20, 1929.

64. Izvestiya Akademii Nauk SSSR, otdelnie ekonomiki i prava, no. 4 (1951), pp. 286-93; and Voprosy filosofii, no. 3 (1954).

65. See Protsess prevrashcheniya nauki v neposredstvennuyu proizvoditel'nuyu silu (Moscow: Nauka, 1971).

66. Filosofskie nauki, no. 6 (1974), p. 127.

67. Sovremennaya nauchno-tekhnicheskaya revolyutsiya, pp. 161-67.

68. Maizel', op. cit., p. 180.

69. V. G. Marakhov, Struktura i razvitie proizvoditel'nykh sil sotsialisticheskogo obshchestva (Moscow: Mysl', 1970), pp. 88-116.

70. Chelovek—nauka—tekhnika, op. cit., pp. 72-78.

71. L. I. Uvarova, Nauchnyi progress i razrabotka tekhnicheskikh sredstv (Moscow: Nauka, 1973).

72. Partiya i sovremennaya nauchno-tekhnicheskaya revolyutsiya v SSSR, op. cit., pp. 97-101.

73. Filosofskie nauki, no. 3 (1975), pp. 90-97.

74. Danilin, Filosofskie nauki, no. 2 (1974), p. 102.

75. Sotsialisticheskaya industriya, March 4, 1973.

76. G. I. Karkhin, Svyazi nastoyashchego i budushchego v ekonomike (Moscow: Ekonomike, 1970), p. 51.

77. See for example, Dvorkin in <u>Mirovaya ekonomika i mezh-dunarodnaya otnosheniya</u>, no. 2 (1967); and Frolov in <u>Voprosy filos-ofii</u>, no. 3 (1973).

78. See for example, <u>Sotsial'naya filosofiya frakfurtskoi shkoly—kriticheskie ocherki</u> (Moscow and Prague: Mysl' and Svoboda, 1975), especially pp. 143-55 and 200-08.

79. August Bebel, <u>Society of the Future</u> (Moscow: Progress, 1971), p. 150.

TECHNOLOGY TRANSFER AND TECHNICAL INNOVATION IN SOCIALIST COUNTRIES

4

TECHNOLOGY TRANSFER AND CHANGE IN THE SOVIET ECONOMIC SYSTEM
John P. Hardt
George D. Holliday

AN OVERVIEW

In the 1970s, importation of advanced technology from Western industrial nations is perceived by the Soviet leaders as an important contributing factor to attainment of their high-priority economic goals. In a wide variety of economic sectors, such as production of automobiles and chemicals, energy development, metal processing, shipping, and animal husbandry. Western machinery and industrial processes have made a significant impact on Soviet production. Official Soviet pronouncements indicate a continuing and expanding commitment to use of Western technology in these and other sectors.

The traditional Soviet arrangements for importing Western technology are being challenged, and in many cases there is evidence of evolution toward a "modified systems approach" to technology transfer. The new approach is characterized by (1) a long-term or continuous connection; (2) complex or project-oriented industrial cooperation; (3) systems-related construction, production, management, and distribution; (4) Western involvement in training and in the decision-making process both in the Soviet Union and abroad. The modified systems approach contrasts with the traditional approach employed by the Soviets in the Stalinist period and by the tsarist regimes in pre-Revolutionary Russia. The traditional approach relied on short-term arrangements designed to rapidly

Special acknowledgements to a number of readers are in order: Joseph Berliner; Frederic J. Fleron, Jr.; Robert Fraser, Philip Hanson, Paul Marer, Carl McMillan, and Henry Nau. The final responsibility of the contents is that of the authors.

achieve specific domestic production goals with minimal personal
contacts with Western managers, engineers, and technicians. The
old policy, which aimed at Soviet economic and technological independence from the West, appears to be giving way to a new policy
that accepts a greater degree of technological interdependence.

To maximize the benefits of Western technology imports, the
Soviet leadership may have to accept a degree of change in the Soviet
economic control system. In order to gain Western levels of efficiency, they may have to go beyond simple imports of machinery and
equipment and accept Western management methods and foreign involvement in the operation of the Soviet economy. Such a change
would tend to subvert the traditional Soviet control and information
system. Moreover, the efficient absorption of technology may require
a concentration of high-quality Soviet goods, personnel, and other
research and development resources in Western-assisted projects.
In addition, substantial Soviet investment in complementary industries and infrastructure may be necessary to bring about the desired
results.

This chapter describes the changing Soviet need for Western
technology and provides a more detailed explanation of what we have
called the modified systems approach to technology transfer. A case
study of Western technology transfer to the Soviet automotive industry in two periods of Soviet economic development—the First Five-
Year Plan (1928-32) and the current period (mid-1960s to present)—
highlights some of the changes that have occurred in the Soviet orientation to Western technology. The case study also provides a basis
for discussing possible changes in Soviet domestic economic policies
and institutions that might follow from prolonged interaction between
the Soviet and Western industrial economies. The central point of
this study is not that Soviet absorption of Western technology inevitably leads to changes in the Soviet economic system, but rather it
suggests the rationale for such change and describes a new Soviet
flexibility, evidenced in part by evolutionary changes in Soviet institutions and in part by active Soviet consideration and discussion of
alternatives to traditional methods.

THE CHANGING SOVIET NEED FOR WESTERN TECHNOLOGY

The Traditional and Modified Systems Approach
to Technology Transfer

Sometime between the December 1969 Party Plenum and the
Twenty-Fourth Party Congress in March-April 1971, when the Ninth
Five-Year Plan was unveiled, the Soviet leadership apparently had

made the decision that the lagging economic performance required a
more explicit modification or abandonment of the Stalinist principle of
technological and economic independence and a turn toward a policy
of selective interdependence with the industrially developed nations
of the West, including the United States.[1] In retrospect it appears
that the decision was based more on a Brezhnev-led consensus than
on a formal and explicit action by the General Secretary, although
public statements indicated a willingness to shift from independence
to interdependence.[2] This coincided with the broader Soviet discussions on a scientific and technological revolution.[3] While the general
need to draw on Western expertise, products, and processes had
been recognized by the Soviet leadership during Nikita Khrushchev's
regime, technology imports had been affected basically within the
traditional Stalinist economic framework. It was left to Khrushchev's
successors, Leonid Brezhnev and Alexei Kosygin, to shift the Soviet
economy toward a new degree of technological interdependence with
the West.[4]

Western economists such as Abram Bergson and Stanley Cohn
have noted the long-term problems of Soviet growth retardation and
the need to improve factor productivity, especially to lower capita-
output ratios.[5] A selective inflow of Western capital goods could add
a critical margin of effectiveness to Soviet investment. It appears
that a similar assessment by the Soviet leadership provided a rationale for a new approach to economic and technological interaction with
the West. The use of Western technology is especially attractive to
Soviet economic planners when long-term credits defer repayment
of foreign investment to future time periods and when payback agreements tie repayments to the incremental productive capacity provided by Western investments in specific Soviet projects.

Some such general calculus probably has been the basis for a
reassessment by Soviet leaders of their strategy of Western technology imports. This general logic was probably reinforced by the
specific economic requirements of Soviet economic planners. For
example, among the most important goals of recent Soviet economic
plans have been the following:

1. Modern regional oil and gas complexes in West
Siberia, including not only increased energy supply but a significant expansion of the related chemical and petrochemical industries. The stepped-up development of these regional energy
complexes is intended to ensure adequate supplies of efficient
energy for domestic, CMEA, and hard-currency export needs.
Foreign capital and technology were essential to meeting the
time and quality standards of this objective.[6]

2. A modern metallurgical industry based on new processes of steel output, such as pelletized steel and higher-qual-
ity output and utilization of other metals. The Krasnoyarsk-
East Siberian aluminum-hydro development, the Yudokan copper development, and the Kursk metallurgical development are
major projects in this modernization effort. The Baikal-Amur
railroad development (BAM), a featured development of the
Tenth Five-Year Plan (1976-80), will correlate with the East
Siberian-Far Eastern metal modernization effort. [7] Western
capital and technology seem to be critical to meeting the time
and quality criteria of the planned expansion.

3. Computer-assisted systems for processing national
economic data and operation of a number of critical sectors in
transportation and industry, such as Intourist and Aeroflot
bookings, port operations, and air traffic control. Western
computer and peripheral equipment was purported to be necessary to provide the basis for transition to a new system of
national economic reporting and enterprise planning and management.

4. Animal husbandry complexes, based on the latest
Western agribusiness techniques to provide a significant increase in meat and poultry output.

5. Construction and operation of modern truck and passenger car complexes to provide the basis for Soviet entrance
into the automobile age in cargo and passenger transport. The
mammoth Kama River truck project and the FIAT-Soviet passenger car plant, started in the Ninth and Eighth Five-Year
Plans, respectively, are the central projects of this step-up in
Soviet automotive capability. Each project has been based
heavily on foreign technology and capital inflow. Attainment of
this objective is the subject of a more detailed assessment in
the second part of this paper, a case study from which we may
draw inferences of potential validity for attaining the other objectives.

In attaining or making a major beginning on the process of accomplishing such economic tasks, there seems to be a changing Soviet view on the appropriate form of technology transfer. In spite of
the path-breaking FIAT example in the Eighth Five-Year Plan, one
might say that the Soviet planners began the Ninth Five-Year Plan
in 1971 with a traditional Soviet concept of a narrow, restricted form
of technology transfer and ended the plan period in 1975 with a much
more flexible, systems-oriented view. [8] These views may be referred to as the traditional Soviet model of technology transfer and
the modified systems form of technological interchange, respectively.

The possible forms of technology transfer range from a narrow, short-term, discontinuous, politically-insulated process to a broader, longer-term, continuous, less institutionally constrained process. In earlier cycles there have been temporary, short-term, controlled openings to the West. The special relationships with the United States and other Western nations were considered temporary re-treats from the basic policy of technological and economic independ-ence. The current policy, in contrast, may be a cautious, case-by-case movement along a scale from economic independence toward economic and technological interdependence. This is a view that appears to be shared by most U.S. corporations involved in the Soviet trade; that is, each agreement is expected to be followed by another, or several others, of at least equal value. Moreover, the conventional U.S. corporate wisdom seems to be that increasing So-viet flexibility may lead to more conventional direct investments in the Soviet Union.

The two variants of technology transfer, the traditional and modified systems approaches, represent points in the spectrum of minimum to maximum Western involvement in Soviet industrial cooperation. Those Soviet leaders who argue for political and insti-tutional stability tend to favor the former; while those who are most concerned about improved economic performance tend to favor the latter. Some of the characteristics of the traditional approach were exceeded in historical cases, such as the Ford-assisted Gorkiy Automobile Plant built in the early 1930s, but during the interim period, from the early 1930s through the 1960s, Soviet policy was to isolate the Soviet economy from Western influence. Technology imports from the West tended to be relatively small in scale and accomplished through passive mechanisms, such as simple imports of machinery and equipment. Some of the characteristics of the mod-ified systems approach were not adopted in the major projects of the Ninth Five-Year Plan, such as the Kama River truck plant, but have been the subject of recent discussions in the Soviet press and of nego-tiations with Western firms. [9]

The traditional Soviet model of technology transfer has charac-teristically minimized all aspects of Western involvement in the So-viet economy in order to maintain Soviet independence of foreign capital, technology, and influence. In the modified systems approach, the Soviet concern for independence is tempered by a recognition of the economic benefits of more active technology transfer mechan-isms. The differences in the approaches can be highlighted by refer-ence to three stages in building and operating an industrial project: design and construction; operation and production; and distribution, marketing, and pricing.

Design and Construction. The traditional model minimizes foreign involvement in the design of production facilities and products. Soviet planners and engineers control the choice of location and the actual construction of the project and specify which machinery and equipment are needed. The modified systems approach encourages the use of Western consultants for a variety of planning, design, and construction activities; for the use of Western designs or the adaptation of Western designs to meet Soviet conditions; for the planning of regional complexes or specific production facilities; and for the supervision of construction, installation, and start-up.

Operation and Production. The traditional model minimizes foreign involvement in the management of Soviet production facilities. The history of tsarist and early Soviet foreign concessions, which resulted in dependence on foreign managerial expertise, has made this a paramount concern for Soviet leaders. However, the modified systems approach allows Western involvement in management to the extent that it is deemed necessary for the rapid reproduction of Western levels of technology and performance. Western involvement includes training by Western specialists in Western facilities and some degree of Western decision-making power in Soviet-based projects.

Distribution, Marketing, and Pricing. The traditional model minimizes foreign involvement in the distribution and pricing of the products of Western-assisted projects. Soviet central planning practices made it necessary to retain this power in Soviet hands; however, the modified systems approach does permit Western managerial advisors to participate in decisions that influence the ability of a new facility to meet foreign and domestic demand, such as matters concerning advertising, servicing, and maintenance. The Soviet need to export competitive products to Western markets creates special requirements for continuing Western involvement.

The transition from the Soviet traditional form of technology transfer to the modified systems approach has not yet been accomplished as a standard or norm of technology transfer or industrial cooperation. Indeed, the norm is still closer to the traditional form. However, all of the aspects of the modified systems approach appear to have been subject to active Soviet study and discussion, and many have been introduced into the negotiation process among Soviet and Western industrial interests.

The Soviet leaders have broadened their view of Western technologies that may have applications in the Soviet economy. Technology embodied in management techniques, computer applications, and economic analysis systems has been added to the range of technologies transferred. Examples of these new forms of technology borrowing include (1) greater use of Western consultant firms for management assistance and computer applications; (2) increased participation in Western research activities, joint management projects, and joint East-West trade research efforts; (3) intergovernmental bilateral exchanges with Western nations, focusing not only on production techniques but on complex applications of management techniques; and (4) increased participation in multilateral forums, such as the International Economic Association and UN research activities.

The Time Dimension in the Transfer of Western Technology to the Soviet Economy

A central question in assessing the significance of the transfer of Western technology to the Soviet economy is the time dimension. Has the Soviet economy become linked to the industrially advanced Western economies on a long-term, expanding trend, or is the Western technology bridge a short-term catch-up expedient that will peak in the not-distant future and give way to earlier patterns of independence?

In the past, certain Soviet and Russian leaders—Stalin, Peter the Great, Catherine—have temporarily opened their Western windows to bring in the latest industrial techniques and shortly thereafter closed them. The political desire for independence from Western influence or domination was an apparent rationale for this policy. Modifications of the traditional insular policy led to cycles of Western exposure. Morevoer, the economic costs of the short-term policy of technological catch-up seemed to have been modest or at least manageable.

Historical patterns, however, may no longer be a valid guide. The Soviet leaders now seem confident in their Great Power status. They may perceive an ability to limit the impact of critical Western influences to their "in-system modernizers." They have publicly stated that the old Stalinist policy of independence and isolation has ended. International division of labor, a form of comparative advantage, has been espoused. Ideological and political control may no longer override economic advantages. The economic advantage of progressively joining the world economy may become greater over time.

The general trend toward a modified systems approach to technology transfer seems dictated by a desire to copy Western measures of efficiency in output, for example, to produce a car or truck model that may be efficient and competitive in the Western market,

including model changes under mass production conditions, or to
duplicate U.S. levels of feed-grain conversion, shorter gestation
periods for marketing animals, and other agribusiness measures.
Technology absorption, diffusion, and domestic innovation—the whole
Western cycle of technological interchange—compel the Soviet Union
toward the systems approach, including Western involvement in
management. In technologically dynamic areas this systems approach,
involving a broad pattern of technological interchange, tends to be
iterative and more efficient through successive iterations. This
tends to accelerate Western involvement over time.

The Soviet leadership's concern with broad economic objectives such as an efficient automotive transport system, modern
hydrocarbon energy complexes, and an efficient meat supply sector,
creates incremental needs for expansion of infrastructure and other
investment. The development of modern truck plants, such as the
Kama River truck plant, may generate requirements for better high-
ways, repair facilities, warehouses, and another truck plant. Likewise, the next large truck plant based on improving Western technology may be more, rather than less, tied to the Western partners.
As the Soviet economy modernizes and closes the technology gap
(even to the point of exporting under competitive conditions), the
Soviet Union may import more rather than less. Thus the traditional
progressive process of international trade among industrialized
economies, based on comparative advantage, may affect the Soviet
economy. [10]

The political calculus may involve a weighing of the pressures
for improvement in economic performance promised by Western
technology imports, against the institutional and political changes
that could result from accommodations to Western standards of efficient organization and management. The latter risks may be considered more containable than they would have been in earlier periods. A strong, mature Soviet superpower may be able to sort out
the advantages of Western technology without exposing itself to undue
Western economic leverage. It therefore may not consider Western
commercial contacts subversive to its ideological system.

By modernizing basic industries such as energy, metals, and
machine building; entering the automotive age; and developing an
agribusiness base of modern agriculture, the Soviet leaders appear
to want not only to catch up but to stay up with the economically
developed nations. The domestic need for a new trend in civilian
technology is reinforced by the marginal but significant requirements
that must be met in order to export in a competitive world market.

In the past, especially in the 1930s, the Soviet leadership was
content to import only enough technology to establish a mass-produc-
tion capability in selected high-priority industries. At that time the

benefits of keeping up with the modest technological changes occurring
in the depression-ridden West were apparently overridden by the
political cost perceived in limited dependence on the West. Moreover,
overtaking the West in physical levels of output was perceived by
Stalin as more important than improving the efficiency of output that
might result from a continued pattern of Western technology transfer.
Closing the technology gap in selected economic sectors was enough;
keeping up was neither necessary nor worth the political risk.

In order to get on the world trend lines for technological change
in the current period, the Soviet economic sectors require more than
the ability to duplicate the current or recent Western models. In the
modern automotive, computer, petroleum, chemical, metallurgical
ages that Soviet officials wish and probably need to enter, their
industries must be able to keep up with the Western rates of technological change. Worldwide technological changes must be imported
and quickly and efficiently reflected in mass production model changes. Lewis Branscomb, a vice-president of IBM, and Western corporate executives in other fields have noted that this mass production capability is a serious deficiency in Soviet industry. [11] The perceived need for Western systems analysis, management, and new
economic forms in the Soviet economic system seems to flow from
the need to keep up and become competitive by world standards.
Western plans, designs, management and production methods, and
marketing techniques are a part of the modified systems approach.
The truck and passenger car facilities to follow KamAZ and Tol'iatti
may well proceed far beyond their current pattern of industrial cooperation.

Another indication of the long-term, continuous, expanding
nature of the Soviet market are the apparent long-term commitments
of major Western corporations to the Eastern market. Implicit in
Western firms' commitments to economic relations with the Soviet
Union is the notion that it is a unique market. In the short run the
Soviets may demand and receive some preferential prices and credit,
and profits may be low. However, in the long run, early Western
entrants to the Eastern market may be in a strong competitive position in an expanding, large, profitable market. At the same time the
political costs and security risks of Soviet commercial relations
might limit the advantages of normal predictable trade. For example,
Western computers with potential military applications may be subject to unpredictable export controls. The Soviet planners may
place large orders in one year and no orders in the following year.
Difficulties in financing trade or domestic political factors affecting
trade may lead to sharp changes in Soviet import policy.

Among the other indications of a Soviet commitment to long-
term, expanding interdependence with the West are long-term scien-

tific and technological agreements with various corporations; the web
of bilateral governmental exchanges; [12] construction of a trade center in Moscow; and the apparent projection of expanding Western involvement in the Tenth Five-Year Plan (1976-80).

THE TRANSFER OF WESTERN TECHNOLOGY
TO THE SOVIET AUTOMOTIVE INDUSTRY*

In the two periods of intensive Soviet interest in Western technology, the First Five-Year Plan (1928-32) and the current period
(the mid-1960s to the present), the automotive industry has been one
of the high-priority areas of Soviet technology borrowing. This case
study is intended to provide a basis for evaluating the hypothesis
that the Soviet orientation to the international economy has undergone a fundamental change since the 1930s. Specifically, Western
technology transfers to major Soviet automotive projects in the two
periods are analyzed in order to determine whether there is movement toward what has been termed a modified systems approach to
technology transfer, characterized by more permanent technological
ties and more active involvement of Western firms in the Soviet
economy. In addition, evidence is examined of changes in Soviet
economic institutions induced by technology transfer. The case study
concentrates on three major projects in the Soviet automotive industry: the Gorkiy automobile plant, which was built with the assistance
of the Ford Motor Company in the late 1920s and early 1930s; the
Volga automobile plant, which was built during the Eighth Five-Year
Plan with the assistance of FIAT; and the Kama River truck plant,
which is now under construction with assistance from a number of
Western firms.

In some ways the use of foreign technology by the Soviet automotive industry has been typical of Soviet industry as a whole. The
contractual arrangements in both periods—technical assistance contracts in the earlier period and various industrial cooperation arrangements in the 1960s and 1970s—were similar to those used in
many branches of Soviet industry. Moreover, the rationale for borrowing foreign technology and the domestic environment into which
the technology was transplanted were similar for the automotive and
other Soviet industries. In the 1920s and 1930s Soviet economic
planners sought foreign assistance to transform a backward domestic industry with insignificant production into a modern mass-produc-

---

*This case study is based on research by George Holliday for a
Ph. D. dissertation in preparation at George Washington University.

tion industry capable of meeting the needs of a rapidly industrializing economy. In the 1960s and 1970s, purchases of foreign technology have been viewed by the Soviet leadership as a means of modernizing a large but in many ways inadequate industry and overcoming the increasingly evident technology gap between the Soviet Union and the industrial West. In both periods, efforts in the Soviet automotive industry paralleled developments in other sectors of the economy.

In the scale of Western technology transfers to the Soviet Union, the automotive industry may be regarded as somewhat atypical. During the two periods studied, the Soviet automotive industry has been the recipient of more Western technology than most other branches of Soviet industry. According to one Soviet source, the Soviet Union spent 311.4 million rubles of scarce foreign exchange for machinery and equipment for the Gorkiy and Moscow automobile factories during the First Five-Year Plan (189.2 million rubles for Gorkiy and 122.2 million rubles for Moscow).[13] These two factories alone accounted for over 4 percent of all Soviet imports during the First Five-Year Plan and exceeded the hard-currency expenditures for such huge Western-assisted projects as the Magnitogorsk metallurgical works and the Dnepr hydroelectric station. Additional funds were spent for expansion of the Yaroslavl automobile plant and for various supplies for the automobile industry, such as glass, metal, and electrical equipment. These expenditures continued, though at a reduced rate, during the Second Five-Year Plan.

Similarly, large expenditures have been and are being made for purchasing Western technology for the Soviet automotive industry during the 1960s and 1970s. The construction of the passenger automobile plant at Tol'iatti, for example, was assisted by purchase of about $550 million of Western machinery and equipment.[14] The Kama River truck plant is expected to result in over $1 billion in purchases from the West.[15] The Tol'iatti and Kama projects represent the major industrial undertakings of the Eighth and Ninth Five-Year Plans respectively. In addition, to modernize other parts of the Soviet automotive industry, large purchases of Western technology have been made during the current periods. Thus it appears that the Soviet automotive industry has been the beneficiary of a disproportionate share of Soviet hard-currency expenditures.

One implication of the high priority given to foreign automotive technology is that the evidence of changes induced by technology transfer may be more pronounced in this sector than in others. However, as research by Antony C. Sutton[16] and others has shown, many Soviet industries have benefited from Western technology transfers. Moreover, the experience of the automotive industry does appear to be representative of a Soviet pattern for using foreign technology that is characterized by the concentration of purchases of foreign technology in large new "showcase" projects. This pattern has been evident in the Soviet chemical, metalworking, and other industries. The large scale of automotive technology transfer during both periods makes it a useful case study because it highlights the differences and continuities of the Soviet approach to economic ties with the West.

The Gorkiy Automobile Plant

On May 31, 1929, the Ford Motor Company signed a contract with the Soviet Supreme Economic Council to assist in the construction of an automobile plant at Nizhni-Novgorod (renamed Gorkiy in 1932). The initial agreement provided for Ford assistance in building a factory to produce annually about .1 million vehicles of two types: a passenger car modeled after the Ford Model A (the Soviet version was called GAZ-A) and a light truck modeled after the Ford Model AA (the Soviet GAZ-AA).[17] The 1929 contract was followed by supplementary agreements with Ford to increase the capacity of the plant and by contracts with other Western firms providing for their assistance in various specialized operations at the plant. Western assistance to the automotive industry was intended to coincide with the First Five-Year Plan, though the contract with Ford continued into the Second Five-Year Plan.

The Soviet contracts with Ford and other Western firms for assistance in automobile production were among the many "technical assistance agreements" concluded by the Soviets in the late 1920s and early 1930s. The technical assistance agreements involved Soviet payments to Western firms for technical data, patents, know-how, and other assistance, to be provided over a specified period of time. They differed from the concessions agreements that the Soviet government had more commonly signed with Western firms in the 1920s. Under concessions, Western firms invested capital equipment in designated areas of the Soviet economy to develop resources or to exploit other economic opportunities. Typically, a Western firm managed the project and was allowed to repatriate profits after making royalty payments to the Soviet government. Ownership of the capital was transferred to the Soviet government. Concessions were gradually phased out in the 1930s, when technical assistance contracts became the preferred means of cooperating with Western companies.

Technical assistance agreements, unlike concessions, did not provide for repatriated profits or royalty payments to the government. Instead the Soviet government purchased machinery and equipment and paid a set fee for the services provided by the West-

ern partners. In addition, the technical assistance contracts provided no management role for the Western firms. While technical
assistance inevitably involved some Western advice on managerial
matters, the contracts were essentially vehicles for transferring
engineering skills. The Western firms generally showed Soviet
specialists how to set up a factory and operate machines and then
left the management of the completed factories to the Soviets. In this
important respect—the absence of a foreign managerial role—the
technical assistance contracts represented a step back from the Soviet policy of allowing selective Western involvement in the economy
and a reassertion of the industrial bureaucracy's absolute control in
Soviet industry. Another key feature of these agreements was the
provision of a schedule according to which the Soviet factory would
achieve progressive independence from the Western partner. The
ultimate success for the Soviet enterprise or industry involved was
ridding itself of the need to import from the West or to rely on Western technology.

The Ford arrangement with the Soviet government was typical
of the technical assistance contracts and is generally cited in the
Soviet literature as one of the more successful agreements with
Western firms.[18] Indeed, it was a well-conceived device for transferring technology to a country that lacked the economic and technical infrastructure needed for such a massive undertaking. In collaboration with other Western firms, which helped to set up certain
parts of the production process, Ford assisted in every phase of the
creation of the plant, from design to start-up of production.

Ford specialists developed the designs for a complete factory
and provided detailed specifications for machinery and materials,
operating instructions for the factory, and designs for the automobiles to be produced. Drawings of all the tools, machines, and fix-
tures at the Ford River Rouge plant were also provided. The Gorkiy
factory was not an exact replica of the River Rouge plant, though
many of the operations were essentially the same. The plans that
the Ford specialists provided contained modifications designed to
meet the conditions under which the Soviet factory would operate.
This was accomplished by working with a team of Soviet specialists
who had the authority for final approval of the factory's design and
for selection of the machinery and equipment to be purchased in the
West. During the planning process for the factory, several Ford
engineers traveled to the Soviet Union to consult with Soviet engineers. The Soviets, in turn, sent a team of technicians to the United
States, where they were allowed to study production processes at
the Ford plant and also at the plants of Ford suppliers.

Ford was not a general contractor for the entire Gorkiy plant.
The Soviet engineers and managers jealously guarded their preroga-

tive in matters of design and selection of machinery. Their reliance on Ford and others was clearly a matter of necessity, to be ended at the earliest possible opportunity. Moreover, the Soviet specialists showed no compunction in rejecting or changing the proposals offered by their foreign counterparts.

The Soviet government signed contracts with other U.S. firms to perform specialized tasks in building and equipping the factory. Contracts were signed with companies such as the Timken-Detroit Axle Company, the Brown Lipe Gear Company, and the Austin Company. [19] The Austin Company, which had built several U.S. automobile plants (including Ford plants) signed a contract with the Soviet government in August 1929 to design and direct the construction of the buildings housing the factory. This was to be completed not later than the fall of 1931 and would accommodate a revised planned capacity of 120,000 vehicles. [20] A number of Austin engineers traveled to the Soviet Union to supervise the work. The Soviet engineers were dissatisfied with Austin's initial design and made changes in it;[21] however, Austin's contract was successfully executed.

The contract with Ford provided for Soviet automobile production to start up in phases. Initially the Soviets merely assembled the vehicles from parts produced by Ford in the United States. For this purpose there were two assembly plants, one at the Gorkiy site and the other in Moscow. The Moscow plant, called the Kim Works, was an unused railroad shop that the Soviets, with Ford's assistance, converted to auto production. The Moscow plant assembled the first vehicles, while the Gorkiy plant gradually phased in production of various parts. After the first year, bodies, fenders, hoods, and all sheet-metal parts were to be produced. Over the next four years, fittings, engines, axles, instruments, batteries, and electrical equipment would be phased in; so that after five years the Gorkiy plant would be working at capacity and producing most of the parts needed for the two vehicles it would produce. In fact, the production schedule proceeded much slower than planned; but in the end this plan succeeded in giving the Soviets the largely self-sufficient automobile industry they wanted.

An integral part of the contract was Ford's agreement to train Soviet workers and technicians, both in the Soviet Union and the United States. Ford agreed to allow 50 Soviet specialists per year, over a period of five years, to study operations in his factories in the United States. Ford sent a number of engineers and foremen to the Soviet Union to train the Soviets. The training was rapidly phased out as the factory neared completion. By 1932 only three Ford specialists remained as instructors at the Gorkiy factory. [22] Thus, after only three years, the involvement of Ford technicians at Gorkiy was virtually ended.

The Soviets attempted to insure that once in operation the Gorkiy factory would represent the latest word in Western technology. The agreement required Ford to place all of its patents at the disposal of Soviet specialists. It further required that any innovations or improvements that would be introduced in Ford automobiles during the life of the contract (nine years) were to be made available to the Soviet plant. [23] Some evidence suggests that Ford took this stipulation seriously. For example, Ford offered to help the Soviets introduce its new V-8 engine, probably the most important Ford innovation during the life of the contract, at the Gorkiy plant. [24] (The new engine was still on Ford's drawing boards when the contract was signed.) The Soviets declined, preferring to produce the simpler and proven Model A. In 1932 Ford discontinued production of the Model A and put the V-8 engine into production in the United States. Soviet specialists noted the development, pointing out that they had the option to acquire the new technology, but they did not do so during the life of the contract. [25]

The V-8 episode reflected a soberness among some Soviet specialists about their technological capabilities that contrasted sharply with the boastfulness about the Gorkiy plant that was often exhibited in the Soviet press. To be sure, the production facilities at Gorkiy were as modern as any automobile plant in the West. Gorkiy's engineers even maintained that the plant was technologically superior to Ford's River Rouge plant, which was generally considered to be the most advanced in the West. [26] The Soviet technicians claimed that the Soviet plant was more carefully planned, had more modern machinery, and was more automated than the Ford plant. Nevertheless, the Soviets had great difficulty in mastering this new technology. The factory produced its first vehicles in 1932, but production was interrupted numerous times because of a variety of problems. Among the problems in the first year were the production of many defective parts, frequent accidents on the assembly line, inadequately equipped laboratories, and insufficient supplies. [27]

The supply problem was perhaps the most difficult. By 1934 the Soviets had achieved their goal of independence from Western suppliers—all parts and materials were supplied internally. [28] However, these were frequently of poor quality and, especially in the early years, seldom in sufficient quantities. As a result the Gorkiy plant was not producing to capacity when its contract with Ford expired. In fact, total Soviet automobile production (from all Soviet plants) did not reach .1 million until 1936. [29]

The Ford-Soviet contract was a relatively "active" technology transfer mechanism in that it provided frequent and specific communications between Soviet engineers and their Ford counterparts. However, the effectiveness of the arrangement was limited by the

provision for an abrupt cutoff of commercial ties with Ford and with
Western industry in general. Soviet economic independence involved
not only an end to imports of materials and parts but also substantial
isolation from technological developments in the Western automotive
industry. Between the termination of the Ford contract and the mid-
1960s, the Soviet automotive industry's technological ties to the West
consisted only of sporadic and relatively passive technology transfer
mechanisms.

The massive transfer of Western technology to the Soviet automotive industry and to other industries in the 1930s brought important changes to Soviet economic institutions. The construction of the
Gorkiy automobile plant was part of the abrupt shift away from small-
batch production in small, local factories to modern mass production
techniques that had been associated primarily with U.S. industrialization. This shift obviously necessitated changes in Soviet industrial
organization. However, the Gorkiy plant was not a simple recreation
of a U.S. factory. Gorkiy emerged as a Soviet factory, which like
other new Soviet factories developed a uniquely Soviet solution to the
problems of mass production. The differences in the Soviet plant
were most apparent in the emerging Stalinist system of enterprise
management, with its emphasis on meeting plan directives for physical output. Henry Ford's renowned attention to consumer demand had
no role in the Soviet manager's world.

There were other important differences between the Gorkiy
factory and Western factories such as the Ford River Rouge plant.
First, there were differences in the technological characteristics
of machinery and equipment. In some cases the Ford plant did not
have the most modern machinery available in the West. When Gorkiy
engineers believed that superior technology was available, they purchased it from other firms in the West.[30] In other cases the Soviets
rejected what they considered "too specialized machinery," apparently motivated by the belief that, under Soviet conditions, more labor-
intensive operations would be efficient.[31]

The Gorkiy factory was also much more vertically integrated
than Western automobile factories. Gorkiy not only assembled automobiles but also manufactured most of the parts and even some of
the machine-tools it needed. This was a departure from the system
of subcontracting that had developed in the Western, especially the
U.S., automobile industries. The absence of complementary industries in the Soviet Union and the consequent problem of an unreliable
supply system made the Gorkiy approach necessary.

A unique feature of the Gorkiy plant was the combined construction of the factory and of an entire new city to provide housing and
services for the factory's employees. The Soviets chose not to locate the factory in a large metropolitan area where workers and an

urban infrastructure would already be in place. The plant was actually constructed outside of Gorkiy (then Nizhni-Novgorod), where no infrastructure existed. Although the construction of auxiliary facilities required additional allocation of scarce capital resources, Soviet planners seemed determined to create a completely modern island within the backward Soviet economy. This pattern was copied for future "avtogiganty" in Tol'iatti and Kama.

Finally, an important difference between Gorkiy and plants in the West was the lack of attention and resources that the former paid to technological progress. The research and development facilities at Gorkiy, as in other Soviet factories, were kept to a minimum. Some Soviet specialists objected to this deficiency. For example, E. A. Chudakov, a prominent Soviet automotive engineer, pointed out that Western methods of producing automobiles were constantly changing, resulting in more efficient production and improved vehicles. In the Ford plant, he wrote, over 4,000 changes in production techniques had been introduced in 1929 and 1930 alone.[32] Chudakov believed that Soviet industry could maintain this pace of technological progress only by spending considerable funds on research and development:

> Thus, mere copying of foreign production, although it
> might be the most rational approach at present, is in
> practice impossible and dooms us to falling immediately
> behind the general tempo of production abroad. Parallel
> with the development of production, it is necessary to
> establish at the factory a research organization for improving production and making it more efficient.[33]

The subsequent retardation of technological change in the Soviet automotive industry suggests that Chudakov's advice was not accepted. Chudakov noted in 1936 that the GAZ-AA truck had already fallen behind the technological levels of comparable Western models. The GAZ-AA, he wrote, "is not the most modern model and has a comparatively weak engine. The most modern trucks of this tonnage have better dynamic qualities."[34] Chudakov's approach, while it was undoubtedly ideal from the Soviet engineer's viewpoint, could not be accommodated to the overall needs of the Soviet economy during the period of rapid industrialization. The economic development strategy of the first two five-year plans placed priority on maximizing physical output, not on improving quality. For automobile production, maximization of output was particularly important because of the extremely small existing automobile park in the Soviet Union, the importance of the automobile to other sectors of the economy, and the high cost of importing them. To expand the production of automo-

biles at the necessary rate, the Soviets had to concentrate scarce
capital on tooling up on the basis of existing technology and mass
producing a few standardized vehicles—primarily trucks. With this
goal in mind, research and development and retooling for new models
had to be considered a luxury. Likewise, continuing contracts with
the West were considered too costly, both in economic and in political
terms.

The Legacy of the Stalinist
Economic Growth Strategy

In view of the priorities of economic planning during the period
of rapid industrialization, the performance of the Soviet automotive
industry in the Stalinist period must be considered a partial success.
A mass production industry was established in an extremely short
period of time. While the ambitious output goals of the economic
planners were not met, the level of production rose at an impressive
rate—sufficient to meet many of the needs of the economy. The industry attained a reasonably high level of technology in the prewar per-.
iod, although it proved incapable of keeping pace with the automotive
industries in the West. Perhaps most importantly, from the vantage
point of the political leadership, it was a self-contained industry,
independent of the industrial West.

However, the structure of the Soviet automotive industry was
not suitable for the needs of an increasingly complex post-Stalinist
Soviet economy. Predictably, the Soviet emphasis on maximizing
output on the basis of a given technology and the drive to isolate Soviet industry from the West resulted in a backward, stagnant industry. The state of the industry became increasingly evident to Soviet
specialists, who in the post-Stalinist era began to offer public criticisms. [35]

Efforts to spur technological progress were also thwarted by
factors other than the Stalinist growth strategy and the industry's
isolation from the West. It was also recognized that organizational
problems, particularly the high degree of vertical integration in
Soviet automotive plants, were partially responsible for its backwardness. [36] On the model of the Gorkiy factory, each Soviet automobile plant tended to produce as many of its own components,
parts, and tools as possible and to develop networks of specialized
suppliers that were primarily responsible for supporting production
of one type of vehicle. As a result, the industry is plagued by a lack
of standardization, resulting in inefficient production of a large number of parts in small quantities for the different types of vehicles in
the various factories.

The creation of large, independent enterprises generated other problems. First, these enterprises tend to duplicate each others' efforts, particularly in the field of research and development. Technology that is developed in one plant is not always shared with other enterprises. Small, self-contained R&D facilities have proven inadequate for keeping abreast of new technological developments. Moreover, the automotive industry tended to grow primarily by expanding old enterprises. This practice, Soviet specialists claimed, brought about growth without modernization. [37] The expanded plants tended to produce at the same level of technology as the parent plants.

This state of affairs was also recognized by the political leadership. In a speech to the 22nd Party Congress, Nikita Khrushchev singled out the Moscow Likhachev automobile factory as an example of how slowly new technology was being introduced to Soviet industry. [38] According to Khrushchev, the factory was producing four-ton trucks that had been put into production 14 years earlier and had had no significant improvements during that period. Substantial resources and time (about six years) had been spent to design and organize production of a better truck, but no progress had been made.

Khrushchev himself bore responsibility for continuing the Stalinist neglect of the Soviet passenger car industry. On a number of occasions he expressed his disdain for widespread private ownership of cars in the West and advocated further development of mass transit and car rentals as an alternative for the Soviet Union. Apparently this was a controversial position. Some Soviet engineers criticized the existing Soviet passenger cars as obsolete and wasteful of resources. [39] A substantial lobby advocating a transition to mass production of inexpensive, small cars, developed in the industry. A half-hearted attempt to produce such a car began with production of the "Zaporozhets" in 1962. However, the Zaporozhets (which is still being produced) has proved to be an unsuccessful venture, both in terms of its ability to incorporate the latest technology and its appeal to the Soviet consumer. Its lack of success, which was apparently a result of inadequate experience and opposition from supporters of Khrushchev's position, probably contributed directly to the decision to seek foreign help in building a new small car factory at Tol'iatti.

In a 1965 speech to the State Planning Committee, Khrushchev's successor as Premier, Alexei Kosygin, criticized the previous leadership for stubbornly adhering to the idea that the Soviet Union did not need to develop production of passenger cars on a large scale. [40] Kosygin suggested that the new leadership would change this approach. In the same speech, Kosygin criticized the automobile industry for manufacturing obsolete trucks that did not meet the needs of the Soviet economy. He claimed that Western man-

ufacturers had long ago ceased production of some of the types of
trucks still being produced in the Soviet Union. He expressed pessimism about the Soviet automobile industry's ability to improve the situation: "We are reconstructing ZIL and GAZ for output of vehicles
with greater capacity, but I am not certain that everything has been
done properly."[41] Kosygin's speech reflected an awareness on the
part of the new leadership of two elements in the stagnation of the
Soviet automotive industry. Not only was it falling behind Western
industry technologically—a state of affairs that had been recognized
by Khrushchev—but it was also failing to meet the growing and
changing needs of the Soviet economy. These needs included fulfilling
consumer demands as well as modernizing the freight transportation
system.

In his 1965 speech, Kosygin did not mention the possibility of
turning to Western automotive firms for assistance. However, his
assessment of the state of affairs in Soviet passenger car and truck
production suggested the rationale for the leadership's future decisions regarding the Tol'iatti and Kama plants. One aspect of the new
leadership's approach has been an attempt to satisfy at least a part
of the Soviet consumer demand for passenger cars. The leadership
has recognized a need to provide quality consumer goods as incentives for Soviet citizens, and Soviet searchers have found that the
average citizen desired a passenger car above all other consumer
goods.[42] Initially, production plans could only meet the needs of
relatively well-to-do Soviet citizens. The cost of the new Zhiguli—
the passenger car produced at Tol'iatti—is prohibitive for most
Soviet citizens, and the waiting lists are still long. While long-run
production plans suggest an effort to provide passenger cars for a
wider spectrum of the population, it is unlikely that cars will be
available for most Soviet citizens in the near future.

The other important goal of the new approach to automobile
production is to provide a flexible, comprehensive automotive
freight transport system. The Soviets have long recognized the need
for trucks to complement their rail and marine transport systems.
Their present truck park is considered inadequate, both in terms of
numbers and of technological sophistication. Perhaps equally important is the shortage of specialized vehicles for the many different
jobs required of truck transport in a modern economy.[43]

One glaring deficiency recognized in the early and mid-1960s
was the shortage of heavy-duty trucks with large load capacities, a
problem that will be ameliorated by the start-up of production at
Kama. However, Kama will not meet the needs for other types of
vehicles. For example, there will still be an unsatisfied need for
various types of specialized vehicles, such as trucks to be used on
construction sites with very rough terrain, which is found in Siberia

and elsewhere. Even more important is a steadily growing need for trucks with a high cargo carrying capacity (larger than Kamaz trucks) to be used on the small Soviet network of first-class roads. [44] The engines and bodies of Kamaz trucks are specially designed with good cross-country capabilities, making them suitable for roads without good foundations, that is, for the vast majority of Soviet roads. However, they will not be the most efficient vehicles for intercity superhighway freight transport. The latter accounts for a growing percentage of Soviet automotive freight transport. The need for such vehicles will presumably be met by further expansion of existing facilities and construction of new truck plants.

The current expansion of the Soviet automotive industry appears to be only a first step. To meet the economy's need for automobiles, as perceived by Soviet specialists, a continuing rapid expansion can be expected in the foreseeable future.

The Volga Automobile Plant at Tol'iatti

Within four months after Kosygin's speech to Gosplan, the Soviet government signed a protocol for scientific and technical co-operation with the Italian automobile manufacturer FIAT. This type of agreement was unusual in 1965 but has since become a commonly used Soviet device for initiating long-term contacts with Western firms. The protocol led to discussions between FIAT and Soviet officials that culminated in the signing of a contract on August 15, 1966, providing for FIAT assistance in the construction of a massive new passenger car factory in Tol'iatti.

Under the contract, FIAT agreed to provide designs for a factory to produce 600,000 passenger cars [45] Included in the contract were the license to manufacture the vehicles in the Soviet Union, technological and organizational studies for the factory, and assistance during the start-up period. The agreement foresaw production of the first autombiles in 1969 and attainment of capacity production in 1972. This ambitious schedule was not met because of a variety of problems not unlike those that had been experienced by the Gorkiy plant in the 1930s. Once again the major problem was deficiencies, both quantitative and qualitative, in the Soviet supply system. [46] The first cars were produced one year behind schedule (in August 1970), and full production capacity, which had been revised upward to 660,000, was attained late in 1974.

Tol'iatti's products are three modified versions—standard, luxury, and family—of the FIAT 124, named the "Zhiguli" in the Soviet Union and the "Lada" for export. Production was scheduled to begin on another model, the "Niva," in 1976. [47] FIAT's engineers

were forced to make extensive modifications in order to make the
vehicle suitable for Soviet conditions. Many parts, the suspension
system, and the frame had to be reinforced, and the frame had to be
raised to withstand rough Soviet road conditions. All the mechanical
parts had to be adapted to the extremely low temperatures of some
regions of the Soviet Union. Gas tanks were enlarged because of the
small number of service stations. In the end, 65 percent of the parts
were different from those of the standard FIAT 124.[48]

Like Ford's role at Gorkiy in the 1930s, FIAT participated in
every phase of the project, from designing to initial start-up of pro-
duction. However, FIAT's advisory role went beyond the role of
Ford in several respects. First, compared to perhaps a few dozen
Western specialists at the Gorkiy plant of the 1930s, about 2,500
Western personnel went to Tol'iatti, including 1,500 from FIAT.[49]
During the same period, over 2,500 Soviet technicians went to Italy
for training and technical work—about ten times the number of Soviet
personnel who traveled to the United States in the earlier period.
Moreover, foreign involvement at Tol'iatti continued for a much
longer period of time than at Gorkiy. Thus the personal contacts
accompanying the technology transfer were far more numerous in
the FIAT-Soviet transaction. In Western countries, such personnel
exchanges are generally considered to be an essential element of
effective technology transfer. The Soviet political leadership, while
apparently aware of the need for personal contacts, has generally
tried to limit them because of real or imagined harmful side effects.
Thus the scale of personnel exchanges in the FIAT-Soviet transaction represents a significant political concession and an important
new development in Soviet economic relations with the West.

FIAT also had a different role as a supplier of capital equipment and licenses for the plant. The contract provided not only for
FIAT to sell machinery and equipment to the Soviet plant but for
FIAT to act as a consultant for other Soviet purchases in the West.
Thus a large percentage of the Western machinery installed in the
Tol'iatti plant was produced for FIAT by other Western manufacturers on a subcontract basis. FIAT specialists selected and purchased
the equipment and supplied it to the Soviet plant. FIAT also acquired
licenses to produce components manufactured by other Western firms
and sold them to the Soviets. The assembly and installation of all
Western machinery and equipment were supervised by FIAT, and
Soviet manufactured materials were sent to FIAT's factory in Turin
to be tested for quality control. The degree of FIAT's involvement
at Tol'iatti appears to be unparalleled in Soviet foreign economic
relations. A similar foreign involvement was considered but could
not be arranged in the initial planning of Kama and may be considered
for future industrial cooperation arrangements.

Another important aspect of the FIAT-Soviet arrangement is the prospect for a continuing long-term relationship. The traditional Soviet agreements with Western firms, including the agreement with Ford, provided a definite cutoff date, followed by complete independence from the West. FIAT, on the other hand, has established a relatively permanent working relationship with the Soviet Union. The 1965 scientific and technical cooperation agreement provides a basis for negotiating contracts for FIAT involvement in other parts of the Soviet economy. The original five-year agreement has been renewed twice, in 1970 and 1975. Moreover, consideration has been given to a new contract for FIAT assistance in expanding the capacity of the Tol'iatti plant to perhaps twice its present size,[50] though FIAT's willingness to expand the capacity of a potential competitor is questionable. The Soviets are clearly interested in maintaining this relationship. One Tol'iatti engineer, citing the development of new equipment at FIAT's Italian plant, remarked, "This experience cannot be ignored; we must simply use the established USSR-Italy channel more actively and on a larger scale."[51]

A major new development in the Tol'iatti project has been Soviet solicitation of Western assistance on an industrywide basis. Western technical assistance is involved not only in the automobile production but in building and modernizing Tol'iatti's supply network, developing a domestic service network for the new Zhigulis, and marketing the cars in the West. Western assistance in these areas parallels Tol'iatti's divergence from the traditional Soviet pattern of building isolated, vertically integrated plants responsible for all phases of production but having inadequate ties to their suppliers and little responsibility for the ultimate disposition of their products.

To be sure, the plant is a highly integrated operation by Western standards, combining all the basic production processes in Tol'-iatti: casting, forging, stamping and pressing, engine production, assembly, and tooling.[52] However, a large network of suppliers—much more extensive than previous Soviet automobile plants—has been developed for Tol'iatti. Two-thirds of all the parts and materials for the Zhiguli come from other plants,[53] many of which have been newly constructed or modernized with the assistance of Western firms.[54] In addition, many parts and components are being supplied by East European countries. Poland and Yugoslavia, which also produce FIAT-designed cars, are major suppliers, while Bulgaria and Hungary also supply some parts.[55] The factory might have been even more decentralized. Before the Tol'iatti plant was built, there was a debate among Soviet planners over whether to disperse it by building smaller factories in several towns. This variant lost out because of the leadership's insistence on starting production as soon as possible. It was decided that an early start-up could best be accomplished by building the entire plant at one location.[56]

In 1972 Tol'iatti introduced a "company system" for servicing its cars—an important first in the Soviet automotive industry.[57] The system, which is apparently patterned after similar operations in the West, includes presale preparation, technical maintenance, and warranty and general repairs. For the first time, the Soviet automobile purchaser receives a service booklet that describes maintenance schedules, and the purchaser is entitled to free warranty repairs for a year or 20,000 kilometers. The purpose of this system is to correct a chronic problem of Soviet car owners—inadequate servicing facilities and a lack of spare parts.

A large spare-parts production department has been put into operation at Tol'iatti, and a nationwide network of auto centers is being developed. Of the 33 such centers planned by the end of 1973, however, only one-third were completed on schedule.[58] Western firms are playing an important role in equipping these centers. The service network, along with the production facilities at Tol'iatti, the suppliers of some parts and components, the engineering and design sections, and the training facilities, are all supervised by the production association (proizvodstvennoe ob'edinenie), AvtoVAZ.

Tol'iatti is also departing from traditional Soviet practice by earmarking a large part (30 percent) of its production for foreign sales. Most of its foreign sales have gone to Eastern Europe, but an effort is underway to market a significant number of Ladas in Western Europe and North America. Ladas and other Soviet cars, particularly the Moskvich, are exported by a foreign trade enterprise, which has developed a novel approach to marketing these vehicles in the West. Joint stock companies have been created with foreign firms that have experience in meeting the special needs of Western markets. Two of the best-established of these joint ventures are Konela in Finland and Scaldia-Volga in Belgium.

Tol'iatti's managers have shown an awareness of the need for continued technological progress that is uncharacteristic of past Soviet industry officials. Tol'iatti's general manager, A. A. Zhitkov, recently complained to a Pravda correspondent of the tendency of Soviet suppliers to "lower the technical level of equipment offered to us," which, he said, "is a retreat by some branches associated with us from positions already won."[59] He asserted that their ability to improve the Zhiguli depended on improving the quality of the machinery and materials supplied to the plant. The management's concern with maintaining technological progress at the plant has resulted in continued purchases of foreign technology, such as a 2,000-ton press and a set of mechanical conveyors, including operational know-how,[60] from the Japanese firms and a license to manufacture a new automatic ignition device from a French subsidiary of Bendix Corporation.

A Soviet economist, E. B. Golland, has suggested that it is time to formulate a complete program for reconstruction and modernization of the Tol'iatti plant. [61] He noted that the world level of automobile manufacturing technology is progressing at an extremely rapid rate and that the Tol'iatti machinery and equipment are already becoming obsolete and worn out. Golland recommended that the Tol'iatti's managers proceed on two fronts: creation of a domestic industry capable of producing modern automobile manufacturing machinery and equipment, and purchase of foreign equipment and licenses. Thus, foreign involvement at Tol'iatti reflects a continuing pattern of technological interdependence, in sharp contrast to the Gorkiy project.

The Kama River Truck Plant

The Kama River truck plant (KamAZ) was undertaken to boost rapidly the production of trucks in order to provide a more balanced freight transport system for the Soviet economy. The project was also designed to bring about another massive infusion of Western automotive technology to complement Tol'iatti's contributions to technological progress in passenger car production. KamAZ is being built at Naberezhnye Chelny with a capacity to produce 150,000 heavy-duty, three-axle trucks and 250,000 diesel truck engines a year. Western technology transfers consist of machinery and equipment shipments and engineering and design assistance for various parts of the complex. The Soviet hard currency payments to the numerous Western firms providing assistance are expected to total over $1 billion.

In the construction and equipping of KamAZ, the Soviets are following a markedly different approach than that of the FIAT contract. The most important difference is the absence of a Western general consultant to select foreign technology and coordinate the deliveries of Western machinery and equipment to the Soviet site. The new approach is dictated by necessity, not choice. In the initial planning stage, Soviet officials approached several Western firms, including Ford and Mack Trucks in the United States, Daimler Benz in West Germany, and Renault in France. These firms declined the role of general consultant for a variety of reasons. Ford decided against involvement after the U.S. Department of Defense opposed the transaction. Mack Trucks believed that the project was too large and would tie up too much of the company's resources. Apparently all of the Western firms were influenced by problems that had been encountered by FIAT in its role as general consultant for the Tol'iatti plant.

Faced with the unwillingness of Western firms to undertake the job, KamAZ's managers were forced to do it themselves. To assist the project's directors in Naberezhnye Chelny, a special purchasing commission (Kamatorg), with permanent offices in New York and Paris, was established. The commission's purpose is to search for the best Western technology and to sign contracts with suppliers. Western businessmen who have dealt with KamAZ's specialists have been impressed with their expertise in general and their knowledge of Western manufacturers in particular. [62] Most Western observers believe that the Soviets have done a good job in selecting the best Western technology for various production processes at KamAZ.

However, the absence of a general consultant has contributed to serious problems. In general these problems have been related to the task of blending various technologies—those from various Western countries and that of the Soviet Union—into a consistent, integrated manufacturing process. A dramatic example of this kind of problem surfaced in the dispute between Soviet officials and representatives of Swindell-Dressler, the U.S. firm that has assisted in designing and equipping the foundry at KamAZ. At one point, Soviet officials charged that Swindell-Dressler was not fulfilling its contracts on time. Swindell-Dressler spokesmen, in turn, complained that they were not given sufficient information about related machinery supplied by other firms or about the buildings in which the foundry was to be housed. [63] These problems were exacerbated because the Soviets initially did not allow Swindell-Dressler's engineers adequate access to the construction site. In some cases Western machinery was delivered but would not fit into the buildings that had already been constructed, necessitating modifications in the buildings. In other cases machinery purchased from one supplier had not met the specifications required by the machinery and equipment supplied by other firms. The job of coordinating the infusion of foreign technology, one of the most difficult tasks in any technology transfer, had been a vital part of FIAT's assistance at the Tol'iatti project.

Confronted with delays that have put KamAZ's schedule back at least two years, Soviet officials have shown an awareness of the shortcomings at the project. Without attributing their problems to the lack of a Western general contractor, M. Troitskiy, the Party regional secretary in the province where KamAZ is located, identified the major problem in the construction of KamAZ as the absence of a "systems approach." Troitskiy indicated that large numbers of sophisticated machines have been brought to KamAZ without careful planning of the way the different parts of the plant would fit together. "In short," he concluded, "for projects such as KamAZ, what is needed is not simply many machines and mechanisms, but systems

of complementary machines."[64] This is precisely the contribution
that the Soviets had sought from a Western firm. Since the experience at KamAZ, Kamatorg officials have publicly indicated that they
prefer Western general consultants for future large projects.[65]

The size of KamAZ appears to be the major cause of many of
its problems. When completed, it will be the world's largest heavy
truck plant. Like FIAT and other Soviet automotive plants, it will be
a highly integrated facility, combining all of the main processes for
producing trucks and diesel engines. In fact, the finished complex
will be considerably larger and more integrated than the Tol'iatti
plant. Moreover, Soviet engineers have more responsibilities at
KamAZ than they did during construction of previous Western-assisted
projects. Consequently there was no previous experience or model
from which KamAZ's planners could learn. Troitskiy pointed this out
as follows:

> Even the construction of such a modern and in every
> respect progressive plant as VAZ (Tol'iatti), was not
> an adequate model. In erecting that plant, the type and
> design of the future vehicles and the technology for pro-
> ducing them were already known. At KamAZ, the models
> for the vehicles and the technology were being created
> at the same time that the construction was proceeding.[66]

Some Western businessmen believe that the Soviets made a
mistake in deciding to concentrate such a large production facility at
one site.[67] The decision was made only after extensive debate (which
paralleled the earlier debate over the location of the Tol'iatti plant)
among Soviet economic planners and engineers.[68] Apparently the
opposition to the KamAZ complex was strongest among the economists at the State Planning Committee. Its opponents argued that
truck production should be more dispersed, along the lines of the
U.S. automotive industry. Specifically, they advocated placing only
the plant for production of diesel engines in Naberezhnye Chelny,
while locating the main truck plant in another city in Siberia and
plants for various parts and components in other cities. A major
argument for this approach was that the more dispersed industry
would assist in providing employment for the surplus labor existing
in some small cities. This "American" approach was successfully
opposed by the proponents of a single complex in Naberezhnye Chelny.
Apparently the victors were primarily engineers from the automotive
and construction ministries. They argued that the Naberezhnye
Chelny site was ideal from the standpoint of availability of hydroelectric power, water transport, and labor and because of its proximity
to the major Soviet automotive centers.

While Troitskiy does not identify foreign technology as a consideration in the debate, it is interesting to consider the advantages of the two variants from the standpoint of facilitating the absorption and diffusion of foreign technology. Considering the importance of foreign technology at KamAZ, this may indeed have been an element of the debate that Troitskiy, a strong advocate of the victorious variant, conveniently ignores. With the advantages of hindsight and in view of the problems the project is experiencing, one is tempted to conclude for several reasons that the Soviets made the wrong choice. First, the construction and equipping of several smaller plants would have been easier to manage. It seems likely that the Soviets could have attracted Western firms to act as general consultants; if not, they probably would have had an easier time managing the separate projects. In either case, there were models, particularly in the West, that could have provided practical experience in truck production. Second, Western technology is logically more suited for the dispersed industry that exists in the West. By taking this into account, the problems of coordinating and blending Western and Soviet technological inputs might have been minimized. Third, the less-concentrated variant probably would have facilitated the diffusion of KamAZ's modern technology to other parts of the industry and the economy. Fourth, Soviet needs might better have been served with something less than the largest, latest, and most complex technologies. There is little evidence that Soviet specialists agree with this assessment, but it is interesting that Troitskiy does not rule out the "cooperative," or dispersed, approach for future projects.

> Of course, the KamAZ experience is not the only possible solution of such problems. A detailed study of all of the factors of production in the conditions of our country allows us to decide in each concrete case which is more advantageous—concentration or cooperation. [69]

Troitskiy's discussion of such issues, which is part of a more general debate that has surfaced during the discussion of the Tenth Five-Year plan and the Fifteen-Year Plan, indicates that Soviet officials are continuing to actively consider different variants of technology transfer and domestic economic organization.

KamAZ diverges from the pattern established by Ford and FIAT in another important way. Its products, the diesel engines and trucks, were originally designed by Soviet engineers, without assistance from the West. They are basically modifications of other Soviet vehicles, redesigned from other parts of the Soviet automotive industry. Although the Soviet officials were initially inclined to seek assistance in building a new engine through a licensing arrangement with a Western firm, they decided that their own engineers at the Yaroslavl Engine Plant could provide a better design. [70] However, in 1972 they enlisted the help of Renault to make improvements on the engines that had been designed for KamAZ trucks. [71]

Soviet officials have placed high priority on developing managerial techniques at KamAZ that will insure efficient production and maintenance of a rapid pace of technological progress. According to one Soviet source, the mangers of the complex will use "the leading domestic and foreign experience in organizing the management of the big production complex. "[72] The Soviets hope to achieve a new style of management, partially by organizing the complex in accordance with the latest institutional changes in the Soviet economy and partially by seeking assistance from the West. On the one hand, KamAZ is organized as a production association, as are the Tol'iatti plant and several other Soviet automotive enterprises. This form of management will theoretically give KamAZ managers a degree of independence from the central ministry and also control over some of the specialized enterprises that provide vital inputs to KamAZ. On the other hand, the KamAZ managers will be assisted by imports of foreign managerial techniques and hardware. Although direct Western managerial assistance appears to be more limited at KamAZ than at other Soviet projects, the Soviets do plan to import a computerized management and automated control system from IBM. Moreover, KamAZ may be a testing ground for new management techniques that are imported through other channels, such as formal study of Western management science.

THE TRANSFER OF WESTERN TECHNOLOGY
AND SOVIET ECONOMIC CHANGE

The Limits on Change

Technology transfer from the West to the Soviet Union may lead to significant change in the Soviet economic system. Technology transfer is broadly interpreted to include the use of Western systems of attaining economic objectives as well as the importation of products, techniques, and knowledge associated with specific production goals. The time for assessing change is not limited to the upcoming Tenth Five-Year Plan (1976-90) but extends to the turn of the century. Economic changes may include modifications of both policies and institutions. While it might be assumed that changes in the Soviet economic system lead to changes in other parts of Soviet culture, these are outside the scope of this chapter. [73]

The changes induced by technology transfer may not be revolutionary. Some may suggest that the absorption of foreign technology
leads inevitably to the destruction of the old regime, after the lesson
of the Paris Commune, but we do not think this is true. Significant
change, in our view, might occur within a more flexible but essentially Leninist system. Likewise, we do not assume that economic,
technological transfer will act as an Archimedes-like lever, forcing
a dialectic process of change on the reluctant managers of the system.

Perhaps "in-system modernizers" (to use a term employed by
Marshall Shulman) may, within Party guidelines and in their own
institutional self-interest, take actions that gradually lead to political and institutional change. The motivations of the leaders (nachal'
niki)[74] may lead them toward change in the interest of improved
economic performance and strengthening of the Party's role in the
economy. Even though trade in technology is a small part of total
output, it may represent the critical margin necessary for attaining
the priority economic goals of the leadership.[75] Even though Soviet
leaders say, and probably believe, that they are engaged in a process
leading to significant change, this may be the unintended long-term
result.

Interdependence and Modified Systems Transfer

The case studies of automotive technology transfer in the 1930s
and in the 1966–75 period indicate some movement in overall policy
from independence to technological interdependence and, more
specifically, from the traditional Soviet model of technology transfer
to a modified systems approach. No longer is independence of the
Western supplier a primary criterion of success; companies such as
FIAT and Swindell-Dressler are encouraged to expect long-term,
expanding relations. Moreover, the policy of the earlier period of
producing a Soviet plant in the indigenous administrative setting has
been challenged and modified. There appears to be increasing
acceptance of the idea that improved performance requires not only
broad Western involvement in the entire cycle of technology transfer
but also new kinds of production facilities that more fully adapt
Western managerial and technical methods to Soviet conditions. The
new kinds of facilities, in turn, are not expected to fit into the
existing Soviet administrative hierarchies; new organizational forms,
such as regional complexes and production associations, are in order. Such changes in organization suggest a shift in power and control from the established ministries and regional Party organizations to the central governmental and Party organs—probably the
State Planning Committee (Gosplan), the Academy of Science Insti-

tutes, and the Central Committee Secretariat departments. The modified systems approach, especially through joint management and joint production decisions, opens the Soviet system to more Western influence.

The new organizational forms in Soviet industry may be unlike both traditional Soviet and modern Western institutions. Just as Western technology was combined with the Soviet conditions of the 1930s to produce new but uniquely Soviet institutions, the current influx of Western technology may produce still another variant. Thus the case study of the Soviet automotive industry suggests only that traditional methods are perceived by Soviet leaders as inadequate and in need of change. Some of the broad outlines of that change are emerging, and the absorption of Western technology appears to be influencing the direction of change.

In the short run the changes resulting from the process of economic interdependence are likely to be selective and limited. Even in the long run the Party and the government may succeed in insulating key sectors of change from the system as a whole. Among the key policy problems that require accommodation to the impact of Western technology are resource allocation priorities,[76] the role of the state trading monopoly, and the economic information control system.

In order to effectively absorb Western automotive production technology, it may be necessary to give higher priority to a domestic supply of high-quality goods, personnel, and research. More important to the attainment of the presumed leadership objective of developing a modern automotive transport system would be extensive investment in an automotive system infrastructure, such as roads and repair facilities. The effectiveness of Western technology transfer to the Soviet Union will depend not only on the systems approach to absorbing the technology but on the development within the Soviet Union of an automotive transport system to effectively utilize modern trucks and passenger cars to provide maximum economic utility. The discussion of the "Auto BAM"—the transcontinental highway from Brest to Vladivostok, a discussion that was quietly, even secretly, begun in 1967, is illustrative of this larger resource commitment.[77]

Resource allocation policy is also likely to be influenced by balance-of-payments considerations, particularly the need to pay for the Western technology. In view of the difficulty experienced by the Soviet Union in maintaining its hard currency balance of payments, Soviet planners are confronted by hard choices. For example, they will have to apportion the expanded output of industrial cooperation ventures between domestic claimants and foreign markets. Will the export passenger car from the Tol'iatti plant, the Lada, be given priority in quality and delivery schedules over the domestic product, the Zhiguli? We already note aggressive European sales efforts for the Lada. A future variant of such preference for foreign over domestic markets might be the establishment of a new plant or a separate line at Tol'iatti that would be designed to meet the foreign market's special demands for high-quality products and timely delivery. For example, the Soviets may be forced to imitate the Japanese auto producers, who have made special export arrangements to meet U.S. environmental standards. Such attention to the requirements of the export market might be a step toward establishing export branches of Soviet industry that might even rival the Ministry of Defense as a claimant for high-quality inputs.

The percentage of total economic activity represented by Western trade and industrial cooperation is likely to be a small but critical margin. Much of the new investment in the upcoming plans will be in Siberian raw materials, transportation, and industrial development. Attainment of the various modernization objectives will be keyed to Siberia and to Western technology transfer—"the biggest programs in the history of the U.S.S.R."[78] A large portion of the new investment for the Tenth Five-Year Plan and the concurrent Fifteen-Year Plan will be in Siberian modernization projects. The time for completion, the efficiency, and indeed the feasibility of many of these projects are likely to depend on the effectiveness of the Western technology bridge and on the priority given to related Soviet supply plans.

One important institutional change that may occur is erosion of the dominance by the Ministry of Foreign Trade over Soviet foreign economic relations. A major purpose of the State Trading Monopoly has been to insulate the Soviet domestic economy from the outside influence of powerful capitalist nations and to maintain the influence of the domestic Soviet enterprises and ministries on foreign commercial policy. This concept is now being eroded or modified. For example, the Ministry of Foreign Trade and its subordinate foreign trade organizations and related agencies no longer monopolize commercial negotiations with foreign firms. At the center, the State Planning Committee (Gosplan) has begun to play an important role. Likewise, the ministries of key industries such as metallurgy, chemicals, gas, and oil increasingly have direct contact with Western firms. The State Committee on Science and Technology, especially through Dzherman M. Gvishiani, its ubiquitous deputy chairman, has made agreements on technology exchanges that narrow the scope or infringe on the mission of the Ministry of Foreign Trade's monopoly. To be sure, the Ministry of Foreign Trade has resisted a dilution of its power and has reorganized to adjust to changing conditions. However, the system of foreign trade administration is in flux.[79]

Payments in kind out of subsequent output by the industrial cooperation ventures have been modified. Concurrent rather than sequential payments are now possible. Now ministry lines are crossed in repayment. Current or concurrent payment is possible, and either hard currency or product may be the form of payment. Thus the dominance of the State Bank (Gosbank) and the Foreign Trade Bank (Vneshtoargbank) has also been eroded. The direct quota control of the Soviet state trading monopoly has limited Soviet end-users from participating in the choice of firms with cooperative advantage and otherwise profiting from direct contact. It has also left the Western firms in a more restricted position than have Common Market-type quotas. [80]

Another consequence of the new approach to technology imports may be modification in economic information control systems. The exchange of economic information has become part of the bilateral, government-to-government exchange program. The exchange of agricultural data, such as current and future crop forecasts, was a subject of summit agreements with Washington in June 1973. Data related to creditworthiness, such as hard currency indebtedness and gold stocks, have been the subject of considerable discussion. Successive presidents of the U.S. Export-Import Bank have stressed the necessity for Soviet disclosure of the information normal to a determination of creditworthiness. However, in spite of numerous discussions, no significant data has been provided. The formal agreement between the Export-Import Bank and the Foreign Trade Bank of April 1973 apparently did not require disclosure. Moreover, the formal and solemn agreement to provide agricultural data did not lead to disclosure, which makes it seem unlikely that there will be general disclosure of the more sensitive monetary data.

The reasons for lack of general disclosure may be traced to several sources: the continued legal barrier to disclosure of a wide range of economic data (the state secrecy laws); the lingering Soviet view that foreign knowledge of the inner workings of the Soviet economy, such as information on stocks of grain, petroleum, and gold, is intelligence information that might reveal strengths and vulnerabilities to a putative enemy; the apparent view of the leadership that availability of information and statistics represent mechanisms of control within the Soviet society; and the habit of secrecy. V. N. Starovskii, former head of the Central Statistical Agency, seemed to treat economic data more as a treasure to be guarded and stored than as a common property to be freely circulated. If he is truly a man of the Stalinist past, his successor may take a less restrictive view on data disclosure. [81]

Despite the Soviet penchant for secrecy, there have been marked changes or exceptions made for some foreign commercial arrangements. The economic and technological ties to the West that have been established in the 1970s require a more flexible attitude toward disclosure of economic information. For example, the Soviet desire to obtain equal and nondiscriminatory prices and credit terms may lead to more responsiveness to Western pressures for more specific information. On-site exploration of the West Siberian gas fields by Western firms was permitted, to allow them to make an objective assessment of the Siberian gas reserves.

The modified systems approach to technology transfer provides much more access to the Soviet economy. As Western companies become involved in the construction and design of projects, the supply of plants, and the distribution of products, the specific "need-to-know" within those particular branches of the economy increases. the FIAT relationship has become a long-term one, and it is likely that Italian specialists in Soviet auto production have become very knowledgeable about domestic Soviet economic matters that the general secrecy system usually proscribes. Moreover, companies such as McKinsey Management Consultants and Control Data Corporation, which provide advice and guidance on Western management techniques and computer applications, are likely to be given greater access to Soviet economic data. Perhaps management and computer consultation will provide a better basis for interpreting and understanding Soviet economic practices than the traditional sources of information and economic data. The intergovernmental exchange programs are another source of data exchange and disclosure. The information exchanged with Western colleagues on research and development in the USSR may be greater in many cases than that exchanged among research institutes within the USSR.

The implication of these foreign disclosures through specific private commercial and governmental channels is that the traditional general system of secrecy is being breached, however selectively and modestly. Certainly the Western corporations protecting industrial secrets or information that provide market advantage may be closed-mouthed and discrete; however, the specific disclosures are made largely in order to obtain more competitive terms and more efficient operations. The latter criteria for wider disclosure might become persuasive within the Soviet Union, especially as the old guard passes from the scene.

Modification of the Administration of Soviet Enterprises
with Western Technological Connections

Perhaps coincidentally with these expanding Western ties, some economic sectors appear to be exploring new administrative forms or variants of the old. What seems to be involved is a removal of these Western-connected enterprises from the traditional bureaucracy and relaxation of the old ministerial ties and of the control by the local Party organizations. The establishment of regional complexes and production associations is a part of this apparent new trend.

The regional complexes, such as the Tyumen petroleum complex, the West Siberian gas development, and the Baikal-Amur railroad development, appear to require considerable Western economic involvement and seem to be moving away from traditional lines of control. Referring to the regional complexes, a Soviet writer noted the following:

> They require a new approach to the creation of an organizational management mechanism, for their effective implementation requires the specific coordination of thousands of organizations and establishments. Such programs are not included within the limits of individual ministries and departments or territorial administrative organs; their management, i.e., the organization, coordination, and control of the joint activities of a large number of scattered enterprises and establishments, could be effective and rational only on the basis of a complex approach. [82]

The large regional complexes tend to upgrade the role of the central Party and governmental organs—the departments (otdel) of the CPSU Secretariat of the Central Committee, the Gosplan, and the Council of Ministers. More direct involvement of important ministries and Party leaders is characteristic of these projects. For example, Western corporate leaders have found that discussions with Brezhnev, Kosygin, and important ministers appear to be essential links in negotiation about industrial cooperation ventures. Moreover, the heads of departments in the Central Committee secretariats, such as Victor Bushuyev in chemicals, Vasily Frolov in machine building, Fedor Mochalin in light and food industry, and Fedor Kulakov in agriculture, may become more important if the roles of subordinate ministries and regional branches of the Party decrease. It is not surprising to find the latter officials arguing for the traditional bureaucratic approach of the past. [83]

Lev Vasiliev, general director of the Kama River truck complex, is reported to have special and high government and Party access. A Western writer commenting on Vasiliev's unique position noted the following:

> What is important is that the Russians seem finally to have got the point that industrial efficiency requires that a manager be given operating authority commensurate with his responsibilities. In the West this is traditional; in the U.S.S.R. it is almost revolutionary. [84]

The role of the local Party in industrial management has been the subject of considerable debate in recent years. According to Darrell P. Hammer, the Leningrad view, expressed by G. Romanov while he was Leningrad Party Secretary, was that the economic role of the Party organization should be enhanced. This would be accomplished by more economic training of the younger Party leaders. Romanov's call for more economic training is concerned with the economics of management rather than with engineering skills. He is said to have had more support among local and regional Party secretaries than among the central Party officials, who have less concern with emulating Western economic practices. In this sense Romanov's new emphasis on managerial over traditional engineering favors decentralized reform. That is, he advocates better-trained industrial managers and management-oriented local branches of the Party, operating within the traditional bureaucracy. [85]

The Party has some difficult problems in deciding whether the new Western-oriented complexes are to be given some autonomy from traditional ministerial and local Party direction and controlled more by the central government and Party organs. The training of local managers and Party officials, from the shop leaders up, would probably involve retraining several million people. Converting those trained as engineers, over half of whom are probably over 50 years old, into effective managers by modern management science criteria would be a formidable task. [86] Although the Romanov view seems to have merit, the short-run solution of removing the large Western-assisted complexes such as Tol'iatti and KamAZ from the control of local branches of the Party and traditional ministerial hierarchy seems to be more effective and expedient.

A third variant to the centralized approach, the decentralized upgrading of Party and managers, is a mixture. Some ministers, such as chemicals, have been strengthened—a "head" ministry approach—and some have been weakened, as in the centralization of the automotive industries. This would be a blend of the two variants: some more regional power to complexes, some more central control by the Central Committee.

To date the debates on organization and control are waged within the parameters of Soviet party guidelines acceptable to the leadership. The dominant position of the Party is not in question. The Leninist concept of democratic centralism is kept intact. Whether progressive forms of Western contacts and technology transfer can be contained within the traditional Party and governmental bureaucratic frameworks remains to be seen. The ripple effect of modest institutional change may lead to more profound substantive change, especially in the long run.

NOTES

1. John P. Hardt and George D. Holliday, U.S.-Soviet Commercial Relations: The Interplay of Economics, Technology Transfer, and Diplomacy, U.S., Congress House, Committee on Foreign Affairs, Subcommittee on National Security Policy and Scientific Developments, 93d Cong., 1st sess. (Washington, D.C.: Government Printing Office, 1973); U.S., Congress, Joint Economic Committee, Soviet Economic Prospects for the Seventies, 93d Cong., 1st sess. (Washington, D.C.: Government Printing Office, 1973, hereafter Soviet Economic Prospects for the Seventies). John P. Hardt, "Soviet Commercial Relations and Political Change," in The Interaction of Economics and Foreign Policy, ed. Robert A. Bauer (Charlottesville: University Press of Virginia, 1975, hereafter "Soviet Commercial Relations and Political Change").

2. Brezhnev speech on West German Television, Pravda, May 22, 1973; Philip Hanson, "Import of Technology" in The USSR Since the Fall of Khrushchev, ed. A. H. Brown and M. C. Kaser (London: Macmillian, 1972); N. K. Baibabkov, Gosudarstvennyi pyatiletnyi plan razvitiia narodnogo khoziaistva SSSR na 1971-1975 gody [State five-year plan for development of the USSR national economy for the period 1971-1975] (Moscow: Politizdat, 1972).

3. See Julian M. Cooper in Chapter 3 of this book.

4. Hardt, "Soviet Commercial Relations and Political Change," op. cit.

5. Abram Bergson, "Soviet Post-War Economic Development," Wicksell Lectures 1974 (Stockholm: Almqvist and Wiksell International, 1974); Stanley Cohn, "Economic Burden of Defense Expenditures," in Soviet Economic Prospects for the Seventies, op. cit., pp. 147-62. See also U.S., Congress, Joint Economic Committee, Soviet Economy in New Perspective, (Washington, D.C.: Government Printing Office, 1976).

6. John P. Hardt, "West Siberia: The Quest for Energy," Problems of Communism, April-May 1973, pp. 25-36; Planovoe khoziaistvo, no. 10 (1974), p. 52 ff.

7. "Directives for the Tenth Five-Year Plan," Pravda, December 14, 1975.

8. The FIAT-assisted Volga Automobile Plant in Tol'iatti, built during the eighth five-year plan, seems in some ways to be the most advanced example of the new approach. In retrospect, as noted below, it appears to be the forerunner of an approach to technology transfer that became more widely accepted during the ninth five-year plan.

9. V. Sushkov, "O torgovo-ekonomicheskom sotrudnichestve s kapitalisticheskom stranami v stroited'stve v SSSR krupnykh

promyshlennykh ob"ektov," Vneshniaia torgovlia, no. 2 (1976) pp.
8-11; N. P. Shmelyov, "Scope for Industrial, Scientific and Technical Cooperation between East and West," paper delivered at the International Economic Association Round Table in Dresden, German
Democratic Republic, 1976.

10.   Hardt, Soviet Commercial Relations and Political Change,
op. cit.

11.   Lewis M. Branscomb, "Science, Technology and Detente,"
Occasional Paper No. 17 (Washington, D.C.: George Washington
University, Program for Policy Studies, 1975).

12.   U.S., Congress, House, Committees on Aeronautics and
Technology, Background Materials on U.S.-U.S.S.R. Cooperative
Agreements in Science and Technology, 94th Cong. 1st sess. (Wash-
ington, D.C.: Government Printing Office, 1975).

13.   D. D. Mishustin, Vneshniaia torgovlia i industrializatsiia
SSSR (Moscow: Mezhdunarodnaia Kniga, 1935), p. 174.

14.   Imogene U. Edwards, "Automotive Trends in the U.S.S.R.,"
Soviet Economic Prospects for the Seventies, op. cit., p. 296.

15.   Chase World Information Corporation, KamAZ, the
Billion Dollar Beginning (New York: the Corporation, 1974).

16.   Antony C. Sutton. Western Technology and Soviet Economic
Development (3 vol., Stanford, Calif.: Hoover Institution Publications,
1968, 1971, 1973).

17.   Details of the contract are provided in Amtorg Trading
Corporation, Economic Review of the Soviet Union, July 1, 1929, pp.
230-31.

18.   L. Mertts et al., "Gaz i Ford," Planovoe khoziaistvo,
nos. 6-7 (1932), p. 258; V. Kasianenko, How Soviet Economy Won
Technical Independence (Moscow: Progress Publishers, 1966).

19.   Sutton, op. cit., vol. 1, p. 248.

20.   Amtorg Trading Corporation, Economic Review of the
Soviet Union, November 15, 1929, p. 378.

21.   Polina Aleshina, et al., Gor'kovskii avtomobil'nyi (Moscow: Profizdat, 1964), p. 20.

22.   Mertts et al., op. cit., p. 259.

23.   Amtorg, July 1, 1929, op. cit., p. 230.

24.   Charles E. Sorenson (with Samuel T. Williams), My Forty
Years with Ford (New York: Norton, 1956), p. 198.

25.   N. Osinskii, "Novyy 'Ford; v Amerikanskoi i nashei
obstanovki," Za rulem, nos. 9-10 (1932), p. 9.

26.   Mertts et al., op. cit. p. 239.

27.   Ibid., pp. 2160-2261.

28.   Sutton, op. cit., p. 247.

29.   U.S.S.R. Tsentral'noe staticheskoe upravlenie pri Sovete
Ministrov SSSR, Promyshlennost' SSSR; statisticheskii sbornik,
1957, p. 223.

30. Mertts et al., op. cit., p. 239.

31. David Granick, "Organization and Technology in Soviet Metalworking: Some Conditioning Factors," American Economic Review, 47, no. 2 (1957): 632.

32. E. A. Chudakov, "Problemy avtotransporta," Sotsialisticheskaia rekonstruktsiia i nauka, nos. 2-3 (1931), p. 154.

33. Ibid., p. 155.

34. E. A. Chudakov, "Razvitie dinamicheskikh kachestv avtomobilia," Sotsialisticheskaia rekonstruktsiia i nauka, no. 3 (1936), p. 34.

35. See, for example, Promyshlenno-ekonomicheskaia gazeta, February 3, 1957, and November 14, 1956, cited in Barney K. Schwalberg, "The Soviet Automotive Industry: A Current Assessment," Automotive Industries, January 1, 1958, p. 69.

36. N. Khartsiev and G. Bazylenko, "Kakie avtomobili nuzhny narodnomy khoziaistvu?" Pravda, May 18, 1965, p. 2; William P. Baxter, "The Soviet Passenger Car Industry," Survey 19 (1973): 228.

37. Ibid.

38. Nikita S. Khrushchev, speech to the 22nd congress of the Communist Party of the Soviet Union, October 17-31, 1961 (Moscow: Gosudarstvennoe izdatel'stvo politicheskoi literatury, 1962), p. 62.

39. V. Papkovskii, "Kakogo tipa legkovye avtomobili nam nuzhny," Kommunist, 36, No. 14, 1959, pp. 126-28.

40. Aleksei N. Kosygin, "Povyshenie nauchnoi obosnovannosti planov—vazhneishaia zadacha plannovykh organov," Planovoe khoziaistvo, no. 4 (1965), p. 6.

41. Ibid., pp. 9-10.

42. U. A. Zamozikin, L. N. Zhilina, and N. I. Frolova, "Sdvigi v massovom potreblenii i lichnost'," Voprosy filosofii 6 (1969): 33.

43. A. A. Anders, "Problems of the Automotive Industry for 1972 and the Development of New Automotive Technology," Avtomobil'naia promyshlennost', no. 1 (1972).

44. D. Velikanov, "Needs of National Economy in Technical Progress in Development of Motor Transport Facilities," Avtomobil'nyy transport, no. 11 (1974), translated by Joint Publications Research Service, USSR Trade and Services: the Service, 1975, pp. 25-26.

45. Some of the details of this contract are provided in Antony C. Sutton, Western Technology and Soviet Economic Development, 1945 to 1965. (Stanford: Hoover Institution Press, 1973), pp. 200-203; and V. Buffa, "Economic and Commercial Cooperation between East and West," draft of a speech, November 3, 1973, provided by Italian Embassy, Washington, D.C. (Buffa was in charge of FIAT's operations at Tol'iatti.)

46. "Why the Volga Automobile Plant's Production Schedule Has Been Disrupted," Radio Liberty Dispatch, November 8, 1972.

47. Sotsialisticheskaia industriia, September 10, 1975, p. 4.

48. Buffa, op. cit.

49. Ibid.

50. Edwards, op. cit., p. 296.

51. "Organizatsiia nauchno-tekhnicheskikh razrabotov na Vaze," Ekomika i organizatsii promyshlennogo proizvodstva, no. 1 (1976) p. 162.

52. Ibid., p. 296.

53. Izvestiia, December 18, 1974, p. 3.

54. Edwards, op. cit., p. 296.

55. Ibid,, p. 290.

56. Aron Katsenelinboigen, "Soviet Sciences and the Economists/Planners," paper delivered at the Workshop on Soviet Science and Technology sponsored by George Washington University and the National Science Foundation, Airlie House, Airlie, Virginia, November 18-21, 1976.

57. Izvestiia, March 3, 1974, p. 3.

58. Andreas Tenson, "Too Few Service Stations for Soviet Cars," Radio Liberty Dispatch, August 20, 1974.

59. Pravda, August 28, 1975, p. 2.

60. Business International, Eastern Europe Report, September 19, 1975, p. 266, and January 9, 1976, p. 5.

61. E. B. Golland, "Tekhnicheskaia snova vysokoi proizvoditel'nosti truda," Ekonomika i organizatsiia promyshleninogo proizvodstva, no. 1 (1976), pp. 84-86.

62. Donald E. Stingel, speech delivered at George Washington University, Washington, D.C., on February 25, 1975.

63. Ibid.

64. M. Troitskii, "Na novom etape," Novyi mir, no. 1 (1975), p. 177.

65. East-West Markets, January 27, 1975, p. 11.

66. Troitskii, op. cit., p. 176.

67. Peter Osnos, "The Soviets at Kama River: Big Complex, Big Problems," Washington Post, November 24, 1974, p. B-2; Donald Stingel, op. cit.

68. Some details of the KamAZ debate are given in Troitskii, op. cit., pp. 170-71 and 178-79.

69. Ibid., p. 178.

70. L. Bliakhman, "Glavnyi vyigrysh—vremia; zametki o problemakh uskoreniia nauchno-teknicheskogo progressa," Neva, no. 1 (1973), p. 173.

71. Edwards, op. cit., p. 309.

72. B. Mil'ner, "On the Organization of Management," Kommunist, no. 3 (1975), translated in Joint Publications Research Service 64452, April 1, 1975, p. 50.

73. See especially the introduction; Chapters 1, 2, and 9, and the Afterword of this book.

74. The nachal'niki are defined as a Soviet social group— "those in positions of authority and management whose main work is the control of men." Z. Katz, "Insights from Emigrés and Sociological Studies of the Soviet Economy," Soviet Economic Prospects for the Seventies, op. cit., pp. 101-102.

75. A multiplier effect of about three is suggested in several recent studies, including the econometric assessments of Donald Green and Herbert Levine, "Macro Econometric Evidence of the Value of Machinery Imports to the Soviet Union," in US-USSR Technological Interaction, ed. J. Thomas (Washington: National Science Foundation, forthcoming). Philip Hanson, "The Impact of Western Technology: A Case Study of the Soviet Mineral Fertilizer Industry" in East European Integration ed. Paul Marer and Montias (Bloomington, Ind.: University of Indiana Press, forthcoming).

76. See especially Hardt, Soviet Commercial Relations and Political Change, op. cit.

77. East-West Markets, June 1975.

78. Mil'ner, op. cit.

79. L. Brainard, "Soviet Foreign Trade Planning", in Soviet Economy in a New Perspective, (Washington, D.C.: Government Printing Office, 1976), pp. 695-708.

80. See Oleg Bogomolev's discussion paper of G. Haberler and John P. Hardt "Integration by Market Forces and Through Planning" at World Congress of International Economic Association, Budapest, Hungary, August 19-24, 1974.

81. V. G. Treml and John P. Hardt, ed. Soviet Economic Statistics (Durham: Duke University Press, 1972).

82. Mil'ner, op. cit.

83. Troitskii, op. cit.

84. Herbert E. Meyer, "A Plant that Could Change the Shape of Soviet Industry," Fortune, November 1974, p. 155; see John P. Hardt and T. Frankel, "The Industrial Managers," in eds. H. Gordon Skilling and Franklyn Griffiths, Interest Groups in Soviet Politics (Princeton: Princeton University Press, 1971), pp. 171-208.

85. Romanov was elevated to the Politburo in 1973. Darrell P. Hammer, "Brezhnev and the Communist Party," Soviet Union Vol. II, Part 1, 1975, pp. 8-12.

86. Hardt and Frankel, op. cit., pp. 198-208.

ECONOMIC DEVELOPMENT AND MODERNIZATION IN CONTEMPORARY CHINA: THE ATTEMPT TO LIMIT DEPENDENCE ON THE TRANSFER OF MODERN INDUSTRIAL TECHNOLOGY FROM ABROAD AND TO CONTROL ITS CORRUPTION OF THE MAOIST SOCIAL REVOLUTION
Robert F. Dernberger

INTRODUCTION

The Problem

Economic development is a primary goal of all societies, both communist and noncommunist. Regardless of the wide variety of cultural values, patterns of social behavior, ideological objectives and constraints, political and administrative institutional organizations, and even specific economic priorities to be found in these societies,

---

Due to space limitations and the comments of readers, this is a significantly revised and reduced version of the research paper, "The Resurgence of 'Chung-hsueh wei-t'i, Hsi-hsueh wei-yung' (Chinese learning for the fundamental principles, Western learning for practical application) in Contemporary China: The Transfer of Technology to the PRC," which I presented to the Conference on Technology and Communist Culture held at Bellagio, Italy, in August 1975. I wish to thank the participants in that conference, especially the discussants of my paper, for their many helpful comments.

All of the data cited in this chapter, unless otherwise noted, are taken from a 29-page statistical appendix prepared for the version of the paper presented at Bellagio. Unfortunately, limits of space do not permit the inclusion of the statistical appendix in this article. That statistical appendix, however, is used as the basis of a statistical analysis of China's machinery and equipment trade that is in preparation. Those readers who are interested in obtaining a copy of this appendix should write to the author.

the results of empirical research and theoretical reasoning by economists indicate that the accumulation and effective implementation of technological innovations is perhaps the most important and difficult of the necessary conditions for any successful economic development program. By definition, the developed countries are the repositories of advanced technology. The developing countries must rely to a significant extent on borrowing this technology in their efforts to achieve economic development.[1] Simon Kuznets states the argument clearly as follows:

> No matter where these technological and social innovations (i.e., those innovations which are the source of the "high rate of aggregate increase and of the high rate of structural shifts that characterize modern economies") emerge—and they are largely the product of the developing countries—the economic growth of any nation depends upon their adoption. In that sense, whatever the national affiliation of resources used, any single nation's economic growth has its base somewhere outside its boundaries.[2]

Historically this intercultural transfer of technology, a necessary component of modernization for the less-developed countries, has involved serious pernicious effects on the borrowing country's social and cultural system. How the Communist countries have coped with this problem and their success in doing so is a major theme of this volume.

Although seriously concerned with the historical tendency for borrowed technology to bring along with it the germs of undesirable social change, the Chinese communists argue that "national science and technology bear no class characteristics"; that is, whatever its origin, foreign technology can be useful in China's attempt to modernize, and it should be possible to sanitize the borrowed technology so it does not lead to undesired changes in the borrowing country's society.[3] The real danger is to be found in the unquestioned and slavish adoption of modern Western technology; the process of defusing its harmful effects lies in its careful adaptation to fit China's needs and environment. Mao's words are as follows:

> China has suffered a great deal from the mechanical absorption of foreign material. . . . We should assimilate whatever is useful to us today not only from the present-day socialist and new-democratic cultures but also from the earlier cultures of other nations. . . . We should not gulp any of this foreign material

down uncritically, but must treat it as we do our food—first chewing it, then submitting it to the workings of the stomach and intestines with their juices and secretions, and separating it into nutriment to be absorbed and waste matter to be discarded. [4]

The Chinese have encountered severe problems in their attempt to "digest" foreign technology and history tells us that previous attempts to separate the good from the bad in this manner have often lead to the demise of the would-be gourmets. In an allegorical argument remarkably similar to Mao's, but much less optimistic, Arnold J. Toynbee concludes as follows from his detailed study of contacts between civilizations:

The truth is that, if once the besieged have permitted even one isolated member of the besiegers' storming column to force his way inside their enceinte, their only remaining chance of saving their fortress from ultimately falling is to take the intruder prisoner before any of his eagerly following comrades-in-arms have had time to rejoin and reinforce the audacious pioneer. An intrusive alien culture-element cannot be purged of its dangerous capacity for attracting to itself other elements, of the same provenance, with which it was associated in its original cultural setting. The rash recipient's only chance of demagnetizing his formidable acquisition is to metabolize and assimulate it to a degree at which it becomes amenable to being worked into his native cultural pattern as an enrichment and not a dissolvent of the prevailing harmony. If the intrusive alien element succeeds in defeating the operation of its host's digestive system by retaining its magnetic alien quality after lodgement, the unhappy host will find himself condemned to look on helplessly while the defiantly intrusive culture-element behaves in his body social like a loose electron disintegrating an atom. [5]

In this chapter I shall show that the Chinese communists have relied rather heavily, despite policy statements to the contrary, on technology borrowed from abroad in their economic development efforts. Furthermore, they are well aware of the possible pernicious effects of this borrowed technology on the Maoist culture they are trying to create in China, and they have actively attempted to limit and neutralize these pernicious effects. I shall provide a tentative judgment about their possible success or failure in these efforts.

The specific organization of the chapter should be self-evident from the headings for each section. There will be a discussion of China's unique and unhappy experience in attempting to control the disruptive effects of modern technology on the indigenous culture in the pre-1949 period. Then there will be a summary review of post-1949 Chinese policy statements regarding the transfer of technology, followed by an analysis of the empirical record of their actual behavior in this regard over the past 25 years. A description and evaluation of contemporary Chinese attempts to insulate domestic efforts to achieve new socialist (that is, Maoist) behavioral attitudes and values from the corrupting effects of modern Western technology is then presented in the final sections of the chapter. [6]

A LESSON FROM HISTORY: THE FAILURE OF EARLIER MODERNIZERS TO INSULATE CHINA'S CULTURE AGAINST THE CORRUPTING EFFECTS OF MODERN INDUSTRIAL TECHNOLOGY

Whatever the outcome of the contemporary attempt by the Chinese Communists to digest foreign technology while avoiding any ill effects on their social body, they are well aware of the utter failure of an earlier generation of Chinese who tried to accomplish this same difficult task.

By the middle of the nineteenth century, the oldest and most stable cultural and political system in the world's history had begun to crumble. Responsible Chinese leaders, serving an alien rule, went through a considerable period of anguish and soul-searching in the attempt to save China's traditional culture and institutions. [7] These Chinese believed in the superiority of their cultural tradition but were forced to recognize, following a disastrous series of wars and "unequal" treaties, the superiority of Western technology and economic productivity. Thus the solution many of them believed possible was in the adoption of Western "things" to sustain and develop the Chinese "way of life." The popular slogan used to convey the argument was "Chung-hsueh wei-t'i, Hsi-hsueh wei-yung," which can be translated as "Chinese learning for the fundamental principles, Western learning for practical application."[8]

The efforts of these 19th century reformers were in vain. Not only did it prove most difficult to transplant Western technology, even on a limited scale, into an unmodified traditional Chinese cultural and institutional environment without greater official support than they had in these efforts, but these inexperienced indigenous efforts to introduce Western industry also were exposed to unrestrained foreign competition when China's domestic economy was finally opened to the forces of "imperialism."

The resulting foreign trade and investment were concentrated in a few major areas of China, but the capital inflow of gross private and public foreign investment between 1902 and 1930 totaled over 6 billion U.S. dollars. [9] Much of this foreign investment was directly related to the foreigners' trading activities and residential facilities (transportation, banking, public utilities, and real estate), and only 18 percent of the total was private direct investment in manufacturing. Thus the output of foreign-owned factories in 1931 accounted for less than one-third the total output of China's modern manufacturers.

Quite simply, although earlier reformers had been unable to preclude a Western economic invasion by developing their own domestic industrial base, indigenous entrepreneurs did emerge, especially after the revolution of 1911, and were able to hold their own in the face of foreign competition. [10] The important feature of this development, however, is not that the Chinese were able to learn from the Westerner and successfully begin their own indigenous industrialization, but that in doing so the borrowed Western technology brought with it its own complementary values and institutions, as follows:

> In the end, the remnants of the old China—its dress
> and manners, its classical written language and intri-
> cate system of imperial government, its reliance upon
> the extended family, the Confucian ethic, and all the
> other institutional achievements and cultural ornaments
> of a glorious past—had to be thrown into the melting
> pot and refashioned. The order was changed within the
> space of three generations. [11]

This experience of failure in trying to cope with the undesirable effects of foreign technology is an important part in the heritage of China's present leaders, who are in a significant sense the product of the early reformers' failures. According to Mao, "the Chinese learned a good deal from the West, but they could not make it work and were never able to realize their dreams." In other words, their digestive system was unable to absorb the nutriments and discard the waste matter. [12]

An important contributing reason for the failure of China's early reformers to achieve the objective of "Chung-hsueh wei-t'i, Hsi-hsueh wei-yung" was the Chinese government's inability to control the foreigners. [13] In the West the normal channels of trade and investment were the successful transmission belt for the foreigners' modern technology. Not only did the foreigners encounter limited resistance to their activities in host cultures with cultural, social and political environments similar to their own, but there often was an eager solicitation and acceptance of their activities.

In countries with alien cultures, however, the Western purveyors of modern technology encountered significant resistance. If the "limited aggression" implied by the Westerners' access to the economic and military superiority of their home countries did not succeed in creating a more friendly environment for their activities in the host countries, then this period of "limited aggression" often produced "open aggression" and colonization. Colonization made it possible for the Westerners to directly transplant not only their modern technology, but their own cultural, social, legal, and political institutions as well.

Given this traditional problem in the transfer of modern Western technology to the non-Western countries, why were Russia, Japan, and even the People's Republic of China relatively successful in coping with this problem, while traditional China was not? A brief review of these countries' experiences indicates that the role played by their governments was critical. Popular sentiment in all four cases would appear to have been strongly antiforeign, but unlike the case of traditional China, the governments in Russia, Japan, and the Peoples' Republic (1) actively pursued the objective of economic development, (2) recognized the need for and advantages of heavily borrowing foreign technology, and (3) effectively controlled and limited the activities of the foreigners within their economies. The fragile balance of control over domestic antiforeign sentiment with simultaneous heavy borrowing of technology from abroad via foreign trade has been one of the striking features of their economic development. In the case of Russia and Japan, this transfer of technology has been eminently successful; these two countries now rank as the second and third largest economies in the world.

It would be premature to claim that the Chinese have been successful, but their prospects for success are very good and their record of past success and expectations of future success owes a great deal to their practice of active borrowing of modern technology from abroad and their ability to control its impact on the domestic economy and society. The empirical record of their borrowing of modern technology from abroad and an evaluation of their attempts to control its impact on the domestic economy and society are presented in following portions of this chapter. First, however, it can be shown that despite their frequent arguments concerning the need for self-reliance in achieving economic development, Chinese economic development policy statements have always allowed for and even emphasized the equal importance of borrowing technology from abroad.

THE DOMINANT THEME OF SELF-RELIANCE
IN THE POLICY PRONOUNCEMENTS
OF CHINA'S CONTEMPORARY MODERNIZERS

Policy statements on economic development in China over the past 25 years can be compared to a great symphonic work. Self-reliance, the dominant theme, provides the basic framework and the ideological spirit of the piece; heavy reliance on borrowed technology, the minor theme, is an ever-present haunting tune in the background. By definition, the dominant theme is loudly emphasized at certain times, but the minor theme never completely disappears. In fact, at times it threatens to take over as the dominant theme. The merit of the work, however, is the intricate and ingenious weaving together of these two themes.

Thus, during some periods over the past 25 years, Chinese policy statements could be interpreted as calling for extreme self-reliance or autarky and, at other times, calling for heavy borrowing of foreign technology from abroad. Furthermore, the advocates of these two conflicting points of view have continued to fight over these differences in determining what particular policy should be adopted. Nonetheless, both a careful reading of their policy statements and an analysis of their actual behavior make it clear that, with the possible exception of the early 1950s, the Chinese communists have continuously followed a policy that represents a compromise: a policy of dual technological development. On the one hand there is the modern sector—the core of China's industrialization, consisting of large-scale, capital-intensive projects, relying heavily on imported technology. On the other hand, there is the rural, small-scale sector, which is very significant in both its contribution to total supply and to China's development potential. The Chinese recognize, however, that this rural industrial sector alone is not a sufficient condition for successful economic development, consisting as it does of smaller-scale, more labor-intensive projects that rely to a greater extent on indigenous technological innovations, which are mostly adaptations of technology available in the modern sector. Although at times they definitely appear to be separated in the thinking of the Chinese economic policy makers, and although Chinese economic development policy may place greater stress on one of these sectors at a particular time, there is considerable interaction between them. It is their emphasis on both sectors that represents, I believe, the evolution of a rational and wise approach to the economic development problem in China today. I shall return to a discussion of the distinction between these two sectors in the concluding section of this chapter.

As for the modern sector, however, three very representative and important examples of the Chinese appreciation of the need for and benefits to be derived from borrowing foreign technology can be cited here: the Chinese First Five-Year Plan, the three short essays by Mao that were required reading during the 1960s, and the authoritative statement on China's economic development policies published at the end of the 1960s.

The First Five-Year Plan (1953-57) represents the most explicit statement of the Chinese leaders' decisions about the means and objectives of China's economic development program following the restoration of the economy in 1952. The language of the plan itself is as follows:

> Our industrial capital construction plan which puts the main emphasis on heavy industry is designed to set our technically backward national economy onto the road of modern technology and lay an up-to-date technical foundation for our industry, agriculture and transport. To achieve this aim our plan of industrial capital construction provides for the establishment of new industries equipped with the most up-to-date technique, and for the similar reequipment of existing industries, step-by-step. This plan is the core of our Five-Year Plan, while the 156 projects which the Soviet Union is helping us to build are in their turn the core of our industrial construction plan. [14]

Following their open break with the Soviet Union in 1960 and their agreement that the unquestioned borrowing of the Soviet approach to economic development during the First Five-Year Plan period had been wrong, the Chinese leadership placed much greater emphasis on self-reliance in their public statements of economic policy. Nonetheless, throughout the last decade or so, the three most emphasized required readings from the works of Mao—the brief gospel for one-fourth of mankind—are "Serve the People" (September 1944); "The Foolish Old Man who Removed the Mountain" (June 1945); and "In Memory of Norman Bethune" (December 1939). These brief essays crystallize the three major "thought of Mao"; the socialist virtue of dedicating one's life to working for the people; the ability of the people to overcome any obstacle through self-reliance and sacrifice; and the life of Norman Bethune, a Canadian, as an excellent example of not adopting something new just because it is new, but also not ignoring the contributions modern technology (meaning technology brought by a foreigner) can make to China's future. Thus the "thoughts of Mao" stress both self-reliance and borrowed technology.

Finally, an article in the October 1969 issue of Hung Ch'i (Red Flag), entitled "China's Path of Socialist Industrialization," was the most explicit statement of China's economic policy in the period after the Cultural Revolution. [15] This article does indeed stress self-sufficiency as the proper means for achieving economic development. Nonetheless, as always, it admits that lessons can be learned from other countries and are desirable; it is the mere imitation of foreign technology that is wrong, and the Chinese must learn to rely on their own initiative in generating technological progress.

This simultaneous commitment to both rural, small-scale, "native" industries and urban, large-scale, modern industries is neither schizophrenic behavior nor dishonest propaganda. It is merely sound development policy for the central government of a country with scarce capital to tell the local authorities in underdeveloped rural areas to develop their areas by utilizing the resources and technology available to them in small-scale, labor-intensive industrial projects and not look to the central government for help while the central government is importing advanced technology for large-scale industrial projects in the urban, modern sector. [16]

This ability of China's leaders to conceptually separate these two sectors and advocate dissimilar technological policies in each is related, of course, to their ability to control the flow of technology borrowed from abroad and its utilization in China. In this regard, the institutional organization of the Chinese economy, as in other socialist economies, places considerable control in the hands of the central government. For all practical purposes, since the mid-1950s at least, all industrial enterprises in China are owned by the state and run by managers appointed by the state. [17] Investment in new industrial projects and the acquisition of new capital in existing enterprises on any significant scale are also controlled through the central budgetary process and require the explicit permission of central authorities, that is of the State Capital Construction Commission.

What foreign technology is obtained from abroad, and who uses it in China, are determined largely, at least in the first instance, by economic agencies directly under the control of the central government.

Although over the past 25 years the development policy of the Chinese has always combined elements of an effort to develop a domestic industrial sector built through their own efforts while simultaneously building a modern industrial sector incorporating technology imported from abroad, this dual industrial-sector development was made possible by the state's centralized control over the importation, distribution, and utilization of foreign technology. Changes in economic and in domestic or international political circumstances have resulted in episodic changes in emphasis from one aspect of this dual policy to the other.

For example, with the creation of the PRC in 1949, the continued success of the Chinese communists depended upon their rapid restoration and development of all industries, but especially the producer goods industries. Self-sufficiency was out of the question, as was the piecemeal grafting on of imports to the domestically produced supply of producer goods, given the magnitude of the new industrial capacity required and the time limit for acquiring it if the Chinese hoped to accomplish their goals of national security and industrialization. Thus, even during the period of recovery in 1950-52, the Chinese actively sought and obtained imports of complete and modern plants from their new Socialist allies. As pointed out earlier, these imports of complete plants were the core of the First Five-Year Plan for the industrialization of China in 1953-57. At the end of the plan period, due to their failure to achieve significant increases in agricultural production, as well as Mao's desire to speed up the pace of the socialist revolution, the Chinese adopted a new approach in their general attack on the economic development problem. [18]

Known as the Great Leap, this new policy emphasized reliance on the mass mobilization of China's rural labor force in county-sized political and economic units—commune—in a guerrilla-type effort not only to increase agricultural output but also to develop small-scale native industries throughout the countryside that would not rely on imports of modern technology, that is, of producer goods. Nonetheless, this new policy also called upon the Chinese to "walk-on-two-legs." Thus large-scale imports of complete plants continued as the Chinese also pursued the expansion of the modern industrial sector, signing agreements in late 1958 and early 1959 that called for additional Soviet deliveries of complete plants in the belief their new development policy had been successful.

By the end of 1959 the failure of the Great Leap became obvious to even the most optimistic of Mao's supporters. The severe agricultural crises of 1959 and 1960 greatly reduced the supply of inputs for industry. These shortages soon generated excess capacity in industry and, in addition, the domestic shortage of foodstuffs created a need for large-scale imports of foodstuffs in order to maintain a minimum standard of living for the Chinese. At the same time, China's foreign exchange earnings were rapidly declining due to the shortage of raw and processed agricultural products for export. Thus both the need for and ability to obtain imports of machinery and equipment, especially complete plants, declined sharply in 1961, regardless of the existing Chinese policy toward the transfer of technology from abroad or the unwillingness of the Soviet Union to supply complete plants to China after 1960.

There was a considerable time lag between the failure of the Great Leap and the adoption of a new economic policy to correct the consequences of that failure. A series of secret documents (articles) calling for specific readjustments in policy were finally issued in 1961 and were summarized in a speech by Chou En-lai in March 1962. These new policies called for a retrenchment in the pace of investment, while the priorities of the previous ten years were to be turned upside down, with agriculture (the foundation) to receive the highest priority in development. In regard to the transfer of technology, policy statements indicated that self-sufficiency was to be an essential principle.

Despite the emphasis given to self-sufficiency in policy statements, the new program of readjustment actually supported the continued borrowing of foreign technology from abroad. China's scientific and technological establishment was to be strengthened for the purpose of achieving the desired self-sufficiency, but the efforts of these scientists were to be rewarded and left relatively free from ideological pressures in their work. That is, emphasis was once more placed on their being experts, although lip service was paid to the desirability of being both "red and expert." This attempt to increase China's scientific and technological capacity, therefore, kept the door open for these scientists to acquire their expertise by borrowing foreign technology. In addition, imports of foreign technology by commodity trade were explicitly recognized as an important contribution to China's economic development.

As the level of domestic economic activity and investments in fixed industrial capital revived in the 1960s, the Maoists' hopes for the socialist transformation of Chinese society were becoming more and more frustrated. With the approval of guidelines in the "revisionist" economic program and the active encouragement of those administering that program, bourgeois tendencies stressing skills, increased income differentials, individualism, a vertical chain of authority and responsibility rather than group responsibility and decision making, enlargement of the market sector, and all the other complements of "economism" and "efficiency" became common features of China's economy. In an attempt to revive the goals of their continuous socialist revolution, the Cultural Revolution in 1966 and 1967 was an open confrontation between the followers of Mao and the Chinese "revisionists."[19]

As a result of this campaign, there was a significant change in China's policy in regard to the transfer of technology. The policy of self-sufficiency was emphasized to a much greater extent than previously; that is, it was more widely and frequently expressed as an operational rule in the short run, rather than as a guiding principle in the long run.

Discussions in the Chinese press during 1970 made it obvious that many of the several radical changes in economic policy that had been proclaimed following the Cultural Revolution either were being seriously reconsidered or had not been effectively carried out. [20] In any event, the economic developments of the early 1970s clearly indicated a return to the policies of the 1950s, at least in the area of transfer of technology. There was a renewal of the decision to strongly push for the simultaneous development of both rural, small-scale industry and modern, large-scale industry. In the 1970s, however, greater emphasis has been placed on the need for improvement in the level of technology utilized in the small-scale industries and for the creation of better ties to the modern industrial sector for this purpose. [21] The simultaneous development of these two types of industry is now proceeding in a much more integrated fashion than was true in the 1950s and early 1960s, when the small-scale industries were a more purely local and indigenous effort.

This most recent episode in China's policy regarding the transfer of technology provides strong support for the Chinese reaffirmation of the need for and desirability of large-scale borrowing of modern technology from abroad. As far as the emphasis on self-sufficiency is concerned, the growth of China's foreign trade in the 1970s has rapidly increased China's participation in the world market, to the point where China is currently the largest purchaser of modern technology among the less-developed countries of the world. [22]

This brief review of China's policy in the area of technology transfer clearly indicates that despite the repeated emphasis on self-sufficiency, the large-scale transfer of technology from abroad could easily be considered the dominant theme of that policy, except perhaps in the early 1960s, when economic conditions greatly reduced the need and ability of the Chinese to pursue that policy, and the late 1960s, when zealous Maoists temporarily gained control and began to implement a program of extreme self-sufficiency. This conclusion is made much more convincing by a review of the empirical record of the transfer of technology to China over the past 25 years, organized according to the episodic swings in emphasis in policy described above.

THE EMPIRICAL RECORD OF THE PAST 25 YEARS: LARGE-SCALE TRANSFERS OF MODERN TECHNOLOGY FROM ABROAD

The transfer of technology from abroad can accurately be described as including the entire range of contacts and intercourse between the two societies. Even when limited, however, to a few specific means of transmission such as publications, exhibitions, meetings, delegations, foreign experts, and training abroad, as well as the importation of technology by means of licensing agreements and/or imports of machinery and equipment embodying modern technology, the definition still remains too broad to allow for a meaningful analysis of the transfer of technology if the objective of that analysis is the identification and quantification of the specific causes and effects of the technology transferred. [23] Therefore, we chose to concentrate our analyses of the empirical record on the technology transfer involved in China's commodity trade, but strongly emphasize that the Chinese have relied on the other means for the transfer of technology to a considerable extent as well. [24]

Despite the importance of the means outside the commodity trade for transferring technology from abroad, a very strong case can be made for identifying the flow of technology embodied in imported producer goods in normal commodity trade as the major means by which the Chinese have obtained foreign technology over the past two decades. That argument can be summarized briefly, and I present it below, before turning to the quantitative analysis of this import of technology from abroad.

First of all, there is the conceptual basis for the argument: the contribution of modern technology to an economy's economic development and growth lies in its contribution to increasing the productivity of labor. For the most part, it only achieves this effect when it is embodied in the physical capital the labor works with in production. Thus, as some economists argue, there are very few disembodied technological innovations that contribute to increased output without a simultaneous adoption and use of modern physical capital. Rather than be treated as a separate source of increased production in the production function, technological innovation should enter as an increased value of the complementary physical inputs. [25]

Equally important with this conceptualization of the process is the actual extent to which the Chinese have relied upon this particular means of technology transfer over the past two decades. In 1952-73 China imported over $8 billion worth of machinery and equipment, accounting for more than one-fifth of China's total imports. In terms of domestic capital accumulation, these imports were over one-tenth of the total domestic supply of new machinery and equipment over these same two decades. In 1952-60, China's imports of machinery and equipment accounted for over one-third of total imports and over one-fourth of the total domestic supply of new machinery and equipment, compared with less than one-fifth and less than one-tenth, respectively, in the 1961-73 period. Nonetheless, after weathering the ill effects on their industrialization program of the

agricultural crisis at the beginning of the 1960s and those of the Cultural Revolution in the mid-1960s, imports of producer goods increased by approximately 40 percent a year between 1969 and 1973,
and in 1974 they reached the highest level of any year since 1949.

Even these impressive summary statistics for China's reliance
on imported technology by means of commodity imports fail to indicate the significance of these imports on China's economic development effort. These statistics treat one dollar's worth of imported
machinery and equipment embodying modern technology as if it were
equivalent to one dollar's worth of domestically produced machinery
and equipment; that is, they are additive to domestic supply on the
margin. Domestic and imported machinery and equipment are not
perfect substitutes for one another, however, and to the extent that
the imports are essential complements to the domestic supply in the
construction of domestic production facilities, China's inability to
acquire these imports would greatly reduce the productivity of the
domestically produced machines. China's development program
could well have suffered an irreparable setback for want of those
imported machines, which are included as a necessary component of
most modern factories; even most of the machines in those factories
were produced domestically. [26]

Table 1 traces China's transfer of technology, using commodity trade figures, through five successive stages between 1952
and 1973. Not all of these imports of machinery and equipment
represent embodied modern technology that the Chinese do not have
available domestically. They simply represent modern machinery
that the Chinese cannot produce in sufficient quantity domestically.
Nonetheless, they do embody modern technology, whether new to
China or not, and do increase the intensity of the impact this modern,
"foreign" technology has on Chinese social norms and behavior. This
is the third justification for concentrating on the Chinese borrowing
of foreign technology by means of commodity trade that has been
given in this chapter: the technological imperative of major concern
in this book results from the interaction of the Chinese labor force
with these imported machines. [27] It is through the use of these
machines in the production process that a society is pressured into
recognizing not only the tremendous contribution modern technology
can make to increased productivity, but also the necessity to create
and develop a host of complementary conditions so that this potential
contribution can be realized.

These necessary complementary conditions often involve
fundamental changes in a whole host of social and economic policies,
with a resulting change in social values and behavior. If they desire
to generate and implement their own modern technology, in their
educational system the Chinese must put significant emphasis on a

TABLE 1

Suggested Periodization of China's Transfer of Technology via Commodity Trade, 1952–73
(annual averages, absolute values in U.S. dollars)

Imports of Machinery and Transport Equipment	Transplants (1952–60)	Transition (1961)	Piecemeal Grafts (1962–66)	Hothouse Cultivation (1967–69)	Revival of Transplants (1970–73)
Total	540	272	220	261	550
Percent of total imports	35	18	14	14	18
Percent of total investment	27	17	8	6	7
From Communist Country X	501	246	123	126	236
Percent of China's total M of machinery and equipment	93	90	56	48	43
Percent of communist country total X to China	47	34	26	39	45
From Noncommunist Country X	39	26	99	136	314
Percent of China's total M of machinery and equipment	7	10	45	52	57
Percent of noncommunist country total X to China	8	3	9	9	12
Percents by largest communist suppliers					
USSR	56	40	26	8	12
Czechoslovakia	11	12	6	7	5
East Germany	15	19	9	12	8
Hungary	3	6	3	3	3
Poland	4	9	5	7	5
Rumania	3	3	5	12	10
Percents by largest noncommunist suppliers					
Japan	1*	—	12	14	21
France	1*	2	6	8	9
Great Britain	1*	2	10	5	5
West Germany	2*	1	8	11	6
Percent by all ten largest suppliers	97	94	90	87	84

*1955–60

Source: Summary of the annual data for "Chinese Imports of Machinery and Transportation Equipment, 1952–73," which is Table A1 in the statistical appendix given in the paper presented at Bellagio, Italy, in August 1975. Other tables included in the statistical appendix are Table A2: "Communist Country Supply of Complete Plants, 1950–73," Table A3: "List of 200 Complete Plant Projects in China Supplied by Socialist Countries," Table A4: "Commodity Composition of China's Imports of Machinery and Equipment from the Noncommunist Countries, 1961–73," Table A5: "China's Purchases of Complete Plants from the Noncommunist Countries, 1963," and Table A6: "Commodity Composition of China's Import Trade, 1928, 1950, and 1953–73," and Table A7: "Output of Selected Producer's Goods Industries in PRC."

238

wide range of scientific knowledge, most of which is devoid of any ideological content, since it is apolitical. To achieve progress in the acquisition, spread, and effective use of this knowledge, the knowledge and those who use it must become specialized. To obtain the effective implementation of modern technology, some system of material rewards must be introduced. To obtain its effective utilization, a hierarchical form of management with fixed responsibilities and authorities must be introduced with the necessary natural incentive differentials to go with these responsibilities and authorities. As for the work force that directly interacts with these modern machines in production, the need for regularity in use, maintenance, and care and the acquisition of manual skills naturally leads to worker discipline, job specialization, and wage differentials. Finally, the economies in scale, the large externalities to be gained from a cluster of producers who produce inputs for each other, and the high cost of the necessary social overhead capital for modern industry lead to the concentration of these factories in urban industrial centers.

Even though optimum efficiency does not appear to be one of China's top economic objectives, all of these forces are at work in contemporary Chinese society and bring modern technology into direct conflict with Maoist ideological goals. Thus the desire of China's leaders to integrate town and country and especially to narrow the difference in income between these two sectors, to elevate "reds" over "experts" as the elite class with decision-making power; to reduce income differences within the industrial labor force as far as possible; to foster group instead of individual responsibilities and job assignments; to make education "practical" and nonelitest, that is, not based on talent and ability but on social merit; and to generate and implement new technology and innovations from and by the masses instead of only among specialists—all are subject to the undermining forces unleashed by the use of modern technology. Thus, in concentrating on China's import of modern technology via commodity trade, we are emphasizing not only the most important source by which the Chinese borrowed modern technology but that source that sets loose the greatest counterproductive pressure in the form of modern technological imperatives on the social values and patterns of behavior the Chinese leaders are simultaneously pursuing in their attempt to transform Chinese society into their form of socialism.

In the final section of this chapter, I shall return to this topic and describe how the Chinese have tried to thwart these negative consequences of modern technology imported from abroad. In the remaining portions of this section I shall show that the level of these imports has been quite significant. The discussion is organized according to the episodic swings in emphasis in Chinese policy. However, our earlier argument should not be forgotten: over the past 25 years the most important feature of China's economic development policy has been the ever-present attempt to develop both sectors simultaneously.

The Wholesale Transplanting of Technology, 1950-60

In the first 11 years of their rule, the Chinese communists imported over \$5 billion of machinery and equipment (M&E). These imports, for the period as a whole, exhibited a growth that was faster than the growth in total imports. [28] This growth in M&E imports, rapid though it was, did not keep pace with the growth in domestic investment in machinery and equipment during the 1950s. [29] As a result, China's rate of self-sufficiency in machinery and equipment was increasing by approximately .5 percent each year in 1952-60.

The Western embargo on shipments of producer goods to China was fairly effective during the 1950s, with only 7 percent of China's M&E imports coming from these countries. [30] Despite the importance of these suppliers in filling the gaps in China's domestic supply on an item-by-item basis, they were but a trickle compared with China's M&E imports from the socialist countries. For example, Poland and Hungary, China's fourth- and fifth-largest suppliers in the socialist block, together provided China with more machinery and equipment during this period than did all the countries in the noncommunist world. The socialist countries as a whole supplied China with 13 times the amount of machinery and equipment supplied by the Western nonsocialist countries in the 1950s.

The data for the commodity composition of China's imports of machinery and equipment from these Socialist countries are limited, but enough are available to indicate that less than half of these imports were piecemeal or item-by-item M&E imports, [31] which would still leave the socialist bloc as China's major supplier of single-order machinery and equipment for filling the gap between domestic production and the needs of China's investment program during the 1950s.

The gap between domestic needs and supply created by China's investment program during the 1950s was not, however, met by the piecemeal importation of individual machine tools, electrical machinery, power equipment, and so on, but by the importation of complete plants. In the 1950s these complete plants, which made up more than 50 percent of their M&E exports to China, were the major

contribution to China of the socialist suppliers of machinery and
equipment, especially in regard to the transfer of technology.

Perhaps the best means to convey the importance of these complete plants is to quote from a Chinese book written for the purpose
of illustrating to the Chinese how important this contribution was in
their development efforts. Written at a time when expression of
such appreciation was still encouraged and directed specifically to
Soviet assistance, this book clearly identifies the crucial role the
Soviet Union and East Europeans played in transferring technology to
China by means of these complete plants, as follows:

> In regard to these enterprises, the Soviet Union renders
> assistance from beginning to end. In the process of the
> new construction or reconstruction of these industrial
> enterprises, from the collection of construction data,
> surveying, the clearing of the construction site, plan-
> ning, provision of necessary materials, management
> of construction and operation, training of technicians,
> and provision of necessary technical data and plans to
> the production of the new product, the Soviet Union com-
> pletely and systematically provides our country with sin-
> cere assistance. [32]

During the 1950s China probably imported over $2.5 billion
of complete plant projects, more than three-fourths of the total
being supplied by the Soviet Union. After the Sino-Soviet split in
1960, less than $50 billion dollars worth of complete plants was sent
to China from the Soviet Union. Fewer details are available concerning the 68 complete plants supplied by the East European members of the Soviet bloc during the 1950s. The information that is
available indicates that they were smaller than the projects supplied
by the Soviet Union and that they included several light industrial
projects.

Of the 11,000 Soviet technicians working in China during the
1950s, about half were estimated to have been directly involved in
the complete plant project. Over 25,000 Chinese technicians and
workers received training in the Soviet Union. [33] These personnel
and the work they did were obviously at the core of the technology
transfer process during the 1950s. The abrupt disruption of this
process in 1960 placed a severe strain on China's development efforts. The Chinese have not been able to reestablish a similar relationship with any single source of modern technology, at least not on
the same scale. Quite the contrary, their experiences with the Russians during the 1950s are used as arguments in their calls for self-

sufficiency and in their hesitancy and caution in accepting large numbers of foreign technicians to work in China, now that they are buying complete plants in the West.

Whatever the effect of the technological imperative on China's society since the early 1950s, it was certainly set loose by these complete plant imports and the foreign technicians who accompanied them, a massive attempt to transplant Soviet and East European modern production units onto Chinese soil. In addition to the magnitude of this technology transfer by commodity trade, however, its generation of the technological imperative was reinforced by the sectoral and geographical distribution of these complete plant projects.

The contrast with the waves of technology transfer to China before World War II is quite significant in this regard. The treaty port system that evolved during the 19th century limited the foreigners' residence and business activities to several ports along the coast and the navigable rivers. [34] Shanghai accounted for almost half the total direct foreign business investment in China, the remainder being Japanese and Russian investment in Manchuria. [35] This geographical concentration of foreign economic activity served to severely limit the points of contact between the foreign and domestic sector, and these contacts were restricted even further by the legal restrictions on the movement of foreigners.

The Chinese communists have also severely restricted and controlled foreigners' access to the domestic producers and consumers of China's exports and imports, but the significant difference between the pre-1949 period and the 1950s is the fact that while foreigners may not have had access to the internal economy in the 1950s, the producer goods they sold, which embodied modern technology, did have this access, and they had it on a large scale. Equally important was the significantly different sectoral and geographical distribution of these producer goods. Not only were the foreigners' residences and economic activity concentrated in the coastal treaty ports, especially Shanghai, but their direct investments, as noted earlier, were concentrated in activities associated with their residences and foreign trade businesses. Of the total of direct foreign investment in 1931, only 17 percent was in manufacturing. Even here the foreigners invested in activities closely associated with their foreign trade activities, which were connected with tobacco (an import substitute), cotton spinning mills (an import substitute), the processing of egg products for exports, shipbuilding, saw mills, and skin products. [36] In any event, an almost negligible share of the foreigners' total direct investments was in the producer goods sector.

A casual glance at the Chinese industrial investment program during the 1950s, which generated the large demand for imports of producer goods, and at the list of complete plant projects clearly shows the contrast between the 1950s and the pre-1949 period in the geographical and sectoral distribution of technology transfer via commodity trade. Of the total capital construction investment in industry during the First Five-Year Plan period (1953-57), over 75 percent was in enterprises under the Ministries of Heavy Industries, Fuel Industries, and Machine-building, while only 7 percent was in enterprises under the ministries of Textiles and Light Industry.[37]

As for the geographical distribution of fixed industrial capital during the 1950s, the traditionally developed regions still accounted for over two-thirds of the industrial capacity in China at the end of the 1950s.[38] The same can be said of the complete plant projects supplied from abroad, a large number being located in the traditionally industrialized Northwest and North coastal provinces. Nonetheless, very few of these complete plant projects were located in Shanghai, and even those were in the heavy industrial sector. Furthermore, those that were located in the interior were the key heavy industries in the development of new industrial centers.

The active search for the large-scale supply of this transplanted technology (from socialist countries), obtainable by commodity trade during the 1950s, changed dramatically after 1960 as a result of the open break between China and the Soviet Union and because of the domestic agricultural crises at the end of the 1950s and the resulting greater emphasis the Chinese placed on self-sufficiency during the 1960s.

The Transition Period, 1961

In a true sense the Chinese were without any active economic policy in 1961. They were merely trying to cope with the simultaneously interacting consequences of their break with the Soviet Union and the agricultural crises. The agricultural crises created excess capacity in industry and thus a significant reduction in the Chinese investment program because of a reduced demand for machinery and equipment. Both were necessary and sufficient explanations for the drastic decline in China's M&E imports from all foreign sources in 1961. Using simple correlation estimates, the changes in domestic fixed construction investment in 1958-62 can explain almost 100 percent of the variance in M&E imports over the same period.

These economic consequences of the agricultural crises alone would explain most of the decline in the level of M&E imports by two-thirds in 1961, although the Sino-Soviet split may well explain the somewhat larger than proportionate decline (almost 80 percent) in M&E imports from the Soviet Union, along with the slightly smaller

than proportionate declines in M&E imports from the East European
countries (slightly less than 50 percent). Even so, the Soviet Union
continued to be China's largest supplier of modern technology by
commodity trade, supplying 40 percent of China's M&E imports in
1961. The real impact of the Sino-Soviet split was the failure of
China's M&E imports from the Soviet Union to revive during the
1960s as China turned to other sources of supply, especially the
noncommunist countries.

Based on China's trade with the Soviet Union and Poland, the
only socialist-bloc countries for which detailed data are available for
1961, imports of complete plants—the major catalyst for the transfer
of technology by commodity trade during the 1950s—continued to
account for over 70 percent of China's M&E imports from the
socialist countries. Thus the import of complete plants continued to
play a dominant role in the transfer of technology by commodity
trade in 1961, although at a much lower level due to the major retrenchment in China's investment program.

Economic Revival and the Piecemeal Grafting of Foreign Technology onto the Chinese Stock, 1962–66

It is very difficult to determine the extent to which China's
development policies during the early 1960s were forced on the Chinese by the harsh dictates of the economic realities they faced or
were due to the advocacy of those in the leadership who championed
the cause of agricultural development, favored the Chinese consumer,
and promoted self-reliance. Whatever the cause, and both causes
reinforce each other, China's foreign trade in 1962–66 reflected a
significant reduction in the pace of investment in heavy industry and
in the importance of M&E imports, especially complete plant imports, in the domestic accumulation of fixed capital.

A close examination of the data, however, indicates that the
switch in emphasis to greater self-sufficiency was neither complete
nor stable during this period, growing considerably weaker as
China's economic revival gathered momentum. For example,
starting from their extreme lows of 1962–63, M&E imports were
increasing at an annual rate of more than 60 percent a year, much
faster than total imports and total domestic investment in machinery
and equipment. Thus, although it was still lower than during the
1950s, M&E imports were rapidly reestablishing their former position as China's dominant import commodity and were becoming a
more significant ingredient in China's domestic investment program.

The dynamics of China's import trade during the early 1960s, there-fore, indicate the policy of self-sufficiency; although it was actively being pursued, it was becoming less effective as time went on.

This argument is further supported when we look at the im-ports of complete plants. Following its break with the Soviet Union, China began shifting the direction of trade from the Soviet bloc to Western Europe and Japan. In 1961 China obtained 90 percent of its M&E imports from the socialist Countries, but by 1966 their share of China's M&E import market had declined to less than 50 percent. Not only were the Chinese shifting from the socialist countries to the Western industrial countries for imports of individual pieces of equipment and machinery to provide the necessary supplements and complements to their domestic production of machinery and equip-ment, but they were also shifting their orders for complete plants.

Between 1963 and 1966 the Chinese purchased 46 complete plants from firms in 10 West European countries and Japan. The total value of these purchases amounted to almost $.2 billion. The share of these imports of complete plants in total imports in 1962-66, of course, was much smaller than during the 1950s, just as the share of M&E imports was a smaller share of total imports and of total domestic investment in machinery and equipment. Nonetheless, this relatively aggressive acquisition of complete plant deliveries for the heavy industrial sector, many of which included provisions for the supply of Western technological information and for the training of Chinese technicians in the West, does not indicate that the Chinese had turned their backs on this vital method of acquiring modern technology.

After their split with the Soviet Union, self-sufficiency was an important slogan for the Chinese to use in order to mobilize their enforced indigenous assault on the economic development problem and to assert their position of independence in dealing with foreign-ers. Self-sufficiency did not operate to deny the very important past contribution of, or their continued need to rely upon, the borrowing of foreign technology.

Intensive Efforts at Self-Sufficiency, 1967–69

The Maoists' victory in the Cultural Revolution introduced a brief period when emphasis on self-reliance as an operational policy was at its greatest level of any period in the preceding 25 years. [39] In fact, in a meaningful way the Cultural Revolution itself can be seen as the Maoists' last stand against the technological im-peratives that had been generated in China's socialist revolution over the previous two decades. [40]

The seriousness of the campaign for self-sufficiency during this brief period can be seen in three major developments, two in the domestic economy and the third in the foreign trade sector. In the domestic economy, the rural, small-scale industries—the showpieces of China's self-sufficiency—were no longer to be isolated from the large-scale modern industries—the showpieces of transferred technology. Quite the contrary, the modern sector was now urged to serve and assist the small-scale sector in its acquisition of technology and training of the labor force. Thus these small-scale industries emerged from their status of a neglected and self-supporting stepchild of economic development to a key position in the acquisition and distribution of technology, foreign as well as indigenous, in China.

A second major institutional reform with significant implications for the transfer of technology and, especially, for China's ability to generate its own self-sufficient technological base was the drastic changes made in the educational system. In essence, formal disciplinary and elitest education was to be abandoned. Institutions of higher learning were ordered to suspend their operations in June 1966 and were not reopened until the latter part of 1970. The changes made in China's educational system in the interim were truly one of the most revolutionary social innovations in the 20th century. Basically, book learning and "useless" theory were out, and practical training came into command. While studying, students are expected to divide their time between reading and study in the classroom and practical experience and application in the field. The curriculum is designed to meet China's practical needs, and not the mere acquisition of impractical knowledge. The time spent in school has been reduced. Most of these reforms represent an attempt to make education an egalitarian exercise in learning how to produce.

Finally, the seriousness of the campaign for self-sufficiency during 1967-69, at least as far as the transfer of technology is involved, is revealed by the developments in China's foreign trade. M&E imports experienced a steady decline at an annual rate of more than 20 percent between 1966 and 1969. These declines continued after the economy had revived following the disruptions of the Cultural Revolution. Moreover, this rate of decrease led to a significant decline in the share of total imports accounted for by M&E imports. More important as a reflection of the self-sufficiency campaign, however, was the rapid decline in the share of imports in total domestic investment in machinery and equipment. This reached the lowest level for any year in the history of the People's Republic, with a rate of self-sufficiency of over 95 percent. The absolute level of M&E imports was so low in 1969, and the obvious downward trend so strong, that this result can only reflect the effectiveness of the policy of self-sufficiency that had been followed during the previous few years. With no new contracts for complete plants, a virtual absence of foreign technicians, an interruption in the flow of scientific journals received from abroad, a dwindling share of imports in the domestic investment program, and reform of the educational system, the most zealous Maoists had cause to hope that they could stem the perverse effects of the technological imperative.

The Chinese, however, were not yet capable in 1969 of providing their own modern technology, that is, of pursuing extreme self-sufficiency in their efforts to industrialize. The harsh dictates of reality, therefore, would force the Chinese to abandon self-sufficiency as an operational principle in the transfer of technology, and they soon revived their attempt to transplant foreign technology on a large scale when they rapidly increased the pace of the investment program in the early 1970s.

Reemergence of the Wholesale Transplanting,
1970-75

By the end of 1969 almost all of Mao's most outspoken opponents had been removed, and local, small-scale industries were accepted as a key to China's economic future. Nonetheless, the more moderate economic leaders remained in power, especially Chou En-lai and Li Hsien-nien, and others reemerged during the early 1970s. As one report notes, [41] a sort of "old-boy" network protected the modern industrial sector from attempts to make it completely subservient to the small-scale rural sector and from the repeated press attacks on the large investments and wastes involved in the past development of modern, large-scale industry. As the Chinese began work on the Fourth Five-Year Plan, scheduled to begin in 1971, pragmatism and a generally hardheaded attitude to development reappeared, with the result that the state attempted to gain greater centralized control over the economy, due to the realization that the rural industrial systems would compete directly with the modern sector for inputs of raw materials, capital, and trained labor. Thus, statements appeared in the Chinese press emphasizing that national needs would require the fulfilling of state targets in the modern sector before satisfying local demand and recognizing the state-owned and -supervised factories as "the economic lifeline of the state."[42] In short, the pendulum was swinging back toward the modern sector.

Thus the early 1970s saw the rapid increase in the level of investment and heavy industrial production in another round of rapid industrialization. It is unlikely that China's leaders adopted this new policy of rapid industrialization in the Fourth Five-Year Plan without knowing its implications concerning the borrowing of foreign technology. Rather, their pursuit of rapid industrialization was an explicit commitment, based on the lessons of the previous two decades, to a renewal of a policy of borrowing foreign technology on a large scale.[43] Thus, beginning in 1970, China's M&E imports increased rapidly, although the share of these imports in the total investment in machinery and equipment increased slowly due to the very rapid rate of increase in the domestic production of producer goods over the same period. In 1974 China's M&E imports reached their highest level in the history of the People's Republic.

Most of the rapid increase in M&E imports after 1969 came from the Western industrialized countries (the United Kingdom, the Federal Republic of Germany, France, and the United States) and Japan. China's M&E imports from the noncommunist countries increased in 1969-73 at a rate of 50 percent a year. Although Japan clearly emerged as China's dominant supplier of machinery and equipment during this period, a more significant development was the opening of trade between China and the United States, for the first time in over twenty years. The Chinese acted quickly to secure supplies of machinery and equipment from this new source.

Despite these rather surprising developments in the transfer of technology from the United States to China in the early 1970s—a transfer that had been prohibited by U.S. laws before 1971 and was still under rather stringent control by the U.S. government—the United States was only China's third-largest supplier of machinery and equipment in 1974 because of the equally surprising increase in China's imports from the Soviet Union. Quite simply, in the early 1970s China was rapidly increasing the transfer of technology by commodity trade from all sources, especially those sources most able to provide it, regardless of any political differences that might exist.[44] This is only another reflection of the influence of pragmatism or moderation among China's leaders in the early 1970s. In general, however, the socialist countries were losing out to China's Western suppliers as the major source of China's imports of technology by commodity trade.

The Western, noncommunist countries' replacement of the socialist countries as the dominant source of transferred technology by commodity trade in 1969-73 was not a continuous process but consisted of two distinct stages. In 1970 the Western noncommunist countries increased their share of China's M&E import market to 63 percent, from 46 percent in the previous year, due to the restoration of M&E imports to their previous peak level in 1966. This restoration did not rely extensively on the import of complete plants but was largely due to a very sizeable increase in transport equipment imports, especially trucks, and—to a lesser extent—to increases in metalworking machinery imports. Thus the revival of Western supplies of machinery would appear to be the reestablishing of the pre-Cultural Revolution pattern of piecemeal grafting on of Western supplies to fill in the gaps of China's domestic supply. No contracts had been signed by the Chinese with Western firms for the supply of complete plants in 1969, and none were signed in 1970 or 1971. Furthermore, once the pre-Cultural Revolution peak had been restored, the level of Western noncommunist country M&E exports to China remained relatively stable (1971-72); in 1972 the level of Western, noncommunist country M&E exports actually declined.

This decline in 1972, however, hides the emergence of the most startling and significant story in the transfer of technology to China in the history of the People's Republic. Beginning in 1972, the start of the second stage in the growing Sino-Western trade after 1969, the Chinese revealed their explicit decision to borrow foreign technology on a massive scale through the purchase of complete plants in the West. The volume of these imports in the 1970s is comparable to the flow of technology via complete plant projects imports in the 1950s. What is more important, however, is that the level of technology being transferred during the 1970s period of transplanting complete units of foreign technology is considerably more advanced than in the earlier period.

Both periods of massive technology transfer have played a vital role in China's economic development efforts. In the 1950s the socialist countries supplied China with much-needed technology in the basic industries (power, steel, mining, metallurgy, machine building, and so on) when China was faced with the need to restore and expand those industries at the core of the producer goods sector. In the 1970s, after the Chinese have accomplished a considerable expansion of those basic industries, the Western countries are supplying China with much-needed technology in what might be called "advanced" industrial sectors, such as the chemical industry. Another contrast between the two periods is the use of foreign technicians. The plants supplied by the socialist countries were accompanied by large numbers of technicians, but despite the much higher level of the technology involved, the Chinese are limiting the number and strictly controlling the activities of the foreign technicians assisting in the construction of the complete plants supplied by the West.

China began purchasing complete plants from the West in the fall of 1972 with the purchase of two thermoelectric power stations from Hitachi Ltd. (Japan), worth $16 million, and a chemical plant from Mitsui, Toatsu, and Toyo Engineering (Japan), worth $11 million. These relatively small purchases preceded a flood of major

contract negotiations in 1973. China purchased 32 chemical plants
and 5 electric power projects, worth $1.25 billion. In 1974 the Chi-
nese continued these large-scale purchases of chemical plants and
electric power stations, but they also signed several very large contracts for deliveries of a cold strip steel mill, a hot strip steel mill,
a silicon steel plating facility, and a continuous casting facility. The
value of the deliveries negotiated during 1974 was approximately $.9
billion. The volume of these purchases continued in 1975. Thus,
despite the often repeated emphasis on self-sufficiency and the actual
embodiment of that slogan in the development of rural, small-scale
industry throughout the countryside, as well as its significant role
in stemming the blind reliance on and copying of foreign models and
expertise, China has again emerged as one of the world's leading
borrowers of foreign technology.

MAO'S SOCIALIST CULTURAL REVOLUTION
AND THE CORRUPTING EFFECTS OF
MODERN, WESTERN INDUSTRIAL TECHNOLOGY

Imports of machinery and equipment, of course, are not the
sole means by which China borrows technology from abroad, and not
all these imports embody technology that is newly introduced in
China. Since the early 1960s, however, these imports have been the
principal carriers that in some areas introduced, and in other areas
reinforced, the germ of the technological imperative associated with
the disease of modern industrialization. Thus far in this chapter my
purpose has been to present and analyze the statistical evidence to
show that the Chinese communists have actively and willingly engaged in this form of technological transfer on a large scale, despite
the emphasis given to self-sufficiency in their policy statements.
Although the principle of self-sufficiency did emerge as a dominant
element in China's operational economic policy in the latter half of
the 1960s, the volume of China's transfer of technology by commodity trade during the 1950s and in the 1970s must rank among the
largest such efforts in the world's history.
    This attempt to describe the means by which foreign technology
was transferred to China and an indication of the magnitude of that
transfer was the major assignment I accepted in agreeing to write
this chapter—that is, an attempt to disprove or at least balance the
popular belief that China's economic development effort was representative of an autarkic development policy with very limited
dependence on modern technology borrowed from abroad. In this
concluding section, however, I desire to specifically address myself
to the central question in this volume, which is the compatability of

modern industrial technology with the communist cultural values in China. There are three major reasons why I believe it is useful to include this discussion here in my chapter.

Reactions against the Technological Imperative

The first of these reasons is that a failure to present an explicit statement on the extent to which the transfer of modern industrial technology from abroad has corrupted Mao's socialist, cultural revolution may imply a conclusion from the arguments already presented that I believe to be wrong. Quite simply, if my efforts in the preceding sections of the chapter have been to argue that the Chinese have relied very heavily on borrowed technology in their industrialization program over the past 25 years, a reasonable reader could easily conclude that this large-scale borrowing implies the corollary large-scale corruption of the Maoist socialist, cultural revolution.

Whatever the validity of the technological imperative in other societies, the massive and ever-growing flow of technology from abroad has presented the Chinese leaders with a serious dilemma. Faced with their own inability to provide the necessary technology and with the role of that technology as a necessary condition for successful industrialization, their hopes for immediate success have left them little choice but to import this technology from abroad by commodity trade and on a large scale. Their unhappy experience with the borrowing of Western technology during an earlier period in history; their status in 1949 as leaders of an inferior economic power that had to rely on foreign assistance; and their program of social change, that which called for the rejection of almost all the implications of the technological imperative generated by modern foreign technology, created serious conflicts within the leadership that have erupted into the open periodically over the last 25 years.

For example, the technological imperatives set loose and reinforced by the transfer of modern technology led to a reaction that found its focus in the Cultural Revolution; however, the need for modern technology in the process of industrialization worked to erode the extreme position of self-sufficiency that was a result of the Cultural Revolution. Once again, the transfer of technology by commodity trade is being carried out on a massive scale, once more raising the serious question of whether or not the technological imperatives of this borrowed technology can be absorbed and controlled by China's leaders. The important point to be made here, however, is that the renewed decision to engage in the transfer of modern industrial technology on a massive scale in the 1970s does not simultaneously imply the abandonment or failure of the Maoist socialist, cultural goals. Although they recognize the many contradictions that exist between the technological imperatives of that technology and those goals, the cohabitation and interdependence of this technological borrowing and social revolution is a key feature of contemporary China. Thus I do not believe that the presently available evidence enables us to use China's experience over the past 25 years to support any particular answer to the central question in this volume; the attempt to make modern industrial technology and Maoist socialist culture consistent is being carried out with great intensity at the present time.

Richard Baum's Evaluation from Observations in Urban Areas

This brings me to the second major reason for including a discussion of the impact of modern industrial technology on Chinese society in this article, the inclusion in this volume of Richard Baum's chapter on technological development and social change in Chinese industry, which strongly argues that this attempt has failed in China. Based on his reading of the Chinese press and his observations during a recent visit to factories in the modern, urban industrial sector in China, Baum believes that the technological imperatives of modern industrial technology have indeed had their hypothesized effect in China. Material incentives or wage differences based on skills, and management and worker assignments with specialization and specific lines of responsibility and authority—all the characteristics of Western industrial activity that the Maoists attacked as indicative of the restoration of capitalism or socialist revisionism in the early 1960s have reemerged as the dominant characteristics of Chinese industry in the 1970s. Even if correct, Baum's conclusions are specifically restricted to the large-scale, modern, urban industrial sector, which is the direct recipient and user of imported machinery and equipment and the modern technology it embodies. That sector, however, is a relatively small segment of China's total society. [45]

My Own Evaluation from Observations in Rural Areas

During my own visit to China in the summer of 1975, when I visited over 50 rural, small-scale factories in the countryside—the countryside is the heartland of the Maoist socialist, cultural revolution and the bulk of China's population—I became convinced of the clear-cut distinction that exists between the rural, small-scale industrial sector and the urban, large-scale industrial sector in the economic development policies of China's leaders. [46] Nonetheless, the distinction made between these two sectors is not made on the basis of the scale or technology utilized, as will be explained below, but on the different degree to which an attempt is being made to neutralize or contain the impact of the technological imperative upon the goals of the Maoist socialist, cultural revolution. This recent personal experience in observing what I believe to be a unique and explicit attempt to cope with the undesirable effects of the technological imperatives of modern technology in a socialist culture—the major theme of this book—is the third and most important reason that I have included a discussion of the topic in this chapter.

The Chinese obviously have appreciated the need for the large-scale borrowing of modern industrial technology from abroad if the industrialization, that is, the socialist revolution, in China is to succeed. This technology is transferred largely by means of imports of machinery and equipment, and these imports are almost exclusively destined for the urban, modern, large-scale industrial sector, located in a relatively limited number of urban centers and employing a relatively small segment of the total labor force. The Chinese define the modern, large-scale industrial sector as those industries owned and operated by the central government, the provincial governments, or the municipalities, regardless of their scales of operations or the technology utilized. Thus the direct effects of the technological imperatives are felt in the most isolated, smallest, and most directly controlled industrial sector in the economy.

The rural, small-scale industrial sector is defined as all industry owned by the counties, communes, brigades, and production teams, that is, by the lowest units in the government and economy. Again, this is regardless of their sizes of operations or the technology utilized. [47] Obviously it is true that the rural, small-scale industries are somewhat smaller, on the average, and utilize less modern technology than the modern, large-scale industries. Nonetheless, we were startled to learn that these rural, small-scale industries, especially those owned by the county government (and these were the dominant type in this sector in terms of employment and output) could not be described as small-scale in an absolute sense and were utilizing relatively modern technology on a considerable scale. The showpiece crude workshop, with a few workers using a few crude hand tools or simple machines to produce elementary agricultural implements, still exists. Probably these workshops were more typical of the small-scale industrial sector in its formative days during the late 1950s, however. On the other hand, the county-run factory that employs between 250 and 500 employees and uses modern machinery and equipment is very representative of rural, small-scale industry in China in the late 1970s.

If both sectors tend to utilize modern technology, how then does the distinction made between the urban, large-scale sector and the rural, small-scale sector serve any purpose in the attempt to weaken the negative effect of the technological imperative of modern technology on the Maoist socialist, cultural revolution during the course of China's modernization? For one thing, a major feature of the distinction made between these two sectors is the "nationality" of the modern technology they use. The presence of imported modern industrial technology is quite obvious in the modern, large-scale sector. This sector is the direct recipient and user of the imported machinery and equipment, which embodies the modern technology and clearly displays a foreign name plate. Once borrowed, however, this same technology is supplied to the rural, small-scale sector embodied in a "Chinese"-made machine, either carrying a nameplate from a factory in China's ever-growing modern, large-scale industrial sector or produced by one of the well-equipped machine shops in the rural, small-scale industrial sector itself, having been produced according to blueprints supplied by a national or provincial design bureau. This is the real meaning and common use of the term "we built it ourselves," which is frequently heard in China today; this machine was made in China, or perhaps in the same province or county, and even more frequently today, in the same plant. Rarely if ever did our delegation encounter a foreign-made piece of machinery or equipment in the rural, small-scale factories we visited.

The "nationalization" of the modern technology before its introduction into the rural, small-scale industries may serve to increase the rural labor forces' receptivity to modern technology and their pride and efforts to develop the local industrial capacity to supply local needs for cement, electric power, iron and steel, nitrogenous fertilizer, agricultural implements, and consumer goods; but this "nationalization" does not remove the technological imperatives associated with the modern technology. In other words, the engineering characteristics of the technology are without nationality. Rather, it is the use of that technology or the social organization of the work place in which it is used that differs from nationality to nationality.

Those who believe that static efficiency in its narrow economic definition is a necessary and absolute objective of modernization would of course argue that there is only one "best" way to utilize this modern technology, and that would be the way it was designed to be used in the Western industrialized countries.[48] Presumably if the technological imperative is a valid concept at all, it is the economic gains of this one "best" way to use this modern technology that force a society to give in to the technological imperatives and accept the "inevitable" need for material incentives and income

differences related to technical skill levels, these skills being
apolitical and based on a classless rationality of cause and effect.
This "best" way entails recognition of the increases in productivity
that come from the ever-increasing specialization in both machine
use and operator tasks; the creation of a hierarchy of individual
responsibility in decision making, also related to technical expertise;
and integrated placement of machines and workers so as to enable the
production process to be coordinated in a continuous flow, that is,
serial production on an assembly line.

It is in this area that the rural, small-scale industrial sector
in China represents a unique approach to industrialization, despite
the use of modern industrial technology. Even in the area of social
organization of the work place, however, the differences between the
urban, large-scale industrial sector and the rural, small-scale
sector are more a matter of degree than of form. For example,
material incentives and money wages are also utilized in the rural,
small-scale industrial sector, which commonly employs the same
eight-grade wage system as is used in the urban, large-scale industrial sector. At the same time, however, the rural, small-scale
sector employs some temporary employees, especially in the com-
munal and brigade factories and workshops. These employees are
paid in work points, receiving a share of the collective units of income along with those who work in the fields. In addition, these
temporary workers in the factories also work in the fields during
peak seasons of planting and harvesting. Thus the income received
by these peasant-factory workers does not differ greatly from the
normal distribution of income to other members of the collective
unit.

The permanent labor force employed in the county-run factories in the rural small-scale industrial sector are paid differential
wages according to the eight-grade wage scale. One gets the impression, however, that the major differences in wages in Chinese
factories in both the large-scale and the small-scale sectors are
due as much to age and experience as to skill differences. In addition, the variations in the distribution of wages would appear to be
decreasing over time, especially in recent years. Many of the rural,
small-scale factories we visited had eliminated the lower wage
grades and were reducing the relative number of workers in the highest
grades through the normal process of retirements, along with limitations on promotions. If this procedure were to become widespread
in the rural, small-scale industrial sector, income differences due
to skill differences would become insignificant even if the eight-
grade wage system were to remain in existence. Furthermore, considerable debate continues at all levels in China about why the Chinese need to use the eight-grade wage system within industry and

also why there is a need for a difference between the income paid to
the factory worker and that paid to a peasant. This problem has become even more important as the local units in the countryside are
creating their own industrial factories and transferring some of the
peasants to work in those factories. Thus the question, Why should
those transferred be paid more income? In other words, the problem is far from being solved, despite the continued existence of differential wages related to skill differences in the rural, small-scale
industrial sector. The technological imperative of the modern technology used in that sector has not eliminated the Maoist attempt to
pursue its socialist, cultural goals. At least not yet, anyway.

The practice in regard to specialization in job assignments
varies widely in the rural, small-scale industrial sector, but the
use of machinery and workers in a wide variety of tasks rather than
for specific assignments is rather common. Not only are individual
machines and workers shifted from task to task, but workers and
machines are frequently grouped as a team and the team assigned
first one task then another without much specialization within the
team. Finally, even the entire factory will often devote its efforts to
producing first one product, such as tractors, and then switch to the
production of another, such as water pumps. [49] In short, repeated
and continuous production of a single item, or the assignment of
workers and machines to specific tasks for long periods of time, is
not very common in many of the rural, small-scale factories. Quite
the opposite, this lack of assembly line production processes means
that a large amount of time is spent in merely setting work up on the
machines in a job lot fashion and moving the work from machine to
machine by hand. Despite the reduction in efficiency from this lack
of causes for specialization in regard to the production of any one
particular good, these factories are very versatile in their ability to
produce a wide variety of products for the local area, which is one
of their major objectives. Thus this failure to push specialization
very far may be due not only to their attempt to eliminate the technological imperatives of the modern technology being used, but it
may be a necessary feature of the output mix these plants are designed to produce.

The above remarks are directly related to those rural, small-
scale factories that do not produce a standard product on a continuous basis. Although the difference was much more noticeable in
these plants, the work effort was also much less specialized, intensive, and continuous in the other Chinese factories we visited than
it is in comparable Western factories. In other words, although they
work with similar machines and technology, the work assignments,
work attitudes, and work behavior of typical Chinese workers, especially those in the rural, small-scale sector, are substantially

different from those of their Western counterparts. The Western
workers' experience has been described as a reduction to a simple
cog in a mammoth and complex machine; this is definitely not applicable to the Chinese worker in the rural, small-scale sector, and due
to the organization of work in the factories, it is unlikely to become
applicable in the near future.

The social organization of work is perhaps the greatest distinction between industries, especially the rural, small-scale industries,
in China and those in the Western industrialized societies. This distinction is obviously one of the most important means by which the
Maoists hope to thwart the negative impact of the technological imperative on their socialist, cultural revolution. [50] Managerial and technical decisions are still largely the responsibility of those possessing
the requisite skills. Nonetheless, these decisions are the subject of
considerable discussion among the workers and are implemented
with a significant degree of worker participation. In formal organizational terms, this popular participation is provided for by the many
committees appointed for this very purpose, from the Revolutionary
Committee at the top, which is responsible for running the factory,
down to the shop-level committees for safety, innovation, and so on.
The important aspect of the degree of popular participation in decision making and implementation in these rural, small-scale factories, however, is not the system of worker representation on these
committees or the actual decision-making power held by the workers,
inasmuch as this aspect of the workers' participation is undoubtedly
rather limited. Far more important and impressive is the average
worker's rather extensive and detailed knowledge about, involvement
in, and concern for the various different social, political, and
economic activities of the factory. This in itself must be considered
as one of the important goals in the Maoist socialist, cultural revolution.

The extent to which these various Maoist policies are being
implemented in the rural, small-scale industries in China undoubtedly varies greatly from place to place. Nonetheless, the existence of
these policies and the extent to which they are carried out cannot be
denied. They add up to an active campaign specifically designed to
eliminate the technological imperative of the modern industrial technology of the Western industrialized countries, as that technology is
being introduced and used in China's rural, small-scale industrial
sector. Furthermore, this campaign continues to be an important
element in China's economic development policy even though Mao
himself has gone to meet Marx and four of the prominent radical
leaders have been purged. Whether or not these policies—the
greater equalization of wages, the downgrading of economic status
and decision-making power associated with technical skills, the

reduction in emphasis on job specialization and serial production in favor of teamwork and job lot production, and the greater involvement of the average worker in the total activities of the factory—will realize Mao's vision of a modernized society utilizing modern Western industrial technology and enjoying a socialist culture of social, political, and economic equality, that is, whether or not these two objectives can coexist or, as Mao believed, can reinforce each other, must await the outcome of the present experiment in China. I believe that the presently available evidence is insufficient to allow for conclusions of either success or failure. Furthermore, the hypotheses of a technological imperative would be a logical necessity, if it were a necessity at all, only for those societies in which short-run static efficiency is a very important objective. Otherwise, a host of alternative socialist organizations, values, and behavior, including the Maoist socialist, cultural revolution, would appear to be potentially compatible with modern industrial technology. The Maoists, at least, believe this to be the case, and based on my visit to over 50 rural, small-scale industries in June–July 1975, I see no evidence that they will give up their attempt to achieve their objective. They would argue, and their argument is a logical one, that only by achieving the objectives of the Maoist socialist, cultural revolution can the Chinese achieve true long-run economic efficiency in the use of Western industrial technology to achieve their socialist goals. Whether their argument is realistic remains to be seen.

NOTES

1. China is a most unique example of this flow of technology from the "advanced" to the "backward" societies. At one point in history, China was the most advanced or developed nation in the world and Europeans "borrowed" from the Chinese treasure chest of inventions. After contributing to the world's stock of technology in the premodern period, however, the Chinese entered the modern period as an underdeveloped country without a modern technological base. Borrowing R. H. Tawney's excellent way of capturing this unique phenomenon, China's peasants "ploughed with iron when Europe used wood, and continued to plough with it when Europe used steel." R. H. Tawney, Land and Labor in China (Boston: Beacon Press, 1966), p. 11.

2. Simon Kuznets, Modern Economic Growth: Rate, Structure, and Spread (New Haven and London: Yale University Press, 1966), p. 287.

3. The phrase quoted in the text comes from a serious discussion of science and technology contained in several articles pub-

lished in Hung Ch'i (Red Flag) in October and November of 1962. For our purposes here, an even more appropriate quote from these articles is, "Thus, the point is not whether we need or do not need to learn good things from foreign countries, but how to learn them." Hung Ch'i, no. 20 (Oct. 16, 1962), p. 4.

4. Selected Works of Mao Tse-tung (1967 edition), Vol. 2, p. 380.

5. Arnold J. Toynbee, Contacts between Civilizations in Space, vol. 8 in A Study of History (New York: Oxford University Press, 1963), pp. 548-49.

6. For my earlier attempts to deal with the question of the transfer of technology to China, the reader should see Robert F. Dernberger, "The Role of the Foreigner in China's Economic Development: 1840-1949," in The Chinese Economy in Historical Perspective, ed. Dwight Perkins (Stanford, Calif.: Stanford University Press, 1975), pp. 19-47; and Robert F. Dernberger, "The Transfer of Technology to China," Asia Quarterly, 1973-74, pp. 229-52.

7. For an excellent survey of "the way in which the scholar-official class of China" tried to "take action to preserve their own culture and their political and social institutions," see Teng Ssu-yü and John K. Fairbank, China's Response to the West (Cambridge: Harvard University Press, 1954).

8. Three of the most famous reformers who preached and practiced this slogan were Tseng Kuo-fan (1811-72), Ling Hung-chang (1832-1901), and Chang Chih-tung (1837-1909). The Kiangnan Arsenal, founded jointly by Tseng and Li in 1861, can be considered the first Western-style factory in China. Although they differed on the definition of the Chinese culture to be saved by borrowing the fruits of Western technology for the "self strengthening" of that culture, the two most notable descendants of these earlier reformers were Chiang Kai-shek and Mao Tse-tung.

9. Unless otherwise noted, these statistics and those in the immediately following paragraphs are from Robert F. Dernberger, "The Role of the Foreigner," op. cit.

10. This is the consensus emerging from recent attempts to reexamine the received argument that the forces of imperialism completely killed off nascent attempts by the Chinese to industrialize. See Chi-ming Hou, Foreign Investment and Economic Development in China (Cambridge: Harvard University Press, 1965); John K. Chang, Industrial Development in Pre-Communist China, (Chicago: Aldine, 1969); Robert F. Dernberger, "The Role of the Foreigner," op. cit.; and Bruce Reynolds, "The Impact of Trade and Foreign Investment on Industrialization: Chinese Textiles, 1875-1931" (Ph.D. diss., University of Michigan, 1975).

11. Teng and Fairbank, op. cit., p. 1.

12. Quote from Mao Tse-tung, On the People's Democratic Dictatorship.

13. The following argument is put forward here as a tentative hypothesis of why some cultures are able to absorb foreign technology more readily and with less ruinous effects on their indigenous cultures and institutions than others. The argument was first suggested to me by Simon Kuznets.

14. First Five-Year Plan for Development of The National Economy of The People's Republic of China in 1953-1957 (Peking: Foreign Languages Press, 1956), p. 38.

15. This article drew heavily from two of Mao's works written in the mid-1950s, "On Ten Major Relationships" and "On the Correct Handling of Contradictions among the People."

16. For example, even when telling the workers and peasants to rely on their own devices in the "native" sector, the Chinese leaders point out the obstacles to using these same techniques in the modern sector and the need to continue to rely on modern technology in the modern sector. See report, New China News Agency (NCNA), May 11, 1963, and in Hsin Chien-she (New Construction), no. 1-2 (1966).

17. I use the phrase "for all practical purposes" because there have been several different forms of ownership in effect and different types of management formats employed over the past two decades. Nonetheless, the conclusion that the state (that is, political authorities at various levels) owns and manages industrial enterprises in China is a valid one, especially for the purpose of this chapter.

18. For a discussion of the economic factors contributing to the need for adopting a new approach to China's economic development problem in 1957-58, see Robert F. Dernberger, "Foreign Trade, Innovation and Economic Growth in Communist China," in China in Crisis, ed. Tsou Tang and Ping-ti Ho (Chicago: University of Chicago Press, 1968), vol. 1, book 2, pp. 739-52.

19. There is a voluminous literature on the Cultural Revolution, but for an interpretation of the economic issues involved, see Robert F. Dernberger, "Radical Ideology and Economic Development in China: The Cultural Revolution and Its Impact on the Economy," Asian Survey 12, no. 12, (1972): 1048-65.

20. "The fact that . . . traditional institutions and attitudes continued to flourish despite the drastic measures instituted by Mao in 1966 to purify the nation, must have been a bitter blow." Leo Goodstadt, China's Search for Plenty: The Economics of Mao Tse-Tung (New York: Weatherhill, 1973), pp. 202-203. "In retrospect, the Cultural Revolution demonstrated that the economic society developed under the Communists in China since 1949 had sunk fairly

strong roots. In spite of the political turbulence during the Cultural
Revolution, the institutional organs in the economy continued to function. . . . Mao and his radical cohorts never were disposed to, or
perhaps never able to, push the Cultural Revolution beyond a certain
state of disruption. Towards the end the sting had gone out of their
blows, and their initiatives met almost universal resistance." Arthur
G. Ashbrook, Jr., "China: Economic Policy and Economic Results,
1949-71," in People's Republic of China: An Economic Assessment,
a compendium of papers submitted to U.S., Congress, Joint Economic Committee (Washington, D.C.: Government Printing Office, 1972),
p. 30.

  21. See Jon Sigurdson, "Rural Industry—A Traveller's View,"
China Quarterly, no. 50 (April-June 1972), pp. 315-32, and his
forthcoming monograph on the technology of China's small-scale industries.

  22. This is my own judgment, based on the fact that China's
import trade ranks seventeenth in the world, ahead of all the other
less-developed countries except for Spain and Brazil, and the fact
that one-fifth of China's imports consists of machinery and equipment.

  23. "Sometimes, the concept [transfer of technology] is so
loosely defined as to be analytically nearly useless." Charles Cooper,
"The Mechanisms for Transfer of Technology from Advanced to
Developing Countries," (mimeographed, Science Policy Research
Unit, University of Sussex, 1970), p. 1.

  24. The version of the paper delivered at Bellagio included a
detailed discussion of China's importation and dissemination of
Western and East European technical books and journals, industrial
exhibitions held in China by Western and East European industrial
countries, China's participation in the research activities of the
socialist bloc's Council of Mutual Economic Assistance as an
"observer" member, the Soviet and East European scientists and
technicians who were assigned to work and teach in China during the
1950s, the technical data and designs those countries supplied to
China, and the Chinese sent abroad for study and training. Limitations of space have required the exclusion of that discussion from
this chapter.

  25. This adjustment of the value of the physical inputs would
not just apply to the machinery and equipment used, but would also
apply to the value of labor, to the extent that labor acquired greater
skills.

  26. Elsewhere, using a very simple economic model with
fixed coefficients, assuming that domestic production was a perfect
substitution for imports and restricting the analysis to the First
Five-Year Plan period (1953-57), for which sufficient data is available, I have estimated that the loss China would have suffered if

denied these imports of machinery and equipment would have been a 20 to 30 percent reduction in its official rate of growth. Using a similar model, Alexander Eckstein estimated that the loss would have been a 20 to 50 percent reduction in China's estimated rate of growth. Robert F. Dernberger, "The Foreign Trade and Capital Movements of Communist China," (Ph. D. diss., Harvard University, 1965). Alexander Eckstein, Communist China's Growth and Foreign Trade (New York: McGraw-Hill, 1966), pp. 123-24.

27.　Inasmuch as this book is devoted to the technological imperative resulting from borrowed technology in the socialist societies, it is necessary to emphasize here that this result is effected mainly by the interaction of the indigenous society with the imported producer goods, which embody the foreign technology. Nonetheless, it is important not to overlook the much more significant technological imperative at work in these societies due to the entire program of modernization and industrialization adopted in these countries, regardless of what particular modern engineering technology is borrowed from abroad, from whom, and how or whether or not the producer goods embodying that "borrowed" foreign technology are produced domestically or abroad.

28.　The annual rate of growth of M&E imports was 18.3 percent in 1952-60, while the rate of growth of total imports was 9.7 percent.

29.　The annual rate of growth of investment in machinery and equipment was 24.3 percent in 1952-60.

30.　The largest market share attained by the Western industrialized countries during the 1950s (1952-60) was in 1957, when supplies from these sources accounted for 12 percent of the total.

31.　This is based on a sample, admittedly biased, of the commodity trade returns for the Soviet Union in 1952-60, Hungary in 1952-59, and Poland in 1958-60.

32.　Huang Chen-ming and Huang Jun-t'eng, The Extraordinary Sino-Soviet Peoples Friendship Looked at from the Standpoint of Sino-Soviet Cooperation (Peking: Finance and Economics Publishers, 1956). The quotations in the following paragraphs are taken from my typed translation of the original in Chinese.

33.　Chu-yuan Cheng, Scientific and Engineering Manpower in Communist China (Washington: Government Printing Office, 1965) pp. 194 and 196.

34.　A more extensive discussion of the geographical and sectoral concentration of foreigners' economic activities in the pre-1949 period is presented in Robert F. Dernberger, "The Role of the Foreigner in China's Economic Development: 1840-1949," in China's Modern Economy in Historical Perspective, ed. Dwight Perkins (Stanford, Calif.: Stanford University Press, 1975), pp. 19-47.

35. C. F. Remer, Foreign Investments in China (New York: Howard Fertig, 1968) p. 97.

36. Remer, op. cit., p. 86. A paper could be written on the technological imperative set loose by the substitution of machine-spun for hand-spun yarn in China's cloth weaving industry, a technological imperative that led to tremendous economic and social unrest in China's countryside.

37. Chu-yuan Cheng, China's Allocation of Fixed Capital Investment, 1952-1957, Michigan Papers in Chinese Studies, no. 17 (Ann Arbor: Center for Chinese Studies, University of Michigan, 1974), p. 48.

38. Yuan-li Wu, The Spatial Economy of Communist China (New York: Hoover Institution Publications, Praeger, 1967), Chapter 3.

39. For a brief but good discussion and interpretation of the events in the Cultural Revolution, see William Hinton, Turning Point in China, (New York: Modern Reader, 1972).

40. Almost every reform or institutional change ensuing from the Maoists' victory in the Cultural Revolution can be readily identified as an attack on a particular result of the way these technological imperatives were working to thwart the continuing socialist revolution. More will be said concerning this point in the concluding sections of this chapter.

41. "China Economy," in Far Eastern Economic Review, 1971 Yearbook, pp. 137-39.

42. For a very good analysis of the many press reports during 1969, 1970, and 1971 concerning the very subtle tug of war between the advocates of the rural, small-scale sector and the advocates of the modern industrial sector, see Leo Goodstadt, China's Search for Plenty, op. cit., Chapter 9.

43. The decision to renew their search for modern technology was also intertwined with the almost simultaneous decision to seek improved political and economic relations with the United States.

44. Ranking China's major sources of machinery and equipment during the early 1970s according to the increase in those imports between 1969 and 1973 yields the following results. The increase from the United States (the third largest) was infinite, since the United States did not trade with China in 1969; from Great Britain (fifth) there was more than a tenfold increase; from the USSR (second) the increase was 350 percent; from Japan (first), it was 300 percent; from Bulgaria (tenth), 300 percent; from France (sixth), 300 percent; from West Germany (seventh), 250 percent; from Poland (tenth), 150 percent; from Romania (fourth), 150 percent; from East Germany (seventh), 67 percent; and from Czechoslovakia (ninth), 50 percent.

45. The limited statistical evidence (estimates) available for the 1960s indicates that the urban population was less than 15 percent of China's total population, while factory employment itself accounted for less than 3 percent of the total.

46. I visited China for four weeks during June 1975 as a member of the Delegation on Rural, Small-Scale Industry. The report of that delegation will be published as a monograph in the near future. Many of the points made on the following pages are discussed at greater length in this forthcoming monograph.

47. Jon Sigurdson estimates that the rural, small-scale industrial sector includes approximately .5 million plants, accounting for approximately one-half of the total employment in industry and mining in China. See Jon Sigurdson, "Rural Industrialization in China, " in China: A Reassessment of the Economy, a compendium of papers submitted to U.S., Congress, Joint Economic Committee, (Washington, D.C.: Government Printing Office, 1975), pp. 411-35.

48. For example, many of those who use factor productivity comparisons to compare countries by their economic success implicitly, or even explicitly, assume that there is one most-efficient technology in existence, that it is available to all economies, and that it has one "best" use throughout the world.

49. Those rural, small-scale factories that produced such standard items as cement and nitrogenous fertilizer did utilize a technology that required a continuous production process; that is, there was constant input at one end of the process and constant output of a final product at the other. Our observations during our visit to these plants, however, indicated that they had considerable down time: they were producing at considerably less than full capacity, compared to similar factories in the urban, large-scale sector. In addition, it is reported that in a few cases factories producing standard products such as cement or nitrogenous fertilizer in the rural, small-scale sector have been converted to production of new and completely different products. Presumably this has occurred when a cheaper source of the original product has been introduced in the vicinity.

50. The discussion in this paragraph touches on one of the most important features of the Maoist socialist, cultural revolution and one of the reasons why Mao labeled the Russian Revolution as having become revisionist. This feature is the primary importance of the relations in production rather than of the ownership of the means of production and the productive forces themselves in carrying out the true transformation to socialism. In other words, the revolution would fail if the state were to replace the capitalist and carry on business as usual. What is essential is the creation of equality in status and material rewards for the workers, technicians, and bosses in the work place.

CHAPTER

6

MASS INNOVATION AND COMMUNIST CULTURE: THE SOVIET AND CHINESE CASES
Rensselaer W. Lee, III

Soviet and Chinese communist managerial doctrines share a commitment to broadly based participation in technical problem-solving within the industrial enterprise. The commitment, as such, is not unique to these countries (or to communist as opposed to other systems): enterprise managers in the West, including the United States, have adopted various schemes to encourage basic-level employees to suggest ways of improving or rationalizing production. What is significant about the Soviet and PRC cases, however, is the extent to which nonspecialist or mass participation in technical change-producing activity has been linked to goals articulated by the

─────────────

The Soviet part of this chapter is largely based on a year's research in Moscow in 1973-74, supported by the International Research and Exchanges Board. The host institution in Moscow was the Moscow Institute of Railway Engineers. Special thanks go to G. A. Platonov, G. V. Ashin, and G. S. Gudozhnik of the institute for helping to provide a stimulating framework for research and discussion.

While in Moscow I interviewed people at the following enter-prises and institutions: the Likhachov auto works, the Lenin Komso-mol (Moskvitch) auto works, the Lyublino casting-mechanical plant, the Perovo locomotive repair plant, the All-Union Society of Inven-tors and Rationalizers, and the State Committee on Inventions and Discoveries.

Preparation of this chapter was facilitated by an American Council of Learned Societies-Social Science Research Council Grant in Soviet Studies for the academic year 1975-76.

political elite. A major objective of this paper is to analyze this
linkage in the People's Republic of China and the USSR and compare
the effects of ideology upon the organization of technical innovation
at the enterprise level, as well as the constraints placed on ideology
by specific patterns and circumstances of technological development.

The argument presented in this chapter will draw most heavily
upon Soviet materials gathered in the course of a year's research in
Moscow, which means that the weight of the comparison will be on
the Soviet side. There are two main reasons for this decision. First,
the Soviet concept of mass innovation antedates by many years that
of the People's Republic. By all indications, it served as a starting
point for PRC development. Second, Soviet source materials in this
area are highly differentiated. They deal with problems of technical
creativity from economic, technical, legal, and sociological as well
as ideological standpoints. The PRC materials, by contrast, tend to
be heavily ideological in their orientation, reflecting both the PRC
"campaign" approach to technical modernization and also the fact
that technical policy has been an area of bitter and protracted conflict between Mao and his rivals within the Chinese Communist Party.

In the light of these considerations, this chapter will be organized along the following lines: The first and major section (from the
point of view of original research) will discuss several important
dimensions of mass technical creativity in the USSR: its technical
significance, its legal-administrative context, its relation to extrabureaucratic or "social" control functions in Soviet society, and its
significance in terms of Soviet ideological goals. The second section
of the paper will evaluate the Soviet contribution to PRC concepts of
mass innovation and analyze the evaluation of these concepts in
light of the patterns of technical and cultural development adopted
by the People's Republic after 1958. Scarcity of data on technical
trends, administrative systems, and "social" organizations in China
makes comparisons with the Soviet Union in these areas somewhat
difficult. While the PRC equivalents, or the lack of them, will be
discussed wherever possible, the major aim of this section will be
to identify similarities and differences in the PRC and Soviet ways
of linking ideology and innovation and from this to draw some general
conclusions regarding the nature of "communist culture" in the two
societies.

THE SOVIET CASE

Mass Innovation and Communist Technical Rationality

Broadly based participation in technical problem-solving is an
explicit and long-standing political commitment of the Soviet regime.
This commitment was already apparent in the late 1920s—a period

that saw the formal recognition, in Soviet law, of a sphere of technical creativity that was likely to be accessible to the ordinary factory worker. This sphere included ideas that did not qualify as inventions, but were only "novel" in terms of the enterprises or branches in which they originated. Compared to inventions, these ideas tended to involve relatively minor changes in products or technical processes. [1] In modern Soviet terminology such ideas are called "rationalization proposals" and are praised both for their mass character and for their cumulative technical importance. As a 1975 article remarks, "Rationalization, as distinct from invention, participation in which requires special training, is the most mass form of creativity. Technical creativity of the masses—that is the basis on which is realized the reconstruction of production. "[2]

Mass innovation in the USSR is a multidimensional concept— one that embodies legal, social, and ideological as well as technical principles. To the extent that it serves purposes and involves agencies that are external to the technical-administrative components of the productive system, it may be seen as a form of "communist" technical rationality.

The political context of Soviet innovation is reflected in several areas. One of these is the broad (by Western standards) coverage of invention legislation, specifically its extension to include rationalization measures, which means useful but unpatentable technical ideas. Soviet legislation provides two main guarantees for would-be rationalizers: the right to a hearing from the factory administration on their technical suggestions and the right to rewards for proposals that create measurable economic advantages for the enterprise. The law, in fact, is fairly explicit, defining a time limit for examining technical claims and establishing a scale of reward based on the percentage of yearly savings created by the innovation. [3] An outgrowth of this legislation, moreover, has been the establishment in many Soviet enterprises of an institution that is relatively unique by Western standards—a full-time staff capability for handling the administrative work connected with innovation. This institution, known as the BRIZ (Bureau of Rationalization and Invention), is responsible for organizing the movement of proposals through the factory hierarchy for decision, implementation, and calculation of reward. In law and in administration, in other words, the Soviets have made a strong formal commitment to protect the authors of "minor" innovations that do not meet the technical standards of invention. Such a commitment is clearly political in nature, and hence broader in scope than the enterprise-specific employee incentive programs of Western countries.

A second manifestation of "Communist technical rationality" lies in the realm of what might be called "social control"—use of "extrabureaucratic" (and extralegal) agencies to promote mass in-

novation and to assure the flow and implementation of technical
novelty within Soviet industry. Social control, which is the responsibility of the party and the trade unions, represents partly a reaction
against "bureaucratism," that is, against instances of apathy or
resistance on the part of the technical-managerial elites toward the
introduction of new technical solutions. It represents an attempt to
place "on social foundations" those functions related to innovation
that cannot be adequately performed by the technical-administrative
staffs of the enterprises. Viewed in these terms, social control is
"an appendix and corrective to the system of state planning," a kind
of internal (to the enterprise) substitute for market mechanisms in
stimulating technical change. [4] On a more political level, however,
it is designed to mobilize mass participation in the technical sphere
and, by implication, to ensure some degree of control by the Party
and the trade unions over the processes of technical innovation in
Soviet industry.

The third, and possibly the most explicit example of communist technical rationality in the sphere of innovation is the linkage, in
Soviet thought, of creative labor to the ideological "goal culture"—
to the normative order that reflects the legitimating political values
of the Soviet regime. Mass technical creativity is hailed as a vehicle
for creating the outlines of the future communist society, a society
in which social distinctions between intellectual elites and manual
laborers have been abolished and in which the productive process is
dominated by a new type of individual, the "worker intellectual."
The Soviets, however, also view the transition to communist society
as contingent on changes in the technical system of production—
specifically on the advance of automation in industry. Hence, while
official promotion of mass participation does contribute to the "unification of mental and manual labor," in the eyes of many Soviet
scholars it is not the only or even the decisive determinant of this
process in the long run. Rather, mass innovation is seen as a
limited effort to reduce social class differences within the constraints created by the technical system at each stage of development.

That the mass innovation concept is an expression of "Communist technical rationality" seems beyond doubt; implicit in the
concept, however, is a technical as well as a social or political
dimension. This dimension, however, is elusive. Most Soviet
writers agree that rationalization is distinct from the creation of
new technology, since it is designed to "improve the use of new
equipment" and to "raise the effectiveness of obsolescent equipment." [5] Moreover, it is obvious from published statistics that the
savings created by the average rationalization proposal (RP) are
only about 850 rubles per year, or less than one-tenth of the savings

created by the average invention. For workers' proposals, that is, for those in which engineering-technical personnel have no authorship role, the figure for a rationalization is less: between 100 and 500 rubles per year. [6]

Critics of rationalization argue that by prolonging the life of obsolescent machinery it tends to divert energy from substantive technical solutions (inventions) and in general to slow down the pace of innovation in the economy. [7] Moreover, they argue that the practical value of rationalization may be outweighed by the administrative costs involved in processing proposals. This argument finds expression in efforts to remove some categories of "minor" proposals from coverage under Soviet law. Such efforts have been partly successful; prior to 1973, "organizational" improvements, such as changes in the division of labor, were covered under Soviet law, but since then they have been excluded. [8]

Possibly the most significant argument of the critics, however, is that rationalization activity has positive effects on enterprise performance, it actually reflects the "low technical culture" of many enterprises. As one writer notes, rationalization is largely the "rectification of an ordinary engineering mistake in design or technology." Hence its practical value does not denote technical progress in the real sense of the term. Rationalization, in other words, is symbiotically related to engineering failures—an argument that implies that its targets are more often new than obsolescent machinery and equipment.

The empirical work of Soviet sociologists tends to confirm this argument. Various studies show that rationalization activity is inversely proportional to the period of functioning of new technology. An especially large number of proposals are submitted when a new machine or automatic line is introduced, but after debugging "it becomes harder ultimately to notice the need to modernize one or another assembly and to propose ultimately how to improve it. "[9]

This argument is crucial to the understanding of Soviet technological innovation and of "communist technical rationality" as well. It illustrates a frequent tendency in Soviet R&D to overlook designing errors in earlier phases of the innovation cycle, passing these on until they finally appear in the actual end use of a new product or process. Such a tendency is compatible with the regime's insistence on worker participation in technical problem solving.

The technical dimension of mass innovation is a fascinating subject in itself; a detailed exploration of it would be an important contribution to the study of technological change in communist states. The focus of the research reflected in the Bellagio Conference papers, however, is on the interface between technology and communist culture; therefore the following pages are designed to highlight the political and social elements of "communist technical rationality, " rather than the technical elements. The former, however, cannot be examined in isolation from the technical-administrative context of the Soviet factory. The study, accordingly, will try to provide a partly empirical approach to the analysis of mass innovation and will emphasize three themes: the implementation of authorship rights in the factory context, the role and effectiveness of "social control" agencies within the enterprise, and the relationship of mass technical creativity to Soviet ideological goals and also to the imperatives of technological change.

Authorship and Administration in the Enterprise

As a mass form of technical creativity, the Soviet concept of rationalization reflects an inherent conflict between authorship rights and bureaucratic practice. As a legal entity, rationalization implies recognition of and, where utility is confirmed, reward for creative effort. Translated into bureaucratic terms, however, it represents a series of decisions that encompasses the entire "life cycle" of a technical innovation, from formulation to final realization in production. Innovation, in other words, is a collective enterprise, and in the Soviet factory context it represents a chain of technical and administrative dependency.

The articulation of a new technical idea often requires different or complementary skills. The common Soviet claim that innovation fosters the unification of "mental and manual labor, " for example, partly reflects the worker-rationalizer's reliance upon the engineer to make drawings and technical calculations. In another, broader sense, the collective nature of technical novelty is embodied in the entire assemblage of factory services that participate, in one way or another, in the examination and evaluation of proposals. It involves not only workers and engineers, but also administrators, economists, and even bookkeepers. [10] Virtually all innovation proposals travel a rather carefully defined route through the factory, a route that involves at least the following stages: registration, examination, introduction, and calculation of author's reward, as well as a number of bureaucratic checkpoints or "instantsii. " The number of checkpoints varies according to several factors: the technical complexity of the idea, the skills and resources available to individual shops, and the allocation of managerial authority within the enterprise. Some proposals are realized almost entirely within the confines of the shop, while others require what is virtually a factorywide effort, involving the approval and cooperation of several shops as well as factory-level technical and economic services. [11]

Authorship rights are circumscribed by organizational relations that determine the success or failure of technical novelties. This is a constant source of conflict within Soviet enterprise. Two broad areas of conflict are apparent, one involving the decisional sequences that comprise the life cycle of a new technical idea and the other involving the parameters of authorship within the innovation process. In practice these areas may overlap (as will be shown below), although they are legally distinct in terms of the formal mechanisms provided for conflict resolution.

Conflicts over the organizational processing of proposals generally derive from: (1) administrative delays in the examination or, following acceptance, in the implementation of proposals; (2) underpayment or delayed payment of authors' rewards; or (3) unfair (from the author's point of view) rejection of a technical idea. In such cases authors do not normally serve as their own advocates before the factory administrations; in Soviet law and political practice this role is assigned to the Party and the mass organizations, particularly the trade unions. Trade union affiliates are the most active extrabureaucratic "watchdogs" over the organizational life cycles of proposals, ensuring timely passage through the instantsii and accurate calculation of authors' rewards and reviewing technical suggestions that are initially rejected by the administration. The advocacy functions of these bodies will be discussed in more detail in the next section of this paper; it suffices to say here that the tension between authorship rights and bureaucratic imperatives is a source of roles and practices not ordinarily seen in Western enterprises.

Authorship conflicts center on the definition of creativity within the total innovation process and are truly the bane of Soviet technical management. In theory such disputes are subject to review by the courts, but in practice they are largely self-resolving—in ways that may violate the rights of the "real" inventors or rationalizers but that often succeed in getting the task of innovation accomplished. This trade-off is known in Soviet literature as the "coauthorship craze" and deserves special attention in the contexts of "conflict resolution" and of the practical organizational arrangements that accompany technical change within the Soviet factory. [12]

Problems of authorship arise to the extent that innovation is a collective product, that is, usually when the innovator cannot formulate and realize a technical proposal on his own. On the technical level the innovator needs an engineer to provide drawings and mathematical calculations and other workers to help in "embodiment in metal." On an administrative level the innovator needs the instantsii to examine and approve the proposal, authorize facilities for its introduction, and calculate the savings it will bring to the factory.

These dependency relations may require the innovator to include as
"authors" all those whose action, or inaction, is likely to affect the
fate of the proposal. This broadening of the authors' collective and
the consequent infrigement of authorship rights, in other words, may
be the necessary price of technical and administrative cooperation.
A good illustration of the bureaucratic pressures faced by rationalizers is seen in the following dialogue in a radio factory between a
BRIZ representative and a worker-innovator named Semyenova, over
the latter's RP (to modify the grid support assembly for electronic
tubes):

> BRIZ: "A golden idea! Molodets! . . . Now, find your-
> self a brigade of co-authors and get to work. Get ahold
> of one of the designers and a fitter . . . somebody
> from the administration—just five or six people, no
> more than necessary. "
> Semyenova: "What Co-authors? I thought of the
> idea myself. I wrote it down and described how the
> supports should be designed. "
> BRIZ: "What? You want to go it alone? [If so,]
> others, on whom the resolution of your proposal de-
> pends won't lift a finger. "[13]

The overall impression gained from reading the Soviet literature on innovation is that authorship rights create expectations of
reward that are in turn responsible for a high level of intra-enter-
prise conflict. An obvious solution would seem to be to vest all of
the rights associated with new technical ideas in the enterprise, as
is typically the case in capitalist enterprises. Authorship rights,
however, are part of a complex system of political controls over
the enterprise and are probably unlikely to be eliminated in the near
future. Still, efforts have been made at the enterprise level to
rationalize the management of mass innovation—efforts that may be
described as "innovation by design. "

Innovation by design includes two principal concepts: thematic
plans and task forces. The former are announcements by the enterprise administration of the "most important and pressing problems
of production. " They are designed to discourage submission of
proposals that are peripheral to production or that affect equipment
that the factory plans to replace in the near future. Thematic planning, which is often a joint effort of the factory administration and
of local trade union organs concerned with "social control" over
factory innovation (see below), is supposed to reduce the administrative costs of processing proposals and increase the success rate of
those submitted. [14] Task forces are worker-engineer teams in "com-

plex brigades" formed on the initiative of the factory administrations
to solve particular technical problems (generally problems identified
in the thematic plan). [15] They represent an effort to fix the parameters of the authorship collectives at the outset of the innovation
process. They do not eliminate the dependency relations that
characterize the life cycles of technical proposals, but they restrict
and formalize them, avoiding the conflicts that characterize the
spontaneous growth of authorship collectives. Moreover, the members of the task force, being selected by the administration, are
likely to get quicker and more favorable treatment in the evaluation
and implementation of their suggestions than the innovators are.

Innovation by design implies management-solicited innovation,
the establishment of better channels of communication between
managers and innovators, and the preemption by management of the
conflicts that derive from spontaneous arrangements in technical
problem solving. Though it may eliminate some conflicts or mis-
understandings over authorship or over rejected proposals, the
loss of spontaneity in the innovation process may contribute to
formation of cleavages between those who are brought into the
innovation process and those who are excluded from it. Such cleavages are already reflected in the fact that some teams are, in fact,
quasipermanent entities: they do not dissolve after accomplishing
their tasks. The fact that these "complex brigades" often include
workers prevents these potential divisions from becoming purely
class divisions; nevertheless, managerial efforts to organize and
to restrict access to the creative process may run counter to the
political goal of maximizing the scope of mass technical participation.

Social Control and Social Creativity

The Concept of Social Control

Much has been written by Western scholars about the constraints imposed by Soviet central planning and "social ownership
of the means of production" upon technical innovation at the enterprise level. The high priority assigned to the basic production plan,
price setting, and marketing by agencies outside the enterprise and
the lack of licensing arrangements for technology transfer between
firms do indeed conspire to make the introduction of any but simple
or ready-made technical solutions a risky proposition for the Soviet
factory manager. The very dysfunctions of Soviet planning, however,
call into being certain countervailing mechanisms—extrabureaucratic

correctives designed to promote the flow and implementation of technical novelty within Soviet industry. These mechanisms are embodied in the concept of "social control." This concept, like that of social ownership of the means of production, provides a useful starting point for analyzing the relationship between technology and politics in Soviet society.

"Social control" refers to participation by unofficial or voluntary bodies in promoting, implementing, and diffusing new technical ideas. The principal, or at least the most direct, instruments of social control have traditionally been the trade unions, although elements of the CPSU and to a limited extent of the Komsomol have also acted as "lobbyists" for risk taking and innovation.

This "innovation lobby" is a direct product of the Stalinist heritage in economic organization. It is not a lobby of spokesmen for fundamental changes in the planning system that might improve overall performance in innovation. It would not advocate fewer planned indicators for an enterprise, for example, or better horizontal links among enterprises.

Basically this group is a "conservative" force, in the sense that it accepts the inevitability of state planning and tends to assess the constraints on innovation, including mass innovation, in Soviet society primarily in terms of "bureaucratism," that is, by noting instances of administrative resistance or apathy toward technical novelty. Because its role, in fact, is partly to combat bureaucratism, its relation to the planning mechanism is essentially symbiotic. Hence the innovation lobby represents no real force for change in Soviet economic organization. Moreover, although it includes (as will be shown) a "specialized structure of interest articulation," it cannot be viewed as comparable to an interest group in the Western sense, since it represents part of an elaborate system of political controls over the bureaucracy.

The activities of these control bodies may be distinguished roughly according to whether they relate to advocacy or to organizational-mass work. Advocacy functions are those that tend to run counter to the short-run interests of managers and planners, that is, those that imply an adversarial relationship between "social" organizations and the official bureaucracy. The major advocacy functions include sponsoring of inventions and important rationalization proposals for inclusion in state, ministerial, and enterprise plans; criticism in official publications of poor invention or rationalization records in individual enterprises and entire branches of industry; defense of the rights of innovators against abuse by factory instantsii; establishment of experimental facilities and protection of those facilities from absorption in normal production routines; and procurement of "release time" for inventors and rationalizers.

Organizational-mass functions, by contrast, are less directly concerned with monitoring bureaucratic behavior or with diverting resources from routine production to innovation. They include activities related to technical mobilization or popularization, thematic planning, legal consultation, technical assistance and training, publicity for the achievements of factory innovators, arrangement of exhibitions and conferences, and sponsorship of technical komandirovki and "exchanges of experience" among factories (a particularly important function because of the sluggishness of ministerial and territorial channels of technical communications).

Most of these activities, moreover, duplicate at the enterprise level the assigned responsibilities of staff bodies such as BRIZ or staff technical information services—a responsibility that these bodies are seldom in a position to discharge effectively, if at all. In many enterprises staff technical information services do not exist, and BRIZ organs are generally very small. Their "recommended" size is as follows:

Number of Employees	Number of BRIZ Staff Members
500–5,000	1–3
5,000–10,000	3–5
Over 10,000	1 for each additional 5,000 employees

In this sense, organizational mass functions are more an extension of formal administration than a corrective of it.

The advocacy and organizational-mass functions described above are designed as a check on and supplement to the activities of managers and planners. In practice, however, they are susceptible to cooptation and exploitation by the official bureaucracy. Advocacy, for example, raises problems of role differentiation at the enterprise level, since the agencies most directly responsible (currently Trade Union affiliates) do not, except in the rare case of a paid staff head of a primary organization, exist apart from the enterprise collective. On the contrary, they hold formal positions in the collective, usually in the technical-managerial hierarchy. Like all managers, they are necessarily concerned with enterprise production and profits. Such role conflicts as might occur between administrators and innovators (or supporters of innovation) are likely to be resolved in favor of the former, particularly where a proposed technical innovation would divert important resources from production.

Organizational-mass work may closely parallel the "official" functions of the factory administration. Sometimes it amounts simply to an involuntary extension of the working day. Some evidence for this point is provided by a 1966 survey of participants in "social creative unions" (trade union affiliates and subordinate groups) in several Chelyabinsk factories. [16] (More evidence will be provided in a discussion of "social design bureaus" below.) When asked why and when they work in such unions, the respondents replied as follows (in percentage):

Why do you work in a creative union?

	Wanted to	Appointed	Elected
Workers	39	35	26
Engineering and technical	26	49	25
Service workers	31	34	35
CPSU members	32	48	20
Komsomol members	28	44	28
No affiliation	36	26	38

When do you work in the creative unions?

	After Work Only	Lunchtime and After Work	After Work and during Work	Only during Work	No Response
Workers	33	12	27	4	34
Engineering-technical	18	10	22	9	41
Service workers	12	15	36	10	27

On the basis of the above arguments, social control activities in the technical sphere may be criticized as being at best an adjunct—sometimes a compulsory one—to managerial functions. Such a conclusion, however, is probably one-sided; despite the obvious limitations, social control undoubtedly helps to promote the value of change-producing activity in what is frequently an unsympathetic environment. There is, in fact, an "innovation lobby" in the Soviet Union that, although perhaps not comparable to the (Western) associational interest groups in structure or effectiveness, constitutes a set of interests that are distinct from those of the planning-managerial bureaucracy. To the groups that comprise the Soviet "innovation lobby" we shall now turn.

The Social Control Network

Komsomol, CPSU, and NTO. On a day-to-day basis the most active social control agency in the USSR today is the All-Union Society of Inventors and Rationalizers (VOIR), a trade union affiliate set up in 1959 (VOIR and its activities will be discussed in the section below

on "specialized structure of interest articulation" for innovators).
However, other voluntary organizations are engaged in various aspects of social control and must be considered as part of what I
collectively call the Soviet "innovation lobby." These include
Komsomol, the CPSU, and the Scientific-Technical Societies (NTO).
The latter, like VOIR, are under the overall supervision of the
trade unions. Komsomol, as one might expect, is primarily concerned with mobilizing the creative energies of youth for technical
innovation. Typical vehicles for this are the "youth soviets of scientific-technical creativity," the "youth complex brigades," and
specialized exhibitions (at the factory, regional, and All-Union
levels) of scientific-technical achievement by young people.
Komsomol's role in social control is not influential, partly because
of the relative smallness of its constituency—not youth but youthful
innovators. Statistically speaking, most innovators are over 30,
which is a reflection of the considerable (11 to 20 years according
to one estimate) factory service required for successful participation in technical change. [17]

Far more influential, at least in terms of overall authority, is
the Communist Party. The CPSU is formally committed to "promote
in every way the development of invention and rationalization work
in all areas of national construction," and to combat bureaucratic
delays in realizing innovation. How these commitments are translated into practical efforts at social control, however, is often
difficult to determine. Party organizations above the primary level
(especially raikom, gorkom, and obkom "Technical-Economic
Soviets" or "Commission for Assistance to Technical Progress")
play an active role in technical diffusion by organizing intra-regional
seminars, conferences, exhibitions, and the like. [18]

At the enterprise level the Party maintains a low profile with
regard to technical policy. Beyond sponsoring particular items of
new technology and requiring managers to report occasionally on
factory innovation (on the number and economic value of the proposals
introduced), the primary party organs (PPOs) seem content to leave
social control to the Trade Union affiliates. This was not always the
case. In the late 1950s and early 1960s, partly because of the
ideological tone of party policies and partly because VOIR was then
in an embryonic stage of development, the PPOs became directly
involved in innovation-related activities. Special commissions to
deal with invention and rationalization work and invitations to
rationalizers to discuss complaints regarding the administrative
processing of proposals became common features of PPO work
during this period. Moreover, primary organizations sponsored and
guided the work of a broad infrastructure of "social" adjuncts to

factory technical-economic services ("social design bureaus" and
"social bureaus of economic analysis"). These adjuncts had been
set up largely as support structures for mass innovation.

Today such activism is scarcely visible; the commissions
have apparently evaporated, and party organs seldom get involved in
conflict resolution over innovation (this is now a legally-defined
activity of VOIR). Authority over the network of factory social
control activities has formally passed to VOIR and the NTO. Party
influence is, of course, by no means absent at the primary level,
but it is intermittent and, when exercised, tends to supplement the
regular work of the trade union affiliates (see Figure 1).

The Scientific-Technical Societies probably exert the most
influence on technical policy in research organizations above the
enterprise level. They also, however, engage in a variety of
control functions with the enterprise. In particular they sponsor
technical innovations to be included in factory plans, popularize
technical achievements of interest to the factory or branch, and
monitor economic calculations and production costs. In many factories technical innovations are sponsored by so-called "Technical-
Production Soviets," which are NTO soviets that have acquired the
status of permanent organs advising the director and chief engineer
on factory technical policy.

Technical achievements are entrusted to "Social Bureaus of
Technical Information" (OBTI), and economic calculations and
production costs are the responsibility of "Social Bureaus of
Economic Analysis" (OBEA). These are NTO-supervised adjuncts
to factory offices that were set up on party initiative in the early
1960s. OBTI, created where staff Bureaus of Technical Information
(BTI) are undermanned or absent, are responsible for informing
innovators about relevant technical novelties as reflected in branch
information bulletins or technical literature. They also popularize
the technical creations of factory innovators and organize exchanges
of experience among enterprises. The OBEA, which are the social
counterparts to the enterprise planning-economic office, monitors
the calculations of economy and authors' rewards for proposals and
help to orient innovators by compiling and disseminating information about production costs.

NTO functions are sometimes more extensive than those
described above, and they are not always clearly differentiated
from those of other voluntary organizations, particularly VOIR (the
degree of duplication seems to vary inversely with the size of the
enterprise). Taken as a whole, however, NTO organizations, even
at the primary level, are associations of specialists more than they
are agencies of social control. The distinction is important to bear
in mind. Except in the economic realm, NTO organizations are not

FIGURE 1

Primary-Level Infrastructure of Social Control Organizations
Involved with Innovation

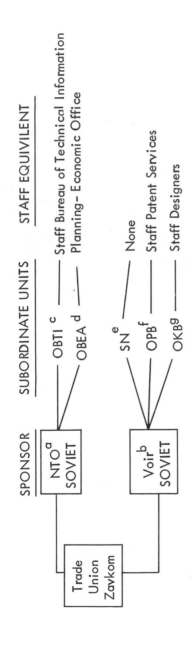

aNauchno-Technicheskoye Obshchestvo = Scientific-Technical Society
bVsyesoyuznoye Obshchestvo Izobretatelei i Ratsionalizatorov = All-Union Society of Inventors and Rationalizers.

cObshchestvennoye Byuro Technicheskoi Informatsii = Social Bureau of Technical Information.
dObshchestvennoye Byuro Ekonomicheskovo Analiza = Social Bureau of Economic Analysis.
eSoviet Novatorov = Council of Innovators.
fObshchestvennoye Patentnoye Byuro = Social Patent Bureau.
gObshchestvennoye Konstruktorskoye Byuro = Social Design Bureau.

Source: Compiled by the author.

279

watch dogs of administrative behavior; nor are they explicitly concerned with mass technical innovation. [17] These are the areas distinct, if not unique, to VOIR, which will be discussed in the following paragraphs.

VOIR. Though VOIR is a relatively recent phenomenon, in a sense
its history is inseparable from the history of social control itself.
Prior to 1930 social control had not been structurally differentiated
from the administrative processing of proposals. Both had been
performed by joint administration-trade union bodies called "Commissions for Assistance to Factory Invention." These bodies were
abolished in 1930, and all powers of technical decision making were
transferred to the factory administration.
        In 1932 a separate trade union social control structure was
established. The so-called All-Union Society of Inventors (VOIZ)
was charged generally with "mass technical propaganda and en-
lightenment," with combatting bureaucratism and red tape in the
factory "instantsii," and with thematic planning for innovators. [20]
Though officially VOIZ was a "mass voluntary organization" open to
all trade union members, it was always primarily a society of
inventors. As such, it was never particularly successful in exercising social control over innovation at the mass level. In the mid-
1930s VOIZ was accused of "lagging behind" the development of
mass forms of invention called forth by the Stakhanovite movement,
and in 1937, its ranks depleted by the purges, it was dissolved.
        New bodies with social control functions were created in 1945,
the so-called Commissions for Assistance to Mass Invention and
Rationalization. [21] It was only in 1959, however, that a true successor to the earlier Society of Inventors was founded: the All-Union
Society of Inventors and Rationalizers (VOIR). The more inclusive
title was undoubtedly designed to reflect the society's commitment
to promoting "mass" as well as elite forms of technical innovation.
        The new (or resurrected) society is a mass membership
organization of 7 million people, 54 percent of whom are workers,
organized along branch-territorial lines. At the center a "presidium" and staff preside over a descending hierarchy of regional
soviets and branch (by industry) sections and about 50,000 primary
VOIR organizations. The apparat or "staff" membership of VOIR,
as mentioned above, tends to create conflict between social control
and self-interest where an innovation would constitute a risk for the
enterprise.
        Two other structural features of VOIR must be considered in
evaluating its role as an innovators' advocate. First, the upper
echelons of the society are staffed primarily by apparatchiks who
have not acquired credentials as technical innovators. In this

respect VOIR differs from other Soviet creative organizations. One
Soviet critic noted this fact in the following terms:

> At the head of the Writers' Union, there stands a famous
> writer, at the head of the Artists' Union, famous "mas-
> ters" of art. And in the creative organization of invent-
> ors, the leading position is held, for some reason, by
> comrades who have never created anything new in tech-
> nology. [22]

Second, though VOIR is a mass membership organization, it
is anything but proletarian in its leadership structure. Only 2 of its
21 presidium members are workers, and almost 97 percent of all
"elected posts" in the society (the figure is over 90 percent at
primary levels) are held by engineering-technical personnel. [23]
Such facts tend to depict VOIR as a bureaucratic organization differing in composition and outlook from its innovator-members, especially those basing their proposals upon practical experience in
prediction.

The central, regional, and local VOIR organizations perform
the full range of advocacy and organizational mass functions mentioned at the beginning of this section. These may be divided roughly
into those that VOIR tends to share with other voluntary organizations
and those that are distinctive in the sense that the society plays the
major or exclusive role. The former includes, first of all, the sponsorship of new technical ideas. VOIR soviets, like other voluntary
organizations (possibly together with them), "lobby" for inclusion of
inventions and rationalization proposals in the enterprise plans of
new technology and of organizational-technical measures. (The plans
for new technology, despite the title, often include almost everything but that. For example, they may be comprised of repair work,
recreational facilities, and the like.)

Above the enterprise level, VOIR participates in sponsoring
certain inventions recommended to ministries by the State Committee on Inventions and Discoveries. (Use of this recommendation
system is itself an interesting commentary on technical diffusion in
a planned economy.) The committee recommendations are just that;
that is, they carry no official weight. Backing by social organizations can therefore mean the difference between success and obliv-
ion for new technical solutions.

A second "shared" function is that of economic control, or
specifically, that of monitoring the calculation of economy and of
authors' rewards. VOIR's role here may directly overlap that of the
NTO-controlled OBEA, although VOIR retains formal powers of conflict resolution in economic matters, according to current legisla-

tion. A third activity, in which VOIR is only one of the participants,
is that of disseminating and popularizing new technical ideas. VOIR
organizations use various instruments for this purpose, depending
upon the level of diffusion involved. These instruments may be
schematically represented as follows:

Factory	Branch	Region	All-Union
lectures	exchanges of	conferences	exhibitions
wall newspapers	experience among	seminars	mass-media
exhibitions and	related enter-	exhibitions	
practical	prises	mass-media	
demonstrations			

There are many functions that are distinctive or unique to
VOIR. This category must be broken down into advocacy and organizational-mass subgroups. The functions of the advocacy subgroup
include resolving conflicts over technical decisions, monitoring the
bureaucratic processing of technical novelties, and extracting from
factory administrations what might be called the "means of creativity." VOIR's role in technical decision making has a formal legal
status, guaranteed in current legislation. Any author can refer a
rejected proposal to the joint VOIR-administration technical soviets
for review.

VOIR's monitoring role, which is aimed at both enterprise
and (aggregate) branch levels, is essentially a matter of identifying
and popularizing abuses. Izobretatel i Ratsionalizator, for example,
might publish articles naming ministries that are guilty of inordinatly
high rejection rates or long delays in examining proposals. Local
VOIR organs might set up electrified "stands" showing—for all to
see—the name of the innovator, where his or her proposal sits in
the instantsii, and who is responsible for examining it.[24]

The efforts of VOIR to provide "means of creativity" center
first of all on experimental facilities. Society "lobbying" has
resulted in the creation of so-called social shops of introduction
designed exclusively for realizing technical novelties. A similar
area of VOIR concern is release time for innovators. "Why wait,"
said an Izobretatel i Ratsionalizator article "until an author tears
several hours out of his family life for studies and tests in order to
economize for the enterprise several thousand rubles or man-
days."[25] Local VOIR units have not often succeeded in securing
release time. Where they have, it has usually been in the context
of quasiofficial agreements between management and innovators to
solve problems in the thematic plan.

The organizational-mass functions that are largely or exclusively the sphere of VOIR include thematic planning, legal aid, tech-

nical education, and assistance in formulating new technical ideas—
all of which are primarily aimed at mobilizing and channeling the
technical initiatives of workers. Thematic planning involves not only
suggesting themes for factory "tyemniks" but also sponsoring thematic contests at the enterprise and branch levels. An example of
an all-union contest organized on a specific theme was one sponsored
in 1971 by the Central Soviet of VOIR and the Ministry of Pulp and
Paper Industry that posed the problem of how to produce more paper
from wood by using less water. Legal aid is primarily an educational
function, designed to inform innovators about specific problems of
invention law, such as authorship rights, definitions of invention and
rationalization proposals, and conflict resolution procedures. The
main role is played by local legal "activists"; also important, however, is the society organ Izobretatel i Ratsionalizator, which
devotes a special section each month to legal advice for a range of
highly typical conflict situations.

VOIR educational activities are aimed at upgrading capabilities
for formulating new technical ideas and at teaching advanced work
methods based on the use of new techniques. The vehicle for the
former is a network of spare-time schools dignified by such titles
as "Social Patent Institutes" and "Social Universities of Technical
Creativity." The Social Patent Institutes are designed to provide
instruction in formulating invention claims and rationalization
proposals, For the Social Universities of Technical Creativity it is
the so-called Council of Innovators (SN), primarily (though not
exclusively) an enterprise-level organ that serves as a final link in
the chain of popularization. That is, it instructs workers in the use
of technical novelties developed within and outside the factory.

Such a role is not an unimportant one, since many innovations
founder on the resistance of their potential users; however, it
represents a dilution of the earlier purposes and pretensions of the
SNs. At one time the councils seem to have been prototypes of true
worker-innovators' organizations, originally set up independently of
VOIR. These organizations were attached to the Central Bureaus of
Technical Information of Sovnarkhozy in major industrial cities.
They duplicated most of the "social control" functions performed by
VOIR.

What made them distinctive was their leadership structure.
Unlike that of VOIR, the leadership structure consisted predominantly of workers, who were often distinguished innovators, representing the metalworking trades (turners, grinders, millers, and so on).
High worker representation remains a characteristic of the SNs,
making them unique among the social control organs described here.
In 1963 efforts were made to create an all-union structure of SNs;
this, however, collapsed along with most of the urban SNs by 1965.

Apparently they were victims of administrative recentralization and perhaps also of the retreat from egalitarianism in Party policies. [26] By the late 1960s the SNs had become an appendage of VOIR, with relatively modest social control functions—a situation reflecting, in a sense, the ascendancy of the bureaucratic principle in interest articulation—of indirect as opposed to direct representation of "mass" interests in the technical sphere.

The technical assistance functions performed by VOIR may be categorized according to whether they are primarily oriented toward inventions or toward rationalization proposals. Responsibility for inventions is entrusted to "Social Patent Bureaus," which like SNs are subordinate to primary VOIR organizations. Often composed of graduates from "Social Patent Institutes," these bodies help draft invention claims for submission to the State Committee on Inventions and Discoveries and also review technical solutions created by factory innovations—originally submitted as rationalization proposals—for possible upgrading to the level of invention.

Technical assistance to rationalizers (excluding that aimed at uncovering inventions in their proposals) is the task of so-called "Social Design Bureaus" (OKB), which are adjuncts to staff-designing organs initially set up to "overcome the contradiction between the rapidly developing technical creativity of workers and the possibilities for timely formulation and embodiment in technical documentation [of their proposals]. "[27] As such, the are a key link between the social control infrastructure and technical innovation within the Soviet factory.

Like SNs, the OKBs were originally independent of VOIR. Created on Party initiative at the beginning of the Seven-Year plan, they did not become formally subordinate to VOIR until the late 1960s. The OKBs, most Soviet writers agree, have over the years acquired functions other than formulating workers' proposals; today they are also engaged in long-range technical projects that are often related to complex mechanization and automation. Like most other social organizations, however, OKBs tend to perform their functions outside of ordinary working hours.

Final Comments on Social Control

The broad panoply of "social organizations engaged in promoting and popularizing new technical ideas lends credence to the idea of a Soviet "innovation lobby. " Although innovators are not a functional group like artists or steel producers, they do have distinct interests—distinct at least from those of the economic bureaucracy. As an appendix and a corrective to the planning system, this supportive effort deserves more recognition than it has received by scholars in the West. This effort, nevertheless, is subject to severe limitations, one of which is inherent in its "social" definition: social control over innovations, like innovation itself (especially its mass forms) is often a spare-time activity. This must impose physical constraints upon the "controllers" themselves, particularly at the enterprise level, since it is difficult to believe that even the most highly articulated control infrastructure could begin to perform competently all of the functions outlined in the preceding pages.

The further limitations, already mentioned, are that those responsible for social control at the basic level are also paid members of the administration. Workers are poorly represented not only in the leadership of local VOIR and NTO organs, but also in their subordinate bodies—the sole apparent exception being the SNs. Their will or ability to place pressure on plant managers is therefore restricted, especially where a proposed innovation involves a high element of risk.

Work in social creative organizations, especially in organs subordinate to NTO or VOIR, may also suffer from poor motivation and morale. Fragmentary evidence from a Chelyabinsk study (mentioned before) indicates that participation in social control is not necessarily a matter of free choice, since it many constitute an involuntary sacrifice of the individual's spare time. The same source also reveals that the great majority of employees polled in the Chelyabinsk factories saw no connection of their unofficial duties with professional advancement or with such nonmonetary advantages as better housing, entrance to rest homes, or day-care centers for children. Also brought out in this study was the lack of moral incentives. For example, most respondents felt that "voluntary" work was not rewarded by mention in the factory "honor roll" or in the local media, or even by thanks from the administration.[28] By such accounts, the edifice of social control constitutes an unwelcome burden upon many members of the factory collective and hence may not serve as an effective support structure for innovation.

Quite obviously the Chelyabinsk figures can be disputed. Other regions and other factories give glowing accounts of their social control infrastructures and of the dedication of their participants. It is well to remember, however, that in Soviet parlance "social" may carry the connotation of "chore."

Ideology, Creativity, and the Scientific and Technical Revolutions

Creative labor in the Soviet Union, and in other communist cultures as well, stands at the interstices of the technical system and the Marxian goal culture (or some indigenous version of it). Its

importance to communist goals is defined in both "sociological" and
"psychological" terms. One argument that is long familiar to students of Marxist ideology stressed the significance of technical
participation in breaking down the distinctions between mental and
manual labor and in raising the cultural-technical level of the
workers, as follows:

> Rationalization activity broadens and deepens the creative
> side of work, speeds the process of elimination of dis-
> tinctions between labor of workers, on the one hand,
> and that of engineers and technicians on the other, and
> contributes to the formation of a worker (truzhenik) of
> a new type—the worker intellectual. [29]

Another, perhaps less familiar, line of argument stems from
the proposition that "feelings of obligation to the society" do not
constitute a sufficient motive to work under communism: the motivation must derive partly from the content of the work itself. "The
stimulation of labor by labor itself" is, moreover, linked to the
formation of the individual personality. More explicitly, creative
labor "motivates" individuals by providing them, in effect, with an
identity distinct from that of the collective. One Soviet theorist puts
it as follows:

> Social interest in the form of moral stimuli will continue
> to be one of the decisive influences on the labor of the
> members of Communist society—but personality (lichnost)
> does not dissolve in the collective; it will continue to ex-
> press its distinctiveness from other people first of all in
> creativity, which carries the stamp of individuality and
> at the same time binds man to society. [30]

The concept of creative labor, however, presents problems
for Soviet ideology because the innovation process cannot be independent of changes in the technical system itself. Much ideological
commentary is, in fact, devoted to "reconciling" mass participation
in the technical sphere with the so-called scientific-technical revolution (STR) in industry. The question of compatability arises because
complex, automated production, as one source puts it, leads innovation "from partial, spontaneous, empirically-derived changes to the
planned, complex improvements of production on the basis of new
scientific achievements."[31] The result of automation is to "narrow
the scope for minor corrections" in factory technology—to make
technical advance increasingly contingent upon "scientific knowledge
of the entire system of production to be rationalized."[32] Such

changes tend to exclude the technical initiatives associated with
physical labor, that is, those based mainly on direct observation of
a particular machine or process. However, in the Soviet view they
do not eliminate mass innovation as such. The crux of the Soviet
argument is that the STR raises the intellectual level of the labor
force, both by creating new social forms of innovation and by
changing the content of labor itself.

The new social forms of mass technical participation engendered by the STR are the so-called complex creative brigades,
which are problem-solving task forces that include engineers,
workers, and sometimes scientists. Complex brigades are described
in the literature on innovation as a response to the "contradictions"
between individual forms of technical creativity and the scale of
technical problems characteristic of modern mechanized or automated production. They are vested with enormous ideological significance. One writer depicts them as helping to "strengthen psycholog-
ical-social links between workers and engineers,"[33] to transmit
designing skills to workers, to "develop their theoretical knowledge,"[34] and—as a consequence—to "eliminate the difference between
mental and manual labor."[35] They serve in Soviet eyes as building
blocks of the goal culture, as vehicles for the intellectualization of
the working class as well as for problem solving under conditions of
high technological complexity.

Central to this conception is a comparison of two factory
worker roles, that of the "naladchik," a supervisor of automatic
lines, and that of the "stanochnik," or ordinary machine operator.
The latter performs narrowly specialized and intensively manual
functions "connected with introducing the blank to the machinery
point, removing it, and passing it on." Naladchiks, by contrast, are
broad-profile workers who encompass "the professions of all the
workers who originally serviced the [individual] machines now included in the line." Their functions, as described in Soviet accounts,
are largely "mental" in the sense that they involve more observation
of than direct participation in a production cycle and require "scientific" knowledge of instrument design, thermal treatment, and interaction of equipment during the processing stages.[36]

Soviet sociologists have conducted a variety of studies,
particularly in the early 1960s, that have attempted to show (1) that
in any given shop the naladchiks, because of the relatively substantive nature of their functions, are several times more likely to
participate in rationalization than stanochniks, and (2) that the STR
has the net effect of improving the "creative profile" of the labor
force by promoting the numerical ascendancy of innovative professions over noninnovative ones. As an extensive study of technical
participation among naladchiks, stanochniks, and other groups in

Gorky factories summarizes the argument, "The incidence of rationalizers is greatest among those professional categories of workers which increase under the influence of technical progress."[37]

Soviet efforts to reconcile complex mechanization and automation with mass technical creativity reflect a concern over the consequences of technical advance for democratic forms of management— a concern that is shared by many scholars in the West. That the Soviets depict these consequences as essentially optimistic hardly seems surprising, given the egalitarian emphasis of the goal culture. Whether the STR makes innovation less spontaneous, more complex, more science-based, but (under socialist conditions) also more open to mass participation, however, is certainly debatable. Questions arise, for example, concerning the adequacy of "complex creative brigades" as vehicles for mass involvement in the technical sphere. One of these may be a matter of definition. Soviet writers sometimes compare the modern factory with the cruder technical conditions of the 1930s and 1940s, under which the entire creative process from the birth of the idea to its practical implementation was realized by the inventors or rationalizers themselves. Whether "team" innovation can offer creative satisfaction to its worker-members is an empirical question that cannot be resolved on the basis of available evidence, but nevertheless, the danger exists that a complex brigade may merely express in formal terms the separation between mental and manual labor, concentrating creative functions in the hands of engineers and consigning workers to the role of embodying new ideas in metal. The creative participation of the worker-members in such brigades is undoubtedly proportionate to their levels of education and skills; this leads to the conclusion that these organizations, to the extent that they are true social forms of innovation in the modern factory, are by no means accessible to all workers. References in Soviet accounts to administration-formed or quasi-permanent complex brigades would tend to confirm the impression of their exclusive, nonmass character.

A further difficulty arises in relation to the assertion that at higher levels of complex mechanization and automation the STR promotes the ascendancy of "creative" functions over less "creative" ones. A more likely outcome of automation, in my view, is the removal of the workers too far from the production cycle to be concerned with creativity, at least in the "production-technical" sense implied by the rationalization concept. The Soviets' preoccupation with the naladchik may reflect their limited experience with automation thus far; the typical worker of advanced automation may be not the naladchik but the control panel operator, whose job would seem to offer little opportunity for technical participation but whose functions, ironically, can be considered largely mental.

Some Soviet writers seem able to grasp the ultimate implications of automation for creativity. For example, a 1974 dissertation in Moscow argued that rationalization should be legally redefined to include as its "objects" not only production technology but also algorithms and computer software. [38] For most, however, rationalization remains a kind of metallic embodiment of the goal culture, a conception that is appropriate to the low level of automation in most Soviet factories and also, perhaps, to the continuing, if largely vestigial, role of the proletarian cult in Soviet politics.

THE CHINESE CASE

The Chinese communists, like the Soviets, have sought to mobilize mass participation in the technical sphere. Their efforts, however, reflect a set of political concerns that differ on the whole from the Soviet ones. The Maoist leadership has had an intense preoccupation with eliminating, or at least containing, evidence of stratification in Chinese society. Unlike the Soviets, at least since the 1930s, the Chinese communists have felt that the disappearance of major social distinctions such as those between mental and manual labor and between city and village can be immanent in the industrializing process itself. That is, these changes need not await a "postindustrial" stage of high automation and vast material wealth. The result has been a kind of inverted Marxism that legitimizes the resettlement of urban dwellers in the countryside and, most important, regular participation in manual labor for intellectual elites. This inversion has affected the purposes of mass innovation in China. It is often seen as a way for the engineer to "get down" to the level of the worker and not only as a way for the worker to "rise" to the level of the engineer.

A second important consideration motivating PRC policies toward mass innovation is nationalism of a form more virulent and culturally more encompassing than anything comparable in the USSR. The Chinese have not regarded the establishment of communist power in 1949 as the culmination of the revolution for national independence. On the contrary, this revolution has continued, as the People's Republic has sought to incorporate uniquely indigenous elements into its own path of modernization. Efforts to restrict or even eradicate foreign influence have been apparent in many areas, including art and literature, science, medicine, technology, and industrial management—in nearly all fields, in fact, with the exception of nuclear and rocket research and development.

In the realm of technology, the so-called technical revolution, which is not to be confused with the scientific-technical revolution

in the USSR, is merely an extension of the national revolution. Moreover, it is closely linked to the egalitarian concerns of the PRC
leadership. A key assumption of the ideology since 1958 has been
that the concentration of technical power in the hands of an elite
fosters "slavish" imitation of foreign technical doctrines, whereas
the broad sharing of such power fosters industrial and technological
change according to distinctively Chinese patterns. This dual thrust
of the ideology—this equation of native and mass—has opened the
technical sphere to the "masses" in the PRC to a degree unparalleled
in the Soviet Union or anywhere else.

The themes of equality and "cultural" nationalism have a high
political visibility in the PRC, since if one is to believe Chinese
accounts, they have been a focus of violent inner-party struggle
since the late 1950s. At the risk of some oversimplification, the
argument could be made that there has been a fair degree of unanimity on these issues within the Soviet elite at least since the 1930s.
Few Soviet spokesmen, for example, have questioned the policies
of large-scale and sustained technological borrowing adopted by the
regime since the early 1920s (and by the Czarist regime before
that).

It is interesting to note in this connection that even during the
Stalinist purges, with all of their antiforeign overtones, Western
specialists continued working in Russia. [39] No comparable group
remained in China during the Cultural Revolution. More recently,
however, foreign technicians have been invited to China in connection with purchases of plants and technology.

The Soviets, moreover, have generally been in agreement on
the nature of equality. They have viewed the socialist "transfer culture," although including elements of it, as the preceding discussion
of worker innovation shows. The Soviets, in other words, accept
hierarchies of status and reward as a necessary precondition for
building a communist society. As far as the factory and innovation
are concerned, engineers are viewed as distinct from workers,
although the latter are elevated to the level of engineers as technology becomes more automated and more complex.

The political salience of equality and nationalism in China has
linked the question of mass technical innovation directly to struggles
within the PRC politburo. Liu Shao-ch'i, for example, is depicted
as the advocate of "management of factories by experts" and of
seeking PRC dependence on foreign technical and industrial models.
Mao, on the other hand, is hailed as the advocate of mass initiative
in the technical sphere and of China's "independent road" of
development.

This linkage, however, creates problems for research, and
particularly for making any useful comparisons between PRC and

Soviet concepts of creative labor. Soviet source materials in this
area are highly differentiated. They deal with problems of technical
creativity from economic, technical, legal, and sociological as well
as ideological standpoints. PRC sources, by contrast, tend to be
heavily politicized and intensely ideological, focusing on the "struggle between two lines" and on the thought of Mao as embodied in the
creative spirit of the working masses. [40] Partly as a consequence,
there is a dearth of information about the actual mechanics of the
"innovation cycle" in PRC factories. This is not the entire story,
however: the PRC has consciously repudiated or has simply failed to
adopt many elements of the Soviet experience in managing innovation. For example, the complicated system of "instantsii" for
processing proposals has been greatly simplified—how much, we do
not know. Moreover, probably wisely, China seems to have greatly
deemphasized monetary rewards for most innovation, although
other forms of reward are practiced, such as publicity or promotion opportunities. Finally, the infrastructure of "social control,"
as it exists in the USSR, has been largely preempted in the People's
Republic by the mass campaign approach to technical change. To the
extent that social control devolves on specific institutions, in China
it is the Party rather than the trade unions that plays a predominant
role.

Because of these considerations, the focus of the essay that
follows will be on political, as opposed to institutional, ideology, as
reflected in the technical sphere. The evolution of PRC policies
toward innovation will be traced from the early 1950s to mid-1970s,
showing the relationship of these policies to the two themes of
equality and nationalism discussed above.

From the Soviet Model to the Great Leap

As a formula of communist technical management, the concept of creative labor seems to have been introduced to China in the
late 1940s by Soviet specialists working in Manchurian enterprises.
Its Soviet origin, as well as China's obvious dependence on Soviet
aid, has partly dictated its early forms. For example, the legal
framework of mass innovation was based on the Soviet regulations
on inventions, technical improvements, and organizational proposals
of 1941. Moreover, the administrative processing of proposals bore
certain similarities to the Soviet patterns. Proposals were apparently routed to a bureau or office in charge of innovation, similar to
the Soviet BRIZ, and then through various bureaucratic kuan k'ou,
which were equivalent to the instantsii, for decisions on feasibility
and reward. [41]

"Social control" over innovation was, following the Soviet
pattern, largely a trade union responsibility consisting largely of
popularizing workers' achievements and sponsoring (along with
Party committees) their proposals before recalcitrant factory administrators. Even at this time, however, an important vehicle of
social control was the mass campaign, which was a prominent feature of industrial life in China even in the early 1950s. [42]

Finally, because China obviously was following a Soviet model
of industrialization, mass innovation in the early 1950s did not reflect the juxtaposition of egalitarianism and technological nativism
characteristic of later years—the distribution of technical power was
coterminous with established technical hierarchies. Moreover, the
ideological justification for mass involvement in the technical sphere
was simply that the workers had become "masters" of the factory
and their machines with the communist accession to power in 1949.
This theme had also been stressed in Soviet communist writings of
the early and mid-1920s.

In the early 1950s the People's Republic followed a two-track
technical strategy that, in effect, divided technology into "elite" and
"mass" spheres. The latter included enterprises or parts of enterprises that had been inherited from the pre-1949 days; these were
thrown open to mass "invention and creation" in the hope of bringing
about the "fullest utilization of existing industrial potential and the
rapid increase in labor productivity." The "elite" sphere included
enterprises that were being built or resupplied with large amounts
of Soviet machinery and equipment. The guiding theme in this "core"
industrial sector was not mass invention and creation but rather
"learning and grasping Soviet advanced experience." In practice,
the mass campaigns of the period tended to spill over from the
"mass" into the "elite" sector—a phenomenon that in the mid-1950s
caused the regime to moderate its enthusiasm for worker innovation. [43]

In 1950, however, the worker-innovator reemerged with stun-
ning force, this time as an essential ingredient in a new PRC cultural self-image. The innovation policies of the Great Leap Forward
(GLF) which began in that year, differed from earlier versions because they now fully encompassed the technological conditions created by the introduction of Soviet aid. In this period Soviet advanced
experience lost its sacrosanct position as the PRC shifted from a
two-track strategy of technical modernization to an integral strategy.
Along with this shift the Party, rather than the trade unions, became
the primary agent of "social control" (if one can describe a mass
phenomenon like the GLF in such limited terms), with primary party
organs assuming the major role in mobilizing the masses for innovation.

Fundamental to the GLF technical strategy was an ideology that now stressed creativity in both class and national terms. This emphasis was most apparent in the campaign to break down "superstition"—meaning, in communist parlance, an unquestioning reverence for scientific theories, authorities, and foreigners. The immediate objective of the campaign was to legitimize mass participation in science and technology, which communist writers argued were no mystery but were "the fruit of many years' practice by the laboring people" and could easily be grasped by them. Experts were viewed as both the perpetrators and the victims of superstition: on the one hand, they attempted to delude or intimidate nonexpert outsiders by surrounding their work with mysterious scientific jargon; on the other, they worshipped "foreigners, foreign books, and foreign methods" and denied the scientific basis of any ideas or techniques that did not originate in foreign countries. Seemingly under attack in the polemics against superstition was a kind of class hierarchy of ideas, a hierarchy that placed the expert above the nonintellectual and the foreign above the indigenous. To break this chain of dependency, the government now declared that productive practice was the source of scientific-technological theory. This meant, in the context of the GLF, that PRC practice could correct, modify, or further develop those foreign theories that had guided China's industrialization in the past. [44]

The attempt to destroy blind faith in the technological experience of foreign countries—to subordinate, in ideological terms, "foreign" theory to "native" practice—was one of the more distinctive elements of Maoist doctrine as it emerged during the GLF. The impact of this new configuration upon the politics of the industrial enterprise may be stated quite simply: the workers gained in technical power over PRC development what the experts lost as a result of their association with foreign influence. Not only did scientific and technical personnel suffer a loss of prestige and status under such conditions, but also Soviet advisers working in PRC industry. That their ordinary functions were difficult to perform in the ideological climate of the period is indicated by a Soviet statement of July 1960 announcing the recall of Soviet advisers from China, as follows:

[The Chinese] did not follow the counsel of the experts in the technical realm. They did as they pleased, often the opposite of what they were told. This attitude showed prejudice against the Soviet government and sapped the authority of the experts whom it sent to China.

Very often, the Chinese scorned the written instructions of the Russian technicians; they made era-

sures in the documents, or contented themselves with
tearing them up and throwing them away. [45]

Maoist technical policy during the GLF may be viewed partly as a
nativist reaction to the Soviet model that had guided China's industrial development under the First Five-Year Plan. One might say
that the studied dependence upon "advanced Soviet experience" had
provoked its dialectical counterpart, which was hostility to things
foreign, as the nation groped its way toward a new technological
identity.

Major Technical and Managerial Themes

The overriding theme of communist technological policy during
the GLF was "native and mass" reliance upon mass participation in
technological decision making, to break down "superstition," create
new techniques, and promote the rapid all-around development of
the nation's economy. Essentially there were two sides to this policy, one stressing innovation in large modern enterprises using advanced equipment and complex production sequences and the other
stressing innovation in small enterprises with few capital commitments and simple production technologies. The first involved a
"direct" campaign against modernity in the form of foreign equipment, product designs, and technical regulations, and the second
involved an "indirect" campaign against modernity that relied on a
broad industrial front to generate new technical ideas and experiences. This front was to "act as pioneers for the modern, large
enterprises."
    The following pages will deal with three subjects that together
comprise the essence of the communist concept of innovation as it
evolved during the GLF: (1) managerial reform (the reform of "irrational" rules and systems); (2) the rationalization and simplification of technical design; and (3) the promotion of mass experimentation in small-scale economic units and the affirmation of "native
methods" as a significant element in PRC industrialization.

Managerial Reform

The mass movement for the technical transformation of
"modern and large" enterprises during the GLF resulted in the
introduction of radically new doctrines of industrial management,
epitomized by the system of "two participation, one reform, and
three combination." This system provided that persons at all
hierarchical levels within the enterprise should participate in both

labor and routine management, that everyone should contribute to reforming irrational conventions and regulations, and that leadership should be combined with the masses, labor with technique, and theoretical knowledge with production practice. This latter innovation was the basis of the so-called "three-in-one combination," a formula partly reminiscent of the Soviet "complex brigades" but designed as much as an experiment in democratic technical management as a collective problem-solving body. Moreover, unlike the Soviet counterpart, it became a vehicle for institutionalized participation in productive labor by technical-managerial elites.

An important aspect of managerial reform involved the reform of rules and systems. This was an essential adjunct to the technical innovation campaign of the period. Communist rhetoric in the GLF stressed that the advanced technology and the complex production sequences of the "modern" sector of industry were a source of both "technological superstition" and "a pile of detailed systems, rules, and regulations" that "weighed heavily on the workers' shoulders." The official rationale for revising or eliminating rules and systems reflected the standard Maoist preoccupation with laboring practice as a corrective of theory—in this case procedures relating to technical management and operations. Many such procedures, the communist workers argued, were irrational on technological grounds and, moreover, did no justice to the practical knowledge of tools and machinery acquired by workers in the course of production. Managers tended to exaggerate the necessity of controls over workers and to regard rules, institutions, and forms as "dogmas which may only be observed but which must be developed." To make the masses "masters and not slaves of regulations" was, in the Communists' view, an essential way of overcoming technical conservatism and liberating the productive forces within enterprises.

The rules and systems subjected to scrutiny or criticism during the innovation campaigns of the GLF were essentially of two types. The first were managerial systems that defined the distribution of technical power within the enterprise and reflected "the relation of one man to another." The second were technical norms that reflected "the objective laws involved in processes of production." The first indicated who had the right to make decisions on technical matters, and the second defined the scientific-technological parameters of these decisions and indicated whether they could or should be made.

The managerial systems that the Communists seemed most anxious to change during the GLF were those concerned with the processing and approval of technical innovations and those involving inspection or quality control within workshops. The former, according to communist accounts, required that innovators submit

detailed blueprints of their proposals—even rationalization proposals
—and that these documents be channeled through as many as ten different departments (kuan k'ou) before receiving approval. "If we do
not get ourselves out of this ensnaring tangle," commented one
writer, "we will never succeed in the technical leap forward."[46]
Another, in describing the Changchun automobile plant prior to the
technical modernization campaigns of the Leap, wrote as follows:

> Certainly the workers were encouraged to make propos-
> als. But if such a proposal touched on design, even so
> minor a change as altering the angle of a tool had to be
> approved by the designing department, which would take
> months—if you made it without this okay, you were med-
> dling with "standard operating procedure." A worker
> named Kao Yung-chuan said: "In the past, we never set
> foot in the engineering building. If you wanted to save
> yourself endless fuss, it was better not to bother your
> brains about things which belonged there."[47]

Such attacks on the bureaucratization of innovation indicated
that prior to the GLF the workers still retained the "right to innovate" in a formal sense. However, the size of the bureaucratic
apparatus involved in processing the workers' proposals seems to
have deprived them of this right in actuality. Hence one aim of the
campaign to reform managerial systems was to restructure the
hierarchy of decision making on technical issues and to transfer the
power to implement some suggestions—at least those for rationalization or for minor technical improvements—to lower levels.

Also transferred to lower levels, along with powers of judgment over technological innovation, were controls over actual production itself, particularly controls over the quality of products.
During the GLF, according to several accounts, a number of people
advocated doing away with the inspection section—that unit of professional management charged with quality of production—on the
grounds that "since the consciousness of the workers had been
raised inspection was something dispensable." Whether or not the
inspection function—or rather the managerial unit responsible for
performing it—was ever completely abolished at any time during
the GLF is unclear. However, the policies of the GLF indicated
that technical inspections would no longer be the exclusive prerogative of managerial elites. Jen-min Jih-pao noted the following in
1958, commenting on the pre-GLF situation in technical management:

> As to the question of quality of products stress was laid
> on workers' supervision; for this reason 147 test and

> inspection personnel were employed [In the Shanghai Diesel Oil Engine Plant] as if only these personnel would attach importance to quality. These personnel came into conflict with and stood against the workers. . . .
>
> In a word, management meant the formulation of institutions and rules. Its striking feature was "to control man" strictly. [48]

The delegation of technical control powers to lower levels did much to demean the role and status of technical personnel within enterprises. Since official policy now stressed that production workers could play a substantive role in technical management, technical personnel were required to go down to the workshops to consult the workers and to seriously consider their suggestions. Prior to the decentralization of technical powers, said one article, "technical persons had no contact with workmen and ignored their suggestions, believing they were superior to the workmen." This attitude "did much to damage the workmen's enthusiasm."[49] After decentralization, however, some technical personnel were transferred to shops—a move that reportedly helped to remold the ideology of technicians, to heighten worker activism, and to promote an all-around leap forward in production.

Other rules and systems that fell under attack during the GLF were concerned with technical as opposed to managerial policy. The technical norms covered all phases of the manufacturing process and dealt with such matters as order of production, product specifications, care and handling of equipment, work methods, safety, and use of raw materials. Communist writings, particularly in the initial phase of the GLF, characterized the bulk of these norms as archaic and "irrational" and as obstacles to the development of production. The revision or abolition of "irrational" regulations took the form of a mass movement, one closely linked to the mass movement for technological innovation and designed to "promote the activism of the masses and expand the productive force."[50]

The campaign against rules and systems occurred on many technical fronts; perhaps its most widespread manifestation, however, was in the area of machine utilization and maintenance. Because of the overriding emphasis of the GLF upon increasing production, the reform of regulations often meant the introduction of "shock" measures designed to increase the productivity of capital. In a sense, machines were forced to perform shock work by running at higher speeds and for longer periods than those for which they had been designed. According to a typical account, workers and technicians broke through the "superstition" that the maximum electric current applied to a certain type of lathe could not exceed 80 amps., greatly increased the rotation speed of the lathe, and shattered all production records in the manufacture of wheels.

Such success stories are somewhat overshadowed, however, by others appearing later on in the GLF that pointed to serious damage done to the machinery by running it beyond designed capacity and by ignoring periodic maintenance and timely repairs. It is wrong, said one article, "to assume that the machine's efficiency can be brought higher and higher without any limit. To ignore the existence of maximum speed completely is . . . often the cause of breakdown of machinery."[51] Another article stressed the need to "curb skyrocketing zeal within the bounds of science and to reduce the strain on equipment by maintaining or overhauling it at frequent intervals."[52] The impression left by these accounts is that violation of the norms regarding the rate of utilization of equipment—that is, how fast and how long it should be operated—may have had serious long-term effects upon industrial productivity within enterprises.

Simplification

In the earliest stages of the GLF, communist writing described the "technical revolution" as encompassing trends from small size to large size, from simplicity to complexity, from a lower stage to a higher stage, and from semimechanization to full mechanization in the development of technology. This view, however, was partly in conflict with the nativist posture of the People's Republic in the technical realm, and specifically with its defense of native methods as "advanced, scientific, and vital" and as an essential ingredient in China's technological modernization. To impart "scientific" qualities to native methods required a modification of evolutionary perspectives that equated relatively simple technologies with relatively backward ones. "Generally, indigenous methods are more simple," asserted a Jen-min Jih-pao article of May 1960, "but to assume from this that they are unscientific, inferior, or backward would be a rather superficial view." The article went on to state that the criteria determining whether or not a method is scientific, advanced, or superior "must be based on the method's actual achievements in production." Some machinery, it said, "may be simple in structure but more advanced and superior from the standpoint of the results that it achieves." Hence, the article concluded, it is "obviously erroneous to consider simplicity as backwardness" and to adopt a "lukewarm and wavering attitude" toward native methods.[53]

Simplification, as a concomitant of nativization, generally involved reducing the size, weight, and number of parts of machin-

ery. Its aim was to increase efficiency, calculated as a ratio between the "inputs" just described and total performance. Communist claims for simplification are far-reaching, as the following
article on the machine-building industry indicates:

> For example, the innovated single axle automatic lathe,
> the perpendicular drilling machine, the power generator,
> and various kinds of pumps all continue to perform the
> same functions as they did, but the number of accesso-
> ries attached to them have been greatly reduced, their
> size reduced, their weight lightened, so that a great
> economy in raw materials has been effected in manu-
> facture. [54]

Some of the more drastic examples of rationalized structures
mentioned in the article included electrical equipment reduced from
1,387 parts to 600 and a "native type" welding machine reduced
from 382 kilograms to 17. Such "new small, light, and efficient
items," the article claimed, "led to the economy of raw materials,
working time, and floor space, as well as to the shortening of the
production cycle;" moreover, it said, they served to break down
"many former superstitious beliefs connected with designing, such
as: 'the more materials we use in building the stronger the machine
will become,' and 'equipment of the higher levels cannot be simplified.'"[55]

The simplification or rationalization of machinery during the
GLF reflected, at least in the eyes of some communist spokesmen,
the workings of "laws" governing the development of technology. In
a highly sophisticated effort to place technical simplification within
an evolutionary framework that could give scientific legitimacy to
simple, that is, native, techniques, one communist leader remarked
as follows:

> Judging from a mass of facts, the development of produc-
> tion techniques proceeds from the simple to the complex.
> But, when a certain stage is reached, development often
> returns from the complex to the simple. For example,
> the spinning of cotton was done by hand at the beginning.
> Later, hand looms were invented and still later, mechan-
> ical looms appeared. As work became more complica-
> ted, with a large number of accessories, there began a
> process of simplification. This resulted in increased
> efficiency, and production since then has gone up, in
> some cases more than 100%. [56]

The above argument finds an interesting parallel in the writings of a Western "historian" of technology, Lewis Mumford, who describes the evolution of technology in the West in terms of the "growth of functionalism" and the development of a "sound machine aesthetic." The aim of sound design, he argues, is to remove from the object "every detail, every moulding, every variation of the surface, every extra part except that which contributes to its effective functioning." The purification, or stripping down to essentials, of industrial technology reflects the increasing dominance of "aesthetics" in machine design—a historical process of repudiating the "conspicuous waste" and "technical virtuosity" of early industrialization. Machine aesthetics, according to Mumford, means a capacity to choose rationally among a number of alternative mechanical solutions to a given problem and so achieve a "complete integration of the machine with human needs and desires."[57]

The argument that rationalization is a key aspect of technological development is, as the above citation indicates, by no means unique to the Chinese communists. The communists, however, conceive the process and the instrument of rationalization in terms that reflect both their ideological commitments and their experience as late-comers to modernization. In their view, the process of rationalization has highly specific historical application. It involves the introduction of foreign technological inputs to the People's Republic and their transformation, through the conscious activities of the masses, into something both native and superior.

Walking on Two Legs

A major variant of PRC technological strategy in the GLF was epitomized by the concept of "walking on two legs"—referring to the simultaneous use of foreign and indigenous methods in the development of industry. Walking on two legs was subject to widely varying interpretations during the Great Leap. One "conservative" interpretation viewed foreign and indigenous methods as separate entities, and the latter as crude or inferior—valuable only in terms of political mobilization, utilization of scattered local resources, adaptation to specific natural conditions, and quick increases in production where foreign or modern facilities were lacking.

A different interpretation, which I assume was shared by Mao and his followers, was that indigenous was not necessarily synonymous with backward and that home-grown methods often contained original and unique advantages that could be brought out and developed in integration with foreign ones. Spokesmen for the integrationist position claimed that native techniques were, in a number of cases, more advanced and scientific than Western ones and that their use represented not a temporary economic expedient but a long-term strategic policy. Such techniques, developed largely in medium-/and small-scale enterprises with relatively few capital commitments and simple production technologies, were claimed to have "a great and promising future" and even to be capable of serving as pioneering examples for more capital-intensive plants. PRC industry as a whole, in other words, would benefit from the lengthening of the production front and increased scope for mass innovation that this implied.

Innovation campaigns in technically backward enterprises derived from a different set of propositions than those of campaigns to reform tools, processes, and managerial systems in the modern sector. One of these was that the relative deprivation of production factors (equipment, supplies, raw materials, or "technical forces") fostered moral virtues, expressed in terms of self-reliance, and that self-reliance engendered improvisation. A second was that such improvisation could serve as a stimulus to technological changes in more "modern" industries in the same branch. The latter argument related specifically to poorly equipped enterprises commissioned to produce relatively complex products, such as steel, machinery, or chemicals, that were initially beyond their technological means. Such enterprises would engage in "technical revolution" on the basis of the facilities and equipment at their disposal and succeed not only in producing the desired product but also in developing "pioneering" ideas and techniques that could usefully be employed in "modern" capital-intensive enterprises. Communist writings during the GLF claimed that many of the "bootstrap" methods of production, developed in technologically deprived conditions, had "overtaken and outstripped foreign methods of production" on account of being "more economical, easier to operate, employing fewer people and less raw materials." Simplicity of equipment and smallness of scale, they argued, increased the scope for technical experimentation, making the enterprises "rich in revolutionary creativeness"— rich sources of techniques that would "overthrow authoritative technical theories" and "propel the technical revolution" within entire industrial branches. [58]

From the Great Leap Forward
to the Cultural Revolution

As is well known, the mass technical mobilization during the GLF had a variety of ill effects: mismanagement of projects, planning errors, technical errors in production and capital construction,

and others. Aside from inflicting damage on the economy, the GLF—
to the extent that it repudiated Soviet technical and managerial experience—was a contributing factor in the withdrawal of Soviet experts (and their blueprints) in July-August 1960. The need to restore
balance in the economy, to raise the quality of products, and to
continue the operation and expansion of the modern sector in the
absence of Soviet advisers had the effect of shifting the locus of
technical power upward within the enterprise. In January 1961 the
Ninth Plenum of the Party Central Committee adopted the slogan,
"Readjustment, Consolidation, Filling Out, and Raising Standards,"
which reiterated the emphasis of the preceding year and formally
signalled the end of the Great Leap Forward. In June the Party
adopted the so-called "70 Articles in Industry," which among other
things reaffirmed the prerogatives of technical staffs in matters of
technical supervision and control.

     The new policy line resulting from these decisions called upon
enterprises to "fully develop the positive functions of technical personnel" and to practice democratic centralism (min-chu chi-chung chih) in
the formulation and execution of technical policy. According to this
formula, projects under consideration would be open to democratic
discussion, but actual decisions would be made by the technical or
administrative agencies involved. Workers were admonished that
differences of opinion on technical matters "could not be made into
an excuse for disobedience."

     It would be incorrect and misleading to say that the masses
ceased to play a role in technical innovation in the post-GLF years.
Their innovations, however, were, as in the 1950s, subject to
strict bureaucratic controls. According to a 1968 account, a worker
introducing an innovation might have to fill out a form stating, for
example, the "theoretical basis" of his idea, its "expected result,"
and the "required investment." Then his proposal would be circulated through 10 or 12 different departments, where it would await
ratification by the "experts" and, more likely than not, be shelved.
If approved, at this stage the innovation would undergo a prolonged
period of scientific testing. [59] These barriers could be viewed as a
restoration of Soviet managerial practices within the modern sector.
Outside of this sector, mass innovation declined in intensity as the
regime retreated from the "walking on two legs" policy. Construction of small-scale, labor-intensive industries was curtailed, and
many of the existing ones—including iron and steel, machine building, motor vehicle and chemical—were put out of commission.

     The relatively conservative technical policies that emerged
in the early 1960s reflected, according to conventional wisdom, a
loss of influence of Mao Tse-tung in favor of his more "pragmatic"
rivals within the Chinese Communist Party. The ascendancy of the
"pragmatists," however, was only temporary. The years 1964-65

saw what could be regarded as a Maoist counterattack in the technical realm—the so-called designing revolution aimed at opening industrial and plant design to the "wisdom and creativity" of the masses. As this campaign wore on, it acquired distinctly antiforeign overtones. Designers were told that separation from the masses caused them to entertain a superstitious belief in foreign books and that creation of truly "new," that is, uniquely Chinese, technology depended on close integration with productive practice. The designing revolution thus reestablished the native-and-mass ideological formula of the Great Leap and set the stage for a new round of technical mobilization in the Cultural Revolution.[60] Mass innovation in the CR represented, in most ways, a replay of the GLF. The original ideological preconditions of the GLF were thus reestablished, and the Cultural Revolution, with which the designing revolution finally merged, reaffirmed the broad outlines of the technical mobilization policies of the GLF. The modern sector was again thrown open to mass "rationalization" of equipment, products, and technical norms. Bureaucratic controls over mass initiative evaporated, and technical personnel suffered a loss of status and prestige. At the same time, the Cultural Revolution (at least in its later stages) renewed the GLF "walking on two legs" strategy in industrialization. As in the GLF, "poor and blank" enterprises were hailed for their ability to "give full play to the wisdom and ingenuity of our working people" and to "serve as pacesetters in the search for new techniques of all kinds."

What distinguished the CR from the GLF, however, was that the factory became a kind of microcosm of inner-party struggle, of the conflict between Mao and his "revisionist" enemies in the Chinese Communist Party. References to the "seizure of technical power by the working class" and to the "overthrow of bourgeois technical authorities" echoed the massive purges taking place in China at the time. Technical elites suffered more than they had during the GLF, simply because any exercise of technical authority could be linked to "revisionism" and, hence, to Lin Shao-ch'i and his "agents." Some hint of the atmosphere in PRC factories at this time is provided in complaints since the Cultural Revolution that many engineering-technical personnel simply abdicated their functions on the theory—not unreasonable under the circumstances—that "labor is safe and technique is dangerous."[61]

Chinese Innovation in Comparative Perspective

In recent years Chinese communist technical strategy has repudiated some of the "ultraleftist" excesses of the Cultural Revolution. On the one hand, an effort has been made to upgrade the role of engineering-technical personnel in technical decision making. Formal scientific training, in some accounts, is regarded as a prerequisite for innovation. "Experience is no substitute for theory nor is practice for reading," asserted a recent article. "To master modern science and make innovations one must not only have revolutionary drive and specific production experience but must also strive to read and acquire theoretical knowledge of natural sciences."[62]

Learning from foreign experience has acquired a limited acceptability: according to a <u>Kuang-ming Jih-pao</u> account, a technician in designing an important device for a car found a similar device in a foreign technical magazine and wanted to accept and imitate the good parts of this. He was worried about criticism, however, and hesitated to start this work. The Factory Party Committee helped to "liberate" him from this thinking, and finally, with the backing of the Party and his fellow employees, he made the device.[63]

Antiforeign themes, however, are still rife in the PRC media; accounts still recall the "slavish compradore philosophy" of Liu Shao-ch'i and stress the need for independence and self-reliance in the technical and industrial spheres. Moreover, retreat from the Cultural Revolution has not resulted in a return to the "Soviet model" of the 1950s. Technical decision making in the factory is highly decentralized compared to the Soviet pattern and is characterized by a high degree of elite-mass intersubjectivity—what the Chinese themselves call "technical democracy."

Technical democracy in the People's Republic represents a useful contrast to the Soviet concept of creative labor—a contrast offering insight into Sino-Soviet ideological differences as well as reflecting on the difference in the stages of growth of the two societies. There are superficial similarities between the two concepts: both share a commitment to Marxist doctrine—notably to the "unification of mental and manual labor"—and both view this principle as partly realizable (that is, in conditions short of universalized equality) in a fairly broadly-based problem-solving procedure within the factory—the vehicle in the People's Republic being the "three-in-one" combination and in the Soviet Union the so-called "complex brigade" mentioned above.

Hereafter, however, the resemblance fades. First, the Chinese writers are not concerned with the role of technical participation in the formation of the "personality" or in the individualistic sense used by some Soviet authors. In fact, the entire question of the relation between technical change and the development of the individual is avoided in the PRC. This in itself is an interesting commentary on the difference between Western and Asian Marxist traditions.

Second, although the Chinese, like the Soviets, regard the elimination of the difference between mental and manual labor as a precondition for the establishment of a communist society, they have ascribed an instrumental significance to it that is relatively absent in Soviet writings. The impact of this Marxist principle in its Maoist translation has been to legitimize the massive redistribution of change-producing functions from the technical-managerial elites to the masses, as well as the downward transfer of the elites themselves to the front lines of production.

To the Soviet Union, by contrast, the unification of mental and manual labor means, not the proletarianization of elites, but rather the elevation of workers to the level of engineers through the increasing automation of technological processes in industry. The following is a typical formulation from a Soviet work:

> Technical progress will lead to the elevation of the
> voluntary technical creativity of the masses to that
> of scientific work of the level of the professional en-
> gineer or technician, involving the solution of major
> and complex technical problems. [64]

The determinist emphasis of Soviet ideology presents a useful contrast to the voluntarism of Maoist doctrine. At the same time, it suggests certain imperatives of technical change that may eventually force a retreat from Maoist precepts of technical mobilization.

As has been shown, such precepts are closely tied to the PRC revolution for national independence. The extraordinary incidence of mass technical participation, however, is also conditioned—made possible, even—by the semimechanized character of much PRC production. At higher levels of modernization, the imperatives of technology, at least in Soviet and Western experience, are likely to establish increasingly rigid constraints upon the contributions that purely practical knowledge can make to the further modernization of industry. The Soviet sociology of innovation points to an essential concomitant of change in industrially advanced societies, which is the increasing mediation by science of human transactions with the natural or technological environment. An excellent example of this developmental "law" is afforded by our own industrial revolution, which can be divided roughly into "early" or "late" stages, depending on the relative importance of theoretical knowledge in the generation of new techniques. One historian of U.S. science notes the following:

> One looks in vain for actual applications of theoretical
> science, as opposed to products of mechanical ingenuity

before the middle of the nineteenth century. By the
last quarter of the century, such applications were
so obvious that it was no longer necessary to make
a point of them.[65]

The industrial revolution in China may similarly move from a "practical" to a "theoretical" phase in accumulating indigenous technical
experience. As modernization proceeds, one may argue, the epistemological framework of Maoist doctrine will be less able to encompass the modes of creating and applying new knowledge. This is not,
however, to deny the particular relevance of Maoist principles to the
specific historical and industrial circumstances of the People's
Republic; to do so would be to confuse the requisites of maintaining
a relatively industrialized society with the prerequisites of achieving
it.

NOTES

1. Unlike novelty (by world standards), technical or economic
importance is not a legal attribute of invention. An average invention, however, is far more important than an average rationalization proposal. In terms of the economy created, the ratio of the
former to the latter is about eleven to one, 9,300 rubles to 850
rubles.
2. P. A. Sedlov, "Economics and the Management of Invention and Rationalization," Voprosy Izobretatelstva 2 (1975): 3.
3. USSR Council of Ministers, "Regulation on Discoveries,
Inventions, and Rationalization Proposals," Voprozy Izobretatelstva
10 (1974): 74-75.
4. E. Zaleski, J. P. Kozlowski, H. Wienert, R. W. Davies,
M. J. Berry, and R. Amann, Science Policy in the USSR (Paris:
Organization for Economic Cooperation and Development, 1969),
p. 441.
5. I. I. Fisher, "Activity of the CPSU in Developing the
Technical Activism of the Working Class in the Struggle for Technical Progress in the Years of the Seven Year Plan" (candidate
dissertation, Leningrad State University, 1971), pp. 130-31.
6. All-Union Society of Inventors and Rationalizers (VOIR),
Information Handbook on the Work of the Central Soviet of VOIR
between the 3rd and 4th Congresses (Moscow: Profizdat, 1973),
p. 6. On specifically workers' proposals, see for example Yakov
Stul, Creative Labor in Socialist Industry (Chelyabinsk: South Urals
Publishing House, 1970), p. 106; and L. T. Makarov, "Raising the

Cultural-Technical Level and Developing the Scientific-Creativity of Workers in the Period of Building Communism" (candidate dissertation, Voronezh State University, 1968), p. 169.

7. B. F. Danilov, Life Is a Search (Moscow: Moscow Worker, 1971), pp. 310-12.

8. Soviet Council of Ministers, op. cit., p. 66.

9. V. V. Volkov, "Automation and the Creative Productive Activity of the Soviet Worker" (candidate dissertation, N. G. Chernishevsky University, Saratov, 1964), p. 198.

10. The discussion here refers to rationalization proposals. Inventions follow a different route, ending in the State Committee of Invention and Discoveries for determination of the novelty (by "world" standards), usually after determination of usefulness has been made by the factory at which the claim originated.

11. For discussion of the routes followed by rationalization proposals through the factory, see A. S. Volokin, "New Methods in the Work of the BRIZ," Voprosy Izobretatelstva 3 (1973): 38-39; A. B. Georgiev, "Great Paths of Krasnoye Sormovo," Voprosy Izobretatelstva 10 (1971): 4; A. G. Bukin, "Organization of the Work of the BRIZ," Voprosy Izobretatelstva 10 (1971): 38-41; V. G. Kurileva, "NOT in the Work of the BRIZ," Voprosy Izobretatelstva 7 (1971): 46.

12. V. Ovchinnikov, "The Coauthorship Craze," Izobretatel i Ratsionalizator 4 (1966): 20.

13. L. Teplov, "Who Are These Co-authors?," Izobretatel i Ratsionalizator 12 (1969): 13-14.

14. State Committee on Inventions and Discoveries (SCID), Central Institute for Raising the Qualifications of Economic Leaders and Specialists in the Area of Patenting, Long Range and Current Thematic Planning of Invention and Rationalization (Moscow: SCID, 1970), pp. 5-7.

15. State Committee on Inventions and Discoveries, Central Institute for Raising the Qualifications of Economic Leaders, Methodological Guidelines for a Course Program on Planning and Organization of Invention and Rationalization (Moscow: Patent, 1971), p. 89. See also discussion in Yu. G. Chulanov, Collective Technical Creativity and Its Effectiveness (Leningrad: Knowledge, 1971), pp. 8, 12.

16. E. D. Oreshnikova, "Development of the Creative Initiative of Soviet Workers," (candidate dissertation, Moscow Oblast Pedagogical Institute, 1968), pp. 148-50.

17. Makarov, op. cit., p. 150.

18. Z. I. Ryzhkovo, "Invention and Rationalization: Under Control of Party Organizations," Voprosy Izobretatelstva 3 (1974): 3-4.

19. G. V. Sheplov, "Role of the Factory Trade Union Committee in Managing Production (1966-70)," (candidate dissertation, Moscow, Higher School of the Trade Union Movement 1973), pp. 162-80.

20. See Resolution of the First All-Union Congress of the Inventors' Society, "On the Problems of Mass Invention in Socialist Construction and the Future Tasks of the Inventors' Society," Izobretatel 2 (1932): 29-33.

21. V. Terekhin, The Work of Factory Commissions for Invention and Rationalization (Moscow: Profizdat, 1951), pp. 5-6.

22. Danilov, op. cit., p. 302.

23. I. F. Suvorov, Engineering-Technical Cadres—Support of the Party in the Struggle for Technical Progress (Moscow: Sovietskaya Rossiya, 1973), p. 207. Figure on Worker Composition of VOIR Presidium from "Composition of Presidium of Central Soviet of VOIR Elected at the Plenum of the VOIR Central Committee," Izobretatel i Ratsionalizator 5 (1973): 17.

24. For criticism of ministries see I. M. Vladychenko, "The Work of VOIR—On the Level of New Tasks," Izobretatel i Ratsionalizator 8, (1968): 2-3. On electrified stands, see V. Karpushchenko, "Short Routes," Izobretatel i Ratsionalizator 6 (1964): 13.

25. V. Abdullayev, "We Should Improve Conditions for Creativity," Izobretatel i Ratsionalizator 7 (1971): 2.

26. On Councils of Innovators see Danilov, op. cit., pp. 151-97, 301-14. Also B. F. Danilov, "Unify the Efforts of Innovators," Kommunist 4 (1963): 126-28.

27. Makarov, op. cit., p. 189. On Social Design Bureaus, see also Chulanov, op. cit., p. 6.

28. Oreshnikova, op. cit., pp. 155-60.

29. V. V. Volkov and V. I. Smolin, Technical Progress and Formation among Soviet Workers of a Creative Relationship to Work (Moscow: Knowledge, 1966), p. 21.

30. R. I. Kolosanov, Communist Labor—Nature and Stimuli (Moscow: Thought, 1968), p. 185.

31. A. V. Vinocur and R. V. Rivkina, "Socio-Economic Problems of the Socialist Rationalization of Production," Soviet Sociology (in English) 3, no. 3 (1965): 6.

32. Ibid.

33. B. I. Yeremeev, Socio-Economic Problems of Technical Creativity in the USSR (Moscow: Thought, 1967), pp. 60-62. also Chulanov, op. cit., p. 16.

34. Ibid, p. 16.

35. Ibid, for additional discussion, see B. I. Yeremeev, Socio-Economic Problems of Technical Creativity in the USSR (Moscow: "Thought," 1967), pp. 60-62.

36. Volkov, op. cit., pp. 127-28, 158.

37. Yeremeev, op. cit., p. 93. Technical participation is a multidimensional phenomenon reflecting such factors as length of service, education, type of production (unit or series), levels of automation, and age (length of use) of factory technology, as well as content of labor. Unfortunately, I did not come across any good methodological analysis of the problem. There is a piecemeal quality to much of the Soviet sociological research on mass innovations. Studies drawn from various shops in various factories show how technical participation is individually related to various factors, for example, positively to intellectual content, education, length of service, and levels of automation (for all professions), and negatively to age of technology and series (as opposed to unit) production. The studies do not show the percentage of variance accounted for by each factor in a given factory or group of factories.

38. G. I. Smirnov, "Legal Questions of Using Technical Achievements in the National Economy of the USSR," (candidate dissertation, Plekhonov Economics Institute, Moscow, 1974), p. 180.

39. Antony Sutton, Western Technology and Soviet Economic Development, 1930-1945 (Stanford: Hoover Institution, 1971), pp. 73, 82-85, 105, 133, 162, 246, 251. Soviet engineers also visited the United States for training during the 1936-38 period. Ibid., pp. 275-77. Sutton notes, however, that most of the Western specialists accompanying the transfer of technology to the USSR had left by mid-1932.

40. A Soviet scholar with whom I talked in Moscow remarked, ridiculing Mao, that the "thought of Lenin" is not immanent in the creativity of the individual Soviet worker.

41. "All-China Federation of Trade Unions' Explanation of Certain Problems concerning Provisional Regulation for Rewarding Production-Related Discoveries, Technical Improvements, and Rationalization Proposals," Jen-min Jih-pao, August 28, 1954, p. 2. See also Chao Erh-lu, "Produce More and Better Machines to Ensure High Tempo of Socialist Construction," Survey of the China Mainland Press, no. 1793 (1958), p. 133; also Jen-min Jih-pao, May 31, 1958, for a retrospective comment on Soviet styles of technical management in the 1950s.

42. For example, "For National Industrialization, Unfold the Technical Innovation Movement," Jen-min Jih-pao, editorial, April 16, 1954, p. 1.

43. Rensselaer W. Lee III, "Ideology and Technical Innovation in Chinese Industry, 1949-72," Asian Survey 7, no. 8 (1972): 648-49.

44. Ibid., pp. 649-50.

45. Mikhail Klochko, Un Russe en Chine, translated from the Russian by Stepan Chripounoff (Paris: Gallimard, 1964), p. 180.

46. Chen Hsin-cheng, "All Together—For 150,000 Cars a Year," China Reconstructs (in English) 8, no. 2 (1959): 6.

47. Ibid.

48. Chen Hsin-cheng, "Rely on the Masses for Reforming Industrial Management," Survey of the China Mainland Press, no. 1914 (1958), pp. 2-4, from Jen-min Jih-pao, November 27, 1958.

49. Op. cit.

50. Wu Wen-pin, "Unreasonable Regulations and Systems Must Be Reformed," Selections from China Mainland Magazines, no. 146 (1958), pp. 9-11, from Che Hsueh Yen Chiu, no. 4 (August 10, 1958).

51. Lu Tien-hung, "Concerning the Raising of Industrial Labor Productivity," Selections from China Mainland Magazines, no. 179 (1959), p. 18, from Li Lun Chan Hsien, no. 5 (May 10, 1959).

52. "Maintenance of Equipment is a Matter of Great Importance in Industrial Production," Survey of the China Mainland Press, no. 2077 (1959), p. 7, from Liaoning Jih Pao, June 19, 1959.

53. Lu Tien-hung, "Massively Consolidate, Promote, and Elevate Technological Revolution," Joint Publications Research Service, no. 5349 (1960), p. 6, from Jen-min Jih-pao, May 26, 1960.

54. "Workers of Machine Building Industry Revolutionize Old Products," Joint Publications Research Service, no. 7135 (1960), p. 3, from Kuang-ming Jih-pao, September 23, 1960. On simplicity of indigenous methods, see Lu Tien-hung, "Massively Consolidate, Promote, and Elevate Technological Revolution," op. cit., p. 6.

55. Ibid., pp. 3-7.

56. K'o Ching-shih, "Leading the Advance of Technical Revolution along the Correct Scientific and All-People Road," Joint Publications Research Service, no. 5245 (1960), p. 135, from Chieh Fang, no. 7 (April 5, 1960), pp. 8-9.

57. Lewis Mumford, Technics and Civilization (New York: Harcourt-Brace, 1963), p. 350.

58. Wang Hou-shou, "Raise Aloft the Red Flag of 'Small, Modern, Mass' Iron and Steel Works," Current Background, no. 618 (1960), p. 13, from New China News Agency, Peking, April 10, 1960.

59. Wang Hou-shou, "Cultural Revolution Releases Productive Forces in Clock Factory," Survey of the China Mainland Press, no. 4222 (1968), p. 19, from New China News Agency, Shanghai, July 15, 1968.

60. Rensselaer W. Lee III, "The Politics of Technology in Communist China," in Ideology and Politics in Communist China, ed. Chalmers Johnson (Seattle: University of Washington Press, 1973), pp. 309-310.

61. Ibid. , pp. 318 and 323.

62. "Workers Must Strive to Master Science and Technology," Selections from China Mainland Magazines, no. 751 (1973), p. 75, from Hung Chi, no. 4 (April 1, 1973).

63. "Emphasize Not Only Daring but Also Education," Kuang-ming Jih-pao, May 5, 1972, p. 1.

64. Vinocur and Rivkina, op. cit., p. 6.

65. George V. Daniels, Science in American Society (New York: Knopf, 1971), p. 271.

THE IMPACT OF TECHNOLOGY AND TECHNICAL RATIONALITY ON SOCIALIST SOCIETIES

7

DIABOLUS EX MACHINA:
**TECHNOLOGICAL
DEVELOPMENT AND
SOCIAL CHANGE IN
CHINESE INDUSTRY**
Richard Baum

Philosophers of history and social critics from Karl Marx to Marshall McLuhan, from Karl Mannheim to Lewis Mumford, have reflected on the relationship between technological development and social change in industrial societies. Within the relatively new field of comparative communist studies, this question has generated considerable debate and disagreement, centering upon the highly controversial theory of technobureaucratic convergence.

In its simplest form, convergence theory consists of three interrelated propositions: (1) that technological development is essentially unilinear, that is, that there exists a relatively fixed path or sequence of technological innovation over which all industrializing societies must travel in their quest for modernity; (2) that modern industrial technology tends to impose similar organizational constraints upon all societies, regardless of differences in culture, ideology, or political institutions; and (3) that in the process of adapting to these universal constraints, human values and behavior patterns tend to converge in a technobureaucratic ethos of "amoral instrumentalism."[1]

In this chapter I shall assess the industrial experience of the People's Republic of China in an effort to determine whether and to what extent that experience has conformed to the expectations of convergence theory. Specifically, I shall examine the impact of modern industrial technology upon the organization, management, and social relations of Chinese industrial enterprises.

China provides a particularly interesting test of convergence theory because in China, perhaps more than anywhere else, the assumptions of the technobureaucratic model of industrial organization and management have been vigorously challenged and rejected in favor of a nondeterministic ethos of "revolutionary activism."

Almost alone among industrializing nations, China has seemingly defied, or at least sought to "bend," many of the putative organizational and behavioral imperatives of technological development. It has been widely observed, for example, that The Thought of Mao Tse-tung contains numerous precepts that are either explicitly or inferentially antagonistic to such ostensibly universal attributes of modern industry as extreme labor specialization, task routinization, bureaucratic formalism, and technocratic instrumentalism. A number of trained observers have claimed to detect in the Chinese industrial experience a significant departure from the conventional organizational and managerial practices that characterize Western and Soviet industrial enterprises. [2]

The Maoist ethos of revolutionary activism stresses the primacy of the subjective "human factor"—leadership, morale, political consciousness, and so on—over the objective material factors of production. In an oft-quoted essay published in 1938, Mao wrote that "objective factors make change possible, but it requires correct directives and efforts on the subjective side to turn this possibility into actuality. . . . It is man, not material that counts."[3]

Once "correct directives and efforts on the subjective side" have been firmly grasped by the masses, they are putatively transformed from a subjective force to an objective force, or "spiritual atomic bomb," capable of bringing about qualitative "leaps forward" in economic and social development. It was precisely such a belief that led Mao to attempt a massive substitution of human labor for physical capital during the Great Leap Forward of 1957-59. It was similarly this belief that led to the ill-fated adoption of the "Paris Commune" model of municipal government—marked by a virtual abolition of the division of labor in administration and management—during the early stages of the Great Proletarian Cultural Revolution in 1967.

In order to fully mobilize human initiative in pursuit of voluntaristic "leaps forward" in socioeconomic development, Maoists have consistently stressed the need to place "politics in command" of economic work. With respect to the goal of industrial modernization, this has meant the following:

> Unlike the modern revisionists who one-sidedly stress
> the material factor, mechanization and modernization,
> [we] pay chief attention to the revolutionization of man's
> thinking and, through this, we command, guide and
> promote the work of mechanization and modernization. [4]

In the realm of industrial organization and management, Maoist voluntarism has been manifested in repeated campaigns to oppose the "conservative thinking" that typifies the technobureaucratic mode of enterprise management. Industrial intellectuals, office-bound bureaucrats, and narrow technical specialists have frequently been derided in China for their lack of bold initiative, their "slavish devotion" to established routines and procedures, and their alleged tendency to lose sight of the human factor while "chasing only after the latest technical equipment."[5]

The source of Mao's concern with such phenomena lay in his deep-seated fear of a possible "capitalist restoration" in China—a fear rooted in his observation of the evolution of Soviet organizational and managerial practices in the 1950s and 1960s. In Mao's view, the capitalistic mode of production, which is characterized by fragmentation of work, material incentives, hierarchy, and inequality, is neither automatically nor inevitably destroyed when the means of production are socialized. On the contrary, the contradiction between socialist ownership and bourgeois production relations continues to exist, according to Mao, throughout the transitional stage of socialist construction. It is the continued existence of this contradiction that makes it necessary to place "politics in command" of industrial management.

The French socialist writer K. S. Karol has clearly elucidated the nature and origins of Mao's concern over "spontaneous capitalist tendencies" in Chinese industry as follows:

> The proletariat, after its victory, . . . must keep the old mode of production and transform it by degrees, while continuing to make it work. . . . Since they must continue to produce, the workers must continue to be workers, subordinated to the productive rhythm of the factory; . . . they cannot do without the machine they have inherited. But if they continue to use it, do they not risk contaminating the new society? As long as economic growth is based on this system, will it not be necessary to preserve the fragmentation of work, the social division of labor, hierarchy and inequality? . . . Mao Tse-tung realized that it is necessary at all costs to control the deep and inevitable tendency to perpetuate the capitalist mode of production, which the revolution inherited from the past and is compelled to use. And this must be done without destroying the productive apparatus, but by using it while defeating its own logic, bending it to priorities other than its own. . . . Until the transition to true communism, ideological and egalitarian counterpressures must be set in motion . . . to prevent the hierarchy of the technical division of labor from being translated directly into distinctions of social status.[6]

Herein lies the crux of Mao's "voluntarist" deviation—not in any opposition to industrial modernization and technological progress as such, but rather in his belief that the technobureaucratic mode of industrial organization and management, with its built-in hierarchics and occupational inequalities, is a bourgeois remnant, a transitional carryover from capitalism, rather than a technologically determined imperative of industrial modernization itself. It is this belief that divides Mao from the convergence theorists.

Although some of Mao's apologists, including K. S. Karol, acknowledge that the tendency to perpetuate technobureaucratic industrial production relations is inevitable, they nevertheless hold that through the exertion of "ideological and egalitarian counterpressures," such tendencies can be successfully combatted.

There can be no doubt that Mao Tse-tung actively sought to exert such counterpressures. He firmly insisted, for example, that managerial cadres, engineers, and technicians must regularly participate in industrial labor in order to avoid becoming "divorced from production." He constantly demanded that ordinary industrial workers must participate in various aspects of enterprise management and technical innovation; he repeatedly attempted to restrict occupational pay differentials between mental and manual workers; he consistently sought to reduce nonproductive midlevel management; and he launched a series of mass political movements—including the Socialist Education Campaign and the Great Proletarian Cultural Revolution—that were designed to innoculate the Chinese people against the corrupting virus of bourgeois mentality.

How successful was the Chairman in combatting the "capitalist tendencies" that inhere in conventional technobureaucratic relations of production? In what ways and to what extent have such production relations been successfully modified or substantially altered by Maoist voluntarism in the course of China's industrial development? Has Maoist ideo-logic provided a viable alternative to the techno-logic of convergence theory? Just how different is China?

In seeking to answer these questions, we shall examine four aspects of the technological-organizational-managerial nexus in Chinese industry: (1) the "state of the art" of productive technology in the modern, heavy industrial sector; (2) the technical organization of work and work processes in modern industrial enterprises; (3) managerial policies and practices; and (4) the informal social structure and interpersonal relations of the factory. By focusing our attention on these critical aspects of organizational structure and behavior, we may hope to shed additional light on the convergence controversy that currently engulfs the field of comparative communism.

THE TECHNOLOGICAL "STATE OF THE ART"

According to a typology officially adopted by the Soviet State Committee for Instruments of Measurement, Means of Automation and Control Systems, technologies of industrial manufacture may be classified in the following evolutionary sequence:

1. <u>mechanized manual production</u>, in which manual labor is used to perform complex tasks with the assistance of relatively simple tools or machinery, powered manually, electrically, hydraulically, or by compressed air;

2. <u>mechanized production</u>, in which the work of loading, direct processing, and unloading is performed automatically by complex machines powered electrically, hydraulically, or by compressed air;

3. <u>integrated mechanized production</u>, in which the entire cycle of the production process is performed by complex, manually operated machinery;

4. <u>automated production</u>, in which all basic and ancillary operations are performed by machines and mechanical devices; and

5. <u>integrated automated production</u>, in which even the regulatory operations are carried out automatically, through cybernetic servomechanisms, so that the complete production cycle is governed without human intervention. [7]

According to this evolutionary typology, Chinese industrial technology in the modern sector is currently approaching the threshold between Stage 2 and Stage 3, with certain vanguard industries (primarily in the strategic defense sector) having already achieved Stage 3 production capability.

In the vital machine-building industry, semiautomated equipment (that is, machines that perform automatically all operations involved in the direct processing of the work piece but require human intervention in loading, unloading, setting, and regulating the apparatus) are in widespread use in China, with a few of the largest machine tools having automatic (program controlled) setting and adjusting devices. In most cases, transfer lines conveying semifinished or finished pieces from one work station to another are manually or semimanually operated. [8]

This last-noted feature, the manual or semimanual operation of transfer lines, illustrates a key feature of Chinese industrial enterprises, which is the technological bifurcation between <u>primary</u> manufacturing processes, such as metal casting, milling, and machining, and secondary processes, such as transport, assembly, and inspection. It has been widely noted that many Chinese factories display a curious combination of highly mechanized, capital-intensive primary technology and semimechanized, labor-intensive secondary technology. This phenomenon of technological bifurcation seems to have evolved in response to China's particular constellation of available production factors and the relative scarcities thereof: a relative excess of unskilled and semiskilled labor, coupled with a severe shortage of investment capital and basic design and engineering expertise. Hence, secondary production functions that by their nature do not require a high degree of mechanized standardization tend to remain largely labor-intensive. In a labor-surplus economy it is simply more feasible (and cheaper) to employ several semiskilled workers to transport work pieces on hand carts from machine to machine than to design, build, and install expensive automatic transfer lines. While such a technological mix may not seem terribly modern, it does appear to be quite rational at China's present stage of development. [9]

The Shanghai turbine plant provides a good example of this type of technological mix—a combination of Stage 2 primary technology and Stage 1 secondary technology. This factory, the first in China to series-produce a .3 million kilowatt steam turbine, has an impressive array of some 1,300 relatively modern machine tools, many of which are semiautomatic in nature. The very largest lathes, those used to machine the enormous turbine and valve housing assemblies, are program controlled, but the vast majority of smaller machines have hand-operated verniers for setting and adjusting machine tolerances. Transfer of semifinished work pieces is accomplished by means of a combination of overhead cranes (for heavy, bulky pieces) and manually operated flatbed trucks (for smaller, lighter pieces). Inspection of processed work pieces is manually governed. The workers use templates and micrometers to check each individual tolerance. Finishing and final assembly are also semimechanized; teams of workers perform the tasks of fitting and joining the various pieces with the assistance of manually operated cranes, winches, and power tools.

By current world standards, metal forging and casting techniques in the Shanghai turbine plant are not particularly advanced. Much of the precision machining done by semiautomatic lathes in the factory would be considered obsolescent in Western or Soviet enterprises of a similar nature, where the required tolerances are now attained directly in the casting process—a step-saving innovation made possible by recent advances in metallurgical and sand casting technology.

Although the Shanghai turbine plant reportedly began to convert from production of steam turbines to more technologically sophisticated gas turbines in 1973, the plant has yet to go into series production of the new-type engines. The primary explanation for this delay lies in the higher-heat-resistant finishes and more precise machine tolerances demanded of materials used in the manufacture of gas turbines. According to a mechanical engineer who toured the plant with me in May 1975, the metallurgical, sand-casting, and machining technologies utilized in the factory were not refined or sophisticated enough to meet the precision requirements of gas turbine production.

In terms of physical output and productivity, the Shanghai turbine plant cannot be regarded as highly efficient by contemporary Western or Soviet standards. With a total labor force of 8,300 workers and technical staff and 1,300 machine tools, the plant's total output in 1974 was ten steam turbines with an aggregate capacity of 1.4 million kilowatts. The chairman of the factory's revolutionary committee frankly acknowledged to me that this output figure was not particularly impressive for such a large, highly mechanized plant as follows:

> Although we have made some progress, our plant is
> still lagging behind. We are unable to cope with the
> demands put forward by the Party and the people.
> . . . [For this reason] we are currently undergoing
> a process of adjustment and filling in gaps. . . .
> Our productivity is still low.

In the opinion of one U.S. expert, a likely explanation for low productivity in the factory was the fact that continued reliance on labor-intensive secondary technologies, such as the need for constant, time-consuming checking and rechecking of machinery and for setting and resetting of machine tolerances on each work piece at each stage of the production cycle and the difficulty of finishing and assembling the giant turbines without automatic machinery, necessarily had an adverse effect upon the rhythm of the productive cycle, with the result that the cycle was neither smooth nor continuous.

Judging from the reports of several foreigners who have visited various Chinese machine-building enterprises, the technologies of manufacture utilized in the Shanghai turbine plant are rather typical of the nonstrategic sector of Chinese heavy industry. There is some evidence, however, that in certain key national-defense-related industries, such as the production of MIG 21 jet

fighter aircraft, more sophisticated main-line and secondary-line
technologies, of the Stage 3 variety, are in operation, including
advanced metal-forging and casting techniques, fully automatic
program-controlled machine tools, and mechanized transfer lines. [10]
Published data on such security-sensitive manufacturing processes
are extremely sparse, however, [11] and the Chinese defense industries are not subject to direct scrutiny by foreign observers. Hence
our primary observations about Chinese industrial technology must
be limited to the nonstrategic civilian sector.

One interesting feature of Chinese machine-building technology
that has been the subject of much discussion in the mass media in
recent years is the technique known generically as "ants gnawing at
a bone." In the absence of advanced forging and casting technology,
large automated machine tools, or mechanized continuous flow
transfer lines, many extremely large pieces of industrial equipment
are manufactured by breaking down the primary production and
assembly-processes into component units, with a series of small,
manually-operated lathes, cranes, and finishing machines utilized
in modular fashion rather than in continuous sequence. The various
semifinished modules are then joined in the final assembly process
by welding or by screws. Using such "intermediate" techniques, the
Shanghai heavy machine building plant reportedly built a twelve-ton
hydraulic forging press without any large-scale, heavy-duty machine
tools. [12]

Two obvious advantages of this "gnawing" technique are, first,
that small, relatively simple and inexpensive tools can be used to
produce large, complex equipment and, second, the modular nature
of the finished product obviates the need to scrap the whole piece in
the event of partial malfunction. The major limitation on this type
of manufacturing process is that it is ostensibly best suited to the
production of bulky, but not particularly sophisticated or high-pre-
cision machinery. Moreover, it is extremely difficult to ensure the
standardization of machine components through such a process. [13]

Despite the Maoist exhortation that China display basic "self-
reliance" in technological innovation, it appears that most of the
heavy machine tools currently in use in China are either of foreign
manufacture or foreign design. At the Shanghai turbine plant, for
example, all of the large, heavy-duty lathes bore foreign brand
names, with Russian, German, and Japanese machines being most
numerous. Many of the smaller lathes were of Chinese manufacture,
although in the opinion of the aforementioned expert, they appeared
to closely resemble Western and Soviet machine tools of a similar
nature. Indeed, the secretary of the plant's revolutionary committee acknowledged that "a certain number" of the factory's machine
tools had originally been copied from Soviet prototypes. A tour

through the industrial machinery exhibit at the Canton Trade Fair
subsequently confirmed the impression that Chinese machine tools
were largely copies or modifications of Soviet, European, Japanese,
and American designs.

Not technological innovation, but rather technological adaptation seems to be the primary mode of industrial self-reliance in
China today. This is reflected in the fact that most of the publicity
given to "native" technical innovations in the Chinese media pertains
to the successful modification of foreign machinery rather than to
the original design of wholly new-type equipment.

The Chinese desire to break away from foreign stereotypes
and conventions and to avoid "mechanical application of foreign
experience" in industrial technology has been widely noted in the
literature.[14] At least three reasons have been advanced to account
for this seemingly stubborn Chinese insistence on technological independence. First, China's past experience with technological dependency proved disastrous—particularly in the early 1960s, when
the abrupt withdrawal of Soviet technical assistance left the Chinese
unable to complete half-finished construction projects (they lacked
the blueprints and basic design and performance data), unable to
manufacture spare parts for completed factories, and unable to
modify existing industrial facilities to meet China's changing needs.

Second, China's available pool of production factors—labor
skills, investment capital, raw materials, and productive technology—differs appreciably from those of the more advanced industrial
nations, thus rendering "blind imitation of foreign techniques" undesirable in terms of the optimal utilization of available resources.
Thus, for example, the extreme scarcity of investment capital
means that China simply cannot afford to discard obsolete machinery
and "chase only after the latest [that is, foreign] technical equipment." Outmoded equipment must be either "transferred downward"
or salvaged and recycled into new equipment; industrial waste
products must similarly be saved and reprocessed wherever possible. (A good illustration of the latter practice is provided by a
Shanghai machine tool factory that has organized a "housewives'
brigade" to pick metal chips out of discarded work rags. The metal
chips are collected for subsequent smelting in the plant's foundry,
while the rags are cleaned and sent on for reprocessing into usable
industrial-grade cloth.)

Wheelwright and McFarlane note that the primary economic
rationale for the Chinese policy of industrial self-reliance is the
idea that "no equipment should be scrapped and no method rejected
so long as the materials and the labor used with them cannot find a
better use elsewhere."[15] Indeed, the ubiquitous internal transfer

and recycling of obsolescent equipment and waste products is perhaps the most widely visible manifestation of industrial self-reliance
in China today.

Finally, there is a widely noted ideological aversion to technological dependency in China. This aversion stems from two main
sources. On the one hand, China's initial response to the impact of
Western industrialization in the last half of the nineteenth century
was a "self-strengthening" movement characterized by the ethnocentric slogan, "Chinese learning as the foundation; Western learning for practical application." This formula, with its built-in
rejection of "barbarian" values and its extreme cultural nationalism,
finds its contemporary analogue in the Maoist exhortation to "use
foreign things for Chinese purposes." On the other hand, there is a
distinctly modern, uniquely Maoist ideological aversion to the
extreme technobureaucratic production relations engendered by the
most advanced foreign technologies—an aversion born of Mao's
distrust of narrow specialists and bureaucratic hierarchies and his
extreme faith in the creative technical and managerial potential of
the Chinese masses. For all of these reasons—bitter experience
with Soviet technical patronage, economic scarcity, traditional
nationalistic "culturism" and modern ideological egalitarianism—
Mao insisted that the Chinese people must "keep the initiative in our
own hands" in the process of industrial modernization. [16]

In practice this emphasis on technological self-reliance has
been tempered by the realization that technological borrowing, if
not done "mechanically" or "slavishly," can be of tremendous
benefit to China's modernization. Thus Chinese leaders have not
closed the door to foreign technology. On the contrary, recent years
have seen dramatic increases in Chinese imports of foreign technology, ranging from precision machine tools to commercial airplanes,
from synthetic fiber plants to entire steel mills, from oil-drilling
rigs to chemical fertilizer factories.

What is different today is that China now seeks to import more
than merely the finished means of production. Wherever possible,
China also seeks to import the basic design technologies, including
blueprints, engineering specifications, test and laboratory reports
on materials performance, and so on, in order to master the arts
of prototype copying and design modification. [17]

It is design modification that is the key element in China's
current drive to retain technological initiative. If there is one single theme that dominates the mass campaign to avoid "blind imitation" of foreign techniques, it is the demand that Chinese workers,
technicians, and engineers become adept at modifying imported
technology to meet Chinese requirements. A typical article in the

Chinese press thus states that "an important aspect of . . . technical innovation . . . [is the need to] make bold changes in the design of production [in order to create] new Chinese-type products characterized by their small size, lightness, high efficiency, and simple structure."[18]

Thus not innovation but adaptation is the primary mode of technological self-reliance in the modern industrial sector in contemporary China. The very latest foreign machines, and even entire factories, continue to be imported in ever-larger quantities and continue to dominate China's heavy industry. Such machinery is increasingly subject to "native" modifications in design and utilization, however, thus insuring at least a modicum of self-retained technological initiative. Rather than renounce the acquisition of foreign technology as such, Chinese leaders have exhorted engineers and technical personnel in all industrial enterprises to "make a concrete analysis of foreign things, select their essence, and discard their dregs."[19] Somewhat paradoxically, it may be noted that such exhortations would seem to embody a basic reversal of the nineteenth century dictum: "Chinese learning as the foundation; Western learning for practical application." Today the operative slogan would seem to be, in effect, "Western learning as the foundation; Chinese learning for practical application."

China's continued reliance upon foreign prototypes and basic design technologies points up a fundamental weakness in its current scientific and engineering research and development. As Hans Heymann has aptly noted, there is a world of difference between the "technology of the laboratory" and the "technology of the factory," between the art of prototype copying and the development of independent production capability, and between minor design modification and major design innovation.[20] While the Chinese have been relatively successful in copying and modifying many foreign machines and techniques, they have had less success in basic research and development.

In their insistence that the laboratory must be responsive to the immediate needs of the factory, that engineers and technicians must humbly "learn from the masses," and that mental workers must become integrated with manual workers, the Chinese have arguably made great strides in breaking down the traditional barriers between theory and practice, between mental and manual labor, and between "book learning" and "learning by experience." In so doing, however, they have, in Heymann's words, "neglected to nurture a corps of highly qualified experimental development, design, and engineering talent."

This shortcoming has not gone unnoticed within China, and in recent years Chinese policy makers have subtly redefined the con-

cept of technological self-reliance. While continuing to oppose the
"revisionist" line of "worshipping foreign things, trumpeting the
slavish comprador philosophy, and promoting the mentality of
trailing behind at a snail's pace," the new emphasis is clearly on
selective borrowing to enhance China's capacity for independent
design and engineering. Recognizing that a prototype "reveals only
what was produced; it does not reveal how it was produced,"[21] Chinese policy makers argue as follows:

> The introduction of a bit of foreign technology is permis-
> sible . . . [but] we can only use it as a reference and
> must actively catch up with it. We must make discoveries,
> inventions, and progress. Otherwise we shall always be
> trailing along at a snail's pace behind other people.[22]
>
>   . . .
>
> Purchasing sample machines from others can only be for
> the purpose of increasing our knowledge and knowing how
> others have taken their road. We cannot open up a road
> for ourselves merely by copying from others.[23]

To sum up the "state of the art" of industrial technology in
China, the People's Republic is currently at an intermediate stage
of development between mechanized manual production (Stage 1) and
semiautomated production (Stage 3). Primary production functions
tend to be more highly mechanized than secondary functions, which
continue to display considerable labor-intensity. Emphasis in the
vital machine-building industry is on lightweight, variable-perform-
ance machine tools, the majority of which have been imported,
copied, or modified from foreign designs and prototypes. Prototype
copying and functional modification of imported technology have been
stressed over theoretical research, with a corresponding emphasis
on factory-centered technical innovation rather than laboratory-
centered experimentation. Acquisition of industrial technology from
abroad has centered around procurement of the most sophisticated,
up-to-date processes, equipment, and designs. The policy of self-
reliance has been implemented primarily in nonstrategic sectors,
both as a pragmatic response to endemic problems of economic
scarcity and as an ideologically inspired (nationalistic and egalitarian) response to both the dangers of excessive technological dependency and the ascribed evils of technobureaucratic production relations.

THE STRUCTURE OF TECHNICAL ORGANIZATION

Industrial organization in China is divided into three distinct
but complementary functional spheres, the technical, the administra-

tive, and the social. Technical organization is described by one authoritative Chinese source as "reflecting the objective laws of the production process," that is, the physical arrangements for converting the forces of production into the means of production. Administrative organization on the other hand, is described as "reflecting the production relationships and management order within the enterprise"—the structural relationships of subordination and superordination, authority and supervision, involved in the process of coordinating technical organization. [24] Both technical and administrative structures belong to the realm of formal organization, insofar as they comprehend the physical specifications of work processes and the institutionalized production relations pertaining thereto.

Social organization, by contrast, is informal insofar as it deals with the complex network of human relations that parallels, but is not necessarily congruent with, an organization's formal technical and administrative structures. Social organization thus comprehends questions of social stratification (as opposed to the functional division of labor), worker motivation, labor-management relations, group dynamics, and various other aspects of noninstitutionalized intraorganizational behavior.

In the modern sector of heavy industry, technical organization in China is largely determined by the nature of the enterprises' primary production functions and the types of manufacturing technologies utilized. For example, in the No. 2 steel rolling mill at Anshan, which is one of the more modern industrial plants that has been visited in recent years by foreign observers, the factory, which employs over 3,000 workers, is divided into 13 workshops, corresponding to the various stages and processes used in the manufacture of rolled steel, including hot rolling, cold treatment, plating, and so on. The machinery utilized in the various workshops is generally of the Stage 2 variety and, as in the case of the Shanghai turbine plant, is largely of foreign manufacture or design. [25]

The technical force of the Anshan rolling mill consists of some 350 technicians, many of whom were graduated from the Shenyang Industrial College, and "more than ten" trained engineers. Each of the plant's 13 main workshops is internally divided into production groups (on the average, 8 to 12 groups per shop), with the membership of each production group determined by functional task, such as roller operators, machinists, or shearers, rather than by workshift assignment or work-post proximity. (The plant operates around the clock on three eight-hour shifts.)

The technical division of labor within each of the plant's various workshops is highly specialized. Each worker normally performs a single task or a series of related tasks at a single piece of machinery. The subdivision of each workshop into task-oriented production groups serves further to reinforce the functional specificity of the technical division of labor.

The phenomenon of Chinese industrial workers specializing in a single task or working at a single type of machine is clearly prevalent throughout the country. Moreover, and somewhat suprisingly, there does not seem to be a great deal of intersectoral variation in this pattern of technical job specialization. Thus, at three of the "native" and intermediate-technology enterprises of various sizes that I visited, a medium-sized, labor-intensive ceramics factory in suburban Canton, a small commune-run farm tool factory in suburban Shanghai, and an electrical circuit assembly plant run by a secondary school in Peking, the workers in each enterprise were assigned to fixed work stations, where they repeated the performance of a single, specialized task, with or without the assistance of mechanized tools. At the electrical assembly plant run by the Peking No. 35 Middle School, for example, each student spends one month per year in the school factory, which manufactures light-flashing units for trucks and automobiles, learning to perform one specific task. Labor is finely divided in this semimechanized enterprise. The machining of the various components and stamping of the electrical circuits are done with small, flexible Stage-1 type machine tools, while the wiring, final assembly, inspection, and regulation of the finished units are done by hand, with long rows of student-workers sitting at benches, each performing a single wiring, fastening, soldering, or adjusting operation.

When I asked several students in the wiring line of this factory if they ever exchanged jobs with coworkers up or down the line or in the other workshops, they responded in the negative—they performed the same task on the same line for the entire duration of their stay in the factory. When I asked a group of assembly workers whether their work, which appeared quite tedious and repetitive, might not be more interesting if it involved more variety and less simple, mechanical repetition, they did not respond at all. My strong impression was that they had simply never considered such an alternative.

During the Great Leap Forward (1958-60), Chinese leaders sought to break away from conventional (Western and Soviet) patterns of labor specialization by advocating that laboring people should seek to become "all-around hands" (to-mien shou), as in Marx's vision of the abolition of the division of labor in communist society. For a brief time, occupational distinctions were indeed at least partially obliterated, as peasants were mobilized to undertake water conservancy construction and/or iron smelting work (in backyard blast furnaces); as industrial workers and soldiers engaged in agricultural production; and as intellectuals, technical workers, and

administrative cadres were "sent down" to do manual labor in farms
and factories. This pattern of multifunctional labor all but disappeared, however, in the aftermath of the economic crisis of 1959-60,
and by 1961 the "all-around hand" had been supplanted once more by
the "master of one technique" as the model worker in Chinese industry. Line workers returned to the line; engineers returned to the
drawing boards; technicians confined their activities primarily to
the solution of technical problems; and administrative cadres were
sent back to do administrative work.

   With some modification (for example, there have been continued exhortations for technical and administrative personnel to spend
a certain portion of their time on the factory floor and for ordinary
workers to be given augmented roles in such matters as technical
innovation and workshop management), this post-Great Leap pattern
of increasing industrial labor specialization has remained largely
constant since the early 1960s (excluding temporary aberrations
during the Cultural Revolution). By and large, there is little evidence
that the Chinese have successfully abolished, or even significantly
attenuated, conventional patterns of functional specificity in the
industrial division of labor.

   One potentially significant caveat must be raised in this connection, however. Since 1972 there have been quite a few references in the Chinese media to a new-type model industrial worker
who combines the best features of the "all-around hand" and the
"master of one technique." This is the worker who has "one specialty and many abilities" (i-chuan, to-neng). Based on this hybrid
model, machine operators in some industrial enterprises have been
encouraged to learn maintenance and repair work in their spare
time in order to help overcome the bottlenecks that periodically
arise when malfunctioning machinery causes disruptions in the
production cycle. One highly publicized case, the Tach'ing petrochemical plant, gave rise to the following report:

> In the past, machinery repair workers only took care
> of machinery inspection and repair, and line workers
> only took care of production, so when a piece of equip-
> ment suddenly developed trouble . . . it was always
> "The repair workers are busy; the line workers must
> wait." This adversely affected production. . . . Now
> the plant's [line] workers not only can run their equip-
> ment, but can also protect and take care of it. . . .
> [Some] of them are also able to repair and rebuild.
> Since we began advocating "one specialty and many
> abilities," everyone is able to use the equipment more
> effectively. [26]

Other media sources have discussed the institution of a system of volunteer labor transfers, wherein temporarily idle workers from one shop are mobilized to help solve problems or overcome production bottlenecks in another shop. In one such case, workers in the Shanghai electrical appliance plant were reportedly able to build a new enamelling machine through an intraenterprise transfer of labor, as follows:

> As manpower was insufficient, the various workshops voluntarily sent some of their production workers to help. Moreover, the boundaries of work were removed, with everyone learning to do many jobs. The plating worker could do tho job of the welder; the grinder could do the job of the turner; even the mason and carpenter came forward to attend the lathes. Coming off their regular shifts, the production workers enthusiastically took part in voluntary labor. [27]

Such reports of skilled laborers in relatively modern (Stage 2) enterprises being transferred to new tasks involving different specialized skills are relatively infrequent. For the most part, multifunctional industrial labor of the "all-around hand" variety is virtually extinct in such enterprises, while the hybrid worker who combines "one specialty with many abilities" is most frequently encountered in enterprises utilizing semimechanized manufacturing technologies of the Stage 1 variety.

Any given technical division of industrial labor can be characterized by four distinct, variable functional dimensions: (1) the degree of requisite physical skill and manual dexterity (a function of the simplicity or complexity of each individual task); (2) the degree of requisite technical knowledge (a function of the simplicity or complexity of the machinery); (3) the degree of requisite skill differentiation (a function of the universality or particularity of the productive machinery); and (4) the degree of requisite task differentiation (a function of the simplicity or complexity of the total manufacturing process). Since each of these variables, as well as the manifold interrelationships among them, are subject to both qualitative and quantitative change at successive stages in the process of technological evolution, it is both unwise and unwarranted to make long-range predictions of wholesale, unilinear increase in the functional specificity of the Chinese industrial division of labor. As reported in a 1966 study of Soviet industrial organization, for example, there have been significantly enhanced opportunities for job enlargement and multiskilled technical competence among machine workers, tool setters, fitter-repairmen, and electricians

in Stage 4 industrial enterprises, as compared with similar occupational categories in Stage 2 and 3 enterprises. [28]

More important for our present purposes is the fact that
changes in intra-occupational labor mobility within a factory do not
necessarily vary in direct proportion to changes in inter-occupational
mobility. For example, skilled machine-tool operators in a Stage
1 enterprise, who perform relatively complex tasks using relatively
simple machines, would have a more difficult time learning to perform new line operations within the same job classification than
their counterparts in a Stage 3 enterprise, who perform relatively
simple tasks using relatively complex and sophisticated machines.
Conversely, machine operators in a Stage 1 enterprise would have
less difficulty learning to repair and maintain their own machines
than their counterparts in a Stage 3 enterprise.

It is not particularly surprising, therefore, that the vast
majority of Chinese media reports pertaining to the phenomenon of
line workers learning to repair and maintain their own equipment
come from Stage 1 enterprises, while most reports of line workers
moving laterally about the factory (that is, from machine to machine) tend to come from more technologically sophisticated enterprises. [29]

Finally, there is evidence to indicate that some of the rigidities in job classification that characterize Western industrial
enterprises have been reduced, or in some cases eliminated, in
Chinese enterprises. In the West, such rigidities frequently stem
not from "rational" technical imperatives but from the insistence of
labor unions that the exact specifications of each particular job be
minutely defined in the work contract. Thus, for example, line
workers in a U.S. automotive assembly plant are not permitted,
under current union contracts, to change so much as a light bulb at
their own work stations. While such rigidities in job classification
are ostensibly intended to prevent workers from being exploited by
management, the effect has often been to perpetuate, and even
exacerbate, irrationalities in the technical division of labor. In
order to overcome such tendencies, the Chinese in recent years
have sought to reform or abolish "irrational rules and regulations"
governing industrial job specifications. In one factory, for example,
it was reported that due to an "excessively fine division of labor,"
line workers "often stood around with nothing to do" while awaiting
materials, repairs, or maintenance personnel. After reforming
"irrational systems" of labor allocation, line workers in the factory
reportedly undertook daily care and minor maintenance themselves
and even assisted in various nonline tasks on a voluntary basis,
after hours and on weekends. [30]

In summary, the technical structure of modern industrial enterprises in China largely conforms to conventional patterns of increasing functional specificity in the division of labor. Industrial occupations are clearly differentiated, and clear distinctions of primary function exist between technical and nontechnical personnel, between line workers and nonline workers. Some attempts have been made to integrate manual and mental labor, to involve ordinary workers in the process of technical innovation, and to modify irrational regulations governing the division of labor. (I shall seek to evaluate the impact of these attempts later in this chapter.) Nevertheless, based on the observations of a number of recent foreign visitors to Chinese industrial enterprises, few factories have yet displayed more than a modicum of multifunctionality in either intraoccupational or interoccupational labor mobility. The size of the enterprise may vary, as may the modernity of its equipment, the number and size of its workshops, the internal organization of its production groups, the educational level of its labor force, and the ratio of technical personnel to production workers; but the basic principles of functionally-specific technical organization and semirigid occupational and task specialization are virtually universal. In these purely technical respects, there is nothing terribly unique about Chinese industrial organization. [31]

THE STRUCTURE OF MANAGEMENT

Managerial organization in Chinese industry has gone through a series of profound structural alterations over the past two decades. [32] In this section I shall concentrate on developments in industrial management since the Great Proletarian Cultural Revolution (1965-69).

In one form or another, the principle of "dual rule" (or functional dualism) has been observed in Chinese industrial enterprises since the Great Leap Forward, with "expert" factory managers, engineers, and technicians sharing decision-making authority with "red" Party secretaries and cadres. During the Cultural Revolution, when the Party was in a state of virtual paralysis under the onslaught of antiestablishmentarian Red Guards and "revolutionary rebels," this dualism was temporarily abandoned in favor of a system of unified enterprise management by revolutionary committees—tripartite combinations of experienced managers and technicians, military representatives, and workers. In 1970-71, however, the Party committees at the enterprise level were reconstituted, and managerial organization returned to the double track, with revolutionary committees maintaining authority over technical planning and operations while Party committees resumed authority in the fields of organization, propaganda, and control.

One new trend that has emerged since 1971 (when the army's role in enterprise management began to decline) is the tendency for the chairman of the factory's revolutionary committee to become concurrently chairman of its Party committee. While the two committees are nominally separate and distinct, the implicit merging of political and administrative authority at the highest level within the enterprise represents a significant shift away from functional dualism toward unified management. This shift has been further accelerated since 1973 by the gradual merging of the various functional departments and administrative staffs of the revolutionary and Party committees, with the result that in many respects Party committees are now virtually indistinguishable from revolutionary committees.

In large, state-owned enterprises, revolutionary committees, which are generally composed of a chairman, two to five vice-chairmen, and ten to twenty-five "ordinary" members, are responsible for meeting the cost targets and output quotas established by the state plan. As a senior official of the Anshan No. 2 steel rolling mill recently put it to a U.S. visitor, "We must finish certain quantities of certain categories at a certain quality and under a certain cost."[33]

In order to facilitate intraenterprise coordination of effort in accomplishing the tasks specified by the state plan, revolutionary committees in each factory have set up a number of specialized functional departments, or sections. In the case of the Anshan rolling mill, which has a revolutionary committee consisting of 17 members, 15 such sections were established, with a total administrative staff of 73. Production planning accounted for 7 members; technology for 5 members; maintenance and repair, 10 members; capital construction, 6 members; safety, 4 members; labor and wage allocation, 4 members; welfare, 5 members; propaganda and education, 4 members; organizational work, 3 members; finance, 7 members; people's militia affairs, 2 members; supplies and raw materials, 6 members; secretariat, 3 members; and inspection and quality control, 7 members.

Apart from its relative complexity, what is interesting to note about this administrative division of labor is the fact that key political, organizational, propaganda, and militia functions, once a virtual monopoly of Party committees, have now been at least partially absorbed by revolutionary committees, which is a further indication of the continuing erosion of the principle of functional dualism.

Each workshop in a factory has its own administrative office, headed by a director and two or more assistant directors, generally including at least one trained technician and one Party cadre. The total number of full-time staff personnel in each workshop is variable, generally from four to six in a relatively large shop. In the Shenyang transformer factory, for example, workshop offices have four administrative subsections: production, administration, technical work, and safety. [34] Each of these subsections is headed by a full-time administrative cadre, with an additional three to ten "ordinary" members selected from among the shop's workers and technicians. The technical innovation section of the factory's coil workshop consists of seven members. Four are workers, one is the office director, and the remaining two are technicians.

Selection of revolutionary committee members and functional staff at the enterprise and workshop levels is done through a combination of democratic participation and higher-level appointment, and the entire process is supervised by the enterprise's Party committee. Thus, for example, while the two technicians serving on the staff of the technical innovation section of the Shenyang coil shop were appointed by the shop office (with Party approval), the four worker members of the section were selected on the basis of recommendations made by the shop's rank and file workers. [35]

Despite the considerable turnover of administrative personnel that reportedly occurred in many enterprises during the Cultural Revolution, there has been a clear tendency for revolutionary committees in many factories to be near replicas of pre-Cultural Revolution management committees. At the Shanghai turbine plant, for example, an administrative cadre acknowledged to me that the current chairman and vice-chairman of the revolutionary committee had held comparable posts on the old management committee. Similar observations have been made by numerous other foreign visitors to China in recent years, leading to the tentative conclusion that the newly created revolutionary committees may not be so new or so revolutionary after all.

Each heavy industrial enterprise has a chief engineer, who is also normally a "responsible member" of the enterprise revolutionary committee. At the Shanghai turbine plant, the chief engineer is concurrently a vice-chairman of the revolutionary committee and head of the enterprise's technology section. At the Anshan rolling mill, the chief engineer is head of the production planning section. In each of these enterprises, the chief engineer is the highest-paid official in the plant.

The technical and administrative division of labor in Chinese industrial enterprises is clearly reflected in the industrial wage scale, which is generally characterized by a top-to-bottom ratio of approximately 5:1 (excluding apprentice workers; if the latter are included, the ratio increases to about 8: or 9:1). [36]

Since about 1956 the principle of straight time wages has been universally adopted in state-owned industrial enterprises, replacing the more inequitable ("revisionist") piece-rate system that had been introduced by Soviet advisors in the early 1950s. Wage scales are established according to the transitional socialist distribution principle, "to each according to his work."

In the Anshan steel rolling mill, the monthly wages of technical and administrative staff (mental workers) range from 58 yuan (about $32) for a recent college graduate to 154 yuan (about $82) for the plant's chief engineer. Manual workers, on the other hand, are paid according to an eight-grade wage scale (excluding apprentice workers, who are below scale), ranging in this enterprise from 34.5 yuan for a first-grade, semiskilled worker to 110 yuan for an experienced, highly skilled eighth-grade worker. Apprentice workers earn between 19 yuan and 21 yuan per month during their two- to three-year apprenticeships. The wage scale at this factory is somewhat lower than that of the Shanghai turbine plant, where the ratio of first to eighth grade workers is 42 yuan to 130 yuan.

In most of the heavy industrial enterprises that have been visited by foreign observers in the 1970s, the "average" industrial worker reportedly earns between 50 yuan and 70 yuan per month although it is not specified whether this "average" comprises a mean or a median figure. Interenterprise variations in wage scales and average wages tend to be positively correlated with variations in type of industry, level of technological modernization, and local living costs, which do, in fact, vary at least marginally from region to region.

The increments between wage grades tend to be smaller at the lower end of the scale and larger at the higher end. Howe thus reports the following wage coefficients for each of the eight grades of manual labor in the Chinese machine-building industry: Grade 1, 1.00; Grade 2, 1.16; Grade 3, 1.35; Grade 4, 1.57; Grade 5, 1.82; Grade 6, 2.12; Grade 7, 2.48; and Grade 8, 2.90. Howe also notes that the wage increment coefficients for both workers and administrators tend to be higher in the modern sector ("class one" enterprises) and proportionally lower in the intermediate sector ("class two" and "class three" enterprises). [37]

While the total wage bill of a state-owned enterprise is fixed by the state plan and is therefore nonnegotiable, each enterprise retains a certain amount of discretionary authority in the assignment of job classifications and wage grades to its workers.

As reflected in the occupational-wage classification scheme adopted in the machine-building industry, interoccupational wage differentials (that is, differentials based on the distinction between

high-skill and low-skill occupations) are at least partially offset by
intraoccupational differentials, which are generally seniority-related.
Thus, for example, crane drivers (low skill) generally start at Grade
1, and metal smiths (high skill) start at Grade 5. Over a period of
many years a veteran crane operator with a good work record may
attain a Grade 6 classification. [38] Seniority continues to be a major
factor in wage determination. It is by no means uncommon for
veteran workers in low-skill occupations to be earning more money
than younger workers in high-skill occupations.

The existence of significant inter- and intraoccupational wage
differentials continues to be a subject of considerable controversy
within China. Following the Fourth National People's Congress, held
in January 1975, a nationwide press campaign was launched—ostensibly on the personal initiative of Mao Tse-tung—that was designed to
restrict the growth of "bourgeois rights" in industry and agriculture.
Prominent among the phenomena targeted for criticism in this campaign was the eight-grade wage system. Early in 1975 Mao stated
that as follows:

> Before liberation [China] was much the same as a capital-
> ist country. Even now she practices an eight-grade wage
> system, . . and this differs very little from the old
> society. . . . The wage system is unequal. . . . Under
> the dictatorship of the proletariat such things can only
> be restricted. [39]

Although it is still too early to tell what effect this campaign
will ultimately have on the industrial wage structure, as of November
1976 no precipitous action had been taken to substantially reduce or
eliminate wage differentials. In a very revealing comment made to
me in May 1975, in response to a question about the way the new
campaign was affecting wage policy in his enterprise, a high official
of the Shanghai turbine plant stated as follows:

> It will take some time. It is a gradual process, and can-
> not be done all at once. . . . We are very cautious in
> taking any practical decisions [to restrict wage differen-
> tials] because we don't want to upset the economic order
> unless it is demanded by the overwhelming majority of
> the masses. . . . We must not take hasty measures.

Despite such manifest cautiousness on the part of industrial
managers, it is apparent that a certain amount of grassroots pressure for wage-scale equalization was exerted in 1975. For example,
in mid-March a letter from a Chinese industrial worker published

in the journal <u>Study and Criticism</u> hinted that inequities in the wage system were responsible for work slowdowns and violations of labor discipline in his enterprise, as follows:

> Under the eight-grade wage system different kinds of
> work are categorized in grades and even for the same
> kind of work there are different types of pay. That was
> why some [workers] were reluctant to do this or that
> kind of work, and disobeyed transfer orders. . . . We
> must advocate communist labor on a voluntary basis,
> without consideration for pay. [40]

Such manifestations of extreme egalitarianism have been officially discouraged in the Party press and labeled as a premature "communist wind." [41] Particularly revealing in this connection is the following report published in the authoritative ideological journal <u>Red Flag</u> in June 1975:

> A young worker who became a cadre after entering the
> [Kirin lard extraction] factory was entitled to the wages
> of a regular worker according to a state decision. But
> she felt that she, together with the young people who
> had entered the factory with her, should receive appren-
> tice wages, and that she should not be given special
> treatment when she became a cadre. So she returned the
> extra wages issued to her. . . . [After being educated
> by plant officials] she learned that in a socialist enter-
> prise . . . <u>the positions of cadres and workers are</u>
> <u>not the same, and the division of labor is not the same,</u>
> <u>so that there cannot but be some distinctions.</u> [42]

Judging by the publication in 1975 of numerous offical exhortations calling on all industrial workers, particularly young, unskilled workers recently recruited from the countryside, to observe labor discipline and refrain from making "unreasonable" wage demands (read: demands for either upward or, as in the above example, downward equalization of wages), the potential for divisive inter-occupational and intergenerational conflict within the industrial labor force must be regarded as significant. This conclusion is reinforced by the fact that the structure of China's nationwide industrial labor union, which was dismantled during the Cultural Revolution and officially reestablished only in 1973, has not yet become fully operational at the enterprise level in many industries. An official of the Shanghai turbine plant thus told me bluntly that "we have not yet established [criteria for] trade union operations." When I tried to press him for further details, he changed the subject. Such examples of retarded union reorganization can reasonably be attributed to a condition of increased polarization among industrial workers, a situation that official media sources openly acknowledge as posing a "serious obstacle to the unity and stability of the proletariat."

Closely related to the question of occupational wage differences in Chinese industry is the question of managerial policy—the operational principles and procedures, lines of authority, and formal channels of communication established to ensure efficient coordination, supervision, and feedback in the production process.

The basic problem faced by industrial managers everywhere is the need to strike a series of "rational" balance between central authority and local initiative, between unified policy and dispersed operations, between collective leadership and individual responsibility, and between labor discipline and labor motivation. In China the search for such managerial balance has also been affected by a series of ideological considerations that are not generally encountered in Western societies. These are the desire to avoid extremes of hierarchical stratification; the desire to enlist the talents of ordinary workers in the tasks of technical innovation and operational management; and the desire to integrate mental and manual labor.

Following a series of pendulum-like swings in management policy during the 1950s and early 1960s, [43] industrial management in China underwent a radical, albeit temporary, transformation during the Cultural Revolution. Functional dualism gave way to political monism. Industrial "experts" (engineers, technicians, and administrative cadres) were denigrated and downgraded in favor of the "red" masses. Specialized management committees were supplanted by revolutionary committees dominated by professional soldiers and worker "activists." Individual responsibility gave way to collective responsibility (in some cases, collective irresponsibility). Mid-level management was drastically reduced. Intraenterprise administrative structures were consolidated and simplified. Various rules and regulations governing such things as industrial job specifications and classifications, labor discipline, safety standards, and promotional criteria were either significantly attenuated or scrapped altogether. All of these measures were ostensibly taken in order to "unbind" the laboring masses from the fetters imposed by "bourgeois authorities" and industrial "experts."

Two examples will serve to illustrate the antibureaucratic, antitechnocratic bias that underlay such reforms. Prior to the Cultural Revolution, factory workers in the Shanghai bicycle plant had been isolated from technical personnel. If a worker had an idea for a technical innovation, "It required initial approval from six departments, then thirteen additional seals of approval were necessary before the worker could begin to work on his idea."[44]

In a similar example, the Peking No. 1 machine tool plant had instituted a series of regulations restricting worker participation in innovation to the point that "in order for a worker to undertake an innovation, he had to obtain permission from 28 different groups. If he did not do so, his tools would be taken from him. . . . [Plant authorities] defended this system on the grounds that 'The workers have had no education; they are stupid.' "[45] During the Cultural Revolution such "irrational rules and regulations" were scrapped in order to "mobilize the masses and arouse their enthusiasm."

In virtually every case such reforms conformed to the ideological imperatives of radical egalitarianism rather than the techno-bureaucratic imperatives of conventional industrial rationalism ("scientific management"). Somewhat paradoxically, the eight-grade wage system, which is currently regarded as a major vestige of "bourgeois right," was not eliminated during the Cultural Revolution, although it did come under criticism from certain radical groups.

Despite the intense "red tide" of the Cultural Revolution, and despite the many organizational reforms initiated therein, neither the tide nor the reforms associated with the Cultural Revolution endured very long. By 1971, with the reconstitution of Party authority at the enterprise level, and the not unrelated purge of Defense Minister Lin Piao, there was a noticeable movement back in the direction of pre-Cultural Revolution "normalcy."

Overall, events since 1971 have seemed to point toward an eclectic compromise between Maoist ideo-logic and conventional managerial techno-logic. While functional dualism, as noted previously, has been undermined by the tendency to merge Party and administrative offices and staff at the enterprise level, this has not involved a return to the political monism of the Cultural Revolution. Industrial experts are now being given at least conditional authority over important technical and operational decisions within the enterprise—conditional, that is, upon their willingness to "consult with the masses and listen to the masses." Industrial workers are being officially exhorted to "let the engineers and technicians play their part to the full."[46] The drastically simplified, streamlined administrative structures of the 1968-71 period have gradually been creeping back to their pre-Cultural Revolution levels of complexity. One example of this latter trend is provided by the Dairen steel mill, where more than 50 technical and administrative posts (out of a total of 370) were eliminated during the Cultural Revolution. This reduction in personnel, however, reportedly led to production problems. "So we strengthened our technical and managerial force, increased our scientific study, and strengthened our production management system by increasing the number of management personnel."[47]

The once-odious "responsibility systems" (denigrated during the Cultural Revolution for ostensibly engendering elitism and bureaucratism) have been at least partially revived, with the "chief leading personnel" and "personnel in charge of production" assuming direct personal responsibility for meeting output quotas, enforcing quality control standards, and so on.[48] As one official media source put it, there must be "clear responsibility of individual posts, changing shifts, systems of equipment, production and maintenance, and systems of product quality control."[49] Another source stated that the purpose of such "responsibility systems" was to ensure that "for every type of task and in all matters the division of labor will be clear and precise, and responsibility will be clear."[50]

There has been a marked swing back in the direction of establishing such "rational rules and regulations" as govern job specifications and classifications, labor discipline, safety standards, technical innovation, and repair and maintenance of machinery.

The clear effect of these various post-Cultural Revolution reforms has been to strengthen the specialized management function in Chinese industrial enterprises. The excesses of participatory democracy that spawned in the late 1960s have been curbed; organizational authority and discipline have been restored; and the once alien concept of "scientific management" has been revived and stripped of its putative "revisionist" connotations, as follows:

> Industrial production, particularly modernized large-scale industrial production, is an extremely complicated process. The higher the standard of socialized production, the more finely will labor be divided, the more necessary it will be to have closer coordination between the different links of production, and the more necessary it will be to have a more careful and scientific system of management.[51]

Although the above summary of post-Cultural Revolution reforms in industrial management tends to point in the direction of technobureaucratic convergence, nevertheless there are some counterindications that are potentially significant and worthy of mention.

In the first place, the elitism that is inherent in technobureaucratic stratification has been partially ameliorated in recent years by a strong emphasis on the recruitment and technical training of previously disadvantaged classes and strata into high-skill, high-responsibility occupations. Thus, for example, college entrance examinations have been modified to give preferential treatment to less sophisticated students of worker and peasant background. As a prerequisite to college enrollment, aspiring intellectuals (in all but a very few top-priority fields of study) must spend a minimum of two or three years after high school graduation doing productive labor on a factory or farm, where their work records and labor enthusiasm are taken into consideration (along with their entrance examination scores) in evaluating their suitability for college entrance.

Moreover, many large industrial enterprises have begun to operate their own industrial colleges and spare-time schools to raise the technical and administrative competence of ordinary workers, thereby making them eligible for promotion to higher-skill, better paying jobs. At the Shanghai turbine plant, for example, a "July 21st Workers' University" was established in 1971 and has trained over 100 "worker-technicians" in the basic principles of turbine theory and industrial design, as well as in the more practical skills of simple blueprint reading and machine repair and maintenance. Many of these worker-technicians received promotions to higher job classifications following their graduation, and four of them are currently serving on the plant's revolutionary committee.

In the second place, increasing functional specialization in the division of labor has been tempered in recent years by the institutionalization of a system of "two participations," wherein technical and administrative cadres are required to spend a certain amount of their time on the shop floor learning how to operate machinery, carrying out first-hand investigations into working conditions, and soliciting the opinions and suggestions of the "masses" with respect to the various policies and operations of the enterprise. For their part, shop workers are encouraged to participate actively in certain aspects of enterprise management, including evaluation of cadre (and fellow worker) performance, discussion of production plans, and representation on shop committees.

In the third place, and perhaps most important, workers are encouraged to participate in the process of technical innovation. This latter aspect of technical democracy is typified by the "three-in-one" innovation teams that exist in virtually all Chinese industrial enterprises. The basic premise underlying the concept of the "three-in-one" team is that ordinary workers, by virtue of their intimate familiarity with the machinery and processes of production, are in a position to offer practical suggestions for simplifying technical operations, modifying equipment, and otherwise economizing in production costs. In order to mobilize this latent resource, the technology section in each workshop is comprised of a "three-way alliance" of veteran workers, skilled technicians, and administrative cadres.

Working in close mutual collaboration, members of these teams spend much of their time—frequently after hours and on weekends—on the workshop floor or in the shop office, designing labor-saving process modifications, trial-producing new machine parts, and consulting production workers on various questions pertaining to the refinement of technical equipment and operations. The plant engineers are consulted by these groups whenever the contemplated modifications or refinements might require significant alteration in the basic design, material composition, or performance specifications of industrial equipment.

Through the operation of such "three-in-one" groups, much of the secondary designing and renovation work normally done by professional engineers in industrial laboratories in Western societies is conducted on the "front line" or production in China. Members of the "three-in-one" groups do not generally receive additional wages for such participation, but they are frequently given token bonuses—and a great deal of positive publicity—when their efforts result in significant labor-saving or cost-saving innovations. [52]

Obviously the efficacy of technical democracy at the workshop level depends upon both the complexity of the productive technologies utilized and the technical skills of the labor force. Rensselaer W. Lee III thus hypothesizes that, other things being equal, "The less the capital outlay within a given enterprise, the greater the scope for [mass] technical innovation."[53]

With respect to the relationship between the technical skill level of the labor force and the efficacy of technical democracy on the shop floor, Chinese industrial managers appear to be fully aware of the manifold problems associated with the generally low technical competence of the average factory worker. In one fairly modern enterprise, for example, the plant's revolutionary committee made a study of why the workers in one shop had been unable to come up with any practical suggestions for technical innovations over a fairly long period of time. The investigators found the following:

> Large numbers of workers had no idea of the technical
> principles of production and had no suggestions to make
> in discussions of production. The contradiction between
> rapid production expansion and a weak technical force
> could have been solved by adopting methods of technical
> training. [54]

Because of the continuing difficulties posed by the relatively low level of educational and technical training of the industrial labor force, in recent years Chinese leaders have inaugurated an intermediate system of technical innovation combining aspects of mass participation with "expert" technical leadership.

Finally, despite the many strides made by Chinese "worker-technicians" and "three-in-one" innovation teams in recent years, it remains true that the vast majority of technical innovations successfully designed and implemented by ordinary workers have been relatively simple, relatively unsophisticated, relatively inexpensive, and only marginally useful. It should be noted, however, that such mass-oriented "mousetrap technology" may be marginal only in a short-term, narrow economic sense, since there may well be significant social and educational utilities inherent in the process of participating in innovation that are not easily reflected in short-term economic calculations. Also, the opportunity costs of workers participating in innovation efforts after hours and on weekends, at no appreciable cost to the enterprise, are low enough to make such efforts "rational" even in the narrow economic sense.

SOCIAL STRUCTURE AND HUMAN BEHAVIOR

In any complex organization, formal technical and managerial structures (production relations) are paralleled by, and interact reciprocally with, informal patterns of culturally conditioned social behavior (human relations). In the preceding discussion it was noted that in purely formal, institutional terms the organizational structure of modern Chinese industrial enterprises diverges only moderately from more conventional patterns of functionally-specific, occupationally-stratified technobureaucratic organization. It was also noted that many of the ostensibly unique features of technical and administrative organization found in Chinese enterprises can reasonably be attributed as much to varying optimal factor proportions and differential opportunity costs as to purely ideological considerations.

More difficult to assess is the psychological and social impact of Maoist ideo-logic. In this section I turn from the subject of production relations to that of human relations in an effort to determine whether, and to what extent, Maoist "ideological and egalitarian counterpressures" (to use K. S. Karol's phrase) have succeeded in "bending the productive apparatus to priorities other than its own," thereby serving to "prevent the hierarchy of the technical division of of labor from being translated directly into distinctions of social status."[55]

E. L. Wheelwright and Bruce McFarlane correctly observe that in a political system geared to the transformation of human thought and behavior, an industrial enterprise "is not viewed as a purely economic unit where economic performance takes undisputed priority."[56] The enterprise is also viewed as an agency of political and cultural socialization that may exert considerable influence on

the attitudes, values, and cognitions of its workers, thereby affecting
the attainment of broader societal goals, including the creation of the
selfless, egalitarian "new communist man." It is precisely this dual-
istic character of industrial-societal objectives (characterized in the
parlance of organization theory by the distinction between the "closed
system" and "open system" perspectives) that has caused the ideo-
logic of "redness" to come increasingly into conflict with the techno-
logic of "expertise" in modernizing communist systems.

The basic parameters of this conflict have been extensively
analyzed in the literature. For present purposes I am concerned
primarily with those aspects of the "red-expert" contradiction that
pertain to the social behavior of Chinese industrial cadres, technicians, and workers. Wherever possible, I shall also seek to draw
inferences pertaining to the subjective attitudes and motivations of
the industrial labor force.

The task of assessing the degrees of cooperativeness, egalitarianism, labor enthusiasm, and selflessness that prevail within Chinese industrial enterprises is rendered extremely difficult by the
paucity of reliable data. For example, there are simply no aggregate
or quantitative data linking variations in physical output, product
quality, and labor productivity to variations in technical or managerial democracy. Similarly, we have no way to confidently assess the
effects of various industrial wage or welfare reforms upon the overall motivation of the work force.

Of course, intuitive, qualitative judgments can be made about
such co-variable relationships based on direct observation, refugee
accounts, official policy statements, and press and radio reports.
Moreover, certain behavioral hypotheses can be offered, based
either on analogous research conducted in other communist systems,
such as the Yugoslav system of worker-management, or on experimental research conducted in Western industrial enterprises, such
as the Hawthorne experiments and the Scanlon Plan. [57] Such hypotheses, however, cannot be adequately tested in the absence of reliable
behavioral data from Chinese industrial enterprises. Hence the
qualitative judgments, inferences, and hypotheses put forward in
this section must be treated as highly tentative and impressionistic.

Many students of industrial labor relations have noted the
beneficial motivational effects of technical and managerial democracy.
Workers who are in some sense "involved" in technical planning and
operational decision making tend to be, ceteris paribus, less alienated, more cooperative, and more enthusiastic—and hence more
productive—than workers who are not so involved. [58] Extrapolating
from such experimental observations, a number of China scholars
have argued that because Chinese industrial enterprises ostensibly
practice the "two participations" and "three-in-one" method, Chi-

nese workers must, by that very fact, display higher levels of labor motivation and productivity than their counterparts in other, less "democratic" industrial milieus. [59] Such deductions may or may not be warranted; but they clearly stand in need of empirical verification.

Many, if not most, foreign visitors to China are quite favorably impressed by the appearance of diligent, contented workers openly professing their selfless, unending devotion to the Party, to Chairman Mao, and to "the people." Such impressions tend to be rather superficial, however, and may be somewhat misleading. An example drawn from my personal experience in China will serve to underscore the difficulty in trying to distinguish between words and deeds, between theory and practice, and between shadow and substance in the evaluation of China's egalitarian "new communist man."

At the Shanghai turbine plant we were given a formal briefing, which included the standard litany about the workers' unflagging devotion to socialism and their enthusiasm for production. Subsequently, however, during a tour of one of the plant's workshops, I paused to read a wall poster written by a "responsible comrade" of the shop's Youth League branch. The poster alluded to recent breakdowns in labor discipline and exhorted all young workers to "staunchly oppose all sorts of schemes of using money and material incentives to seduce young people." Another poster in the same shop stated that there had been "a certain number" of recent cases of line workers not taking proper care of their machines, which had led to mechanical breakdowns and consequent disruptions in production. The poster contained a plea to "strengthen proletarian stability and unity," and concluded that: "to make a success of the work of caring for machinery, we must foster the spirit of not being afraid of difficulty."

Such an experience, which is by no means unique to myself, illustrates the difficulties involved in trying to evaluate the efficacy of "ideological and egalitarian counterpressures" in contemporary China. They also serve to reinforce the conventional wisdom, which holds that in a controlled society, things may not always be as they seem.

In 1975 official government sources in China openly acknowledged the existence of certain "serious problems" in industrial labor relations. Numerous incidents involving industrial work stoppages, sabotage, "bourgeois life styles," theft, and corruption of various sorts were reported in the public media. While no aggregate statistics or detailed breakdowns of aberrant behavior were published, the frequency of these reports and the apparent seriousness with which they were treated in the course of the campaign to restrict bourgeois rights would seem to indicate that the problems were both widespread and critical.

Lack of labor discipline among the industrial cadres and workers was one widely cited problem. In a diesel engine plant, for example, lax discipline reportedly manifested itself in "certain undesirable practices such as pilfering and gambling; later it resulted in a wave of major and minor accidents."[60] In another enterprise it was claimed that a wave of absenteeism had occurred, wherein "some people went to the doctor without any symptoms of illness, took a long period of time to recuperate when they were only slightly ill, and went around pretending to have hallucinations."[61]

Laziness and complacency among the work force were frequently cited as impediments to proletarian "unity and stability." In one factory, for example, "Some of the masses . . . schemed to avoid troublesome labor, fearing the bother of production, and consequently neglected quality."[62] In another enterprise "some comrades, afraid of difficulty and trouble . . . do not dare struggle with phenomena that endanger the people's interests, but rather think that 'peace is disturbed by revolution.'"[63]

Worker opposition to high output quotas was another problem candidly discussed in the press. In one plant, for example, a group of workers "advocated lowering the target in order to 'maintain some leeway.' . . . They were afraid that 'if plans are set too high they will be difficult to achieve; if we don't complete our tasks we will receive terrible criticism.'"[64]

Even more serious were widespread reports of a rising tide of "bourgeois decadence" in the industrial labor force. In one enterprise master workers were said to have "exerted a bad bourgeois influence on apprentice workers. They trumpet the bourgeois style of living."[65] In another factory some "bad elements" reportedly used "vicious methods of telling sexual stories, scattering the putrid thought of the bourgeoisie to win over the corrupt workers."[66]

Economic corruption and graft were similarly cited as major problems adversely affecting China's industrial performance. In one instance some "bourgeois elements" of the staff of a certain enterprise allegedly "carried out mutually advantageous, unauthorized use of capital, equipment, and products belonging to the state and the collective."[67] In another instance a cadre in a shipbuilding plant "made use of his authority to purchase state-controlled building materials and built a house for himself."[68] Other people with "bourgeois mentality" were scored for "talking not about revolutionary principles but about 'human feeling.' They said, 'You do me a little favor, and I'll do you a little favor.'"[69] This latter problem was said to be particularly rampant among new workers recently recruited from the countryside, many of whom reportedly "carry with them the bourgeois mentality of the small producer."[70]

The desire for bourgeois privilege and material comfort was said to have motivated a "certain number" of industrial cadres to "lord it over others, live in comfort . . . and lead the life of an official. . . . [They] fear hardship, love pleasure, and always ask others to help them obtain special privileges. "[71] In other cases "new bourgeois elements" among Party and state industrial cadres allegedly "tried their best to replace socialist relations between people with relations based on money or rank, relations between employer and employee, and relations between rivals. "[72] Some of these "new bourgeois elements" also reportedly "used funds under their control to . . . practice usury, open 'underground factories,' or carry out speculation. "[73]

Socialist labor incentives were also said to have been undermined by neobourgeois influences. In one plant a system of providing bonuses for overfulfillment of output quotas was criticized for having "created disunity between various shops, teams, and individuals, and between cadres and masses. "[74] In another plant the introduction of bonuses to technical personnel allegedly led to slack discipline and resentment among the workers. [75] The nature of this problem was further illustrated in one enterprise wherein certain "bad elements" had spread the "bourgeois notion that 'the division of people into three, six, or nine classifications is a way of saying that some people are superior to others.'"[76] In order to counteract such nonproletarian thinking, it was stated that "we must criticize the . . . traditional concept that regards the division of labor as an expression of hierarchy . . . and such exploiting class filth as bureaucracy and ideas of privilege. "[77]

Individual examples of deviant behavior in Chinese industrial enterprises could easily be multiplied. However, the relative frequencies of such behavior are impossible to determine in the absence of statistical data from a significant sample of enterprises. Nevertheless, there could be no doubt that Chinese government officials were extremely concerned about this situation. The degree of their concern was clearly revealed in a June 1975 editorial published in the authoritative ideological journal, Red Flag as follows:

> In both city and countryside, there exists a bourgeois trend. A variety of capitalist tendencies in the life of the people is seriously undermining our state plan and the principled policies of the Communist Party, as well as gravely impairing mutual socialist relations among the people. [78]

If such statements are accepted at face value, it would seem reasonable to conclude that despite the steady exertion of "ideological and egalitarian counterpressures," human relations in Chinese industrial enterprises continue to be characterized by a considerable amount of self-interested behavior, status consciousness, and improper ("backward") attitudes toward labor, leisure, and fellow man. The "new communist man" in a Chinese factory may have proletarian hands, but he appears also to have certain unreconstructed bourgeois appetites and attitudes.

This is not to imply, however, that the "typical" Chinese industrial worker is severely alienated in the classical Marxian-Durkheimian sense. On the contrary, there is good reason to believe that factory workers on the whole are considerably less alienated than some other occupational groups in Chinese society—most notably younger peasants, "intellectual youths," and demobilized soldiers who have been sent down to the countryside.[79]

There are a number of possible explanations for this phenomenon. The most frequently cited factor is that industrial workers, particularly those employed in state-owned enterprises, comprise a relative socioeconomic elite in contemporary China. Workers generally enjoy a standard of living, a life style, and certain fringe benefits that are unmatched in the countryside. Riskin thus observes that the real income of urban industrial workers is on the order of 10 to 70 percent higher than that of peasants, with an average differential of perhaps 15 to 25 percent.[80] One possible categorical exception to this generalization comprises apprentice workers, whose living standard may be only marginally, if at all, superior to that of the average peasant.

In addition to higher wages, industrial employment also offers certain life-style attractions, including a greater variety of available consumer goods and services, relatively wider opportunities for educational and occupational advancement, and a more stimulating cultural environment. Social welfare services are also more comprehensive in the industrial sector. Workers and their dependents in state-owned enterprises generally receive subsidized medical care, housing, and child care, as well as sick leave, disability and retirement pay, and paid maternity leave.

For all of these reasons, worker alienation probably has not been a significant problem in the modern sector of Chinese industry. This in turn may well account for the otherwise rather puzzling fact that Chinese leaders and industrial managers do not seem particularly concerned with making the content of work more varied, more interesting, or more challenging for the average wage earner. As Carl Riskin points out, "Most observers feel . . . that the issue [of job enrichment] is one to which they have shown no great sensitivity in responding to queries, or in the technologies of plants actually observed."[81]

It is, of course, possible that the high intensity of the 1975 campaign to restrict bourgeois rights might be indicative of the first significant manifestations of widespread worker alienation. Based on the conventional notion of a "revolution of rising expectations," it may be hypothesized that as China continues to industrialize at a fairly impressive rate (the average annual industrial growth rate since 1953 has been approximately 9 percent), workers may feel that improvements in their standard of living, which in the past have generally been gradual and quite modest, are not keeping pace with their heightened expectations, thus leading to a "revolution of rising frustrations." Such a possibility cannot be discounted in a society that continues to pursue a "rational low wage" policy that calls upon workers to live austerely, forgoing current consumption in the interest of maximizing capital accumulation for investment in national construction. [82]

In such a situation, it will not be surprising if Chinese authorities encounter increasing resistance in their attempts to persuade industrial workers to continue subordinating their immediate material interests to the long-term interests of the state. In this respect the new PRC constitution of January 1975 is noteworthy for its explicit recognition of and ostensible concessions to, the increasing popular demand for expanded consumer goods production, for augmented opportunities to engage in supplemental, spare-time self-employment, and for relaxation of restrictions on "small-scale" private commerce. [83]

Also significant in the new constitution is a provision explicitly guaranteeing industrial workers the right to strike. This latter provision, which is ostensibly intended to enable workers to rebel against "revisionist tendencies" displayed by industrial managers, is in reality a two-edged sword. From what we know of the increasing frequency of work stoppages and slowdowns in the critical iron and steel and transportation industries in China in the past few years, it appears that some of these disturbances have their origin in the workers' desire to expand, rather than restrict, bourgeois rights, while others are directly related to the self-interested demands of younger, lower-paid workers for an immediate, total equalization of wages.

Finally, and closely related to the question of the workers' right to strike, we must consider the role of industrial labor unions as a link between the formal technical-administrative structures of an enterprise and the informal social relations of its employees. Here, too, the evidence is mixed. On the one hand there is some indication that in the 1950s and 1960s unions served a positive function in helping to facilitate mutual communication between management and labor, as well as between the Party and the masses. Moreover, the "small-group" structure of union organization at the basic level of the workshop ostensibly contributed to the primary-group solidarity of the union members. [84]

On the other hand, however, because Chinese labor organizations are, in effect, "company unions," their functions have tended to be more symbolic and ritualistic than substantive. Based on interviews with a number of former trade union members, Martin K. Whyte thus concludes that "in the 1960s unions played only a peripheral role in factory life" and that most workers felt little sense of identification with worker congresses or trade union organizations. Moreover, union activities were generally confined primarily to periodic political and ideological education, routine discussion of production targets and shop operations, and certain welfare work. [85]

During the Cultural Revolution, labor union leaders were heavily criticized, and the All-China Federation of Trade Unions was formally dismantled, because of the alleged union tendency to pay more attention to the material welfare of the workers than to the politicoideological welfare of the Party and the state. The formal reconstitution of the union structure, which began in 1973, has undoubtedly served to revive this issue, although the paucity of substantive data on the functions and operations of the newly reorganized unions makes it impossible to verify this. We may hypothesize, however, that in those industrial enterprises in which unions were back in operation by 1975, they were probably in the thick of the heated debate over the restriction of bourgeois rights. This hypothesis may well explain the previously-noted reluctance on the part of a leading cadre at the Shanghai turbine plant to discuss with me questions pertaining to union membership, organization, or activities in the plant.

CONCLUSION

Throughout this chapter I have posed the question of Maoism vs. industrial technologism in terms of the problematic efficacy of antibureaucratic, antielitist ideological counterpressures in "bending" the imperative techno-logic that convergence theorists claim governs the relationship between the forces and means of production, on the one hand, and the relations of production, on the other. In my brief and necessarily impressionistic survey of technical, managerial, and social structures and relations in Chinese industrial enterprises, I found little evidence to support extreme claims that substantial numbers of new communist men have been successfully resocialized in what are still essentially old technobureaucratic institutions, or that ideologically induced voluntarism, unsupported by substantial differential material benefits, has provided an effective, long-lasting antidote to more conventional ("bourgeois") patterns of incentive and motivation.

This is not to deny or to belittle the remarkable progress in industrial development achieved by the People's Republic in the relatively short span of 27 years; nor is it to deny either the rationality or the efficacy of the Maoist development strategy. Indeed, judged by contemporary third-world standards, China's rate of industrial modernization has been rather impressive. Moreover, this progress has been accomplished by the institution of a broad range of progressive social welfare services, by a deep commitment to raising the economic and cultural level of the peasantry (a sadly neglected social class in most developing nations), and by the inculcation of a new sense of national pride and self-respect in the Chinese people. These are no small accomplishments.

Nevertheless, in terms of my original question concerning the presence or absence of significant convergent tendencies in Chinese industrial organizations, my primary conclusion must be that such tendencies clearly do exist, though not to the total exclusion of certain innovative departures from the technobureaucratic model.

These latter departures—the various ideological and organizational "counterpressures" discussed earlier—may be likened to a prism, refracting the primary rays of convergent light and thereby ensuring at least a modicum of secondary spectral divergence. Such secondary refraction notwithstanding, however, there seems to be little reason to dispute Robert L. Heilbroner's contention that "we cannot say whether the society of the computer will give us the latter-day capitalist or the commissar; but it seems beyond doubt that it will give us the technician and the bureaucrat."[86]

Indeed, in contemporary China, as elsewhere in the industrialized world, the portentous figures of the technician and the bureaucrat have become prominent, if not dominant, features of the organizational landscape. And in view of official revelations made in connection with the 1975 campaign to restrict bourgeois rights, there is reason to believe that substantial numbers of Chinese industrial technicians and bureaucrats, (as well as ordinary workers) continue, despite repeated and prolonged "socialist education," to think and act in ways not altogether unlike their "bourgeois" counterparts in other industrial societies.

While it is surely too soon to render a confident verdict on the ultimate shape of China's emerging industrial order, the available evidence suggests that industrial technology, organization, management and human relations in the PRC are currently evolving in directions that are neither so fundamentally unique and innovative nor so radically egalitarian as China's more ardent apologists have asserted. China may indeed be "different"; but the difference appears to be diminishing, rather than growing, over time. Plus ça change, plus c'est la même chose.

NOTES

1. For an elaboration of the theory of technobureaucratic convergence, see Alfred G. Meyer, "Theories of Convergence," in Change in Communist Systems, ed. Chalmers Johnson, (Stanford: Stanford University Press, 1970); also Zbigniew K. Brzezinski and Samuel Huntington, Political Power: USA/USSR (New York: Viking, 1965), pp. 10-11.

2. See for example, Stephen Andors, "Revolution and Modernization: Man and Machine in Industrializing Societies," in America's Asia, ed. Edward Friedman and Mark Seldon (New York: Vintage, 1971), pp. 393-438; also John Gurley, "Capitalist and Maoist Economic Development," in ibid., pp. 324-56.

3. Mao Tse-tung, "On Protracted War" (June 1938), in Mao Tse-tung, Selected Works, (New York: International Publishers, 1954), Vol. 2, p. 192.

4. Mao Tse-tung, quoted in Peking Review, November 11, 1966, pp. 19-20.

5. Liu Shao-ch'i, "The Present Situation, the Party's General Line for Socialist Construction and It's Future Tasks" (May 1958), in Communist China 1955-59: Policy Documents with Analysis, ed. Robert R. Bowie and John K. Fairbank (Cambridge: Harvard University Press, 1962), p. 432.

6. K. S. Karol, The Second Chinese Revolution (New York: Hill and Wang, 1973), pp. 79, 81, 89.

7. The preceding discussion is adapted from Labour and Automation: Technological Change and Manpower in a Centrally Planned Economy (Geneva: International Labour Office, 1966), pp. 5-9.

8. These observations were made by me in the course of a 16-day visit to China in May 1975, during which time I visited six industrial enterprises of varying size and technological complexity.

9. On this point see E. L. Wheelwright and Bruce McFarlane, The Chinese Road to Socialism (New York: Monthly Review Press, 1970), p. 167.

10. See Joint Publications Research Service, no. 52653 (1969), p. 24.

11. On the limitations on our knowledge of the technology of China's aircraft industry, see Hans Heymann, Jr., China's Approach to Technology Acquisition (Santa Monica: RAND, 1975), Part 1.

12. Wheelwright and McFarlane, op. cit., pp. 164-65.

13. This conclusion was reached by a U.S. mechanical engineer who observed the "gnawing" technique in operation at a machine tool plant in Shanghai.

14. See for example, Rensselaer W. Lee, III, "The Politics of Technology in Communist China," in Ideology and Politics in Contemporary China, ed. Chalmers Johnson (Seattle: University of Washington Press, 1973), pp. 301-25.

15. Wheelwright and McFarlane, op. cit., p. 169.

16. See Lee, op. cit., p. 325 and passim.

17. On this point, see Heymann, op. cit., Part 1, pp. 47-53.

18. Quoted in Lee, op. cit., pp. 320-21.

19. Hung-ch'i, no. 6 (June 1972), p. 30.

20. Heymann, op. cit., Part 1, pp. 51-53 and passim.

21. Ibid., p. 52.

22. Quoted in ibid., p. 5.

23. Kuang-ming Jih-pao, April 8, 1965.

24. Cited in Franz Schurmann, Ideology and Organization in Communist China (enlarged ed., Berkeley and Los Angeles: University of California Press, 1971), pp. 232-33.

25. I would like to thank Robert A. Scalapino and Robert Vincent for providing data on the Anshan No. 2 steel rolling mill.

26. Hung-ch'i, no. 10 (October 1972), p. 51.

27. Hung-ch'i, no. 11 (November 1974), p. 97.

28. Labour and Automation, op. cit., pp. 35-38.

29. This observation, while admittedly impressionistic and based on a limited sample of media reports, is consistent with the findings of Barry M. Richman in his 1966 study of industrial management in China. See Barry M. Richman, Industrial Society in Communist China (New York: Vintage, 1969), especially chap. 9. See also Hung-ch'i, no. 4 (1973), p. 40.

30. Hung-ch'i, no. 12 (December 1972), p. 19.

31. For further elaboration, see Richard Baum, "Technology, Economic Organization, and Social Change: Maoism and the Chinese Cultural Revolution," in China in the Seventies, ed. B. Staiger (Wiesbaden: Otto Harrassowitz, 1975), pp. 131-92.

32. For a summary and discussion of these structural alterations, see Schurmann, op. cit., pp. 241-308; Richman, op. cit.; Andors, op. cit.; Stephen Andors, "Factory Management and Political Ambiguity, 1961-63," in China Quarterly, no. 59 (July-September 1974), pp. 435-75.

33. Robert A. Scalapino, communication to the author.

34. For a detailed study of the administration of this factory, see Mitch Meisner, "The Shenyang Transformer Factory," China Quarterly, no. 52 (October-December 1972), pp. 717-37.

35. Ibid., p. 728.

36. See for example, ibid., p. 731; Christopher Howe, Wage Patterns and Wage Policy in Modern China, 1919-1972 (Cambridge: Cambridge University Press, 1973), Chapter 3; Christopher Howe, "Labour Organization and Incentives in Industry, before and after the Cultural Revolution," in Stuart R. Schram, ed., Authority, Participation, and Cultural Change in China (Cambridge: Cambridge University Press, 1973), pp. 233-56; Richman, op. cit., pp. 798-804; and Charles Hoffmann, The Chinese Worker (Albany: State University of New York Press, 1974), pp. 98-104.

37. Howe, op. cit., p. 71. Similar differentials are reported in Hoffman, op. cit, p. 98.

38. Howe, op. cit., p. 71.

39. Quoted in Peking Review, no. 22 (May 30, 1975), p. 8.

40. Selections from PRC Magazines (U.S. Consulate General, Hong Kong), no. 818 (May 22, 1975), pp. 5-6.

41. See, for example, Vice-Premier Chang Ch'un-ch'iao's article in Peking Review, no. 14 (April 4, 1975), pp. 5-8.

42. Emphasis added.

43. See Schurmann, op. cit., pp. 241-308; Richman, op. cit.; Andors, "Revolution and Modernization," op. cit., and Andors, "Factory Management and Political Ambiguity," op. cit., pp. 435-75.

44. Peking Review, no. 30 (July 27, 1973), p. 6.

45. Hsinhua Weekly, no. 45 (November 5, 1973), p. 40.

46. Jen-min Jih-pao, November 17, 1971.

47. Hung-ch'i, no. 4 (April 1972), p. 30.

48. Jen-min Jih-pao, October 8, 1971.

49. Jen-min Jih-pao, June 16, 1972.

50. Hung-ch'i, no. 4 (April 1972), pp. 31-32.

51. Jen-min Jih-pao, August 28, 1972. See also Jen-min Jih-pao, March 21 and October 24, 1972.

52. See Howe, op. cit., pp. 123-25. Although payment of bonuses has been minimized in recent years, there is some evidence that such incentives are still in use. See for example, Hung-ch'i, no. 5 (May 1975), p. 41.

53. Lee, op. cit., p. 257.

54. Jen-min Jih-pao, August 23, 1972.

55. Karol, op. cit., p. 89. Emphasis added.

56. Wheelwright and McFarlane, op. cit., p. 163.

57. On the Hawthorne experiments, see F. J. Roethlisberger and William J. Dickson, Management and the Worker (Cambridge: Harvard University Press, 1947); on the Scanlon Plan, see Fredrick Lesieur, The Scanlon Plan (Cambridge: MIT Press, 1958).

58. See for example, Jaroslav Vanek, General Theory of Labor-Managed Market Economies (Ithaca: Cornell University Press,

1970). See also, "Who Wants to Work?" Newsweek, March 26, 1973, pp. 79-89.

59. See for example, Carl Riskin, "Maoism and Motivation: Work Incentives in China," in China's Uninterrupted Revolution, ed. Victor Nee and James Peck (New York: Pantheon Books, 1975), pp. 415-61; also Gurley, op. cit.; Andors, "Revolution and Modernization," op. cit.

60. Hsueh-hsi yu P'i-p'an, no. 3 (1975), in Selections from PRC Magazines, no. 818 (May 22, 1975), p. 18.

61. Ibid., p. 10.

62. Hung-ch'i, no. 5 (May 1972), p. 31.

63. Hung-ch'i, no. 3 (March 1975), p. 55.

64. Hung-ch'i, no. 4 (1973), pp. 42-43.

65. Selections from PRC Magazines, no. 818 (May 22, 1975), p. 21.

66. Hung-ch'i, no. 9 (September 1973), pp. 69-74.

67. Hung-ch'i, no. 4 (April 1975), p. 34.

68. Selections from PRC Magazines, no. 818 (May 22, 1975), pp. 10-11.

69. Hung-ch'i, no. 4 (April 1975), p. 41.

70. Hung-ch'i, no. 5 (May 1975), p. 37.

71. Selections from PRC Magazines, no. 818 (May 22, 1975), pp. 10-11.

72. Peking Review, no. 28 (July 11, 1975), p. 12.

73. Hung-ch'i, no. 4 (April 1975), p. 33.

74. Hung-ch'i, no. 5 (May 1972), p. 41.

75. Hung-ch'i, no. 5 (May 1975), pp. 60-63.

76. Hung-ch'i, no. 4 (April 1974), pp. 58-59.

77. Peking Review, no. 24 (June 13, 1975), p. 13.

78. Hung-ch'i, no. 6 (June 1975), p. 5.

79. On this point see Carl Riskin, "Workers' Incentives in Chinese Industry," in China: A Reassessment of the Economy, U.S., Congress, Joint Economic Committee, 94th Cong. 1st sess. July 10, 1975 (Washington, D.C.: Government Printing Office, 1975), pp. 199-224.

80. Ibid., p. 205.

81. Ibid., pp. 222-23.

82. See ibid., pp. 216-22; also Howe, op. cit., Chapter 3 and passim; Hoffmann, op. cit., pp. 98-104.

83. The 1975 State Constitution appears in Hsinhua News (special issue), January 22, 1975, pp. 7-12.

84. On the role of labor unions in China, see Paul Harper, "Workers' Participation in Management in Communist China," in Studies on Comparative Communism, July-October 1971; Charles Hoffmann, Work Incentive Practices and Policies in the People's

Republic of China, 1953-1965 (Albany: State University of New York Press, 1967); Martin K. Whyte, Small Groups and Political Rituals in China (Berkeley and Los Angeles: University of California Press, 1974), Chapter 8.

85. Ibid., pp. 172, 187.

86. Robert L. Heilbroner, Between Capitalism and Socialism: Essays in Political Economics (New York: Random House, 1970), p. 158.

8

THE SOCIAL CONTEXT OF TECHNOLOGY ASSESSMENT IN EASTERN EUROPE
William N. Dunn

The organization is the form of mediation between theory and practice.

G. Lukács, History and Class Consciousness (1922)

Technology is embedded in social structures and cultural patterns that exert a politically decisive influence on the production, distribution, and utilization of technical knowledge in socialist societies. The meaning, uses, and consequences of an assembly line, tool, or management information system are therefore fundamentally different in countries as unlike as the Soviet Union, China, and Yugoslavia. While the production and utilization of technology presupposes cultural values that legitimize technical rationality and knowledge generated within the empiricoanalytic sciences, it is nonetheless all too evident that the social organization of work shapes different ways of viewing the physical and social world (theory) and alternative courses of action designed to control the material and human environment (practice). For this reason any adequate account of the relations between technology and socialist culture must proceed from dialectical assumptions about the social context in which specialized technical knowledge is produced and applied: society is a human product; society is an objective reality; man is a social product. [1] A dialectical approach to problems of technical rationality in socialist societies thus avoids the passive recording of presumed "functional requisites," "evolutionary universals," and "technological imperatives," while at the same time rejecting futile attempts to transcend the "cult of technical specialization . . . by abstract and irrelevant humanistic demands added by way of complementary addenda." [2]

This chapter proceeds from several interrelated assumptions that have a direct bearing on problems of assessing the reciprocal impact of technology and socialist culture in Eastern Europe, as follows:

1. Science and technology are political. Claims about technical knowledge and its application always involve conflicting interests and values in the domain of epistemology, theory, and methods, and not merely in the sphere of the social and political consequences of science and technology.[3] The nature of the social sciences is such that claims to the valid explanation and understanding of social processes necessarily include values that are in principle incapable of empirical corroboration.[4] For this reason theories of "scientific and technological revolution" put forward by various socialist writers—who have freely applied the category of false consciousness to their adversaries, but seldom to themselves—must be examined in light of what they conceal. The methodological necessity of ideology-critique is quite as evident when we consider the assessments of technology and socialist culture made by external interpreters, whose epistemological frameworks, theories, and methods likewise derive from particular ideals and images of science and society, and not from the assumed "facticity" of technical rationality, technological change, or modernization in socialist systems.[5]

2. Cultural values are essential for understanding the social context of technology in socialist systems. If we adopt a broad definition of culture as inclusive of technical rationality, technology, and technique,[6] it becomes evident that narrow technical approaches are likely to prove inadequate to problems of relations between technology and socialist culture. Nevertheless, it is essential to clarify and make operational those concepts that give concrete meaning to elements of culture.[7] Culture may be broken down into its general features, including world views, beliefs about nature and humankind, and social values, as well as specifically socialist components involving a commitment to science, sociohistorical progress, industrialization, egalitarianism, and the emancipation of labor. General and specifically socialist components must nonetheless be examined in the concrete social settings in which they arise, which suggests the necessity for a diachronic approach to culture change.[8] Thus, for example, approaching culture in terms of different types or spheres of rationality that intersect one with another in a relation of potential complementarity and conflict, prevents us from making static

assumptions about our subject matter. Furthermore, a diachronic approach permits us to avoid the fallacy of misplaced
concreteness (Whitehead), according to which abstractions
such as "technical rationality," "modernization," and "scientific and technological revolution" are improperly employed
as a basis for making ostensibly concrete generalizations
about culture change in Eastern European societies.

    3. Culturological perspectives on science and technol-
ogy, however much guided by a diachronic approach, fail to
provide a convincing or satisfactory account of the cultural
variations and value conflicts found within and between Eastern
European societies. Indeed, in their pure form culturological
explanations of technology and socialist culture represent one
form of collective psychological reductionism that dismisses
profound differences in social organization such as those
captured by ideal types of state capitalism, state socialism,
and self-managing socialism. [9] Social organization governs the
ways in which cultural values serve as a basis for the institutionalization of new patterns of behavior and social interaction.
General and specifically socialist elements of culture are
governed by and reciprocally related to differences in the
social organization of work and authority in Eastern European
societies.

    4. Culturological and structural perspectives, when
employed separately, distort our understanding of technology
and socialist culture. Attempts to place technology in a dynamic
sociohistorical context have thus far run aground, both in
Marxist and nonMarxist accounts, at precisely that point at
which it becomes necessary to construct satisfactory explanations based on some combined assessment of objective and
subjective factors. Four major theoretical viewpoints on technology and social change—technological determinism, technological imperativism, sociotechnical systems, and modernization—each contain characteristic weaknesses as frameworks
for interpreting the production and utilization of technical
knowledge in socialist societies. It is essential to recognize
that identical empirical generalizations can be interpreted in
alternative ways, depending on the use of theoretical viewpoints that are in all cases partially "ideological."[10] Explanations of technology and social change are therefore external to
empirical data; the "facts" never speak for themselves.

    5. Contemporary evolutionary theories of technology
and culture, from "scientific and technological revolution" to
"post-industrial society," tend to project a depoliticized vision
of imperative historical progress, a vision that is naive, unre-

flective, and ideological. Developments in Eastern Europe,
particularly Yugoslavia, tend nonetheless to challenge the key
assumptions on which such evolutionary theories are based.
Self-managing socialism, elements of which may be found in
other Eastern European societies at different points in time
since 1956, provides a concrete historical instance of objective
possibilities for the emancipation of labor under conditions of
rapid technological change. The Yugoslav case, contrasted
with those of Poland and Czechoslovakia, suggests that dominant patterns of nonhierarchical social organization, egalitarian cultural values, and a socialist market-planned economy
have exerted politically decisive influences on the development,
importation, and uses of technology.

In summary, "technology assessment" is necessarily a political
and ideological activity. The choice of explanatory theories and inter-
pretive frameworks requires the adoption of philosophical and value
positions that consciously or inadvertently project different preferences concerning the distribution of legitimacy and rewards in society.
No existing account of technology and culture in socialist systems is
free from such influences, as follows:

> All epistemologies are, at base, derived from ontolog-
> ical postures which are themselves a prioristic in
> nature, predicated as they must be on cosmological-
> teleological suppositions which are perforce deductive
> and non-apodictical in character. [11]

Theoretical explanations of technology and socialist culture are
therefore based on a priori assumptions about man, nature, and the
production and uses of knowledge in society. The essential difference
between competing explanations is the degree to which they embody a
self-reflective awareness that all theories are necessarily grounded
in concrete human values with political consequences in the domain
of action. In short, "empirical studies" of technology and socialist
culture are grossly incomplete by themselves, and perhaps irrelevant, so long as the absence of ideology-critique prevents us from
recognizing the pseudoscientific character of the theories that have
thus far deterred us from recognizing that science and technology
are human projects.

THE POLITICS OF TECHNOLOGY

Both socialist and capitalist interpreters often ignore the
social context of technology assessment in accounts of scientific and

technological revolution. Thus recent accounts of technological
change in late capitalist societies reflect the essentially depoliticized framework and assumptions of the observers, such as those
associated with the Harvard Program on Science and Technology. [12]
The treatise by Radovan Richta and colleagues, while guided by a
different set of concerns, also depoliticizes technology, insofar as
progressive consequences are assumed to follow scientific and technological revolution so long as knowledge and its use are somehow
harnessed by the socialist organization of society. [13] One of the
major works on scientific and technological revolution in Yugoslavia
proceeds from a different starting point, but in the end argues much
the same point as Richta. [14] Self-managing socialism provides opportunities for adapting to scientific and technical revolution that are
shared by no other system of social organization, establishing conditions for the emancipation of labor and the democratization of work
under conditions of rapid scientific and technological progress.

Each of these theoretically distinguishable views on technology
and sociohistorical change might be reduced to simple expressions
of technical rationality; yet such a reduction overlooks fundamental
differences in these theories of scientific and technological revolution and the social contexts to which they are reciprocally related.
Thus it is one thing to argue that the leading theories of intellectuals
in socialist and capitalist societies embody beliefs in technological
progress that ignore politics, [15] but it is quite another matter to
make inferences about the cultural patterns of socialist societies on
the basis of theories that have their roots in the special technical
perspectives and interests of particular groups. [16] Science and technology are products, but they are also grounded in political processes
that reflect different cultural values and modes of organizing work
and authority in society. [17]

In a context of concern with a critical theory of society, [18] it is
appropriate to question the tenability of different assertions about the
capacity of socialism to pacify science and technology, that is, to
maintain or recover the intended relations between socialist theory
and practice under conditions of rapid scientific and technological
change. Thus, while self-managing socialism may well share a
comparative advantage over rival forms of social organization in
maintaining the authenticity of socialist development, it is nonetheless apparent that contemporary Eastern European socialist theory,
including that of self-managing socialism in Yugoslavia, shares
marked tendencies toward economism and other elements of technical rationality. [19] Within Eastern Europe there are identifiable
groups whose orientations toward technology and social organization
vary considerably. At one end of a continuum we can place critical
Marxists, comprised largely of intellectuals, students, and a small
contingent of workers, who have adopted the position that one form

or another of organizational reform and cultural revitalization is necessary to subdue the growth and domination of privileged strata in the economy and in scientific and technical institutions. [20] At the other extreme are establishment Marxists, found in positions of political authority throughout Eastern Europe, who see no serious incompatibility or conflict between industrialization, technological progress, and the cultural values of socialism. [21] Between these two groups are a variety of liberal reformers, comprised mostly of technical intelligentsia and managers, who tend to see technological development, economic growth, and industrial autonomy threatened both by politicized economic decision making and by the cultural values of egalitarianism and the emancipation of labor. [22] Hence throughout Eastern Europe there is considerable variation in the social values and political influence of various functional groups, ranging from intellectuals and leaders within the mass media to personnel in industrial organizations, state administrations, and party and trade union bodies. [23]

In Yugoslavia and elsewhere in Eastern Europe, the problem of the relationship between technology and socialist culture may be amplified and rendered more precise by conceptualizing technical rationality, technology, and technological artifacts as several important variables of social organization, including the social structures, social values, and configurations of work organizations in society. A critical approach to technology assessment requires that problems of technological prerequisites, requisites, and consequences are investigated in a context of concert with variations in social organization such as those that characterize different systems in Eastern Europe. Postwar Yugoslav development, for example, suggests that nonhierarchical forms of social organization, when supported by egalitarian social values, can effectively guide scientific and technological change while at the same time maintaining high levels of material production, personal welfare, and consumption. Nevertheless, the unanticipated consequences of industrial, scientific and technological development create recurrent conflicts between different social groups. Efforts to resolve such conflicts, which assume the form of successive attempts to repoliticize the context of industrial and technological decisions through political mobilization, have been directed toward the intensification of involvement of workers in the processes of economic and political decision making.

The processes of politicization, depoliticization, and repoliticization, which are closely associated with the conflicting demands of revolution and modernization in socialist societies, strongly suggest more or less regular phases of conflict, change, and adjustment. This phase hypothesis appears to be applicable primarily to those socialist societies that have successfully undergone social revolutions followed by periods of independent national policy making, during which indigenously generated forms of social organization could be institutionalized. Recognizing that there are great differences in social organization between Yugoslavia and other socialist systems, it appears nonetheless that the phase hypothesis is primarily or exclusively applicable to only two or three socialist societies. [24]

The problem of the reciprocal impact of technology and socialist culture is essentially an empirical question. While multiple perspectives can and should be applied to issues associated with scientific and technological change, such perspectives range from the philosophical to the strictly empirical. [25] Thus, for example, a synchronic perspective may assist the investigation of the logical structure of theory, permitting conclusions about the relative dominance of logical positivist and functionalist paradigms in socialist societies. [26] A diachronic perspective, on the other hand, would permit historical analysis of the growth of science, although there are few such studies about socialist societies. [27] Two additional perspectives, the axiothetic and the critical, permit analysis of the relationships of science and technology with two critical facets of life in socialist societies: goal-seeking behavior associated with societal guidance and activities directed toward ascertaining the meaning of science and technology for projected societal conditions, including the potentiality for full equality and the emancipation of labor in socialist communities. [28] Lastly, a sociological perspective, in the widest sense, employs a variety of social science disciplines to investigate producers, interestees, and users of knowledge in society. [29]

Each of these five perspectives on science and technology informs and mediates others; they are interdependent, not mutually exclusive. Nevertheless, it is essential to distinguish the kinds of questions for which each perspective is appropriate. Synchronic, axiothetic, and critical perspectives cannot directly answer empirical questions about the differential impact of technology on cultural patterns in different socialist societies. The answers to such questions can only proceed from diachronic and sociological analyses, which are concerned with empirical phenomena investigated with the tools of history and the social sciences. The three remaining perspectives—synchronic, axiothetic, and critical—deal with the essential nonempirical problems associated with philosophical anthropology, epistemology, and ethics.

ORGANIZATION AND TECHNOLOGY

In the absence of efforts to undertake a systematic investigation of the historical growth of science under socialism, it is still possible to employ a sociological perspective to examine the production, dissemination, and use of knowledge in particular socialist societies. One is nevertheless confronted with several conceptual dilemmas, as follows:

1. When technical rationality, technology, and technique are conceptualized and defined as elements of culture, and culture itself is taken as constitutive of knowledge, belief, art, morals, laws, customs, habits, traditions, and symbolic capabilities, it is difficult to relate science and technology to the structural variations exemplified in different forms of social organization.

2. Formal definitions of technical rationality, technology, and technique as elements of culture often tend to emphasize the subjective dimension of scientific and technological change.

3. A conceptualization of science and technology at the level of global culture tends to stress the imposition of cultural patterns on social organization, as distinguished from their generation in social groups.

These conceptual problems may be illustrated by considering the theoretical viewpoints associated with two principal dimensions of technology and socialist culture: objective versus subjective behavior relations and imposed versus generated conditions. (See Figure 2.) Objective and subjective behavior relations are conceptualized as alternative explananda of theory, while imposed and generated conditions are viewed here as the explanantes of various theories related to technology and socialist societies.

FIGURE 2

Theoretical Viewpoints on
Technology and Socialist Societies

		Behavior Relations that Define Societies	
		Objective (Materialist)	Subjective (Idealist)
Technological phenomena that explain societies	Imposed (determined)	technological determinism	technological imperativism
	Generated (free-willed)	sociotechnical systems	modernization

Source: Adapted from Walter Wallace, Sociological Theory (Chicago: Aldine, 1969), pp. 5-13.

While drawing admittedly exaggerated distinctions, the above classification scheme allows us to identify the essential differences among four somewhat idealized theoretical viewpoints on technology and socialist societies. Thus technological determinism emphasizes conditions that are imposed on societies by the presumed nature of technology and its effects on objective behavior relations associated with changes in the mode of production. [30] By contrast, technological imperativism stresses such conditions as technological complexity as universal explanations of changes in other elements of socialist society. Ideology and cultural patterns must themselves adapt to technological changes if socialist societies are to develop or even survive. [31]

In contrast to explanations based on imposed conditions, two additional theoretical viewpoints emphasize socially generated factors. Sociotechnical systems theory, for example, posits that technical and social systems are interdependent, contributing to patterns of mutual influence that accommodate processes of innovation and invention as well as the resultant social changes. [32] Modernization, which stresses the generation of such individual attitudes as scientific rationality, empathy, and beliefs in instrumental reason, looks toward changes in individual subjective behavior relations that are believed to accompany processes of societal differentiation, specialization, and integration, particularly through changes in production organizations. [33]

The assumptions of logical independence underlying the classification of theoretical viewpoints (Figure 2) conflict with a dialectical conception of knowledge and action, thereby reducing subject and object to separate and self-sustaining categories. An emphasis on imposed conditions of any kind lends to theories of technology and socialist culture a degree of certainty and finality that is untenable. Such theories contribute to the hypostatization of history and societal change. By contrast, theoretical viewpoints based on generated conditions successfully capture the complexities of socialist societies in which different options and strategic choices are exercised in efforts to resolve diverse social, economic, and political problems. At the same time, such viewpoints allow for the possibility of imposed conditions and sociocultural adaptations. An emphasis on both subjective and objective factors generated within social groups is consistent with critical and sociological perspectives on the creation and use of knowledge in society.

The application of a sociological perspective to problems of technology and socialist culture can be accomplished with the concepts and tools of organizational analysis. Complex organizations in socialist societies, particularly work or production organizations, may be conceptualized in terms of three sets of interdependent variables associated with organizational, social, and technical systems. [34] The relationships among these systems may be conceptualized as both generated and imposed, inclusive of subjective and objective behavior relations at once. An organizational system, which includes structures of authority and control, group interaction, and attitudes of individual members, is situated in a technical and social system. Social systems, which comprise other organizations, groups, and sociocultural values, may be more or less salient in influencing variations in organization. A technical system similarly influences and is influenced by organizational and social systems. Technical systems may be conceptualized in terms of process-embodied (operations), product-embodied (materials), and person-embodied (knowledge) technologies. [35]

The rationale for conceptualizing organizational, social, and technical systems in the manner described above is threefold:

1. Organizational control structures and forms of technology are distinguishable sets of interdependent variables.

2. Relationships between different organizational control structures, technologies, and social systems govern the degree to which organizations promote conditions for efficient production and the humanization of work.

3. Variations in social structure and social values establish boundaries around different types of organizational control and mediate technology in the fulfillment of societal and organizational goals.

This conceptualization avoids defining technology as coextensive with social control; thus it avoids the tendency to equate organizational control with technology, which is itself defined as the control of human and material resources. [36] Moreover, conceptualizing organizational, technical, and social systems in this fashion allows us to treat socialist "transfer culture" as a multidimensional construct that includes aspects of technology, but also aspects of social organization. Indeed, variations in the organizational dimension of transfer culture may be such as to mitigate or neutralize the unanticipated consequences of technology for socialist goal culture. [37]

The utility of the above conceptualization may be illustrated by comparing organizational and technical systems in different socialist societies. As a form of social organization, workers' self-management in Yugoslavia extends to all industrial and service organizations in the country. Despite variations in the number of workers' councils and management boards in various industries, a common legal regime establishes more or less uniform norms for all work organizations in the socialized sector. The practice of self-management nonetheless suggests differences that are partly governed by technology. Thus the salience of self-managing norms, including worker control over various spheres of decision making, is greatest in small handicrafts industries with low technological complexity, high flexibility, and largely self-generated technological processes. [38] In mechanized enterprises, norms of self-management are relatively less salient, while automated firms lie somewhere in between.

In China, while there are differences between the systems for organizing work in agriculture (Tachai) and industry (Tach'ing), both systems appear to involve technologies that are low to moderate in complexity, highly flexible, and largely self-generated. [39] The group basis of Tachai and Tach'ing, which promotes a measure of technological flexibility and worker control, shared perhaps only by handicrafts firms in Yugoslavia, involves technological design by work groups composed of party cadres, technicians, and production workers. Therefore organizations in both societies differ in the extent to which socialist norms of associated labor are salient in guiding the social uses of technology. The relationships between technological complexity and the salience of socialist production organizations, the latter operationalized in terms of worker control over the decision-making processes, are suggested in Figure 3.

In summary, an organizational perspective on technology and socialist culture permits us to treat organizational, technical, and social systems as variables of global social organization. The investigation of differences in social organization among and within socialist societies assists in the empirical determination of the prerequisites, requisites, and consequences of technology. Given similar technologies, such as those that appear to characterize the mechanized production processes in the iron and steel industries in China and Yugoslavia, organizations nonetheless differ in effectively mediating technology in accordance with socialist values. Technical rationality or purposive rational action, however, is a constant that underlies all forms of technology, whether imported, diffused, or self-generated. While essential as a philosophical category, technical rationality is only indirectly applicable to empirical investigations. Social organization mediates technology and governs the character of socialist praxis.

TECHNOLOGY AND CULTURE

The development of comparative communist studies may be characterized largely in terms of linear approaches to history and societal change, together with broad dichotomous categories in which different socialist societies are typed for purposes of compar-

FIGURE 3

Organizational Salience and Technology

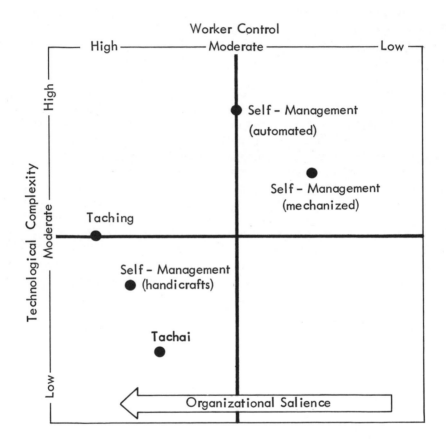

Source: Compiled by the author.

ison. China, Cuba, and North Korea are typically placed at one end of a continuum described in terms of egalitarianism, moral incentives, revolutionization, politicization, ideological radicalism, and relative international isolation. The socialist societies in Eastern Europe, particularly Yugoslavia, are regularly assigned a position at the opposite end of the same continuum; elitism, material incentives, modernization, rationalization, ideological pragmatism, and international integration are among the characteristics of more highly industrialized and economically developed forms of European socialism. Schemes that permit such contrasts are of obvious importance for the comparative analysis of technology and socialist culture. The cultural values that underlie different conceptions of rationality and variations in the use of material incentives within production organizations define the social contexts in which knowledge is produced and applied in the form of various technologies and techniques.

Nonetheless, the social context of technology assessment may be systematically obscured by the reification of properties thought to characterize cultural patterns in different socialist societies. Contrary to conventional descriptions of Yugoslavia as the most "capitalist" of contemporary socialist societies,[40] its social organization has mediated technology in a manner not dissimilar to descriptions of "technological nativism" in China.[41] The dominant pattern of technological change in Yugoslavia suggests largely self-generated technical processes and selective borrowing from abroad, not a linear process of modernization according to models and to historical experiences of socialist or capitalist systems.[42] As the dominant form of social organization since the early 1950s, self-management is inextricably linked with egalitarian cultural values formed in a peasant society under conditions of successful guerrilla warfare and social revolution.

Compared with other socialist societies, the Yugoslav experience accentuates the importance of three critical factors affecting postwar social organizations. (1) Its presocialist social structure and cultural patterns were largely consistent with socialist egalitarianism, as compared with the social structures and values that fostered forms of socialist elitism elsewhere in Eastern Europe. (2) Its national liberation and social revolution were accomplished through an indigenous popular movement (Partizans) that depended only marginally on foreign military, technical, and economic assistance. (3) After a short period of administrative socialism (1946–50) modelled after that of the Soviet Union, its foreign and domestic policies became comparatively independent of outside influence. They included the maintenance of high levels of domestic savings, labor-intensive production, and a low level of imposed technological change, whether imported from abroad or fostered by specialized ministries and research institutes within the country. [43]

When these critical factors are employed in a reconstructed conceptual framework that includes two major dimensions, which are elitism versus egalitarianism and imposed versus generated technological change within production organizations (see Figure 4), we may be compelled to reassess comparative statements about technology and culture in socialist societies. Thus, for example, most of Eastern Europe and the Soviet Union might well be described in terms of "technological modernization," while China and Yugoslavia might well be characterized in terms of "technological development."[44] Such descriptions raise a series of new and problematic questions regarding the impact of culture and social organization on technological change within socialist societies. Moreover, the classification scheme itself raises what would appear to be a critical question about socialist societies—the question of the meaning of scientific and technological "revolution" in societies committed to egalitarianism and the emancipation of labor as central revolutionary values.

Egalitarian cultural values are largely responsible for the degree of success manifested by self-managing socialism as the institutionalized mode for organizing work in Yugoslavia. Self-management in Yugoslavia, when compared with efforts to establish workers' councils and other forms of direct producers' involvement elsewhere in Eastern Europe, has sustained itself and become more intense over a period of some 25 years. Nearly all major studies indicate that the values of self-managing socialism have been firmly institutionalized in Yugoslav society. [45] Egalitarianism, defined in terms of expressed preferences for the principle that the allocation of social rewards should reflect minimal income differentials, is a dominant value of Yugoslav society. [46] Egalitarianism has been identified in a cross section of groups in the working population including party members, youth, and various categories of personnel in production organizations.

The results of surveys point to the salience of egalitarianism and raise questions about the official ideology of self-management. In the period between the economic reform of 1965 and the ideological offensive of 1971, official spokesmen strongly emphasized the principle "to each according to his work." Challenging egalitarianism in the form of wage-leveling (uravnilovka), these official spokesmen in effect supported values of equal opportunity, not egalitarianism. While survey research suggests strong preferences for egalitarianism at the level of implicit or behaviorally manifested values, the same surveys also disclose a broad commitment to equal opportunity (social equity) at the level of explicit or verbally enunciated values. [47]

FIGURE 4

Technological Change and Cultural Patterns
in Socialist Societies

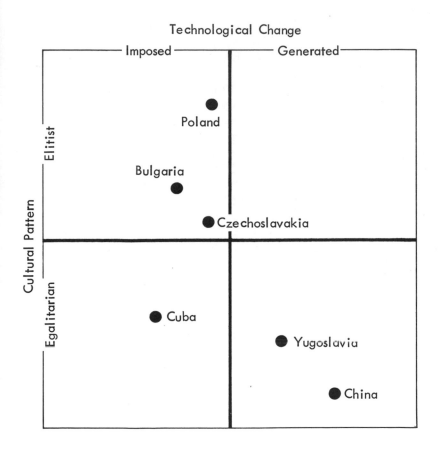

Source: Compiled by the author.

Among the prominent characteristics of implicit egalitarianism
in Yugoslav society is a manifest preference for highly compressed
wage differentials. While there is strong support for the regulation
of wage differentials, as evidenced by findings in a cross section of
the population, there is also a marked tendency among production
workers to prefer wage differentials that do not exceed 2 or 3:1, a
ratio that parallels actual wage differentials immediately after the
war. The results of one large survey of employees in ten Croatian
industrial organizations suggest that the majority of personnel in all
categories except managers—production workers, administrative
employees, supervisors, and experts—support the further compression of wage differentials. [48]

These attitudes toward wage differentials are even more significant when related to other indicators of equality, including actual
wage differentials and income distribution. While the gap in per-
capita incomes in the six republics and two autonomous provinces
has increased since 1947, earnings differ little within separate
enterprises. The average intrafirm wage differential is 1:3.4 in 75
percent of enterprises and 1:4 in 25 percent. The average intersectoral differentials in the social sector approached 1.7:1 in 1963,
falling to 1.3:1 in 1971. [49] The average interskill wage differentials
in various sectors fluctuated marginally in 1957-69. The distribution
of individual and household incomes reflects a distribution in which
the upper 5 percent of the population receives approximately twice
the share of the lowest 25 percent, although the distribution of
household incomes is less equitable than that of individual incomes. [50]

The available evidence on egalitarian values and social structure suggests a strong association between cultural values and social
organization, particularly the capacity to sustain and develop self-
managing bodies in industry, educational institutions, scientific
institutes, health and welfare organizations, and housing. One of the
factors underlying recurrent efforts at ideological mobilization in
the period since 1954 is the conflict between workers, who share
egalitarian values, and experts and technicians, who are increasingly
achievement-oriented and inclined toward principles of equity. The
League of Communists, which has recurrently supported changes in
policy designed to benefit workers, has nonetheless been largely
unsuccessful in maintaining high levels of party membership among
workers. The proportion of party members among all categories of
workers has been less than among university and college-educated
employees, as well as party members with primary and secondary
education. [51]

While egalitarianism is a dominant value, there are nonetheless
differences among various groups in the relative importance
assigned to egalitarian values. Thus, for example, a major finding

of the International Study of Opinion-Makers is that occupational function is the most important single variable associated with differences in the attitudes and behavior of Yugoslav opinion leaders. Barton writes as follows:

> In a modern society without a capitalist class, the major source of differentiation among leaders lies in the common experiences of and identification with one's particular social function, as a mass organization leader, legislator, federal administrator, economic leader, mass communicator, or intellectual.[52]

Wage egalitarianism among the above groups varies. Over 50 percent of intellectuals, mass organization leaders, and legislators express the view that wage differentials among various groups should not exceed 4.5:1. Among mass communicators, federal administrators, and economic leaders, a significantly lower proportion (34 to 49 percent) responded that wage ratios should not exceed 4.5:1.[53] The results reported by Bolčić suggest similar low levels of implicit egalitarianism among managers and correspondingly high levels among workers.[54]

The dominance of egalitarianism in Yugoslav society cannot be separated from history and societal change; it is particularly related to the prewar culture, which provided the social context in which the Communist Party came to power. In contrast to Poland, Czechoslovakia, and East Germany, industrial capitalism and a relatively crystallized class structure had not developed. Moreover, agrarian or peasant cultural values were heavily oriented to an ethic of redistribution at the level of global society.[55] The presocialist elements of culture and social structure fused after 1946 into what has been described as an "egalitarian syndrome." This includes several interdependent dimensions: antipathy toward private ownership, distrust of acquisitiveness, antientrepreneurship, antiprofessionalism, and antiintellectualism.[56]

The tensions between egalitarianism and cultural patterns supportive of conventional approaches to modernization and industrial development, whether based on the experience of the capitalist West or that of the Soviet Union, may be summarized in several major propositions.

1. Egalitarianism places emphasis on redistribution, as distinguished from acquisition, conferring social prestige and status on the political leaders and organizations that are responsible for maintaining egalitarian patterns in the distribution and redistribution of economic resources.

2.   Egalitarianism imposes limits on incomes as well as on individual economic aspirations, establishing a motivational struture different from that based on unlimited aspirations and insatiable needs.

3.   Egalitarianism circumscribes professionalism, particularly in the sphere of management, by emphasizing the democratization of decision making at the local level. At higher levels, executive authority in functionally organized political groups is emphasized as a vehicle for societal guidance.

4.   Egalitarianism tends to emphasize labor-intensive production processes and the quantity of human inputs, checking or thwarting the growth of the technical intelligentsia and technological developments in areas of organization, management, and planning.

TECHNOLOGY AND SOCIAL CHANGE

The presocialist social structure and cultural patterns, together with a communist party capable of effectively leading a popular guerrilla movement through a successful war of liberation, made possible the introduction, implementation, and continuous development of self-managing socialism. In the period following Yugoslavia's rupture with the Soviet Union and expulsion from the Cominform, a series of organizational reforms occurred in a social context of egalitarianism, and not as a result of a paradoxical turnabout of communist leaders who engaged in the self-abnegation of their own power. The establishment of workers' councils in 1950, together with successive efforts to decentralize the state administration and the economy, were therefore not the product of a unitary political elite that suddenly discovered that economic benefits could be derived from decentralization and a socialist market economy. The view that holds that political leaders purposefully convened in 1949-50 to calculate the probable economic benefits to be reaped from self-management overlooks the fact that a departure from central investment planning was at that point economically irrational, since heavy guided investments would probably have produced optimal rates of growth well into the 1950s.[57] More important, such an interpretation fails to recognize that the motivation for establishing self-management was essentially political. The motives included nonalignment in foreign affairs, but also the development of institutions that fostered legitimacy in a predominantly egalitarian society, most of whose politically active members were youthful veterans of a successful guerrilla war. Self-management was broadly legitimized among the workers and

the broad mass of the population, a pattern that did not occur elsewhere in Eastern Europe, including East Germany, Hungary, Poland,
and Czechoslovakia. [58]

The two dimensions of egalitarianism and elitism are of central
importance for scientific and technological revolution in socialist
societies. A somewhat crude classification scheme can be used to
generalize the ideological positions of various groups in Eastern
Europe: liberal reformers who seek greater autonomy in science,
technological development, and the economy; establishment socialists
who seek to maintain or reform central investment and production
planning for purposes of balanced growth and social development; and
humanists who are concerned with transcending the negative consequences of programs supported by established leaders and other
ideological groups. [59] The values associated with scientific and technological revolution are typically supported by liberal reformers and
younger and more highly educated members of the establishment. In
Yugoslavia such groups tend to be occupied with issues associated
with insulating science and technology from political influence and
problems of modernizing or professionalizing the management of the
economy and other spheres of production. Liberal reformers are
also among those who call for changes in cultural values, including
egalitarianism, so as to provide greater incentives for scientific
advance, technological growth, and modernization.

Egalitarian values have sustained the workers' self-management; both have served as the effective mode for exercising political
control over the pace and direction of technological change. There
have been at least the following major characteristics of the overall
pattern of self-generated technological change since 1950:

1. Low external dependence on foreign technological
products, processes, and knowledge, particularly in the period
preceding the 1965 economic reforms.

2. Selective technological borrowing under conditions of
maximum organizational control provided by self-management.

3. Decentralized and locally generated technological
innovation, reflected by the structure of scientific and technical
institutions and the volume and sources of patents and inventions.

4. A system of industrial management that provides for
significant involvement of managerial personnel, political
leaders, and production workers in decisions regarding technology and modernization.

In the period since 1950, the rates of economic growth in Yugoslavia have been among the highest in the world. In 1950-64, rates

of growth averaging between 7 and 8 percent placed the country
second or third in the world, following Japan (8.6 percent) and Israel
(7.5 percent). The average rate of growth of GNP has been calculated
at 6.8 percent for 1960-68, compared with 2.3 percent in the period
of central planning (1946-53).[60] Estimates of the growth rates of 29
high-growth countries rank Yugoslavia sixth, behind Japan, Bulgaria,
Spain, Taiwan, and Greece. More important, Yugoslavia and Japan
have successfully employed a strategy of economic development with
low levels of external capital and high rates of domestic savings.[61]
Comparisons of gross domestic capital formation among selected
socialist countries in the 1950s suggest a very high comparative
reliance on domestic savings.

The structure of imports in the 1952-70 period reflects low
dependence on external product-embodied technology in the form of
imported machinery and transport equipment. Product-embodied
technological imports, which accounted for 33.5 percent of total
imports in 1970, were slightly above the 1952-70 average of 30.5
percent.[62] At the same time, total import content as a percentage
of production increased from 11 percent in 1962 to 13.4 percent in
1970, which indicates a growing total import dependence in 1962-70.
This dependence on industrial imports nonetheless reflects increases
in raw materials and semimanufactures only, with investment and
consumer goods declining as a share of the total.

Imports of mechanical equipment, the principal indicator of
changes in product-embodied technology, fluctuated according to
product in the period following the economic reforms of 1965. The
rate of growth of mechanical equipment in four categories—nonelec-
tric power-generating machinery, agricultural machinery, construction and mining machinery, and office machinery—declined in
1965-71. In three other categories, including metalworking machinery, industrial processing machinery, and general industrial machinery, the rates of growth increased.

Imports of product-embodied technology, which are primarily
capital or investment goods, declined as a proportion of total
imports in 1954-71. At the same time, process-embodied technology,
imported through various licensing arrangements between Yugoslav
and foreign firms, increased throughout the 1960s. In 1970 over 100
licensing agreements regulating the use of various processes, from
the production of soft drinks, cigarettes, and cosmetics to the production of electric semiconductors, automobiles, and trucks, were
in force between Yugoslav and foreign firms.[63] Many licensing
agreements also involve direct investments in Yugoslav enterprises
through joint ventures, which since 1967 have been institutionalized
through various legal arrangements.[64] Among the perceived advantages of joint ventures are access to foreign markets, additional

investment capital, industrial and business engineering skills, and advanced technology. "The joint venture system," observes Sukijasović, "seems preferable to the license system as a way of getting technology. Past experience with licenses was not very encouraging since the purchase of a license did not mean . . . the newest technology."[65] Foreign investors are likewise expected to apply engineering skills "to improve the organization of work and the process of production and to train the personnel of the home enterprise."[66]

Joint ventures are regarded as a more effective means than licenses for transferring process-embodied and person-embodied technologies. More than eight foreign firms registered as partners in joint ventures in 1968-74, with the bulk of activity concentrated in Slovenia and Croatia.[67] Joint-venture capital, which is limited to a 49 percent share by foreign partners and excluded from the areas of banking, insurance, communications, commerce, public utilities, and social services, has thus far been largely confined to the motor vehicle industry. By the end of 1972, joint-venture agreements had been signed with some 68 partners, committed to provide some $20 million of investment capital annually, which amounts to 1 to 2 percent of annual capital movements.[68] Joint ventures with U.S. firms comprise a small part of a total investment pattern in which West European firms play a dominant role, investing in varied industries: printing, electronics, appliances, acrylics, contact lenses food flavorings, cellulose, polyesters, petroleum, steel, and metal processing. In a survey of 10 U.S. firms engaged in joint ventures, four responded that their primary motivation for investing in Yugoslavia was to generate revenue from technical and managerial know-how, while the remaining firms sought to obtain raw materials, cheap labor, and an expanded market in Eastern Europe.[69] The transfer of person-embodied technology through joint ventures and international organizations has increased significantly since 1968. Joint ventures, together with investments in training and research, transportation planning, and industrial development by the United Nations, account for a sizable inflow of person-embodied technology.[70] While documentation is generally lacking, it is known that the larger Yugoslav enterprises employ Western management consultants to assist with problems of organizational planning and production.[71]

An overall pattern of low external dependence on capital and technology began to shift toward increasing external dependence in the aftermath of the economic reforms of 1965. The economic reforms, which promoted greater decentralization of enterprises, freed a large number of commodities from price controls, altered foreign currency and trade provisions, and made firms more competitive in international markets. The reforms also called attention

to demands for increased productivity and efficiency through the
importation of new technologies. Technological change appeared to
be particularly critical, given the country's increasing involvement
in world markets and its relatively antiquated technological stock,
much of which was installed prior to World War II or imported in the
immediate postwar period. In addition, labor-intensive techniques
of production and a comparatively low level of technological innovation also provided a rationale for technological modernization through
external borrowing.

The technological modernization thesis, according to which
Yugoslavia is described as a backward or underdeveloped country
incapable of pursuing self-sustained growth and technological development, has often been overstated. Given high rates of growth in the
early period of self-management, a substantial portion of which can
be attributed to increases in technical progress, the technological
modernization thesis overlooks the fact that rapid postwar development was accomplished under conditions present in few other countries: worker control, decentralization, and the democratization of
industry. [72] Comparisons of efficiency and technical progress under
three major periods of social organization in 1911-67 suggest that
self-management, while failing to meet the criteria included in
typical checklists of modernization, has nonetheless contributed to
economic, technological, and social development.

As the dominant form of social organization since the early
1950s, self-managing socialism is intimately tied to egalitarianism,
but also to a decentralized and largely self-generated pattern of technological change in which production workers have played a dominant
role. Thus, until the end of the 1960s technological imports were of
marginal significance for economic and social development, as were
loans and grants-in-aid from Western powers. U.S. aid came
primarily in the form of agricultural products and foodstuffs, contributing little to the successive structural changes in the economy
and marginally to technological progress. The development of new
technological processes and knowledge was based principally on the
activities of production workers in self-managing organizations.

In the postwar period the social control of science and technology has been reflected in a tendency toward deprofessionalization
in society at large. [73] Indicators of deprofessionalization include
controls over the functional autonomy of experts, withdrawal of
professional titles, relaxation of criteria for access to professions,
depression in the cost of professional services, and a negative attitude toward the professions generally, including industrial design
and management. While there are advanced schools for the organization of work in Slovenia, Croatia, Serbia, and Vojvodina, there has
been public concern that their admissions procedures will result in

TABLE 2

Comparative Analysis of Efficiency under
Three Forms of Social Organization, 1911–67
(rates of growth)

Social Organization	Gross Domestic Product	Employment	Fixed Capital	Technical Progress
Capitalism				
(1911–32)	3.28	1.87	3.52	0.71
(1932–40)	4.67	0.72	2.59	3.16
Etatism				
(1940–54)	5.91	4.76	9.99	−1.04
Self-Management				
(1956–67)	10.31	4.44	7.84	4.44

Source: B. Horvat, _Privredni Sistem i Ekonomska Politika Jugoslavije_ (Belgrade: Institut Ekonomskih Nauka, 1970), p. 32.

the development of elitism among industrial managers. [74] Since late 1972 there have been regular public attacks on bureaucratic-technocratic tendencies among managers, and a large number of directors and technical staff members have been replaced or demoted in a number of firms.

The area of technological innovation and invention reflects the decentralization of scientific and research and development activities. The 1963 and 1974 constitutions confer equal status to scientific and technical institutions as self-managing organizations, while the 1965 General Law on the Organization of Scientific Activity and Research governs their establishment and operations. Research units may be established whenever necessary, either in universities or in work organizations, and function according to principles of self-management. Workers' councils as well as scientific councils, the latter of which are comparable to the management boards in self-managing firms in industry, are elected by members of the collective. More important, research and development activities are carried out primarily by industrial enterprises and economic associations, with some 70 percent of the funds provided by decentralized organizations themselves. In the period since 1970, the budgetary support for research efforts formerly funded by federal and republican bodies has been shifted to those local organizations and bodies that are most directly interested in the products of research.

The decentralized form of social organization characteristic of self-managing socialism has also affected technological change in the form of patents and inventions. The number of registered patents increased from 90 to 246 in 1964-66, rising to 1,000 in 1968. [75] Nonetheless, the annual average of persons per registered patent is some four to twelve times lower than those of the other socialist countries in Eastern Europe. (See Table 3.) Of the patents registered in 1968, 83 percent were filed by individuals, with 14 percent submitted by enterprises and 3 percent, scientific institutions. [76] A survey of 22 enterprises, conducted by the Economic Chamber of Serbia, disclosed that only 4.47 percent of 1,274 registrants possessed advanced educational preparation. More than 78 percent of the patent registrants were qualified or highly qualified workers. [77] The characteristics of technological change thus suggest that inventions and innovations are largely separated from formally organized scientific activities, pointing once more to a pattern of decentralized and self-generated technological development.

The average number of patents in Yugoslavia may well be considerably higher than official registration data suggest, principally because legal regulations carefully limit the classes of inventions that may be registered. The Law on Patents and Technical Improve-

TABLE 3

Persons per Registered Patent
in Selected European Countries
(annual averages)

Country	Persons per Patent
Switzerland	692
Belgium	778
France	1,351
Austria	1,352
Sweden	1,729
Great Britain	2,376
Italy	2,635
West Germany	2,665
United States	3,986
Czechoslovakia	5,716
Finland	6,476
Greece	8,429
Rumania	12,197
Poland	19,058
Yugoslavia	83,558

Source: M. Pečujlić, Budúčnost koja je počela: naučno-tehno-
loska revoljucija: samoupravljanje [The Future Which Began: The
Scientific-Technological Revolution and Self-Management] (Belgrade:
Institute for Political Studies, 1969), p. 78.

ments (1960), for example, restricts the definition of a technical
improvement to areas other than planning, administration, accounting, and statistics. The 1960 law further limits potential patents by
providing that submissions that result from the performance of
regular professional tasks are excluded from its provisions. While
members of work organizations receive small sums for inventions,
technological innovation is regarded as part of the work obligation
of members of collectives, particularly members of the technical
intelligentsia.[78]

SELF-MANAGEMENT AND THE
POLITICS OF TECHNOLOGY

Technological change in Yugoslavia cannot be properly understood outside the context of self-management as the particular form

for the organization of work in society. While it is not possible here
to review or systematize the large number of sociological and economic studies of self-managing production organizations, [79] it is
nonetheless useful to consider the dimensions of self-management as
an ideal-type. [80] An ideal-type of self-managing production organization, which can be described as a form of "intermediate association,"
differs markedly from other forms of work organization. [81] As tech-
nology-mediating organizations, self-managing enterprises share the
following distinctive characteristics:

1. Structural Duality. Work organizations have sociocultural as well as economic objectives. Economic objectives,
which include production, exchange, maximization of income,
and the manipulation of price and monetary policies, are equal
in importance to social and political objectives. The latter are
pursued primarily through the workers' participation in major
areas of enterprise policy, which permits the exercise of
influence in the production process and in distributing the
results of work in the form of personal incomes and nonmonetary benefits (housing, recreation, and vacations). Comprehensive objectives promote complex interactions between
"representative" and "administrative" structures, which are
analogous to "natural" and "rational" forms of social organization.

2. Polyfunctionality. Multiple objectives are related to
polyfunctional roles, which are designed to satisfy a wider
scope of individual needs than conventional economic organizations but a narrower scope than "natural" forms of social
organization. The latter satisfy a full range of economic,
social, cultural, political, and emotional needs. The scope of
activities of intermediate associations is far greater than
"enterprises," greater than "segmentary association," but
less than "total association."

3. Role Dedifferentiation. The interaction and interdependence of representative and administrative structures is
reflected in dedifferentiated role structures. Individuals perform multiple tasks as electors, representatives, policy
makers, administrators, and production workers. The distinctions between manual and intellectual labor are reduced. The
ratio of multiple roles per individual is much greater than that
of "enterprise," greater than "segmentary association," but
less than "total association," in which all or nearly all perform every task.

4. Optimal participation. Full participation in performing all tasks is constrained by the dual structure and objec-

tives of intermediate associations. While the distribution of
organizational power tends to be polyarchal and relatively equal
within the representative structure, it is oligarchical within
the hierarchical structure. Intermediate associations do not
manifest the scope and intensity of involvement of "total associations" but support participation in a broader scope of activities than either "segmentary associations" (Scanlon Plan companies, comites des enterprises, comitati del fabbrica, works
councils, Mitbestimmung) or conventional "enterprises."

  5. Environmental interdependence. The high degree of
autonomy characteristic of "enterprise," "segmentary association," and "total association," which develops strong group
cohesiveness and outward aggressiveness in a competitive
social system, is constrained by political and administrative
regulations designed to control social inequalities, autonomous
price setting, interindustry income differentials, and monopoly
formation. The interdependence between external bodies and
enterprise policy is institutionalized through constitutional and
legal norms that derive their legitimacy from egalitarian social values and a broad societal commitment to self-managing
socialism. Intermediate association is characterized neither
by market autonomy nor total external control, as in "perfect
competition" and "state" and "monopoly" capitalist variants of
enterprise and segmentary association. Intermediate association has a comparative advantage in assuming social responsibility when compared with "enterprise" and "segmentary association."

  6. Organizational Dynamics. Structural dualism and
social values that legitimize multiple objectives, polyfunctional
roles, and selective external controls promote a relatively
uniform division of social power. Polyfunctional role relationships facilitate the emergence of different functional groups,
including professional managers, technical staff, and members
of sociopolitical organizations. Given discrepancies between
social values and organizational structure and behavior,
recurrent social conflicts occur between the members of the
administrative structure and the members of the representative structure, the latter deriving power from the Party, trade
unions, and youth organizations. An unstable equilibrium in
organizations capable of social redirection results in recurrent
cyclical trends in worker participation and influence. Organizational objectives are periodically realigned with different
sources of social power.

Ideal-types, of course, are neither utopian idealizations nor
simple pictorial statements about reality. Instead they express "a

synthesis of a great many diffuse, discrete, more or less present and occasionally absent concrete phenomena, which are arranged according to those one-sidedly emphasized viewpoints into a unified analytical construct. "[82] The ideal-type of intermediate association, which is closely related to the objective possibilities of socialist development under conditions of technological change, assists in making judgments about the adequacy of imagination to reality. [83] In this context it should be added that empirical studies of self-management also provide insights into organizational power, attitudes, and technology. Thus research suggests that self-management under varying technological conditions does not immediately promote markedly increased levels of satisfaction, motivation, and self-realization. [84] Studies also indicate that the development of complex technology creates parallel structural changes, [85] that is, increasing authority of the technical hierarchy and a concurrent enlargement of the workers' involvement in self-managing bodies. In organizations in which the workers are "most alienated or subordinated to technological requirements of work, such as mechanized labor, group or collective identifications are most expressed. On this level the workers feel most strongly the need to compensate the work situation by an intensified group involvement. "[86]

CONCLUSION

Scientific and technological revolution, together with the processes of societal change conventionally described in the rhetoric of modernization, call into question the authenticity of socialist development. The case of Yugoslavia nonetheless demonstrates that pre-socialist cultural patterns and social structure, when followed by an authentic social revolution, can promote conditions for the continuous development of forms of social organization that effectively mediate technology and socialist values. The case of postwar Yugoslav development indicates that social revolution and egalitarianism may be necessary for the effective control of technology; the Yugoslav case also suggests that decentralized forms of social organization are the sufficient condition for maintaining the authenticity of contemporary socialism. Self-management, despite its contradictions and insufficiencies—including regional disparities, a high level of unemployment, and extensive labor migration—may hold one of the keys to the recovery of socialist praxis under conditions of rapid scientific and technological change.

Demands for industrialization and economic development, which are intimately tied to the theme of scientific and technological revolution, have promoted strong tendencies toward the rationalization of production and management throughout Eastern Europe. Thus far Yugoslav society has nevertheless proved capable of achieving high rates of growth under conditions of minimal and selective external dependence on capital and technology. Further, this has been accomplished through nonhierarchical forms of social organization and significant levels of worker involvement in production decisions. Nevertheless, apparent strains between socialist egalitarianism and the ideologies of industrialization and modernization are reflected in periodic conflicts between the party and technical and managerial groups, thus raising questions about the meaning and historical implications of liberal economic reforms undertaken since 1965. Nonetheless, recurrent successful efforts to repoliticize the social context of organization and technology suggest that self-managing socialism retains a capacity to maintain social responsibility in directing socialist development. The case of Yugoslavia thus demonstrates that social organization is the form of mediation between technology and socialist practice.

NOTES

1. P. L. Berger and T. Luckmann, The Social Construction of Reality: A Treatise in the Sociology of Knowledge (Garden City, N.Y.: Doubleday, 1967), p. 61. See also R. Lichtman, "Symbolic Interactionism and Social Reality: Some Marxist Queries," Berkeley Journal of Sociology 15 (1970): 75-95.

2. Frankfurt Institute for Social Research, Aspects of Sociology, with a preface by Max Horkheimer and T. W. Adorno (Boston: Beacon, 1973), p. 127.

3. R. V. Burks, "Technology and Political Change in Eastern Europe," in Change in Communist Systems, ed. Chalmers Johnson (Palo Alto: Stanford University Press, 1970).

4. See for example, G. H. von Wright, Explanation and Understanding (Ithaca: Cornell University Press, 1971); G. Radnitzky, Contemporary Schools of Metascience (2 vols., Chicago: Regnery, 1973); J. Habermas, Knowledge and Human Interests (Boston: Beacon, 1971). Note that this proposition about the nonapodictic character of scientific values is not based on a commitment to Weberian value-freedom, according to which certain ultimate values are presumed to lie outside the realm of rational discourse; nor does it express the limited notion, still popular among positivists, that social values can be treated simply as "data."

5. The most pointed example of a controversy surrounding the theoretical status of alternative explanations of technology occurred in the context of the conference discussions of papers pre-

sented by Richard Baum and William Leiss. These two papers express most clearly the fundamental differences between critical and
traditional empirical theory. Baum's paper (Chapter 7) tends to
assume that functional explanations of technology and social change
in China are self-evident, while Leiss's paper (Chapter 2) questions
the grounds on which certain value assumptions external to empirical
generalizations may be employed as satisfactory explanations of
sociohistorical change. Similarly, there are no inductive grounds
whatever for the ontological and epistemological assumptions that
underlie the particular form of modernization theory employed by
Rensselaer W. Lee III (Chapter 6), who concludes, "As modernization proceeds, one may argue, the epistemological framework of
Maoist doctrine will be less able to encompass the modes of creating
and applying new knowledge." Julian M. Cooper's paper (Chapter 3)
traces the official Soviet account of sociohistorical change, which is
identical to that of Baum and Lee insofar as a nomological (covering
law) model of historical changes in technology and culture is employed as a self-evident mode of explanation. In commenting upon the
use of nomological models in historical explanation, von Wright observes, "In retrospect, it seems almost an irony of fate that the
fullest and most lucid formulation of the positivist theory of explanation should have been stated in connection with the subject matter for
which, obviously, the theory is least suited, namely history." Von
Wright, op. cit., p. 10. While von Wright is chiefly concerned with
Hempel's formulation of the covering law model in historical explanation, the same point is nonetheless relevant here: values are not
simply employed as data, but enter into explanations of data themselves, sometimes by projecting the illusion that certain choices are
"imperative." On strictly inductive grounds one wonders whether
events such as the Cultural Revolution do not provide a plausible
empirical basis for adopting one of the preferred positivist modes of
theory development—that is, changing theories to reflect newly discovered "serendipitous" findings (Merton)—if not actually engaging
in an ideology-critique so as to uncover pseudoscientific assumptions.

    6. See the introduction to this volume by Frederic J. Fleron,
Jr.

    7. Operational definitions of concepts, which should not be
confused with the methodological doctrine of operationism, according to which the only meaning of a concept derives from the procedures by which it is measured, are essential for linking language
and experience. In the course of the conference discussions it became apparent that a lack of agreement on the meaning of elements
of culture (including technical rationality) compelled nearly all the
participants to accept a narrow definition of technology as a pro-

visional solution to unresolved theoretical problems. In a context of concern with papers by Joseph Berliner, Colin C. Gallagher, and Julian M. Cooper (Chapter 3), it became uncomfortably clear that theoretical issues had been conveniently set aside, or dismissed altogether, in the belief that better definitions, instruments, and measurement procedures might promote better interpretations. The adequacy of empirical generalizations—for example, the validity and reliability of observations—obviously has nothing to do with explanations of why certain empirical regularities occur. At the same time, theoretical constructs exercise a coercive effect on what is observed by establishing the problem domain and concepts through which experience is filtered. Given the a priori and nonapodictical character of theory, it is surprising and somehow amusing that some of the contributions to this volume reflect the belief that explanations derive their legitimacy from "empirical observations."

8. Diachronic refers simply to that method that seeks to locate two (or more) sets of cultural values which stand in a relation of complementarity and conflict at points in time. In contrast, synchronic analysis stresses a particular set of similar cultural values at one point in time. J. Habermas's essay on "Science and Technology as 'Ideology' " provides a particularly good illustration of diachronic analysis applied to problems of science, technology, and culture. See J. Habermas, Toward a Rational Society (Boston: Beacon, 1970), pp. 81–122.

9. See B. Horvat, Towards a Theory of Planned Economy (Belgrade: Institute of Economic Sciences, 1964). Ideal types, it should be emphasized, are not coextensive with idealizations of the social world; they are accentuations of structural and cultural properties that have been synthesized from concrete historical instances. See H. H. Gerth and C. W. Mills, From Max Weber: Essays in Sociology (New York: Oxford University Press, 1946), pp. 59–60.

10. In discussing Marxian and non-Marxian social science, von Wright (op. cit., p. 203n) observes, "They [parallel types of social science] differ not so much in that they hold conflicting views about facts as in the paradigms which they adopt for purposes of description and explanation. This difference in paradigms reflects a difference in ideology. 'Revolutions' in social science, therefore, are the results of ideology-critique. " (Emphasis in original.)

11. J. W. Sutherland, "Axiological Predicates of Scientific Enterprise, " General Systems 19 (1974): 4.

12. Emmanuel G. Mesthene, Technological Change: Its Impact on Man and Society (New York: New American Library, 1970).

13. Radovan Richta, et al., Civilization at the Crossroads: Social and Human Implications of the Scientific and Technological Revolution (White Plains, N.Y.: International Arts and Sciences Press, 1969).

14. M. Pečujlić, Budučnost koja je počela: naučno-tehnološka revoljucija i samoupravljanje [The Future which Began: The Scientific-Technological Revolution and Self-Management] (Belgrade: Institute for Political Studies, 1969).

15. See for example, William Leiss, "The Social Consequences of Technological Progress: Critical Comments on Recent Theories, " Canadian Public Administration 13, no. 3 (1970); T. B. Bottomore, Sociology as Social Criticism (New York: Pantheon, 1974), pp. 181-93.

16. This unresolved problem influenced the course of many conference discussions surrounding the issue of technical rationality. Some contributors, such as Fleron and Leiss, tended to view technical rationality as the product of capitalism. Some, such as Cooper and Feenberg, viewed it as an element of a dialectical transcendence (Aufhebung) of capitalism under socialism. Others, such as Baum, Lee, and Field, saw it as a characteristic of an evolutionary process of convergent modernization. Still others, including Berliner and Gallagher, approached the issue primarily in terms of market exchange and optimal decision making. Dernberger and Hardt approached it in terms of the transfer of technology. While different theoretical perspectives were employed by Baum and Lee, on the one hand, and Hoffmann, on the other, only these three papers sought to explore the group basis of conflicting views of technology and technical rationality (as distinguished from efforts to link technology and technical rationality to different systems of social organization). The conference discussions took a surprisingly "apolitical" turn, inasmuch as the group basis of culture conflict was somehow replaced by universal categories or levels of analysis or by descriptive accounts of finished technological products and machine processes.

17. The common practice of viewing science and technology as finished products, which is no less characteristic of positivism in Eastern Europe than it is in the West, seriously impedes the recognition that science and technology are part of a societal process of production, distribution, and utilization of knowledge. Accordingly, science and technology may be investigated in terms of several components: products, producers, distributors, interessees, and users. See Radnitzky, op. cit. , pp. x-xii. For an effort to apply metascientific perspectives to administrative theory, see William N. Dunn and B. Fozouni, Toward a Critical Administrative Theory (Beverley Hills: Sage Professional Papers in Administrative and Policy Studies, 1976). Colin C. Gallagher's paper observed that the relations between basic science and technological development are fundamentally different in centrally planned and market economies, thus challenging the assumption of the unity of science and technology as finished products.

18. A critical theory of society is one "designed with a practical intention: the self-emancipation of men from the constraints of domination in all its forms." T. McCarthy, translator's introduction to J. Habermas, Legitimation Crisis (Boston: Beacon, 1975), p. xviii.

19. Technical rationality refers to the belief that sociohistorical progress is possible primarily or solely through the application of strategic and instrumental rules designed to control man and nature. To assume its intended meaning, technical rationality must be contrasted with other forms of rationality. The historical problem of "rationality" has arisen in a context in which purposive rational action increasingly dominates the forms of interaction associated with emancipation, whether expressed in the language of equality, democracy, or civil liberties. Among the several ways of contrasting different types of rationality, we note those of Max Weber (substantive versus formal rationality), Mannheim (substantive versus functional rationality), and Haberman (technical rationality versus institutional rationality). The tendency toward a dominance of technical rationality in Marxian theory has led Habermas to criticize "the reinstatement of the political innocence of forces of production." Habermas, Toward A Rational Society, op. cit., p. 89.

20. See for example, various Eastern European contributors to Marxism and Sociology: Views From Eastern Europe, ed. P. Berger (New York: Appleton-Century-Crofts, 1970); Eric Fromm, ed., Socialist Humanism (New York: Doubleday, 1967); and the Zagreb, Yugoslavia, journal Praxis.

21. For a conceptual overview of the differences among various groups, particularly social scientists, see B. Denitch, "Sociology in Eastern Europe: Trends and Prospects," Slavic Review 30, no. 2 (1971): 317-40. On Czechoslovakia see I. Svitak, The Czechoslovak Experiment, 1968-1969 (New York: Columbia University Press, 1969); on Yugoslavia, see D. Milenkovitch, Plan and Market in Yugoslav Economic Thought (New Haven: Yale University Press, 1971).

22. On the role of liberal reformers in Czechoslovakia, including their opposition to self-management and worker control, see K. Kovanda, Labor in Management, Czechoslovakia, 1968-1969: A Study in Radical Democracy (Ph.D. diss. MIT, 1974); E. Gellner, "The Pluralist Anti-Levellers of Prague," Dissent, Summer 1972, pp. 471-83. On Yugoslavia, see B. Denitch, "Notes on the Relevance of Yugoslav Self-Management," Politics and Society 3, no. 4 (1973); William N. Dunn, "Ideology and Organization in Socialist Yugoslavia: Modernization and the Obsolescence of Praxis," Newsletter on Comparative Studies of Communism 5, no. 4 (1972); 21-56. For an excellent treatment of the ways different cultural values and social structures have influenced industrial management in Poland and

Yugoslavia, see S. J. Rawin, "Social Values and the Managerial Structure: The Case of Yugoslavia and Poland," Journal of Comparative Administration 11, no. 2 (1970): 131-59.

23. The most complete empirical investigation of the group basis of social values in a socialist society, to the author's knowledge, is A. Barton, B. Denitch, and C. Kadushin, Yugoslav Opinion-making Elites (New York: Praeger, 1974). Results of surveys carried out in Czechoslovakia are reported in Kovanda, op. cit.

24. Elsewhere an attempt has been made to extend the Amitai Etzioni-E. Skinner-W. Winckler hypothesis concerning compliance cycles to socialist industrial organizations, including Yugoslav, Chinese, and Cuban enterprises. See William N. Dunn, "Revolution and Modernization in Socialist Economic Organizations," in Comparative Socialist Systems: Essays on Politics and Economics, ed. Carmel Mesa-Lago and Carl Beck (Pittsburgh: University of Pittsburgh Center for International Studies, 1975), pp. 147-91. For the original statement of the cyclical hypothesis, see E. Skinner and W. Winckler, "Compliance Succession in Rural Communist China: A Cyclical Theory," in Complex Organizations: A Sociological Reader, ed. Amitai Etzioni (New York: Holt, Rinehart and Winston, 1969), pp. 411-38. See also Carmelo Mesa-Lago, "A Continuum Model for Global Comparison," in Mesa-Lago and Beck, op. cit., pp. 92-120.

25. See Radnitzky, op. cit. p. xi.

26. For example, Z. Golubović, "Why is Functionalism More Desirable in Present-Day Yugoslavia than Marxism?" Praxis 9, no. 4 (1973): 357-68.

27. Denitch, "Sociology in Eastern Europe, op. cit., provides a sketch of the potentialities in this area, although his analysis is admittedly schematic. The work of Radovan Richta, Pečujlić, and various Soviet writers analyzed by Julian M. Cooper (Chapter 3) is essentially synchronic. Their inferences about projected and past developments are based on beliefs about the logical properties of science and technology, including a belief in their "neutral" character.

28. On axiothetic and critical perspectives in Yugoslavia, see for example, various contributions to the management journal Moderna Organizacija (Kranj, Slovenia) and Praxis (Zagreb).

29. See for example, R. Supek, Sociologija i Socijalizam (Zagreb: Naprijed, 1966); and J. Županov, Samoupravljanje i Društvena Moć (Zagreb: Naše Teme, 1969).

30. This viewpoint is of course associated with certain forms of mechanistic Marxism (as distinguished from Marx's own views).

31. This viewpoint is emphasized in Alexander Eckstein, "Economic Development and Political Change in Communist Systems," World Politics 22, no. 4 (1970): 475-95.

32. See A. Matejko, "The Sociotechnical Principles of Workers' Control—Industrial Democracy: Myth and Reality," in Participation and Self-Management (Zagreb: Institute for Social Research, 1973), vol. 3, pp. 25–56.

33. See A. Inkeles, Becoming Modern: Individual Change in Six Developing Countries (Cambridge: Harvard University Press, 1974), pp. 299–300.

34. S. H. Udy, "The Comparative Analysis of Organizations," in Handbook of Organizations, ed. J. G. March (Chicago: Rand-McNally, 1965), pp. 678–710.

35. D. J. Hickson, D. S. Pugh, and D. C. Pheysen, "Operations Technology and Organization Structure: An Empirical Reappraisal," Administrative Science Quarterly 14 (1969): 378–97.

36. C. Perrow, "A Framework for the Comparative Analysis of Organizations," American Sociological Review 32 (1967): 194–208.

37. See Fleron, "Introduction: Basic Issues."

38. See for example, V. Rus, "Influence Structure in Yugoslav Enterprises," Industrial Relations 9, no. 2 (1970): 148–60; J. Obradović, "Participation and Work Attitudes in Yugoslavia," Industrial Relations 9, no. 2 (1970): 161–69.

39. See Chapters 6 and 7.

40. It is instructive to compare North American capitalists and socialists on the issue of "capitalism" in Yugoslavia, for they reach similar conclusions. See Paul Sweezy and Charles Bettelheim, On the Transition to Socialism (New York: Monthly Review, 1971); G. Buck, "A Socialist Enterprise that Acts like a Fierce Capitalist Competitor," Fortune (January 1972), pp. 82–86.

41. For example, Rensselaer W. Lee III, "The Politics of Technology in Communist China," Comparative Politics 5, no. 2 (1973): 301–25.

42. Among prominent spokesmen for an evolutionary thesis, according to which Yugoslav production organizations have become increasingly specialized, differentiated, depersonalized, and bureaucratized in a process of modernization, see A. Meister, Socialisme et Autogestion: l' Expérience Yugoslave (Paris: Seuil, 1964). On the modernization of individual values, see G. Bertsch, "A Cross-National Analysis of the Community-Building Process in Yugoslavia," Comparative Politics 4, no. 4 (1972): 438–60. For contrary views by Yugoslavs, see J. Županov, "Enterprise and Association: Real and Illusory Dilemma," in Sociologija: Selected Articles, 1959–1969 (Belgrade: Yugoslav Sociological Association, 1970), 71–92; and F. Bučar, "The Participation of State and Political Organizations in the Decisions of the Working Organization," Participation and Self-Management, (Zagreb: Institute for Social Research, 1972), Vol. 1, pp. 41–61. See also William N. Dunn,

"The Economics of Organizational Ideology: The Problem of Dual-Compliance in the Worker-Managed Socialist Firm," Journal of Comparative Administration 5, no. 4 (1974): 395-441.

43. See G. W. Hoffman and F. W. Neal, Yugoslavia and the New Communism (New York: Twentieth Century Fund, 1962); B. Denitch, "Violence in Yugoslav Society," paper presented at the annual meeting of the American Association for the Advancement of Slavic Studies, Dallas, Texas, March 1972; Rawin, op. cit.

44. Modernization may be defined as the process whereby national policy makers seek to improve their relative positions in relation to countries perceived as prestigious or "well placed." Development refers to the organizational capacity of a society to respond effectively to changes in its material and human environment according to national goals and values. See J. P. Nettl and R. Robertson, International Systems and the Modernization of Societies (New York: Basic Books, 1958), pp. 56-58. With the exception of Yugoslavia, the placement of countries in Figure 3 is suggestive only.

45. See for example, Denitch, "Notes on the Relevance of Yugoslav Self-Management," op. cit.; and Stvaraoci Javnog Mnenja u Jugoslaviji, ed. F. Džinić, 4 vols., (Belgrade: Institut Društvenih Nauka, 1969).

46. See J. Zupanov, "Egalitarianizam i Industrijalizam," Sociologija 12, no. 2 (1970); S. Bolčić, "The Value System of a Participatory Economy," Participation and Self Management, (Zagreb: Institute for Social Research, 1972), Vol. 1, pp. 97-112. Both of these authors view the relationship between egalitarian values and industrialization as contradictory, an interpretation that is rejected in this chapter. Županov's paper may be found in J. Obradović and William N. Dunn, eds., Workers' Self-Management and Organizational Power in Yugoslavia (Pittsburgh: University Center for International Studies, 1977).

47. Županov, in "Egalitarianizam," op. cit., observes that "at the explicit level there is an emphasis on allocation according to 'merit,' while at the implicit level stress is placed on distribution according to elementary needs (uravnilovka)."

48. See also Denitch, "Notes on the Relevance of Yugoslav Self-Management," op. cit., Tables 12-14, in which similar relationships are found. Denitch's data are compiled from Slovenian firms, while Županov's are drawn from Croatian samples. It is important to note that Slovenia and Croatia are the most economically developed and technologically advanced republics in the country.

49. Yugoslavia: Development with Decentralization (Baltimore and London: published for the World Bank by the Johns Hopkins University Press, 1975), p. 108, Table 4.5.

50. Ibid., 102-103.

51. See B. Denitch, "Mobility and Recruitment of Yugoslav Leadership: The Role of the League of Communists," in Barton, Denitch, and Kadushin, op. cit., pp. 95-119.

52. A. Barton, "Determinants of Leadership Attitudes in a Socialist Society," in Barton, Denitch, and Kadushin, op. cit., p. 230.

53. Ibid., p. 234, Table 8.1.

54. Bolčić, op. cit., p.111, Table 11. Research was conducted in 1971-72 in 16 industrial enterprises throughout Yugoslavia (two from each republic and autonomous area). The sample of 916 respondents includes members of workers' councils (one-third quota).

55. Županov, "Egalitarianizam," op. cit. pp. 21-23. There are, of course, other dimensions of culture that will not be treated here, including the values of combativeness and individual consumption at the national and individual levels, respectively. See D. Rihtman, Kulturna Tradicija i Vrednote: Neke Pretpostavke i Jedno Pilot-Istraživanje (Zagreb: Institut za Društvene Istraživanje, 1967); Denitch, "Violence in Yugoslav Society," op. cit.; V. St. Erlich, Yugoslav Family Life in Transition (New York: Columbia University Press, 1967).

56. Županov, "Egalitarianizam," op. cit., pp. 25-38 Županov, whose analysis juxtaposes egalitarianism and industrialism, operates largely within a conventional paradigm of modernization. His central proposition is that the "dysfunctionality of the egalitarian complex or syndrome is beyond doubt." Ibid., p. 39.

57. See D. Milenkovitch, Plan and Market in Yugoslav Economic Thought (New Haven: Yale University Press, 1971); and Carmel Mesa-Lago, review in Economic Development and Cultural Change 21, no. 2 (1973); 364-70. Milenkovitch and Mesa-Lago call attention to the fact that the rationale for decentralization in Yugoslavia was essentially political, while the motives for similar reforms in Eastern Europe more than a decade later were economic. This difference seems essential for understanding the particular social context in which the ideas of Radovan Richta and his colleagues were advanced. The dominance of economic and technical values in the Czech reform movement is well documented in George S. Wheeler, The Human Face of Socialism: The Political Economy of Change in Czechoslovakia (New York: Lawrence Hill, 1973).

58. Demands for greater involvement in production decisions came from among the workers themselves in East Germany, Hungary, and Poland. Nevertheless, a relatively crystallized social structure, elitism, and the vested interests of the technical intelligentsia obstructed efforts at implementation. The movement for reform in Czechoslovakia, however, proceeded largely from demands of

intellectuals and the technical intelligentsia, who were supported by workers. Kovanda, op. cit. convincingly shows that the critical factor in the demise of the Councils of Labor in 1968-69 was opposition by technocrats.

59. The classification scheme can be extended to include several other groups, including orthodox (Stalinist) and antisocialist groups. See Milenkovitch, op. cit., pp. 281-88; and Dunn, "Ideology and Organization," op. cit.

60. B. Horvat, "Yugoslav Economic Policy in the Postwar Period: Problems, Ideas, Institutional Developments," American Economic Review 61 (1971): 91.

61. H. Chenery, "Growth and Structural Change," Finance and Development 8, no. 3 (1071): 24, Table 2.

62. Yugoslavia: Development with Decentralization, op. cit., p. 273, Table 12.5.

63. The firms include Coca-Cola, Pepsi-Cola, Lorillard, Helena Rubenstein, General Electric, Westinghouse, KHD, Fiat, and Mercedes-Benz.

64. See W. Friedmann and L. Mates, eds., Joint Ventures of Yugoslav Enterprises and Foreign Firms (New York and Belgrade: Columbia University and the Institute of International Politics and Economics, 1968); M. Sukijasović, Foreign Investment in Yugoslavia (New York and Belgrade: Oceana Publications and the Institute of International Politics and Economics, 1970); and R. B. Glickman and M. Sukijasović, "Yugoslav Worker Management and Its Effect on Foreign Investment," Harvard International Law Journal 12, no. 2 (1971): 260-311.

65. Sukijasovic, op. cit., p. 12.

66. Ibid.

67. See Yugoslavia: An Introduction to the Yugoslav Economy for Foreign Businessmen (New York: Chase Manhattan Bank, 1974); Sukijasović, op. cit., Appendix I, pp. 167-73; Glickman and Sukijasović, op. cit., Appendix, pp. 309-11.

68. Yugoslavia: Development with Decentralization, op. cit. p. 291.

69. Yugoslavia: An Introduction, op. cit., pp. 29-30. In late 1972 the Overseas Private Investment Corporation began to provide investment guarantees to U.S. companies investing in Yugoslavia. The majority of the joint ventures with U.S. firms have originated since 1973.

70. The budget for projects undertaken by the UNDP mission in Yugoslavia amounted to some $14 million in the period 1966-72. The UNDP's projected budget for 1973-77 is approximately $5 million. See Partners in Cooperation: Yugoslavia, the United Nations and Its Specialized Agencies (Belgrade: UNDP, 1973), Tables 1 and 2.

71. Buck, op. cit., provides a brief description of foreign consultants' activities in Energoinvest, Sarajevo, which is one of the 10 largest enterprises in the country.

72. See R. Franke, "Critical Factors in the Postwar Economic Growth of Nations," Participation and Self-Management (Zagreb: Institute for Social Research, 1973), Vol. 5, pp. 107-20. Franke contends that "authoritarianism in economic and other organizations . . . may be moderated by participative organization, which for at least one nation [Yugoslavia] has proven compatible with a high rate of economic growth." Ibid., p. 107.

73. See Županov, "Egalitarianizam," op. cit., pp. 28-29.

74. For a discussion of elitist tendencies in advanced schools, see Moderna Organizacija 4 (1970): 237-43. These advanced schools, which are compared with Pittsburgh's Carnegie Institute of Technology and the Sloane School at MIT, were initially established in 1965. In 1970 a Faculty for Organizational Sciences was established at the University of Belgrade. Three major types of programs are offered: Personnel Stream (two years); Organization-Production Stream (two years); and the Organization-Cybernetics Stream (four years). The four-year program includes training in mathematics, economics of the firm, technology, economic systems, marketing, interpersonal relations and social psychology, quantitative methods, and systems analysis (cybernetics). It also includes a practicum in model building based on the problems of the student's own firm.

75. Pečujlić, op. cit., p. 78.

76. Ibid. Pečujlić also notes in this connection that the proportion of national income allocated for research and science (.85 percent in 1967) is some four times less than the proportion allocated in Western Europe. S. Dedijer estimates that in the 1960s the per capita expenditures on research and development in Yugoslavia were some four times less than in Poland and Hungary. See S. Dedijer, "Underdeveloped Science in Underdeveloped Countries," in Criteria for Scientific Development, ed. E. Shils (Cambridge: MIT Press, 1968), pp. 143-63.

77. Županov, "Egalitarianizam," op. cit., pp. 32-33.

78. Ibid., p. 33; S. Pretnar, "Zaštita Industrijske Svojine," Moderna Organizacija 6 (1969).

79. See Participation and Self-Management (6 vols., Zagreb: Institute for Social Research 1972, 1973); B. Horvat, Mihailo Marković and R. Supek, eds., Self-Governing Socialism: A Reader (2 vols., White Plains: International Arts and Sciences Press, 1974); I. Adizes, Industrial Democracy: Yugoslav Style (New York: Free Press, 1971); Obradović and Dunn, op. cit.

80. See R. Supek, Longitudinalno Istraživanje Strukture Utjecaja u Radničkom Samoupravljanju (Zagreb: Institute for Social

Research, 1971). B. Horvat, Towards a Theory of Planned Economy (Belgrade: Institute of Economic Sciences, 1964); J. Županov, Samoupravljanje i Društvena Moć (Zagreb: Naše Teme, 1969).

81. Among other ideal types we include "enterprise," "total association," and "segmentary association." "Enterprise" refers to hierarchical or bureaucratic organizations, while "total association" is coextensive with administratively structureless organizations. "Segmentary association" refers to hierarchical organizations with limited worker participation in market economies. Examples of these constructs are, respectively, organized monopolies or oligopolies in state socialist and capitalist countries; small work units with little or no administrative structure within larger organizations, such as functional task groups; and organizations with limited participation and hierarchy in market settings, such as Scanlon Plan companies, codetermination, and works' councils.

82. Max Weber, On the Methodology of the Social Sciences (Glencoe: Free Press, 1949), p. 90.

83. A. G. Ramos, "Modernization: Towards a Possibility Model," in Developing Nations: Quest for A Model, ed. W. Beling and G. Totten (New York: Van Nostrand, 1970), p. 29.

84. See J. Obradović, Participacija i Motivacija u Radničkom Samoupravljanju Obzirom na Tehnološki Nivo Proizvodnje (Zagreb: Institut za Društvena Istraživanja, 1967); Obradović, "Participation and Work Attitudes in Yugoslavia," op. cit.

85. R. Supek, "Two Types of Self-Managing Organizations and Technological Progress," Participation and Self-Management, (Zagreb: Institute for Social Research, 1972), Vol. 1, pp. 150-73.

86. Ibid., p. 173. See also the case studies by I. Adizes of modernization and technological innovation in two Belgrade firms. Adizes, op. cit. Informal group processes reflect significant joint involvement of three major groups: technical experts, sociopolitical organizations (League of Communists), and production workers, particularly the skilled workers who are most directly involved in maintaining machine processes (majstori).

9

TECHNOLOGY, VALUES, AND POLITICAL POWER IN THE SOVIET UNION: DO COMPUTERS MATTER?

Erik P. Hoffmann

The aim of this essay is to deepen understanding of some important reciprocal relationships between the scientific-technological revolution (STR) and the Soviet political system. The central questions to be studied concern the dynamic interaction between technological change and policy formation—that is, the impact of technological innovations on policy making, and the influence of politics on the introduction and use of new technologies. Attention will be focused on modern information-processing technology and on the changing power relationships, if any, that this technology has produced and can produce in socialist one-party systems. Also to be examined closely are the values, attitudes, and beliefs of political leaders, which are the key intervening, or mediating, factors that shape the complex interaction between scientific-technological and social-political change. Significantly, contemporary Soviet leaders and social theorists view computerization and automation as crucial elements of the STR. In conclusion, some thoughts will be offered on the reciprocal relationships among computer technology, values, and fundamental political change in the USSR.

The author wishes to thank Loren Graham, Erik Lindell, and the members of the Bellagio conference on "Technology and Communist Culture" and of Columbia University's Research Institute on International Change for their helpful comments on an earlier draft of this chapter. The final version was prepared while the writer was a Senior Research Fellow at the Research Institute on International Change and the Russian Institute of Columbia University. Support from these institutes and from the American Council of Learned Societies and the Social Science Research Council is appreciatively acknowledged.

Which "technicians of power" and "managers of technique" will rule in developed socialist societies?[1] What are the prospects of "control by a knowledge elite, " and what are the problems of "control of the knowledge elite"?[2] Specifically, how will modern information technology alter power relationships within and among the major Soviet bureaucracies? Will Soviet computer specialists attain greater political influence in certain issue areas, or will their skills serve the traditional interests of the traditional elites? Is it likely that computerized information systems will produce changes in the values, attitudes, and beliefs of Communist Party leaders, who may in turn make significant adjustments in substantive policies, policy-making procedures, and institutional arrangements in the Soviet political system?

"The computer age" has just begun in the Soviet Union and Eastern Europe. Western sources estimate that approximately 6, 000 computers were installed in the USSR in 1971.[3] Since then Soviet scientists have designed and manufactured new "third generation" (Riad) computers, and different Soviet institutions have made small but rapidly increasing hardware and software purchases from various East and West European countries, including Japan. Soviet planners optimistically scheduled the installation of 31, 500 computers by 1976. Although official spokesmen frequently bemoan the underutilization of existing computer facilities, Soviet political and economic officials have made persistent, but largely unsuccessful, efforts to obtain the most advanced U.S. technology. The U.S. Office of Export Administration approved the sale of 903 Western-made computers (679 of U.S. design) to Eastern Europe between 1967 and 1973, but very few licenses for computer exports to the Soviet Union have been granted.[4] Sooner or later, however, the USSR will probably be able to import the latest U.S. information technology—perhaps chiefly through multinational corporations. This equipment, together with Soviet and East and West European products, will then be increasingly used for economic and social planning, the automation of industry, and many other purposes. Hence, computer-assisted information systems may eventually play a major role in various aspects of Soviet policy making and administration.

THE ARGUMENT THAT USE OF COMPUTERS
WILL BRING POLITICAL POWER
FOR COMPUTER TECHNICIANS

One hears it argued in the West and the East (infrequently in the latter, and mostly in private) that the wider and more efficient use of computers will significantly influence the policy-making procedures and substantive policies of socialist one-party systems. Decision-making practices, the relative importance of cadres with certain skills, power relationships within and among party and state organizations—all allegedly will be reshaped by the new information technology and by the expansion, redirection, and "rationalization" of information flows. Knowledge is power, it is argued explicitly and implicitly, and the consultant or technical expert—for example, the computer specialist who generates, processes, and interprets quantitative economic and social data—can wield considerable power by controlling information and by shaping the perceived alternatives and eventually even the problem-solving approaches and thought patterns of professional politicians. [5]

The top leaders of the Communist Party of the Soviet Union (CPSU) have alledgedly relinquished their monopoly over information. Previously they had less policy-relevant data at their disposal, but they had nearly total control over the interpretation and use of those data. Now Party leaders are thought to consider it in their own best interests and in the public interest to loosen their tight control over "acceptable" political ideas and to broaden the "legitimate" arenas for debating policy alternatives and adjustments, especially about operational, rather than strategic, questions. The reasons are several. They include the increasing complexity and volume of public policies; the national leadership's quest for improved economic and social planning; the need for much more pertinent, diverse, and timely information to cope with pressing and ongoing problems; the appeal of systematic approaches to the study of complex interdependencies and uncertain policy outcomes; and the capacities and availability of the computer technology itself. Thus, recent scientific and technological innovations, changing elite perspectives about the nature of effective societal guidance, the greater distribution of key data and skills, and the "objective" need to broaden and deepen specialist elite participation at all stages and levels of decision making are believed to make the diffusion of political power likely or even "necessary" to sustain social and economic development. [6] The deconcentration of power within and among the major Soviet bureaucracies (including the CPSU) may gradually but profoundly alter the present role of the Communist Party in the Soviet polity and economy.

A second and more systematic argument concerns the impact of computers on career patterns in the USSR. Computer technology is thought to produce a situation in which a substantial part of the present generation of middle-level Soviet leaders will become irrelevant, or at least expendable, and will not be able to rise to prominent positions because the standards of promotion will be radically changed by the new requirements of a political elite capable of dealing with computer management techniques. The argument goes something like this:

1. The drift to central decision making in the allocation of all resources has already produced a considerable demand for accurate information and/or projections at the Central Party apparatus level. This information demand can best be met by computer technology.

2. The technology itself is sophisticated and requires a substantial commitment of time in order to master it. Those already in the middle-management level will not have that time at their disposal. (Ironically, they are too valuable to spare at present.) Thus it will be necessary to train younger people, probably of university age, in the techniques of computer technology and in the use of that technology to provide the necessary information for centralized decision making.

3. Those who are trained in this technology will, perforce, be attached to the central Party and state organs, thereby enjoying maximum exposure, as technologists, to the upper echelons of decision makers. Hence computer experts will be given the opportunity to demonstrate their technical competency, administrative skills, and political reliability far sooner than would otherwise have been the case. That is, they will not have been required to have proven themselves "in the field" before they will have access to people in a position to see to their rapid promotion into the upper echelons.

4. As technical specialists, they will not threaten the highest CPSU leadership because their initial assignments will be to provide information based on policies that they will not, at first, be required or invited to formulate or challenge. Moreover, their skills are, to a large degree, adaptable to numerous policies. This is especially true in the initial uses of computer technology, which in most cases will be limited to keeping good records and giving requested factual information. However, as the service they perform for a limited number of top-level officials becomes recognized and valued, they will probably be invited to participate in the formulation of certain policies, or in economic and social planning, because they "understand the issues." This is perhaps especially true of economic rather than social planning.

5. To the extent that the technology itself is useful and becomes more widely adopted, those who have mastered it will become involved in more sectors of the polity and have an impact on the style and the form of dialogue about it. Thus, in a process that feeds on its own successes, those who lack the

technological skills will become less essential to central management and less capable of participating in the dialogue with ranking central officials.

6. The conclusion, then, is that the impact of the successful introduction of computers into any sector of the polity will create an almost irresistible attraction to similar sectors to follow the successes of their bureaucratic "competitors." From this it follows that those who can provide this particular service will be given access to power and decision makers, both because the service they perform is valuable and because the service they perform requires it. [7]

FACTORS THAT WILL LIMIT
THE POLITICAL POWER
OF COMPUTER TECHNICIANS

My own view, briefly stated, is that modern information-processing technology will almost surely not produce major changes in the central values of the Soviet leadership or in the most important characteristics of the Soviet political system, for at least the next decade or so, and probably longer. For centuries many different societies have demonstrated considerable capacity to adapt new technologies to existing social structures and values, and there are numerous reasons to think that the highly centralized Soviet system will not prove to be an exception. Computers have indeed come to the USSR, just as they earlier came to the United States; but electronic data processing has not dominated politics or reduced the importance of political leadership in the United States, where sophisticated technology and a fragmented decision-making process make politics perhaps unusually susceptible to technocratic influences. Like their U.S. counterparts, Soviet political leaders will probably continue to be able to "contain" new technologies and scientific-technical specialists.

The chief reasons for these conclusions lie in the political context in which economic and social information and computer technology are used. Soviet society is highly bureaucratized. Bureaucratic politics is a conflict-ridden process, and in the Soviet Union an administrative culture exists that has had a tremendous impact on the development, manufacture, and above all the practical application of the new technologies. Policy makers and bureaucrats are not dependent upon even the highest quality quantitative data and computer technology to inform or to legitimize their actions. Also, administrators have many sources of power, many competing values, and many incentives for resisting technological innovations.

In short, Soviet elite political culture may be particularly resistant
to dislocative change, and modern information technology is likely
to be integrated or absorbed into the existing bureaucratic value
systems and behavioral patterns rather than precipitate fundamental
changes in Soviet politics. What is most likely to happen in the USSR
is that electronic data processing will reinforce and intensify centralized control of strategic decisions by "generalist" politicians and
by well-trained technical specialists who are also Party officials or
who work directly for central Party agencies. In the foreseeable
future, the top CPSU leadership will probably continue to encourage
computerization in many state and economic institutions, and perhaps especially at the national and primary Party organization levels
of the CPSU, for the purposes of helping to formulate the most
feasible and informed national policies and promote the most efficient
and "creative" implementation of the center's directives.

      These, then, are the central themes to be developed below.
Let us begin by scrutinizing the lines of argument presented above.

      The present Soviet leadership almost certainly looks to com-
puters as an important means of improving centralized decision-
making and planning, especially on economic and technical matters.
It is generally believed in the West that the greatest high-level support for the central mathematical economics institute (TsEMI) comes
from the Politburo's most conservative (most Stalinist) members.
There may also be conservative support for quantitative techniques
in different areas of social control, where Party sociologists, professional propagandists, and no doubt KGB officials have for some
time been conducting survey research on public opinion (for example,
on the "effectiveness" of ideological work), and have been gathering
and quantifying many kinds of social and social-psychological data.
Information-processing skills may well prove to be an increasingly
important criterion for deciding which Party cadres will reach top-
level positions quickly.

      It is quite likely, too, that the CPSU's computer specialists
and mathematical economists will be "recruited" largely from the
younger apparatchiki or "co-opted" from the ranks of the non-Party
scientific and technical intelligentsia. Efforts to "retool" upper-
and middle-level Party and state officials in new management and
computer science techniques have only recently been initiated in
several newly established institutes. Thus CPSU cadres with quantitative data skills are likely to play a gradually increasing role in
political decision-making administration at various stages and
levels, to rise faster than others with comparable qualifications
(such as political judgment), and sooner or later to gain influence
in national decision-making organs such as the Politburo, the
Secretariat, the Central Committee apparatus departments, the
Council of Ministers, and the Supreme Soviet standing committees.

The foregoing developments will not automatically or speedily occur; nor is the process irreversible, as has been shown by East Germany in the 1960s and 1970s. Most important, major changes in Soviet administrative behavior and in the uses of political power will not necessarily result from any technological innovation, including modern information technology. The reasons for this include the following:

1. Top leaders may ignore the new quantitative or "better" information in their political calculations and policy making.

2. Politicians may only be influenced by those quantitative data that reinforce preexisting values, attitudes, and beliefs or that help them to legitimize to themselves and to others policy preferences based on very different considerations (such as bureaucratic infighting).

3. Despite the fact that it is quantified, the quality and practical value of the information generated may not prove to be particularly good, and top-level officials, individually or collectively, may become well aware of this and be unwilling or unable to remedy the situation. To be useful, computers need accurate and significant quantified data, and these are in relatively short supply in socialist countries for various political-bureaucratic, social-economic, and technical reasons (the absence of standardized statistical procedures).

4. National officials will be likely to use quantitative data in conjunction with other more conventional sources of information such as personal observations, evaluative reports from trusted sources, and military and police intelligence.

5. New computers may or may not reshape the larger "information culture" and information systems of which they are a part. Computers may produce significant organizational, perceptual, and even cognitive change, or they may simply be injected into existing information systems and have little or no influence on current behavioral patterns or modes of thought. Information systems may also undergo significant change for essentially normative-political, rather than technical, reasons.

6. While computer specialists may gain greater influence, many of these men and women will be central and regional Party officials, and their power relative to that of other apparatchiki will not necessarily increase because there are many sources of bureaucratic power (for example, patronage and secrecy) other than scientific and technical knowledge. Nor will the power to make basic policy choices—"the politics

of principles" as distinguished from "the politics of details"—
necessarily drift away from the Communist Party to other
institutions in society, for the same reason.

The impact of technological innovations on the power of the
CPSU vis-a-vis other major Soviet institutions is difficult to analyze.
It seems likely that the same technology can have very different
political consequences in different issue areas. For example, a
Western writer asserts that "there can be no doubt that the continuing progress of automation in industry and the recent emergence of
computerization in the USSR have strengthend the position of industrial and state administrators." He also contends that computerization has "vastly reduced" the political influence of professional
sociologists and their institutions. "This has come about because
computerization makes possible the objective analysis of social
information directly by the party apparatus. . . . New means of
data processing thus transfer the burden of social modernization
methods from the shoulders of the sociologist to those of the party
technocrat."[8]
Moreover, the suggestion that young technical specialists will
gain access to central Party organs with little experience "in the
field" implies a high degree of "recruitment," rather than "co-optation," of information specialists. Western scholars seem to disagree
about whether there is a trend toward co-optation of mid-career
technical experts into the CPSU or whether the Party will be increasingly staffed by better-educated technical and management specialists who work their way up the Party ladder (often with experience
in state organs) immediately after leaving the Komsomol aktiv.[9]
Implications of the "recruitment" thesis are that it will probably
take longer (maybe decades) to utilize more fully the available
computer technology and skills (domestic and foreign) in national
policy making; that the influence of the recruited quantitative data
specialists, whether they rise quickly or slowly through the Party
hierarchy, will probably be greater than that of the co-opted computer specialist; that the trend toward computerization of decision
making will be stronger in the long run and less easily reversible;
and that the devolution of power to the major non-Party bureaucracies will be less likely because CPSU committees will have their
own data banks and data processing experts.
Everything depends on the attitudes of the highest-level Soviet
leaders toward the promise and pitfalls, achievements and shortcomings, of the new technologies. It is problematical whether
national and provincial CPSU officials will be willing to take the
risks inherent in unqualifyingly promoting technological innovations
the political consequences of which neither they nor anyone else can

confidently predict. Also, it is open to question whether the present
or next generation of Politburo officials (and Western presidents who
lack the training of a Giscard d'Estaing) can clearly comprehend the
normative and technical advice of even the most "responsible" automated systems analysts and mathematical economists, not all of
whom agree with one another, not surprisingly.[10] Most likely, the
highest political leaders will encourage, even institutionalize,
alternative technical elites and multiple sources of technical information that are pertinent to important policy questions. That is, a
greater amount of controlled conflict will probably be deliberately
built into the policy process, and new technologies and technical
expertise will be significant instruments, or resources, in that conflict. The CPSU leadership will, of course, insist on its right to
arbitrate and orchestrate this competition; but its organizational
and intellectual ability to do so, for the purpose of achieving policy
outcomes that are reasonably popular or acceptable to key elites
and the general public, will be a most important factor in shaping
the development of the Soviet polity.

　　Furthermore, both the "diffusion of power" and the "power-to-
the-computer-specialist" arguments seem to rest on the assumptions
that (1) Party leaders will recognize the need to improve policies on
how to make policy (that is, the policy-making system); (2) top CPSU
officials are earnestly striving to develop feasible national policies
and to implement centrally determined goals; and (3) successful
policies are essential to maintaining the power positions of the
national Party and government leaders, individually and collectively.

　　The first two assumptions probably accurately reflect the
thinking and behavior of the Politburo and Secretariat leadership,
but they may be much less valid immediately below this level in all
of the major Soviet bureaucracies, including the Party. Significantly,
many prominent CPSU officials, economists, social theorists, and
cyberneticists seem to be well aware of the changing nature of
effective policy making and societal management (upravlenie) and of
the vital role that innumerable types of information and communication play in these processes. Also, the present CPSU leadership is
apparently making serious and modestly successful efforts to improve the quality and processing of social, economic, and "inner-
Party" (vnutripartiinaia) information and to develop their distinctly
non-Khrushchevian interpretation of "democratic centralism."[11]

　　The third assumption, however, raises broad and intriguing
questions, including the question of how much political power is
based on achievement in the Soviet system. My own view is that
Khrushchev's power and prestige were to a large extent dependent
upon the success of his policies,[12] but that this has become much
less true under the present "collective leadership." There is now

prior consultation of bureaucratic elites on the policy alternatives that affect them. Major compromises are made before new policies are enunciated. National leaders mobilize bureaucratic support to facilitate the implementation of central directives and do not usually harangue or threaten officials who diligently attempt to carry out the tasks entrusted to them. In addition, many Soviet bureaucrats may be well aware that the Politburo's choices are becoming more and more circumscribed; that it is increasingly locked into its past political, economic, social, military, and international commitments; and that national policies are becoming more complex, interrelated, and interdependent. Their success hinges on countless contributions and contingencies and on coordinated and cooperative efforts among numerous Soviet and sometimes foreign institutions. Few horizontal coordinating agencies exist in the USSR, even at the national level, and the lack of strong integrating and coordinating mechanisms provides innumerable opportunities for parochialism and "buck-passing" at the center and in the provinces. Also, the departmental esprit de corps cannot be minimized. The Soviet Soviet bureaucratic elites, especially at the national level, enjoy remarkable job security. Hence credit, blame, and responsibility can be and are being spread around much more evenly than before.

How, and by whom, are the fruits of technological progress ascertained and evaluated in the USSR? Success—for instance, the short- and long-term benefits of new technologies—is very difficult to define, measure, and assess in many fields. Scientific-technological advances in one area may subvert other policies and priorities. This necessitates choices and trade-offs among such competing values as control, efficiency, and ideological considerations. These conflicts must be resolved in a highly politicized and bureaucratized context. For example, powerful national leaders can simply proclaim major domestic and international accomplishments, aided greatly by modern technological breakthroughs in telecommunications and the printed word.

Many technical benefits derive from the introduction of electronic data processing into national, regional, and local governments. These improvements lie chiefly in the quantity and quality of the data generated and in their speedier transmission and greater availability for various potential uses. There are also a number of technical costs, which most computer experts consider negligible in comparison with the advantages of automated data systems. [13] The salient views about benefits and costs are those of the central political leaders, however, and these officials are likely to be interested first and foremost in the policy and power implications of the new technologies. For the professional politician there is no distinction, and no reason to distinguish, between choices of value, strategy, and tactics, on the one hand, and technology, on the other. And for the politician or bureaucrat, there is every reason and opportunity to dispute the success of specific policies and the role that new quantitative data and data processing technology have played in policy outcomes or impacts. (The quantification or improved quality of data, of course, are not ends in themselves.)

My hunch, then is that under the Brezhnev administration the powers of the major bureaucracies are not highly dependent on the success of their collectively agreed-upon policies or on the efficient use of new technologies, perhaps not even in economic policy areas in which achievements and failures are relatively easy to determine, such as agriculture. Instead, organizational goals may be the operative "success criteria" of national policies and the decisive reasons why access to decision makers by Soviet computer specialists will not necessarily bring influence, and why better policy-relevant information will not necessarily be used for what the Soviet technical specialists or disinterested outsiders would consider to be productive or rational uses. Traditional organizational values would seem to be especially important in a highly bureaucratized society such as the Soviet Union, which is still encumbered by a considerable amount of conformity, caution, and coercion.

THE "INFORMATION CULTURE"
IN THE SOVIET BUREAUCRACIES

This brings us to the whole question of the "information culture" of Soviet bureaucracies and of the Soviet political system. In trying to assess the impact of computers on policy making and administration, one must give serious consideration to the elements of secrecy, orthodoxy, official ideology, arbitrariness, bureaucratic inertia, sanctions, evasiveness, confusion, and mendacity—in short, the Stalinist legacy—in contemporary Soviet politics. CPSU leaders have recently permitted and encouraged more intra-elite discussion of many policy questions, but they continue to suppress criticism of Stalinism and its consequences, which greatly reduces the effectiveness of their renewed emphasis on the "democratic" side of "democratic centralism" in Party and state activities. Traditional, but not necessarily Stalinist, bureaucratic patterns (for example, loyalties) and communication pathologies (for example, blockage of accurate upward communication) also persist. [14]

In brief, many factors other than technology influence Soviet administrative behavior and the bureaucratic information culture, and many of these patterns would have to change before a culture-transforming process could be sustained. The Soviet leadership is trying to make some important changes, such as widening specialist participation in decision making and reducing the sanctions on constructive criticism of policy details at official CPSU meetings, but there is little evidence that the central leaders wish to change the basic bureaucratic incentive and reward structure or the fundamental elite values and institutional arrangements of the present political system. Thus it seems more likely that the new Soviet information technology will reinforce the existing information systems or be grafted onto them without substantial changes rather than spur a culture-reshaping process or significant changes in organizational behavior and power relationships within and among the major bureaucracies.

Before developing this view further, some additional observations must be made about Soviet elites, elite political culture, and the "power-to-the-computer specialist" argument. [15] First, there are competing elites at the highest Party and state levels. Also, it is unlikely that middle-level officials will become a cohesive grouping, with shared values and group consciousness. As Michel Tatu and others have demonstrated, the political alliances in the Soviet Union run up and down the Party and state hierarchies rather than across the "top." [16] Khrushchev's, and now Brezhnev's, support is anchored at different levels in the various bureaucracies. If Khrushchev had not had such strong support below the Politburo level, he would never have been able to hold on to power until 1964, as his authority in the Politburo and Secretariat became increasingly tenuous. To suggest that the "top" and "middle-management" elites are in sharp conflict with one another is to distort the complexity and impermanence, and the often vertical nature, of post-Stalin coalition alignments and bargaining relationships.

Second, computer technologiests will not easily "edge out" middle-management-level groups on the career ladder. Regional and national middle-level officials, in the Party and in the ministries, provide considerable support for various Central Committee and central Party apparatus groupings. T. H. Rigby has aptly described the cooperation between high-ranking CPSU officials and their supporters at lower levels as "patron-client" relationships. [17] The client supplies support for the patron and his policy preferences, while the patron provides job protection and security, and possibly promotion, for the client. For the highest political leaders to ignore their clients at subordinate levels might be politically disastrous.

It would seem, then, that the structure of leadership in the Soviet Union is a crucial variable to consider before concluding that the whole category of middle-management personnel will be bypassed by a younger, less politically influential group. It is doubtful that the computer experts, because of their rather specialized knowledge and because of their youth, could serve as the political "functional equivalents" of Party cadres in middle-level positions, many of whom have other technical skills, considerable power in political arenas, and various sources and kinds of information and experience.

In short, the top Party leaders will probably not be willing to sacrifice the support and expertise of provincial and middle-level officials for the "unknown quantity" of the computer technologists. Their sophisticated new skills may eventually become "known" and valued to some extent, but this development will take place in the context of competition among shifting CPSU groupings, and the risks of jeopardizing present sources of bureaucratic support, such as the support of traditional ideological specialists, would seem to be high and the counterincentives (job security, increased opportunities to be consulted on decision alternatives, peer-group pressure not to undermine the post-Khrushchev "collective" policy-making proce- dures) would seem to be compelling.

Third, it is highly questionable whether computer experts will emerge as a reasonably cohesive elite grouping to which power will "gravitate." Power is, of course, relational; it is not something that a group possesses as if it were a material item. Data process- ing specialists may gain more power vis-a-vis the middle-level cadres, but what about their relationships with central Party offi- cials? One cannot simultaneously argue that power will accrue to the computer experts and also that the young technologists will not challenge the top officials because of their youth.

The skills of the computer specialists threaten to upset the existing power relationships and policy-making procedures through- out the Party and state. My guess is that national CPSU and govern- ment leaders understand this fact and, rationally or instinctively, are acting accordingly. Computer experts make possible and may eventually stimulate some political and administrative changes, but these changes are not likely to be in the essentials of the system. The central Party elites probably have it within their power to utilize the skills of the computer technologists at little or no political "cost."[18] That is, the fast-rising young computer and management specialists may be asked to participate in planning and decision making, but may soon be asked to leave if they do not pro- vide practical assistance to policy makers or if they prove expendable for other reasons. Despite, or perhaps because of, high-level policy disputes, there is no reason to believe that central Party elites would not or could not act in this arbitrary manner.

To argue the opposite would be to suggest that the power of a group's function is the crucial determinant of political authority in modern industrial societies, as if power flows from function. It does, in a sense, but organizational relationships, not economic-technical functions, are probably still the key determinants of political power, especially in the USSR. "Dual executives" or "red-experts"—people who combine political, administrative, and technical (such as engineering and computer) skills and who probably reach positions of real authority late in their careers—are likely to have the most lasting impact on the values, priorities, programs, and policy-making practices of the CPSU. [19]

Moreover, as a group, "dual executives" will probably not exercise political power. As technical specialists they will not only be employed at the central apparatus and ministerial level but at regional and local levels as well, and they will also be "scattered" throughout the different state committees and agencies, R&D institutes, and public and economic organizations. This further diminishes the experts' ability and desire to achieve collective professional consciousness, common goals, organizational solidarity, and the capacity to mobilize support for shared objectives.

One finds it difficult to imagine any occupational grouping in the Soviet Union, with the possible exception of institutionalized professional alignments in the "military-industrial complex," [20] to be so indispensable to the central authorities that it could dominate policy making in even one issue area. Some Western observers assumed that the industrial executives and factory managers would become a powerful "interest group" in the USSR because of their important skills and experience. Like the computer experts, the managers of Soviet industry were once considered to be likely candidates to play a crucial role in Soviet policy making because of their technical functions. However, as Jeremy Azrael has capably demonstrated, the industrial managers are presently not much more powerful than they have ever been. [21] In a word, their valuable technical skills have not been transformed into political power and have not been sufficient to ensure them a prominent role in national policy making.

Whether the expertise of computer specialists or factory managers is more essential to various decision makers, and whether one "group" has or will have a greater sense of identity and common interests, are moot questions. Computerization in the USSR, except in the military and the economy, is still in its early stages, and the profession of the data-processing specialist is a very new one. In any event, there seem to be good reasons to expect that computer experts will not develop a shared group "interest" or the capacity and will to promote it, any more than, say, economists, and probably less than industrial managers.

Furthermore, there seems to be nothing inherent in the computer technologists' skills and training that would suggest that they will challenge, rather than serve, the basic values, priorities, and

directives of political leaders (national, regional, and/or local) and
pursue in a unified manner similar, coherent policy alternatives.
Rather, it is much more likely that quantitative data skills will be
utilized by individual leaders and bureaucratic units for all sorts
of partisan, and possibly nonpartisan, purposes. The chief consequences of this would be the breaking up of any embryonic "group"
of information specialists and probably enhancement of the power
of the central Party leadership or segments of that elite (more on
this later). In short, individual computer technologists are likely to
end up joining the traditional types of bureaucratic patron-client
relationships that already exist. [22]

Fourth, it is all too easy to overemphasize the importance of
quantitative and technical data, neither of which can satisfy the
important needs of central policy makers, even those whose basic
goals are relatively set and agreed upon. What is always necessary
is "normative" communication, which is constantly circulating at all
levels of the different hierarchies. That is, CPSU leaders must
determine how "things are going," how various cadres and state
officials are doing their jobs, who is creating problems, and so on.
Some data of this kind will be fed into computers, and the results
and the interpretation of these results will probably be considerably
influenced by Marxist-Leninist categories of analysis and by salient
political and organizational values, attitudes, and beliefs (explicit
and implicit). Many kinds of nonquantifiable feedback are essential
to national policy makers, however, and it is these types of information that, with varying degrees of completeness and accuracy, are
being largely supplied by, or can be periodically elicited from, both
scientific and technical experts and middle-level political and administrative officials (who are often the same people).

It is unlikely, therefore, that middle-level CPSU and government officials will be pushed aside by the young computer technologists. If this were really to happen, an interesting dilemma might
face the Soviet leadership: it might have to choose among different
information needs and to favor various groups, depending upon what
types of information were sought. It is much more likely, however,
that Party leaders will seek to generate and obtain numerous kinds
of normative and technical primary and feedback information from
a wide variety of sources. [23]

More important, top officials will almost surely strive to
preserve their authority to interpret and evaluate the policy implications of these data and to make political choices accordingly. Changes
in the style of leadership are quite possible, including less central
interference in day-to-day operational questions and more efforts to
generate information that can significantly assist national leaders in
long-range economic and social planning. Quantitative and nonquan-

titative data about the environment that are fed back to the political
leadership do not in themselves contain "imperatives" for action.
Politicians, individually and collectively, must ascribe meaning to
these data and, to the extent that this process is a conscious or
rational one, Soviet officials will probably determine the significance
of these data in reference to organizational goals. Therefore newly
generated data do not themselves change leadership goals and
behavior in preordained directions. These data will be filtered
through the existing values, attitudes, and beliefs of political leaders
and through the rational and extrarational elements of their cognitive
orientations. Only by considering these mediating social-psychological factors, then, can one speak meaningfully about "goal-changing"
feedback.

Fifth, the process of computerization may have more far-
reaching effects in the USSR than in the United States, because an
institutional differentiation between political and economic power
does not exist in the Soviet Union. Once again it must be contended
that there are very few technologically determined relationships in
politics and that a computerized information system will probably
only be as important as the Soviet leaders desire it to be or can
induce middle- and lower-level officials to make or let it be. This
is not to deny that computerization will have some important effects
of its own, but rather to suggest that the central Party elite may
have ample resources (nontechnical and technical) to control its
uses and to cope with its unintended consequences.

Zbigniew K. Brzezinski and others maintain that major
changes in the USSR will most likely be leader-initiated. [24] Since
top Soviet officials seem well aware that most kinds of knowledge
carry political implications that are usually in dispute, computerization at different decision-making stages and levels will amost certainly be introduced with considerable caution and monitored with
exceptional care. My guess is that one of the major reasons for the
much greater mechanization of information processing outside of the
Communist Party is the desire of CPSU leaders to ensure control of
the adaptation of the new technology to the Party's existing organizational procedures, and vice versa (more on this later). In any case,
an evaluation of the impact of modern information technology on
policy making and administration must give very serious consideration to the values, goals, and capabilities of the powerful central
Party leadership (Politburo, Secretariat, Central Committee, and
Central Committee apparatus department) and also of the regional
and local Party apparatchiki.

CPSU leaders have various goals, policy preferences, and
priorities. Ongoing conflict among competing ideas and bureaucratic
interests, inside and outside the Party, is a cardinal fact of Soviet

politics. There is virtually no evidence to suggest, however, that any group within the CPSU is advocating the weakening of Party power ("the withering away of the Party"), or the voluntary devolution to state and public organs of its ultimate policy-making authority (such as its monopoly over "the politics of principles"). In other words, there is no reason to anticipate the "radical democratization" of key political functions, such as the determination of national goals, the setting of priorities, and the establishment of criteria and standards to evaluate alternative programs, that Mihailo Marković and others have advocated. [25]

Nor are there more than the beginnings of a trend toward ensuring that the views of Party members who are in the minority on a given issue will be given careful consideration both before and after a decision is made. Surely there have been no serious efforts to establish "mechanisms" for a sustained "dialogue" between non-Party dissenters and the bureaucratic elites, as Roy Medvedev urges. Medvedev, for one, is striving to create a highly just and productive socialist society within the framework of a more responsive and less repressive and bureaucratized one-party system. [26] Nevertheless, the traditional Russian idea that great power should be concentrated at the center so that it can be used for constructive purposes, remains an important part of the Soviet elite and mass political cultures, even among many of the dissenters who question, as Medvedev is increasingly doing, the fairness as well as the wisdom of various government policies.

Briefly stated, there is every reason to believe that CPSU leaders will continue to try to enhance their capacity to direct Soviet society. Few will challenge their right to do so, although they will meet with some institutional and societal resistance to specific policies. They will cautiously attempt to enlist new technologies in the service of presently-held values, such as maintenance of the social order and the primacy of the Party, institutional flexibility, and bureaucratic responsiveness to new opportunities and problems. They are more likely to be successful if they seek out and utilize technocratic counsel to improve the effectivenss of substantive public policies and the efficiency of policy-making procedures. One gains the clear impression from the Soviet literature on the STR and "the scientific management of society" that the Party leadership will jettison or do without any technologies it thinks it cannot harness.

More important, Communist Party leaders and social theorists seem confident that the Soviet people can and will tailor native and imported technological innovations to the tasks of constructing a more socially and economically developed socialist society and (less convincingly) that this society eventually will be transformed into a communist one. [27] Soviet writers recognize that there <u>will</u> be unanticipated political and cultural changes and pressures, but it is apparently thought that few of these social side-effects will be undesirable and that all can be corrected, adjusted, or managed by effective societal guidance from the CPSU.[28]

A typical official Soviet view of the role of the "scientific and technological intelligentsia," and of the political implications of its increasing size and prominence, is the following:

> As for political decision making, there has never been any manifestation of real political authority of technocrats. As soon as the problems of management go beyond the competence of this or that specialist, he immediately becomes powerless as far as exercising real authority is concerned, and submits to the political ideology prevailing in the given society.[29]

The author immediately makes it clear that there is an inherent contradiction (my word) or tension in the relationship between the Soviet policy maker and the scientific or technical specialist and that members of both groups are dependent upon each other and influence one another, as follows:

> The experience of socialism shows that the increasing influence of the STI [the scientific and technological intelligentsia] on the elaboration, adoption and practical implementation of political decisions, i.e., on the real execution of power, is effected through a social mechanism radically differing from the elitarian models of power. The socialist intelligentsia . . . does not seek to "monopolize" all intellectual activity with the aim of turning it into a factor of power, but, on the contrary, spares no efforts to make intellectual wealth accessible to all working people, so that by obtaining up-to-date knowledge and acquiring education and culture they will be better equipped for exercising democratic state power. And the more the intelligentsia succeeds in fulfilling this task, the greater becomes its moral and political authority in socialist society, its influence on the political decisionmaking.[30]

In short, the Soviet technical intelligentsia is exhorted to apply "all its abilities and knowledge to the solution of the key economic and socio-political tasks."[31] In return, scientific and technical specialists (individually and perhaps collectively) are promised increasing, but still very circumscribed, power to determine the basic purposes and nature of those tasks.

THE IMPACT OF
MODERN INFORMATION TECHNOLOGY

What impact will the introduction of modern information technology have on these shifting and perhaps delicately balanced power relationships? My own view is that computerized information systems will produce considerable bureaucratic conflict in the Soviet Union and that computers are likely to increase the concentration of power at the center. That is, the new technology will heighten competition among the predominantly vertically-structured alliances within and among the major Soviet bureaucracies. It will also enhance the collective capacity of national Party leaders to exercise effective and efficient societal leadership, in accordance with whatever fundamental values they can agree upon, most likely the ones they presently hold, including important understandings about "the rules of the game" and acceptable levels of conflict among these values. With the Radovan Richta of the 1970s, I too challenge the assumption that "where power is armed with knowledge, it is eo ipso knowledge that controls power."[32]

As discussed earlier, the ultimate results and effectiveness of modern information technology are not self-evident; they will always be the subject of political controversy, which is likely to be resolved in favor of important centrally-led groups or coalitions whose power derives from various technical and nontechnical (such as organizational) sources. In a word, government leaders determine the political and technical advantages and disadvantages of the new technologies, and both kinds of calculations shape the eventual uses of the quantitative data and data processing equipment, their impact on information systems and policy outcomes, and the role of computer specialists in policy making, planning, and control.[33]

It is eminently practical for a politician to calculate the effects of technological innovations on politics. As Anthony Downs insightfully suggests, automated data systems produce at least seven important power shifts, or institutional changes in decision making, at different levels of government. These changes all tend to centralize political power, and in an already highly centralized polity such as the USSR, they are likely to consolidate the existing leadership structure further as follows:

1. Lower- and intermediate-level officials tend to lose power to higher-level officials and politicians.
2. High-level staff officials gain power.
3. Legislators tend to lose power to administrators and operating officials.
4. The government bureaucracy as a whole gains power at the expense of the general population and nongovernmental groups.

5. Well-organized and sophisticated groups of all kinds, including government bureaus, gain power at the expense of less well-organized and less sophisticated groups.
6. Those who actually control automated data systems gain in power at the expense of those who do not. Therefore, much of the controversy that is sure to arise about the proper design and operation of data systems will reflect a power struggle for control of those systems.
7. Technically educated officials gain power at the expense of old-style political advisors. However, men who possess both technical sophistication and wisdom will acquire increasing power. [34]

There is no reason to repeat Downs's argumentation in support of these conclusions. Suffice it to say that it rests heavily on the assumption that computer-assisted systems enable central officials to bypass middle- and lower-level officials in the pursuit of policy-relevant data and to improve thereby the quality and quantity of the information communicated from "bottom to top." Also, this increased technological capacity to generate and transmit information to national policy makers may reduce the distortion of upward communication within the bureaucracies. Middle-level officials will know that national agencies have the equipment and personnel to augment the usual sources of normative and technical information, and the intermediate officials will therefore be more likely to transmit ample, accurate, and timely intelligence to their superiors.

Middle-management executives, in terms of their capacity to influence the formulation and administration of national and regional policies and to remain relatively independent of central authority, would seem to have the most to lose from a trend toward computerized decision making and automated data processing systems. More and better information of all kinds enables the highest central leaders to plan better, to develop clearer and more feasible national policies, to coordinate the work of diverse governmental units more effectively, and to supervise the implementation of programs more efficiently. All of these factors reduce departmental or "subsystem" autonomy.

If numerous national and regional political institutions possess their own computers, does this not fragment, rather than consolidate, political power? "Yes," replies the technological determinist. "Not necessarily" or "no," responds the observer who stresses diverse sources of organizational power and diverse technical skills and who can reasonably demonstrate the ability and will of a specific elite to control the distribution of the new technologies and ensure that these technologies are used to pursue centrally prescribed goals. Effective use of computers in operational decision making would serve precisely these purposes.

There is nothing inherent in information technology that produces a greater concentration of political power in the hands of top national officials. "Centralization of machines does not necessarily imply centralization of power, decision, or information";[35] nor does it ensure integrated, coordinated, and complementary policies. Some federal agencies might conceivably use computers to increase their power vis-a-vis the highest central political authorities. Regional governmental units might utilize computers to increase their autonomy from the center, for example by freeing officials' time for policy-relevant, rather than routine, tasks. Middle-level bureaucrats might play a major role in shaping the kinds of data that go into central computers and thereby diffuse power. National leaders might voluntarily disseminate the information they have to assist other bureaucratic units at various stages and levels of policy making and administration. In a word, the new information technology could redistribute or consolidate government power.

Modern information-processing technologies must operate in bureaucratic contexts, however, and this fact alone strongly suggests that the technical potential for "rationalizing" decision making and information flows will be far from realized, especially in very centralized political systems like the USSR. Institutional and personnel changes are essential to the effective use of computers; but incumbent officals at all levels will be reluctant to initiate these changes. National policy makers, especially in highly bureaucratized one-party states, oversee the manufacture and/or importation of the modern equipment by governmental agencies, approve the design of computerized information systems, and authoritatively evaluate the results. Members of "collective" leaderships will approve the uses of the new information technologies only when they are confident, to the best of their understanding, that the likely shifts in bureaucratic power will strengthen central authority generally and further centrally-determined goals (or benefit their institutional units or coalitions, or promote their own policy preferences).

If central policy makers are sharply or evenly divided, or merely disorganized and inefficient, the chances are that the introduction of sophisticated new information technology will be disjointed and delayed or that technological innovations will be given "trial runs" at the lowest hierarchical levels, in outlying geographical areas, and in the least controversial policy fields. As Downs concludes, the real and perceived technical and power payoffs from automated data systems probably will induce many national, regional, and local governments to develop these information systems "in a piecemeal, department-by-department fashion. "36 Thus the creation of comprehensive and integrated scientific-technical, economic, and especially social information systems is likely to be a prolonged and quite competitive process. "The rationalizing effect which the new procedures should theoretically have upon decisional processes (albeit within rather narrow technical boundaries) finds other strong limits in the particularistic needs of the actors who manage such processes. "37

The U.S., West and East European, and Soviet experience to date tends to confirm these conclusions and to support Downs's hypotheses. Alan Westin and his colleagues quickly found that, despite the burst of high-level U.S. government enthusiasm for the promised planning and efficiency benefits of "the new economics," PPBS, and the "social indicators" movement in the early and mid-1960s, "there was still hardly any [computerized] information system [in 1970] that was having any significant effect on strategic or tactical decision making in executive branches of government at any level. "38

Studies of the West European experience come to the same general conclusion, but they credit computers with having some impact on routine administrative tasks and, more important, with alterations in power relationships within and among governmental units, especially at the municipal level. 39

Significantly, Jeffrey Straussman concludes provisionally from the U.S. experience that (1) "technocratic counsel accepts the strategic options supplied by policymakers as given and beyond discussion" and (2) "willing producers who aspire to some degree of influence in the policy process invariably must accept the strategic positions of the powerful consumers. "40

Briefly stated, Western computer and management experts seem to accept the prevailing values and goals of the professional politicians and bureaucrats they serve and of the political systems in which they live and work. Westin concludes that in the United States "there [is not] the slightest sign of a displacement of the traditional leadership elites of top and middle management in government by the information specialists. "41 Franco Ferraresi likewise concludes that "in none of the [West European] administrative systems examined have the different categories of informaticians taken on dominant power positions. "42

Evidence concerning the political impact of modern information technology in the Soviet Union and Eastern Europe43 is sparse and speculative, and it is surely premature to consider "testing" Downs's hypotheses in socialist contexts. However, Downs's conclusions do help to explain some important, and perhaps otherwise inexplicable, facts about recent Soviet experience with information processing.

Foremost among these is the remarkable degree to which the CPSU is lagging behind other Soviet bureaucracies in the introduction and utilization of modern information-processing technology. Economic, military, security—even legal and educational—institutions all seem to be far ahead of the Party in the day-to-day use of computers and electronic and even manual punch card systems. [44] Add to this the intriguing possibility that the computerization of information and decision processes is taking place primarily at the primary Party organization level and that the use of the new technologies may be slowly working its way up the CPSU hierarchy. The head of the Party Information sector of the Central Committee's Organizational-Party Work department clearly implied this in a recent article, in which he tersely described the "first steps" toward introducing computerized information technology into several "Party organizations of the largest factories" and the wider use of less sophisticated [that is, usually nonelectronic] data retrieval equipment in the local CPSU committees up to the union republic level. The writer was silent about the use of new information technology in the departments of the Central Committee apparatus, and very little is known about this. [45]

Most probably, the present plan or tacit policy is to employ computers in the Communist Party, first, for very routine tasks at the national level, and for monitoring, control, and decision-making assistance at the production unit level (urban and rural). After that, computers will probably be used more and more for social planning— they are now used extensively for economic planning—and personnel matters at the national level and for "housekeeping, " such as inventory control; for coordinating, such as regional planning; and eventually for decision-making operations at the middle and lower levels of the CPSU.

The entire foregoing discussion about the politicized nature of technological progress suggests that computers may be introduced very slowly even into national CPSU organs and may be used only for the most mundane tasks in the foreseeable future. This would be a sensible response to the nonprogrammed nature of much of national policy making, and it would also be responsive to the highly bureaucratized character of the central Party apparatus and to the possibly acute sensitivity of its different divisions to the political implications of the new technologies, such as their effects on policy alternatives and their potentially disruptive effects on power relationships among Central Committee departments, and between these departments and the state ministries whose work they oversee.

Why would the Party leadership allow the CPSU to fall behind all other major bureaucracies in the deployment of this potentially fruitful and powerful new technology? Would not the top CPSU leaders

and central apparatus officials have a common interest in strengthening their capacity to direct Soviet society and to maintain their power
vis-a-vis other institutions, particularly the regional Party organs
and the sprawling, fragmented state ministerial complex? This
question cannot be answered with confidence, but Downs's hypotheses
suggest some answers, or at least some reasons for the manifest
caution and slowness with which the CPSU is employing the new
information-processing technology.

Social theorists like S. V. Shukhardin and V. G. Afanas'ev
may extol the societal benefits of the modern information technology
ogy,[46] but full-time Party apparatchiki cannot be insensitive to the
power and policy implications of the new managerial techniques and
skills analyzed by Soviet writers on the STR and advocated by the
would-be "rationalizers" and "scientific managers" of society. For
example, many CPSU officials may vividly recall Khrushchev's
attacks on the Party's ideological specialists and on Party cadres
who lacked the necessary technical skills to manage a modern
economy. If the national CPSU elite were really unified, and if the
coalitions in Soviet politics were not more vertical than horizontal,
computers would probably soon be widely used in the central Party
apparatus, as well as in economic institutions and in the military-
industrial, security, and scientific-technical branches of the state.
One could speculate that the Afanas'evs speak chiefly for powerful
Politburo and Secretariat groups and their partners in the most
technologically sophisticated state ministries and that there may be
cleavages between these alignments and the Central Committee
department officials who nominally serve as powerful agents of the
center or as "honest brokers" between key Party and governmental
organs.

Darrell Hammer suggests that the really important differences
are between those industrial executives who share an "engineering"
outlook and those who share a reformist "managerial" outlook,
regardless of their positions.[47] Significantly different perspectives
also exist between technically trained Party apparatchiki and many
ideological specialists. One suspects that cadres with "ideological"
and "engineering" attitudes, for example about the proper functions
of the Party and its role in the economy, have managed, so far, to
block most "managerial" efforts to introduce systems approaches
and new information technology into national policy making.

One might hazard the guess that there is now a tacit understanding among various departments of the Central Committee that
modern information processing technology will not be introduced
into important Party work at this time, will be used only in very
limited competition among departments, or will be employed only by
their non-Party coalition partners. This understanding, if it exists

at all, is no doubt temporary and fragile; but it could be based on mutual acceptance of Brezhnev's serious effort to regularize policy-making practices and institutional arrangements; on the belief that the present "collective" and consultative procedures provide somewhat greater automony, that is, influence, at least over one's own work, for all Central Committee departments; and on a common interest in minimizing the potentially destabilizing and disruptive effects of adapting technological innovations to the post-Khrushchevian policies on formulating policy.

In brief, the introduction of the new information technology into policy making and administration will make possible and probably generate increased bureaucratic conflict in the Party and the state. The top CPSU leaders are very likely aware of this possibility and perceive it as a significant, but certainly as not an insurmountable or unnegotiable, problem. Many national CPSU and government officials may also be keenly aware of these contingencies and view them as either opportunities or threats. Those who are most sensitive to the political disadvantages of the new technologies from a national or departmental point of view may well be coping with their respective problems by forming an alliance that, to date at least, has succeeded in very gradually introducing modern information-processing technology into the least controversial stages and levels of Party decision making.

This general interpretation may also help to explain the flexibility or ambiguity of centralized directives concerning the use of computers and new punch card systems in the regional Party committees. The present method is clearly "piecemeal"; indeed, it may be haphazard. In effect, central officials seem to be saying to the local Party bureaus, "Introduce any of this new equipment (orgtekhnika) you can obtain in whatever ways you choose, and to whatever extent you think it will enhance your ability to fulfill centrally determined objectives, without disrupting valuable existing political relationships, especially at the regional and local levels. "

The present cautious approach to the training of information specialists within the Party is also more understandable in this light. Here, too, local CPSU bureaus have been given considerable authority to determine the role of the information specialist, and they also have the responsibility to train that specialist in whatever ways they wish. To date, most regional Party organizations have carefully limited the scope of the work of the new "information sectors, " and, especially at the city and district levels, have employed many "nonstaff" workers, such as retired cadres, to perform largely clerical information-gathering tasks. [48]

Briefly stated, many CPSU leaders believe that computers have great potential to benefit the Soviet people by creating new opportunities to enhance economic and social planning and development and by helping to cope with the economic and social problems of managing a developed socialist society. The political trade-offs of institutional flexibility, stability, and efficiency are real, and the present CPSU leaders are gingerly introducing new information technologies into the upper and middle levels of the Communist Party. The top Party leadership appears to be encouraging the installation of computerized data systems chiefly at the production unit level, particularly for automated process control and for repetitive, programmed economic decisions that are made in accordance with the basic plans, policies, and priorities established at the center.

Even more important, the cautious approach of the Party leadership to modern information technology may reflect its common interest in controlling, or not having its choices unduly pressured or manipulated by, the new technology, the types and forms of information it produces, and the technical specialists—especially in the central industrial ministries—who generate and process this information. To be sure, the highest CPSU leaders are encouraging the use of more and better expertise at virtually all stages and levels of decision making. The central Party apparatchiki, however, have a particularly strong vested interest in maintaining the legitimacy of other sources and types of information. Most important, of course, is the traditional Soviet claim to knowledge of "the laws of social development" and of truths ascertained by a Marxist-Leninist cognitive orientation and by "theory-directed" empirical observation.

If the legitimacy and power of the Brezhnev administration were based primarily on economic, social, diplomatic, or military "success indicators" and accomplishments, the legitimizing and self-legitimizing functions of the official ideology might be less important. As suggested earlier, however, the power and prestige of the present "collective leadership" may not be highly dependent upon the success of its policies, even though its top leaders are clearly "achievement oriented" and strongly motivated to use bureaucratic power for constructive, substantive purposes. Appropriately, one current policy priority is the significant improvement of political education work, or the centrally directed reshaping of the mass political culture. In pursuit of this goal, national Party officials are increasingly utilizing recent technological innovations in mass communications and are conducting public opinion surveys and data-based research on the social and psychological consequences of ideological work.

Hence the appeal to "rationalize" information flows does not imply the democratization of decision making or the significant diffusion of political power. [49] That is, the central Party leadership

maintains its prerogative of making the truly important value-,
institution-, and resource-allocation choices for society and of using
or ignoring the new technologies and data as it sees fit. The national
CPSU leaders are trying to alter certain aspects of the existing
bureaucratic information culture (with mixed success), but they
appear to be reluctant or unwilling to make appreciable changes in
the larger information systems, of which computer technology is
only a part.

Soviet elite attitudes toward modern information-processing
technology have virtually nothing in common with fear of "bourgeois
technical rationality." Soviet officials and writers seem to be
increasingly sensitive to the cultural implications of applying Western management techniques to Soviet conditions and needs. However,
the Manichaean official Soviet view of cultural diffusion and technology transfer persists: Western ideas are very harmful, but Western
technology and trade are very beneficial.

Succinctly stated, the chief domestic policy aims of the present Communist Party leadership apparently are (1) to enhance its
societal guidance and problem-solving capacities; (2) to mobilize
organizational and material resources to accomplish centrally
determined ends; (3) to utilize more and better technocratic counsel
in formulating and periodically reevaluating these ends; and (4) to
adjust substantive policies and policy-making procedures "to combine organically the achievements of the scientific-technological
revolution with the advantages of the socialist economic system."[50]

CONCLUSION

Will computerized information systems help to bring fundamental political change to the Soviet Union? The thrust of this
analysis is that computers, by themselves, do not matter much. My
best guess is that recent technological developments in electronic
data processing and telecommunications will reinforce, rather than
undermine, the existing bureaucratic information culture and the
essentials of the Soviet political system. Technology cannot be substituted for political and social choices,[51] and technical equipment
is not necessarily the predominant factor in shaping these choices
or in ensuring the effectiveness of the decisions reached.

One's conclusions depend, of course, on a subjective identification of the basic characteristics of the Soviet polity. John Hazard
suggests that if there is to be systemic transformation in the USSR,
it must come through changes in the following key areas: (1) the
Soviet leaders' "sense of infallibility"; (2) one-Party rule; (3) the
nomenklatura system; (4) the proscription of factions in the CPSU;

(5) the proscription of associational interest groups; (6) restrictions on freedom of expression; (7) a judiciary that is subject to Party domination in political cases; and (8) a security police with few limitations on its power. [52] Significantly, Hazard does not consider "an expansion of the circle of the ruling elite" by broadening and deepening specialist participation and consultation in policy making to be among these areas of potential systemic change.

Of these eight crucial characteristics of the Soviet system, only the first seems to have undergone considerable change as a result of the STR. Party leaders and social theorists repeatedly stress the increasing complexity of situations and problems, the intricacies of effecitve decision making, the need to find satisfactory solutions (some call for "optimal" solutions), and the difficulties of coping with uncertainties, interdependencies, and an ever-changing environment.

How are modern information technologies shaping the values, attitudes, and beliefs of socialist elites? How are various scientific and technical innovations altering power relationships within and among the major bureaucracies in one-party systems? How is technological progress affecting the "legitimacy claims" of ruling parties? These are very important questions for future research, which will only be briefly discussed below.

One need not assess the role of computer specialists in terms of elite conflict between knowledge elites and political elites, or between distinct ascending and descending elite groupings that perform different functions and possess different skills. Rather, the problem may be conceptualized as one in which technocratic consciousness becomes pervasive and subtly influences policy makers' and information specialists' thinking about politics. This has almost certainly begun to happen in the Soviet Union, for example, through the influence of cybernetics and systems analysis, through the professionalization of economic thought, and in the persistent official emphasis on the concepts of "rationality," "efficiency," and "the scientific management of society." Computers are indeed merely a part of larger information systems, which may or may not predispose their users (or participants) to new problem-solving approaches and innovative modes of analysis. [53]

My hunch is that the newer attitudes and beliefs of Soviet leaders have yet to produce any major changes in their central values. Scientific and technological innovations might eventually precipitate a major shift of values that will significantly alter the political and information cultures, and the fundamental public policies, policy-making procedures, and priorities of the Soviet bureaucratic elites. An educated guess is that contemporary information technology is least likely to change the leaders' cognitive orientations and basic values; more likely to change selected substantive policies and attitudes; and most likely to change specific policy-making procedures and beliefs. In a word, the nature and substance of political discourse is evolving.

Also, computerized information systems will undoubtedly bring some changes in the distribution of political power among the major Soviet bureaucracies. It is very likely that there will continue to be gradual shifts of power to competing bureaucratic groupings that have mastered key technical and analytical skills, such as weapons technology or optimal economic planning and that are located in certain geographic areas, such as Siberia. In turn these evolving institutional arrangements may adjust the perceptions, motivations, and expectations of various bureaucratic elites. However, basic changes in elite values and institutional relationships do not seem imminent. A major redistribution of organizational power would almost certainly produce significant changes in the uses of power, but this too does not seem likely in the next decade or so.

Prominent Soviet writers and officials, it is worth noting, have expressed views similiar to those above. V. G. Afanas'ev asserts the following:

> Computerization is an essential factor in the social-economic, technical, and spiritual development of man. Computers are more deeply and broadly entering into all spheres of human activity, including the intellectual. The computer today is not only a powerful calculating instrument and a means of storing and processing vast amounts of information, but it is also a means of shaping man's intellectual activity. Through the influence of computers, new structures of human thought are formed, the organization of physical and mental labor, cognition and learning, the spiritual world of man, are changed.[54]

Iurii Volkov declares the following:

> The STR unquestionably has an influence on the system and mechanism of power, but, in the first place, its impact on different types of society is by far not the same, and in the second place, it is not in any case a decisive factor capable of radically changing the system of power. . . . [The STR produces] new factors in public life, and in the system of management in particular, [but] they do not introduce any fundamental changes in the system of power under socialism. . . .
>
> In the course of the STR, technocratic and bureaucratic tendencies can arise. [But] it is not fatally inev-

itable that they become stabilized. However, their
neutralization should not be considered an easy or almost automatic matter. [55]

Iurii Tikhomirov states the following:

> Under socialism the latest electronic computers do not
> interfere with state management and do not try to take
> its place. . . . Naturally, we must not simplify this
> process and exclude the possibility of some or other
> contradictions arising. The introduction of electronic
> computers will work the necessary changes in the sys-
> tem of the management links, in the content and methods
> of their activity, and in the structure of state bodies.
> New equipment inevitably adds new features to the very
> style of work, requires better legal arrangements for
> it, enables the management bodies to save time on the
> collection and transfer of information and to spend
> more time on evaluation. The main thing, however,
> is that it releases the creative power of people for the
> analysis and accomplishment of major socio-economic
> tasks, stimulates their initiative, activity and conscious-
> ness, helps to ensure greater publicity, more exact
> evaluations and comparisons of the results of social
> activity. The new technological basis of management
> promotes the scientific approach to the management of
> social affairs and extends the democratic principles
> of management. [56]

Viktor Glushkov adds the following:

> A systems approach presupposes not only the mere
> purchase and installation of the computer but also the
> planning of the entire system of the collection and proc-
> essing of information, in the cost of which the computer
> itself accounts for a comparatively small share. . . .
>   It has been found that it is often more profitable
> to use a single big data bank, based on computers, than
> it is to use many smaller ones. In other words, there
> is a trend toward the centralization of reference-in-
> formation services. [57]

My chief conclusion is this: the STR, and modern information
technology in particular, seem to be bringing some changes in Soviet
elite perspectives and in the structure of political power in the USSR,

but not <u>major</u> changes in the most significant characteristics of the Soviet polity. The changes that have taken place under the present "collective leadership" appear to be highly conservative forms of adaptation, that is, pragmatic adjustment to new conditions of traditional Soviet values such as economic growth and the primacy of the Party and old principles such as "democratic centralism. "

Modern information-processing technology may contribute to significant modifications in policy-making procedures, however. Societal and organizational "learning" are important dimensions of pragmatism, and the ability to learn from past experience and mistakes is an essential component of leadership. The practical-minded men who direct the CPSU seem to be increasingly aware that empirical primary and feedback information (nonquantitative and quantitative) is crucial to the effective making and remaking of policy and to "rational" and national economic and social planning.

Also, the current CPSU leaders are probably well aware that improved policy making and planning necessitate more careful analysis of values and priorities, and hence, without a Stalin and in a complex modern society, greater conflict is generated within and among political institutions and among other sources of scientific, technical, and social knowledge. Better information makes possible better-informed policies, but it often creates more choices, reduces uncertainty, and threatens informal (and sometimes illegal) behavior patterns. Moreover, experienced Soviet politicians surely know that efforts to "rationalize" information flows can produce changes in power relationships and that trade-offs of political control, economic efficiency, institutional stability, and technological progress will almost certainly have to be made.

Richard Lowenthal perceptively links policy-making changes to the present Soviet leaders' real and perceived need to maintain, and develop new sources of, political legitimacy, as follows:

> In fact, for modern societies there is no long-run alternative to legitimacy based on institutional procedures.
> . . . A long-term legitimacy, based not only on a value consensus between rulers and ruled and a doctrinaire self-legitimation of the party that satisfies its own cadres, but on the plausibility of the claim that its procedures of leadership selection and policy decision are likely to meet the needs of a [mature industrial] society.[58]

Lowenthal's analysis lends added significance to the new policy-making procedures of the Brezhnev administration, and it would seem to support my earlier contention that substantive policy successes such as scientific-technical, economic, and international

achievements are becoming relatively less important sources of the
power and legitimacy of the post-Stalin leadership. Thomas Baylis
thoughtfully notes that "a shift in the basis of legitimacy claims may
profoundly affect power relationships within the elite itself."[59]
Major changes in the structure of Soviet power do not seem to have
taken place in the first half of the 1970s, however.

My own belief is that the top CPSU leadership is not voluntarily
relinquishing its power to key state ministries, and in fact it is
probably not dissipating its authority by seeking to improve the
learning and coordinative capacities of the political system by such
means as using new information-processing technology, encouraging
more constructive criticism through official channels, or recruiting
the most important state officials into the Politburo.

The Politburo and Secretariat may be diminishing their power
to make arbitrary decisions that affect the major bureaucracies.
The highest leaders' commitment to incremental change and the
constraints of past decisions certainly reduce the scope of viable
and perceived policy alternatives. More important, central Party
officials are striving to enhance their capacity to direct societal
development in a planned and "conscious" way (in the Leninist sense)
toward more clearly thought-out and feasible national goals. In so
doing, the current Soviet political leaders may be able to mobilize
more bureaucratic support for these goals and thereby legitimize
more effectively whatever policy outcomes ensue. The following
significant observation by Samuel Huntington applies with particular
force to the USSR:

> A complex society requires both increased functional
> autonomy for managerial specialists and increased
> political authority for the central political leadership.
> Meeting this latter need is the principal function of the
> party apparat. It is as essential to the system as the
> expert bureaucracy.[60]

Most likely, the highest CPSU leaders are cautiously trying
to augment their problem-solving and coping powers through the
application of any and all new technologies, while at the same time
debating and bargaining over the appropriate uses of that power,
and collectively and individually attempting to minimize the risk of
losing their traditional sources of bureaucratic authority. At least
two kinds of pragmatism are at play here: organizational learning
and power maintenance; and the highest Soviet leaders are attempting to reduce the potential conflict between the two. If faced with a
choice, the national Party elite will surely opt for power maintenance, but this is not a "zero-sum" game, and members of all com-

peting groups in the Politburo seem to be stressing the importance of organizational learning—for various purposes, of course. The chief constraint on systemwide planning and the "rationalization" of information flows is not a powerful and hostile environment, but rather the highly differentiated bureaucracies, whose various units, and the alliances among them, are reluctant to risk relinquishing any of their own power in the "national interest" of improving societal and organizational learning—unless, of course, they have what they consider to be an appropriate say in shaping public policies and the uses of this knowledge.

To conclude, native and imported information technology is not likely to alter the fundamental characteristics of the Soviet political system and the central values of the national Communist Party leaders. Rather, computerized information systems are among the important new means of pursuing traditional values and goals under contemporary scientific, technological, economic, social, and international conditions.

Medvedev, for one, rejects out of hand the possibility that the new technologies will modify the overcentralization and "undemocratic" essentials of the system. [61] Official Soviet spokesmen likewise reject projections based on technological determinism. A U.S. researcher provocatively argues that the Western literature on "post-industrial" society is chiefly concerned with the "tactical" political implications of technological innovations, [62] and the same can surely be said of the recent Soviet literature on "the scientific management of society."

Soviet political leaders and social theorists would almost certainly agree with the Harvard University scholars who conclude as follows:

> The challenge to research and inquiry—and eventually to policy—is to find out why the old economic and political forms are not working, and to modify them or design new ones that will both preserve the fundamental values of society and yet be adequate to modern technological realities. [63]

Whether fundamental Soviet values will change, and to what extent technological innovations will induce these changes in elite and mass behavior and attitudes, are crucial but unanswerable questions. Recent Soviet experience and theory suggest that limited cultural transformation and carefully controlled adaptation of the style and substance of politics, rather than a technologically determined "cultural revolution," are the most likely prospects for the foreseeable future. Political "consciousness" will be shaped, but not mastered, by technological "spontaneity."

NOTES

1. This is my formulation of a key question raised in Daniel
Bell, The Coming of Post-Industrial Society: A Venture in Social
Forecasting (New York: Basic Books, 1973), pp. 339-67 ff.;
Barrington Moore, Jr., Terror and Progress—USSR (New York:
Harper & Row, 1966), pp. 179-231 ff. The quoted phrases are
attributed to Boris Meissner in Ernst Kux, "Technicians of Power
versus Managers of Technique," in The Soviet Political Process, ed.
Sidney Ploss (Waltham, Mass.: Ginn, 1971), pp. 145-83.

2. Frederic J. Fleron, Jr., in the introduction to this book.

3. Jiri Slama and Heinrich Vogel, "Die Verbreitung neuer
Technologien in der UdSSR—Fallstudie I: Elektronische Datenverar-
beitung," in Jahrbuch der Wirtschaft Osteuropas, (Munich: Günter
Olzog, 1975), Vol. 6, pp. 123 ff.; John Stein, Estimating the Market
for Computers in the Soviet Union and Eastern Europe (Santa Monica,
Calif.: RAND, 1974), pp. 6 ff.; Stefan Possony, "The Real Revolution in Warfare: The Computer Impact," Orbis 17 (1973): 853.
These sources illustrate the diversity of Western estimates of the
military use of computers in the Soviet Union. Stein estimates that
6,100 computers were in nonmilitary use in 1971; Possony contends
that "virtually all" of the 6,000 computers installed in the USSR in
1971 "were allocated to the military and arms industry." Possony,
op. cit., p. 853. Slama and Vogel cautiously sidestep the issue. The
present chapter analyzes computerized information systems in nonmilitary sectors only.

4. For example, an IBM 360/50 was exhibited in Leningrad in
1971 and sold directly to the Ministry of the Chemical Industry in
1972. See Stein, op. cit., p. 27; Bohdan Szuprowicz, "Eastern
Europe's Thirst for Computers," Computer Decisions 5 (1973): 23-
28; Josef Wilczynski, Technology in Comecon (New York: Praeger,
1974), pp. 109-39.

5. For example, Radovan Richta, et al., Civilization at the
Crossroads: Social and Human Implications of the Scientific and
Technological Revolution (White Plains, N.Y.: International Arts
and Sciences Press, 1969), pp. 238-43.

6. "Most of the arguments that attempt [to support] the notion
that postindustrial society will witness the flow of power from politicians to experts seem to be derived from the 'axiom' that knowledge
and information are scarce resources. From this, the following
propositions are developed:

PROPOSITION 1. Knowledge in advanced industrial systems
                is an instrument of political power.

1.1 Societal complexity and rapid rates of change have the
     effect of making existing forms of knowledge and infor-

mation obsolete. This increases the demand for new
knowledge and information.

1. 2   The problems of advanced industrial society require
specialized knowledge and information. This establishes
the primary social role of experts.

1. 3   The problems of industrial society are increasingly
amenable to solution through the application of existing
knowledge and information.

1. 4   Because of the technical complexity of most policy
decisions, experts are increasingly brought into the
decisionmaking process to supply specialized information and advice.

1. 5   The political power of experts increases due to this
social role. Politicians, because they are dependent on
experts for knowledge and specialized information,
witness an erosion of political power.

Variants of these propositions can be found in the writings of
such diverse theorists of industrial and postindustrial society as
Daniel Bell, Zbigniew K. Brzezinski, Jean Meynaud, Alain Touraine,
John Kenneth Galbraith, Raymond Aron, and, most obviously,
Jacques Ellul. " Jeffrey Straussman, "Technocratic Counsel and
Societal Guidance, " in Politics and the Future of Industrial Society,
ed. Leon Lindberg (New York: McKay, 1976), pp. 150-51. Italics
in original.

7.   This argument is a condensation of a private communication to the author by Joseph H. Hennessy, December 3, 1973.

8.   Samuel Lieberstein, "Technology, Work, and Sociology in
the USSR: The NOT Movement, " Technology and Culture 16 (1975):
65-66.

9.   See, for example, Frederic J. Fleron, Jr., "Systems
Attributes and Career Attributes: The Soviet Political Leadership
System, 1952-1966, " in Carl Beck, et al., Comparative Communist
Political Leadership (New York: McKay, 1973), pp. 43-85; Robert
Blackwell, "The Soviet Political Elite—Alternative Recruitment
Policies at the Obkom Level, " Comparative Politics 6 (1973): 99-121;
Darrell Hammer, "Brezhnev and the Communist Party, " Soviet
Union 2 (1975): 1-21. Fleron and Hammer analyze recruitment pat-
terns at the national level, and Blackwell analyzes them at the pro-
vincial level.

10.   For example, see Richard Judy, "The Economists, " in
Interest Groups in Soviet Politics, ed. H. Gordon Skilling and
Franklyn Griffiths (Princeton, N. J.: Princeton University Press,
1971), pp. 209-51.

11.   See Erik P. Hoffmann, "Soviet Information Processing:
Recent Theory and Experience, " Soviet Union 2 (1975): 22-49; Erik

P. Hoffmann, "Soviet Metapolicy: Information Processing in the Communist Party of the Soviet Union," Journal of Comparative Administration 5 (1973): 200–32.

12. Carl Linden forcefully makes this case in reference to Khrushchev, in Khrushchev and the Soviet Leadership, 1957–1964 (Baltimore: Johns Hopkins University Press, 1966).

13. For lists of the technical benefits and costs of computerized data systems, see Anthony Downs, "The Political Payoffs in Urban Information Systems, " in Information Technology in a Democracy, ed. Alan Westin (Cambridge: Harvard University Press, 1971), pp. 312–13.

14. See Hoffmann, "Soviet Information Processing, " op. cit.; Hoffmann, "Soviet Metapolicy, " op. cit.

15. The five following observations draw heavily from an unpublished essay by Erik Lindell.

16. Michel Tatu, Power in the Kremlin from Khrushchev to Kosygin (New York: Viking, 1969).

17. T. H. Rigby, "The Soviet Leadership: Towards a Self-stabilizing Oligarchy?" Soviet Studies 22 (1970): 167–91.

18. On the concept of political "cost, " see Fleron, op. cit., pp. 44 ff.

19. On "dual executives, " see George Fischer, The Soviet System and Modern Society (New York: Atherton, 1968).

20. On the effectiveness of Party control over the military in the formulation of national policy, see William Odom, "Who Controls Whom in Moscow?" Foreign Policy 19 (1975): 109–23; William Odom, "The Party Connection, " Problems of Communism 22 no. 5 (1973): 12–26.

21. Jeremy Azrael, Managerial Power and Soviet Politics (Cambridge: Harvard University Press, 1966); Jeremy Azrael, "The Managers, " in Political Leadership in Eastern Europe and the Soviet Union, ed. Barry Farrell (Chicago: Aldine, 1970), pp. 224–48. See Albert Parry, The New Class Divided: Science and Technology versus Communism (New York: Macmillan, 1966).

22. Richard Judy wrote in 1968, "Although part of a supposedly centralized and planned economy, the Soviet computer industry displays an amazing degree of fragmentation and lack of coordination. Responsibilities for design, manufacture, installation, maintenance, operations, and software development are distributed among a multitude of organizations. The result is that no single organization has overall responsibility for satisfactory research, development, and operation of computing systems. " Richard Judy, "The Case of Computer Technology, " in East-West Trade and the Technology Gap, ed. Stanislaw Wasowski (New York: Praeger, 1970), p. 67. Judy's conclusion would seem to corroborate my analysis above. In 1972 a

"super computing agency" was created—the All-Union Scientific Research Institute of Problems of Organization and Management—which was subordinated to the State Committee on Science and Technology of the USSR Council of Ministers and headed by D. G. Zhimerin, First Deputy Chairman of that committee. This is not an all-powerful agency, however, for instance, the Ministry of the Radio Industry still produces the complex hardware, and various agencies are responsible for training computer experts, staffing computer centers, and assigning and monitoring computer work. In short, an important step has been taken toward alleviating the coordination problems described by Judy, but all of the same problems still seem to persist in present-day efforts to utilize the new "third generation" Riad computers. Thus effective centralization of the computer industry and group cohesiveness in the computer profession almost surely do not exist. See, for example, Soviet Cybernetics Review 2 (1972): 2-29; Soviet Cybernetics Review 3 (1973): 2-17; Soviet Cybernetics Review 4 (1974): 2-10.

23. For example, see Donald Schwartz, "Decisionmaking, Administrative Decentralization, and Feedback Mechanisms: Comparisons of Soviet and Western Models," Studies in Comparative Communism 7 (1974): 146-83.

24. Zbigniew K. Brzezinski, Between Two Ages (New York: Viking, 1971), especially Part 3.

25. Mihailo Marković, From Affluence to Praxis: Philosophy and Social Criticism (Ann Arbor: University of Michigan Press, 1974), pp. 229 ff.

26. Roy Medvedev, On Socialist Democracy (New York: Knopf, 1975), pp. 30-47 ff.

27. For example, Leonid Brezhnev, "Otchetnyi doklad Tsentral'nogo Komiteta KPSS XXIV s'ezdu Kommunisticheskoi Partii Sovetskogo Soiuza," in Materialy XXIV s'ezda KPSS (Moscow: Politizdat, 1971), pp. 3-106; G. E. Glezerman, Istoricheskii materializm i razvitie sotsialisticheskogo obshchestva (Moscow: Politizdat, 1973).

28. One of the most cautious and insightful statements on this subject is offered by Dzherman M. Gvishiani. "The intensive rationalization and technicalization of decisionmaking results in decisions becoming not only more adequate but also more impersonal, lacking any imprint of individuality, intuition or value preferences of the persons making them." D. M. Gvishiani, "Scientific and Technological Revolution and Scientific and Technological Policy," paper presented at the VIII World Congress of Sociology, Toronto, August 17-24, 1974, pp. 4-5.

29. E. M. Babosov, "Scientific and Technological Revolution: The Growing Role of Scientific and Technological Intelligentsia,"

paper presented at the VIII World Congress of Sociology, Toronto, August 17-24, 1974, p. 14.

30. Ibid., pp. 15-16. My emphasis.

31. Ibid., p. 16.

32. Radovan Richta, "Scientific and Technological Revolution and Prospects of Social Development," paper presented at the VIII World Congress of Sociology, Toronto, August 17-24, 1974, p. 25.

33. "An alternative explanation of the social role of experts focuses on the process of legitimation . . . [or] symbolic ratification. Stated in propositional form, this alternative assessment states:

> PROPOSITION 2. The primary social role of experts is to legitimize policy decisions made by the real holders of power.
>
> 2.1 Major policy alternatives pose value choices that are inherently conflictual.
>
> 2.2 Value disparities reflect the balance of power within the political system.
>
> 2.3 Choice, therefore, symbolizes the 'victory' of a particular structure of power.
>
> 2.4 After the decision is made, policymakers look for ways to legitimize their decisions. Technical explanations and justifications serve to diffuse conflict.
>
> 2.5 The image of the expert who is 'above politics' is a useful legitimizing tool. Moreover, since they are expendable, experts serve as convenient scapegoats for policies that have failed.

Straussman, op. cit., pp. 151-52. Italics in original. See note 6.

34. These seven points closely paraphrase Downs, op. cit., pp. 316-18.

35. Franco Ferraresi, "Structure, Power, and Technology in Complex Organizations: The Case of Automated Data Processing in Public Administration," paper presented at the eighth World Congress of Sociology, Toronto, August 17-24, 1974, p. 4.

36. Downs, op. cit., pp. 320-21.

37. Ferraresi, op. cit., p. 27. See above.

38. "The distant future may tell a different story, but in the early 1970s it requires a powerful flight of ideological or philosophical imagination to go from the current pedestrian uses being made of computers to move paper and perform basic transactions to anything resembling sophisticated, data-rich decisionmaking" [in the civilian agencies of the national, state, and local governments] of the United States. From Alan Westin, "Information Technology and Public Decision-Making," abstract in Harvard University Program

on Technology and Society, 1964-1972: A Final Review (Cambridge, Mass.: Harvard University Press, 1972), pp. 60, 65-66. See also Kenneth Laudon, Computers and Bureaucratic Reform (New York: Wiley, 1974).

39. For example, Ferraresi, op. cit., pp. 8-17.

40. Straussman, op. cit., pp. 144-45.

41. Westin, op. cit., p. 66.

42. Ferraresi, op. cit., p. 15.

43. On Eastern Europe, see for example, Thomas Baylis, The Technical Intelligentsia and the East German Elite (Berkeley: University of California Press, 1974); David Kraus, et al., National Science Information Systems: A Guide to Science Information Systems in Bulgaria, Czechoslovakia, Hungary, Poland, Romania, and Yugoslavia (Cambridge: MIT Press, 1972); Longin Pastusiak, Komputery a polityka (Warsaw: Wiedza Powszechna, 1975).

44. See for example, Medvedev, op. cit., p. 300; Hoffman, "Soviet Information Processing," op. cit., p. 41.

45. I. A. Shvets, "Vnutripartiinaia informatsiia—instrument rukovodstva, sredstvo vospitaniia i kontrolia," Partiinaia zhizn' 12 (1975): 26.

46. See, for example, the important collective works Man, Science, Technology (Moscow-Prague: Academia, 1973); Partiia i sovremennaia nauchno-tekhnicheskaia revoliutsiia v SSSR (Moscow: Politizdat, 1974). See also, V. G. Afanas'ev, Sotsial'naia informatsiia i upravlenie obshchestvom (Moscow: Politizdat, 1975); V. G. Afanas'ev Nauchnoe upravlenie obshchestvom, Izdanie 2 (Moscow: Politizdat, 1973); V. G. Afanas'ev Nauchno-tekhnicheskaia revoliutsiia, upravlenie, obrazovanie (Moscow: Politizdat, 1972).

47. Hammer, op. cit.

48. See Hoffmann, "Soviet Information Processing," op. cit.; Hoffmann, "Soviet Metapolicy," op. cit.

49. The concept of "rationalization" of information flows is a flexible one. It is instructive to compare the sections on this topic in Richta, et al., op. cit., pp. 240-43 and the revised Russian-Czech version, Nauchno-tekhnicheskaia revoliutsiia i sotsializm (Moscow: Politizdat, 1973), pp. 290-93. The two sections are virtually identical.

50. Brezhnev, op. cit., p. 57. Emphasis in original.

51. Jean-Jacques Salomon, Science and Politics (Cambridge: MIT Press, 1973), pp. 60 ff.

52. John Hazard, The Soviet System of Government (4th ed., Chicago: University of Chicago Press, 1968), pp. 201-14 ff.

53. See for example, Loren Graham, Science and Philosophy in the Soviet Union (New York: Vintage, 1974), especially Chapter 9 on cybernetics; Moshe Lewin, Political Undercurrents in Soviet

Economic Debates (Princeton, N.J.: Princeton University
Press, 1974); John P. Hardt, et.al., Mathematics and Computers
in Soviet Economic Planning (New Haven: Yale University Press,
1967). On Eastern Europe, see especially Peter Ludz, The Changing
Party Elite in East Germany (Cambridge: MIT Press, 1972).

54. Afanas'ev, Sotsial'naia informatsiia, op. cit., p. 307.

55. Iurii Volkov, "The System of Power and Democratic Institutions," Social Sciences (Moscow), 6, no. 3 (1975): 118-19, 122.
See also Man, Science, Technology, op. cit.; Partiia i sovremennaia nauchno-tekhnicheskaia revoliutsiia v SSSR, op. cit.; Afanas'ev,
Sotsial'naia informatsiia, op. cit.; Afanas'ev, Nauchnoe upravlenie
okshchestrom, op. cit., Afanas'ev, Nauchno-tekhnicheskaia, op.
oit.; Hammer, op. cit. Soviet and Western scholars differ, of
course, in their identification of the fundamental characteristics of
the Soviet system.

56. Iurii Tikhomirov, "The Socio-Political Nature of Management," Social Sciences (Moscow) 4 (1973): 73. Soviet appeals to
strengthen "the democratic principles of management" are essentially calls to broaden specialist elite participation in operational
decision making, rather than strategic policy making, at all levels
of economic management.

57. Viktor Glushkov, "Scientific and Technological Progress
in Management," Social Sciences 4 (1973): 56, 59.

58. Richard Lowenthal, "On 'Established' Communist Party
Regimes," Studies in Comparative Communism 7 (1974): 353, 356 ff.

59. Baylis, op. cit., p. 18.

60. Samuel Huntington, "Social and Institutional Dynamics of
One-Party Systems," in Authoritarian Politics in Modern Society,
ed. Samuel Huntington and Clement Moore (New York: Basic Books,
1970), p. 33.

61. Medvedev, op. cit., pp. 300 ff.

62. Straussman, op. cit., pp. 143-45 ff.

63. Emmanuel G. Mesthene, "The Study of Technology and
Society: Methods and Issues," in Harvard University Program on
Technology and Society, op. cit., p. 9. For a forceful critique of
Mesthene and the Harvard project, including some observations
pertinent to contemporary Soviet social theory, see William Leiss,
"The Social Consequences of Technological Progress: Critical Com-
ments on Recent Theories," Canadian Public Administration 13, no.
3 (1970): 246-62.

10

TECHNOLOGY, MEDICINE, AND "VETERINARISM": THE WESTERN AND COMMUNIST EXPERIENCE

Mark G. Field

A casual perusal of almost any Western medical journal is likely to yield an abundance of advertisements by pharmaceutical firms touting the virtues of their wares. In recent years the psycho-active drugs in particular have been peddled to physicians[1] with great vigor and great profits to the industry. The emphasis in the copy is usually on the radical transformation of the patient's condition or mood: he or she, crippled by despondency, paralyzed by emotional problems, or neurotically unable to face daily tasks at home or at work, is restored to "normal" functioning. The message also often hints that the patient will be eternally grateful to the physician who, with his magic pill, has solved his or her "problems."

The pill must be considered, in the context of our discussion, "technology"; it is an instrument, an artifact, a tool, a piece of capital equipment that, we assume, performs at least two functions: (1) it has some effect on the disease or dysfunction or, as the case might be, on the symptomatology, and (2), like any other piece of capital equipment it is often, but not necessarily,[2] labor saving—that is, it substitutes capital for labor intensity. In psychiatric (and general medical) practice, for example, instead of spending hours

This paper is part of my general work in the sociology of medicine, and more particularly of my interest in the comparative study of health systems with special emphasis on the U.S. and Soviet health systems. In the last few years this work has been, in part, supported by Grant R01HS 00272 from the National Center for Health Services Research, Health Resources Administration, Public Health Service, U.S. Department of Health, Education and Welfare.

fathoming the roots of the patient's "trouble" and providing the
emotional support and sympathy that has traditionally been associated
with the healer's role, a few minutes are devoted to rapid conversation, accompanied by scribbling on the prescription pad, and the
patient is on the way. The next one can be processed just as expedi-
tiously. The number of patients the physician can see increases; and
science, technology, and medicine have scored another triumph.

The above sketch is obviously a caricature. It is not meant to
downgrade the "miracles" wrought by medical equipment and the
"wonder drugs." In a life-and-death situation, an antibiotic will be
preferred over sympathy and reassurance. However, my intention
is to draw attention to an area of human activity in which technology
plays an increasingly important role in the West as well as in communist countries, but where relatively little attention has been paid
compared, for instance, to technology in industry and in the military.
It is my contention that this is also an important domain for testing
the congruence, or lack of, between Western-style technology, its
derivative technical rationality, and communist goal-culture. Medicine, by its very nature, is both a "humane" occupation concerned
with the well-being of individuals and groups and with the application
of scientific knowledge and technical rationality to the handling of
morbid conditions.

This concern is entirely consistent with the avowed goals of
communist society. The argument I will advance later on is that the
impact of technology and technical rationality upon medicine has
immensely increased its ability to deal with an ever-wider range of
conditions and problems, East and West. At the same time, this
very technology and rationality have introduced into the clinical
setting a disturbing element that interposes itself between the pro-
vider of services and the emotional and psychological needs of the
patient. It thus affects that "humane" aspect mentioned earlier. I do
not find, at least in the Soviet Union, that communist goal culture
has mitigated the consequences of the introduction of technology into
medicine in any perceptible way. Indeed, I would add that I find concern about that problem to be more salient in the West than in Soviet
society, though not unnoticed there.

In this chapter I shall briefly sketch, as background, the history and development of the Soviet health system[3] and raise certain
questions about the nature of that development, and particularly
about the consequences, in the organization and management of the
Soviet health service, of the introduction not only of technical
rationality but also of such goals as universal coverage, equity in
treatment, gratuity of services, and controlled deployment of health
resources (particularly personnel).[4] I shall then turn my attention
to the specific case of the organization of the Soviet pharmaceutical

system, and particularly to some of the consequences deriving from
a rational, bureaucratic blueprint for attending to the pharmaceutical
needs of the Soviet population. This will be contrasted to the situation of the United States, with its "capitalist" and profit-motive orientation. Finally, I will venture for a few moments into the Communist
Chinese medical scene, point to some of the present differences
between the Soviet and Chinese health systems, attempt to account
for some of these differences, and then try to look into the future of
health systems and technology in industrial societies, whether "communist" or not.

SOVIET MEDICINE

When the Soviet regime seized power in the fall of 1917, Russia
was in the third year of a ruinous war. Its economy was in shambles;
its transportation system was crippled; and the health of its population was rapidly deteriorating. Russia was suffering from the epidemics and pandemics that were the usual travel companions of war
and famine. Their very existence posed a problem of major magnitude to the new regime, which was precariously attempting to rule
the immense empire it had seized (or inherited) from tsarism and
the Provisional Government. It would be fair to say that the problem
was almost one of physical survival. "Either the lice destroy socialism or socialism destroys the lice, " Lenin tersely declared in 1919,
referring particularly to typhus.[5] Thus, the first years of the Soviet
regime, until about 1924-25, were dominated by the devastating
impact of epidemic diseases and a subsequent high mortality rate
caused by the lack of adequate food, the weakened condition of the
population, and the absence of drugs (formerly produced and imported from abroad) and of even such simple disinfectants as soap.[6]

It is under these circumstances that the Soviet health system
was born (officially in July 1918), and it was natural that its original
orientation was to mass epidemics, and thus eventually to the prevention of conditions that would lead to, or facilitate, the spread of
such epidemics. This orientation, born of necessity during the early
years, was thus much more to public health than to clinical medicine.
Although over the years some important shifts have taken place in
the direction of much greater emphasis on clinical medicine, the
basic institutional features of the Soviet health system, forged in the
early years of the regime, have remained more or less the same
until today. These aspects, which I have outlined in some detail
elsewhere,[7] are worthy of brief summation here:

1. Public health, as well as clinical medicine, medical
research, health manpower training, and the design and pro-

duction of medical equipment and pharmaceuticals, are the
responsibility of the polity and of the community and not left
to voluntary, charitable, or private initiative and action. This
means, among other things, that all health resources—hospitals, clinics, laboratories, medical and nursing schools,
pharmacies and pharmaceutical plants, and so on—belong to
the state (nationalized) and are managed and financed as public
institutions. It also means that all health personnel, including
and particularly physicians, are state employees and members
of a civil service. The medical profession, which under tsarism had enjoyed a fair amount of autonomy, politically and
occupationally, was destroyed as a corporate group, as were
other "liberal" professions, such as the legal profession, and
reduced to "medical workers," salaried by the state and subject, of course, to state-determined postings. It may be noted
for the historical record that the early years of the Soviet
health system were characterized by a "class approach" in
medicine. This meant that old regime physicians, except
those few who had cast their lot with the new regime, were
considered as the former exploiters of the medical proletariat
(nurses, feldshers, orderlies) and often found themselves subordinate to, and taking orders from, that proletariat, who
were supposed to know better where the peoples' interests lay.
This drive against the medical (and other) professions must be
seen through the optic of a leftist revolutionary ideology that
tends to regard professions as a conspiracy against the public,
shrouding their activities in mystery, immune to public control, and basically exploitative of the people. Such hostility
and suspicion toward physicians as professionals and as specialists has disappeared from Soviet society but can be seen
operating in other societies, for example in contemporary
China and in Allende's Chile, and gives fuel for the antimedicalism in the West, which is best epitomized by Illich's Medical Nemesis, [8] and to which I will return later. Although
Soviet physicians have regained their undisputed leading positions over subordinate health personnel, their political power,
and for the most part their financial status, remain relatively
and absolutely low. There is indeed, in the Soviet Union, no
medical profession as a corporate group with political power
and the right to negotiate or bargain with the polity. [9]

We must look upon the Soviet health system as it has
evolved and as it exists today, as a national system of socialized medicine that is financed, organized, and managed by the
state as a public service and not as an insurance system (as
in France, Japan, or Germany), a prepayment health service

system (as in England), or a mixed, pluralistic system (as in the United States).[10] The centralization of the health system, its standardization, its bureaucratization, and its governmental management and control thus make the health system a fairly pliable instrument of governmental policy and action.

2. In theory the health system and all the measures it implements regarding the health level and health care of the population are closely articulated with the policies and programs of the government and are thus integrated into the national and subnational planning schemes. Planning for health is expected to be in line with general planning. It must be compatible with other sectors of the society that also require scarce resources in facilities and personnel. It must also contribute to the general programs and priorities of the regime. The responsibility of the health system is to decrease, insofar as possible, the impact of morbidity, trauma, invalidity, and premature mortality on the work capacity of the population.

3. As noted earlier, health and almost all related services are provided to the population as a public service, and thus are gratuitous at the time of use; it is in this respect that they are "free". Since nothing in the real world is free, however, these services are financed from general revenues, particularly from the turnover tax imposed on all consumer goods. In essence, the Soviet citizen pays or prepays for health services through involutary contributions to the state treasury and the loss of discretionary income. The only major exception to this rule of gratuity is for pharmaceuticals purchased by patients and prescribed for outpatient ambulatory use. For a certain specified list of chronic conditions (diabetes, for example), the necessary drugs are available to the patient free of charge. In addition, members of the Soviet political, intellectual, artistic and other elites receive their medical services in so-called "closed" institutions reserved for them and their families as perquisites of rank, for which they make no additional payments.[11] Functionally, these "closed" medical installations are the equivalent of either the private pavilions of Western hospitals or of the medical facilities placed at the disposal of members of the U.S. Congress. Access to these facilities ceases when the individual does not hold the position anymore.

4. Prevention is always prominently mentioned as the keystone of Soviet health services. This is hardly surprising, particularly in view of the conditions prevalent at the birth of Soviet socialized medicine as mentioned earlier. I must add, however, that from observations and general knowledge, the

weight of preventive activities in the total activities of the
health system seems relatively modest and probably not radically different from what we see in the West. At present the
major preventive program being promoted is called "dispensarization." Dispensarization means the constant supervision
of the health of the population, the healthy as well as the sick,
through periodic examinations and checkups. The purpose of
dispensarization is the early detection of morbid and premor-
bid conditions on the assumption that these forms are easier
to treat and reverse than advanced ones. The Soviets claim
that at the present time only certain groups of the population
are completely covered by that program (school children and
workers in occupationally dangerous industries) but that by
1990 the entire population will be "dispensarized."

5. The policy of unity of theory and practice, which is
derived from Marxism, holds that medicine, and particularly
medical research, must be oriented to the "real" problems of
the population and should not be frittered away into intellectually interesting but pragmatically sterile research. This
pragmatic injunction, of course, runs into the core of the
usual dilemma in medical research between basic and applied,
or directed and programmed, efforts. It is my impression
that since the mid-1960s the medical research establishment
(particularly the Academy of Medical Sciences USSR) has been
increasingly free to indulge in basic medical research on the
assumption that eventually the breakthroughs will have practical implications and that short-term, applied research does
not necessarily hold out the promise of eventual solutions. At
the same time, and this goes without saying, the orientation
of Soviet medicine and of the Soviet health system is to science
and technology in the sense in which it is understood in the
West, and not as far as I can see to any specific Soviet interpretation of scientific and technological rationality.

6. The need for popular support brings up the left-wing,
populist, and socialistically derived principle that the health
system and the physicians are really incapable of helping the
population if they are "detached," or set apart from and above
the population. The population, in turn, must help manage the
health system. It must assist the physicians and the nurses;
the health system is "theirs." It is set up for their benefit:
they must participate in it and make it a genuinely popular
endeavor. I would say, as I have noted earlier, that these
views were certainly prominent in the early years of the Soviet
regime and health system; that they approximate (in their
ideological formulation) what we now see in Mainland China

and Castro's Cuba; but that over the years actual participation of the people in the management of their health services has become more symbolic than real; that as the Soviet health system has become increasingly professionalized (in the narrow sense of the word), specialized, bureaucratized, and hierarchic, that principle has had little manifest impact on the system.

It is true, of course, that every health ministry or department, national or republican, is administratively a component part of the Soviet governmental structure, from which it derives its specific mandate and from which it receives its logistic support. If by the Soviets we mean the "people," then the health system is run by the people. In effect, however, I see little evidence of genuine popular participation or even of the type of consumerism or community participation that has recently developed in the West, and in the United States particularly. This is perhaps because such activities are difficult to mesh with an increasingly technical and complex area such as modern medicine, and with reference to the Soviet Union to the deep respect and awe in which specialists and specialization are held. This makes genuine cooperation between health personnel and the general public difficult.

7. An implicit priority order is observed. As long as health services remain a relatively scarce and expensive commodity, the regime will allocate these services on a priority basis, the highest priority going to those who, in the eyes of the regime, perform the most important tasks. Roughly speaking, it means, as seen earlier, that the elites (political and intellectual) get the best that is available (or if not available, imported from abroad), followed by qualified workers in critical industries, and so on down the line, with the peasant population receiving (probably quite differently from the Chinese case), the short end of the medical stick.

These features or principles constitute the basic framework of the Soviet health system. It would take us too far afield to describe how well they are implemented in practice and the manner in which the system makes primary, secondary, and tertiary care available to the population either by the territorial or the occupational networks. I have described these at length elsewhere.[12]

What I want to do is come back to the theme of the use of equipment and technology in modern medicine.

There is little doubt that, over the last hundred years, medicine as a process of intervention in illness and other health-related conditions has achieved a high level of effectiveness and that the

greater part of that effectiveness is due to the application of scientific knowledge to morbid conditions by way of technology. It has been
said that up to about 1910 the average American visiting the average
physician had only one chance in two of benefiting from the encounter.

Since then the odds have changed drastically in favor of the
benefits, as I suggested in the early part of this paper, the increased
use of technology and medical equipment, the increased division of
medical labor that accompanies specialization and superspecializa-
tion, the bureaucratic structures that emerge for the management,
financing, and provision of health services and the employment of
health personnel have tended to alienate the patient from the
provider(s) of care. No computer knows how to hold hands! Furthermore, it seems that most patients suffer primarily from simple and
self-limiting conditions. What they seek from the medical encounter
is a kind of emotional support and reassurance, traditionally associated with the "pastoral" functions of the physician.

This support is often not forthcoming. Often a technological
fix is offered the patient instead of personalized concern. In addition,
the seemingly inexorable growth in the division of medical labor not
only depersonalizes the clinical encounter but, in the light of the
disappearance of generalists, leads to the lack of integrative mechanisms and agents that could knit together the increasingly narrow
outputs of specialists into a comprehensive "medical product." This
latter problem is a technical one, probably most evident in the highly
instrumented, research-oriented university hospital but in general
endemic throughout the health system.

Without going as far as Illich,[13] who claims that society would
be better off without a specialized health system (he claims that the
system as presently constituted is "counterproductive", that is, that
it causes illness and mortality), I would say that the existence of
technology and an advanced division of labor sometimes conspire to
create a kind of medicine of the absurd, a Kafka-like situation in
which technological abundance coexists with therapeutic poverty.

Given this concern in the West[14] about some of the consequences of technological rationality in a field in which human emotions are so heavily engaged, I have on several occasions looked at
the Soviet health system to see whether a different approach might
be detected there. In the course of more than 20 years of studying
the Soviet health system, including seven visits to the USSR between
1956 and 1975, I do not find much, if any, evidence that the Communist goal-culture has had an impact in altering or softening the brunt
of technical rationality in the health care area. Indeed, in terms of
an evolution of the health system, the Soviets seem to be still at the
stage in which the belief is overwhelming that science, technology,
and rationality, if properly applied, will solve most of the health

problems of their society. Medical equipment is endlessly mentioned
and exhibited with pride to foreign visitors; it is held to be the hallmark of medical progress and modernity. Equipment is also the
element that Soviet medical visitors to the United States seem most
eager to see and learn about and if possible import or emulate.

At the same time, it is fairly clear that the organization of
medical services in the Soviet Union is bureaucratic to its very core.
In June 1975 I met with a deputy Health Minister USSR in Moscow.
His first words were to the effect that the Soviet health system was
governmentally run, that it was centralized, and that the Health
Ministry was the "general-staff of the medical system." The military analogy is perhaps not accidental; it tallies with Lenin's conception of the Party and also that of Stalin: not only centralized and
militarized, but hierarchical, rational, specialized, and so on. As
such, this bureaucratic organization suffers from the usual problems of such structures everywhere: "formalism," inordinate red-
tape, slowness in decision making, avoidance of responsiblity,
"bunching up of bureaucrats for mutual protection," and frequently
indifference to those it is mandated to serve. Even though the Soviet
health system has a highest per capita supply of physicians in the
world[15] (although such figures must be interpreted very carefully
before comparisons with other countries can be made[16]), and even
though one might assume on this basis that Soviet medicine can
afford to be labor-intensive, reports from the Soviet Union suggest
that the ordinary Soviet patient is subjected to the same problems as
with regard to other consumer goods and services: long waiting
lines, inordinate red tape and formalities, insufficient time with the
physician, rudeness and often cruelty on the part of providers, lack
of equipment and amenities, "assembly-line" methods, and so on.[17]

From time to time, but not too often, one will see in the Soviet
press letters or articles complaining about the situation, which
often has tragic implications for the victims,[18] but if I read the
literature correctly, the "ideal" against which the contemporary
medical scene is held is not derived from the communist goal-culture as such, as much as it is from the code of behavior and ethics
of the progressive Russian physicians of the second half of the
nineteenth century and the early part of the twentieth, particularly
the sense of dedication, devotion, and humaneness of the Zemstvo
physicians or of such idealized clinicians as Botkin or Chekhov.

SOVIET PHARMACEUTICALS

I have referred to the highly rational and bureaucratic nature
of the Soviet health system, and I began this paper with a discussion
of the significance, in contemporary medical practice, of pharma-

ceuticals. Since pharmaceuticals do represent an important aspect
of the armamentarium of medicine in any society, I would like to
briefly discuss the background and major findings of a series of
studies I conducted (at times in cooperation with Raymond A. Bauer)
on the U.S. and the Soviet pharmaceutical systems.[19] The impetus
for such studies was the fact that in the United States the pharmaceutical industry has come under severe attack and criticism for
many of its practices. Among the targets of such criticism are the
relatively (some would say unconscionable) high profits of the industry; the tendency to rush into large-scale production and distribution
of pharmaceuticals before they have been thoroughly tested in clinical practice; the production of drugs that are only a slight variation
or a combination of already available products, which are presented
as innovations; the very high costs of promotional practices, and
particularly the existence of a large body of detail men who visit
physicians and sell their firms' products; and, as perhaps the most
important consequences of such a system, the high costs borne by
the consumer at the time of purchase—time when the consumer is
presumably least able to afford them. If the major problems inherent in the U.S. pharmaceutical scene are seen as the result of a
special form of economic organization, or as the organizers of this
conference might call it, "capitalistic rationality," which means
that it derives from a commercial and profit-oriented entrepreneur-
ial system, then one important alternative for a basic restructuring
of the pharmaceutical system might entail such elements as greater
governmental (that is, nonprivate, federal) involvement and supervision of the pharmaceutical system for the benefit of the people
rather than of private firms. Another might be the discouragement,
if not outright elimination, of current promotional practices, including detail men, to be replaced by a "rational" system of informing
physicians of the availability of new pharmaceutical products, their
indications and contraindications, and so on. There might be a
rationalization of research, to be conducted in federal laboratories,
separate from manufacturing. There might be better supervision of
clinical testing, with elimination of costly and unnecessary duplication and the development of redundant products. All these would
result in a radically cheaper product to the consumer and a better,
more intelligent use of scarce societal resources.

This blueprint, which seems to evolve logically, if not dia-
lectically, from a critical examination of the major failings of the
U.S. (or capitalist) pharmaceutical system and the removal of most
of its "negative" features, resembles the Soviet approach to the
question in many, if not most, respects. This approach thus constitutes an already available experiment in a radically different (and
noncapitalistic) arrangement for supplying the pharmaceutical needs

of a large population. The Soviet pharmaceutical system (research, testing, manufacturing, distribution, retailing, and promotion) is governmentally owned, planned, operated, financed, and managed. It is centralized, bureaucratic, and theoretically rationally operated. Its parts are integrated with each other. It does not, of course, embody as its primary rationale a profit orientation; it is aimed at economizing resources and investments and the maximization of social utility. It does not embody a philosophy of aggressive promotion and advertisement but relies on the good sense of physicians in keeping abreast of new developments and in reading sober announcements in the medical press about new items. It includes the principle of fixed and relatively low or subsidized prices to the consumer.

An examination of the Soviet pharmaceutical system as it works in practice, based solely on Soviet sources, reveals very serious flaws in its operations.[20] Newly discovered and successfully tested preparations are slow, and sometimes fail altogether, to effect the transition from research and development to mass production. The institutional separation of research from mass production is one of the major obstacles to a swift move from one to the other. The lack of financial incentives for manufacturing plants to undertake retooling for new products and the difficulty of recovering the start-up costs in the selling price often motivate managers to continue producing the same drugs they have in the past rather than risk not fulfilling their fiscal plans. In other words, they risk being penalized for innovating. Additional complaints center on the fact that not only are new items often unavailable in the pharmacies, but that this is also true of long-established and familiar preparations, which for a variety of reasons are in short supply.[21] Thus, while the overriding concern of the U.S. consumer is the high cost of pharmaceuticals at the purchase point, the Soviet consumer worries more about the sheer availability of the product.

There are other aspects of the Soviet system that were quite unexpected. For example, the Soviet sources note that the lack of an aggressive promotional policy or advertising techniques means that busy physicians simply do not learn of the availability of new items and keep prescribing the same old remedies they learned about in school, thus wasting sizeable investments in the development, production, and distribution of new drugs. Just as the U.S. system is criticized for wasteful practices associated with detail men and the cost of these practices to the ultimate consumer, Soviet sources complain of a lack of direct channels of effective personal communication between the pharmaceutical system and physicians. They urge, for example, that pharmacists make it their business to maintain liaisons with the clinics and appear periodically before physi-

cians' meetings or clinical conferences to brief them on what is
available in the pharmacies, what is new, what can be substituted
for what, and so on. Indeed, a survey of the specialized sources
indicates that they urge, time and again, that they (the Soviets) borrow devices and ideas from the "capitalistic" world to improve their
own operations within the pharmaceutical system. The upshot of
these studies is that most of the criticisms made of the U.S. system
were "mirrored," so to speak, in the Soviet situation. The Soviets
were criticizing their system precisely for not adopting many of the
structural and institutional features that are often criticized in the
United States.

In conclusion, this comparative examination of a "capitalistic"
and "socialistic" system for provisioning a population with pharmaceuticals fails to reveal any new approaches or a new "socialist"
technical rationality. One might suggest, at least from the discom-
fort sometimes expressed in the West about the interposition of
technology between the patient and the physician, that the Soviets
might suggest that an inadequate provision of pharmaceuticals might
be a positive trade-off in the name of socialist technicality. If this
is so, I must report I have found no evidence of it in any of the
studies conducted. What I have found are a series of complaints
about how inadequately the system works and suggestions for changes
that would bring the system more in line with the situation under
capitalism.

THE CHINESE AND SOVIET HEALTH SYSTEMS

I would like in this last section to briefly highlight some similarities and differences between the Chinese and the Soviet health
systems. [22] Let me deal with the similarities first, as follows:

1. The health systems of both countries, as well as
those of the Eastern European countries of the Soviet block and
Cuba, are "socialized" or "public" in the sense that I defined
above in examining the basic characteristics of the Soviet
health system.
2. The two regimes look upon the health systems "in-
strumentally," because health means the capacity to perform
occupational and other tasks and is thus seen as a natural and
national resource. It is this view that justifies the considerable
manpower and material resources the two regimes have been
willing to invest in that sector, in view of many competing
claims and the overall scarcity of resources.

3. Both countries early ceased to outlaw physicians
with presumably "bourgeois" prerevolutionary associations
as political entities.

The areas of difference are more numerous. Following are
some of the distinctive ones:

1. The most dramatic or visible difference is the
absence, in the Soviet Union, of a charismatic personality
such as Mao and, in the context of the present discussion, of
his interest in health and medicine.

2. The overt dislike shown by Mao for the city and
urban life, when compared to the land and the village, has
certainly contributed to the official antiurban cast of the Chinese health system and to the apparently successful shifting
of manpower and resources away from the city to the countryside. The Soviet Union, on the other hand, is definitely
oriented to the city, and from all evidence the health services
in the countryside and at the village level have been neglected
from almost all points of view. The Soviet regime has tried to
shift manpower to the countryside and originally was all set
to phase out the feldsher system as a kind of second-class
medicine unworthy of equal Soviet citizens. It has, however,
never been successful in providing physicians for the villages
and it has continued to rely on the feldshers. It is now structuring a health system in which the rural populations will be
directed from the villages, by semiprofessional health
screening personnel, to more specialized medical installations
in provincial centers, staffed by physicians.

3. The Soviet health system is much more centralized
and bureaucratized than its Chinese counterpart, although the
degree of centralization is somewhat less than it was at the
time of Stalin's death.

4. In the Soviet Union the specialist is held in great
esteem and indeed glorified. This is in contrast to the suspicion and dislike for the specialist, including the Western-
trained physician, in China. This dislike is probably part of
the feeling that specialists in whatever field use their skills
and knowledge to set themselves apart from the rest of the
population, and thus away from the socialist-egalitarian cast
of the regime. As noted earlier, antagonism toward the
specialist was also present in the early years of the Soviet
regime.

5. Perhaps the most revealing and important difference
I find in the two systems, which is apparently also the result

of Mao's personal intervention and suggestions, is in the
emphasis and on the legitimation of traditional Chinese medicine alongside Western medicine. The resurrection, enthrone-
ment, and official support of traditional Chinese medicine is
one of the more intriguing developments in the People's
Republic. This development may well be due to that aspect of
"reactive nationalism" one finds in technologically backward
societies in the throes of development. It is perhaps a kind of
compensating mechanism for a feeling of inferiority. It
asserts itself through the glorification of the cultural past of
the society and the assertion of the essential superiority of
its cultural heritage and past over that of the modern West.
In addition, there is no doubt in my mind that the legitimation
of traditional Chinese medicine, as a parallel medical stream
to Western medicine, has a strongly practical dimension in
making services available to large groups of the rural population that would otherwise be unreachable. I think this is where
the barefoot doctor fits in.

When we look at the Soviet scene, the only phenomenon
remotely resembling it was the famous (and notorious) Russian
"priorities" campaign mounted in the post-World War II years
and mercifully dismantled or toned down after Stalin died. The
major purpose of that campaign was also to wean the Soviet
people from a sense of inferiority toward the West. This well-
orchestrated propaganda effort hit the health system and
particularly medical research, leading, for example, to the
canonization of Pavlov's findings and methods of research and
the obsessive search for "firsts." In the course of that episode
there were certainly many references to popular Russian folk
medicine and calls for increased investigation and clinical
testing of the efficacy of herbal preparations, prompted, one
might suspect, by the perennial shortage of pharmaceuticals
noted earlier. However, there was not, as far as I could
detect, any enshrinement of a popular or folk or "Russian"
medicine equivalent to traditional Chinese medicine, as
equally legitimate and parallel to Western medicine. Indeed,
the Soviet arguments were entirely within the canons of
scientific Western medicine, and the claim for Russian
medicine was that it was as good as, if not superior to,
Western scientific medicine.

The Chinese medical scene thus represents, in my view, a
somewhat different approach to the structuring of health services
and certainly differs, in that technical rationality, from both the
Soviet and the U.S. or Western model. There are, as noted earlier,

certain themes in it that are reminiscent of what obtained in the Soviet Union immediately after the Revolution, and indeed until the beginning of the five-year plans. Some of these themes incidentally also appeared, in a somewhat altered form, in the United States in the 1960s in connection with agitation for a better health delivery system for the urban poor and the black ghettos. Such was the concept of the community (or neighborhood) health clinic or center sponsored by the U.S. Office of Economic Opportunity.

I would suspect that much of this phenomenon in the Chinese context is due first to the lack of sufficient resources, of enough Western-trained physicians, of enough medical technology and pharmaceuticals, combined of course with the emphasis on rural rather than urban settings. This tendency is further reinforced by feelings of national pride and cultural superiority over the West.

It is also true that in the health area, as in many others, the Chinese are still experimenting. They are trying to utilize techniques and concepts that they have inherited from the past, which they feel are better adapted to their situation and certainly more available and affordable. By contrast to the decentralized, innovative, rural-oriented, and experimental Chinese health system, the Soviet scene has crystallized into a deadly administrative bore. The Chinese also, and wisely, have avoided establishing a health system based on the most advanced models of the West, which are singularly inappropriate to developing nations. They are inappropriate because they lead to the investment of extremely scarce resources, in manpower and money, into high-technology facilities benefitting only an infinitesimal number of people and depriving the rest of the population of simpler and fundamental services for common ailments and problems. How much of what we see on the Chinese medical scene is a different type of technical rationality deriving from the goal-culture of communism I am not prepared to say.

It might be interesting to speculate about the future of the health system now that Mao is dead. My own reading would be that his passing away might well signal a decrease in the salience of the health question in the Chinese priority scheme. It might eventually lead to a downgrading of traditional Chinese remedies and personnel, to be replaced by the more conventional and technically oriented medicine of the Soviet or Western type. It may lead to the adoption of some of the organizational devices and patterns used in dealing with the health problems in the Soviet Union and the West. I would not be surprised if Western-type physicians gained the upper hand, not as a politically organized group (or lobby) but in demonstrating and claiming the functional superiority of scientific (Western-type) medicine and the importance of technology and pharmaceuticals. I have recently seen indications[23] that the training of barefoot doctors is becoming lengthier, more specialized, more professional. Indeed, I will not be surprised if, a quarter of a century from now, the bare-foot doctor will be just a fond memory in the pages of the history of the Chinese health system. Neither will I be surprised if, in the long run, both the bureaucratic elements and the technological con-straints of scientific medicine lead to structures resembling those in the Soviet Union and those emerging in the West. With those, the problems outlined earlier, having to do with the alienation of the patient in an increasingly technical medical system, may well also appear in China.

CONCLUSION

What I have hinted at in this paper is the possibility of a con-vergence of the health systems of modern societies despite ideolog-ical, goal-culture, political, and historical differences. This con-vergence is fueled by the twin dynamics of an increasing effective demand for health services for the population under an ever-larger set of conditions and by the universal constraints brought about by medical technology. Indeed, I would presume that the introduction of technology into the health system and the justification for such an introduction follow lines that are quite different from the introduc-tion of machinery and technology in industry. Since medicine deals with human life and with suffering, the strict calculus of costs and benefits often cannot be applied or justified.

The convergence, if there is one, will be in the direction of a health system that many in the West find not wholly desirable and sometimes even thoroughly objectionable. That view manifests itself in the West, at least, in a rising tide of antimedicalism. Ivan Illich, whose name I have mentioned several times, seems to best epitomize that trend (in its non-Marxist incarnation). I see Illich casting him-self in the role of a Martin Luther attacking a powerful and bloated medical establishment whose priests have appropriated and monop-olized the medical salvation of the population and have thus alienated the public from its own health and health care.

No such strong attacks have appeared, to my knowledge, in the Soviet Union, although the concern about the impact of technol-ogy on medicine has been expressed from time to time. This trend is sometimes termed "veterinarism," meaning a highly scientific and technological, but narrow, approach to human beings as physical entities, as organisms, and the neglect of the personal and emotional factors that enter health and illness. A. Bilibin of the Academy of Medical Sciences USSR, has written the following:

> A few scholars remark with sorrow that medicine, to a
> certain decree "veterinarizes itself." Clearly for the
> treatment of an animal a natural science approach is
> sufficient. . . . To treat a human being such an ap-
> proach must be supplemented with experience, taking
> into consideration psychological laws and data obtained
> with methods based on the so-called clinical mentality.
> . . . If during the period of investigation the personal-
> ity of the patient escapes the attention of the physician,
> then in spite of all his erudition, there is a trend
> toward veterinarism. [24]

Professor Bilibin is thus careful to distinguish a scientific approach
to the patient from what he calls the clinical approach, which considers the patient as a person, with his own peculiarities and emotions. Failure to emphasize the latter can only mean clinical failure.

It is strange indeed (or is it?) that at the very moment when
modern society (East and West) is becoming increasingly impersonal, medicine, this humane endeavor par excellence, by becoming
addicted to the rational, scientific, and technological approach to
illness is increasingly alienating itself from the patient as a human
being. Medicine and the health system everywhere seem to be
caught in the same bind as other elements of modern society: the
contemporary, highly instrumented research and the teaching-
oriented hospital, for example, are analogs of the automated industrial plant, the large corporate office, the supermarket, or even
the multiversity. Nevertheless, individuals, when they are sick,
still expect from the physician (or from someone) that kind of
personal attention, emotional support, indeed "love"—support and
reassurance that have been traditional aspects of medicine. They
often find that the modern health system is not equipped to provide
that counter to the alienation noted earlier, that the physician,
trained in the scientific method, is often more at ease in the laboratory than in the clinic. Even psychiatry is following this trend,
particularly in the Soviet Union, where it fits well with the material-
ist ideology, of prescribing pills rather than personal comfort and
sympathy. I would have liked to have perceived different trends in
communist societies, but so far this search has not been very
successful.

NOTES

1. It is a peculiarity of advertisements of "ethical" drugs
that they are aimed at the medical profession and not the general

public. Thus the physician must be "sold," and the patient buys only by direction of the doctor. There is no concept of "ethical" drug advertising in the Soviet Union.

2. The introduction of equipment in medicine essentially means that something can be done that often could not be done before, such as renal dialysis. As such, this equipment usually needs additional personnel to use it, monitor it, maintain it, and so on. It may be health saving, life saving, or life prolonging, but it is usually not labor saving.

3. The term "medical system" and "health system" will be used interchangeably here. "Health system" is a more comprehensive term, and in previous papers I have used it to define the totality of the resources and efforts any society invests in the health of its population. In the Soviet Union, the ministry concerned with that question is called the Ministry of Health Protection (zdravookhranenie). See for example, Mark G. Field, "The Health Care System of Industrialized Society: The Disappearance of the General Practitioner and Some Implications," in Human Aspects of Biological Innovation, ed., Everett L. Mendelsohn, Judith P. Swazey, and Irene Taviss (Cambridge: Harvard University Press, 1971), pp. 156-80; Mark G. Field, "The Concept of the 'Health System' at the Macrosociological Level," Social Science and Medicine 7 (October 1973); 763-85. For a more specific comparison between the United States and the Soviet Union, see Mark G. Field, "Health as a 'Public Utility' or the 'Maintenance of Capacity' in Soviet Society," in Social Consequences of Modernization in Communist Societies, ed. Mark G. Field (Baltimore: Johns Hopkins University Press, 1976), pp. 234-64.

4. For a brief review of Western interest in, and work on, the Soviet health system, see Mark G. Field, "Health as a 'Public Utility'," op. cit, pp. 262-63. To that list one should add Michael Kaser, Health Care in the Soviet Union and Eastern Europe (London: Croom Helm, 1976).

5. Cited in Mark G. Field, Soviet Socialized Medicine: An Introduction (New York: Free Press, 1967), p. 52.

6. N. A. Vinogradov and I. D. Strashun, Okhrana zdorovia trudiashikhsia v Sovetskom Soiuze (Moscow, 1947), pp. 6-7.

7. See Mark G. Field, Doctor and Patient in Soviet Russia (Cambridge: Harvard University Press, 1957); Field, Soviet Socialized Medicine, op. cit.

8. Ivan Illich, Medical Nemesis (New York: Pantheon Books, 1976). A revised version of this book has recently been published as Limits to Medicine (New York: Pantheon Books, 1976).

9. See, on this, Mark G. Field, "Taming a Profession: Early Phases of Soviet Medicine," Bulletin of the New York Academy of Medicine, second series, 48 (April 14, 1971): 83-92.

10. For an attempt at a typology of ideal-types of national health systems, see Mark G. Field, "Prospects for the Comparative Sociology of Medicine: An Effort at Conceptualization," Current Research in Sociology, ed. Margaret S. Archer, Current Sociology, Supplementary Volume 1 (the Hague: Mouton, 1974), pp. 147-83.

11. For a recent reference to closed medical facilities and particularly the "Kremlin Clinic," see Hedrick Smith, The Russians (New York: Quadrangle, 1976), pp. 33 ff.

12. Field, Doctor and Patient, op. cit.; Field, Soviet Socialized Medicine, op. cit.

13. Illich, op. cit.

14. A whole literature on this subject has grown, ranging from the Rousseauian, romantic critique of Illich to left-wing attacks on the exploitation of illness under capitalism, epitomized, for example, in Howard Waitzkin and Barbara Waterman, The Exploitation of Illness in Capitalist Society (New York: Bobbs Merrill, 1974); or Vicente Navarro, Medicine Under Capitalism (New York: Prodist, 1976); and going through literally hundreds of "middle-of-the-road" studies.

15. See Mark G. Field, "Health Personnel in the Soviet Union: Achievements and Problems," American Journal of Public Health 56 (November 1966): 1904-20; Mark G. Field, "American and Soviet Medical Manpower," International Journal of Health Services 5 (1975): 455-74.

16. Ibid.

17. On this, see Mark G. Field, "Soviet Medical Practice: Five Case Histories," Review of Soviet Medical Sciences 7, no. 2 (1970): 1-12.

18. Ibid.

19. See Raymond A. Bauer and Mark G. Field, "Ironic Contrast: US and USSR Drug Industries," Harvard Business Review 40 (September-October 1962): 89-97. Raymond A. Bauer and Mark G. Field, The Soviet and the American Pharmaceutical Systems: Some Paradoxical Contrasts, (mimeographed, Cambridge, Mass.: Arthur D. Little, 1961), also available in U.S., Congress, House of Representatives, Hearings before the Committee on Interstate and Foreign Commerce, 86th Cong., 2nd sess. (Washington, D.C.: Government Printing Office, 1962), pp. 344-55; Mark G. Field, The Soviet Pharmaceutical System: Administration and Operation-1966, (mimeographed, Cambridge, Mass.: Arthur D. Little, 1966); Natasha Lissman and Mark G. Field, The Soviet Pharmaceutical System Revisited—Developments, 1965-1972, a mimeographed monograph for Public Policy Research, Pfizer, Inc., December 1972.

20. Ibid.

21.　Smith also notes the perennial shortage of pharmaceuticals. Smith, op. cit, p. 35.

22.　A fuller version of this can be found in comments on Michel Oksenberg in Mark G. Field, "The Chinese Policy Process and the Public Health Issues: An Arena Approach, " Studies in Comparative Communism 7, no. 4 (Winter 1974): 374–408; and Mark G. Field, "Health and the Polity: Communist China and Soviet Russia," both in Studies in Comparative Communism 7, no. 4 (Winter 1974): 421–25. It is interesting to note how much more attention, comparatively, has been paid in the West to the Chinese approaches in health care than to the Soviet approach and to speculate on the reasons for this. See, for example, the China Health Studies, published for the U.S. Department of Health, Education and Welfare by the Geographic Health Studies Project of the John E. Fogarty International Center for Advanced Study in the Health Sciences, one of which is Medicine in Chinese Cultures: Comparative Studies of Health Care in Chinese and other Societies, ed. Arthur Kleinman, Peter Kunstadter, E. Russell Alexander, and James L. Gale (Washington, D.C.: Government Printing Office, 1975).

23.　From conversations with Peter New of the University of Toronto.

24.　A. Bilibin, "Vrach-eto myslitel," Meditsinskaia Gazeta, October 25, 1968, p. 3.

The foregoing chapters contain a variety of perspectives on
our main concern in this volume, which is the impact of technology
transfer on the development of communist culture. It would be an
enormous task to attempt a systematic comparison of the findings
of these contributions relative to the existing literature on the subject; therefore, to entitle this concluding chapter "The Conclusion"
would be presumptuous indeed. Hence, these sketchy and schematic
concluding remarks bear the title "Afterword." However, in the
spirit of the activities of the ACLS Planning Group on Comparative
Communist Studies and of the intention of the conference to explore
and give impetus to new directions in the comparative study of
socialist systems, these comments are also intended (perhaps even
primarily intended) as a foreword to future studies.

During the conference discussions, it became clear that at
least four distinct theories of the relationship between technology
and society were being propounded, either implicity or explicitly:
the neutrality theory of technology, technological determinism, the
theory of the scientific and technological revolution (STR), and the
ambivalence theory of technology. For present purposes it will be
useful to outline the major points of these four theories, since they
each arrive at different conclusions about the relationship between
communist culture and technology, and then to show their relationship to the historical-cultural approach outlined in the introduction,
which we will refer to here for purposes of identification as the
mediation theory of technology.

THE NEUTRALITY THEORY OF TECHNOLOGY

Theories of technological neutrality view technology as having
no particular consequences for social organization and the nontechnical aspects of culture. Advocates of this position hold that technology itself is therefore neutral concerning its particular applications. It can be used for good or evil purposes or both, but its
particular applications and applicability are not foreordained or
determined or contained within itself. In this view, technology is
technology. There is no such thing as "good" technology or "bad"
technology, "capitalist" technology or "socialist" technology; there
is merely technology. The "good" or "evil," "capitalist" or "social-

ist" depends solely on the uses to which it is put, and the uses are
purely external to it, not predetermined by it. This view is, of
course, eminently compatible with, and in fact historically and
intellectually related to, the so-called fact-value distinction, by
which facts and the material world are seen to stand "out there" in
full view and all readiness for scientific scrutiny and material
progress whereas values and political choices lurk in the shadows
of human emotionality and/or the cloudy rarified regions of spirits
and gods. This fact-value distinction is one of many related and
false dichotomies of the modern Western philosophical tradition that
are crucial to this problem, if for no other reason than that Marxism
claims for socialism and only socialism the ability to transcend
them in reality.

The neutrality theory is epitomized in the following passage
from The Conquest of Nature by R. J. Forbes:

> The technologist can only argue in defense of his art
> that his creative act produces an end that is neither
> good nor bad. Technological problems, like those of
> science, recognize only a correct or an incorrect solu-
> tion; the value judgments of "good" and "bad" come
> only when the solution is applied to the affairs of men.
> It is as a social and political animal that the technol-
> ogist is required to ask himself whether his particular
> technological act is necessary to the common good and
> whether the application of his skills may produce un-
> intended consequences along with the good or neutral
> results he can readily foresee. [1]

The view that technology is neutral with respect to the ends
for which it is employed has found its way into the study of the impact of Western technology on communist societies and was expressed by a colleague in our conference discussions as follows (reported here closely but not verbatim):

> Since it is a confusion to say that the uses of technology
> are necessarily related to the quality or particular
> characteristics of that technology, it follows that mod-
> ern industrial technology can be used in the service of
> capitalism as well as socialism without any necessary
> particular social consequences in either. Granting that
> there may be certain imperatives involved in the use of

computers (such as the technical competence necessary
to make the computer in the first place), that does not
necessarily mean that the computer must dominate social thought or that a society must become dependent
upon the computer. The computer can be a useful tool
just as the hammer can be a useful, or destructive,
tool. In short, technology is neutral with respect to
social goals. We can say that the computer (or any technical hardware) is neutral in that it can be used for
good or evil purposes. Quite simply, it can be used by
good guys or it can be used by bad guys. Or, to make the
same point somewhat differently, lasers can be utilized
for good (medical) ends as well as evil (military) ends.
In the case of technology transfer, very often the patterns of social behavior and social goals that are made
possible by the technology are adopted along with the
technology, but that would be for reasons other than
those connected with the technology itself. (Emphasis
added)

In such a formulation there is an implicit but unclear distinction within technology, and it is further unclear which is viewed as
neutral, the nature of the thing produced or the process of production, or both. The above formulation seems to focus our attention
primarily on the thing produced by the technology—the end product—
rather the social consequences of the technological process itself.
It must be noted that this distinction itself is more and more difficult
to make as what we might call postproduction technologies increasingly become the product of capitalist material and cultural development. These process-entailing "products" fairly fling at us the
implications of their adoption, and in this regard another conference
colleague remarked that he failed to see how a computer is in any
way neutral in terms of social organization and social power, being
one of the most complex and expertise-dependent types of technology
imaginable. In contrast, he suggested, a hammer is a much more
egalitarian instrument.

TECHNOLOGICAL DETERMINISM

One of the most widespread interpretations of the relationship
between technology and society is that of technological determinism,
which holds that there is some form of inner logic or dynamic in
modern industrial technology that results in similar social consequences regardless of the setting. John Kenneth Galbraith and

Jacques Ellul are perhaps the most widely read exponents of this
view. The basic message of Galbraith's work The New Industrial
State is as follows:

> It is part of the vanity of modern man that he can decide
> the character of his economic system. His area of deci-
> sion is, in fact, exceedingly small. He could, conceiv-
> ably, decide whether or not he wishes to have a high
> level of industrialization. Thereafter, the imperatives
> of organization, technology and planning operate simi-
> larly, and we have seen to a broadly similar result,
> on all societies. Given the decision to have modern
> industry, much of what happens is inevitable and the
> same.[2]

Once the decision is made to opt in favor of modern industrial technology, then, the pattern of social consequences will be determined
by these "imperatives of technology." As one observer has summarized this theory, "Something in the 'nature' of modern industry sets
the limits of human options once it is adopted."[3]

In introducing his six major imperatives of technology (increasing span of time, increase in capital commitment, increasing
inflexibility of commitment, specialized manpower, specialized
organization, and planning), Galbraith argues:

> Nearly all of the consequences of technology, and much
> of the shape of modern industry derive from this need
> to divide and subdivide tasks and from the further need to
> bring knowledge to bear on these fractions and from the
> final need to combine the finished elements of the task
> into the finished product as a whole.[4]

All of this involves an increase in the degree of social differentiation, a process that William Taubman insightfully labels "the great
hope of convergence theory.[5]

It must be pointed out here that theories of technological determinism are not usually concerned with the particular social, cultural, or historical sources of elements of the imperatives of technology. Rather, those imperatives are merely taken for granted.
That they exist is all that matters; never mind from whence they
came. To illustrate, another conference colleague made the following point:

> It is unnecessary and even confusing to apply any adjec-
> tive to the term "technology." (In this sense, my col-

league agrees with Galbraith, although contrary to
Galbraith he feels that we have to be explicit about
the goals of a communist society.) For example, suppose a human who landed on the moon returns to earth
with some sort of stuff that has the hardness of steel
and the invisibility of glass. Then suppose we set about
discussing the impact of this stuff on a communist
society. One cannot imagine any purpose for which
one would want to inquire whether it was produced in
a capitalist or a socialist society. The technology has
nothing to do with where it was produced. We are only
interested in its impact on the communist society. For
that reason, it is not necessary to know whether it was
"capitalist" technology or "socialist" technology. Putting the adjective on "technology" serves no useful
purpose and only confuses things. It is the hardware
itself that is important. Now we may also be interested
in the fact that certain types of hardware tend to be
produced in a communist society, but that is of no
interest in trying to answer the question: What is the
impact of this technology on communism? It is not
necessary to know the native origin of the technology
in order to determine its impact on society.

As with our technology-is-neutral colleague, a confusion can be
seen here between technology as a process of production and the end
product of that process. To repeat, with the qualifications already
noted, technology refers to the process, the means and the instruments of production, not to its products.

Four contributors to this volume explicitly accept the concept
of "imperatives of technology" and the technological determinism it
implies. Richard Baum, in his survey of technical, managerial, and
social structures and their relations in Chinese industrial enterprises (emphasis added),

found little evidence to support extreme claims that
substantial numbers of "new communist men" have
been successfully resocialized in what are still essentially old technobureaucratic institutions or that ideologically induced voluntarism, unsupported by substantial differential material benefits, has provided
an effective, long-lasting antidote to more conventional
("bourgeois") patterns of incentive and motivation.
. . . [The result is that] "in contemporary China,
as elsewhere in the industrialized world, the porten-

tious figures of the technician and the bureaucrat have
become prominent, if not dominant, features of the
organizational landscape.

Rensselaer W. Lee III argues that the imperatives of technological change "may eventually force a retreat from Maoist precepts of technical mobilization." The high incidence of mass technical participation in China, he argues, is conditioned and perhaps
even made possible

> by the semimechanized character of much PRC produc-
> tion. . . . At higher levels of modernization, the im-
> peratives of technology, at least in Soviet and Western
> experience, are likely to establish increasingly rigid
> constraints upon the contributions that purely practical
> knowledge can make to the further modernization of
> industry.

Mark G. Field concludes his comparison of Chinese, Soviet,
and Western health care systems by suggesting (emphasis added)

> the possibility of a convergence of the health systems
> of modern societies despite ideological, goal-culture,
> political, and historical differences. This convergence
> is fueled by the twin dynamics of an increasingly effec-
> tive demand for health services for the population for
> an ever larger set of conditions and by the constraints
> brought about by medical technology.

In his analysis of technology transfer into China, Robert F.
Dernberger commented on the technological imperatives "set loose
by these complete plant imports and the foreign technicians who
accompanied them." Accordingly, "the Cultural Revolution itself
can be seen as the Maoists' last stand against the technological
imperatives that had been generated in China's socialist revolution
over the previous two decades."

Dernberger never questions the existence of technological
imperatives. He merely suggests that their impact on China has
been limited to the modern, large-scale industrial sector, which is
relatively small in comparison to the rural, small-scale sector of
the economy. The latter has so far been able to ward off the imperatives of technology. Thus Dernberger's criticism of Baum's analysis
hinges not on the acceptance or rejection of the notion of technological imperatives but rather on the empirical question of how much
these imperatives have pervaded Chinese society and culture. If and

when the Chinese opt in favor of high technology in the rural, small-scale sector of the economy, then presumably the "imperatives of technology" will be felt there as well. There is nothing in Dernberger's analysis indicating disagreement with such a possibility, and his interpretation can therefore be said to fit into the category of technological determinism.

Certainly we must investigate the possibility that particular modes of production and technological hardware place constraints on the range of possible social choices. Robert L. Heilbroner has stated the problem as follows:

> Modes of production establish constraints with which
> humanity must come to terms, and the constraints of
> the industrial mode are peculiarly demanding. The
> rhythms of industrial production are not those of nature,
> nor are its necessary uniformities easily adapted to the
> varieties of human nature. While surely capable of being
> used for more humane purposes than we have seen
> hitherto, while no doubt capable of greater flexibility
> and much greater individual control, industrial produc-
> tion nonetheless confronts men with machines that
> embody "imperatives" if they are to be used at all,
> and these imperatives lead easily to the organization of
> work, of life, even of thought, in ways that accommodate
> men to machines rather than the much more difficult
> alternative. [6]

However, it is important to note that technological determinism does seem to reflect in extreme form the ethnocentric limitations that each of our perspectives has to some degree. (See Andrew L. Feenberg's excellent discussion of the methodological implications of this problem for communist studies, in the section of Chapter 1 entitled "Transition or Convergence?") One's own cultural experience can most easily be seen as the only possible "response" to technological development. This results in the inability to see widely different perspectives on the problem. In this case it has most probably resulted from the fact that the notion of the imperatives of technology is derived from an ahistorical (and noncomparative) analysis of technological development. A more satisfactory approach that can at least entertain the possibility of alternative technologies and technical cultures is one that is based on concrete historical analysis of the interaction (really, the interpenetration) of technology and culture.

THE THEORY OF THE SCIENTIFIC
AND TECHNOLOGICAL REVOLUTION

According to at least the most prominent authors, and most notably the Soviet ones, the theory of the scientific and technological revolution (STR) that has developed in the last two decades holds that the technology developed during the last two centuries of the Industrial Revolution contained both objective and subjective elements. This distinction between objective and subjective elements can be illustrated well with reference to social organization and management. For the limited purposes of these comments it will serve as the only major example: in the STR theory the distinction is widely applied. Dzhorman M. Gvishiani, deputy chairman of the USSR State Committee for Science and Technology, has written as follows:

> Even though the function of organizing combined labor emerged on the basis of capitalist production, it is conditioned not by the specific features of that system, but by the basic objective features of large-scale social production in general. This, however, does not mean that we should regard that function irrespectively of the mode of production: it does not proceed in a social vacuum. The antagonistic relations of production determine the concrete historical form in which it is implemented.[7]

Writing about the period of capitalist development, when the management and ownership functions became separated out and performed by different people, Gvishiani observes that the manager then

> fulfills the entire function of management, including both its aspects: the work of management, stemming from the nature of large-scale social production, and the labour of "superintendence," which reflects the antagonistic nature of production.[8]

In this context the "management" function is objective in that it is required by the very nature of large-scale social production, whereas the "superintendence" function is subjective in that it merely "implements and protects the interests of the capitalists."[9]

In this view capitalism is an historically progressive force, in that it permits the development of these objective elements of organization and management:

Modern American "business management" organically
combines refined exploitation of the working people with
the latest achievements in the field of organization and
management, which reflect the demands of large-scale
machine production. [10]

But these objective elements cannot fully develop under capitalism
because they are in ultimate contradiction with the subjective requirements of capitalist production:

Under capitalism, as Marx pointed out, science stands
opposed to the worker as a force of capital. . . . [While
on the one hand] it would be absured to deny the actual
achievements of science and technology in the conditions
of contemporary capitalism, . . . [it is also necessary
to recognize that] the sole motive force of scientific and
technological progress in bourgeois society has been, and
remains, the quest for profit, the desire of the given
factory or corporation to utilize one or another scientific
achievement to the detriment of its competitors. [11]

Under conditions of capitalist society, therefore,

science and technology advance in an exceptionally contradictory way squandering their potential and ruling
out any possibility of scientific co-operation on the
scale of the entire society. [12]

. . .

A rational organization of production management
on a social scale, similar to that being effected at the
enterprise level, is impossible under the bourgeois
system because of the domination of capitalist relations
of production. This determines also the basic features
of the capitalist theory of organization and management,
and notably the limits within which bourgeois research
is conducted into that sphere. [13]

. . .

It is not surprising that the development of the
scientific and technological revolution further exacer-
bates the basic contradictions of capitalism, bringing
out the incompatibility of all-round development of
society's productive forces with the capitalist system. [14]

In sharp contrast to capitalism, the socialist system "removes all
obstacles" [15] and "creates the most favourable objective conditions" [16]
for the general advance of science and technology.

How does socialism create such favorable objective conditions
in this view? According to Gvishiani:

> Under socialism the social aspect of management does
> not oppose the organizational and technical aspects,
> but forms its basis and promotes its success. . . .
> The socialist mode of production removes the obstacles
> capitalism places in the way of a rational solution of
> the management problem and of bringing the forms
> and methods of management into correspondence with
> the requirements of modern, rapidly developing large-
> scale production. Socialist production relations en-
> gender qualitatively new, consistently progressive
> management methods, corresponding to the require-
> ments of accelerated economic development. [17]

Thus the "rationality" of socialism is said to be congruent with the
"rationality" of large-scale social production, whereas the "rationality" of capitalism is rooted in the profit motive and is therefore
contradictory to the "rationality" of large-scale social production.

Perhaps the crucial link in bringing about this situation is the
changing relationship between the form and the content of technology
as it develops under capitalism. "Production, which under capitalism involves not only the creation of material values, but also
exploitation, acquires a new social content as soon as socialist
economic relations are established."[18] This formulation permits
the utilization of "capitalist forms" during the period of socialism,
as long as these forms are imbued with a new socialist content.
Indeed, as Gvishiani points out, "Lenin attached great importance
to studying and making use of the bourgeois experience of industrial
organization"[19] and even referred to the Taylor system of scientific
management as " 'capitalism's last word' in the organization and
management of production. "[20] Lenin believed that "a distinction
should be made between its scientific achievements, reflecting the
actual nature of large-scale social production, and those of its
standards that were conditioned by the needs of capitalist exploitation. "[21]

Taylorism, then, is said to combine both subjective elements
and the objective characteristics of large-scale social production.
The former are the repressive and exploitative content of Taylorism; the latter are the progressive and potentially liberatory forms.
These two elements of Taylorism represent a contradiction that can
be overcome by replacing the subjective and exploitative capitalist
content with a new socialist content that would have the effect of
bringing the social aspect into harmony with the organizational and

technical aspects, that is, the objective forms of large-scale social
production.

In reply to this particular attempt to locate the development
of modern industrial production technology in the social production
system of capitalism, one could argue that the "objective logic" of
large-scale forms of social organization not only developed from
but were organically rooted in the "subjective principle of the division of labor." In contrast to attempts to separate out progressive
objective elements from the exploitative and repressive subjective
elements, I would deny the ability to make such a dissection of
reality by arguing that the forms were born within a particular
historical-cultural system of production forces and cannot be
separated out from it. Such a view would maintain that capitalism
provided not only the specific content, but also the very forms themselves. I would also in general deny the validity of a rigid distinction between subjective and objective factors, as of between form
and content, positing instead a dialectical interrelationship, if not
an essential identity, with the distinction being the result of the
position of the perceiver.

The "form versus content" question reappears in the ambivalence theory and in fact is central to any effort to understand the
impact of capitalist technology on socialist societies in communist
theories of the STR.

Gvishiani summarizes the role of technology under communism
as follows:

> Communist society . . . is built and developed on the
> basis of the highest achievements of science, technology,
> and organization. The scientific and technological revol-
> ution is historically concrete, definite way of building
> the material and technical basis of communism. [22]

This principle is still so much a part of Soviet thinking that Gvishiani can quote with approval Lenin's claim that

> socialism is merely the next step forward from state-
> capitalist monopoly. Or, in other words, socialism is
> merely state-capitalist monopoly which is made to
> serve the interests of the whole people and has to that
> extent ceased to be a capitalist monopoly. [23]

A major problem, however, is that

> the subjective activity of people will not necessarily
> coincide with the objective trends of social production.

> To make subjective actions conform with the objective
> possibilities of optimizing production under socialism,
> all administrators must fully and clearly understand
> the objective advantages of the socialist economic sys-
> tem. [24]

What this clearly implies is that there is a certain similarity
between some theories of the STR and technological determinism.
Insofar as the STR perpetuates the Cartesian and Kantian subject-
object distinction, it perfectly sets up the problematic for a resolution by an "objective" technology that is the embodiment of reason
itself. As in the United State of Zamyatin's We, human choice no
longer exists, and indeed, is no longer necessary, since subjective
calculations of individual human rationality can only be brought into
alignment with the objective rationality of large-scale social production. Thereby freedom is surpassed.

Gvishiani criticizes "the desire of bourgeois writers to present
the capitalist forms of organization of the production process as universal and unrelated to any definite socio-economic formation."[25]
His own view of the STR, however, is to take certain elements of
those forms and declare them as universal and objective. The net
result is a variation on the theme of technological determinism. In
both cases the result is that some elements of productive relations
in the historical development of technology under capitalism are
given a degree of independence or autonomy from the historical-
cultural forces that produced them. In both cases those isolated
factors are viewed as universal, objective, and natural forces in
the development of technology, resulting in a common theme of
technology fetishism and technological determinism. The determinist element of this Soviet theory of the STR is quite consistent with,
and related to, the long-standing Soviet tendency of a mechanical
and determinist interpretation of the theory of stages.

THE THEORY OF AMBIVALENCE

In an effort to transcend the contradictions and difficulties of
the foregoing interpretations of the relationship between technology
and its cultural context, Andrew L. Feenberg has argued as follows:

> According to the theory with which Lenin was familiar,
> the proletariat could consolidate its class hegemony on
> the basis of the old capitalist technology. But class
> power determines what potentialities in the given tech-
> nical heritage are developed and which others are

stunted. <u>Technique</u> (and culture) <u>is not neutral but ambiv-
alent</u>, capable of various alternative developments, of
growing according to different class criteria. [26]

Feenberg accepts as the central point of traditional discussions
of the transition:

> the capacity of the proletariat to master the old tech-
> nology and administration and improve it, and not its
> ability to create something radically new. . . . The
> main concern is with the possibility of starting out
> from the capitalist heritage. [27]
>
> . . .
>
> It was by reversing the capitalist cultural policy
> that Lenin hoped to <u>instill a new class content in the
> old organizational forms</u> and promote the eventual
> transformation of the infrastructure under commu-
> nism. [28]

Feenberg draws our attention as follows to Claudin-Urondo's
discussion of the significance of three related elements in Lenin's
concept of culture, which were culture as civilization, culture as
knowledge, and culture as ideology:

> "Culture-civilization" is the material and spiritual
> heritage of a society, the ultimate measure of its level
> of development. For Lenin there was one single cultural
> continuum, the advanced capitalist countries located at
> the top of the scale and Russia far below. "Culture-
> knowledge" is the general culture and skills required
> to participate intelligently in the economic and social
> life of a modern nation. This Russia must acquire in
> order to build a high level of civilization, which is a
> pre-condition of socialism. Finally, there is "culture-
> ideology," strictly class-bound world-views in competi-
> tion for the mind of the masses. Only in this area the
> proletariat must not imitate the bourgeoisie, but de-
> feat it.
>
> In these three definitions of culture there are
> two moments of continuity between capitalist and social-
> ist society and one of rupture: civilization and knowledge
> can be taken over directly from the bourgeoisie and
> turned to new uses while ideology alone must be com-
> batted. The peculiarity of Lenin's conception of cultural
> revolution lies in his belief that the ideological struggle

is won at the levels of civilization and knowledge.
Victory over bourgeois ideology will be assured when
the objective pre-conditions of socialism have been
obtained through the application of bourgeois knowledge
to the problem of building civilization.

Claudin-Urondo argues that Lenin's theory of
cultural revolution underestimates the need for criticism in the appropriation of past culture even as it
over-estimates the power of this appropriation to resolve ideological problems. Lenin overlooked the ideological character of all aspects of culture and subordinated the ideological struggle to an objective process
of development. [29]

Feenberg rejects Claudin-Urondo's criticism of Lenin for retaining
capitalist forms of knowledge and civilization (especially, but not
exclusively, science and technology).

In defending Lenin on this score, Feenberg's argument
resembles in some respects the "objectivist" Soviet position. I cite
as one example the 1968 attack by the Soviet philosophers Iu. A.
Zamoshkin and N. V. Motroshilova on Marcuse's "subjectivist"
critical theory of society, in which they accused him of refusing to
make use of the "tools" made available to him by contemporary
scientific research:

> But is it possible fully to identify the internally con-
> tradictory logic of development of concrete social studies
> with the logic that naturally led to the development of the
> empirical means, techniques, and operational procedures
> and principles of functionalism, with that real, histori-
> cally concrete ideological function that these investiga-
> tions take on in the given social environment, under
> conditions in which the state-monopoly bureaucracy is
> becoming more powerful, under the influence of co-
> option by a given social class? Can one simply throw
> out of the window the scientific techniques and methods
> of collecting representative factual information about
> particular concrete situations and mechanisms, and the
> manifestations of the consciousness of real people, only
> because these techniques and methods are employed
> "by factory inspectors," officials, and "social engi-
> neers" for pursposes formulated by the bureaucracy?
> No; impossible. [30]

In Feenberg's terms, this seems to be an effort to reject the culture-
ideology aspects of capitalist social science while retaining the cul-

ture-knowledge elements. Zamoshkin and Motroshilova reject neither the form nor the content of this knowledge; they reject merely the ideological uses to which it has been put by "factory inspectors, officials, and social engineers for purposes formulated by the [capitalist] bureaucracy." Never mind that this "culture-knowledge" results from the same social division of labor, domination, and hierarchy as other forms of capitalist production. [31] The implication for concrete social practice is that bourgeois social science (especially its techniques) can be used under socialism. Hence, the consequences of the theory of ambivalence come to resemble those of the neutrality theory of technology. However, the ambivalence theory is more politically optimistic: that powerful liberating aspect of technology joins socialism's struggle to realize the new human freedom.

This is the crucial difference in the conceptualization of the content of technology between these two approaches, and that difference leads them in two divergent directions. In the neutrality theory there are no particular values inherent in the technology itself, and that is why, according to that theory, technology is said to be neutral with respect to ends or social goals. Hence all of the values associated with a particular technology come from outside of the technology; they are supplied only by those who use the technology to particular ends. The ambivalence theory starts from a very different assumption about the nature of technology. In this case there are both positive and negative elements in the technology itself. That is, there are both liberatory and repressive elements inherent in industrial technology. Under capitalism some positive, liberatory elements are manifest, but it is mainly the repressive elements that predominate. The task of socialism is to struggle to repress these negative elements while attempting to insure that the positive, liberatory elements predominate.

It is in this context that Feenberg can argue that technological development under capitalism is determined "not so much from the logic of technology as from the interests of capital," a central element of which is the capitalist division between mental and manual labor. This is quite similar to Leiss's formulation of socialist theory and practice "as the determinate negation of capitalism, that is, as the social form that would fall heir to the positive accomplishments wrought by capitalism while overcoming its negative aspects."

THE MEDIATION THEORY OF TECHNOLOGY: AN ALTERNATIVE APPROACH

In my view, the four preceding theories of the impact of "Western" technology on socialist societies suffer from serious shortcomings that render them either so pessimistic (technological determinism) that they do not allow humanity any hope of transcending the problems raised by earlier material creations, or they are so optimistic (theories of the STR and the theory of ambivalence) that they cannot present a satisfactory accounting for obvious contradictions in contemporary socialist societies that are quite obviously related to, but not solely caused by, the utilization of foreign technology, or they would have us accept the (to me) bizarre assumption that there is no connection between the material-technical-cultural forms in society and the goals of that society (the neutrality theory). As was mentioned in the Introduction, in order to understand the impact of foreign technology on socialist societies and cultures, we must analyze the impact of culture and society on technology in its formative stages. Only then can we begin to appraise the actual relationship between technology and culture. Only by coming to grips with the question of the extent to which a particular technology (say, capitalist technology) in its formative stages was a material reflection, embodiment, or reification of dominant cultural values will we be able to progress to a solution of the questions about the impact of that technology on other societies and cultures and the likelihood that those societies will be able to develop alternative or qualitatively modified technologies and cultures.

All four of the theories described above are concerned with the question of the impact of technology on society and culture. I am convinced, however, that there is a necessary prior question that must be answered: What is the impact of society and culture on technology, both in its formative and later stages? Technological determinism and the neutrality theory of technology ignore this question as irrelevant. The STR and ambivalence theories consider the question as relevant but, in my view, arrive at conclusions that fatally underestimate the extent of cultural and social reification in technological forms and content.

In the introduction to this volume I presented the broad outline of an approach that I shall refer to here as the mediation theory of technology, a theory that has yet to be fully developed, the essential element of which is that technology as one of the artifacts of culture embodies the dominant values contained in that culture.

As a product of its particular historical circumstances, the technology that developed under capitalism is a reification and concrete material manifestation of the dominant capitalist idea of maximizing control over labor in order to maximize profits. This control function is reflected not only in the machine itself, but also in the accompanying forms of technical rationality and technical infrastructure. Furthermore, not only is this control function in-

fused in these various elements of capitalist technology in its
formative stages, but it continues to be reinforced through later
refinements. We can see the control function built from the outset
into the factory system and its resulting technology. We encounter
the control function again in Her Majesty's Shipyard at Deptford
where in the late eighteenth century Samuel Bentham (described by
Peter Linebaugh as the Frederick Winslow Taylor of the Royal
Navy) developed a technology for the interchangeability of parts
that revolutionized British shipbuilding, eliminated the infamous
"chips," and thereby removed control of the production process
from the workers and centralized it in management.[32] The control
function was most certainly involved in the purposeful introduction
of labor-saving machinery and the resultant redefinition of job
structures in the U.S. steel industry following the Homestead Strike
of 1892.[33] The time and motion studies of Frederick Taylor's
"Scientific Management" and Frank Gilbreth's cyclograph both
contributed to the definition of a division of labor that permitted a
much more highly rationalized and efficient control function, which
was then literally incorporated into the machine technology itself
as well as into the whole system of technical rationality and technical infrastructure employed in the application and utilization of
that machine technology.[34]

To say that the control function and other elements of capitalist production relations and values are embodied in the technology
during its formative stages and thereafter reinforced at each successive stage of development is not to suggest that the substructural
and cultural reinforcement must continue to be present in order for
the technology to retain those elements of capitalist culture. We
must investigate the possibility that, having been reified in the technology, these elements of capitalist culture attain a degree of
autonomy. As Antonio Gramsci so wisely noted, under capitalism
the superstructure, including, of course, cultural forms, has become increasingly "dense" because of the (quite unanticipated by
Marx) long-term interpenetration of capitalist productive forces
and cultural forms—in this case, by technology.[35] For Gramsci
this density factor meant that it is very difficult to overcome the
subjective (exploitative) elements of culture, and the longer the
period of interpenetration, the more difficult will this revolutionary
project become. Certainly, more than 40 years after Gramsci
wrote this analysis, the process of interpenetration has produced
such a "dense" superstructure that the identification of and triumph
over subjective capitalist elements hailed by Gvishiani and the STR
theories is at least very difficult, although perhaps not completely
impossible.

Despite this warning from an earlier generation of "Western
Marxists," a contemporary critical Marxist philosopher (and one

who has been greatly concerned with the culture-technology interface) could still write the following in 1969:

> Is it still necessary to state that not technology, not
> technique, not the machine are the engines of repression,
> but the presence, in them, of the masters who determine
> their number, their life span, their power, their place
> in life, and the need for them? Is it still necessary to
> repeat that science and technology are the great vehicles
> of liberations, and that it is only their use and restric-
> tion in the repressive society which makes them into
> vehicles of domination?[36]

The mediation theory of technology stands in opposition to this
interpretation and argues, in brief, that it is not possible to take
the master out of the machine he has built as his armor.

Such a position does not necessarily lead to a fetishization of
technology or a disguised version of technological determinism, so
long as the dominant cultural forces reified in and mediated by that
technology are not forgotten. This means merely that form cannot
be separated empirically from content, that when a cultural form
such as technology is transferred to another society it brings with
it a particular cultural content. That cultural content cannot simply
be "purged" from the form by the receiving society. Of course,
elements in the recipient society may struggle against what they
consider to be undesirable consequences of this process. These
efforts may have a greater or lesser mitigating effect, depending
on their nature. That is quite different, however, from suggesting
that it is possible merely to infuse a new class content into old
capitalist forms, since there are very basic and important respects
in which those forms themselves are exploitative and repressive. The
precise nature of efforts to mitigate the perceived undesirable
effects of technology transfer on socialist societies and cultures is
an important phenomenon that remains to be explored carefully and
systematically. In proceeding in that endeavor, we must bear in
mind the fundamental caution that societies explaining themselves as
quite different at the level of political theory may nevertheless be
very similar in certain basic respects. This seemingly self-evident
point is frequently forgotten in contemporary studies of the impact
of Western capitalist ideas and technology on socialist societies and
cultures.

This struggle against the undesirable consequences and effects
of imported capitalist technology and technical rationality is not
ignored by theorists of the STR and the ambivalence theory. As
Julian M. Cooper points out, the IIEiT team has argued that "the

realization of the STR itself and the social changes the STR makes
possible is regarded as necessarily requiring conscious, mass
action within a framework of progressively enhanced socialist
democracy. " Thus political and social class power are necessary
during the period of the transition.

Andrew L. Feenberg is adamant on this point in developing
his theory of ambivalence. For him, the exercise of proletarian
class power is crucial in bending capitalist technology to the service of socialist goals. I mention this point here in fairness to advocates of both theories, who are quite aware of the fact that capitalist technology does not automatically lead to the realization of
socialist goals. Feenberg especially would reject N. I. Bukharin's
position that "all technique (the machine, technical method, etc.)
when introduced into the system of socialist production relations by
that very fact becomes socialist technique."[37] For Feenberg the
ambivalent nature of capitalist technology requires that class power
be used to change the very nature of work and technology.

If for the sake of argument we agree with the position of those
advocating the STR and ambivalence theories that capitalist technology can be, and indeed, for some, must be, used by communists
in the transition from capitalism to socialism, we can still ask:
When will the repressive aspects of this capitalist technology be
transcended? At what point in the development of socialism—in the
period of transition—will the limitations of capitalist technology be
overcome and human liberation thereby be made noticable? What
concrete indicators shall we look for, both in the theory and the
practice of socialism, as signs of this transformation? These are
fair questions, and the proponents of these two theories are obliged
to provide us with some direct answers.

The theory of the STR as described by Cooper does not give
us any clear answers. On the one hand, according to Cooper, there
are Soviet theorists such as V. N. Shevchenko who view the main
aim of the STR as "the 'scientification' (onauchivanie) of all aspects
of social life, including the management of all natural, production
and social processes. " In addition, Cooper stresses the emphasis
in recent Soviet theories of a "new technological solution to the
negative and harmful consequences" of the STR. Both of these views—
the scientification of life and the emphasis on purely technical solutions to all technical and concomitant social problems—are key
characteristics of technocratic thinking. Hence, in my opinion, their
implementation will lead the USSR ever deeper into the morass of an
oppressive technical rationality, not essentially unlike that of capitalism. In addition, part of these technical solutions to technical
and concomitant social problems is the "harnessing of science (both
natural and social) in order to enhance human control over all

aspects of human life on earth." Presumably this would include the domination of all nonhuman nature, a theme that Leiss has described as an essential element of the capitalist mode of social reproduction and which we have discussed earlier as an essential element of capitalist technical rationality.

Some Soviet theorists of the STR appear quite sensitive to these issues. V. G. Marakhov, in particular, is aware of the ecological consequences of the STR and even goes so far as to describe the STR as a double-edged weapon, referring to its positive and negative aspects. Rather than concluding that human beings should live in harmony with nature, however, even Marakhov returns ultimately to the domination of nature theme. In the new style of philosophical thought emerging during the STR, he suggests, man will see himself as the "owner" of the planet!

Nevertheless, I sense great significance in some recent works by the Soviet theorists Marakhov, G. Danilin, G. S. Gudozhnik, and Smirnov that the scientific and technological revolution is only a scientific and technological revolution, followed by the clear suggestion that the present STR will be superseded, in Cooper's words, by "yet another new STR, as a necessary stage in the process of building a developed communist society."

The implication of these writings is that too much capitalist rationality and infrastructure have been retained in the period of the present STR. These are startling implications indeed, and important developments can be expected to follow: they add fuel to speculation in the West that the present-day STR has failed to provide a useful guide to the transition from capitalism to communism. Perhaps this new STR, if it materializes, will point the way toward a genuine transcendence of the technical and a broader cultural domination of capitalist industrialism.

A new STR may be a basis for optimism, but insofar as it is, it will have to deal with the undoing as well as the doing of what has heretofore been considered technological progress. I do not wish to be misunderstood as advocating a Luddite position vis-a-vis the totality of modern capitalist industrialism. While I do not reject the possibility of a radically original path of development, I certainly do not view this as the only possible form of technological development under socialism that could avoid the negative aspects of capitalist technology (the position Feenberg attributes to me). Socialism cannot be made to represent a complete break with the historical past; such an effort would reflect an ahistorical utopianism that is quite incompatible with the mediation approach. At the same time, I am not at all clear how the heritage of elements of capitalist technology, culture, and social institutions can, in Feenberg's words, become "the basis for the realization of new social purposes quite

different from those which inspired its creation." I cannot comprehend
the success of Feenberg's formula for the transition that "the old
forms are given a new class content as a step toward their total
dissolution."

Feenberg's "old organizational forms" are the forms of
antagonistic class relationships. André Gorz states in his paper
pointedly titled "Their Factories and Our People":

> To dominate those who are made to produce and those
> who are enslaved to the goals which are alien to them,
> to the tools with which people impose on them their
> minute mode of employment: the will of domination is
> profoundly inscribed in the nature of the machines,
> in the organization of production, in the division of
> labor which it materializes: capital, its representatives
> and functionaries, on one hand, the supervisors of pro-
> duction, on the other.[38]

This problem is related to the ambivalence theory of technology in the following manner:

> The collective ownership of tools can have two dia-
> metrically opposed effects: it can subordinate social
> relations to the exigency of the tools, like putting men
> in the service of machines in a manner more effective
> yet than capitalism. Such is the essence of Stalinism.
> Or, on the contrary, collective ownership of tools can
> signify that the community is engaging in employing the
> tools to promote convival social relations.[39]

Thus even the collective ownership of the means of production does
not solve the problem of the ambivalence of technology; it merely
raises it to another level. For Gorz this ambivalence is perpetuated
in the following manner:

> It is the technology of the factory which imposes a cer-
> tain technical division of labor, which in turn exacts a
> certain type of subordination, of hierarchy and of
> despotism. . . . As long as the material matrix re-
> mains unchanged, "the collective appropriation" of
> the mass of factories can only be a perfectly abstract
> transfer of legal property, a transfer which will be
> incapable of putting an end to the oppression and sub-
> ordination of the workers. If it leaves the organization
> and techniques of production intact, such a transfer

> will also leave intact the matrix of hierarchical rela-
> tions of domination and authority along with the old
> division of labor; in short, the relations of capitalist
> production. [40]

As a result, the essence of production under socialism could remain "their factories and our people."

This is quite obvious when we speak of certain forms. A prison is a prison, and the only way to alter the class content of a prison is (in the trivial sense for purposes of this discussion) to change the occupants of the cells from, say, proletarians to capitalists. Liberation of humanity requires the elimination of prisons, not merely the alteration of their class content. The use of certain forms of social organization under capitalism is no historical accident. Capitalism utilizes those forms of social organization because they can be used to maintain control, either directly or indirectly. In other words, there is an organic (not merely mechanistic) connection between form and content.

In the case of architecture, Samuel Bentham's panopticon is a form of social structure designed for purposes of social control. Whether utilized in the designing of prisons, hospitals, or schools, the purpose is still social control. There is nothing socialism could do to the panopticon as a form of architecture to eliminate the social control function inherent in it. The fact that proletarians might own all panoptical structures (forms) in a socialist society and manage them by workers' councils or even Taching methods would not essentially alter the control function of those structures.

At times it appears that in Chapter 1 Feenberg would agree with this position, when, for example, he defines technologies as developed ensembles of neutral technical elements that are

> greater than the sums of their parts. They meet social
> criteria of purpose in the very selection and arrangement
> of the intrinsically neutral units from which they are
> built up. These social criteria can be understood as
> "embodied" in the technology and not simply as an ex-
> trinsic use to which a neutral tool might be put. (Em-
> phasis added)

Feenberg also suggests that Marx did not regard this bourgeois heritage as neutral, as follows (my emphasis):

> From capitalism the workers would obtain a techno-
> logical apparatus designed to be operated by a disqualified
> labor force under the control of an autocratic management—

in other words, <u>a technology adapted to the culture</u>
<u>of capitalism</u>.

Feenberg agrees with Marx's minimum thesis, which, he
argues, asserts not the inevitability but at least the possibility of
socialism, as follows:

> Industrial technology is compatible with a radically
> different division of labor than that under which it
> first develops. . . . [Hence, while the capitalist tech-
> nological apparatus taken] as a whole introjects cultur-
> al values antagonistic to the goals of socialism, . . .
> [the proletariat could nevertheless make use of it] to
> produce the goods required for their continued sur-
> vival while they changed it to suit their new criteria
> of efficiency and social purpose.

The historical record of socialism in power suggests that this
task has not yet been fruitfully undertaken on a large scale—most
certainly not in the USSR and Eastern Europe (with some conflicting
evidence regarding Yugoslavia). Our effort has been to shed some
light on the reasons why this has not been accomplished. In this
discussion I have attempted to identify some reasons why at least
four current theories addressing this question are inadequate to that
effort. The reader might object that so far I have not made a good
case for my alternative approach—the mediation theory—and that the
example of Bentham's panopticon is hardly an adequate illustration
of the position. Let me proceed with a brief discussion of more
current examples in the development of advanced technology: automation, systems theory, and computers.

In a recent study of the impact of commercial relations on
political change in the USSR, John P. Hardt examined the role of
computer technology and made the following suggestion:

> A reform in the system of planning and management
> is probably more important to performance than com-
> puter hardware is. [41]
>
>   . . .
>
> A sage Western observer once noted that the
> best approach to efficient computer usage would be to
> design the operation as if it were to be converted to
> computer application and then stop short of conver-
> sion. This seems to be the opposite of current Soviet
> thinking, which is likely to overemphasize the change
> in institutions required to make effective use of the
> computer technology. [42]

This is a very revealing statement and also implies, as I argued in
the introduction, that technology involves far more than hardware.
It includes broader cultural factors of infrastructure and rationality,
and these elements must be present in order if the hardware is to
function as it was designed.

Erik P. Hoffmann arrives at the same conclusion as Hardt:
"Computers, by themselves, do not matter much." While Hardt
focused on what he considered to be the more important infrastructural elements, Hoffmann draws our attention to the factors of technical rationality involved in computer information processing, but
he does so only indirectly, as follows:

> Soviet elite political culture may be particularly re-
> sistant to dislocative change, and modern information
> technology is likely to be integrated or absorbed into
> the existing bureaucratic value systems and behavioral
> patterns rather than precipitate fundamental changes
> in Soviet politics.

The specific types of changes he is addressing concern the ability
of computer technicians and information processing specialists to
convert their technical skills into political power. That, of course,
is an important issue that has preoccupied Western analysts (and,
no doubt, the traditional Party professionals) for decades. It is the
old "apparatchik versus technocrat" perception of the problem.

Hoffmann concludes, along with Jeremy Azrael, that the technocrats have not made much political progress, as follows:

> Their valuable technical skills have not been trans-
> formed into political power and have not been sufficient
> to ensure them a prominent role in national policy
> making.

In the realm of computer technology, Hoffmann suggests the following as the reason for this failure:

> There seems to be nothing inherent in the computer
> technologists' skills and training that would suggest
> that they will challenge, rather than serve, the basic
> values, priorities, and directives of national, regional,
> and/or local political leaders, and would pursue sim-
> ilar, coherent policy alternatives in a unified manner.
> Rather, it is much more likely that quantitative data
> skills will be utilized by individual leaders and bureau-
> cratic units for all sorts of partisan, and possibly
> nonpartisan, purposes.

As a result of this reasoning, Hoffmann suggests that in the future

> it is unlikely . . . that middle-level CPSU and govern-
> ment officials will be pushed aside by the young com-
> puter technologists.

Hoffmann's analysis is quite compelling on this score, and it
is easy to agree with his persuasive, case-specific conclusions:
political power does not necessarily flow from newly acquired and
valued technical skills. That is an important conclusion about the
prospects for one dimension of political change in the USSR. However, there is another, broader set of related questions to which
Hoffmann only alludes. In fact, his assumptions on this score may
be somewhat misleading:

> One need not assess the role of computer specialists
> in terms of elite conflict between knowledge elites and
> political elites or between distinct ascending and de-
> scending elite groupings that perform different functions
> and possess different skills. Rather, the problem may
> be conceptualized as one in which technocratic conscious-
> ness becomes pervasive and subtly influences policy-
> makers' and information specialists' thinking about
> politics. This has almost certainly begun to happen
> in the Soviet Union, for example through the influence
> of cybernetics and systems analysis, through the pro-
> fessionalization of economic thought, and in the per-
> sistent official emphasis on the concepts of "ration-
> ality," "efficiency," and "the scientific management
> of society." Computers are indeed merely a part of
> larger information systems, which may or may not
> predispose their users (or participants) to new prob-
> lem-solving approaches and innovative modes of anal-
> ysis.
>   My hunch is that the newer attitudes and beliefs
> of Soviet leaders have yet to produce any major changes
> in their central values. Scientific and technological in-
> novations may eventually alter the political and informa-
> tion cultures and the fundamental public priorities,
> policy-making procedures, and priorities of the Soviet
> bureaucratic elites. An educated guess is that con-
> temporary information technology is least likely to
> change the leaders' cognitive orientations and basic
> values; more likely to change selected substantive
> policies and attitudes; and most likely to change spe-

cific policy-making procedures and beliefs. In a word,
the nature and substance of political discourse is
evolving.

What about the nature and substance of political discourse,
however? We have argued earlier that terms such as "rationality"
and "efficiency" that are devoid of specific content do not tell us
much; they merely perpetuate the mystification of important historical-cultural relationships.

The skills of the information specialists are related to new
quantitative techniques for the processing of information. What may
be more important are the values and skills of those whose task it
is to interpret that data. At least we must distinguish between the
narrow technical skills utilized in the computer processing of information and the broader skills related to the analysis and interpretation
of those results. Hoffmann suggests that

> The interpretation of these results will probably be
> considerably influenced by Marxist-Leninist categories
> of analysis and by salient political and organizational
> values, attitudes, and beliefs (explicit and implicit).

How long, though, will the Party leadership continue to interpret
the output in terms of Marxist-Leninist categories? We have already
indicated in these pages how theories of the STR represent an effort
to rationalize increased use of elements of the capitalist machine
technology, infrastructure, and technical rationality. To the extent
that this continues to happen, it represents a modification of the
system of rationalization or, in Hoffmann's words, "the nature and
substance of political discourse." Shifting the focus to this much
broader set of questions surrounding the system of rationalization
expands the parameters of our analysis of the impact of technology
on socialist societies.

The Chapter 4 case study of the Soviet automotive industry by
Hardt and Holliday points to one very important dimension of this
phenomenon. What they term the traditional Soviet approach to
technology transfer is giving way to the modified systems approach,
which results not only in a Soviet thrust toward technological interdependence with the West but also serves as a conduit for the
increased flow of capitalist infrastructure and technical rationality
into Soviet society. The increasingly widespread acceptance of the
modified systems approach in the USSR indicates that the Soviets
are not developing new criteria of efficiency but rather are opting
increasingly in favor of capitalist measures of efficiency.

At this point in the analysis, the mediation theory of technology, which stresses the impact of culture on technology in its formative stages, provides us with a different perspective on some key issues. Cooper suggests that "a worker may be technologically subordinate to the technical means if his or her movements and actions are determined by the machine itself." There is no quarrel here with the STR theory to the effect that this is indeed what happened under capitalism during the transfer of the technological and energetic functions from man to the machine.

If mechanization forced us to coordinate our bodies to the requirements of the machine, then surely cybernetics and automation force us to coordinate our minds to the requirements of the machine. The mediation theory of technology suggests that this will be the result of applying the cybernetics and automation developed under capitalism, since they, like every other level of capitalist technology, are vehicles for the mediation of capitalist cultural values and patterns. So tainted, this higher level of technological development can be no more liberating in a socialist context than were the earlier forms of capitalist technology.

Some STR theorists have clearly fallen victim to the mode of technocratic thinking characteristic of capitalist technical rationality. The Czech sociologist Ladislav Tondl, for example, has written the following:

> The present scientific-technical revolution is characterized by the enormous increase in the process and equipment in transmitting information, a revolution which has begun to automate the processes of decision-making. [43]

This would be tantamount to eliminating the process of decision making: automatic decisions are obviously nondecisions.

Many STR theorists look to automation of the production processes as the key to human liberation under socialism. According to Julian M. Copper:

> The invention and application of the working machine freed the human race from the direct fulfillment of the technological function, while the use of the mill and later the steam engine freed it from the direct fulfillment of the energetic function. In the opinion of Shukhardin, the STR takes this process a stage further. Now it is the logical and control functions that are being transferred from human to technical means.

The liberatory potential of such a process seems suspect, since in addition to the problems already mentioned, as human functions are taken over by machines there comes a point when the process becomes robbing, not freeing.

Rensselaer W. Lee III suggests that there is a great difference between the Chinese and the Soviets in their perceptions of the possibilities for and the concrete effects of new social and production relations during the postrevolutionary process of industrialization:

> Unlike the Soviets, at least since the 1930s, the Chinese communists have felt that the disappearance of major social distinctions such as those between mental and manual labor and between city and village can be immanent in the industrialising process itself. That is, those changes need not await a "postindustrial" stage of high automation and vast material wealth.

The Chinese see this mistake in the Soviet case resulting in the acceptance of "hierarchies of status and reward as a necessary precondition for building a communist society." The Chinese approach to this problem indicates a keen awareness of the interpenetration of means and ends. It shows an understanding that a socialist society must comprehend the relationship between being and becoming. To do otherwise is merely to invite rationalizing of the failure to attain socialist goals and to continue replicating elements of capitalist superstructure. For reasons already stated, the current theory of the STR appears to be just such a system of rationalization. As such, it casts serious doubt on Robert C. Tucker's formulation of one of the symptoms of the deradicalization of Marxist movements, in which he suggests that "the process of deradicalization has a certain inner 'dialectic.' For deep-seated reasons, theory and practice diverge. The movement intensifies its theoretical adherence to revolutionary goals at the very time when in practice it moves down the path to reformism."[44] In fact, Tucker suggests, "the appearance of a serious discrepancy between revolutionism in theory and reformism in practice is thus one of the hallmarks of deradicalization."[45]

In my view the theory of the scientific and technological revolution does not represent "revolution in theory" at all. Rather, it is a conservative doctrine that describes (and rationalizes) what has in fact been Soviet practice since 1917: the wholesale incorporation of elements of capitalist machine technology, technical rationality, and infrastructure into the transfer culture of communism. I see no great divergence between theory and practice in this process.

The Soviet case therefore gives us small cause for encouragement; yet the lingering doubts that some Soviet Marxists express about the ability of the current STR to liberate humanity leave some room for change, and some policies and practices in China, Cuba, and Yugoslavia provide real hope. Marxism itself continues to hold up higher ideals and a fruitful method of understanding the reality it seeks to transform.

NOTES

1. R. J. Forbes, The Conquest of Nature: Technology and Its Consequences (New York: Mentor, 1968), p. 103.

2. John Kenneth Galbraith, The New Industrial State (New York: Mentor, 1971), p. 380.

3. William Leiss, "The Social Consequences of Technological Progress: Critical Comments on Recent Theories," Canadian Public Administration 13, no. 3 (1970): 251. This article presents an excellent critique of both technological determinism and the neutrality theory of technology, although Leiss does not draw as much of a distinction between these two approaches as does the present analysis.

4. Galbraith, op. cit., p. 32.

5. William Taubman, "The Change to Change in Communist Systems: Modernization, Postmodernization, and Soviet Politics," in Soviet Politics and Society in the 1970's, ed. Henry W. Morton and Rudolf L. Tökés (New York: Free Press, 1974), p. 376.

6. Robert L. Heilbroner, An Inquiry into the Human Prospect (New York: Norton, 1974), p. 78.

7. Dzherman M. Gvishiani, Organisation and Management: A Sociological Analysis of Western Theories (Moscow: Progress Publishers, 1972), p. 50. Emphasis added.

8. Ibid., p. 52.

9. Ibid., p. 53.

10. Ibid., p. 40.

11. Ibid., p. 152.

12. Ibid., p. 40.

13. Ibid., p. 61.

14. Ibid., p. 149.

15. Ibid., p. 150.

16. Ibid., p. 149.

17. Ibid., p. 79.

18. Ibid., p. 78. Emphasis added.

19. Ibid., p. 26.

20. Ibid., p. 27.

21. Ibid., p. 27.

22. Ibid., p. 173.

23. Ibid., p. 57. Here Gvishiani is quoting V. I. Lenin, "The Impending Catastrophe and How to Combat It," Collected Works (4th ed., Moscow: Progress Publishers, 1964), Vol. 25, October 1917, p. 358.

24. Gvishiani, op. cit., p. 116.

25. Ibid., p. 30.

26. Andrew Feenberg, review of Lenine et la revolution culturelle, by Carmen Claudin-Urondo, in Theory and Society 2 (1975): 599. Emphasis added.

27. Ibid., p. 598.

28. Ibid., p. 599. Emphasis added.

29. Ibid., pp. 597-98.

30. Iu. A. Zamoshkin and N. V. Motroshilova, "Is Marcuse's 'Critical Theory of Society' Critical?" Voprosy filosofii, no. 18 (1968). This quotation is taken from the English translation that appeared in The Soviet Review 11 (1970): 11-12.

31. See André Gorz, "Technical Intelligence and the Capitalist Division of Labor," Telos 12 (1972): 27-41.

32. See Peter Linebaugh, "The Passage from Workers' Power in the Period of Manufacture: Samuel Bentham, Technological Repression, and the Eighteenth Century British Shipyards," paper presented at the 1976 annual meeting of the American Political Science Association, Chicago, Illinois, September 2-5, 1976. This theme will be treated in greater detail by Linebaugh in his study, Crime and Class Struggle in Eighteenth-Century London (London: Allen Lane, forthcoming).

33. See Katherine Stone, "The Origins of Job Structures in the Steel Industry," Review of Radical Political Economics 6 (1974): 61-97.

34. Perhaps the most graphic description of this particular phase of the development is presented by Siegfried Giedion, Mechanization Takes Command: A Contribution to Anonymous History (New York: Norton, 1969), especially Part 3, entitled "The Means of Mechanization."

35. See Quintin Hoare and Geoffrey Nowell Smith, eds., Selections from the Prison Notebooks of Antonio Gramsci (New York: International Publishers, 1971), pp. lxvi, 238.

36. Herbert Marcuse, An Essay on Liberation (Boston: Beacon 1969), p. 12.

37. Quoted by Julian M. Cooper in Chapter 3.

38. Andre Gorz, "Their Factories and Our People," Telos 18 (1973-74): 151. Emphasis added.

39. Ibid., pp. 155-56.

40. Ibid., p. 152.

41. John P. Hardt, "Soviet Commercial Relations and Political Change," in The Interaction of Economics and Foreign Policy,
ed. Robert A. Bauer (Charlottesville: University Press of Virginia,
1975), p. 65.

42. Ibid., p. 67.

43. Ladislav Tondl, "The Janus Head of Technology," in
Contemporary East European Philosophy, vol. 4, ed. Edward
D'Angelo, David H. DeGrood, and Dale Riepe (Bridgeport, Conn.:
Spartacus, 1971), p. 295.

44. Robert C. Tucker, The Marxian Revolutionary Idea (New
York: Norton, 1969), p. 192.

45. Ibid.

ABOUT THE EDITOR AND CONTRIBUTORS

FREDERIC J. FLERON, JR., the editor of this volume, is Professor of Political Science at the State University of New York at Buffalo. He is editor of Communist Studies and the Social Sciences (1969), coeditor of The Conduct of Soviet Foreign Policy (1971), co-author of Comparative Communist Political Leadership (1973), and contributor to several other scholarly books and journals on political socialization, Soviet politics, and comparative communism.

RICHARD BAUM is Professor of Political Science at the University of California at Los Angeles. He has authored and edited several books and articles on contemporary China, including China in Ferment: Perspectives on the Cultural Revolution (1971), Prelude to Revolution: Mao, the Party, and the Peasant Question, 1962–1966 (1975), and Maoism and the Chinese Industrial Revolution (forth-coming).

JULIAN M. COOPER is Research Fellow at the Centre for Russian and East European Studies, University of Birmingham (England). He is coauthor of the forthcoming book The Technological Level of Soviet Industry and is currently engaged in research on new forms of organization of industrial R&D in the USSR.

ROBERT F. DERNBERGER is Professor of Economics and Member of the Center for Chinese Studies at the University of Michigan at Ann Arbor. He has published numerous articles on China's economy in both popular and academic journals and has contributed articles to several conference volumes on China.

WILLIAM N. DUNN is Associate Professor in the Graduate School of Public and International Affairs at the University of Pitts-burgh. He received the 1977 Douglas McGregor Award of the Amer-ican Society for Public Administration for the best contribution to theory, practice, and values in applied behavioral science. He is coauthor of Toward a Critical Administrative Theory (1976), co-author of Workers' Self-Management and Organizational Power (1977), and numerous scholarly articles on Yugoslavia, comparative communism, and organization theory.

ANDREW L. FEENBERG is Assistant Professor of Philosophy at San Diego State University (California). He has published widely in the area of Marxist theory and is author of a forthcoming book on the May 1968 events in France.

MARK G. FIELD is Professor of Sociology at Boston University, an Associate of the Russian Research Center at Harvard University, and a Visiting Lecturer at the Harvard School of Public Health. He is author of Doctor and Patient in Soviet Russia (1957), Social Approaches to Mental Patient Care (1964), Soviet Socialized Medicine: An Introduction (1967), Evaluating Health Program Impact (1974), and editor of Social Consequences of Modernization in Communist Societies (1976).

JOHN P. HARDT is Senior Specialist in Soviet Economics and Associate Director for Senior Specialists at the Congressional Research Service of the U.S. Library of Congress. He has authored numerous studies for Congress, and he organizes, edits, and summarizes the annual Joint Economic Committee publications on the Eastern economies. He has authored and edited numerous other books and articles on the Eastern economies.

ERIK P. HOFFMANN is Associate Professor of Political Science at the State University of New York at Albany. He is Coordinating Editor and Managing Editor for Government and Administration of the journal Soviet Union. He is coeditor of The Conduct of Soviet Foreign Policy (1971) and has published several scholarly papers on various aspects of contemporary Soviet politics, especially national policy making and administration.

GEORGE D. HOLLIDAY is an economic analyst in the Congressional Research Service of the United States Library of Congress. He is coauthor of several congressional studies on East-West commercial relations.

RENSSELAER W. LEE III is a Senior Research Analyst at the Analytic Support Center of Mathematica, Inc. (Bethesda, Maryland). He has published several articles on Chinese and Soviet politics in scholarly journals.

WILLIAM LEISS is Professor of Environmental Studies and Political Science and a Member of the Graduate Programme in Social and Political Thought at York University (Toronto). He is author of The Domination of Nature (1972) and The Limits to Satisfaction: An Essay on the Problem of Needs and Commodities (1976). He is also editor of Environment and Politics in Canada (forthcoming) and has published articles in several scholarly journals.

CURRENT RESEARCH IN COMPARATIVE COMMUNISM: An
Analysis and Bibliographic Guide to the Soviet System
Lawrence L. Whetten

EDUCATION AND THE MASS MEDIA IN THE SOVIET UNION
AND EASTERN EUROPE
edited by Bohdan Harasymiw

*THE INTERNATIONAL POLITICS OF EASTERN EUROPE
edited by Charles Gati

*POLITICAL DEVELOPMENT IN EASTERN EUROPE
edited by Jan F. Triska and
Paul M. Cocks

THE POLITICS OF MODERNIZATION IN EASTERN EUROPE:
Testing the Soviet Model
edited by Charles Gati

SOCIAL SCIENTISTS AND POLICY MAKING IN THE USSR
edited by Richard B. Remnek

TECHNOLOGY TRANSFER TO EAST EUROPE: U.S.
Corporate Experience
Eric W. Hayden

*Also available in paperback as a PSS Student Edition